COMPANY SECRETARY
COMPANY LAW
CORPORATE GOVERNANCE
IN NIGERIA

COMPANY SECRETARY COMPANY LAW CORPORATE GOVERNANCE IN NIGERIA

Collins C. Okpanum, PhD

malthouse MP

Malthouse Press Limited

Lagos, Benin, Ibadan, Jos, Port-Harcourt, Zaria

First Published 2012
Second Edition 2024
ISBN: 978-978-51578-9-5

Published by

Malthouse Press Limited

Lagos Port Harcourt Zaria

5 Adele Road, Off Warehouse Road, Apapa
Lagos Mainland, Nigeria
E-mail: malthouselagos@gmail.com
Facebook:@malthouselagos
Twitter:@malthouselagos
Instagram:@malthouselagos
Tel: 0802 600 3203

International Distributors:
African Books Collective Ltd, Oxford, UK
Email: orders@africanbookscollective.com
Website: http://www.africanbookscollective.com

DEDICATION

This edition is dedicated to:
Mrs. Grace Okpanum (My Mother)
and
Mrs. Rosaline Egwuma (My Mother-in-Law)
Two Great Women

ACKNOWLEDGEMENTS

For this book, I still owe and repeat my appreciation to those that made the earlier version, which has now been dramatically changed to a different book, possible.

I acknowledge the unfettered and fatherly support of my mentor, James Ezike Esq, (Nnam Ukwu), who allowed me unlimited and unrestricted access to his rich law library for the research work for this book. I also thank the lawyers at J.C. Ezike & Co (Barristers & Solicitors) for their friendly dispositions, particularly, Barristers Ejezie, Onwukwe and Ologwu, in no particular order. The invaluable services of the office secretary and librarian, Mr. Oriyomi, 'Arewa,' is duly acknowledged, with thanks.

I have benefited, very immensely, from several learned texts, including *Company Law and Practice in Nigeria* by Justice Olakunle Orojo; Gower & Davies, *Principles of Modern Company Law*; Charlesworth & Cain, *Company Law*; Bob Tricker *on Corporate Governance*; Palmers' *Company Law*; Roger Mason's *Company Secretary's Guide*; ICSA's *Manual on Company Secretaryship*; Dr. Fabian Ajogwu on *Corporate Governance*; Bhadmus on *Corporate Law*; Nkiru-Nzegwu Danjuma, *Company Secretary's Role in Corporate Governance*; Brendan Hannigan, *Company Law 3rd* edn, and James Thorne, Butterworths *Company Law Guide*, 4th edn, among others.

I appreciate my wonderful wife, Nkechi, and my children for tolerating my 'isolation' to concentrate on working on this book. The deed is now done, play can resume.

Collins C. Okpanum PhD
Lagos, Nigeria, 30 November, 2023.

PREFACE

Four things, or even five, in the main, made this edition of the book inevitable in this present form, with a changed structure and title.

The first was the coming into effect of the *Companies and Allied Matters Act (CAMA), 2020 (*as amended). The CAMA 2020 made some far-reaching innovations in the area of company law and practice that could not be ignored. The first edition of this book was written based on the CAMA, Cap C20, LFN 2004. Therefore, a new edition that addresses the new developments both in the CAMA 2020 and the corporate and commercial world in general, was necessary.

The second was the volume, nature and sources of the feedbacks that came after the first edition was published, which was titled *Company Secretaryship in Nigeria.* Students from Faculties of Law in Nigerian Universities and the Law School, got in touch to appreciate the book and offered suggestions. One of the surprising suggestions was that they wanted more theoretical arguments and the author's opinions to be expressed in the book, where necessary. In the preface to the first edition, it was indicated that such arguments were deliberately left out. The second edifying feedback was that some university students actually took up final year project topics in the area of company secretaryship after being directed to read the book by their lecturers. It was pleasing to hear such feedbacks. This edition, therefore, has taken university students as one of the target audiences.

The third was on the title of the first edition, *Company Secretaryship in Nigeria*, which a lot of the responses said was restrictive, almost seeming as if the book discussed the law of meetings. The responses opined that the title did not bring out the company law and corporate governance aspects of the issues treated in the book and that this should be done, for balance. This Second Edition is now titled *Company Secretary, Company Law and Corporate Governance in Nigeria.*

The final feedback blamed the printer's devil for some errors in the first edition, which we have corrected and worked very hard to make amends and possibly eliminate any such issues in this edition.

The structure of the Second Edition has changed. From 17 chapters in the first edition, we now have 21 chapters in this edition. There are also the innovative 'checkpoints,' which act as pinpoint reviews at the end of almost all the chapters. The book will be a researcher's delight. It has been updated with current legislations, Codes, and more recent case laws. And yes, there are now more expressed opinions and legal arguments by the author.

Users of the book will notice that in citing the provisions of the CAMA in this book, there are usually 2 citations of the sections of the CAMA. The first citations are for the CAMA 2020, while the second citations are for the CAMA LFN 2004. Wherever there is any material difference(s) made by the CAMA 2020 as against the provisions of the CAMA 2004, those were highlighted, and if necessary, discussed.

The hope is that all those that use this Second Edition will find same even more useful than its predecessor.

Collins C. Okpanum, PhD
Lagos, Nigeria, 30 November 2023.

CASES

Awoyale *v.* Ogunbiyi (1985) NWLR Pt. 10, 861; 300
Awoyemi *v.* Solomon (1976) FRCR, 165; 270
Azuh *v.* UBN Plc (2014) 11 NWLR Pt. 1419, 580; 128
Baffa *v.* Odili (2001) 15 NWLR (Pt. 737) 709, 740; 154, 229, 232, 233
Baillie *v.* Oriental Telephone and Electric Co. Ltd (1915) 1 Ch., 103); 214, 341
Bairstow *v.* Queen's Moat Houses Plc (2001) 2 BCLC, 531; 207, 537
Balkis Consolidated Co. Ltd *v.* Tomkinson (1893) AC, 396; 421
Ball *v.* Metal Industries Ltd (1957) SC, 315); 331
Bamford *v.* Bamford (1969) 1 All ER, 969; 180
Bamgboye *v.* Unilorin & Anor (1999) LPELR-737; 236
Bank of Baroda *v.* Iyalabani Co. Ltd (2002) 13 NWLR Pt. 948, 551; 73
Bank of the North *v.* Akintoye (1999) 12 NWLR Pt. 631, 392; 441
Bank of West Africa Ltd *v.* Fadoul (1960) NNLR 15; 443
Barclays Bank Ltd *v.* CBN (1976) 6 SC, 175; 29
Barnett, Hoares and Co. *v.* South London Tramways Co. (1887)18 QBD, 815; 4
Baroness Wenlock *v.* River Dee Co. (1883) 36 Ch.D, 675; 361
Barton *v.* Staffordshire Rly. Co (1888) 38 Ch.D, 458; 434
Beach *v.* Sullivan (1957) 1 WLR, 1247); 299
Bellerby *v.* Rowland Ltd (1902) 2 Ch, 14; 429
Ben Hasem *v.* Ali Shayif (2009) 1 FLR 115; 77
Bentley-Stevens *v.* Jones & Ors (1974) 2 All ER 653, 655; 277
Bentley-Stevens *v.* Jones (1974) 1 WLR, 638; 339
Birch *v.* Cropper, Bridgewater Navigation Co. Ltd (1889) 14 AC, 525; 395, 397
Black *v.* Homersham (1878) 4 Ex D, 24; 542
Blair *v.* Consolidated Enfield Corp. (1995) 128 DLR (4th), 73; 353
Bloomenthal *v.* Ford (1897) AC, 156; 422
Boardman & Anor *v.* Phipps (1967) 2 A.C. 46; 175
BON *v.* Bello (2000) 7 NWLR Pt. 664, 244; 441
Bond *v.* Barrow Haematite Steel Co. (1902)1 Ch 353; 532
Borland Trustees *v.* Steel Brothers & Co. Ltd (1901) 1 Ch., 279; 393
Bratton Seymour Service Co Ltd *v.* Oxborough (1992) BCLC 693; 102
Bray *v.* Ford (1896) AC, 44; Thorne, 219); 194
Breiss *v.* Woolley (1954) AC, 333; 172
Brewtech Nig. Ltd *v.* Akinnawo & Anor (2016) LPELR-40094; 469
Bristol & West Building Society *v.* Mothew (1996) 4 All ER 698, 711; 159
British and American Trustee and Finance Corporation *v.* Couper (1894) AC 399, 417; 400

Heron Intl Ltd *v.* Grade (1983) BCLC, 244); 177

Panorama Developments (Guildford) Limited *v.* Fidelis Furnishings Fabrics Limited (1971) 2 QB, 711); 5

Re Greymouth Point Elizabeth Railway and Coal Co. Ltd (1904) 1 Ch., 32; 236

STATUTES

FOREIGN

INTERNATIONAL

CONTENTS

CHAPTERS

4. COMPANY'S CONSTITUTIONAL DOCUMENTS: MEMORANDUM AND ARTICLES

5. CONVERSION AND RE-REGISTRATION OF COMPANIES

6 APPOINTMENT AND POWERS OF COMPANY DIRECTORS

8. PROCEEDINGS OF COMPANY DIRECTORS

11. MEMBERSHIP IN A COMPANY

12. MEETINGS OF MEMBERS

13. RESOLUTIONS AND MINUTES OF MEETINGS

14. THE SHARE CAPITAL OF A COMPANY

15. COMPANY SHARES

16. INSIDER TRADING

17. COMPANY DEBENTURES

18. STATUTORY REGISTERS, RECORDS AND RETURNS

19. DIVIDEND

20. THE INTERSECTION OF LAW AND CORPORATE GOVERNANCE: THE ROLE OF THE COMPANY SECRETARY

21. REMOVAL OF THE COMPANY SECRETARY FROM OFFICE

Chapter 1

GENERAL OVERVIEW

Until the year 1980 or thereabouts, company law as a subject of study and area of practice had established solid reputation and its principles virtually fully standardized globally. The same could not be said of the subject of corporate governance, which, until much later, could not have formed or be expected to form a part of the opening chapter of a book that discusses company law and related topics, if at all. The rise to prominence of the concept and practice of corporate governance owes largely to the inefficiencies and corrupt tendencies exhibited over the years by the persons that had the responsibility of implementing the provisions of the relevant company law legislations and managing companies and corporations. In essence, company law and corporate governance are not totally different and unrelated fields as some scholars and analysts may want to argue, although modern trends have developed the concept of corporate governance into an independent field of work and study. We now have corporate governance professionals, which is part of what this book discusses. In the opinion of this book, the urgency of corporate governance came from the failures of company directors and managers to have fidelity to the letters of the laws, principles, rules and regulations that govern modern company administration.

Conceptually, simply put, company law is the field of law that studies and provides the basic laws, norms, rules and regulations that regulate companies and corporations. In themselves, these laws, norms, rules and regulations, hereafter called the cannons of company law, are complete and evolutionary, in the sense of always evolving organic and inorganic solutions, through legislations and the Courts, to take care of emerging issues and problems. The major problems, however, are the acute ill-implementation, non-implementation, and sometimes, deliberate sabotaging of these cannons of company law, by those entrusted with the responsibility to direct and manage company affairs: the directors and senior management team. This scenario, when not effectively checked, has thrown up devastating consequences. It is in a bid to checkmate this possible situation from manifesting that the concept of corporate governance and company law have converged, inevitably, but by design.

The anchor of this convergence between company law and corporate governance has been the company secretary, who is the link between the drivers of the system, that is, the directors, and the beneficiaries of the system, that is, the shareholders and other stakeholders. The company secretary, who is called 'corporate secretary' in some jurisdictions, comes into the picture as the primary tool in the hand of modern companies to efficiently implement the cannons of company law, and doing so in concert with the tenets of corporate governance. The position of the company secretary is, therefore, central to a company's effective implementation of corporate governance ideals, although the policy formulation and strategic direction in that respect rest with the board of directors. As we shall see throughout this book, the devastating effects of badly managed companies, for obvious reasons, are more widespread in effect in publicly quoted companies, than in private companies, especially smaller ones.

This book is about the coming together of the cannons of company law and the principles of corporate governance, under the watch of the company secretary. It is not intended to engage in any deep historical analysis of the development of company law (pre and post the case of *Salomon* v. *Salomon (1897) AC, 22*) or into the divergent theories of corporate governance (agency theory, resource dependence theory, stewardship theory, managerial and hegemony theory, etc). However, the major principles and concepts in corporate governance will be highlighted and discussed. The book will adopt a simple approach, which will evaluate the position and work of the company secretary in modern company law and administration and how they interplay with the laws, rules, and regulations that regulate the application of company law and corporate governance principles in Nigeria, seen through the tripod mechanisms of the *Companies and Allied Matter Act (CAMA) 2020* (as amended), the *Nigerian Code of Corporate Governance (NCCG) 2018,* and other *Codes* from around the world, and through case laws.

In terms of structure, the book will open with a substantive chapter on the company secretary and corporate governance, to put them in proper perspectives. Thereafter, the succeeding chapters will then discuss various aspects of company law and company administration starting with the formation of companies. Getting into serious intersections of company law and corporate governance will start from the chapters that discuss company directors (duties, powers, meetings, remuneration, vacation of office, etc) to the chapters on membership of a company (rights, liabilities, meetings, etc.) and meetings of members.

As it must have become obvious by now, this book is not meant to be a company law text, in the traditional sense of the subject. It is meant to be a text that blends the cannons of company law with the principles of corporate governance, as superintended by board of directors and supported by the company secretary. This being the case, traditional company law topics like business names, receiverships, company taxations, mergers, acquisitions and takeovers, capital markets (excluding insider trading), and winding-up, are not dealt with in this book. They are better dealt with elsewhere in standard company law books and there are lots of good ones around.

Chapter 2

THE COMPANY SECRETARY AND CORPORATE GOVERNANCE

INTRODUCTION

The roles of the company secretary in modern business environment and corporate practices have evolved over the years, and understandably so. In contemporary company law and practice, the position of the company secretary has gotten so intertwined with the operations and lives of modern companies, especially large private and publicly quoted companies, to the extent that writing anything meaningful on the roles of the company secretary would, in a sense, appear to be writing on company law as a subject. The two subjects are so inseparable. Considering the central roles that company secretaries now play in modern company administration, such a perception must be appreciated and understood.

The footprints and signatures of the company secretary are firmly rooted across the whole spectrum of company practice: from incorporation of companies, administration, organisation and reorganisation, to winding-up. Therefore, the early jurisprudence on the company secretary being a 'mere servant' and his duties being of 'limited and humble nature,' as was held in the old cases of *George Whitechurch Limited* v. *Cavanagh (1902) AC, 117; Barnett, Hoares and Co.* v. *South London Tramways Co. (1887)18 QBD, 815,* has long been jettisoned from modern business lexicon and consigned to the archives. The company secretary is now considered an important and integral part of the company and a high-ranking officer, who works in concert with the board of directors for the smooth administration of the company's business.

Under the *Companies and Allied Matters Act 2020* (as amended)*(hereinafter CAMA 2020),* which is now the principal legislation regulating company law and practice in Nigeria, in section 864 (*s. 567 Companies and Allied Matter Act, Cap. C20 LFN 2004), hereinafter, represented in bracketed numbers*) it defines an 'officer' in relation to a body corporate to include a director, manager or secretary. The fact that the company secretary is a high-ranking officer of a company has been variously confirmed by the Courts in Nigeria in *Okeowo* v. *Migliore (1979) 11 SC, 138; Wimpey Limited* v. *Balogun (1987) 2 NWLR Pt. 28, 322.* This position had earlier been confirmed in England in *Panorama Developments (Guildford) Limited* v. *Fidelis Furnishings Fabrics Limited (1971) 2QB, 711).* In the *Migliore* matter, Idigbe, JSC, described the company secretary as 'a principal officer of the company.' Meanwhile, in the *Panorama* legal proceedings, Lord Denning M.R., was more elaborate on the place of the company secretary in modern company law and practice, and this was more than 50 years ago, in 1971, when he said:

> but times have changed. A company secretary is a much more important person nowadays than he was in 1887. He is an officer of the company with extensive duties and responsibilities. This appears not only in modern company Acts but also in the role which he plays in the day-to-day business of the companies. He is no longer a mere clerk. He regularly makes representations on behalf of the company and enters into contracts on its behalf which come within the day-to-day running of the company's business. So much so that he may be regarded as held out as having authority to do such things on behalf of the company. He is certainly entitled to sign contracts connected with the administrative side of the company's affairs such as employing staff and ordering cars and so forth. All such matter now come within the ostensible authority of the company secretary.

It is with this current reality and mindset that we must place the rather recent case of *Erinfolami & Anor* v. *Mbagwu & Anor (2018) LPELR-46512 in proper context.* In this case, the Court *of Appeal defined a 'secretary' to be 'an administrative assistant, corporate officer in charge of correspondence, minutes of board meetings, record of stock ownership and transfer'. Also, that the Secretary could be called a 'clerk'.* This is also similar to the line taken by the Court in *Ozoinyi & Ors* v. *Oguama (2017) LPELR-43775,* where the Court simply adopted the *Webster English Language Dictionary's* definition of a 'secretary' and applied same as 'a person employed to keep records, correspondences and handle clerical business for a person or business organisation.'

It is obvious that the Courts in *Erinfolami and Ozoinyi's* cases above were not referring to a modern company secretary, but to an office assistant or clerk. Otherwise, the definition of a 'secretary' in those cases would have been fruitless efforts to return the globally established jurisprudence on the position of the company secretary to the era of the late nineteenth century and early twentieth century. The corporate and commercial world has since moved on from those periods.

The need to separate the modern company secretary from the 'office-clerk' confusion might be one of the reasons why several companies now designate their company secretaries with other nomenclatures, including, Chief Legal Officer, General Counsel, Chief Legal Counsel, Legal Adviser, Legal Adviser and Company Secretary, Head of Legal Services etc. This is not to say that, strictly speaking, there are no differences, semantically, amongst the designations. In practice, however, apart from the companies that separate the roles of the company secretary and legal adviser into distinct baskets, most times, the duties performed by those occupying these variously-designated positions are virtually the same. The exception to this scenario is where the duties and responsibilities are deliberately segregated by the company's board of directors. In *Daily Times Nig. Plc* v. *Akindiji (1998) 13 NWLR Pt. 580, 22*, it was held that whether the company secretary is simply so addressed or addressed as company secretary and legal adviser, it is immaterial, and the protection provided by the law for the company secretary in a public company still avails him. The Central Bank of Nigeria (CBN) had in July 2023 published and circulated the Corporate Governance Guidelines for Commercial Banks, Non-Interest and Payment Service Banks in Nigeria, 2023, effective 1st August 2023 (The CG Guidelines). The CG Guidelines made some new provisions, which although restricted to banks alone, are worthy of mention here:

i. section 3.6.2 of the Guidelines prohibits banks from outsourcing company secretarial functions;
ii. section 3.6.3 prohibits banks, except Payment Service Banks (PSPs), from combining the positions of the Company Secretary and that of Head of Legal Services or Legal Adviser, without the approval of the CBN;
iii. the Guidelines also provide that the CBN will have to ratify the removal of a bank's Company Secretary by the board of directors of the bank, before the removal could be valid and effective.

Although the objective behind the prohibition on the outsourcing of company secretarial jobs is understandable, that is, considering the sensitive materials that pass through that office, it is not clear why the CBN will ban the combination of the roles of the Company Secretary and Head of Legal Services.

In our opinion here, the issue should be an internal matter for the board of the concerned bank to deal with. This is because for smaller banks with small customer base, engaging two different individuals as Company Secretary and Head of Legal Services respectively, would be a waste of both human and material resources. The provision should not be implemented at all, even though the Guidelines say that the CBN could give exemptions. It is submitted that the micro-managing of the issue by the CBN is utterly unnecessary.

On the second issue of the CBN approving the removal of a bank's Company Secretary, in order for the removal to be effective, it is not clear if the provision will stand the test of further scrutiny. This is because it will seem to conflict with the express provision of section 331(1) CAMA 2020, (s. 296(1), which gives the board of a company the powers, without qualifications, to hire and remove the Company Secretary, while only adhering to the provisions of the Act. The CG Guidelines on this matter, therefore, seem to be beyond the powers of the CBN and ultra vires.

As an attestation to the revolutionised roles of company secretaries in the corporate and commercial space in recent decades, a strong case has been made that company secretaries in public companies, especially, have graduated to become distinct organs in such companies. This is because such officers are now imbued with substantial authority in the administrative area of the company with powers and duties derived directly from the company's Articles of Association and the relevant Companies Act (*Gower and Davies' Principles of Modern Company Law 7th ed; 298*). It is instructive to note that in some large corporations in Nigeria, company secretaries have also been appointed simultaneously to the dual position of directors in those companies.

The pivotal role of the company secretary in company law and administration has made both the CAMA 2020 and 2004 to make elaborate provisions, in varying degrees, regarding the qualifications, appointment, duties and removal of company secretaries in Nigeria. The *Nigerian Code of Corporate Governance, 2018 (NCCG)* also took time to make provisions concerning the place and duties of the company secretary in the areas of company administration and corporate governance. This is intended to supplement the provisions of various other governance codes and statutory provisions that apply to the areas of company law, company administration and corporate governance in Nigeria.

Although earlier texts on company law in Nigeria did not pay so much attention to the roles of the company secretary as a stand-alone subject, this book approaches the subject differently. Also, the issue of corporate governance and the roles of the company secretary in company administration seem to be developing in different independent directions (there are increasingly standard texts written on the subject of corporate governance that pay little attention to the roles of the company secretary, while concerning themselves fully with the roles of the board of directors), however, what is intended here is to mirror their mutual areas of intersections.

APPOINTMENT OF A COMPANY SECRETARY IN NIGERIA

Section 330(1) CAMA 2020 (s. 293(1) provides that, except with respect to a 'small company,' every company registered in Nigeria is mandated to have a company secretary. This contrasts with the provisions of the section 291(1) CAMA 2004, which mandated every company registered in Nigeria to have a company secretary and made no provision for 'small company' exception thereto.

Under section 394(1) CAMA 2020, a company qualifies as a 'small company' in relation to its first financial year if the qualifying conditions are met. However, by the provisions of section 18 of the schedule to the *Business Facilitation (Miscellaneous Provisions) Act (BFA) 2022*, which amended section 394(2) CAMA 2020, the qualifying conditions for subsequent years for small companies were amended to read that: 'a company qualifies as a small company in relation to a subsequent financial year, if the conditions qualifying it as a small company are met in that year and the previous financial year.' This amendment simplifies the conditions for qualifying as such for subsequent years, as against those stated in the amended section of the CAMA 2020.

Section 394(3)(a) to (f) CAMA 2020 (s.351) prescribes the qualifying conditions for a 'small company,' exempted from having a company secretary, and for other purposes, as one with the following qualifications in the relevant financial year:

a. it is a private company (common section 22 of both the CAMA 2020 and 2004 describes a private company), (the phrase 'having a share capital' in s. 351(1)(a) CAMA 2004 added to a 'private company' here is omitted by the CAMA 2020);
b. its turnover is not more than ₦120,000,000.00 (One hundred and twenty million naira) or such amount as may be fixed by the Corporate Affairs

Commission (hereafter the Commission, from time to time), (under the CAMA 2004, the turnover threshold was ₦2,000,000.00 (Two million naira only);

c. its assets value is not more than ₦60,000,000.00 (Sixty million naira) or such amount as may be fixed by the Commission from time to time), (the net assets value under the CAMA 2004 was ₦1,000,000.00 (One million naira);
d. none of its members is an alien, defined in section 868 CAMA 2020 (s. 567) as a person or association, whether corporate or unincorporated, other than a Nigerian citizen or association;
e. none of its members is a government, government corporation, agency or its nominee; and
f. in the case of a company having share capital, the directors between themselves hold at least 51%of its equity share capital.

Under section 395(1) CAMA 2020, a parent company will qualify as a 'small company,' as described above, in a financial year only if the group it heads qualifies as a 'small group.' Section 395(4)(a)-(f) repeats the qualifying conditions stated above for a 'small company' as also the qualifying conditions to be satisfied by a group to be termed a 'small group.'

Two things come out from the above provisions of the CAMA 2020 exempting 'small companies' from appointing company secretaries. The first is that small private companies, which are mostly family owned or 'one man' companies, are now exempted from the requirement to appoint a company secretary. The wisdom in this exception is that most of the companies in that genre, though required under the CAMA 2004 to appoint company secretaries, never really appointed company secretaries, in practice. They complied with the previous CAMA requirement in this area in the breach. The 'small company' exception to the appointment of a company secretary is, therefore, a welcome development as made by the CAMA 2020, although, not without its downsides, as we shall see below.

The second thing is that the qualification(s) for being a 'small company' is not static, being that the Commission is given the power and discretion to adjust, as they deem fit, two important criteria relating to turnover and value of assets for a company's qualification as a 'small company.' This would imply that, depending on the action(s) or inaction(s) of the Commission in that regard, a company may qualify as a 'small company' in one financial year and not so qualify in another year. Apart from this, there is another concern on the exercise of this power by the Commission.

The concern is that the CAMA 2020 does not state the basis on which the Commission could exercise its powers and discretion under sections 394 and 395 of the Act to tamper with the qualifications for a company qualifying as a 'small company' or 'small group.' In essence, the question is: are there limits to this exercise of powers and discretion by the Commission in this and other respects or could this power be exercised arbitrarily and without checks? If so exercised, can such exercise of powers and discretion by the Commission be challenged in a Court of law? The answer to the second question is in the positive. Any such exercise of power by the Commission can be challenged in Court by a company aggrieved, being that the right of access to Court is constitutionally guaranteed and cannot be detracted from *(Fidelity Bank Plc* v. *Monye (2012) 10 NWLR Pt. 1307, 1; Global Excellence Communications Ltd* v. *Duke (2007) 6 NWLR Pt. 1059, 22; Ugwu* v. *Ararume (2007) 12 NWLR Pt. 1048, 365; Amadi* v. *NNPC (2000) 10 NWLR Pt. 674, 76.* What is not guaranteed, however, is the outcome of any such legal challenge.

It was noted above that the exemption of entities classified as 'small companies' from appointing company secretaries has its own downside and the reason is not far-fetched. According the global governance think-tank, *Corporate Governance Institute (CGI; www.corporategovernanceinstitute.com),* 'the company secretary is now an integral member of the governance team whose principal responsibilities include making sure the company complies with the law, ensuring specific statutory registers are kept up to date, and filing required documents with the registrar of companies.' What this implies is that the expertise and utility that the company secretary brings to a company in the areas of company administration and corporate governance are totally lost in entities classified as small companies, which do not appoint company secretaries. The effect of this major downside is that, if, eventually such a small company exits from being a small company or converts to a public company, as it is allowed under the law to do, and the appointment of a company secretary becomes mandatory under the CAMA, then, there will be problems. The obvious problem will be that the acceptable level of expertise and culture of corporate governance and company administration that forms part of the general functions of the company secretary would have to be cultivated afresh in such a company. While there may be a positive side to this exemption above, the downside is also worthy of note.

The provisions of the CAMA 2020 and 2004 on the position of the company secretary are follow-ups from the *Companies Act of 1968,* which was the first legislation that statutorily provided for the appointment of a company secretary by Nigerian companies. Since then, the position of the company secretary has grown in importance and status and several conventional initiatives and statutory provisions have been devised, over the years, to formalize the institution and position of the company secretary. This is a departure from older company practices wherein the appointment of a company secretary was optional for any company and their duties and responsibilities were only determined by each company's Articles of Association, as was deemed fit.

Having established the foundation for the appointment of a company secretary by companies, we now turn to the person of the company secretary to be so appointed and the appointment processes.

WHO CAN APPOINT AND WHO CAN BE A COMPANY SECRETARY IN NIGERIA?

The CAMA 2020 and CAMA 2004 seem pre-occupied majorly with the appointment of a company secretary by public companies. For instance, section 330(2) CAMA 2020 provides that where a public company has not appointed a company secretary on the commencement of the Act, the company must do so within six (6) months of the commencement of the Act. The CAMA 2004 had no such mandatory provision on the period deadline for the appointment of company secretary by public companies. There is also no such provision with respect to private companies in the CAMA 2020. Furthermore, the fine imposed on a company and its directors for non-compliance with the provision of section 330 CAMA 2020, are only imposed on public companies and their directors and not on the directors of private companies. The CAMA 2004 did not impose any such fine at all.

It is not clear why both the CAMA 2020 and CAMA 2004 played down, as it were, the importance of the position of the company secretary in private companies. While conceding that most private companies are small and medium enterprises that might not really require the permanent services of a company secretary on a day-to-day basis, it is also true that there are, in Nigeria, large private companies that cannot operate without the appointment of a qualified company secretary. This is especially so in the telecoms, oil and gas, aviation, mining and engineering and construction sectors of the economy. Apart from the 'small company' exception to the appointment of a company secretary as already noted, it is our view, (even if it means raising the threshold for qualification as a 'small company'), that the provisions for the appointment of a company secretary should be uniform or slightly genre-calibrated for all companies, including 'small companies,' on specified terms. This is especially so with respect to the qualifications of the potential appointees.

Section 332 CAMA 2020 (s.295) imposes a general duty on directors of a company to take all reasonable steps to ensure that the person to be appointed a company secretary is a person who appears to have the requisite knowledge and experience to discharge the duties of a company secretary. This is a general duty and would apply to directors of private and public companies. This is more like an admonition to the directors of a company as there are no sanctions prescribed by the CAMA for the failure of any director(s) to take such steps as indicated.

Since no qualification(s) is indicated under the CAMA 2020 and CAMA 2004 for a company secretary in a private company, it is taken that the above provision applies more specifically to the directors of a private company. This is because without specifying any basic qualification(s) for persons to be appointed company secretary in private companies, the CAMA 2020 (and CAMA 2004) gives the directors of private companies wide latitude and discretion with respect to the person to be appointed as such. The directors only need to have in mind the admonition to 'take reasonable steps to ensure that the person (to be appointed) appears to have the requisite knowledge and experience' to function as a company secretary.

Appointment of Company Secretary for Public Companies

In general, section 333(1) CAMA 2020 [s. 296(1)] provides that it shall be the responsibility of the directors of a company to appoint a company secretary and, once complying with the provisions of the Act, they may also remove the person so appointed. *Principle 8.8 of the Nigerian Code of Corporate Governance (NCCG)* agrees with this provision of the CAMA, in providing that 'subject to the provisions of extant laws, the appointment and removal of the company secretary should be a matter for the board.' There are two main reasons for this although the CAMA and the NCCG did not go into such details.

The first reason is that, as was seen above, the company secretary is considered a senior member of the executive management team in the company and the appointment and removal of such a person must be by the entire board. Under principle 8.2 of the *NCCG,* it is provided that 'where the company secretary is an employee of the company, he should be a member of senior management and should be appointed through a rigorous selection process, similar to that of new directors.' The second reason is because of what the company secretary brings or is expected to bring to the company as a commercial going concern. Under principle 8 of the *NCCG,* it is provided that 'the company secretary plays an important role in supporting the effectiveness of the board by assisting the board and management to develop good corporate governance practices and culture within the company.' Apart from dealing with issues of law, therefore, in terms of effectively implementing the principles of corporate governance within the company, the roles of the company secretary in supporting the overall objectives of the company, as stated, cannot be over-emphasized.

For newly incorporated companies, the usual practice is for the name of the nominated company secretary to be submitted alongside the other incorporation documents to the Commission in *Form CAC 8* (Appointment of Secretary). Specifically, for public companies, section 332(a) to (e) CAMA 2020 [s.295(a)-(e) 2004)] provides that to be appointed a company secretary, the candidate shall be a person who is one of:

a member of the Institute of Chartered Secretaries and Administrators (ICSA);

a legal practitioner within the meaning of the Legal Practitioners' Act 1975 (as amended);

a member of any professional body of accountants established from time to time by an Act of the National Assembly; (this provision specifically deletes the express mention of the name of the Institute of Chartered Accountants of Nigeria (ICAN) as it was under section 295(c) CAMA 2004.

There had been running battles between the members of ICAN and other accounting bodies registered in Nigeria, with regard to the former provision, which specifically mentioned only ICAN and then 'or such other bodies of accountants' as are established from time to time by an Act'. The other registered bodies of accountants in Nigerian, especially the likes of the

Association of National Accountants of Nigeria (ANAN), fought over the years to have their names also listed in the Act or to have ICAN's name deleted. This has now been done apparently to assuage the complaints and agitations of the other accounting bodies in that respect:

> any person who has held the office of a secretary of a public company for at least three (3) years of the five (5) years immediately preceding his appointment in a public company; or
> a body corporate or firm consisting of members each of whom is qualified as one of those listed in the first three (3) categories above.

The CAMA 2020 excludes from this last category, those who qualified under section 332(d) that is (s.295(d) CAMA 2004), being those having held office as a secretary of a public company for at least three (3) years of the five (5) years before the appointment. It is not clear why the CAMA 2020 omitted this provision but it would appear that the framers of the legislation were wary of a situation where some persons who were secretaries in public companies but who were not chartered secretaries, legal practitioners or accountants, but could then rely on the provision of sub-section (d) to form and run a firm of company secretaries under the Act.

Although the CAMA has stated what should be the educational or professional qualifications of a person to be appointed a company secretary in a public company, it did not go as far as stating what the other skills-set of the person should be, which is also a very important factor. In this respect, principle 8.1 of the *NCCG* has provided that in addition to the educational and professional qualifications of the potential company secretary, 'the board should ensure that the person appointed has the gravitas and objectivity to provide independent guidance and support at the highest level of decision-making in the company.'

It is therefore clear that skills are important factors, and in-fact equally as important as educational and professional qualifications, in determining who gets appointed as a company secretary. The *Corporate Governance Institute* (CGI) was clear in pointing out some of the needed skills that contribute to enhance the effectiveness of the company secretary as a company law expert and governance professional, as follows:

- knowledge of company law and corporate governance;
- excellent communication skills – both verbal and written;

- influence over colleagues at the highest levels;
- a keen eye for detail;
- capable of processing large amounts of information;
- confidentiality;
- time-management skills;
- being extremely organized and diligent.

The World Bank Group, through International Finance Corporation (IFC), in its 2016 study entitled *'The Corporate Secretary: The Governance Professional'* has indicated that apart from the technical and general professional qualifications required to be an effective company secretary and a governance professional, skills in emotional intelligence (EI)are also crucial for the company secretary to be successful in the position. In this respect, the soft skills indicated in the study are:

- respectful, diplomatic, and effective communication skills;
- active listening abilities;
- bringing issues to the surface, especially those relating to reputational risk for the company;
- describing common concerns and interests;
- generating alternative solutions on matters presented for resolution;
- appreciation for all parties and disagreeing constructively, where appropriate.

The mention of knowledge of company law above by the CGI as one of the attributes of a company secretary is noteworthy. This is because although the CAMA 2020 and CAMA 2004 have made provisions on the qualifications for one to assume the position of the company secretary in a public company, as we have seen above, in practice, it is difficult to find a company secretary in a public company who is not a legal practitioner. In Nigeria, experience has shown, from the distant-past up till now, that even those who were not legal practitioners on their appointment to such a position, would, along the line, acquire law degrees to cement their positions. As will be seen in subsequent chapters, this development seems to be the case considering the intricate nature of the duties and responsibilities of company secretaries in public companies, which involve, more often than not, very complex legal issues.

Also, the mention of knowledge of corporate governance, as one of the attributes of an effective company secretary, is equally instructive. This is because, in modern company law and administration, it is getting increasingly difficult to segregate the essentials of company law and those of corporate governance into distinct baskets. The blur in any attempted segregation is mostly from the fact that the duties and responsibilities of the company secretary have become so multi-dimensional in nature, that trying to pigeonhole them into watertight compartments would not be a useful exercise.

DUTIES AND RESPONSIBILITIES OF THE COMPANY SECRETARY

As already noted, one would be pardoned to posit that it is not possible to isolate and discuss, with exactitude, the duties and responsibilities of the company secretary in a modern business setting. This is especially so when it pertains to large private and big publicly quoted companies, where the diversity of shareholders and other stakeholders could be quite enormous. In this wise, it has been strongly canvassed, and in our view, rightly so, that, in general, the duties of the company secretary vary with the size of the company, the nature of its business, the type of company and the terms of the contract of engagement of the company secretary (*Palmers Company Law 22nd ed. Vol.1, 721*). This does not detract, as will be seen below, from the fact that a general picture of the duties and responsibilities of the company secretary could still be perfectly captured.

In general, the duties and responsibilities of the company secretary can best be described as multi-dimensional and could also be corporate-generic in character. The duties are multi-dimensional in the sense that they encompass elements of administration, human resources management, transactional issues, litigation monitoring and core company secretarial duties, that is, in relation to services to the board and management of the company. They could be also corporate-generic in the sense that a company's Articles of Association or the board of directors could limit or expand the duties of the company secretary in particular cases. For instance, in some companies, the company secretaries also double as the substantive Heads of Human Resource Management or Heads of Compliance, for the companies in question.

With the exception of some aspects of the duties of company secretaries that are prescribed by statute, for instance, the CAMA, the details of their overall duties are not fixed by law but are assigned under the company's Articles, or the contract of engagement of the company secretary or specifically assigned to him by the directors in any specific document made for the purpose (Palmers, 722; *Okeowo* v. *Migliore & Ors (1979) NSCC, 210,*

219). In essence, apart from some of the specific duties mentioned under the CAMA, the company secretary could be directed by the board or the company in a general meeting, to do any act(s) that is deemed fit. Such other duties that do not fall within the express or ostensible authority of the company secretary would need either the board or shareholders' authorization or might be invalid in effect, against the company secretary. For instance, it has been held that the company secretary cannot, without the authorization of the board of directors, borrow any money on behalf of the company or commence litigation in the name of the company without such authorization *(Re Cleadon Trust Ltd (1939), Ch, 286; and Daimler Co. Ltd* v. *Continental Tyre etc Co. Ltd (1916) 2 AC, 307) in Charlesworth & Cain, Company Law, 12ed, 1983, 38).* As further examples, the company secretary cannot call a general meeting of a company without the direction or authorization from the directors *(Re State of Wyoming Syndicate (1901) 2 Ch., 431*); *Orojo, Company Law and Practice in Nigeria 5th ed, 290).*

It is ideal that the limiting or expansion of a company secretary's job scope by the company directors should be formally documented by the company (like in a company's handbook, process manual, specific board resolution(s) or the company's Articles) to ensure certainty. Where such is meant to be a temporary measure, the duration of such a measure should also be made clear in the relevant source document, as indicated.

In terms of scope, both the CAMA 2020 and 2004 did not attempt to give an exhaustive numeration of what the duties of the company secretary should be. In doing this, both Acts used the phrase 'the duties of a secretary include,' and the word 'include' is 'usually used to enlarge the meaning of words or phrases occurring in the body of a statute' *(Rabiu* v. *State (1980) 8-11 SC,130; Uhunmwangho* v. *Okojie (1989) 5 NWLR Pt. 122, 471).* Specifically, section 335(1) CAMA 2020), (s. 298) enumerates the statutory duties of a company secretary, but, as already indicated, they are not by any means exhaustive. The duties of the company secretary are said to include:

- attending meetings of the company, the board of directors and its committees, and rendering all necessary secretarial services in respect of these meetings;
- advising all the above meetings on the issue of compliance with all applicable rules and regulations;
- maintaining all statutory registers and records as required by the CAMA;

- rendering proper returns and giving all requisite notification(s) to the Commission as required by the CAMA; and
- carrying out such administrative and other secretarial duties as directed by the director(s) or the company.

The above are the statutory duties prescribed by the CAMA for the company secretary, while using the word 'include' to acknowledge that the list is not exhaustive, in any way.

On its own part, the *Corporate Governance Institute (CGI)* expanded what should ideally be the work scope for the company secretary, by including, among others, the corporate governance aspects of the company secretary's duties. According to the CGI, a typical company secretary is responsible for:

- developing and implementing all processes to support good corporate governance;
- providing impartial advice to all board members and acting diligently in the company's interests;
- supporting the board and its committees in fulfilling their responsibilities and following best practices;
- ensuring that board members are presented with high quality, up-to-date information in advance of meetings and scheduling meetings accordingly;
- reminding the chair that there should be rigorous annual board, committee, directors and CEO's assessments and ensuring that actions arising from the evaluations are completed;
- supporting the chair through the entire board development process, including board evaluations, inductions and trainings;
- educating management concerning the expectations of, and the value of, the board;
- collaborating with the board and chair to maintain effective relations with the company's stakeholders, such as investors and even creditors;
- creating training plans for individual directors and the board and developing tailored induction plans for new directors;
- making all reports available to shareholders per statutory or regulatory requirements, and drafting the section on governance in the company's annual report;
- being available to all directors for advice and services;

- managing the share register (and other registers) and monitoring share ownership changes in a publicly traded company;
- ensuring that all contractual agreements with suppliers and customers follow company policies;
- managing relations with external regulators and advisors, such as external solicitors and external auditors.

Even with the above elaboration on the roles of the company secretary by the CGI, what have been enumerated above are still not exhaustive. For instance, aspects of the roles of the company secretary in some companies that relate to human resource management, whistle-blowing and related matters are not mentioned at all. This observation notwithstanding, it could be seen that a combination of the duties stated by the CAMA and those listed by the CGI, gives a fair view of the duties and responsibilities of a modern company secretary. This does not suggest, by any means, that all the duties have been captured above, and that is for a reason.

While the duties of the company secretary are not at large and must be defined within the context of the powers reserved for that position, the duties are also not closed, either. This is because when authorized by the board of directors, the company secretary may also exercise any of the powers vested in the directors (s.335(2) CAMA 2020), (s. 298 (2). These directors' powers will be discussed in subsequent chapters.

In trying to explain the structure of the roles of the company secretary, the Word Bank Group (IFC) explains that the company secretary performs a combined role. This is because, due to the compliance element inherent in the company secretary's roles, a lot of companies do combine the roles with that of head of legal services (usually as company secretary and legal adviser or company secretary and head of legal), even without pronouncing the compliance aspect, as such, in the appointment nomenclature. The company secretary then performs such governance and compliance functions either expressly assigned to him or on delegation from the board of directors. This points to one of the problems to be encountered in implementing, if at all, the CBN Corporate Governance Guidelines as noted above, which seek to always keep the positions of a Company Secretary and Legal Adviser separate.' A particular note needs to be taken, that, while the directors of a company are at liberty to delegate any of their duties to the company secretary under the above section, the CAMA 2020, in section 305(7), (s. 279(7), stipulates that no director is allowed to delegate a duty in such a way as to amount to an abdication of the duty imposed on the director.

Abdication of duty, according to the *Black's Law Dictionary, 9th edn, 4,* is to renounce or abandon such a duty. Added to this is that, in general, the company secretary does not, *stricto sensu,* owe a fiduciary duty to the company, unlike the directors. The exception to this is where the company secretary is acting as the company's agent in a particular situation or transaction, then his fiduciary duties to the company will be activated. This will prevent him, for instance, from allowing his personal interests to conflict with the interests of the company, or from being able to make secret profits from so acting (s. 334 CAMA 2020), (s. 297).

The implication of the above provision would appear to be that where a director abdicates his duties and responsibilities to the company in the guise of delegation and the delegate (the company secretary) incurs any liability to the company in the course of carrying out the instructions, the director would still be liable for the breach of duty (*Adedire & Anor* v. *Caretaker Committee Ife Divisional Council & Anor (1963) All NLR, 38; Regal (Hastings) Ltd* v. *Gulliver (1942)1All ER, 378).* This position is fortified by section 305(8) CAMA 2020), (s. 279(8) which stipulates that no provision, whether in the Articles, resolutions of a company or any contract shall relieve a director from the duty to act as a fiduciary or relieve him from the liability incurred for breach of his fiduciary duties to the company. Thus, whether a director delegates his duties under the Act or not, his fiduciary duties and responsibilities to the company enure to him, and the company has the right to enforce same against the director in question, for any breach (s. 305 (9) CAMA 2020), (s. 279 (9).

Finally, whatever be the source(s) of the duties and responsibilities to be executed by the company secretary, whether conferred by the CAMA, the Articles or by his contract, the constant decimal is that the present functions of the modern company secretary make the position almost indispensable, and surely so in large, and especially quoted companies. As will be discussed in subsequent chapters, the signatures and footprints of the company secretary are firmly stamped and entrenched on all aspects and broad spectrum of company activities, from incorporation (when appointed as part of the process) to winding-up and, we predict, that the position of the company secretary will become functionally more complex, in terms of their centrality in the affairs of large companies, in the years to come. This is because of the ever-increasing globalization and digitization of company affairs and the breakdown of the traditional barriers, both in terms of business genre and location in the last decades. This situation is expected to become more urgent and established in the decades to come.

CHECKPOINTS

- ✓ The modern company secretary has evolved over the years and is now, without debates, regarded as a senior member of the management team in modern corporate environment. The old era of equating the company secretary with a company clerk is long gone and forgotten.
- ✓ The requirements for the appointment of a company secretary are now statutory, although the CAMA 2020 excludes a 'small company' from mandatorily having to appoint a company secretary. This is unlike under the CAMA 2004, wherein all companies were mandated to have company secretaries. It is therefore at the option of a 'small company' to make the choice to appoint a company secretary or not.
- ✓ As it was with the CAMA 2004, the CAMA 2020 did not also stipulate any qualification(s) as to who becomes a company secretary in a private company. That responsibility is left to the judgment of the directors in their general direction to appoint a person who appears to them to have the knowledge and experience to competently function in such a position.
- ✓ As with the CAMA 2004, the CAMA 2020 stipulates the qualifications for a person to be appointed a company secretary in a public company. However, the CAMA 2020 went ahead and removed the express mention of membership of ICAN as one of the qualifications and simply states membership of a professional accounting body recognised by an Act of the National Assembly. That issue had been very contentious for years between members of ICAN and the other accounting bodies in Nigeria.
- ✓ The duties and responsibilities of the company secretary have now grown into multi-dimensional proportions, and any attempt to exhaustively itemize them will be futile. Although the CAMA listed some specific duties for the company secretary, the Act also went ahead to say that the directors can delegate any duty and responsibility to the company secretary, as they deem fit.

- ✓ The company secretary is now required to have other emotional intelligence skills, aside professional qualifications, being that the roles they now perform have greatly changed over the years.
- ✓ According to the World Bank Group (IFC) aspects of corporate governance are ingrained into the work of the company secretary, especially from the compliance perspectives and care has to be taken to ensure that one aspect of his job does not overshadow the others.
- ✓ The *Corporate Governance Institute (CGI)* states that apart from having a good knowledge of company law, a sound knowledge of corporate governance is mandatory for a person to be successful and function efficiently as company secretary in a modern business setting.
- ✓ The law is that the company secretary cannot, without the authority of the board of directors, purport to exercise any of the powers vested in the directors.
- ✓ Conversely, where authorized by the board of directors, the company secretary may exercise any of the powers vested in the directors. However, any such delegation of duties does not relieve the directors of their fiduciary duty to the company, if there be any breach of that duty upon being delegated.
- ✓ As a general rule, the company secretary does not, *stricto sensu,* owe fiduciary duties to the company, except where he acts as an agent of the company in a particular situation or transaction, then his fiduciary duty arises. This will prevent him, for instance, from placing himself in a situation where his personal interests come in conflict with the interests of the company and he cannot make any secret profits thereby.

Chapter 3

THE COMPANY INCORPORATION PROCESSES

INTRODUCTION

The processes and procedures leading to a company being incorporated and assuming the status of a distinct legal entity in Nigeria are governed by law, the CAMA. The processes start with the promoters of a company meeting the conditions stipulated by law for incorporating a company of a particular genre. The company could be an unlimited company, a company limited by shares or limited by guarantee. It is the responsibility of the promoters to choose a name for the proposed company, noting the areas of prohibited and restricted names. In practice, some company promoters, in a practice that is recommended by this book, would appoint a company secretary (subject to regularization on the formal incorporation of the company) as part of the initial activities leading to the incorporation of the company. It would then be for the person so appointed to lead the promoters through the whole gamut of processes that will lead to the company's incorporation at the Commission, which is where the major incorporation activities of the company secretary start.

As noted in the previous chapter, the CAMA 2020, which repealed the CAMA 2004 is now the principal legislation that regulates the formation, direction, membership, administration and winding-up of companies, among others, in Nigeria. However, it is noteworthy that the aspects of company administration relating to takeover, mergers and acquisitions (apart from mergers of associations under section 849 CAMA 2020) have been transferred to the *Federal Competition and Consumer Protection Act (FCCPA) 2018*, with the repeal of sections 118 to 128 of the *Investment and Securities Act (ISA) 2007*, which hitherto regulated this area.

THE CORPORATE AFFAIRS COMMISSION (THE COMMISSION)

Section 1 of the CAMA 2020 (s.1) establishes the Corporate Affairs Commission (the Commission). It is a distinct legal entity with perpetual succession, able to sue and be sued in its corporate name and capable to acquire, hold and dispose movable and immovable properties. It has the primary responsibility of administering and enforcing the provisions of the CAMA.

Section 2 of Act, established, for the first time, a governing board, (the Governing Board) for the Commission. The governing board is comprised of a chairman, to be appointed by the President, then, a representative from the business community, the Legal profession, the Accountancy profession, Manufacturers Association of Nigeria (MAN), Securities and Exchange Commission (SEC), Ministries of Trade and Investment, Industry and Justice, with the Registrar-General of the Commission. Other members of the board are representatives from the Institute of Chartered Secretaries and Administrators (ICSA), Ministry of Finance and the Nigerian Association of Small and Medium Enterprises (NASMEs). Members of the governing board are to hold office for a term of three (3) years, renewable only once. All the members are appointed on a part-time basis, except the Registrar-General of the Commission.

Section 4 of the CAMA 2020 stipulates the functions of the board, to include providing general policy guidelines for the Commission to perform its duties, general oversight on the administration of the Commission, reviewing the Commission's strategic plans, determining terms and conditions of service of the Commission's employees, fixing and reviewing the remuneration, allowances and benefits of the Commission's employees, among others.

For the Commission itself, section 8 of the Act (s. 7) stipulates the functions of the Commission, and these are:

- to administer the CAMA, including the duty of regulating and supervising the formation, incorporation, registration, management, striking-off and winding-up of companies, business names and incorporated trustees under the Act. This provision is subject to section 722(2) CAMA 2020 (s. 541) (which excludes the application of the CAMA to trade unions);
- to establish and maintain suitably equipped company registries in all the states of the federation to enable it discharge its functions under all relevant laws;

- to arrange or conduct investigations into the affairs of any company, incorporated trustees or business names where the interests of the shareholders, members, partners or the public so demands. It is important to note that it is the CAMA 2020 that added 'incorporated trustees and business names' to the entities that the Commission can investigate and also added 'members' and 'partner' as those whose interests could trigger such investigations. It was not so under the CAMA 2004;
- ensure compliance by companies, business names and incorporated trustees with the provision of the Act and such other regulation as the Commission may make; (this is an entirely new addition by the CAMA 2020);
- to perform any other act(s) that may be specified by the Act or any other law; and
- to undertake all other activities that are necessary or expedient for giving full effect to the provisions of the Act.

Section 8(2) of the CAMA 2020 (s.7(2) preserves the powers, duties and jurisdiction of the Securities and Exchange Commission (SEC) under the *Investments and Securities Act, 2007* (or any amendment(s) or re-enactment thereof).

Apart from the additions noted above, the CAMA 2020 retained most of the provisions of the CAMA 2004 with respect to the Commission.

In undertaking to give full effect to the provisions of the CAMA, the Commission has drawn up an Operations Checklist for its clients, giving details about its services in fulfilling its mandate. Some of these services are indicated on the Commission's website and include:

- reservation of names for business names, companies or incorporated trustees;
- o incorporation of companies (private or public, limited by shares, guarantee or unlimited; including the availability of names for registration of companies);
- o registration of Business Names;
- o registration of Incorporated Trustees;
- o facilitating Searches of the Companies Registry;
- o issuance of certified true copies of documents in its file;
- o registration of increase or decrease in share capital of companies;
- o registration of mortgages, debentures, charges etc;
- o registration of change of name for companies;

- processing and registration of statutory returns including annual returns, resolutions that require registration, particulars of directors and secretaries and changes thereto; alteration of Articles and Memorandum of Association;
- Partnership (LLP) and changes thereto;
- registration of receiverships;
- conducting investigations into the affairs of companies, business names, and incorporated trustees where the interest of the shareholders, members, partners or the public dictates;
- responding to enquiries and complaints with respect to its services;
- registration of professionals (lawyers, chartered secretaries etc) for accessing its services;
- registration of company charges, which include mortgages;
- generally enforcing compliance with the provisions of the CAMA.

There are presently over seventy-five (75) items specified in the Commission's operational checklist and the list is by no means exhaustive. The company secretary has an enormous role to play in carrying out the activities that are conducted at the Commission on behalf of any company. This is because apart from facilitating these activities at the Commission, the company secretary would also be in a position to advise the board of directors and executive management on the legal implications of effecting or neglecting any of the listed activities. This is important as no company would like to pay unnecessary fines and penalties for breaches, engage in unnecessary and usually protracted disputes or litigation with the Commission, when this could be avoided.

In the above respect, it is helpful, at the outset, to draw attention to the pre-action notice provision of section 17 CAMA 2020, which was not there under the CAMA 2004. By this provision, it is now required that before commencing any action against the Commission, a thirty-day's written notice of intention to sue must have been served on the Commission by the intending plaintiff or his agent. This notice will indicate the cause of action, particulars of the claim, the names and addresses of the intending plaintiff and the potential relief to be sought in Court.

The purpose of this pre-action notice, as in any other instance, is to allow the Commission, when served with such a notice, to determine the nature of the claim and if it is a claim that the Commission may want to settle with the potential plaintiff out of Court, instead of having it litigated. The Courts have held that when a pre-action notice is mandated by law, then it is a condition precedent, the absence of which robs the Courts of jurisdiction to entertain the suit(s) in question *(Nnonye* v. *Anyichie (2005) 1 SC Pt. 11, 96).* The ultimate effect of such non-compliance with the service of a pre-action notice, is, however, not fatal to the case of the plaintiff. It only puts the jurisdiction of the Court on hold until such a notice is served on the defendant, here, the Commission *(Barclays Bank Ltd* v. *CBN (1976) 6 SC, 175; Okotie-Eboh* v. *Okotie-Eboh (1986) 1NWLR Pt. 16, 264; Eze* v. *Ikechukwu (2002) 18 NWLR Pt. 799, 348).*

For the company secretary, the job is cut out in terms of commencing any matter in Court against the Commission, either during or after the process of incorporation. The correct route is that a pre-action notice must be served on the Commission, with the details stated under section 17 of the Act. This is to avoid unnecessary waste of precious time and resources, in having to be directed by the Court to serve the requisite pre-action notice on the Commission. This could be avoided with the necessary advice to whoever is filing the suit, even if firmed out to external solicitors.

We now examine the pivotal roles of the company secretary in the process of incorporation and related processes. In doing this, we take the point, as alluded to earlier in this book, that the company secretary has been appointed during the incorporation process, subject to regularization on incorporation.

FORMATION OF A COMPANY

Under common section 18(1) CAMA 2020 and 2004, any two (2) or more persons may initiate and incorporate a company by complying with the requirements of the Act with respect to the type of company being formed. This was where the CAMA 2004 stopped. However, in a provision which is considered in some circles as a breakthrough for small and medium scale companies (it has its downside also), the CAMA 2020 in section 18(2) provides that one person may form and incorporate a private company, while complying with the provisions of the Act with respect to same.

As will be discussed in subsequent chapters, this provision on 'one man' private company has implication(s) in relation to the effective administration of such companies and related matters.

The CAMA prohibits the formation of any association or partnership consisting of more than 20 persons for the purposes of carrying on any business for profit or gain by the association or partnership, or by the individual members of such an association or partnership, except it is registered as a company under the Act (common section 19(1) CAMA 2020 and 2004. This provision limits the number of persons and the extent to which a group of individuals could undertake to do business as a 'group' without being formally incorporated as a registered company.

The CAMA 2020 removed the word 'company' from the above provision as it was under CAMA 2004, leaving only the words 'association' or 'partnership' as the 2004 provision seemed to contradict itself and other provisions of the Act with that word. This provision should be noted specifically. This is because unlike the CAMA 2004, which imposed a fine of ₦25 per day on every member of the association or partnership anytime the number of persons exceeds the stipulated threshold and they carry on business for more than 14 days with the contravention ongoing, the CAMA 2020 hands over to the Commission the discretion to fix the daily fines payable by such person(s) liable. This trend runs through the whole gamut of the Act.

It should be noted that the prohibition on the number of persons that could form and run an association or partnership does not apply to:

- any co-operative society registered in Nigeria under an existing law;
- any partnership that is formed to practice as legal practitioners or accountants, which must be formed by persons qualified to practice as such (common section 19(2) CAMA 2020 and 2004).

This implies that a legal practitioner and a medical practitioner or an accountant, for instance, the latter who does not have legal training and licensed as such to practice as legal practitioner, are not permitted to form a firm of legal practitioners under this exception. So, also, is true, with a firm of accountants, which cannot be formed by a qualified and licensed accountant and a third party who is not so qualified.

Capacity to Form a Company

The Black's Law Dictionary, 9th ed, 235, defines the term 'capacity' as 'the power to create or enter into a legal relation under the same circumstances in which a normal person would have the power to create or enter into such a relation, specifically, the satisfaction of a legal qualification…' It is from the perspective of 'capacity' as legal qualification in terms of company formation that we discuss the issues below.

This is the point from which the effective expertise and knowledge of the company secretary comes to into play in a much more serious manner. This is because any mistake(s) made in the process of incorporating a company, for instance, by allowing disqualified persons under the Act, to form a company, might have serious consequences for the company. This is especially so with respect to the entity being regarded as having been validly incorporated and reaping the benefits of such incorporation. It is, therefore, advisable to strictly comply with all legal requirements for incorporation from the outset.

Under common section 20(1) CAMA 2020 and 2004, a person shall not qualify to join in the formation of a company, if:

- he is less than 18 years of age; or
- he is of unsound mind and has been so found by a Court in Nigeria or elsewhere; (*Hunpunu-Wusu* v. *Hunpunu-Wusu (1969) 1 All NLR, 62*, where the Supreme Court held that the terms 'unsound mind', 'mental illness,' 'mental disorder' and 'insanity,' among others, are interchangeable. In *Adamu* v. *State (2014) LPELR-22696 (SC)*, the Supreme Court defined 'insanity' to be 'any mental disorder, severe enough that it prevents a person from having legal capacity and excuses the person from criminal or civil responsibility. The Court held that insanity is a legal and not a medical standard. It is important to note that not every allegation of unsound mind will suffice here to disqualify a person under this head, as the person must have been so found to be insane by a Court of competent jurisdiction; or
- he is an un-discharged bankrupt; or
- he is disqualified under section 283 CAMA 2020 (which provides for disqualification for directorship), (s. 254 CAMA 2004 disqualifies any person who has been convicted of fraud in connection with promotion, formation and management of a company from being a director in a company.) The person is also disqualified from being able to be part of a team to form a company. Note that section 20(d) of the CAMA also listed persons disqualified under section 281 of the Act. However, there has been a mistake in the CAMA 2020, as section 281 of the Act is the section that provides for appointment of directors for life and the apparent reference would have been to section 280 of the Act which disqualifies fraudulent persons and is on all fours with section 254 of the CAMA 2004;
- it is a corporate body in liquidation (ss. 20(3) CAMA 2020 and 2004.

A person disqualified as above by reason only of being under 18 years may still join in the formation of a company, if two (2) other persons who are not disqualified have subscribed to the memorandum to form the company in question (ss. 20(2) CAMA 2020 and 2004.

A non-Nigerian may also join in the formation of a company, if he has complied with other laws that regulate the rights and capacity of non-Nigerians to undertake or participate in trade or business in Nigeria (ss. 20(4) CAMA 2020 and 2004. This would include the requirements that aliens would have complied with the relevant sections of the *Immigration Act, 2015*, including the requirements for resident permits and the procurement of appropriate visas.

The role of the company secretary in the area just considered is critical. This is especially concerning the disqualification of persons for past fraudulent activities in relation to the promotion, formation and management of companies and the qualification of an alien for participation. Equally important is the item about persons adjudged to be of unsound mind, being that the issue of running a company is too important to the global economy and to the nation at large to be allowed into the hands of persons with questionable sanity.

Being that most times those who promote and actually run companies do not have any legal training or experience, it presupposes that the company secretary assumes the tasks for any requisite background checks in this area to comply with the requirements of the CAMA.

Registration (Incorporation) of a Company

Before proceeding to register a company, the promoter(s) would have chosen and reserved a name for the proposed company. It must be noted that it is not every name that could be reserved at the Commission, as some names are outrightly prohibited from being used, while the use of others names are only restricted or conditional.

A progressive provision has been added to the process of incorporation of companies in Nigeria by section 8 of the *Business Facilitation (Miscellaneous Provisions) Act (BFA), 2022*. The section mandates the Registrar General of the Corporate Affairs Commission (Commission) to ensure, that14 days from the commencement of the Act, all its application processes are automated from the start to the conclusion. This is a welcome development and it is hoped that when fully implemented, it will be a veritable addition to the increasing digitization of the processes at the Commission.

In another good development, the *Nigeria Startup Act, 2022* has made several innovative provisions to assist startup companies to take-off and consolidate their footholds on the Nigerian business arena. The Act establishes the National Council for Digital Innovation and Entrepreneurship (the Council) to administer the provisions of the Act and formulate polices and strategies for its implementation. Section 47 of the Act defines a startup as a 'company in existence for not more than 10 years, with its objectives being the creation, innovation, production, development or adoption of a unique digital technology, innovative product, service or process.' A sole proprietorship or partnership that meets any of the criteria of a startup is given a six-month window to meet the other conditions of being qualified for startup labelling under section 13(2) of the Act. The conditions are:

- it is registered as a limited liability company under the Companies and Allied Matters Act, and has been in existence for a period not more than 10 years from the date of incorporation;
- its objects are innovation, development, production, improvement, and commercialization of a digital technology innovative product or process;
- it is a holder or repository of a product or process of digital technology, or the owner or author of a registered software;
- it has at least one-third local shareholding held by one or more Nigerians as founder or co-founder of the startup.

Section 30 of the Act also mandates the Council, through its secretariat, to collaborate with the Corporate Affairs Commission (the Commission) to designate a separate section on the startup portal and reserve same to ease the processes for startups that conduct transactions at the Commission. In addition, sections 25 thru 37 of the Act have made provisions for diverse incentives for startups, ranging from tax and fiscal incentives, credit guarantee scheme, access to exports facilities, technology transfer and funds repatriation, accessing government loans, access to crowd funding, among many others. Without doubt, the provisions of the Act, when implemented with vigour and fidelity, without the processes being corrupted, will engender a huge boost amongst startups in the country.

Reverting to the Corporate Affairs Commission, the Commission may, on a written application, either in hard copy or through electronic means, and on payment of the prescribed fees, reserve a name pending registration or change of name by a company. However, this is contingent on the confirmation by the Commission that the name is available for use. This reservation could be for a period as the Commission thinks fit but shall not exceed a period of 60 days. During the period of reservation, no other company shall be registered with the reserved name(s) or the names that closely resemble it (s.31 CAMA 2020), (s.32). The express provision for the use of electronic communication in this respect is a new addition by the CAMA 2020, and was not available to clients of the Commission under the CAMA 2004.

The CAMA 2020 made additional provisions with respect to reservation of names for companies, which were not there under CAMA 2004. Under section 31(3)(5) of the Act, the Commission has the power, at any time before issuing a certificate of incorporation to a company, to withdraw or cancel a reserved name, if it is discovered that it is identical to an already registered name or so nearly resemble it as to be likely to deceive. The Commission may also cancel a reservation if it is discovered that it was fraudulently, or otherwise improperly or unlawfully procured.

PROHIBITED NAMES

As already noted, it is not every name proposed for the registration of a company that would be accepted by the Commission. While some names are outrightly prohibited from usage, others are restricted but could be used only on the fulfilment of certain conditions. Section 852 CAMA 2020 provides that no company, limited liability partnership, limited partnership, business name or incorporated trustees, (the CAMA 2004 simply used the phrase 'no company') shall be registered under the Act by a name or trade mark (this is a new addition), which:

- is identical with that by which a company or limited liability partnership in existence is already registered, or nearly resembles that name as to be likely to deceive. (The exception is where the company in existence is in the course of being wound up and signifies its consent in a manner that the Commission requires), (ss. 1 (a); or
- is a name that contains the phrase 'Chamber of Commerce' except it is a company limited by guarantee (ss. 1(b); or
- is a name that, in the opinion of the Commission, is capable of misleading as to the nature or extent of the company's activities or if such a name is undesirable, offensive or otherwise contrary to public policy (ss. 1 (c); or
- in the opinion of the Commission, the name would violate or conflict with any existing trademark or business name or body corporate formed under the Act in Nigeria, unless the consent of the owner of the trade mark,

business name or trustees of the corporate body has been obtained (ss. 1(d).

The above are the items on which there are concurrent provisions on prohibition of their use by the CAMA 2020 and 2004. However, the 2020 CAMA has gone further to add other categories of names that are prohibited:

- a name that contains any word which, in the opinion of the Commission, is likely to mislead the public as to the nationality, race or religion of the persons who wholly own or control the business (ss. (1)(e);
- a name that is, in the opinion of the Commission, deceptive or objectionable, for containing a reference or suggesting an association with any practice, institution or personage, foreign state or government, international organization or brand or is unsuitable; or (ss. (1)(f);
- a name that is capable of undermining public peace and national security (ss. (1)(g).

RESTRICTED NAMES

Under section 852(2) CAMA 2020, no company, limited liability partnership, limited partnership, business name or incorporated trustees shall be registered by certain names, except with the consent of the Commission. Under the previous provision under section 30(2) CAMA 2004, only the word 'company' was used, principally because there was no limited liability partnership and limited partnership as business genres under that regime. The names are those that:

- include the word 'Federal' 'National' 'Regional' 'State' 'Government,' or any other word which in the opinion of the Commission suggests or is calculated to suggest that the company enjoys the patronage of the Government of the Federation or of a State in Nigeria or any ministry or department of government; or
- contains the word 'Municipal' or 'Chartered' or in the opinion of the Commission suggests, or is calculated to suggest, connection with any municipality or other local authority; or
- contains the words 'Co-operative,' 'Building Society,' 'Group' or 'Holding').

Section 852 CAMA 2020 (s. 30 CAMA 2004) gives the Commission the latitude to exercise its discretion in deciding when to register a name in circumstances where it has to proffer an opinion as to the acceptability of a proposed name. Once the Commission exercises its discretion properly in accepting or refusing to register a proposed name, no action shall lie successfully against such an exercise of discretion *(Corporate Affairs Commission* v. *Ayedun (2005) 18 NWLR Pt. 957, 391).*

In the above case, the Commission acting by its powers under section 30 CAMA 2004, refused to register the name Credit Registry Ltd. The matter went to Court and the High Court, relying on section 36(2) CAMA 2004 (which dealt with applicants for company registration giving notice to the Commission to apply to Court for direction), held that the Commission was obliged to so apply to Court in this instance. On appeal, the decision was overturned and the Court of Appeal held that the Commission's exercise of discretion with respect to prohibited and restricted names under section 30 CAMA 2004 (s. 852 CAMA 2020) does not require that the Commission should apply to Court for any direction in that respect. Furthermore, that nothing extraneous should be imported into the clear and unambiguous provision of section 30 to require the Commission to approach the Court*(Ogbonna* v. *A-G Imo State (1992) 1 NWLR Pt. 220, 647; African Newspapers (Nig) Ltd* v. *FRN (1985) 2 NWLR Pt. 6, 137.*

It has also been held that in its decision to refuse to register a name that is identical to an already existing name, the Commission only needs to do a comparative analysis of the names in its data bank, from the way they look and sound, particularly to the business community. The Commission is not required to conduct an etymology of the words used in forming the names in question.*(Mustapha* v. *Corporate Affairs Commission (2008) 11 CLRN 42).* It is noteworthy that this matter actually went on appeal to the Supreme Court, where it was dismissed on another ground, that the appellant had no *locus standi* to sue in the first place. This was because the appellant had sued the Commission in his personal name instead of the name of his aggrieved client, for whom he was to register the company *(Mustapha* v. *Corporate Affairs Commission (2019) 10 NWLR Pt. 1680, 355).*

For the company secretary, the watchword is due diligence. Once a proper background research is undertaken before submitting proposed names to the Commission for reservation and then registration, there is less probability that any negative issue(s) will be encountered at the Commission.

To make the process more effective, this book recommends that, before approaching the Commission for the process of incorporating a company, the company secretary or the solicitor undertaking the incorporation process, should ensure that all the avoidable teething problems are dealt with. This will include issues of restricted and prohibited names, the particular genre of the company to be incorporated and the requirements for such, the issues of the capacity of the initial members to form a company, the capacity of the initial directors, ensuring that a person(s) disqualified under any of the provisions of the CAMA or other laws does not get involved, either as a member or a director, in the affairs of the company.

In other cases where the disqualifying criteria are remediable, this should be remedied before the incorporation documents are submitted to the Commission. Examples would be where a person who is subscribed to the Memorandum is below 18 years, then, this should be remedied by adding other persons who are adults to remedy the defect. Again, if any of the company's proposed objects is rendered illegal by any statute, common law or public policy, it is better to remedy same by deletion of the object(s) in question before submitting the documents to the Commission for registration.

In all the above scenarios, the company secretary is in a vantage position to advise the company's promoters on the most efficient process to adopt in dealing with the Commission. This is to make the process seamless and not turn same into unending rigmarole.

AT THE CORPORATE AFFAIRS COMMISSION (THE COMMISSION)

When the promoter(s) of a company has decided on the nature of the company to incorporate and the name(s) of the company has been approved by the Commission, the next step is to submit the necessary documents, usually referred to as incorporation or registration documents, to the Commission.

Previously, under section 35(2) CAMA 2004, among others, the key documents to be submitted to the Commission are the Memorandum and Articles of Association which constitute the two key constitutional documents for any company to be registered under the Act. Also, the notice of the address of registered office of the company and the head office (if different from the registered office), statement of the list and particulars, together with the consent of persons who are to be the first directors of the company and a statement of the company's authorized share capital, signed by at least one director.

The CAMA 2020 has taken steps to simplify the process of incorporation of companies in a number of ways.

One, it is no longer compulsory to submit the Articles with the Memorandum to the Commission when applying to register a company. This is because under sections 33, 34 and 36(e) of the Act, a default Model Articles would be adopted when a company did not submit a copy of its Articles for registration; and the company will still be registered.

Two, the requirement under section 35(3) CAMA 2004, making it mandatory to submit to the Commission, a statutory declaration, deposed to by a legal practitioner that all the requirements of the CAMA relating to company formation have been complied with, has been jettisoned. (Note that statutory declaration is re-introduced into the registration process by CAMA 2020 by section 41(3), (s. 36(3) CAMA 2004, where the Commission may require a person to declare that he is not dis-qualified under any of the provisions of section 20). The only difference here is that it is optional at this instance for the Commission to request such a declaration from any person(s) or not.

The utility of the requirement of a statutory declaration above is not clear, or at best, is superfluous. This is because section 41(7) CAMA 2020 empowers the Commission to withdraw, cancel or revoke a certificate of incorporation already issued to a company, if it is discovered that it was improperly, unlawfully or fraudulently obtained, which process the Commission may publish in a Federal Government Gazette. The CAMA 2004 did not provide for this.

In place of *statutory declaration* in the CAMA 2004, section 40 (1) CAMA 2020 introduces a *statement of compliance*, which if delivered to the Commission by either the applicant or his agent, suffices. This helps to simplify the process of company registration under the CAMA 2020, by allowing non-lawyers to easily fulfil this requirement. It should be noted that the Commission still has the discretion under the section to accept a *declaration of compliance* on oath by a legal practitioner confirming that compliance with all registration requirements is complete.

When the Commission Will Not Register a Company

When all the documents of incorporation together with the statement of compliance have been delivered to the Commission, section 41 CAMA 2020 (s.36) mandates the Commission to register the Memorandum and Articles of the company. However, the Commission is not obligated to register a company, if it is of the opinion that it should not register the Memorandum and Articles of a proposed company because:

- the documents do not comply with the provisions of the Act, or
- the businesses which the company is to carry on or the objects for which it is formed or any of them, are illegal; or
- any of the subscribers to the Memorandum is incompetent or disqualified in accordance with section 20 of the Act; or
- there is non-compliance with the requirement of any other law as to registration and incorporation of company; or
- the proposed name conflicts with or is likely to conflict with an existing trade mark or business name registered in Nigeria (s. 41(1) CAMA 2020), (s. 36(1)).

If the Commission refuses to register the Memorandum and Articles of a company for any of the reasons stated above, a person aggrieved by that decision may give notice to the Commission to apply to Court for directions. The Commission shall within 21 days of the receipt of such notice apply to the Court for directions (s. 41(2) CAMA 2020), (s. 36(2)). This is the proper section applicable under which the Commission is required to apply to Court, when requested, and not when the Commission refuses to register a company because of the non-suitability of a proposed name, as was attempted by the applicant in *Corporate Affairs Commission* v. *Ayedun (2005) 18 NWLR Pt. 957, 391.* The Court struck down the applicant's request for the Commission to approach the Court for direction in that instance.

Apart from the above instances where the Commission may refuse to register a company, the CAMA 2020 introduced some new grounds under which the Commission may refuse to register some names as companies. For instance, where misleading information has been given to the Commission to register a company, partnership, business name or incorporated trustees, or the name is misleading as to the nature of the company's activities as to be likely to cause harm to the public, the Commission may withdraw registration and direct the entity concerned to change its name (ss. 855 and 856 CAMA 2020).

Again, under section 857 CAMA 2020, a person may send an objection to the Commission's Administrative Proceedings Committee (the Committee) that a company's name that has been registered by the Commission is the same or sufficiently similar to the name wherein the applicant has goodwill.

This is especially so if the allegation is that the name was registered in bad faith, for instance, in order to prevent the applicant from registering the same name or to extort money from him. The respondent will be given the opportunity to justify why the objection should fail, after which the Committee takes a decision to uphold or dismiss the objection. The CAMA 2004 has no provision to this effect. The CAMA 2020 did not say what will happen after the Committee has made a decision and the applicant is not satisfied with it. The obvious resort, however, will be for applicant to approach the Court for redress.

LEGAL EFFECTS OF REGISTRATION OF A COMPANY

Once the Memorandum and Articles of a company are registered, the Commission shall certify under its seal that:

- the company is incorporated;
- for a limited company, that the liability of its members is limited by shares or by guarantee;
- for unlimited company, that the liability of its members is unlimited; and
- that the company is a private or public company (whichever is applicable) (s. 41(5) CAMA 2020), (s. 36(5).

From the date of incorporation of a company as mentioned in the certificate of incorporation, the subscribers to the Memorandum and any other persons that may become members of the company from time to time, shall become a body corporate by the name contained in the Memorandum. They shall be capable of exercising all the powers of an incorporated company, including the power to hold land (property), have perpetual succession and a common seal (if need be). However, depending on the type of company registered, the members shall also have the liability to contribute to the assets of the company in the event of winding-up (s. 42 CAMA 2020), (s. 37)*(Vassilev* v. *Okegbe (2000) 12 NWLR Pt. 681, 347).*

The above provisions are to the effect, in a nutshell, that registration confers distinct legal personality on the company, allowing it to assume a corporate personality of its own, able to sue and be sued in its own name and do all other things that such a status empowers it to do (*STB Plc* v. *Olushola (2008) 1 NWLR Pt. 561, 23; Onuekwusi* v. *Registered Trustees of the Christ Methodist Zion Church (2011) 6 NWLR Pt. 1243, 347).*

What Type of Company Do We Register?

The natural question that arises when everything is set to incorporate a company is the question as to the type of company to be set up. It is the reality that sometimes, company promoters, while having in mind the type(s) of business they would want to engage in, may not fully understand the intricacies, including the legal and regulatory requirements, for registering the type(s) of company that suits their purpose. The company secretary (if already appointed, or the promoter's solicitors) should be able to advise the promoters on the distinct requirements of the CAMA with respect to the different types of companies under the Act and their suitability or otherwise for the intended purpose(s).

Types of Registrable Companies

Under common section 21 of the CAMA 2020 and 2004, three (3) types of companies could be incorporated in Nigeria and each of these could be incorporated either as a private or a public company. A registered company could be:

- **limited by shares**: this is a company having the liability of its members limited by its Memorandum of Association to the amount unpaid (if any) on the shares held by each of the members (common section 21(1)(a) CAMA 2020 & 2004). The vast majority of the applications submitted to the Commission for registration fall under this category;
- **limited by guarantee**: this is a company having the liability of its members limited by its Memorandum of Association to such amount as each member undertakes to contribute to the assets of the company in the event of its being wound-up (usually used for the promotion of commerce, sports, religion, science, arts, culture, education, research, charity or similar objects (common section 21 (1)(b) CAMA 2020 & 2004.

Companies limited by guarantee would appear to be of a special class, as both the CAMA 2020 and 2004 made detailed provisions regarding their registration and operations. The CAMA 2020 even went further with new and far-reaching provisions on the registration and operations of this category of company. A few instances will suffice for the present purposes:

- Section 26(2)(3) CAMA 2020, like the CAMA 2004 (s.26(3(4), declares void any provisions in the Memorandum or Articles of a company limited by guarantee that purports to give any person a right to participate in the company's divisible profits or to divide the company's undertaking into shares or interests;

- A company limited by guarantee cannot be registered as limited by shares;
- Furthermore, a company limited by guarantee is prohibited from having the object of making profits for distribution to its members. A default in this respect will have all officers and members who are aware of the carrying on of such business liable to pay off the debts and liabilities incurred by the company in carrying on such business. Additionally, the company and every such member and officer shall be liable to a penalty as prescribed by the Commission for every day during which the company carries on such business (s.26(11) CAMA 2020). Note: under section 26(6) CAMA 2004, the penalty was ₦100.00 for every day of default;
- if a company limited by guarantee is wound up, any of its properties remaining, after the discharge of its debts and liabilities shall not be distributed to its members but be transferred to another company limited by guarantee with similar objects or applied to some charitable object as shall be determined by the members prior to the dissolution of the company (s. 26(15) CAMA 2020), (s. 26 (10));
- Under section 26(5) CAMA 2004, the Memorandum of a company limited by guarantee shall not be registered without the authority of the Attorney-general of the Federation. The provision had no qualification or exception.

However, the experiences gathered from the year 1990, when CAMA 2004 was passed into law and became operational until its repeal in 2020, showed that the above provision frustrated a lot of persons and groups that sought to register companies limited by guarantee. This was because communication of the consent or withholding of same by the Attorney-General of the Federation (AGF) never came back, in most cases, from that office to the promoters of the companies. For some of such promoters, it was a dead-end. This should not have been the case, as the AGF would have, and in-fact, should have, delegated the function to trusted subordinates and made it very efficient.

Having realized the above difficulty, the CAMA 2020 made detailed provisions for overriding the requirement of the consent of the Attorney-General of the Federation in the registration process, when unduly delayed.

Firstly, the Attorney-General of the Federation has 30 days within which to give his consent, once there are no objection(s) to the Memorandum submitted by the proposed company or any other cogent reason(s) for not granting approval to register the company, as limited by guarantee. Also, where the office of the Attorney-General requires further information from the promoters, the 30-day period will then start to run from the day the Attorney-General's office receives the additional information (s. 26(5)(6) CAMA 2020).

Secondly, where the promoters submitted all valid documents to the office of the Attorney-General and no decision is made by that office after 30 days, then the promoters shall place an advert in three (3) national daily newspapers and invite objections (if any) to the incorporation of the company. Any objection(s) to the registration shall be forwarded to the Commission within 28 days of the last publication and the Commission shall consider the objection(s) and may either uphold or reject same. The Commission will then inform the promoter(s) accordingly of its decision in that respect (s. 26(7) (a)-(f) CAMA 2020).

Thirdly, if the Commission is satisfied that the Memorandum and Articles submitted by the promoters of the company have complied with the relevant provisions of the CAMA, the Commission shall then place its own advertisement of the application for registration of the company in three (3) national daily newspapers, inviting objection(s) to the registration of the company, also within 28 days of the last publication in the newspapers. If any objection(s) is received, the Commission shall consider same and may uphold or reject same (s. 26 (8)(9) CAMA 2020).

If no objection(s) is received after the Commission's advertisement or the objections(s) received was considered and rejected, the Commission is empowered to exercise its discretion and register the company as one limited by guarantee. The Commission will then issue a certificate of registration, accordingly (s. 26(10) CAMA 2020).

It is important to note the reluctance of the framers of the CAMA 2020 to override the authority of the Attorney-General of the Federation (AGF) to grant approval to register a company limited by guarantee. This reluctance is understandable. Under section 150 of the 1999 Constitution of the Federal Republic of Nigeria (as amended), the Attorney-General is the Chief Law Officer of the Federation with enormous powers and almost not answerable to anybody, in principle *(Elelu-Habeeb* v. *AG Federation (2012) 13 NWLR Pt. 1318, 423; A-G Federation* v. *ANPP & Ors (2003) 15 NWLR Pt. 844, 600).* This explains why the process of overriding the Attorney-General's consent under the CAMA 2020 is so intricate as seen above and would take, if diligently pursued by all concerned, a minimum period of not less than 6 to 8 months to achieve, at the minimum.

Having said the above, the new provision in the CAMA overriding the consent of the Attorney General of the Federation is also an indictment on that office for perceived inefficiency in this respect, over the years. Otherwise, one would wonder what the difficulty is with the office of the Attorney General, as powerful as it is, with its full complement of full-time staff and aides, and the capacity to recruit more staff as desired, that will make it incapable for the office to assent or deny assent to applications to register companies limited by guarantee, for years on end. It is a sad commentary on the work ethic and general inefficiency of the country's civil and public services, in particular, and also the generality of the workforce, in general. One could only imagine the unnecessary additional costs to be incurred by the applicant(s) and the Commission in overriding the consent of the Attorney General in this respect.

- **Unlimited:** this is where a company does not have a limit on the liability of its members (common section 21(1)(c) CAMA 2020 and 2004. Under section 25 of the CAMA 2020 an unlimited company is now required to be registered with a share capital not below the minimum prescribed for other companies limited by shares under section 27(2)(a) of the Act, which is, one hundred thousand naira (₦100,000.00) for a private company and two million naira (₦2,000,000.00) for a public company. The figures were ten thousand naira (₦10,000.00) and five hundred thousand naira (₦500,000.00) for private and public companies respectively, under section 27(2)(a) CAMA 2004.

For whichever type of company to be registered, the primary role of the company secretary would be to ensure that the relevant provisions of the Act with respect to the specific genre of company are complied with and within time, when they are time sensitive. This is important because several provisions of the CAMA in this area have imposed varying monetary penalties on breaches and most of the penalties are continuing fines, which enure, as long as the default persists.

It is now proper to consider in details the implications of choosing to register a company either as a private or public company.

PRIVATE COMPANY

The CAMA 2020 has made tremendous changes to the nature and operations of a private company, apparently in reaction to the emerging globalized business world. Under common section 22(1) CAMA 2020 and 2004, a private company is one that its Memorandum of Association says is private. This is an important provision, being that once a company is a private company by the registered Memorandum and Articles, the Courts are reluctant to use any other extraneous factors to classify it otherwise.

The above issue came up for consideration by the Supreme Court in *Orji* v. *Zaria Ind. Ltd & Anor (1992) 1 NWLR Pt. 216, 124),* where the Court held that the fact that the Kaduna State Government held a 40.9% stake in the company's shares does not, *ipso facto*, make the company a public company for the purposes of turning the employees therein into those whose employment had statutory flavour. The company was registered as a private company and remained so notwithstanding the fact that the highest single shareholder in the company was the State Government. This also underscores the great importance of the contents and provisions of a company's constitutional documents, that is, the Memorandum and Articles of Association, as the bedrocks on which the company is built.

By section 22(2) CAMA 2004, private companies were mandated, without exception, to restrict, by their Articles, the transfer of their shares. The CAMA 2020 has done away with this mandatory restriction and gives a private company a discretion with the use of the phase 'may restrict the transfer of its shares.' In construing a statute, like the CAMA, the word 'may' is mostly used to import discretion or permissiveness *(Edewor* v. *Uwegba & Anor) (1987) 1 NWLR Pt. 50, 313)*, unlike the word 'shall', that was used by the CAMA 2004, which imports obligation or mandatory direction *(NLNG Ltd* v. *ADIC Ltd (1995) 8 NWLR Pt. 46, 677; Kaliel* v. *Aliero (1999) 4 NWLR Pt. 597, 139).*

Having removed the blanket restriction on the powers of private companies to transfer their shares, the CAMA 2020 also gave them the power to provide that:

- the company shall not, without the *consent of all its members*, sell assets having a value of more than 50% of the total value of the company's assets;
- A member shall not sell that member's shares in the company to a non-member(s) without offering other existing members the right of first refusal to purchase such shares;

- A member or a group of members acting together, are not allowed to sell or agree to sell more than 50% of the company's shares to a non-member(s), except the non-member(s) offers to buy all the existing members' interests on the same terms as those being negotiated with those selling their shares (s. 22(2)(a)(b)(c) CAMA 2020).

While the CAMA 2020 tried to ease the restrictions on the powers of a private company to transfer its shares, it also took note that a private company is not a public company and should not, under any guise, have an unfettered right to transfer shares to outsiders, like a public company. The *right of pre-emption*, as seen above, which is a right to buy before others, (*Black's Law Dictionary, 9th ed, 1297)*, is usually used to ensure that a company's shares are retained, as much as possible, within the company by the members, except when no existing member(s) wants to acquire such shares, before same are offered to outsiders.

For the company secretary, certain issues are to be noted from the above considered provisions under section 22 (a)(b) and (c) CAMA 2020.

The first issue is that the regime of the mandatory restrictions by the Articles of private companies under CAMA 2004 on the transfer of its shares, without any qualification or discretion, is gone. Also, gone are all the jurisprudence and judicial affirmations of that regime by some popular Nigerian cases, including *Okoya* v. *Santili (1990) 2 NWLR Pt. 131, 172; New Resources Intl Ltd & Anor* v. *Oranusi (2011) 2 NWLR Pt. 1230, 102,* among many others.

The second issue is that the shareholding threshold of individual members of a private company, especially large shareholders, now becomes critical in determining whether any share transfer among the members can take place. This is in order not to offend subsection (a) and (c) of section 22 CAMA 2020, which would invalidate any such transfer(s) of shares or assets, being mandatory provisions. In this respect, the correctness and proper keeping of the register of members sanctioned under section 109 CAMA 2020, for guidance, becomes critical also.

The third issue is the requirement for offering to members of a company the *right of first refusal* by a member who intends to sell his shares. The above provision does not state the modalities for such offering. However, this book submits that any such offer must be in writing and must state a time limit, which must be reasonable (to be determined on a case-by-case basis), within which any member interested should accept to buy such shares. The company's Articles should make provisions for this. The Supreme Court has held that what amounts to a reasonable time in any occasion is not static and must be determined with respect to the peculiar facts and circumstances of each case *(Pam & Anor* v. *Mohammed & Anor (2008) 5-6 SC Pt. 1, 83; Abiegbe & Anor* v. *Ugbodume & Anor (1973) 1 SC, 103).*

The fourth issue is that section 22(a) CAMA 2020, as noted above, requires the consent of all its members, if a company is to sell assets having a value of more than 50% of the total value of its assets. The provision did not also state the manner or modality for the members' consent to any such sale. However, if 'consent' means, 'agreement' 'permission' 'approval' or 'result of coming into harmony of accord, as affirmed by the Supreme Court in *Abdulkarim* v. *Incar Nig. Ltd (1992) 7 SCNJ, 366,* then, it is submitted that any such consent by the members of a company must be in writing. In this context, however, this book proposes that the members' written consent to the transaction does not have to be individually given by every member, as members' resolution (written or in a general meeting) approving such a sale without any dissent should suffice for the purpose. For clarity, it is better for a company's Articles to provide details for this also.

Apart from the noted innovations by the CAMA 2020, the earlier provision under the CAMA 2004 relating to the items below were retained by the CAMA 2020:

- in a private company, the total number of members shall not exceed 50 persons (excluding *bona fide* employees or ex-employees who continue to be members). It is noteworthy that for purposes of determining the number of members in a company under this sub-section, joint holders are counted as a single member (common section 22(3)(4) CAMA 2020 and 2004);
- a private company shall not, unless authorized by law, invite the public to subscribe to any of its shares or debentures; and shall not deposit money for fixed periods or payable at call, notwithstanding whether such a deposit is interest bearing or not (common section 22(5) CAMA 2020 and CAMA 2004).

It is not clear why the CAMA, both 2020 and 2004, imposed restrictions on private companies depositing money (obviously in financial institutions) for fixed periods or on call. This is even if the funds are to be deposited on interest yielding basis. While we understand the logic behind section 22(5)(a) of the Act that restricts the right of a private company from inviting the public to subscribe to any of its shares or debentures, it is difficult to understand why a private company, duly authorized by its board of directors, cannot fix idle funds for a period or on a call while earning interest thereon, pending when the targeted project(s) execution is finalized.

Another aspect of the issue is that of enforcement of the provision. Laws are not simply made for the sake of perceived correctness, they must be capable of being enforced, otherwise the making of the law becomes an effort in futility. The question is: who will enforce the provision restricting private companies from fixing funds in financial institutions, whereas these institutions actually go out of their ways to solicit such deposits from such companies, while offering attractive interest rates? How will the provision be enforced, if it should, and by whom? It is even doubtful if financial institutions in Nigeria are actually aware that a provision of this nature does exist in the CAMA. This book submits that this provision is an unnecessary hair-splitting by the framers of the Act and should be expunged from Act.

Now, leaving all of the above, if a private company defaults in complying with the provisions of section 22 as stated above, it ceases to be entitled to the privileges and exemptions reserved for private companies under the CAMA. Thereafter, the Act will apply to the private company as if it is not a private company (common section 23(1) CAMA 2020 and 2004).

On the application of a company or a person interested, and where a good cause has been shown that the failure to comply with the provisions of section 22 was due to a mistake or inadvertence, the Court may grant relief. Equally, where it is shown that non-compliance was due to other sufficient cause(s), or that it is just and equitable to grant relief to the company, the Court may grant such relief from the consequences of non-compliance with section 22 (common section 23(2) CAMA 2020 and 2004).

While the provisions of section 23(1) of the Act above seek to make companies comply with the provisions of section 22 of the Act, section 23(2) creates a leeway for companies to escape the consequences of any non-compliance. This would be by applying to and establishing before a Court that the non-compliance was either accidental or an oversight or any just cause is shown that would convince the Court to exercise its discretion in favour of the company.

A person who is appointed a company secretary in a private company should, except where inevitable, avoid getting to the stage where an application would have to be made to the Court to relieve the company of liability under section 23(2) of the Act. Apart from the fact that company resources would have to be spent to rectify the lapse(s), such scenario does not usually impress companies' boards and senior management.

THE PUBLIC COMPANY

A public company is one other than a private company and does not have all the inhibitions of a private company as listed above, for instance, not being able to invite the public to subscribe to its shares.

The Memorandum of a public company shall state that it is a public company (common section 24 CAMA 2020 and 2004). Unlike a private company that can be formed by a single individual under the CAMA 2020, the minimum number of members for a public company is two (2) and there is still no limit as to the maximum number of members. Aside these differences, there are other material differences that should be noted that exist between a private and a public company. A few of them will serve as examples here.

Some Differences between Public and Private Companies Limited by Shares

Apart from the number of persons that could be members of a private company (maximum 50) and public companies (unlimited), it should be noted that unlike a private company, there is no 'small company' classification for public companies under the CAMA 2020. This aside, there are some other differences between private and public companies limited by shares, including:

- under section 235 CAMA 2020 (s. 211), every public company must hold a general meeting of the members (statutory meeting) within 6 months of being incorporated. This is not required for private companies;
- under section 330 CAMA 2020, private companies that fall into the 'small company' category are not mandated to appoint a company secretary, while public companies must appoint a company secretary (ss. 2);
- a private company shall not, unless authorized by law, invite the public to subscribe to any of it shares or debentures; and shall not deposit money for fixed periods or payable at call, whether it is interest bearing or not (common section 22(5) CAMA 2020 and 2004). This restriction does not apply to public companies;
- under section 278 CAMA 2020 (s.252), there is a restriction on the appointment of a person who is seventy years (70) and above as a director of a public company. Such a person must disclose the fact of his age to members of the company in a general meeting. Non-disclosure attracts

penalty as specified by the Commission. This restriction is not applicable to directors in private companies;

- the minimum issued share capital for a private company is one hundred thousand naira (₦100,000.00), while that for a public company is two million naira (₦2,000,000.00). The figures were ₦10,000.00 and ₦100,000.00 respectively under the CAMA 2004;
- under section 287(1) CAMA 2020 (s.261(1), no single motion is allowed to be used to elect two or more persons into office as directors of a public company, except the meeting had earlier resolved that the motion would be moved as such and there was no dissenting vote. A private company does not have this restriction in electing its directors;
- under section 332 CAMA 2020 (s.293), there are statutory requirements for the appointment of a person as the company secretary of a public company: either a legal practitioner, chartered secretary, chartered accountant or other recognized accounting qualifications, etc. There is no such requirement for the appointment of company secretary of a private company. The directors of a private company would simply have to be satisfied that the person to be so appointed appears to them to have the requisite experience and knowledge to function as a company secretary.

CAPACITY AND POWERS OF A COMPANY

The cardinal question now has to be: having been successfully registered, what are those things that an incorporated company can do after being imbued with the powers as noted above?

Upon being registered by the Commission and consequentially being issued with the appropriate certificate of incorporation under the CAMA, a company shall, except in circumstances where its Memorandum or any other enactment provides otherwise, have all the powers of a natural person of full capacity. This should be, however, for the furtherance of its authorized business or objects (section 43(1) CAMA 2020), (s.38(1). As would be seen below, the phrase in 'furtherance of its authorized business' has been redefined, in the context of the modern company law and practice, where the effect of the doctrine of *ultra vires* has been watered down, over the years, in most, if not all, common law jurisdictions.

Apart from the above powers, it should be noted that, in general, a company is usually considered as having implied powers to do anything that is incidental to the realization of its expressed objects, unless any such act is expressly prohibited by law or the company's Memorandum *(Rolled Steel Product (Holdings) Ltd* v. *British Steel Corporation (1982) 3 WLR, 715; Charlesworth & Cain, 86).* For instance, a trading company is considered to have an implied power to borrow money for its businesses and also the power to give security, when required, to borrow such money *(General Auction Estate and Monetary Co.* v. *Smith (1891) 3 Ch., 432; Charlesworth & Cain, 84).*

In Nigeria, even with their acknowledged implied powers as noted above, a company is prohibited from making any direct or indirect donation or gift of its property or funds to a political party or association or for any political purpose. It could be explained that this prohibition is still in accord with a company having powers to do anything only in furtherance of its businesses, being that donating to a political party or association cannot be said to be in furtherance of any company's businesses.

When there is a breach of this provision, the officer in breach and any member that voted for the breach shall be jointly liable to refund to the company the amount or value of the offending donation or gift (s. 43(2) CAMA 2020), (s.38 (2).

PROOF OF INCORPORATION

Sometimes it is not enough to simply affirm that a company has been registered by the Commission and therefore possesses all the powers of a natural person. Situations may arise, especially during litigation or other judicial processes, where it would become necessary to establish that a company has been duly incorporated. This could be in order to enjoy a particular status or to establish or prove a particular point. The certificate of incorporation issued to a company is *prima facie* evidence that all the requirements of the CAMA regarding registration of companies and matters precedent and incidental thereto, have been complied with. It is also evidence that the company is a duly registered one under the Act (s. 41(6) CAMA 2020), (s.36(6).

In order to prove incorporation of a company, therefore, a person has to produce the certificate of incorporation, as a starting point. It should be noted that it is primarily the duty of an incorporated company to prove its legal personality when required to do so, except the other party admits such a status *(Zenith Plastics Ind. Ltd* v. *Samotech Ltd (2007)16 NWLR Pt. 1060, 315; ACB Plc* v. *Emostrade Ltd (2002) 8 NWLR Pt. 770, 501; Reg. Trustees of Apostolic Church* v. *A-G Midwestern State (1972) 7 NSCC, 247).*

In *NNPC* v. *Lutin Investments Ltd & Anor (2006) 2 NWLR Pt. 965, 506; a case* wherein the appellant (NNPC) alleged before the Courts that there were two entities registered as Lutin Investments Ltd and that they only dealt with one of the entities. However, the appellant's inability to produce the certificate(s) of incorporation during the pendency of the suit from the High Court to the Supreme Court, meant that the Supreme Court had no choice but to agree with the lower Courts, that the non-production of the certificate(s) of incorporation to prove incorporation of the other said company was fatal *(House of Reps.* v. *SPDCN (2010) 11 NWLR Pt. 1205, 213).*

It has to be noted that being *prima facie* evidence of registration, the validity of a certificate of incorporation could be impeached, if any of the disqualifying factors stated in the Act is proven to be true. For instance, if misleading information were submitted to the Commission by the company promoters or that the registration of the company was, in any way, procured illegally or otherwise against the express provision(s) of the Act, the certificate of incorporation, though issued, could be withdrawn by the Commission under sections 855 and 856 CAMA 2020. This will be a rebuttal of the presumption of regularity in the registration process, that it was carried out in a manner substantially regular *(Torri* v. *National Park Services of Nigeria (2011) 13 NWLR Pt. 1264, 152.)*

CHANGE OF NAME BY A COMPANY

The process of choosing a name and submitting the relevant incorporation documents have been completed and the company has now been registered. It is important to note that a company already registered by the Commission may, under certain circumstances decide or be compelled by the Commission to change its name. This could happen in the following instances:

Change of a Conflicting Name

If, on its first registration or re-registration with a new name, a company is registered through inadvertence or otherwise with a name that is identical to that of an existing company, or so nearly resembling it as to be likely to deceive, the latter registered company may, with the approval of the Commission, change its name. This is where a company changes its name on its own volition.

If, on the other hand, it is the Commission that directs the company to change its name, the company concerned shall change its name within a period of six (6) weeks from the date of such direction by the Commission. However, the Commission has the discretion to allow a longer time for the name change (section 30(1) CAMA 2020), (s.31(1). The Commission has the power to prescribe a continuing penalty for a company flouting its direction(s) in this respect. This penalty was ₦25 per day under the CAMA 2004 but is now to be prescribed by the Commission under the CAMA 2020.

A classic manifestation of this latter scenario was in the case of *Capital Oil Plc* v. *Capital Oil & Gas Ind. Ltd & Ors (2021) (LPELR-54986),* where Capital Oil Plc, the plaintiff/appellant, was registered in 1985, whereas, Capital Oil & Gas Ind. Ltd, the defendant/respondent, was registered in 2001. On being made aware of the existence of another company with a name likely to confuse the members of the public, and which, according to the Court records, actually confused the public, the appellant wrote to the Commission on this. The Commission directed the defendant/respondent to change its name. The defendant/respondent was said to have refused to do so.

After several engagements between the parties for a resolution failed, in 2008, the plaintiff/appellant went to Court against the defendant/respondent to force the change of name. As legal proceedings began, the parties further explored amicable resolution and this time agreed on terms of settlement to resolve the dispute. The Court entered the terms of settlement as a consent judgment. However, it was Capital Oil Plc, the plaintiff/appellant who actually agreed to receive the sum of ₦100 million naira (which was later re-negotiated to the sum of ₦230 million naira), to change its own name. The initial sum of ₦100 million was later returned to the defendant/respondent due to some complicated developments, which bordered, in the opinion of this book, on lack of proper administrative and legal directions within the respective companies. As at the time of the Court of Appeal's decision on the matter in 2021, the judgment sum had still not been paid to the plaintiff/appellant.

Possible Lessons from the Capital Oil's Case

A few lessons could, in general, be learnt from the Capital Oil's case. However, for the plaintiff/appellant's company secretary, in particular, and the company's senior management in general, there are a few things that should be pointed out from the outcome of that case, as learning points:

- Since the plaintiff/appellant, that is, Capital Oil Plc, notified the Commission of the breach of its registered name and the Commission requested the defendant/respondent to change its name and it refused to do so, what action did the Commission take against the defendant/respondent? This is because under the then section 31(2) CAMA 2004, if a company refuses to change its name when directed to do so by the Commission, the penalty was ₦25.00 (twenty-five naira) per day of default until compliance. The question that arises for an answer is: was this provision of the CAMA or any other one for that matter, enforced by the Commission against the defendant/respondent for failure to obey the direction of the Commission, and if so, what had been the outcome? Or, was the Commission powerless in that respect?

- Why did the Commission not file a suit and get an order of Court to compel the defendant/respondent company to change its name, in the form of seeking the Court's direction in the matter, as allowed under section 742 CAMA 2020, wherein the Commission can approach the Court for directions on any aspect(s) of its operations?
- From the processes filed by the parties, it was disclosed during the legal proceedings that the plaintiff/appellant returned the ₦100 million paid to them by the defendant/respondent as the consent judgment sum. This was allegedly on the ground that the board of directors of the defendant/respondent did not approve the payment. The questions that arise are:
  i. whose duty was it to get the respondent's board approval before the payment was made?
  ii. who complained that the respondent's board did not approve the payment to the appellant?
  iii. to whom was the complaint of the lack of approval of the payment by the respondent's board made?
  iv. who actually ordered a return of the N100Million already paid to the plaintiff/appellant by the defendant/respondent, when the Court's judgment had not been set aside?
  v. again, instead of asking that the judgment sum already paid to the appellant be returned to the respondent, could the respondent's board or general meeting not have exercised their powers to ratify the payment already made to the appellant and closed the matter?
- Finally, since the Court of Appeal ruled that the consent judgment executed by the parties at the High Court was still binding on the parties, what has been the reason(s) why the plaintiff/appellant has not executed the judgment, being a monetary judgment, against the

defendant/respondent through any of the known and effective judgement enforcement mechanisms?

We answer that there is no reason that could have stopped the execution of the judgment, especially since matter ended at the Court of Appeal (even if an appeal has been filed to the Supreme Court, except there has been a stay of execution of the judgement ordered), which re-confirmed the subsistence of the consent judgment.

The above questions are important being that such an uncomplicated matter has been going through the country's Court system for more than 20 years. The company secretary is in a good position to advise the appellant's board and management on the strategy to realize the judgment sum in the suit. (The author is not privy to the internal workings of the appellant company and the advice the company secretary proffered). This is because from the records of proceedings at the Court of Appeal, it would appear that the respondent simply used the legal proceedings to buy time and dribbled the appellant company around. As much as possible this should not be allowed to have lingered as much as it did. Company secretaries have vital roles to play in bringing matters of this nature to final resolutions, much earlier, that is, if the board and executive management listen to and implement their suggestions and advice.

Leaving the above commentaries, the Commission may also require a company to change its name if it is discovered that such a name conflicts with an existing trade mark or business name registered in Nigeria, prior to the registration of the company. This is where the consent of the owner of the trademark or business name has not been received. A classical case on this is that of *Niger Chemists Ltd* v. *Nigeria Chemists Ltd (1961) All NLR, 171,* where the defendant was restrained by an injunction from using the name 'Nigeria Chemists' to trade as chemists in the same area and the same line of business as the plaintiff, being that the names were confusing the public (s.30(4) CAMA 2020), (s.31(4).

We have seen above the difficulties that could sometimes arise when companies are directed by the Commission to change their names, already registered by the Commission. More often than not, the matter ends up in protracted litigation, a situation which we believe, the CAMA wanted to avoid by providing for the initial intervention of the Commission on such occasions. The efficacy of the Commission's intervention in matters of this nature is not clear, being that several cases have gone to Court on this score and dragged on for years. There is, however, a possibility that the Commission settles some cases of this nature administratively, though not brought to the public domain.

Voluntary Change of a Company's Name

Once a company's name has been registered by the Commission, the company is at liberty to change its name whenever it wants. Under section 30(3) CAMA 2020, by a special resolution and with the approval of the Commission in writing, a company is allowed to change its name (s.31(3). No approval is required from the Commission if the change is simply to add the suffix 'Ltd' for 'Plc,' when a public company converts to a private company or vice versa.

The change of name, once approved, shall be reflected in a new certificate of incorporation to be issued by the Commission to the company. In terms of effect, a company's change of name does not, in any way, mean that a new company has been formed or that a new condition(s) has been imposed on the company. The company is perpetually deemed formed on the date of issuance of the first certificate of incorporation *(Oshkosh B'gosh Inc* v. *Dan Marbel Inc Ltd (1989) BCLC, 507; Cross* v. *Aurora Group Ltd (1988) 4 NZCLC 64, 909,* in *Mayson, French and Ryan, Company Law 21st ed., 87).*

Of note also is that a name change does not affect any of the company's rights or obligations, neither does it render defective any legal proceedings by or against the company. Legal proceedings that could have been commenced by or against the company in the old name can proceed with the new name (s. 30(6) CAMA 2020), (s. 31(6) *(Sambawa Farms Ltd* v. *Bank of Agriculture (2015) LPELR-25939; Nagarta Integrated Farms* v. *Nagoda & Ors (2016) LPELR-40266).* In practice, however, where legal proceedings are already pending by or against a company before a change of its name, the company (more suitably) will require the leave of Court to substitute the company's new name for the old one on the Court processes. All the other consequential changes to the processes thereto will follow.

When companies have successfully changed names, the Commission is mandated to periodically publish their names in a national daily and the Commission's website (s. 30(7) CAMA 2020), (s. 31(7). It should be noted that under the CAMA 2004, the Commission was expected to publish the names in a gazette only, which was considered evidence of successful change of name, and there was no provision for publication on its website.

It has been held that a company registry, like the Commission, does not have an independent power of its own to rename a company. The power given to the registry in this respect is to direct the company to change its name as allowed by law. Also, that the registry cannot be ordered by a Court to effect a name change for a company, if not so authorized by the enabling law, here the CAMA, or any other applicable statute. The Commission can and usually, in appropriate circumstances, apply to Court to order a company in question to change its name and the company concerned is duty bound to comply with the order of Court *(Halifax Plc* v. *Halifax Repossessions Ltd (2004) BCC 281, Mayson et al., 71).*

In changing a company's name (whether voluntarily or by the direction of the Commission or otherwise), the company secretary would be saddled with most of the responsibilities in that regard. From calling the appropriate meetings as directed, to working with the board of directors on the requisite resolution, to liaising with the Commission on all aspects of the process, the company secretary is central to the whole process. Added to this will be the post change of name responsibilities. Being the communicating link between the company, its members, stakeholders and the outside world, after a successful change of name, the company secretary is to ensure that the requisite post-change alterations, modifications and notifications are effected accordingly, including:

- changing the names displayed outside the registered office of the company and elsewhere, including its correspondences (letters, emails, etc.);
- reprinting the company's stationeries to reflect the new name, including cheque books, letterheads, memo pads, etc and ensuring the destruction of the old ones;
- ensuring that the company's website and other electronic media outlets are consequentially changed to the reflect the new name;
- make a new common seal (if needed, as this is no longer compulsory for any company under the CAMA 2020), (s.98) (under s.74 CAMA 2004, a common seal was compulsory for all companies);
- send notifications of the change of name to the members, advisers, bankers, external solicitors, consultants, auditors, other stakeholders and all relevant regulatory authorities, aside the Commission;
- make a general advertorial to the general public notifying of the change of name. This could be done through wide-circulating newspapers and the company's website (*Luke Thomas, ICSA Company Secretaryship Handbook 6th ed., 112 (ICSA).*

COMMENCING BUSINESS AFTER INCORPORATION

A company is at liberty to commence business after its incorporation documents have been fully registered and the company issued with a certificate thereby. However, for companies in certain sectors of the economy, other formalities are still required to be fulfilled before they may fully commence business after incorporation:

- under section 733 CAMA 2020 (s.553), every bank, insurance company, or a deposit, provident or a benefit society shall, before it commences business and also on the first Monday in February and the first Tuesday in August of every year, during which it carries on business, submit to the Commission a Statement in the form of the one in the 14th Schedule to the Act or as near to that as circumstances may admit;
- a copy of the Statement shall be put up in a conspicuous place at the registered office of the company and in every branch office or place where the business of the company is carried on;
- in default, a continuing daily fine is to be imposed by the Commission on the company and on every director and manager (under the CAMA 2004, it was a continuing fine of ₦100.00 for every day of default);
- every member in such a company and every creditor shall be entitled to a copy of the Statement on the payment of a sum prescribed by the Commission. Under the CAMA 2004, the sum to be paid was ₦1.00, which explains why the fine is now left to the discretion of the Commission.
- for the purposes of the CAMA, a company that carries on insurance business in common with any other business or businesses is deemed to be an insurance company.

In practice, what the company secretary does is to ensure that the statement required under this section is displayed at the company's head office, as a starting point. Once this has been done, a copy of the statement is then sent to the respective branches of the company for display and compliance. This is also the procedure for replacement statements. This is important because, as seen above, there is a possible continuing penalty that the Commission could impose on companies for non-compliance.

COMPANY WITH FOREIGN PARTICIPATION

Aside from having to be incorporated in Nigeria to carry on business, a Nigerian company that has foreign participation is prohibited from commencing business in Nigeria without registering with the Nigerian

Investment Promotion Commission (NIPC) (s.20 NIPC Act, Cap N117 LFN 2004). The Commission is an agency of the Federal Government responsible for encouraging and promoting investments into the Nigerian economy (ss.17 and 20 *NIPC Act)* Additionally, such a company with foreign participation is not permitted to engage in certain areas of business, including the production of arms and ammunitions, narcotic drugs and psychotropic substances and the production of military and paramilitary uniforms and accoutrements (ss.18 and 31 NIPC Act). Once the Nigerian entity with foreign participation has complied with all the requirements for registration under the Act, the Commission is mandated to register such a company within 14 working days (s.20(2).

There has been a new addition to the relevant provisions of the NIPC Act by the *Business Facilitation (Miscellaneous Provisions) Act (BFA) 2022.* Section 58 of the schedule to the BFA has amended section 20 of the NIPC Act by adding that 'an enterprise registered in Nigeria, which subsequently acquires foreign participation after the commencement of business, shall, within three months of such acquisition, register with the Commission.' This is a lacuna-filing provision.

To further encourage foreign participation in Nigerian enterprises, the Federal Government, through the NIPC Act, has given guarantees to foreign investors for unconditional transferability of their funds through authorized dealers, that is, with respect to dividends, profits (net of taxes), funds for foreign loan service, proceeds of enterprise liquidation, among others. There is also guarantee against nationalization and expropriation of the enterprises that foreigners have invested in (ss.24 and 25 NIPC Act). In simple terms, 'expropriation' is the act of taking away someone's money or property without any compensatory payment to the person *(Statoil Nig. Ltd* v. *Inducon Nig. Ltd (2014) 9 NWLR Pt. 1411, 56).*

PARTICIPATION INVOLVING TRANSFER OF FOREIGN TECHNOLOGY

If the participation of a foreign entity in a Nigerian company involves technology transfer to Nigerians, then there is a mandatory requirement to register the technology transfer agreement or contract with the National Office for Technology Acquisition and Promotion (NOTAP) under the *NOTAP Act, Cap N68, LFN 2004.* This registration enables the foreigner to repatriate profits, dividends and other payables in the future from Nigeria without any difficulty. This registration has to be done within 60 days of the execution of the agreement or contract in question between the parties (s. 5(2) NOTAP Act).

Although 60 days is stipulated under the Act, as above, as the time limit to register the technology agreement or contract, section 48 of the schedule to the *Business Facilitation (Miscellaneous Provisions) Act (BFA) 2022* amends section 5(2) of the NOTAP Act and adds a proviso to the above provision. The proviso is to the effect that 'provided that companies in their first two years of business operation shall not be liable to late registration penalties where such contracts are registered before the end of the second year of their business operation.' This proviso effectively extends the registration period for the agreement or contract to two years, with respect to companies that just started business. This would seem to suggest that companies that have been in business for many years before entering into such an agreement or contract will not be able to enjoy the two-year concession.

Questions have arisen about the effect of non-registration of contracts and agreements that are otherwise registrable under the NOTAP Act. Also, whether or not agreements to transfer technology from Nigeria to entities abroad also qualify for registration under the Act. These questions arose for consideration in *Stanbic IBTC Holdings Plc* v. *FRCN & Anor (2018) LPELR-46507*, where, the trial Court held that agreements and contracts effecting transfer of technology from Nigeria, as with those into the country, are registrable. It was also held that the effect of non-registration in either case is to make the contracts or agreements void, illegal and unenforceable.

On appeal, after reviewing sections 4(d) and 7 of the NOTAP Act that deals with registration of agreements and contracts and the effects of such registration, the Court of Appeal reversed the decision of the trial Court on both points, and held that: (i) the failure to register a registrable contract or agreement under the NOTAP Act does not constitute a criminal offence; (ii) that failure to register a registrable contract or agreement does not render the contract or agreement illegal, null and void or unenforceable, and; (iii) that the effect of non-registration of a registrable contract or agreement under the Act, is to prevent payment of money in Nigeria by the Ministry of Finance, the Central Bank of Nigeria (CBN) or any other bank to the credit of any person outside Nigeria, with respect to the financial obligations of the parties under the contract or agreement. The judgment of the Court of Appeal, in the opinion of this book, is sound on these points in all ramifications. There are few reasons for our opinion:

- section 7 of the NOTAP Act is clear enough in providing that subject to section 8 of the Act, (which deals with the power of the Director to cancel any registration where the parties thereto alter the initial agreement or contract without the requisite approval), no payment shall be made in Nigeria to the credit of any person outside Nigeria by or on the authority of the Federal Ministry of Finance, the Central Bank of Nigeria or any licensed bank in Nigeria in respect of any payments due under a contract or agreement mentioned in Section 4(d) of the Act if such an agreement or contract had not been presented to the NOTAP office for registration.

  In simple terms, therefore, the foreign party that transferred the technology to an entity in Nigeria will not be paid if the agreement or contract for the transfer of the technology is not registered with NOTAP. That is the principal 'sanction' for non-registration under the Act, though the agreement or contract between the parties thereto, is not invalidated thereby.
- the second point is that, as borne out by section 4(d) of the Act, NOTAP is principally concerned with the reception of technology into Nigeria and not the transfer of technology from Nigeria to the outside world. That is why the key words used in the Act is 'foreign technology' which, as was correctly observed by the Court of Appeal, could not be speaking of a Nigerian technology.

With the two points above, the Court of Appeal was therefore right in reversing the decision of the trial Court and holding that: (i) the trial Court was in error in its decision that non-registration of the agreement rendered it unenforceable, illegal and void; and (ii) the lower Court was also mistaken to hold that an agreement to transfer technology from Nigeria to a foreign country is also registrable under the NOTAP Act. The Court of Appeal held, and we agree, that the trial Court's decision would amount to importing extraneous matters into the provisions of the Act to interpret same, which is something, the Courts in Nigeria are not allowed to do *(Adewunmi* v. *A-G-Ekiti State (2002) 2 NWLR Pt. 751, 474; A.T Ltd* v. *A.D.H. Ltd (2007) 15 NWLR Pt. 1086, 118; NURTW & Anor* v. *RTEAN & Ors (2012) 10 NWLR Pt. 1307, 170).*

FOREIGN COMPANIES INTENDING TO OPERATE IN NIGERIA

What was considered above was a situation where a foreigner or foreign entity intends to participate in a Nigerian enterprise or transfer technology to a

Nigerian enterprise. However, there could be instances where foreign companies could intend to come into Nigeria to carry-on businesses. In such situations, the law mandates that the companies should incorporate in Nigeria as separate legal entities for that purpose *(Procter & Gamble Co.* v. *G.S.D. Intl Ltd (2013) 1 NWLR Pt. 1336, 409)* (s.78(1) CAMA 2020), (s.54(1). Until so incorporated, a foreign company shall not carry-on business in Nigeria or exercise any of the powers of a registered company. Such a company is also prohibited from having a place of business or an address for service of documents or processes in Nigeria for any purpose other than for the receipt of notice(s) and other documents that are preliminary to its incorporation. Anything done by a company concerned in contravention of the above prohibitions, is void (s.78(2), (s. 54(2)*(Edicomsa International* v. *CITEC International Estates (2006) 4 NWLR Pt. 969, 114; Watanmal (Singapore)* v. *Liz Olofin & Co. (1998) 1 NWLR Pt. 533, 311).* It is to note that this prohibition does not affect companies that were granted exemptions under previous company laws in Nigeria or under any treaty to which Nigeria is a party. Section 2 of the schedule to the *Business Facilitation (Miscellaneous Provisions) Act (BFA) 2022* has added a third exemption, for a foreign company, 'exempted under any other Act of the National Assembly.'

Where a non-exempted foreign company carries on business in Nigeria without being registered under the CAMA, the company in question shall be liable to a criminal prosecution and also liable to a fine, as stipulated by the Commission. Additionally, every officer or agent of the company who authorized or permitted the default or failure to comply with the law (CAMA 2020 removed the phrase 'knowingly and wilfully authorises or permits) shall be liable on conviction to a fine to be stipulated by the Commission. This is irrespective of whether the company is also convicted of any offence or not (s.79 CAMA 2020), (s.55).

What is 'Carrying-on Business' in Nigeria?

The provisions of the CAMA that require foreign companies that intend to carry-on business in Nigeria to take steps to be registered as separate legal entities are clear enough. What has not been clear, until lately, is the phrase 'carrying-on business' in Nigeria. It cannot be correct to say that any step(s) or activity undertaken by a foreign company in Nigeria would amount to 'carrying-on business.' The issue was complicated by the fact that the CAMA did not define or elaborate on what activities would amount to 'carrying-on business,' within the context of the Act. This lacuna created problems of interpretation for the regulatory agencies, especially, until the Courts finally stepped in to forge a definite direction in that respect.

Judicial authorities have severally held that the phrase 'carrying-on business,' for the purposes of a foreign company coming into Nigeria, means to 'conduct, prosecute or continue a particular vocation or business as a continuous operation or permanent occupation.' In essence, an activity that would qualify as 'carrying-on business' should entail a bit of a continuous, repetitive, commercial conduct by the company concerned, as against one-off incident(s), especially when same is of no direct or contingent commercial value *(Ritz Pumperfabrik and Co. AG* v. *Techno Continental Engineers & Anor (1999) 4 NWLR Pt. 598, 298; EIIa* v. *CIE Ltd (2006) 4 NWLR Pt. 969, 114, 125; Unipetrol (Nig) Plc* v. *Agip (Nig) Plc (2002) 14 NWLR Pt. 789, 312.*

Exemption of Foreign Company from Incorporation

The requirement by the CAMA that foreign companies be incorporated in Nigeria before being able to carry-on business is not absolute. There are some statutory exceptions to the rule. Under section 80(1) CAMA 2020 (s.56(1), it is permitted for a foreign company to apply to the Minister, (under the CAMA 2004, the application was to the President), for exemption from the provisions of the Act requiring mandatory incorporation before engaging in business in Nigeria. Under the present regulatory regime, the application is to the Minister responsible for trade (s.868 CAMA 2020). To qualify for exemption under the Act, the foreign company must fall into any of the categories below:

- foreign companies (other than those specified in section 80(1)(d) invited to Nigeria by or with the approval of the Federal Government to execute any specified individual project(s); or
- foreign companies which are in Nigeria for the execution of specific individual loan projects on behalf of a donor country or international organization;
- foreign government-owned companies engaged solely in export promotion activities; and
- engineering consultants and technical experts engaged on an individual specialist project(s) under contract with any of the governments in the Federation or any of their agencies or with any other body or person where a contract has been approved by the Federal Government.

A written application for exemption by the foreign company shall be addressed to the Minister (responsible for trade) (under the CAMA 2004, the application was to be sent to the Secretary to the Government of the Federation) stating:

- the name and place of business of the foreign company, outside Nigeria;
- the name and place of business or proposed name and place of business of the foreign company in Nigeria. (The question is: why would a foreign company not yet incorporated in Nigeria be required to provide a name and place of business in its application, when it is not allowed to carry on business in Nigeria before incorporation? Although the word 'proposed' is also used in the provision);
- the name and address of each director, partner or other principal officer of the foreign company;
- a certified copy of the charter, statutes, or Memorandum and Articles of the foreign company (or other instrument constituting or defining the constitution of the company, and if not in English, then a certified English translation is required;
- the name(s) and address(es) of a person(s) resident in Nigeria authorized, to accept, on behalf of the foreign company, service of processes and any notice required to be served on the company;
- the business or proposed business of the foreign company in Nigeria and the duration of the business;
- the particulars of any project previously carried out by the company as an exempted company in Nigeria; and
- such other particulars as may be required by the Minister or Secretary of the Government of the Federation (s.80(2)(a)-(h) CAMA 2020), (s.56(2)(a)-(h)).

It could be observed that the last paragraph of section 80 (2) of CAMA 2020 mentions the Secretary to the Government of the Federation as one of the persons who may require 'any other particulars' from the foreign company seeking exemption from incorporation in Nigeria. In the opinion of this book, this is a very unnecessary provision, which seems to indicate that the office of the Secretary to the Government of the Federation is reluctant that the Presidency is being left out completely from the process of foreign company exemption.

It is to be recalled that under the CAMA 2004, applications by foreign companies seeking exemptions from incorporation were submitted to the office of the Secretary to the Government of the Federation. However, in their wisdom, which this book supports, the reviewers of the CAMA 2004 removed the office of the Secretary to the Government of the Federation and replaced same with the Minister responsible for trade, as the approving office for exemptions. Approval of exemption for a foreign company is an administrative decision and that is where the matter should have ended. There is no need to smuggle the office of the Secretary to the Government of the Federation back into the exemption process, as has been done here, by giving them powers to request any particulars from a foreign company seeking exemption. The responsible Minister should be able to request for and receive any particulars needed from the foreign company seeking exemption.

Again, if the application for exemption is to be submitted to the office of the Minister, how would the office of the Secretary to the Government of the Federation be aware of what was submitted by the company, in order to be in a position to request for further particulars? This is because the CAMA 2020 did not assign any role to the office of the Secretary of the Government of the Federation in the whole exemption process.

This book recommends that the above provision that brought back the office of the Secretary to the Government of the Federation into section 80(2)(h) of the CAMA 2020 should be expunged from the Act. There could be no justification for it. Instead of simplifying the process of exempting deserving foreign companies as the CAMA 2020 intended to do, adding another layer of authority, this time, the office of the Secretary to the Government of the Federation, to the process, actually complicates the bureaucratic bottleneck and should be jettisoned.

Grant and Revocation of Exemption

After reviewing a foreign company's application for exemption, if the Minister is satisfied that the application has merits, he may grant the exemption sought and impose any condition(s) thereon as he deems fit. Every exemption granted shall specify the period for which it is granted or the project(s) to be executed by the company. The exemption consequently shall expire at the end of the period or the completion of the project(s), whichever is applicable (s.80(3)(4) CAMA 2020), (s. 56(3)(4).

The Minister may, at any time, revoke any exemption granted to a foreign company, if he is of the opinion that the company has breached any provision of the CAMA or failed to fulfil a condition(s) contained in the exemption order. The details of any grant or revocation of exemption order are to be published in a gazette (s.80(5)(6) CAMA 2020), (s.56(5)(6).

An exempted company is mandated to deliver a notice of such exemption to the Commission with 30 days of being granted the exemption by the Minister. There is a prescribed penalty to be specified by the Commission for a company's default in forwarding the notice of exemption to the Commission (s. 80(7)(8) CAMA 2020). This is a new provision in the Act, as this notification to the Commission was not provided for under the CAMA 2004.

A foreign company exempted from incorporation shall have the status of an unregistered company and the provisions of the CAMA applicable to such genre of company shall apply to it accordingly. Such a company is required to submit a yearly report to the Commission as the Commission may prescribe (ss. 81 & 82 CAMA 2020), (ss. 57 & 58).

Foreign Company Suing in Nigeria

As seen above, the law in Nigeria is that for a foreign company to operate in Nigeria as a business concern, it has to be incorporated under the CAMA. The only exception is where a foreign company has applied to the Minister (for trade) and has been granted exemption.

Notwithstanding the above discussions, a foreign company is permitted by law to commence an action in Nigerian Courts in its own name or the name of its agent, without being incorporated, to enforce its rights. A foreign company can also be sued in Nigeria without being incorporated locally here (Section 84(b) CAMA 2020, (s.60(b)*(NBCI Ltd* v. *Europa Traders Ltd (1990) 6 NWLR Pt. 154, 36; Sodipo* v. *Lemninkainen (1992) 8 NWLR Pt. 258, 229; Olaogun Enterprises Ltd* v. *SJ and M (1992) 2 NWLR Pt. 235, 361; Bank of Baroda* v. *Iyalabani Co. Ltd (2002) 13 NWLR Pt. 948, 551; Ritz Pumperfabrik GMBH & Co. AG* v. *Techno Continental Engineers & Anor (1999) 4 NWLR Pt. 598, 298; EIIa* v. *CIE Ltd (2006) 4 NWLR Pt. 969,114).*

The roles of the company secretary in all what we have discussed above are several and sometimes interconnected. In effect, it is all about compliance with the relevant laws that prescribe what is to be done in every particular circumstance(s), as noted. From the specialized notifications required from companies in the banking, insurance, deposit, and related businesses before they could commence operations after being incorporated, to the registration of companies that have foreign participation with the NIPC; the company secretary's roles therein are crucial.

It was noted above that where a foreign company intends to engage in business in Nigeria, that incorporation as a company in Nigeria is required, or an exemption from that requirement should be sought. The application for exemption should be made to the office of the Minister responsible for trade (actual designations could differ). Also, we established that where a foreign company's participation in a Nigerian entity involves the transfer of technology from the foreign entity to the Nigerian entity, then a compulsory registration with the NOTAP is required. These two instances are areas where the expertise of the company secretary comes in handy, being that success or otherwise of these applications have serious legal (and ultimately financial) implications for the company and those involved with it. Therefore, they are not simple routine processes to be left to anyone to initiate and process to conclusion.

ACTS THAT ARE *ULTRA VIRES* THE COMPANY

A company that has been registered in Nigeria, while meeting all regulatory requirements should be considered ready to commence business. The company must however be engaged in businesses that it is authorized or empowered to do. Most companies now couch the objects in their Memorandum almost open-ended, and there is a reason, or there used to be a reason for that.

In general, under Nigerian law, a company is not permitted to carry on any business that is expressly prohibited (the CAMA 2004 used the phrase 'that is not authorized') by its Memorandum, and shall not exceed the powers conferred on it by its Memorandum or the Act (s. 44(1) CAMA 2020), (s.39(1). The breach of this provision may be cited in bringing representative and derivative actions to protect minority shareholders under section 344 CAMA 2020), (s. 300).

In its classical form, the doctrine of *ultra vires* is to the effect that after incorporation, a company's objects are as stated in its Memorandum and anything the company does outside the objects is *ultra vires*, invalid and cannot be ratified by the members. The doctrine of *ultra vires* was considered to have done more harm than good in several instances. The popular Nigerian case on this is *Continental Chemists Ltd* v. *Ifeakandu (1966) 1 All NLR, 1*, where the company sent the respondent abroad to complete his training as a medical doctor. After his training, the respondent did not complete the 5 years the parties agreed that he would work for the company on his return to Nigeria. The company sued and the suit was dismissed. On appeal to the Supreme Court, the respondent argued, as at the trial Court, that the company's object did not authorize them, being Chemists, to engage in training of doctors or running hospitals. As ridiculous as the argument sounded and still sounds, it was the law at the time and the Supreme Court upheld the decision of the trial Court dismissing the suit. It was obvious to all that the reform of the *ultra vires* doctrine was inevitable.

The *ultra vires* doctrine was eventually reformed in Nigeria as elsewhere. Though a company is still, in general, not allowed to carry on any business expressly prohibited by its Memorandum or exceed the powers conferred by the CAMA, no such act by a company or any acquisition by it or transfer of property shall be invalidated because the act or transfer was not done for the furtherance of any of the objects of the company or that the company otherwise exceeded its objects or powers (section 44(3) CAMA 2020, (s. 39(3). This provision is meant to deal with previous position of the law dealing with *ultra vires* acts, as was inherited by Nigeria from the English common law.

The CAMA still allows a member of a company or a debenture holder of a floating charge over all or any of a company's property (or his trustee) to apply to Court for an injunction to stop a company from entering into a transaction or doing an act that exceeds its powers or objects. On any such application being made, the Court may set aside the transaction and may award compensation to any of the parties to the contract as the Court deems fit (s.44(4)(5) CAMA 2020), (s.39 (4)(5).

In modern business circles in Nigeria, it is difficult, though not impossible, to foresee a situation where an application to restrain a company from exceeding its powers would be made, except in situations where the directors and senior management deliberately intended to oppress a section of the shareholders, by engaging in unauthorized acts. This is because the way and manner modern object clauses are drafted, even with an omnibus clause, a company can virtually venture into any legitimate business, without offending any law(s).

Lifting the Veil of Incorporation

In company law, one of the major, in fact, the central incident of incorporating a company is that it acquires a separate legal personality, distinct from its promoters, directors, managers and members. This also comes with powers to acquire and hold property in its name and to dispose same as deemed fit. The company is also able to sue and be sued in its own corporate name*(CDBI* v. *COBEC Nig. Ltd (2004) 13 NWLR Pt. 948, 376; Union Bank (Nig) Ltd* v. *Penny Mart Ltd (1992) 5 NWLR Pt. 240, 237; Okolo & Anor* v. *UBN Ltd (2004) 3 NWLR Pt. 859, 87; Marina Nominees* v. *Fed. Board of Inland Revenues (1986) 2 NWLR Pt. 20, 48).*

The above-noted attribute of corporate legal personality of registered companies notwithstanding, there are instances where a company's legal personality as a juristic person will be sidelined and the *'veil of incorporation'* lifted or pierced. This is usually in situations where it has become necessary to see those behind the veil (company) and, in appropriate cases, to impose personal liability on them that would have otherwise been borne by the company. In several instances, the lifting of the veil of incorporation is by statutes that impose criminal or civil sanctions on members, officers and directors of companies for acts done by the company in its own name. In other instances, the veil of incorporation could be lifted by the Courts, especially in situations where the company is being used as a vehicle for fraudulent activities.

It has to be noted however, that when the veil of incorporation is pierced for whatever reason(s), it is to solve the particular problem that necessitated it and not for all purposes. In essence, piercing the veil of incorporation does not suddenly treat the company for all purposes as never been incorporated in order to impose personal liability on the members or officers. In the final analysis, therefore, piercing the veil is said to be a limited operation with limited consequences, rather than a wholesale disregard of the fact of incorporation *(Ben Hasem* v. *Ali Shayif (2009) 1 FLR 115; Brenda Hannigan, Company Law, 45).*

Statutory Lifting of the Veil

The CAMA has made several provisions relating to the circumstances whereby the veil of incorporation on a company may be lifted and personal liability imposed on individual members of a company and, sometimes, on its directors and management. A few examples will suffice here:

- under section 110(2) CAMA 2020 (s.84(2), a company is required to send a notice to the Commission of the location of its register of members and change thereof. If this provision is not complied with within 28 days, the company and every of its officers shall be liable to such penalties and additional continuing daily fine as the Commission shall specify;

- under section 271(3) CAMA 2020 (s.246(3), a director or member of a company, not being a 'small company,' (this small company exception was not in CAMA 2004) who knows that a company carries on business after the number of directors had fallen below two (2) for more than 60 days shall be liable for all the liabilities and debts of the company during the period the company so carries on business;
- under section 316 CAMA 2020, (s.290), where a company receives a loan for a specific purpose or receives money or other property as advance payment for the execution of a contract or with intent to defraud fails, to apply the money or property for the purpose, then, every director or officer of the company who is in default shall be personally liable to the party from whom the money or property was received for a refund of the money or property so received and not properly applied. This does not affect the liability of the company itself;
- under section 379 CAMA 2020, (s.336) if, at the end of each year, a company has subsidiaries, the directors shall, while preparing individuals accounts for that year, also prepare a group account for the company and its subsidiaries. A holding company and its subsidiaries are usually treated as one concern in terms of the group account, balance sheet and profit and loss account. There is the tendency to sidestep the separate legal personalities of the various companies within the group and look at the economic entity of the group as a whole. This is especially so where the parent company holds all the shares of the subsidiary and controls all of its affairs *(DHN Food Distributors Ltd & Anor* v. *London Borough of Tower Hamlets (1976) 3 All ER, 462, 467; Harold Holdsworth & Co. (Wakefield) Ltd* v. *Caddies (1955) 1 All ER 725).*
- under section 729(1) CAMA 2020, (s.548 (1), every incorporated company shall:
  i. paint or affix its name and registration number legibly outside of every office or place where its business is carried on, in easily legible letters;
  ii. have its name engraved on its seal, that is, if the company has one;
  iii. have its name and registration number mentioned in legible letters on its business letters, notices, advertisements, official publications, cheques, promissory notes, bills of exchange, invoices, receipts, etc.;

Section 729(3) CAMA 2020, (s. 548(4), imposes personal liability on any officer of the company or any person on its behalf who defaults in complying with the provisions of the section.

- under section 671(1) CAMA 2020, (s. 505(1), where a company is being wound up and it is shown that proper books of account were not kept by the company throughout the period of two years immediately preceding the winding-up, or period between the incorporation of the company and commencement of the winding-up (whichever is shorter), every officer in default shall be personally liable on conviction to a fine to be prescribed by the Commission, (the fine was ₦250.00 under the CAMA 2004) unless he shows that he acted honestly and that the default was excusable in the circumstances;
- finally, under section 672(1) CAMA 2020, s.506(1), where in the winding-up of a company it appears that the business of the company has been carried on in a reckless manner or with intent to defraud creditors of the company or creditors of any other person for any fraudulent purpose, the Court may, on the application of the official receiver or liquidator, or any creditor or contributory of the company, if it deems it fit in the circumstances, declare persons who were knowingly parties to the said transactions personally liable without any limitation for all or any of the liabilities or debts of the company.

Judicial Lifting of the Veil

Apart from situations where a statute has made provisions for lifting of the corporate veil and imposing personal liability on members, officers and directors of a company, there are instances when the Courts also pierce the veil to see those really behind the company. An example is where a Court is convinced by the evidence before it that a company has been established as a sham to be used for other unstated fraudulent purposes. In such cases, the Court usually exercises its powers to lift the veil of incorporation and see those behind the company and the real purpose for its establishment.

A classic Nigerian case where the Court lifted a company's veil for suspected fraud and imposed personal liability on an officer was in *Public Finance & Securities Ltd & Anor* v. *Jafia (1998) 3 NWLR Pt. 543, 602.* In the case, the 2nd appellant who was the chairman and managing director of the 1st appellant, induced the respondent to place funds with the 1st appellant, which funds were not repaid when the investment matured. In Court, the appellants' defence that the inability to pay the respondent was because of the 'general decline in business due mainly to political crises and orchestrated blackmail by some fraudulent staffers' was considered by the Court to amount to constructive fraud on the respondent. The 2nd appellant was ordered by the trial Court to personally repay the investment to the respondent. On appeal, the Court of Appeal upheld the decision of the trial Court. In other cases, like *Alade* v. *Alic Nig. Ltd & Anor (2010) 19 NWLR Pt. 1226,111; Trenco Nig Ltd* v. *African Real Estates & Invest. Ent. Co Ltd (1978) 4 SC, 9; Eboni Finance & Securities Ltd* v. *Wole-Ojo Tech. Serv. Ltd & Ors (1996) 7 NWLR Pt. 461, 478;* the decisions were the same as that of Public Finance above.

In another respect, it has been held that where there is an irregular arrangement between the shareholders and a company, for instance, an arrangement which has the effect of effectively constituting the company as an agent of the shareholders for the purpose of the company's business, the Court will be entitled to lift the veil of incorporation to ascertain the true state of affairs *(Smith, Stone & Knight Ltd* v. *Lord Mayor, Alderman and Citizens of the City of Birmingham (1939) 4 All ER 116; Charlesworth & Cain, 26)*.

From all the discussions above, we could see that the footsteps and signatures of the company secretary are imprinted everywhere from the application to register a company to when the company actually commences business, and everywhere in between. Even after commencing business, if a company decides on its own to change its name or the Commission directs the company to do so, for the appropriate reason(s), it is the duty of the company secretary to initiate the processes of the name change and to effect the post-change formalities, including all notifications and compliance requirements.

From a governance perspective, the company secretary has to be alert to the areas highlighted above where the CAMA or the Courts could lift the veil of incorporation based on the actions of the members, officers or directors of the company and advise on and mitigate same appropriately. In a similar manner, the company secretary should flag, and call the attention of the directors, when the company is exceeding its powers and acting unlawfully. This is to avoid a situation whereby those entitled to apply to Court will do so to restrain the company from exceeding its powers. This will not be good for company and stakeholders' relations.

In addition, where there is an infringement on any of the company's proprietary rights, including real property and intellectual property rights, company's name (as in the Capital Oil's case discussed above) or goodwill, it is within the realm of authority of the company secretary to put machineries in place to redress such situations. There are legions of other examples.

CHECKPOINTS

- ✓ The CAMA 2020 has brought a lot of new innovations to the area of company law and practice, one of which is the introduction of a governing board to have a general oversight on the administration of the Commission, among others.
- ✓ The Act also introduced a 30-day pre-action notice before any action can be instituted in Court against the Commission. This notice is to give the Commission the time to decide on whether to settle such a case with the plaintiff out of Court or to litigate same.
- ✓ Added to the above, the CAMA 2020 also introduced the Model Articles to the company incorporation process. This means that a proposed company can simply send in only its Memorandum of Association to the Commission to register it as a company and the Model Articles will be adopted for the company as default Articles.
- ✓ The need for statutory declaration by a legal practitioner to complete the process of incorporation of a company has been jettisoned under the CAMA 2020. In its place now is required a statement of compliance, which can easily be complied with by a non-legal practitioner.
- ✓ Even where a proposed company has complied with all the prescribed statutory requirements for incorporation under the CAMA, the Commission still has the powers to refuse to register it. This is where there are grounds to do so, for instance, where any of the company's objects was found to be illegal, among others.
- ✓ Where the Commission refused to register a company as above, a person aggrieved may give notice to the Commission to apply to Court for directions in this respect. The Commission has 21 days to do so.
- ✓ Once a company has been registered, a person can apply to the Administrative Proceedings Committee (APC) of the Commission, on the ground that the name with which the company was registered breaches his goodwill. The Committee will then invite the respondent to defend the petition and then make a decision one way or the other.

- ✓ A company is normally registered either as a private or public company. It could also be a company limited by shares, limited by guarantee or unlimited, with each genre having its peculiarities. A registered company assumes the status of a distinct legal personality distinct from its promoters, managers and directors.

- ✓ Once incorporated, a company assumes all the powers of a natural person of full capacity for the furthering of its businesses. This does not, however, entitle a company to make donations to a political party or to a political association.

- ✓ Sometimes it becomes necessary to prove that a company has actually been incorporated. The certificate of incorporation is *prima facie* evidence of the fact of incorporation, and it is the duty of the company to establish that fact, except if the other party admits it. Being *prima facie* evidence, it can be rebutted by superior evidence to the contrary.

- ✓ When a company is registered with a name that conflicts with an existing name or trademark, the company on its own volition (by special resolution) or the Commission may direct the company to change its name. The Commission may also apply to Court to order a company to change a conflicting name.

- ✓ Once a company has been incorporated and issued with a certificate to that effect, it can proceed to commence business. However, for companies in some sectors like the banking industry or the insurance industry, etc, they usually have additional regulatory requirements to fulfil before they can start business, after incorporation.

- ✓ The CAMA 2020 made some far-reaching innovations in the provisions relating to the registration of a company limited by guarantee. The most innovative of them is the provision to override the consent of the Attorney General of the Federation, where same is being unduly delayed. This, however, comes at additional costs to the applicant(s) and the Commission.

- ✓ It is no longer mandatory for private companies to restrict, in their Memorandum and Articles, the transfer of their shares. It is now optional to do so. A private company can transfer its shares but on certain conditions imposed by the CAMA, one of which is pre-emption right to existing members to buy the shares, before offering those shares to outsiders.

✓ A public company does not have most of the restrictions imposed on a private company, and there are other material differences: a private company does not have to hold a statutory meeting within six (6) months after incorporation. Again, a private company classified as a 'small company' is not mandated to appoint a company secretary, and a private company is not mandated to disclose the age of a director(s) who is above 70 years; etc

✓ Where a Nigerian company has foreign participation, it has to register with the NIPC before commencing business. After this registration with the NIPC, the company may commence business but is restricted from engaging in certain businesses and cannot engage in the production of military and para-military uniforms and accoutrements, narcotics, etc

✓ When a foreign company's participation in a Nigerian entity involves the transfer of technology to the Nigerian entity, then the agreement or contract between the parties has to be registered with the NOTAP. This is mandatory although the Courts have determined that non-registration will not invalidate the agreement or contract or make same illegal, but that the financial benefits thereunder cannot be transferred from Nigeria to the entity outside Nigeria.

✓ It is important to note that without being incorporated in Nigeria, a foreign company can still bring an action to enforce its rights, for instance, to recover its debts from entities that are operating in Nigeria.

✓ A company is not, legally speaking, allowed to go outside of its objects or business clauses in carrying on business. However, the CAMA, like the practice in several common law jurisdictions around the world, has watered down the effect of the *ultra vires* doctrine. This, however, does not stop a member in a company from relying on the ground that a company acted *ultra vires* as a ground to get injunctive reliefs or file derivative actions against the company that it is exceeding its powers.

✓ The incidence of incorporation clothes a company with juristic personality and separates it from the owners, managers and directors. The company can then sue in its own name and own and transfer properties its corporate name. However, there are instances when the veil of incorporation would be lifted, either by the Courts or by statute to look beyond the veil and see who is behind the company. This is common in cases where a company has been registered as a sham or a tool for fraud. The Court will then order personal sanctions on those behind the company, while ignoring, in that particular instance, the veil of incorporation.

✓ It has to be noted that when a company's veil of incorporation is lifted, it is for that particular purpose and does not remove the veil for all purposes. In effect, the incidence of lifting the corporate veil does not turn the company into one without juristic personality. That is not the situation. It is usually a one-off lifting of the veil to deal with the particular situation as identified.

Chapter 4

COMPANY'S CONSTITUTIONAL DOCUMENTS: MEMORANDUM AND ARTICLES

INTRODUCTION

A company's Memorandum and Articles of Association, taken together, constitute the company's basic constitutional documents. In sum, a company's Memorandum states the nature of the company, its objects or business, liability of its members, its share capital, among other vital information, mostly meant to inform the outside world about the general structure of the company *(Charlesworth & Cain, 55).* For instance, at the time when the *ultra vires* rule held sway in company law in Nigeria and elsewhere, it was a company's Memorandum that stated the extent of the company's powers and its objects in order to put outsiders on notice when dealing with the company. It could therefore be said that the Memorandum simply concerns itself mostly with the company's external audiences. But this is not all. The Memorandum could also be used to place certain restrictions on the company's powers, where desired, even for some restrictions that could have traditionally been contained in the company's Articles.

THE NATURE OF THE MEMORANDUM OF ASSOCIATION

It has been held, that in terms of functionality, the Memorandum of Association controls the Articles of a company, though the Articles may be used to explain the content of the Memorandum. This is with respect to matters that the relevant company legislation, here, the CAMA, did not require to be in the Memorandum mandatorily *(Guinness Plc* v. *Land Corporation of Ireland (1882) 22 Ch.D., 349, 381; Orojo, 55).*Considering the current trajectory of modern company law, an issue that has arisen and will continue to be debated into the foreseeable future is the extent to which the Memorandum will remain relevant in the scheme of company law and practice. With the watering down of the effect of the *ultra vires* doctrine in company law jurisprudence, coupled with the current situation where the objects of most companies permit them to engage in almost open-ended businesses, apart from members subscribing as such therein, what will be the other utility of the Memorandum of Association, going forward? Hannigan, in fact, has posited that the Memorandum, in no distant future, will have no continuing relevance in the realm of company law and practice *(Hannigan, 9).*

The matter, however, might not be as simple as that, for the Memorandum of Association to simply disappear overnight. If, as has been acknowledged generally that as between the Memorandum and the Articles, that the Memorandum is the dominant instrument that will prevail in so far as their provisions conflict *(Charlesworth & Cain,103).*Then, whatever becomes the fate of the Memorandum might be a case of gradual phasing out, if at all.

THE CONTENT OF THE MEMORANDUM

The CAMA has prescribed some mandatory provisions that are to be contained in a company's Memorandum. According to common section 27(1) CAMA 2020 and 2004), the Memorandum of every company shall state:

- the name of the company;
- that the registered office of the company shall be situate in Nigeria;
- the nature of the business(es) which the company is authorized to carry on, or if not for business, then the objects of its being established;
- the restrictions (if any) on the powers of the company;
- that the company is a private or public company (whichever is applicable);
- that the liability of its members is limited by shares, guarantee or unlimited (whichever is applicable);
- if the company has a share capital, the Memorandum shall state the amount of the minimum issued share capital with which the company is to be registered (not less than ₦100,000.00 for a private company and ₦2,000,000.00 for a public company) and the division into shares of a fixed amount;
- where a subscriber to the Memorandum of a company holds the shares he subscribed or part thereof in trust for any other person, he shall state so in the Memorandum and the name of the beneficiary of the shares (common s. 27(3). A trustee is a person or firm that holds and administers property or assets for the benefits of a third party *(Nwankwo* v. *Nwankwo (2017) LPELR-42832).*

If the company is one that is limited by guarantee, then its Memorandum shall also state that:

- the income of the company shall be applied solely to the promotion of its objects and that no portion shall be paid or transferred to the members of the company, except as permitted by the CAMA; (common s. 27 (4(a);
- each member undertakes to contribute to the assets of the company in the event of winding-up while he is a member or within one year after he ceases to be a member for payment of the debts and liabilities of the company and the cost of winding-up, such amount as may be required not exceeding a specified amount but not less than ₦100,000.00 (One hundred thousand naira) (the amount was ₦10,000.00 (Ten thousand naira) under CAMA 2004 (common s. 27 (4)(b);
- the Memorandum shall be signed by each subscriber in the presence of at least one attesting witness and shall be stamped as a deed.

A notable development is the provision in CAMA 2004 that required the subscribers to the Memorandum to take among themselves not less than 25% of the authorized share capital. This provision has been removed by the CAMA 2020, which has replaced the concept of 'authorized share capital' with that of 'issued share capital.' This presupposes that at incorporation and subscription by members, the minimum share capital, which is now issued share capital, would already have been issued to the members of the company.

Apart from the above observations on the Memorandum of Association, the other area that will deserve attention will be its amendment. This is discussed further below.

THE ARTICLES OF ASSOCIATION

The Articles of Association is the second part of a company's constitutional document, after the Memorandum. Under section 33 CAMA 2020, the Minister (responsible for trade) may, by regulations, prescribed model Articles for different genre of businesses. A company may therefore not register any Articles with its Memorandum and simply adopt the Model Articles, either wholly or in part. Otherwise, the Model Articles will apply as default Articles for the company where none was registered by the company.

The CAMA 2004 had no provision for Model Articles. It remains to be seen how the Commission will synchronize part of a company's Articles and part of Model Articles into a working document, that is, if a company decides to adopt the Model Articles in part. This book proposes that the provisions of the Model Articles should prevail in the event of a conflict between it and a company's Articles, being that the Model Articles is from the sector regulator, the Commission. Also, the company had the opportunity to submit its own Articles in full, but chose not to do so and should have known the provisions of the Model Articles before adopting same, fully or in part.

The major takeaway from the observations above is that it is no longer mandatory to register a company's Memorandum with its Articles of Association. The Articles is the document that complements the Memorandum and prescribes detailed rules and regulations for the administration of the company as a going commercial concern (s. 32 CAMA 2020, (s. 33). It could be said that the Articles is the company's internal regulator, dealing with sundry issues including, membership, quorum for meetings, transfer of shares, alteration of share capital, voting rights, proxy, dividends, accounts, employment of officers, winding-up, directors, and other incidental issues.

Section 34(3) CAMA 2020 stipulates the general form of the Articles for every company in simple terms and that it shall:

- be contained in a single document;
- be divided into paragraphs and numbered consecutively. (This is unlike the CAMA 2004 which stated expressly that, in addition to the two items above, the Articles was to be printed, be signed by each subscriber of the Memorandum in the presence of at least one attesting witness and be stamped as a deed).

The provision of section 34(2), 2004, which requires that the Articles of a company that is limited by guarantee should state the number of members with which the company proposes to be registered with, to enable the Commission to determine the fees payable for such registration, has been omitted by the CAMA 2020.

In practice, as noted above, the Articles usually deal in detail with issues relating to:

- rights of shareholders: (being a member, attending meetings, voting, holding shares, name being in the register, etc.);
- shares: (restrictions, classes, transfer, transmission, rights attaching thereto, forfeiture, conversion, pre-emption right, etc.);

- directors: (appointment, removal, powers and duties, proceedings of directors, rights, quorum, tenure of office, share qualification (if applicable), removal of directors, casual vacancy, written resolution etc.);
- dividends: (declaration, interim and final payment, qualification to receive; etc.);
- company secretary: (appointment, duties, removal, etc.);
- common seal: (uses, custody, authority for usage, etc.); (Note to be taken that CAMA 2020 has made the use of common seal by a company optional);
- capital of the company: (increase or decrease in share capital, borrowing powers of the company, etc.);
- auditors: (appointment, duties, remuneration, removal, etc.).

EFFECT OF REGISTERED MEMORANDUM AND ARTICLES

As the basic constitutional documents of a company, registered Memorandum and Articles are any company's core documents of value. Together they contain the statement and standard of the company's existence and the nitty-gritty of its internal regulation. Under section 46(1) CAMA 2020 (s. 41 (1), when registered, the Memorandum and Articles shall have the effect of a contract under seal between the company and its members and officers and between the members and officers themselves. It is sometimes referred to as 'statutory contract' or section 41 contract (now s. 46) under the CAMA. The implication is that the parties (the company, the officers and the members) have all agreed to perform and abide by the provisions of the Memorandum and Articles, as altered from time to time, in so far as they relate to the company, members, or officers. In essence, therefore, any contravention or breach of the registered Memorandum and Articles is actionable at the instance of the interested party, *qua* member(s) *(Ladejobi* v. *Odutola Holding Ltd (2002) 3 NWLR Pt. 753, 121; NIB Investment (WA)* v. *Omisore (2006) 4 NWLR Pt. 969, 172).*

The above agreement notwithstanding, there are few clarifications that need to be made in terms of the nature, ambit, implications and, some might say, limitations, of the 'statutory contract' referred to above:

- the statutory contract has been held to be binding only in respect of rights and liabilities of the member as a shareholder in the company ('membership rights', which include the right to vote, right to dividend, right to participate to appoint directors, etc.) and not in any of the member's private capacity *(Hickman* v. *Kent or Romney Marsh Sheep Breeders Association (1915) 1 Ch 881, James Thorne, Butterworths Company Law Guide, 4th edn, 35);*

- members of a company may sue themselves based on the contract contained in the Memorandum and Articles and need not do so through the company, as long as the issue(s) pertains to their membership rights *(Hayfield* v. *Hands (1960) Ch 1, Thorne, 35)*;
- the Articles will not act as a contract between a company and someone who is not a member, but it is possible for the Articles to be the basis of an implied or 'collateral contract' between the company and an outsider or with a member *(Re: New British Iron Co, ex parte Beckwith (1898) 1Ch 324, Thorne, 35).*

Having been registered with and being in the custody of the Commission, which is a public institution, it is correct to say that the Memorandum and Articles then become public documents, accessible for inspection, extraction and certification, like all other public records in Nigeria, by anyone paying the applicable fees. This is relevant in view of the abolition of the doctrine of constructive notice of company's official and registered documents in the custody of the company or the Commission, under section 92 CAMA 2020 (s. 68) *(Animashaun* v. *Olojo (1990) 6 NWLR Pt. 154, 111).*

Section 102 of the Evidence Act 2011 (as amended) defines 'public documents' as: (a) documents forming the official acts or record of: (i) the sovereign authority; (ii) official bodies and tribunals; or (iii) public officers, legislative, judicial and executive, whether of Nigeria or elsewhere; and (b) public records kept in Nigeria of private documents *(NAFDAC* v. *Reagan Remedies (2019) 17 NWLR Pt. 1700, 1.* In *House of Representatives* v. *SPDC (Nig) & Anor (2010)* LPELR-50116, it was held that the certificate of incorporation of a company, being a document with a public institution and being always accessible for public inspection and use, is a public document.

The CAMA also provides for other incidences that emanate from the registration of the Memorandum and Articles:

- all moneys payable by a member to the company under the Memorandum or Articles shall be a debt due from the member to the company and shall be of a nature of specialty debt (section 46(2) CAMA 2020), (s. 41(2). As a specialty debt and not a simple debt, this presupposes that the member is entitled for up to twelve (12) years to sue to recover the debt from the company. This is as against the period of six (6) years normally allowed to sue to recover simple debts.

- it is important to note that notwithstanding any limitation(s) that the Articles may have in dealing with outsiders as noted above, where the Memorandum or Articles empower any person to appoint or remove a director or other officer(s) of a company, such power shall be enforceable by that person notwithstanding that he is not a member or officer of the company in question (s.46(3) CAMA 2020), (s. 41(3). *(Longe* v. *FBN Plc (2006) 3 NWLR Pt. 967, 228).*
- a member or an officer of a company who wants to sue the company for an obligation owed under the Memorandum or Articles may, with the consent of other members or officers who also allege breach of that obligation against the company, sue in a representative capacity on behalf of himself and all other members and officers who may be affected. This will exclude any member who is a defendant in the suit (s. 46(4) CAMA 2020, (s. 41 (4);
- the company is bound to its members according to the terms of its Articles *(Salmon* v. *Quin & Axtens Ltd (1909) 1 Ch., 31);*
- the company is entitled to sue its members for the enforcement of, and to restrain them from a breach of its Articles. The company can also sue to declare as irregular anything done in contravention of the Articles *(Pender* v. *Lushington (1877) 6 Ch. D., 70; Charlesworth & Cain, 404).*

In the final analysis, it is clear that the Articles could actually be used by a company to achieve a lot of objectives and even restrict the powers of the company in the Memorandum. It can also be used to confer rights on members. The only limitation to this power is that, the Articles cannot confer a right on any person in any other capacity other than in the person's capacity as a member of the company *(Kung* v. *General Metalware Co. Ltd & Anor (1987) FHCLR 214, 224*).

For the company secretary, the issues that have been discussed above are critical issues, especially as they relate to what the rights of the members are as derived from the Articles. Being that the company secretary is the link between the members, the management and the board of directors, a good grasp of the detailed membership rights in the Articles, their qualification(s) and limitation(s), if any, is crucial. The company secretary should be able to advise members on the one side and the directors on the other on the position of the law, the implications and applications of membership rights across board.

This will obviate unnecessary tensions between the members *inter se* and between the members and the company. This will also help to avoid any unnecessary litigations against the company by members. This issue will be discussed in further details in the chapter that deals with membership.

The roles of the company secretary in this respect do not, however, stop here. As will be shown below, the company secretary's position is interwoven intricately with the operations of a modern company, especially, large private and public companies.

When a company decides to alter either its Memorandum or Articles or both, although there are statutory provisions under the CAMA for these processes, however, there are also entrenched and widely accepted common law principles that guide the processes. When such principles of law are violated by the company in effecting any amendment of any of its constitutional document(s), it could lead to a striking down of any such purported alteration(s) by the Courts.

It is therefore imperative for the company secretary to guide the board and management aright through the whole alteration processes to ensure a seamless flow and avoid any friction between or among any of the critical stakeholders: members, management and directors.

ALTERATION OF THE MEMORANDUM

A company, being a going concern, may have the need, from time to time, to alter its Memorandum in other to meet the demands of its business. In making provisions for the alteration(s) of the Memorandum, the CAMA distinguished between 'conditions' in the Memorandum and other provisions. The 'conditions' in the Memorandum are those provisions that the CAMA expressly stated that they must be in the Memorandum, including, the name of company, registered office, nature of business, liability of members, share capital, etc. (common s. 27 CAMA 2020 and 2004).

To alter any of the conditions in the Memorandum, section 49 CAMA 2020 (s. 44) states that this must be done only to the extent and manner as is expressly provided for in the Act.

The above notwithstanding, under the common law, there are instances when an alteration of the Memorandum (and even the Articles) would be in line with the provision of the Act but is still impeached. A case will be where members that voted in favour of the resolution did not do so *bona fide*, in the interest of the company as whole (for the jurisprudential difficulties associated with determining when actions are taken in the 'interests of the company as a whole,' see *Gower & Davis, 691-696*).

Furthermore, it is possible that the Memorandum or Articles may prescribe a modality for alteration which may conflict with the provisions of the CAMA. Therefore, with this and other like situations in mind, section 723 CAMA 2020 (s. 542) provides that the provisions of the CAMA shall have effect notwithstanding anything to the contrary in a company's Memorandum or Articles, contract, resolution of the general meeting or directors etc.. It might then be doubtful whether an alteration of a company's constitutional documents could still be set aside if done in accordance with the provisions of the CAMA, but conflicts with some principles of common law.

Section 50 CAMA 2020 (s. 45) has prescribed different modalities for the alteration of the different aspects of the Memorandum.

Alteration of a Company's Name

The name of a company registered under the Act can only be altered with the consent of the Commission. That is the law as stated in section 30 CAMA 2020 (s. 30). As discussed in the previous chapter, the section makes detailed provision on the different circumstances wherein a company's name can be changed: ranging from voluntary change by the company itself to a change of name as directed by the Commission. It also means that all the rules relating to the use of prohibited and restricted names are applicable to a change of name scenario as they apply to new registrations.

After a change of a company's name, a new certificate is issued to the company, though, as noted above, the name change does not affect any of the company's rights and liabilities, or any legal proceedings by or against the company. Furthermore, with respect to the new certificate issued to the company, the powers of the Commission to cancel or revoke a certificate for any fraudulent or improper conduct by the company under section 41(7) CAMA 2020 will still be potent.

Alteration of the Object or Business Clause

After a company has been incorporated, its object or business clause could still be amended at any time during its lifetime. However, unlike previously, when the doctrine of *ultra vires* held sway and companies where frequently altering their object clauses in order to make their activities *intra vires*, alterations of object clauses in modern company practice are always for more far-reaching reasons. For instance, when a company is venturing into very new areas of business that were not envisaged at all during its incorporation and which area could not have been covered by its Memorandum, an alteration of its object clause may be necessary, although, non-alteration, as was seen above, will not be fatal to its business.

The CAMA apparently accords high importance to the alteration of object clauses by companies in Nigeria. In this respect, section 51 CAMA 2020 (s. 46) has stipulated detailed procedures for such an amendment:

- for a company's business or object clause to be altered, the company has to call a general meeting and pass a *special resolution;*
- for the meeting above, the written notice of meeting must be sent to all its members (whether they are entitled to such notice or not);
- the same manner of notice to members for the special resolution shall also be given to all debenture holders.

Once a special resolution is passed as provided for by the Act, with the requisite notices to all who should receive same, a company may proceed to alter the object or business clause on its Memorandum. The process of alteration could, however, be challenged by certain classes of persons, by approaching the Court with an application to cancel the alteration. If so challenged, the alteration will not have any effect except as confirmed by the Court.

Those that qualify to make application to Court to cancel an alteration of the object clause under the CAMA are those holding:

- not less than, in the aggregate, 15% of the nominal value of the company's issued share capital, or if the company is not limited by shares, then by not less than 15% of the members of the company; or
- not less than 15% of the company's debentures entitling the debenture holders to object to the alteration of the objects of the company. The debentures entitling a holder to object to the alteration of the objects of a company shall be debentures secured by a floating charge (s. 51(5) CAMA 2020), (s. 46(5).

By the proviso to section 51(2) CAMA 2020 (s. 46(2), it is noteworthy that a person who has consented to or voted in favour of the alteration of the objects of a company is not entitled to subsequently apply to Court objecting to the alteration.

The question here would be whether a person who consented to the alteration of the company's objects or business clause based on fraudulent or other types of misrepresentations by the directors or management can still apply to Court to set same aside, if other conditions are otherwise met? We submit that such an application can still be made, being that a fraudulently induced consent amounts to no consent at all. This is because fraud, when proven, vitiates consent. In fact, the Supreme Court has held that fraud, when proven, vitiates everything, even judgments and orders of Court *(Ugo* v. *Obiekwe (1989) 1 NWLR Pt. 99, 566; Onwudiwe* v. *FRN (2006) 10 NWLR Pt. 988, 383; Vulcan Gases Ltd* v. *GF Ind (2001)9 NWLR Pt. 719, 610).*

An application to Court to cancel an alteration of the objects shall be made not less than 28 days after the date on which the resolution altering the company objects was passed. The persons making an application to Court may appoint any one of them in writing to bring such an application on their behalf (s. 51(3) CAMA 2020), (s. 46(3).

Where Application is made to Court

When an application is made to Court to cancel an alteration of the objects of a company, the Court may confirm the alteration, either wholly or in part, and may permit the alteration on terms, as it deems fit. The Court may also permit an arrangement to buy-off the interests of the dissenting members, provided that no capital of the company may be used for such a purchase (s. 51(4) CAMA 2020), (s. 46(4).

Where a company passes a resolution to alter its object or business clause and application is made to Court by those qualified to do so:

- the company shall forthwith give notice to the Commission that an application has been made to Court, and thereafter shall deliver to the Commission within 15 days from the day the application was made, a certified true copy of the order in the case of refusal to confirm the resolution; and
- a certified true copy of the order in the case of confirmation of the resolution together with a printed copy of the Memorandum as ultimately altered is also to be sent to the Commission in appropriate cases (s. 51(7(a) CAMA 2020), (s. 46 (7)(a).

Where no application is made to Court against an alteration to a company's objects, the company shall within 15 days from the end of the period allowed for making such an application to Court, deliver to the Commission a copy of the resolution that was passed to alter the objects. The Court is empowered to extend the time within which any document(s) is to be delivered to the Commission. If the Commission is satisfied with the resolution delivered by the company as above, a printed copy of the Memorandum as altered shall be delivered to it forthwith, thereafter. If, on the other hand, the Commission is not satisfied with the resolution sent by the company, it shall notify the company in writing of its decision and any person aggrieved can appeal to Court against such a decision within 21 days of receipt of the notice of rejection from the Commission (s. 51(8) CAMA 2020), (s. 46(7)(b).

There is a continuing penalty to be prescribed by the Commission imposed on the company and officer in default for failure of a company to give any requisite notice(s) or deliver any document(s) to the Commission in this respect.

For the purposes of the procedures described above for altering the business or object clause of a company, the definition of a 'member' is extended to include a person who is financially interested in the company, and not necessarily a shareholder in the company (s. 51(12) CAMA 2020), (s. 46(11).

ALTERATION OF RESTRICTION ON THE POWER OF THE COMPANY

Except where a company's Articles place restriction(s) on the objects, the objects are considered unrestricted (s. 35(1) CAMA 2020). Relatedly, any provision contained in a company's Memorandum restricting the powers of the company to do certain act(s) may be altered in the same manner as the business or objects of the company under section 51 of the Act as described above (s. 50(3) CAMA 2020), (s. 45(3).

ALTERATIONS OF PROVISIONS IN THE MEMORANDUM INSTEAD OF THE ARTICLES

Any provision contained in a company's Memorandum which might legally have been in its Articles, may be altered by a *special resolution*. However, if an application is made to the Court for the alteration to be cancelled, such an alteration shall only have effect in so far as it is confirmed by the Court (s. 52(1) CAMA 2020), (s. 47(1). However, this will not apply where the Memorandum itself has made provision for, or has prohibited the alteration of all or any of the said provisions, and shall not authorize any variation or abrogation of the special rights of any class of members (s. 47(2). Section 51 (2), (3), (4), (7), (8) and (9) CAMA 2020, (which relate to the mode of alteration of the business or object clause in a company's Memorandum) shall apply in relation to any alteration and to any application that would be made to Court under this heading, applicable to alterations and applications to Court.

The exclusion of section 51(2)(b) (which talks about debenture holders) by CAMA 2020 (s. 46(2)(b), from the above provision implies that only members can apply to Court to cancel an alteration under this heading. A company's debenture holders are by implication excluded from making any such application to Court for this purpose.

The major role for the company secretary in all the above alterations to the content of the Memorandum is to ensure that the stipulated rules for the alterations are followed, and so, followed to the letter. For instance, where the law requires a special resolution for any alteration to be effected that must be ensured and not substituted with an ordinary resolution, which would then make the alteration susceptible to be invalidated by the Court. Also, when the law has given a particular threshold shareholding, debenture holding or membership (for non-share-holding company) for people to challenge any alteration, the company secretary must ensure that such minimum shareholding or membership base is met before any challenge could be allowed to proceed in Court. Otherwise, it would be for the company itself to approach the Court that the challenge to the alteration(s), as constituted, is incompetent for failure to meet the condition precedent for the challenge, and should be struck out.

EFFECT OF RELIANCE ON RESTRICTIONS IN A COMPANY'S MEMORANDUM

A company's Memorandum may contain some restrictions on its powers and capacity to carry on its authorized business. When this happens, section 45(1) CAMA 2020 (s. 40(1), has stated that such restrictions will not be applied at large, but may be relied upon and have effect only for the purpose(s) of proceedings:

- against the company by a director or member, or where the company has issued debentures secured by a floating charge, over all or any of its properties, by the holder of any of such debentures or the trustee of such a holder; or
- by the company or a member against the present or former officers for failure to observe any such restrictions; or

- by the Commission or a member of the company to wind-up the company; or
- for the purpose of restraining the company or other person(s)from acting in breach of the Memorandum or directing the company or such person to comply with the same.

In proceedings referred to above (except the one restraining the company), a person may not rely on the restriction on the company's power in the Memorandum where he voted in favour or otherwise expressly agreed to the doing of an act by the company or conveyance by or to the company, which is alleged would be contrary to the restriction (s. 45(2) CAMA 2020), (s. 40(2). This section introduces the concept of *estoppel by conduct* against a person seeking to rely on the restriction in the Memorandum *(Abalogu* v. *S.P.D.C. Ltd (2003) 13 NWLR Pt. 837, 308, 335).* Estoppel by conduct, in summary, is that where a person by his words or conduct wilfully causes another to believe the existence of certain things and induces him to act on that behalf so as to alter his own previous position, the former is precluded from averring against the latter a different state of things, as existing at the same time *(A-G Bendel State* v. *A-G Federation & Ors (1981) 10 SC 1; Section 169 Evidence Act 2011).*

THE ARTICLES AS A COMPANY'S CONSTITUTIONAL DOCUMENT

As noted previously, the Articles is the company's 'internal regulator', specifying the intricate details of issues that concern membership rights and general administration of the company. The issues for the Articles include, voting rights, divestment of rights, rights to doing things by proxy, shareholding, including share transfer, directors and their meetings, notices for respective events (though some notices are statutory), meeting of members, appointment of directors, company secretary etc.. In sum, everything about the Articles is always about things that will enhance the general well-being of the company, its members and management.

In construing the Articles of a company, therefore, the overriding principle is usually that it should be regarded as a business document. In essence, any interpretation should approach the Articles in a manner that gives efficacy to the objects of the company as against an interpretation that would make the Articles impractical of implementation *(Holmes* v. *Keyes (1959) Ch. 199, 215).* In line with this understanding, therefore, the Courts will not imply any terms or conditions into the Articles of a company, except those items that are needed to give effect to the language of the Articles in terms of ensuring efficacious business *(Bratton Seymour Service Co Ltd* v. *Oxborough (1992) BCLC 693).* The Courts do this by giving words used in the Articles their ordinary and natural meaning within the context in which they appear (*Towcester Racecourse Co. Ltd* v. *The Racecourse Association Ltd (2003) 1 BCLC 260, Bhadmus, Corporate Law Practice, 58).*

ALTERATION OF A COMPANY'S ARTICLES

A company has an inherent right, subject to the provisions of the CAMA and the conditions and other provisions contained in its Memorandum, to alter its Articles as desired. A *special resolution* duly passed is required to alter a company's Articles. Any alteration made to the Articles shall, subject to the Act, be as valid as if originally contained therein and be alterable likewise by a special resolution (s. 53 CAMA 2020), (s. 48).

Principles on the Alteration of the Articles

Most company law statutes do have provisions on principles regulating the processes by which a company may alter its Articles. The most common that has been seen is usually the provision prescribing a 'special resolution' as a means to any alteration of the Articles. This notwithstanding, over the years, there are certain common law principles, rules and limitations that have crystallized and generally accepted as the basic barometer to guide the process for the alteration of a company's Articles. These include that:

- a company's power to alter its Articles is limited by the provisions of its Memorandum *(Allen* v. *Gold Reefs of West Africa Ltd (1900) 1 Ch. 656, 671; Charlesworth & Cain, 109)***.** For instance, section 53 CAMA 2020 dealing with alteration of the Articles starts with 'subject to the provisions of this Act and to the conditions or other provisions contained in its Memorandum…'
- the alteration of a company's Articles must be *bona fide* for the benefit of the company as a whole. In this respect, an alteration of a company's Articles that was applicable to all members and for the benefit of the company as a whole cannot be impeached on the ground of bad faith, simply because its practical impact was felt by only one member *(Allen* v. *Gold Reefs of West Africa Ltd (1900) 1 Ch 656; Shuttleworth* v. *Cox Bros & Co. (Maidenhead) Ltd (1927) 2 KB 9, Hannigan, 86).*

- a contract made by a company that it will not enforce its statutory power to alter its Articles is unenforceable *(Russell* v. *Northern Bank Development Corporation Ltd (1992) 1 WLR, 588);*
- a company's Articles cannot validly provide that its provisions cannot be altered. This is because a company always has the statutory power to alter its own Articles (s. 53 CAMA 2020), (s. 48). *(Allen* v. *Gold Reefs of West Africa Ltd (1900) 1 Ch. 656, 671;*
- if a thing cannot be done by a company without an authorization contained in its Articles, and there is no such authorization, then a special resolution by the company to do the particular thing would not be interpreted as impliedly altering the Articles to provide the necessary power for such an action *(Hutton* v. *Scarborough Cliff Hotel Co. Ltd (1865) 4 De G J & S 672, all in Mayson et al, 117-9);*
- a company is not prevented from altering its Articles by the mere fact that such an alteration would constitute a breach of contract, even though an action for a breach of contract may lie in favour of the other party to the contract (*Cumbrian Newspaper Group Ltd* v. *Cumberland & Westmorland Herald Newspaper and Printing Co. Ltd (1987) Ch., 1);*
- majority shareholder(s) will not be permitted by the Court to use the guise of alteration of the Articles of the company to perpetrate a fraud on or oppress the minority*; (Menier* v. *Hoopers' Telegraph Works (1874) LR 9 Ch. App., 350; Hannigan, 424);*
- finally, a company's Articles is not one of the documents that a Court can rectify for mistake, duress or other reasons. This is because once registered, the Articles becomes one of the company's constitutional documents, open to the public for inspection and alterable by reference to the procedure in the relevant provisions of the enabling statute *(Scot* v. *Scot F Scot (London) Ltd (1940) Ch., 794; Charlesworth & Cain, 114; Hannigan, 95).*

Limitation of Liability When Memorandum and Articles are Altered

The effect of the alteration of a company's Memorandum and Articles is not at large, that is, where every conceivable end-result could be expected. There are limitations under the Act as to what liabilities, if any, could be imposed upon a member by the fact of alteration of a company's constitutional documents.

Under section 54 CAMA 2020 (s. 49), except to the extent to which a member agrees in writing to be bound, and notwithstanding anything to the contrary in the Memorandum and Articles, a member shall not be bound by any alteration to a company's Memorandum and Articles that requires him, on or after the date of the alteration to:

- take or subscribe to more shares than he held at the date on which he became a member; or
- increase his liability to contribute to the share capital of the company; or
- pay money by any other means to the company.

The above provision is a mechanism aimed at checkmating a company from using the alteration of its constitutional documents for other ends. For instance, any alteration should not be used as guise to oppress a section of the shareholders or to impose terms on members that might be intended to extract unearned moneys from members or to achieve other pre-arranged objectives. This is especially the case in private companies, where the scrutiny from the Commission is not as thorough or far-reaching as with publicly quoted companies.

Notwithstanding the cautious provision in section 54 CAMA 2020 above, the option has been left open to any member(s) who decides to opt into any such arrangement which, though might seem ordinarily suspect in outlook, but which the member(s) decides to still accept and adopt. To be valid, any such acceptance and adoption by the member(s) must be expressly in writing to the company.

In summing the above discussions, a company's Memorandum and Articles of Association are the constitutional documents that define the very existence of the company as a legal and business entity. It is on them that the fact of incorporating or registering the company is based. They are therefore fundamentally important to a company's continued existence and should treated as such.

The company secretary must have a deep grasp, without question, of the company's Articles as this is immensely crucial in his relationship with the members, and with the board of directors. This is especially so in publicly quoted companies, where sundry thorny issues could prop-up for resolution without warning.

The areas in the Articles that should be of particular interest to the company secretary are the areas of membership rights, especially voting rights and where there are pre-emption rights in terms of sale or transfer of shares. These are usually the areas that lead to protracted boardroom and inter-member squabbles, when allegations of side-stepping a company's Articles arise.

Then the issue of the alteration of a company's constitutional documents is also very vital. Here, the major role for the company secretary will be to ensure that laid down procedures are followed in the alteration processes. For instance, for altering the Memorandum, the questions will be: what provisions are proposed to be altered? Are they 'conditions' in the Memorandum (that would require a special resolution) or other provisions? If the alteration involves the name of the company, is the proposed new name available and reserved at the Commission, that is, not being restricted or prohibited?

When altering a company's object or business clause, has the requisite notifications for the meeting (for special resolution) been sent, and sent to all those entitled thereto? (Here, all the members are required to be notified, whether entitled to attend the meeting or not)? So, also, are debenture holders to be notified of the meeting, otherwise the meeting and the resolution outcome will be liable to be set aside. While altering the Articles, apart from the requirement of a special resolution which has been noted above, the common law principles on alteration enunciated above should also serve as a guide.

Finally, in all cases, alteration of the Articles must pass what has come to be known in the company law circle as the 'Allen test', which comes from the principle laid down in the case of *Allen* v. *Gold Reefs of West Africa Ltd (above).* That principle states that any alteration of the Articles of a company must be done *bona fide* and for the interests and benefits of the company, as a whole. Otherwise, such an alteration is liable to be struck down by the Courts on a proper application.

CHECKPOINTS

- ✓ A company's Memorandum and Articles, taken together, constitute the company's constitutional documents. They contain critically important information about the nature of the company and its operations and may also impose restriction(s) on the activities and powers of the company.
- ✓ There are certain provisions that the law mandates to be in the Memorandum, including description of the type of company, capital, object or business clause, how to apply its income (for companies limited by guarantee); company's name etc.. These mandatory requirements are

called the 'conditions' in the Memorandum and are alterable only by a special resolution.

- ✓ On its part, the Articles prescribe the detailed rules and regulations for the administration of the company as a going concern. Things like transfer of shares, voting rights, pre-emption rights, meetings, proxy, quorum, dividends, alteration of capital (also statutory in some respects); directors' shareholding qualification etc. are always in the Articles.
- ✓ When registered, a company's Memorandum and Articles have the effect of a contract under seal between the company and its officers and members, and also between the members themselves. This is usually referred to as the 'statutory contract,' and it has implications.
- ✓ The statutory contract relates only to the rights and liabilities of a shareholder in a company (membership rights) and not in any other capacity, and members can sue themselves on those rights. They do not have to go through a third party or the company to do so.
- ✓ A member who intends to sue on any right granted by the Memorandum and Articles may, with the consent of the other members, bring the action in a representative capacity for all those affected by the issue sought to be redressed in Court.
- ✓ A company's Memorandum and Articles may be altered by laid down rules as prescribed by the CAMA. The important fact is that the conditions in the Memorandum (name of company, object clause, capital, etc.) must only be altered by a special resolution, failing which, any purported alteration will be invalid and liable to be set aside.
- ✓ Even where a company's object clause has been validly altered by a special resolution of the members, any person(s) holding 15 per cent value of the issued capital or 15 per cent of the company's debentures is entitled to approach the Court to set aside the alteration. This has to be done within 28 days of the passage of the resolution that approved the alteration.
- ✓ A person who consented to the alteration or voted in favour of the resolution to alter the Memorandum cannot approach the Court to apply to set aside the alteration. The exception will be where his consent was obtained by fraud or misrepresentation by the company, in which case, such incidents will vitiate the purported consent.

- ✓ A company's Articles is the second part of a company's constitutional documents, complementing the Memorandum. It can only be altered by a special resolution also. Apart from this, there are other common law principles that guide the alteration of the Articles. For instance, that an alteration of a company's Articles must be shown to be *bona fide,* in the interests of the company as a whole, failing which it stands to be aside by the Courts.
- ✓ Again, a company's Articles cannot validly provide that its provisions cannot be altered, being that a company has a statutory power to alter its own Articles.
- ✓ It is noteworthy that, except where a member agrees in writing, he is not bound by any alteration of the Memorandum and Articles that purports to increase his liability to the company, pay more money to the company by any means, or take up more shares that he did not request for.

Chapter 5

CONVERSION AND RE-REGISTRATION OF COMPANIES

INTRODUCTION

From the outset, companies are usually incorporated for particular purposes(s). However, the initial incorporation of a company under a particular category does not stop its conversion or re-registration to another genre, when desired. This is subject to the satisfaction of the conditions stipulated for such a conversion under the CAMA. It has to be noted that the processes of conversion or re-registration of companies are relatively straightforward and closely regulated by the CAMA.

Controversies or disputes in this area of company law and practice are rare and decided cases on the issue of re-registration of companies are also hard to encounter, both locally and otherwise. This is principally because the processes for re-registration of a company from one genre to another hardly involve any third party but are almost exclusively internal affairs within the companies concerned. Secondly and maybe more importantly, is the fact that most re-registrations are usually marketed to the members by the directors as potentially well-thought out and very beneficial and expected to move the company towards better achieving the objectives of the members. This is keying into the provisions of principle 22.1 of the *Nigerian Code of Corporate Governance, 2018,* which stipulates that 'the board should develop a policy that ensures appropriate engagement with shareholders.' Once this is effectively done, most of the time, the re-registration processes are usually solidly backed by the members.

For the company secretary, the duties and responsibilities in this respect are clear cut as his position might virtually be solely responsible in matters of conversion and re-registration of a company. This is because this is not an area where the Courts are keen to intervene or have frequently intervened in the past, being that the processes are usually clearly spelt out in finite details by the Act, here, the CAMA. The board of directors, more often than not, would rely on the company secretary for advice, guidance and implementation, with regards to the regulatory requirements involved in this respect. In most situations, the board of directors and management are usually peopled by those with little or no legal background, and the company secretary would, therefore, have to be thorough in advising and following-through on the processes involved in any re-registration or conversion exercise, which processes are, in most cases, actually not complicated.

Under chapter 2 of the CAMA 2020 (s. 55), (s. 48), there are 5 different types of company re-registrations that could be undertaken by a registered company in Nigeria:

- re-registering of a private company to a public company;
- re-registering of a public company to a private company;
- re-registering of a private company limited by shares to unlimited company;
- re-registering of unlimited company to a company limited by shares;
- re-registering of a public company as an unlimited company (this type is a new addition by the CAMA 2020 and was not there under the CAMA 2004).

RE-REGISTERING OF A PRIVATE COMPANY AS A PUBLIC COMPANY

Under section 60 of the CAMA 2020, (s. 50), a private company, whether limited or unlimited, may be re-registered as a public company limited by shares, if certain conditions are met:

- the members of the company are to pass a *special resolution* that the company should be so re-registered. To be converted to a public company, the company must comply with provisions of section 57 of the Act:
- have a share capital;
- the nominal value of the allotted share capital must not be less than those prescribed under section 27(2) CAMA 2020, out of which at least 25% shall be paid-up and the whole of the premium on it;
- any pending undertaking to pay for shares or share premium with work or services, such undertaking shall have been performed or otherwise, discharged;
- any shares allotted for undertaking otherwise than in cash, then the undertaking shall be performed or discharged and the company shall enter

into a contract to have the services performed within 5 years of the special resolution being passed;

- shares allotted in pursuance of employees' share scheme, by reason of which the company would be precluded from being re-registered as a public company, shall not be regarded for the purpose of determining whether the requirements for re-registration to a public company are met.
- In addition to the above, the company is expected to comply with conditions relating to its net assets and any recent shares allotment for non-cash consideration under sections 58 and 59 CAMA 2020:
- the company shall alter its Memorandum (name, status, etc) and Articles, so that it states that it is a public company and also make other necessary alterations to the Memorandum to meet the requirements of a public company under the Act. Also, if the company is an unlimited company, the necessary changes are needed to make it a company limited by shares.
- the company must not have been previously re-registered as an unlimited company.

When all the above conditions precedents have been met, the company's application for re-registration shall be sent to the Commission. It is notable that the requirement under the CAMA 2004 that the application be signed by at least one director and the company secretary has been omitted in CAMA 2020. Under section 60 (1) CAMA 2020, (s. 50(3), the company's application for re-registration shall contain the following documents:

- a statement of the company's proposed name on re-registration and if the company did not appoint a company secretary as a private company, then statement of the name of the proposed company secretary (with particulars, principally, names, addresses and e-mail address. The statement shall also contain the consent of the proposed company secretary to so act). It is in order to suggest that the company secretary's telephone number is also part of the particulars included in the register;
- a copy of the special resolution, as passed;
- a copy of the Memorandum and Articles as altered (as proposed to be amended) pursuant to the special resolution; and
- a balance sheet (not more than 7 months old), with auditor's unqualified report of same and the auditor's statement that the company's net assets was not less than the aggregate of the company's called-up share capital and undistributable reserves;

- statement of compliance that the requirements of the Act for re-registration as a public company have been complied with.

In an apparent attempt to simplify the process of re-registration in this part, the CAMA 2020 dispensed with the written statement on oath by the directors and the company secretary and their statutory declaration respectively and replaced them with statement of compliance.

If the Commission is satisfied that the company has complied with all the laid down conditions, it shall re-register the company as a public company and issue a new certificate of incorporation to reflect its public status. Once a new certificate of incorporation is issued, the company becomes a public company and the alterations in its Memorandum and Articles shall take effect as such. If the name of a company secretary was proposed with the application, he is deemed to have been appointed on the day a new certificate is issued to the company as a public company (s. 62 CAMA 2020), (s. 50 (4)(5)(6).

The certificate of incorporation issued to a re-registered company shall be *prima facie* evidence that the prescribed requirements for re-registration under the Act and matters precedent and incidental thereto have been complied with; and that the company is a public company (s. 62(5) CAMA 2020), (s. 50 (6). Being *prima facie* evidence presupposes that the process could still be impeached, if facts emerge that will show that the re-registration ought not to have been approved by the Commission. For example, if there were suppression or misrepresentation of material facts by the company in getting re-registered.

RE-REGISTERING A PUBLIC COMPANY AS A PRIVATE COMPANY

The process of re-registering a company from being a public company to a private company appears more intricate, for obvious reasons, though not totally different, from what has been discussed above, that is, converting from private to public. Large public companies have huge shareholders and assets base, huge data base of information on shareholders, directors and other stakeholders. Therefore, due care is taken by the law to closely regulate the processes that seek to convert such companies to private companies, where the level of regulatory oversight by the relevant authorities is not as thorough and sustained as that of public companies.

In terms of the procedure for re-registration, section 63 CAMA 2020, (s. 53), stipulates that a public company may be re-registered as a private limited company if certain conditions are met:

- the members pass a *special resolution* that the company should be re-registered as a private limited company;
- the special resolution is then accompanied by a formal application to the Commission to re-register the company as a private limited company. Also, to be included in the application is a statement of compliance that the requisite conditions have been met;
- a copy of the Memorandum and Articles as proposed to be altered (in line with the special resolution) as to name, status, etc;
- there is no pending application in Court asking that the special resolution be cancelled. If any was filed, it has been discharged or refused.
- For this particular category of re-registration, there is a provision in section 64 CAMA 2020, (s. 53), for certain qualified persons to make applications to Court to cancel any special resolution passed by members to re-register the company. Those who are qualified to make the application to Court are:
- the holders of at least 5 per cent in nominal value of the company's issued share capital, or a class thereof (excluding treasury shares: which are shares held by the company itself in a proprietary capacity for its own legal and beneficial use);
- if the company is not one limited by shares, (for instance a company limited by guarantee), then by at least 5 per cent of its members;
- by at least 50 members of the company, (but excluding any person who had consented or voted in favour of the resolution).

The application to Court to cancel a company's resolution shall be made within 28 days after the passing of the resolution. The class of persons entitled to approach the Court may appoint one of their members to make such an application on their behalf. The question is: what then happens if the application to Court is not made within the mandatory time of 28 days allowed by the Act?

This book opines that those making the application can approach the Court with an *ex-parte* application for extension of time within which to make such an application, with sufficient reasons, and putting relevant materials before the Court. Since it is a matter that will involve the exercise of the discretion of the Court, care should be taken to make sure that convincing reasons and materials are placed before the Court explaining the delay in applying to set aside the resolution.

Although the Courts have inherent powers to extend the time within which any such application as above could be made, the importance of putting enough materials before the Court cannot be over-emphasized. This is because being a matter of exercise of discretion, if the application is refused by the Court, leave of the same Court is required to appeal against such a refusal. Most times such applications for leave to appeal are denied, except fresh pieces of evidence are adduced to convince the Court otherwise *(Chief of Air Staff* v. *Edward & Ors (2019) 14 NWLR Pt. 1691, 183; Dapianlong* v. *Dariye (2007) 8 NWLR Pt. 1036, 239; UBN Plc* v. *Sogunro (2006) 6 NWLR Pt. 1006, 505).*

A Court hearing the application is required to make an order either cancelling or confirming the resolution and may make other orders or give other directions as it may think proper or expedient in the circumstances. The Court may also make an order adjourning the proceedings to allow for arrangement to purchase the shares of dissenting members or for the company to purchase the members' shares and reduce its capital. Consequentially, the Court may also order amendment of the company's Memorandum and Articles in that respect (s. 64 (3-6) CAMA 2020), (s. 53(5).

Once an application has been made to Court to cancel a resolution passed to re-register a company as above, the applicant(s) is mandated to immediately notify the Commission of that fact. On its part, once the application is served on the company, the company is also mandated to immediately notify the Commission. Also, when an order has been made by the Court on the application to cancel the resolution, the company is mandated to send a copy of the order to the Commission within 15 days of the order being made, or as directed by the Court. A daily continuing fine is imposed on the company and each officer for failure to comply with the notification provisions as indicated (s. 65 CAMA 2020), (s. 53 (6).

When a company has fulfilled all the conditions stipulated for registration as a private company, it shall send a formal application to the Commission accompanied with the proposed name on re-registration, the special resolution to re-register as a private company, amended Memorandum and Articles and a statement of compliance that all conditions laid down by the CAMA in this respect have been complied with. On being satisfied with a company's application to re-register, the Commission shall issue a new certificate of incorporation and the company becomes a private company and the alterations in its Memorandum and Articles shall take effect as such.

As noted above, when we were discussing re-registration from a private to a public company, here also, the certificate of incorporation is *prima facie* evidence that the prescribed requirements for re-registration under the Act and matters precedent and incidental thereto have been complied with; and that the company is a private company (ss. 66 and 67 CAMA 2020), (s. 53(9)(10).

Apart from preparing all the internal documents needed for this class of re-registration, the company secretary's other main tasks in this respect are notifications to the Commission. For instance, once a company has been served with an application to cancel the special resolution to re-register the company, it is for the company secretary to notify the Commission of such an application. Again, once the Court decides on the application to cancel the resolution, one way or the other, the company secretary is also to notify the Commission, before proceeding with the regular process to re-register, that is, if the resolution was not cancelled by the Court.

RE-REGISTRATION OF COMPANY LIMITED BY SHARES AS UNLIMITED

A company registered as private limited company can be re-registered as an unlimited company, if the requisite conditions laid down by the CAMA are met. Under section 68 CAMA 2020 (s. 51), a company may be re-registered as such if:

- *all the members* of the company have assented to have it so re-registered (note that a trustee in bankruptcy and a personal representative of a deceased member can attest for them, respectively);
- a formal application will have to be sent to the Commission with a statement of compliance indicating that the conditions stated by the CAMA in that respect have been complied with;
- the company would not have been previously re-registered to the limited status.

The company will make consequential changes to its name and its Memorandum and Articles, in relation to its new unlimited status and its share capital. The application to the Commission shall contain a proposed name on re-registration and an authenticated assented form signed by all the members. Also, to be included in the application are the amended Memorandum and Articles.

The statement of compliance shall contain a statement by the company's directors (under the 2004 CAMA, it was a statutory declaration that was required to do this) that those who assented to the re-registration constitute all the members. Additionally, the directors are to affirm that for those members who did not assent personally, that efforts were made to confirm that the persons who represented them to assent have the authority to do so (s. 69 CAMA 2020), (s. 51(6).

If the Commission is satisfied with the company's application, it will issue the company a certificate on the new company status and the company becomes unlimited and changes to the Memorandum and Articles become effective (s. 70 CAMA 2020), (s. 51(8).

There appears to have been an error in the CAMA with regards to the effect of the certificate to be issued by the Commission in this respect. Section 70(5) CAMA 2020 states that the certificate issued by Commission is conclusive evidence that the requirements of the Act as to the re-registration have been complied with. The actual effect should have been *prima facie* evidence, as it was under section 51(9) CAMA 2004 in similar respect, not conclusive.

Particular note must be taken of this procedure, that it is the first of the re-registration procedures that requires the assent of every member in a company for it to progress. The reason is not far-fetched, as agreeing to submit to the regime of unlimited liability is not something that should be done lightly. The Commission has to be sure and assured that all the members willingly agreed to make their liability unlimited, before approving the re-registration.

RE-REGISTRATION OF AN UNLIMITED COMPANY AS LIMITED BY SHARES

A company registered as unlimited under the CAMA may be re-registered as limited by shares if certain conditions stipulated by the Act are met. Once this has been done, the company will send a formal application to the Commission to effect the registration. The process is not markedly different from the ones discussed above:

- the members of the company shall pass a special resolution that the company be re-registered as limited by shares;
- the company would not have been previously been re-registered as unlimited;

- in this instance, the special resolution shall state whether the intention is to re-register the company as limited by shares or limited by guarantee;
- the company will then make the necessary changes to its name, Memorandum and Articles, and its status as a limited company (whichever genre is chosen).

A formal application is then submitted to the Commission, accompanied with a proposed name on re-registration, and a statement of compliance indicating that all the necessary conditions have been complied with. Also, to accompany the application will be the amended Memorandum and Articles, and a copy of the special resolution to re-register the company. If the choice has been to register a company limited by guarantee, then a statement of guarantee, stating the liability of each member to contribute to the assets of the company on winding-up is also required to accompany the application (s. 72 CAMA 2020), (s. 52 (3)(5).

If the Commission is satisfied that the company has complied with all the laid down conditions for re-registration, it shall re-register the company as limited by shares or guarantee and issue a new certificate of incorporation to it as a limited company, as altered. Once a new certificate of incorporation is issued the status of the company changes from unlimited to a limited company and the alterations in its Memorandum and Articles shall take effect accordingly (s. 73 (1)-(4) CAMA 2020), (s. 52 (6) (7).

The certificate of incorporation shall be *prima facie* evidence that the prescribed requirements for re-registration under the Act and matters precedent and incidental thereto have been complied with (s. 73(5) CAMA 2020), (s. 52 (8).

The CAMA 2020 added a further requirement for a company that has been re-registered under this head. After re-registration, if the company has already allotted its shares, it shall, within 15 days after the re-registration, send to the Commission a statement of share capital indicating therein:

i. the company's total number of shares;
ii. aggregate nominal value of the shares;
iii. rights attached to each class of shares, their aggregate nominal value, total number of shares in the class and amount paid-up and amount unpaid on each share (s. 74 (1)-(3) CAMA 2020).

The company secretary would be responsible for these returns to the Commission. A default to send this notice to the Commission attracts a continuing daily penalty to the company and each officer as prescribed by the Commission.

RE-REGISTRATION OF PUBLIC COMPANY AS UNLIMITED

This class of company re-registration is a new addition by the CAMA 2020 as the CAMA 2004 had no provisions for it. Here, a public company limited by shares may be re-registered as an unlimited company, (with a share capital) if certain conditions are met, under sections 75 and 76 CAMA 2020:

- all the members have consented that the company should be re-registered as an unlimited company (this is the second category requiring all the members to consent) (a member's trustee in bankruptcy and a deceased member's personal representative may assent on their behalf on an authenticated prescribed form);
- the company has not previously been re-registered either as a limited or unlimited company;
- a formal application to the Commission to re-register the company as an unlimited company shall be submitted with a statement of compliance that the requisite conditions for re-registration have been complied with.

The statement of compliance shall contain a statement by the company's directors (i) that those who authenticated the assent form for the re-registration constitute all the whole membership of the company. (ii) Additionally, the directors are to affirm that for those members who did not authenticate the assent form personally, that efforts were made to confirm that the persons who represented them to assent have the authority to do so (s. 76 (4) CAMA 2020).

If the Commission is satisfied that the company is entitled to be re-registered as unlimited, it shall re-register it accordingly and issue a new certificate of incorporation to it as unlimited company, as altered. Once a new certificate of incorporation is issued the status of the company changes from public to unlimited company and the alterations in its Memorandum and Articles shall take effect accordingly (s. 77 (1)-(4) CAMA 2020).

The certificate of incorporation shall be *prima facie* evidence that the prescribed requirements for re-registration under the Act have been complied with (s. 77(5) CAMA 2020.

In sum, although the process of re-registration or conversion of commercial entities from one genre to the other is not an everyday occurrence in the Nigerian corporate and commercial circles, it does take place. A company that has been registered as a particular type of undertaking may, in the future, and for diverse reasons, decide to re-register as a different genre of company. The CAMA has fairly standardized the procedures and processes for re-registering a company. Apart from the addition of a new class of re-registration (from public company to unlimited company) in CAMA 2020, the procedures enunciated in CAMA 2004 and CAMA 2020 are not fundamentally different, though there are few material changes as noted above.

The primary duties of the company secretary in the above respects are to ensure that the conditions laid down for every type of re-registration are met. Also, care should be taken to ensure that a company did not fall within the ambit of prohibited re-registration when this is being sought.

Special attention should be paid to areas where the CAMA 2020 has changed the processes and procedures for any company conversion. For instance, the replacement of the need for statutory declaration on oath in several areas with a statement of compliance should be noted. Again, in an area like re-registering a private company to a public company, the specific new conditions added by CAMA 2020 in sections 58 and 59 should be noted.

The processes for re-registering from a public to a private company is the most intricate of all. Care should be taken to meet the several timelines for doing particular tasks imposed by the CAMA in this respect. Again, the group of persons who are entitled to apply to Court to cancel any resolution passed to re-register a company under this head and the timeline for doing so should be noted.

For re-registration from a public company to an unlimited company under sections 75 to 77 CAMA 2020, being a new addition to the CAMA, attention should be paid to the detailed requirements, being that there is no practice precedent to rely on in this respect.

In all, therefore, as noted early on, the company secretary's main tasks here are to ensure a good compliance with the requirements as per each of the re-registrations and within the timeline prescribed, if any. It needs to be re-emphasized that there are lots of time-sensitive regulatory returns and notifications to the Commission within the whole processes of re-registration. The other tasks relate to ensuring that all the necessary changes to the company's corporate nomenclature incidental to the re-registration are undertaken and promptly: changing the stationeries, signposts, common seal (if any), website, branded vehicles and other of its business paraphernalia could said to be consequential only when the core processes and procedures leading to the re-registrations have been successfully implemented. This is especially important where the re-registration also affected the company's name or designation, for instance, changing from a private limited company (Ltd) to a public company (Plc), or vice versa.

From a corporate governance perspective, the company secretary will have to engage the shareholders, especially institutional shareholders and shareholder groups, and other stakeholders in making any votes that will lead to the passing of the requisite resolution or assent for any re-registration of a company to be seamless. This is especially so in the type of re-registration that requires unanimity of consent of all the members. As the link between the shareholders, the board and senior management, the company secretary has a crucial role to play in communicating the positives of any re-registrations(s) being the position of the board and senior management, to all the stakeholders. In this way, any incident of any section of the membership of the company applying to Court to set aside any planned re-registration, will be reduced to the barest minimum.

CHECKPOINTS

- ✓ A company, once registered, may, along the line, have reason(s) to want to change its genre and operate as another type of company. The CAMA allows this type of conversion, as long as the laid down rules and regulations are followed. Although it is not a routine process in the Nigeria, but it still happens, from time to time.
- ✓ The CAMA 2020 has listed five (5) different types of corporate re-registrations, unlike the CAMA 2004 that listed four (4) possible conversions. The new addition in the 2020 Act is the re-registering a public company into an unlimited company.
- ✓ To re-register from a private company to a public company, a special resolution is required, that is, the company having first met the conditions stipulated under section 57 CAMA 2020. The section stipulates the basic minimum conditions precedent for a private company that wants to re-register as a public company.
- ✓ A company may also wish to re-register from being a public company to being a private company. This process is more intricate than that of re-registering from a private company to a public company, for obvious reasons. The process starts with the members passing a special resolution and then a formal application is sent to the Commission to re-register the company as sought, other conditions being met.

✓ Some classes of persons are entitled to approach the Court to stop the processes of re-registration of the company. The first is those who hold 5 per cent in the nominal value of the company's issued shares, or 5 per cent of the members, for companies not limited by shares. Another group would be 50 members of the company in question acting together. The application to Court will have to be made within 28 days of the passing of the resolution to re-register the company.

✓ The applicants are required to notify the Commission once the application is filed in Court and the company is required to notify the Commission once they receive the Court processes. When the Court makes an order, the company is mandated to send a copy of the order to the Commission without delay.

✓ If the Commission is satisfied with all the processes received from the parties and the company's application, it will re-register the company as a private company.

✓ A company is entitled to re-register from a company limited by shares to an unlimited company. To commence this type of re-registration, all the members of the company will have to assent (unanimous assent) that the company should be so converted. Afterwards, a formal application shall be made to the Commission, attaching the members' verified assent, among other documents. Once the Commission is satisfied with the documents sent by the company, it will re-register the company as an unlimited company.

✓ A company may also apply to the Commission to be re-registered from being an unlimited company to being a company limited by shares. Here the application process starts by the members passing a special resolution to that effect, which will then necessitate a formal application to the Commission to re-register the company. If the Commission is satisfied with the resolution and the documents submitted by the company, it will go ahead and re-register the company as a company limited by shares.

✓ A company registered as a public company may apply to the Commission to be re-registered as an unlimited company. This is a new category introduced by the CAMA 2020 and was not there under the 2004 Act. This will require the assent of all the members of the company (unanimous assent) to kick-start the process. A formal application will then be sent to the Commission with a statement of compliance affirming that all the conditions stated in the CAMA for the procedure have been complied with by the company. If the Commission is satisfied with the members' verified assent sent by the company and the accompanying documents, it will re-register the public company as an unlimited company.

- ✓ The company secretary has crucial roles to play in all the above instances of re-registrations. Apart from the legal aspect of summoning the necessary meetings to pass the requisite resolutions and obtain the needed assents, from a governance perspective also, the company secretary's role is vital. It is the company secretary that will communicate the decision of the board and management of the company to re-register the company to the shareholders and other stakeholders and also engage them with positive reasons for adopting such a procedure by the company. In this way, incidents of dissent by members and other stakeholders will be minimal.

Chapter 6

APPOINTMENT AND POWERS OF COMPANY DIRECTORS

INTRODUCTION

In modern company practice, and it appears to have always been the case since incorporated companies came into existence, the general direction and administration of a company is usually the responsibility of the board of directors. This includes policy formulation, strategic planning, policy direction and general administration of the company. Though the directors are usually assigned individual responsibilities in terms of specific duties in a company, (it is common to hear of positions like director human resource management, director finance, marketing director, etc.), the expectation is that in managing and directing the affairs of a company, the directors act as a unit, that is, the board. The collectivity of the board of directors is key, both in their actions and even in their decision-making processes. In this respect, the World Bank Group (IFC) in their 2016 study entitled the '*Corporate Secretary: the Governance Professional*' submitted that the collectivity of directorship in companies entails that once directors take any decision as a collective (board), whether any one of the directors disagree with the decision or not, he is bound by it and must work with it (47).

The *Nigerian Code of Corporate Governance, 2018* (the NCCG), as released by the Financial Reporting Council of Nigeria (the FRCN), captures well the essence and attributes of a good board of directors:

> a successful company is headed by an effective board which is responsible for providing entrepreneurial and strategic leadership as well as promoting ethical culture and responsible corporate citizenship. As a link between stakeholders and the company, the board is to exercise oversight and control to ensure that management acts in the best interest of the shareholders and

other stakeholders while sustaining the prosperity of the company (Principle 1).

The *UK Corporate Governance Code, 2018* (the UK Code) agrees with the above principles, and states that 'a successful company is led by an effective and entrepreneurial board, whose role is to promote the long-term sustainable success of the company, generating value for shareholders and contributing to wider society' (Principle A, 4).

The CAMA does not seem to attach much importance to the nomenclature used to describe persons directing the affairs of a company. It seems to place more focus on the functions and actions of any such persons within or for the company. It is even possible that a person who has not been appointed or named a director in a company could be treated by the law as such. In essence, the substance would appear to prevail over the form, in terms of determining who is treated as a company director under the law in Nigeria.

WHO IS A COMPANY DIRECTOR IN NIGERIA?

For our present purposes, it is actually germane to start by trying to find out who a company director is. The answer may not be as straight-forward as many will want it to be. As noted above, a person could be considered, in law, a director in a company without even working directly with the company in question.

Section 868 CAMA 2020, (s. 567) defines the term 'director' to include 'any person occupying the position of director by whatever name called, and includes any person in accordance with whose directions or instructions the directors of the company are accustomed to act.' These latter persons are usually referred to as 'shadow directors' (s. 270 CAMA 2020), (s. 245). This description excludes professionals, who offer their professional opinion or advice to the company and on which the directors act. It is therefore immaterial that a director of a company is called 'administrator,' 'governor,' 'trustee,' or any like term. The CAMA is more interested in the actions and functions of the person involved and whether the person, in essence, participates in directing and managing the company. If so, that would qualify the person concerned as a director. This position must be juxtaposed with the provision of section 269(1) CAMA 2020, (s. 244), which states that 'a director of a company is a person duly appointed by the company to direct and manage the business of the company.' In *Olufosoye* v. *Fakorede (1993) 1*

NWLR Pt. 272, 947, a 'director' was described as a person who has been appointed or elected according to law, and authorized to manage and direct the affairs of a corporation or company.' In all events, therefore, the elements of management and direction of the entities involved, are always constant in the classification or description of directorship.

On its face value and on strict construction, section 269 CAMA 2020 (s. 244) may sound misleading, in that it seems to emphasize the fact of 'due appointment' of every person to be properly called a director. This, however, is not the position of the law, because a person may even be regarded as a director of a company by 'holding out' only, having held out himself or being held out by the company, even when not duly appointed as such. The CAMA criminalizes the fact of holding out either by the person himself or by the company, of anybody not duly appointed as a director, but who holds himself out as such. However, once a person has been held out, whether validly or not as a director, his actions are considered regular, especially in relation to third parties, although subsequently, other sanctions may be meted out to him or the company that held him out.

If it is the company that holds the person out as a director without due appointment, then the company, apart from being liable to a fine, may be restrained by any member from such holding out until the person is duly appointed a director (s. 269 (3)(4) CAMA 2020), (s. 244 (3)(4). When it is an individual that holds out himself as a director of a company without due appointment, the company has the standing to restrain such a person, also. In both cases the restraining will be by an order of injunction, which is a judicial order commanding or directing a person or entity to do or refrain from doing an act *(Azuh* v. *UBN Plc (2014) 11 NWLR Pt. 1419, 580; Kotoye* v. *CBN (1989) 1 NWLR Pt. 98, 419).*

For a person(s) to be considered a director in a company, the CAMA also emphasizes persons 'directing and managing' the business of the company and not necessarily their due appointment only. However, section 269(2) CAMA 2020, (s. 244(2), raises a rebuttable presumption of due appointment in favour of a person dealing with persons that have been held out by a company as its directors, and this is irrespective of whether the persons were not actually so appointed. This situation is akin to holding out someone as having an authority, for instance, of an agent when such an agency has not been expressly created or was not intended to cover the particular transaction involved. The law will still input agency to the principal, here, the company *(Fridman, The Law of Agency, 2nd edn. 93).* In all, it will be fair to say that to actually determine who a company director is under Nigerian law, as per the CAMA, the provisions of the Act, especially sections 269, 270 and 868 CAMA 2020 (ss. 244, 245 and 567) would have to be read holistically and liberally, in line with the rules of statutory construction *(Rabiu* v. *State (1980)8-11 SC, 130; Mobil Oil Nig. Plc* v. *IAL 36 Inc (2000) 6 NWLR Pt. 659, 146).* That is when it can be seen that the sections bring out clearly the factors of appointment, holding out and external directions as critical in determining when a person could be said to be a director, for all intents and purposes.

The company secretary is not part of the persons, strictly speaking, that have the duties to appoint directors. Not at all. That is the duty reserved for the board of directors, for casual vacancies, and the general meeting for general appointments and ratifications. However, from a corporate governance perspective, the company secretary has huge roles to play in the process of the appointment of directors, especially, subsequent directors or those to fill causal vacancies. According the World Bank Group (IFC, 57), 'the company secretary should advise the chairman on the size and composition of the board, the tenure of board of the directors and directors' selection and appointment. Policies on all of these should be developed by the company secretary and approved by the board. These policies should be part of a governance manual.' Although the matter of directors' tenure of office is partly provided for in the CAMA and usually fully in the Articles, the company secretary has the duty to keep the chairman of the board up to date on related board issues, for example, the sequence of directors' retirements and the need to maintain a balanced board on replacement.

From what has been discussed above, an issue that should be, and is usually, of further concern to the company secretary is the aspect of holding out as a director, either by a person(s) or by the company itself. It is even worse that the CAMA criminalizes the situation, and a member may restrain the company through a Court action (injunction). Another issue is that of the person(s) on whose instructions and directions the directors are accustomed to act, the person that has been labelled by the law as 'a shadow director.'

For the company secretary, on discovering that the company is holding out an individual as a director, the proper approach is to bring that situation to the attention of the chairman of the board of directors. The board will then have three options open to them for rectification of the situation: (i) to formally appoint the person(s) a director, if the holding out is by the company and is deliberate; or (ii) to cease holding out the person as a director and take all steps to disassociate the company from any legacy image of his directorship already established; or (iii) to restrain the person by an action (injunction) from so parading himself as a director.

In the case of a person(s) on whose instructions and directions the directors of a company are accustomed to act, the situation might be more complicated, depending on what the initial relationship between the company and the person was. This is especially so for small and private companies. What the company secretary could do here is simply to bring to the attention of the board of directors that the law considers the third party a director in the company, considering his influence and affinity to the company. It is left to the company as to what to do with that information, being that the CAMA did not criminalize shadow directorship, the Act will then be ascribing all apparent and ostensible authorities and duties of directors (including fiduciary duties) to the person in question. Considering the legal and other implications inherent in a case of this nature, it will be a situation for the company to really pay attention to and take note of.

APPOINTMENT OF DIRECTORS

Determining the processes for the appointment of company directors would depend on whether one is discussing the appointment of directors at inception, that is, when the company is being incorporated or subsequently, when it is already a going concern. It is important to reiterate that the processes for both are not the same. Even when a company has become operational as a going concern, the processes of appointing directors to replace retiring directors, for instance, or those that died or resigned their appointments, are also different from when the general meeting is statutorily replacing directors. These issues are discussed below.

Appointment of First Directors

The overall prerogative for determining the names and number of the persons to be appointed as a company's first directors is that of the subscribers to the company's Memorandum of Association or majority of them (s. 272 CAMA 2020), (s. 247). This subscription has to be in writing. The use of the phrase 'or majority of them' implies that there need not be unanimity among the subscribers to the Memorandum on the names and number of persons to be appointed as first directors, once a majority of them are agreed on those recommended. This is subject to section 271 of the Act, which regulates the minimum number of directors a company is permitted to have. The first directors may also be named in the company's Articles by the subscribers in the process of incorporating the company along with filing the necessary incorporation forms to appoint directors.

Until recently, that is until the year 2020, every company registered in Nigeria was required to have at least two (2) directors appointed to manage and direct its affairs. Any company whose number of directors falls below that threshold is mandated to appoint a new director(s) to make up the numbers within one (1) month. The company should cease to carry on its business if such replacement appointment is not made after the prescribed period has elapsed (s. 246 (1)(2) CAMA 2004). However, with the coming into force of CAMA 2020, the situation has changed.

Under section 271(1) CAMA 2020, every company, except a 'small company', as defined under section 394 of the Act (as amended by section 18 of the schedule to the *Business Facilitation (Miscellaneous Provisions) Act (BFA) 2022)*, is mandated to have at least two (2) directors. The other provisions in section 246 CAMA 2004 relating to when the number of directors falls below two (2) and what to do and the timeline for doing so still apply under the CAMA 2020. Any member or director in a company, not being a small company, who is aware that a company whose number of directors had fallen below the prescribed minimum still carries on business and does so for more than sixty (60) days shall be liable for the liabilities and debts incurred by the company during the period in question, that is, when the company so carried on business (s. 271 (3) CAMA 2020), (s. 246 (3).

A few words have to be said about the appointment of the managing director. Unless in a situation where the directors are empowered to appoint a managing director by the Memorandum or the Articles, the directors cannot exercise such powers to appoint. Where, however, the Articles authorize the directors to appoint a managing director, the company, in its general meeting, cannot then go ahead to make the appointment, without first amending the Articles to remove the directors' powers of appointment *(Thomas Logan Ltd* v. *Davis (1911) 104 L.T. 914; Charlesworth & Cain, 362).* Further discussions on different aspects of the position of the managing director will be taken in subsequent chapters.

Appointment of Subsequent Directors

While the appointment of a company's first directors is for the subscribers to the Memorandum, subsequent appointments are for the members and directors of the company. Principally, the members have the power at general meetings to re-elect or reject any of the directors and appoint new ones in their stead (s. 273(1) CAMA 2020), s. 248(1); *NIB Investment (West Africa) Ltd* v. *Omisore & 5 Ors (2006) 4 NWLR Pt. 969, 172, 199).* As will be seen below, this appointment by the general meeting is not the only method of appointing directors into a company's board.

It is noteworthy that it is possible for a company's Articles (especially in a private company) to give the power of nominating a director(s) for appointment to a particular person(s) *(Orojo, 252),* or class of shareholders, debenture holders or other third parties (*Gower & Davies, 398*). This was one of the contentions of the plaintiff/appellant in the *NIB Investment case above*, with the appellant alleging, among others, that the O'odua Group actually appointed several directors on the company's board, when it was not a member of the company. Unfortunately, we did not get the benefit of the Court's analysis on this point, being that the matter was decided, both at the trial Court and on Appeal, on the issue of the plaintiff/appellant's *locus standi* and the rule in *Foss* v. *Harbottle* (that where a company, being a legal person, is allegedly injured by acts of other person(s), either members or not, that it is the company alone that has the right, bar a few exceptions, to sue to remedy the injury).

As noted above, a company's Articles could give powers to a class of person(s), shareholders or debenture holders, among others, to appoint directors for the company. Where this is the case, the company's existing directors cannot, in the exercise of their powers to increase the number of directors on the board, appoint the number of directors as to make it impossible for the person(s) specified in the Articles to be able to exercise the power to nominate directors. This book opines, that where the directors act in such a manner, such an appointment(s) is liable to be struck down by the Court on the application of the person authorized by the Articles to so appoint. This is because the action of the directors in that respect would have been seen to breach one of the cardinal principles of their office, which is to always act *bona fide* and in the 'best interest of the company as a whole.'

Casual Vacancy

A casual vacancy occurs in a company's board of directors when a director(s) resigns, dies, retires or is removed before the expiration of his tenure and before the company's annual general meeting. Under section 274 (1) CAMA 2020, (s. 249(1), the board of directors is empowered to appoint a director(s) to fill in the casual vacancy *(DYS Trocca Valessia Ltd & Ors* v. *Sanyaolu & Ors*

(2016) LPELR-40423; Wariboko v. *Imago Group Co. Ent. Nig. Ltd & Ors (2014) LPELR-26428).* Any director(s) so appointed shall be approved by the members at the next annual general meeting, failing which such a person(s) ceases to be a director (s. 274 (2) CAMA 2020), (s. 249(2). This confirms the supremacy of a company's general meeting in matters relating to the appointment and removal of directors, among other matters.

The board of directors may increase the number of directors on the board at any time, provided that the number does not exceed the maximum number of directors allowed by the Articles. However, the general power to increase or decrease the number of directors on the board, even if amounting to the alteration of the Articles, rests with the general meeting. It is also true that the general meeting may use the process of increasing or reducing the number of directors to determine the rotation by which the directors shall retire. In that respect, however, any reduction in the number of directors shall not in any way invalidate any action(s) that had been taken by the removed director(s) (s. 274 (3) CAMA 2020), (s. 249 (3).

If, for any reason(s), all the directors and shareholders of a company die, any of their personal representatives is entitled to apply to Court for an order convening a meeting of all the personal representatives of the shareholders who are entitled to attend and vote at a general meeting to appoint new directors for the company. This provision is mostly important for private companies, especially smaller ones, where all the members are usually also the directors. If the personal representatives of the deceased directors and shareholders fail to convene a meeting for the purpose of appointing new directors for the company in the circumstance described above, the company's creditors, where they exist, shall have the right to do so (s. 273(2) CAMA 2020), (s. 248 (2).

Shadow Directors

We have seen the processes for the appointment of first and subsequent directors for companies. Shadows directors are said to be directors and are so made by imputation of the law. Note should be taken that there is usually no appointment or such a process for them, but the law still recognizes them as directors.

Recall that under section 868 CAMA 2020 (s. 567) a director includes any person occupying the position of a director and includes any person on whose instructions and directions a company's board of directors is accustomed to act. This excludes professionals who are advisers to the directors of a company and on whose advice the directors usually act (s. 270 (1)(3) CAMA 2020), (s. 245 (1)(3). This is without prejudice to the due appointment provision to be a director under section 269 CAMA 2020, (s. 244). Specifically, therefore, it is the aspect of the person(s) on whose instructions and directions that the directors are accustomed to act, that brought about a director who, though not appointed, but could be controlling the company from the 'shadows.'

With specific reference to shadow directors, the CAMA makes four (4) important clarifications:

- if a person who meets the conditions to be considered a shadow director in relation to a company becomes insolvent and while being so keeps influencing the company as a director, such a person shall be liable to a fine to be prescribed by the Commission or a term of imprisonment (not less than six (6) months or more than two years) or both (s. 279 CAMA 2020), (s. 253).
- a company is required to include shadow directors in its register of directors' shareholding (s. 301 CAMA 2020), (s. 275).
- the requirement that a director who holds multiple directorships in different companies shall owe fiduciary duties to all of them and not use information, opportunity or property obtained in the course of managing one company to the benefit of the other companies or himself, is also applicable to shadow directors (s. 307 CAMA 2020), (s. 281).
- furthermore, the restriction on a director holding more than five (5) multiple directorships in public companies also applies to a shadow director (s. 307 (3) CAMA 2020, as amended by section 16 of the schedule to the *Business Facilitation (Miscellaneous Provisions) Act (BFA) 2022*). This restriction was not in the CAMA 2004.

As noted above, the incidence of shadow directorship is one that is imputed to an individual(s) or person(s) by operation of law, which then imposes all the duties and responsibilities of directors on such person(s). This is without the person(s) expressly agreeing to assume those responsibilities and duties. This situation is unlike that of the regularly appointed directors, where consent to act as a director is usually required from the person(s) to be so appointed. Notwithstanding the fact that a person could be imputed with directorship position by the law as a shadow director, it is still important to note, that, generally, a person who acts as a director of a company, but who has not been duly appointed as such, except otherwise held out by the company, shall not bind the company and shall be personally liable for his actions (s. 276 CAMA 2020, (s. 250).

Apart from the statutory provisions by the CAMA as seen above, what has been the judicial approach to the issue of 'shadow directorship' in Nigeria?' Judicial authorities on the issue by Nigerian Courts are very scarce. As a matter of fact, as at the time of writing this page, we have been unable to locate a Nigerian decision that has dealt squarely with the issue of shadow directorship in a company. However, there are persuasive authorities from English Courts that could provide guidance. One of them is the case of *Secretary of State for Trade and Industry* v. *Deverell (2000) BCLC, 133*; (Hannigan, 146), where Morritt LJ, examined the definition of a 'shadow director,' under the English Companies Act 2006, which provisions are on all fours with that in the CAMA, and made the following key propositions, among others:

- that the definition of a 'shadow director' should be construed literally to give effect to the intention of the parliament in addressing the noted mischief;
- that the purpose of the legislation is to locate those, aside professionals, with real influence on the company, which influence does not have to cover all the company's areas of business;
- that whether any communication from the 'shadow director' to the company could be classified as 'instruction' or 'direction' must be objectively ascertained by the Court based on the available evidence;
- that it would be sufficient to show that the properly appointed directors do surrender their own discretions in the face of the instructions and directions from the shadow director.

Elsewhere, there has been a suggestion in another case that it would suffice if a majority of the directors, and not all of them, heeded the 'instructions' and 'directions' of the shadow director *(Ultraframe (UK) Ltd* v. *Fielding (2005) EWHC 1638, 1272; Hannigan, 142-143).* Whatever be the case, the position of the CAMA on the shadow director is clear: it is a person on whose instructions and directions the company directors are accustomed to act.

The above propositions are helpful, though not conclusive on all the issues in this respect. The aspect of the issue of shadow directorship that enjoys consensus is that a one-off instruction or involvement by a person with a company is not enough to make him a shadow director, irrespective of the extent of the engagement. It is necessary to show a pattern of engagement in which the director(s) are accustomed to act on the instructions or directions of the alleged shadow director *(Secretary of State for Trade and Industry -v Becker (2003) 1 BCLC 555; Hannigan, 146fn).*

In the final analysis, questions remain about the essence or effects of the incidence of shadow directorship on a company. While it is a way that the law has tried to prevent a company from being 'remote-controlled' by 'unseen forces' who would eventually be accountable to nobody, there is an opinion that shadow directorship is a bad practice, both for a company and for the directors. This is because the shadow director, while 'invisible' as it were, runs several risks in relation to the company, without being visible to the company, its members and the other stakeholders. This scenario is especially serious if, for instance, the company improperly goes insolvent *(Mason, The Company Secretary's Desktop Guide, 3rd edn, 13).*

LIFE DIRECTORSHIP

Having examined the processes for the appointment of directors in a company, first directors, subsequent directors, casual vacancy appointment and the incidence of shadow directorship, a question now arises: can a person be appointed a director in a company without term limits? Or, put in another way, can a person be appointed a director for life in a company? The answer is in the affirmative. As a general principle of law, a person can be appointed a director for life in a company. The only proviso to that assertion is that such an appointment would not stop the person so appointed from being removable by the company in the same manner as every other director (that is by an ordinary resolution in a general meeting (s. 281 CAMA 2020), (s. 255).

Having noted the above, it is important to put the above provision in proper context to avoid any confusion. The CAMA allows a company to appoint a director for life but does not allow a company to designate a person to a directorship position within the company for life. For instance, while a person may be a director for life in a company, the CAMA does not permit a person to be appointed 'finance director for life', 'marketing director for life,' etc.

The above situation arose for resolution before the Supreme Court in *U.O.O Nig. Plc* v. *Okafor & Ors (2020) 11 NWLR Pt 1736, 409.* In this case, the company, apparently misconstruing the provision of the CAMA on life directorship, purported to have appointed two (2) individuals to the board of directors and designated them 'managing director for life,' and 'board chairman for Life.' Trouble arose and the matter went to Court. On appeal to the Supreme Court, the Court reviewed the relevant provisions of the CAMA and held that the above appointments made by company were unsupportable in law. In fact, it was held that to the extent that clauses in the company's Memorandum or Articles made provisions for such appointments, the clauses are illegal, being contrary to the express provisions of the CAMA. This is because the powers to elect a company's chairman and the managing director and determine their tenure are statutory and vested in the directors and the members in general meeting and cannot be usurped by a company's constitutional documents.

ROTATION OF DIRECTORS

After their respective appointments, the mode of rotation of office for directors (those leaving and those coming into the board) in a company, is primarily determined by the company's Articles. The CAMA provisions in this respect are subject to any contrary provision(s) in a company's Articles. This is one of the instances where the provisions of the CAMA on a particular subject are subordinated to the provisions of a company's Articles. The reason is presumably that the manner of rotation of directors on the board would appear to be, in the main, an internal affair of sort to the company, and better dealt with by the company itself. This must have been the thinking of the framers of the CAMA, in subjecting its provision on this issue to the company's Articles.

Under section 285(1) CAMA 2020, (s. 259), at a company's first annual general meeting, all the directors shall retire from office, although those interested may offer themselves for re-election. Thereafter, in a company's annual general meeting in every subsequent year, one third of the existing directors at that point in time shall retire from office. Where the number of directors is not three (3) or in the multiple of three (3), then the number that is nearest to one-third of the members of the board of directors shall retire from office.

Of the directors in a company, those who are due to retire every year shall be those who have stayed the longest period in office since they were last elected into office. However, for persons who became directors on the same day, their retirement shall be determined by lot, except they otherwise agree among themselves on the modalities to retire (s. 285(2) CAMA 2020), (s. 259 (2).

This book submits that the choice of the system of casting lot to determine the retirement sequence of directors in this time and age should be revisited and actually jettisoned. In its place, the CAMA should adopt a simple process that guarantees certainty and openness, for instance, where the directors who were appointed on the same day should be retiring in alphabetical order or by their respective ages, the older retires before the younger. We believe that this is a better and more systematic approach of rotating directors.

At the meeting where a director(s) retires as is stipulated above, the company may fill the vacancy by electing another person to replace the retiring director. However, where the retiring director is offering himself for re-election and no person has been elected by the meeting to fill his place, the retiring director shall be deemed to have been re-elected, unless the meeting expressly resolved not to fill the vacated office or unless the resolution to re-elect the retiring director was put to the meeting and lost (s. 285 (3) CAMA 2020), (s. 259(3).

Apart from a retiring director in a meeting, no person shall be eligible to be elected to the office of a director in a general meeting, except the person is recommended by the directors. For a person to be eligible to be elected a director in a general meeting, a notice in writing must have been left at the registered office or head office of the company not less than three (3) days or more than 21 days before the date of the meeting. The notice is to be signed by a member duly qualified to attend and vote at the meeting in question stating his intention to propose such a person for election as a director. In addition, the person so proposed by the member is also required to leave a notice in writing at the company's registered office or head office within the period stated above declaring his willingness to be elected a director of the company (s. 285 (4) CAMA 2020), (s. 259(4).

What has been discussed above are the legal positions as provided in the CAMA relating to the rotation of directors on a company's board. However, from a corporate governance perspective the company secretary plays greater roles in this area of company law. According to the *World Bank Group (IFC, 58)*, the company secretary should be very familiar with the directors' tenure and term limits in the organization. With respect to directors' rotation, therefore, the company secretary should keep a record of who has been re-elected, when, and when their next re-election is due and the person who is likely to rotate out of the board at a particular point in time, barring any unforeseen events.

Apart from the above, the company secretary should also be able to advise the board, through the chairman, on the needed mix on the board in replenishing the board with directors with fresh ideas. It was noted above that the company secretary, legally speaking, is not part of those that are saddled with the responsibility of appointing directors. That is still the correct position of the law. However, the vantage position of the company secretary, as the only person who is not a director but who attends all board and committee meetings as secretary of the board, make his position very vital to any process to select directors. He is, therefore, in a good position to offer quality advice to the chairman, in particular, and generally to the board, on sundry issues relating to board successions and replenishments.

RESTRICTIONS ON THE APPOINTMENT OF DIRECTORS

From the appointment of the first directors to subsequent directors, and, we submit, even to shadow directors, it is not everyone that can be appointed a company director in Nigeria. As noted above, the primary responsibility for subsequent appointment of directors in a company rests with the members in general meeting. The board of directors may also fill casual vacancies on the board or increase the number of directors within the limit prescribed in the company's Articles.

However, the CAMA has placed restrictions and qualifications on the class of persons that could be appointed as company directors. Some of these restrictions also come with punitive measures, including fines and terms of imprisonment when breached.

Section 283 CAMA 2020, (s. 257) disqualifies some categories of persons from being made directors of a company, including:

- a person under the age of 18 years;
- a person removed under section 288 of the Act, where such removal was on the ground of fraud, dishonesty or unethical conduct (as amended by section 15 of the schedule to the *Business Facilitation (Miscellaneous Provisions) Act (BFA) 2022*(a person removed from office under s. 288 CAMA 2020 is a director who was removed from office before the expiration of his tenure of office). Note that this is a new addition by the CAMA 2020 as CAMA 2004 had no equivalent provision under this head.
- a lunatic or person of unsound mind. In *Hunpunu-Wusu* v. *Hunpunu-Wusu (1969) 1 All NLR, 62*, the Supreme Court held that the terms 'unsound mind', 'mental illness,' 'mental disorder' and 'insanity,' among

others, are interchangeable. It has to be noted that the person's unsoundness of mind has to be affirmed by a Court of competent jurisdiction to be a disqualifying factor.

- A person disqualified under sections 279 (insolvent persons), 280 (persons convicted of fraud by a High Court in relation to the promotion, management or winding-up of a company); and 284 (those who vacated offices as directors for not meeting share qualification requirements) of the Act.

The CAMA restrains a person who has been convicted by a High Court of any offence in connection with the promotion, formation, management of a company or of fraudulent trading during the winding-up of a company, from being a director in any company (s. 280 CAMA 2020), (s. 254).

For persons convicted under any of the heads above, the Court is enjoined to make an order that the person shall not be a director of any company, or in any way directly or otherwise be connected or take part in the management of a company for a specified period, but not exceeding 10 years. For an order to be made by a Court against a fraudulent person, an application has to be made to the Court by a person who is entitled to do so. Those entitled to make such an application are the official receiver, liquidator, a member or former member of the company, or its creditor.

For clarity, section 280(2) CAMA 2020 provides that the 10-year disqualification period within which a person convicted as above shall not be a company director will start to count after the person might have served the sentence imposed by the Court or paid the fine imposed (whichever is applicable). The CAMA 2004 had no equivalent provision. This is a very good provision that removes the possibility of any disputes as to whether the period a person is serving a jail term, for instance, also counts as part of the waiting period during the person's disqualification. A person intending to apply to Court to make an order as above shall give notice of not less than 10 days to the person against whom the order is sought. During the hearing of the application proper, the person against whom the order is being sought may appear by himself and give evidence or call witnesses on his own behalf (s.280 (4) CAMA 2020), (s. 254 (3). It is arguable that the right given to a person against whom an order is sought to appear to give evidence and call witnesses, if need be, would also include an opportunity to do so through a Counsel of his choice. This is because there is a possibility that the person concerned might not understand the intricacies of legal proceedings in order to fully ventilate his view or get the best out of his witnesses.

The general rule in appointing company directors is that, bar any disqualification as noted above, a person who is 18 years or older may be appointed a director in a company and may hold his directorship for as long as his appointment is renewed by the company, subject to the provisions of the Articles and the CAMA. For a public company, however, the CAMA requires that once a person to be appointed a director has attained the age of 70 years or more, special notice is mandatorily required of any resolution appointing or approving the appointment of such a person as a director (s. 282 CAMA 2020), (s. 256). This presupposes that where the directors themselves appoint a person who is 70 years or more to fill a casual vacancy or to increase the number of directors on the board, a special notice shall be given to the company at the general meeting where such an appointment is sought to be approved or ratified.

The notice to be given to the company or by the company to its members on the age of the proposed director(s), or a director(s) whose appointment is sought to be approved in a general meeting, shall state the actual age of the person to whom it relates.

A company's Articles may fix particular shareholding qualification for the directors, otherwise no shareholding qualification shall be required for any company directorship (s. 277(1) CAMA 2020), (s. 251 (1). This will prescribe the number of the company's shares that a person must hold in order to be appointed or continue to remain a director in the company. Where it is provided for in the Articles, it is usually regarded as one of the restrictions on being appointed or remaining a director of a company in Nigeria.

This provision implies that a company cannot of its own accord, that is, where the Articles did not make any provisions, require a managing director, for example, by his service contract, to fulfil a shareholding qualification. Such a requirement would be invalid as being against the provisions of the CAMA.

Where, however, a company's Articles provide for directors' shareholding qualification, the directors are duty bound to meet that condition, and if not met before being appointed a director, then it must be met within two (2) months after such a person has been appointed. A director who fails to meet the requisite shareholding qualification after two (2) months of being appointed shall vacate his office. Likewise, a director who met the shareholding qualification on appointment but at any time while being a director fails to meet the condition, shall vacate his office (s. 277 (2)(3) CAMA 2020), (s. 251 (2)(3). A director that vacates his office on account of not meeting a shareholding qualification cannot be re-appointed as a director in the company until he has met that requirement (s. 277 (4) CAMA 2020), (s. 251(4).

The avowed purpose for requiring directors to hold shares in a company is to make them to have personal interests in and commitment to the affairs of the company (*Orojo, 252*). The global corporate governance crisis that engulfed much of the corporate and financial world in the early to mid-2000s would seem to challenge the assumption that shareholding by directors in a company makes them to be more ethically inclined. This proved not to be the case before the financial crisis started. What was seen at the beginning of the crisis was that those who were company directors and held shares in their companies, used inside information they got and sold-off majority of their shareholdings before the shares lost value. This is a practice that is criminalized in most jurisdictions of the world and in-fact led to the passing, by the United States' Congress, of the *Sarbanes-Oxley Act,* in 2002. The Act forms an integral part of the United States' corporate governance legal regime and is meant to tighten financial record-keeping and bring more transparency into reporting obligations and auditing for US companies, especially big ones. Several other countries later followed suit.

The CAMA imposes a fine on any person who acts as a director in a company without meeting or having lost the shareholding qualification, if required by the company Articles to have such a holding.

Attributes of Company Directors

The legal requirements stipulated in the CAMA for appointment of persons as company directors are meant to prevent, as much as possible, persons considered as unfit, in any way from being appointed directors. However, this is as far as the legal requirements can go in this respect. The corporate governance considerations for the appointment of company directors are more elaborate and far-reaching. According to Tricker, apart from the legal provisions and the corporate governance codes and company structures, there are other attributes that are key attributes to a person being appointed as a company director. Some of the attributes include:

i. **integrity**: since the directors hold the powers and resources of the company they manage in trust for the members and other stakeholders, the directors owe a fiduciary duty to act openly and honesty in the affairs of the company. This will mean avoiding any conflict of interests and acting in the best interests of the company and not in their self-interests;

ii. **character**: this is also termed 'strength of character' and has been described as the ability to be independently minded, impartial and objective in a director's approach to issues about the company. In this respect, while the ability to work toward consensus is a great virtue, so is also the ability to take a stand, be resilient and be courageous on issues, very useful traits for a director;

iii. **personality**: certain personality traits are listed as very useful for company directors to possess. These include ability for positive interaction with people, flexibility, sensitivity, diplomacy, persuasiveness and inter-personal skills, among others *(Bob Tricker, Corporate Governance, Principles, Policies and Practices, 263, 266).*

It is clear from all of the above that a combination of the legal requirements and corporate governance considerations above, would inevitably lead to a very effective board of directors being assembled for a company.

CATEGORIES OF DIRECTORSHIP

Apart from the provisions for the recognition of 'shadow directorship' in section 270 CAMA 2020, (s. 245), and for the appointment of 'independent directors' by public companies in section 275 CAMA 2020, there are no other classifications, as per genre, of directors to be appointed by companies in Nigeria. It would appear that the CAMA has left the categorization or classification of directors to the respective company's Articles or internal structures. The CAMA therefore makes no mention of the appointment of 'executive,' 'non-executive,' 'assignee,' 'alternate,' 'dormant' 'passive' or any type of directors at all.

It is usually the case that any or all of the above directorships could be created in a company's Articles and responsibilities assigned thereto. In doing this, companies, especially large private or publicly quoted companies, do also have recourse to the existing Corporate Governance Codes, from time to time in force. Any such positions as above created internally by companies would be recognized by the CAMA as valid directorships, once the persons so appointed are not disqualified under any head under the Act. The persons would also have to be contributing to the direction and management of the company in question, within the meaning of section 269 CAMA 2020 (s. 244).

Section 868 CAMA 2020, (s. 567) makes this clear and states that the term 'director' includes any person occupying the post of director by whatever name called.

In the management of companies, there are still other designations for directors, which, as discussed below, are simply peculiar internal company preferences. Sometimes the designations will describe the region(s) over which the director is in charge, but most times, the designations describe the portfolios being superintended by the director in question, or the class of directorship in question.

Executive and Non-Executive Directors

In modern business circles, the appointment by companies of 'executive,' and 'non-executive,' directors seem to be the dominant global practice. In sum, executive directors are normally those that are in the employ of the company, receiving salaries and other benefits, and they have their individual contracts of service and participate in the day- to- day running of the company's business.

In *Longe* v. *FBN Plc (2010) 6 NWLR Pt. 1189, 1*, it was held that executive directors are senior managers appointed by the board of directors under the company's Articles, for convenience and in the interest of running the company *(Mainstreet Bank Registrars* v. *Ukandu (2017) LPELR-50172).* Also, in *Amaye* v. *AREC Ltd (1990) 4 NWLR Pt. 145, 422*, it was held that executive directors (including the managing director) do have contracts of service with the company regulated by the Articles, but that in the case of the managing director, it would amount to a drastic over-simplification of the relationship to simply equate it to a master and servant relationship between the managing director and the company. It goes far beyond that threshold and that a better view would be that directors are trustees, agents and fiduciaries of the company. This accords with section 309 CAMA 2020 (s. 248), which made directors the trustees of the company's money, properties and powers and that they may be regarded as agents of the company.

Principle 5 of the *Nigerian Code of Corporate Governance (NCCG) 2018*, states that 'executive directors support the managing director in the operations and management of the Company.' Additionally, executive directors are to support the managing director in the proper implementation and achievement of the company's strategic objectives, as well as contribute to ensuring the prudent management of the company's finances and other resources. The code also, as already noted above, advised that the terms of the employment of executive directors, including their powers, duties and responsibilities should be clearly spelt out in their contracts of service.

In contrast to the above, the non-executive directors are usually engaged on a part-time basis. They may also hold non-executive directorship positions in other companies, which fact, until CAMA 2020, was not regulated by law, but without being binding, by respective corporate governance codes applicable in Nigeria. In most cases, non-executive directors consist of experienced professionals, businessmen or technocrats who are appointed into the board for their wealth of experience and technical know-how and to add balance and diversity of backgrounds to a company's board. Non-executive directors do not participate in the day-to-day running of the company, even though they are expected to attend board meetings and offer constructive advice to executive directors and the company's management team. The NCCG captures it aptly that 'non-executive directors bring to bear their knowledge, expertise and independent judgment on issues of strategy and performance on the board' (Principle 6).

Non-executive directors do have letters of appointment for their positions in a company but do not usually have contracts of service with the company. This is because, essentially, they serve the company, as directors, but are not in the service of the company, as employees. They receive allowances but no salaries and other employee benefits. The provisions of the CAMA and other soft laws, like the corporate governance codes, that usually attempt to regulate the number of directorships a person may hold simultaneously, are mostly targeted at non-executive directors (the CAMA has now delved into this regulation). This is because a person is not encouraged, sometimes not even allowed, especially in public companies, to hold executive directorship positions in two companies at a time, even if it is allowed in some holding companies and their subsidiaries.

The Managing Director

The managing director is, to say it loosely, the *primus inter pares*, that is, the first among equals, in the directorate cadre and heads the company's executive management team. Under any guise or definition, at all, the managing director is the directing mind, the will and the alter ego of a company, through which the company acts *(Longe* v. *FBN Plc (2010) 6 NWLR Pt. 1189,1; Delta Steel Nig Ltd* v. *A.C.T. Incorp (1999) 4 NWLR Pt. 597, 53; Marine Mgt. Assoc. Inc.* v. *NMA (2012) 18 NWLR Pt. 1333, 506).* The NCCG simply states that the managing director is the head of management delegated by the board to run the affairs of the company to achieve its strategic objectives for sustainable corporate performance. This is, however, not where the corporate governance essentials of this position end.

The fact that the managing director is the head of the company's executive management team has a lot of implications. Under principle 4 of the NCCG, by this position, the managing director is expected to have a broad and deep understanding of the company's business, demonstrate entrepreneurial skills, credibility and integrity and have the confidence of the board and management. He is also expected to lead by example and establish a culture of integrity and performance, which should be assimilated by personnel at all levels of the company. This fact of assimilation of the positive ideals propagated by the managing director and diffused downwards by the other directors and senior management, should be clear from the positive performance results that should emanate from the company's business. In turn, this makes the fact of succession easier, being that the culture of integrity and performance would have taken deep roots in the company and picking a successor(s) to the managing director, or replenishing the board, is made a lot easier.

In theory and practice, a person will have to be a director in a company first, before being appointed to the position of a managing director. (In rare cases, people have been appointed to the managing director position from being general managers, although, this is rare in a closely regulated industry, like the banking or the insurance industry).

In practice, however, it is usually from the rank of a company's existing executive directors that a managing director is chosen, that is, if the board of directors decides to appoint a managing director from within the company. Even where the company (especially large private or public companies) decides to appoint a managing director from outside the company, he is usually appointed from among the executive director cadre from other companies. As noted in *Amaye* v. *AREC (above),* the managing director is an employee of the company and which relationship is regulated by the Articles and his contract of service. Being first and foremost a director in the company, the managing director, therefore, ceases to be one if he ceases to be a director in the company.

Independent and Non-independent Directors

In a company, non-executive directors could be either independent or non-independent directors. The criteria for determining their independence revolve around whether or not the director in question has any form of affinity to the company or its top executive, either presently or in the recent past as to colour his judgment on issues. If this were to be the case, the director ceases to be considered independent and becomes a non-independent director but still able to make meaningful contributions to the board of directors.

In the past, it has always been the different corporate governance codes in Nigeria that tried to specify the details of this aspect of company directorship. The successive company legislations did not bother with such details, until the CAMA 2020, although it related same to public companies only.

Section 275(1) CAMA 2020 provides that a public company shall have at least three (3) independent directors, meaning that a company could elect to appoint more than three (3) independent directors, as the Act stated the basic threshold. This provision has itself been amended by section 14 of the schedule to the *Business Facilitation (Miscellaneous Provisions) Act (BFA) 2022*, to the effect that every public company shall have at least one-third of its total number of directors as independent directors. In the same manner, a person who nominates candidates for the board of a public company, who will form the majority on the board members when constituted, must nominate at least one-third of those candidates who will be independent directors.

Under section 275 (3) CAMA 2020, to be considered as 'independent,' the director in question has to be a person who, or whose relatives, during the preceding two (2) years:

- was not an employee of the company;
- did not make or receive from the company payments of more than ₦20,000,000.00 (Twenty million naira); or own more than 30% share in the company or acts as a partner, director or officer in the company that made or received payment of more than ₦20,000,000.00 (Twenty million naira);
- did not directly or indirectly own more than 30% of the company's shares; or engaged directly or otherwise as the company's auditor.

A juxtaposition of the above provisions of the CAMA with that of the NCCG on the issue of independent directorship, reveals a tilt towards a stricter approach by the NCCG. A few examples of their respective provisions on some aspects of the issue will suffice for our present purpose. Under principle 7 of the NCCG, to be considered 'independent' as a director, the person will have to be one, who:

i. does not possess a shareholding in the company the value of which is material to the holder such as will impair his independence or in excess of 0.01% of the paid-up capital of the Company. The threshold shareholding under the CAMA is 30%, which, we submit is extremely generous, and the NCCG's provision is preferable in this respect;
ii. is not a representative of a shareholder that has the ability to control or significantly influence Management;
iii. is not, or has not been an employee of the company or group within the last five years (the CAMA provision is two (2) years, though the CAMA went further to add relatives of the person in question into the fray;
iv. is not a close family member of any of the company's advisers, directors, senior employees, consultants, auditors, creditors, suppliers, customers or substantial shareholders;
v. does not have, and has not, had within the last five (5) years, a material business relationship with the company either directly, or as a partner, shareholder, director or senior employee of a body that has, or has had, such a relationship with the company;
vi. has not served at directorate level or above at the company's regulator within the last three years. (This provision will disqualify a person who recently left a senior management job at the Commission, or if the company is a bank, a person who recently worked at the Central Bank of Nigeria (CBN) or the Securities and Exchange Commission (SEC), for public companies.

It is clear that the provisions of the NCCG are stricter than those of the CAMA on this subject and apparently geared towards a better atmosphere of corporate governance in companies. In essence, the provisions of the NCCG are preferable as they set higher standards of independence for directors. However, it still has to be noted that the CAMA is an Act of the National Assembly backed by the Constitution of the Federal Republic of Nigeria 1999, as amended, whose provisions are binding on and enforceable against all persons and entities in Nigeria. The NCCG does not have such a status.

To look at the issue from an outsider perspective, recommendation 2.3 under principle 2 of the Australian Stock Exchange's *Corporate Governance Principles and Recommendations, 2019 (Australian Principles)*, maintain that to describe a director as being 'independent' imports a particular connotation that the director in question is not aligned or affiliated with the interests of the company's management or a substantial shareholder. This implies that the director can and will bring an independent judgement to bear on issues before the board. It was, therefore, submitted that calling a director 'independent' is an appellation that gives great comfort to company's security holders, and it is not a classification that should be applied lightly to a director.

The point above having been made, the provisions of the CAMA and NCCG on independent directors are all geared at achieving the central objective of their appointment to the position, which is independence of opinion and judgment. A person whose opinion or judgment is fettered, directly or indirectly, by any factor(s), internal or external to the company, cannot function effectively as an independent director. This is because what is considered as the most important aspect of the contributions of independent non-executive directors in a company is the independence that they bring to the board. Since they are not employees, affiliated to, or recent or former employees of the company, and do not owe loyalty to the company's top executives, at least in principle, they are able to approach issues concerning the company with high level of objectivity. This is the reason they are usually appointed into sensitive committees in companies, such as the audit committee and the remuneration committee.

ALTERNATE AND ASSIGNEE DIRECTORS

There are instances where, as permitted by a company's Articles, vacancies in a company's board are filled by the individual directors themselves, informally, instead of the company as entity. This is when the issues of alternate and assignee directors come into play. The practice is a common law tradition and some company law legislations, like the CAMA, do not actually make express provisions for it.

Alternate Directors

A director in a company may, for several reasons, not be disposed to carrying out his duties and responsibilities to the company, over a specific period of time. There may then be the need for the director concerned to appoint an alternate in his place, to hold his position until he resumes his duties with the company. This is especially the case with respect to non-executive directors. However, the practice is not routine to every company.

The appointment of an alternate director is dependent on the provisions in a company's Articles. Where the practice is allowed in the Articles, a substantive director is entitled to appoint another person to act as his alternate in his absence. The alternate director is to exercise the substantive director's powers and responsibilities in the company in relation to taking decisions for the company and performing other duties. Details about the modalities for such an appointment, the extent of powers the alternate may exert, functions, limitations, and benefits that would be due to the alternate director are usually specified in the company's Articles (*Orojo, 248*). An important point to note is that, except otherwise provided, alternate directors are deemed, for all intents and purposes, to be directors in their own rights, and are liable as such for their own acts and omissions until the substantive director resumes his position. They are also not agents of their appointors or acting on their behalf in the company, within the period of their directorship *(Hannigan, 141).*

Bearing in mind the meaning of a director under section 868 CAMA 2020, as a 'person occupying the position of a director by whatever name called,' (s. 567) this will mean that an alternate director will be entitled to all the benefits and be liable to all the liabilities and restrictions placed on directors by the CAMA, including fiduciary duties. Also, it implies that particulars of alternate directors and their shareholdings (if any) have to be entered in the appropriate registers for directors in the company. Furthermore, all disclosures required from directors, like their interests in any particular contract(s) with the company, would have to be made to the company and the Commission in appropriate cases involving alternate directors.

Assignee Directors

Where a company's Articles permit, a director who is no longer in a position to perform his duties and responsibilities to the company, could appoint an assignee director in his place to take over those duties and responsibilities. However, unlike the situation with the appointment of an alternate director, discussed above, which is a temporary arrangement to take care of the absence of a substantive director, the appointment of an assignee director is usually a permanent arrangement. In this instance, the situation involves the substantive director permanently ceding the performance of his duties and exercise of his powers in the company and transferring same to the assignee director (*Baffa & Ors* v. *Odili & Ors (2001) 15 NWLR Pt. 737, 709).*

In practice, a notice to the company of the appointment of an alternate or assignee director is required from the appointing director. However, a notice to the company is not necessary to terminate the appointment of the alternate director. This is because once the appointing director resumes his duties in the company, the appointment of the alternate ceases to have effect without any further action being required from the appointing director. It is, however, considered a neater process, procedurally, for the appointing director to also inform the company formally, that he has resumed duties and his alternate has ceased to so act.

MODALITIES FOR THE APPOINTMENT OF DIRECTORS

We have now seen the different ramifications of who company directors are and the different categories of directors. Also, we have seen those who can and who cannot be company directors in Nigeria, while others could become directors when meeting certain conditions. Some of the attributes of a good and successful director have also been highlighted. This would appear a good time to consider the modalities for appointing directors into the boards of companies in Nigeria.

In general, it is a company's general meeting that has the primary responsibility of appointing directors to the board. When a casual vacancy occurs due to a director's death, resignation, retirement or removal, the board of directors will then appoint a replacement director(s) to fill the vacancy, subject to approval of the appointment by the company in general meeting. Where the general meeting does not approve the appointment, the director so appointed ceases to be one.

The CAMA seems to have left the issue of the procedures or modalities of appointing directors purely to the companies to decide in their Articles. For a private company, the CAMA does not make any provisions at all relating to the modalities for appointing directors in general meeting.

However, for a public company, there is a restriction in section 287 CAMA 2020 (s.261) against the use of a single resolution to appoint two (2) or more persons as directors of a company. Such a motion can only be taken if the meeting had earlier agreed on a resolution, without a dissenting vote, that such a motion would be moved during the meeting proper. A failure to follow this procedure will invalidate the motion appointing the directors. This is irrespective of whether or not there was any objection during the meeting against the resolution being passed (s. 287(2) CAMA 2020), (s.261(2)). This is about the only restriction placed by the CAMA on the latitude of companies to appoint directors in general meeting. Otherwise, a company will have the right to choose the modalities to adopt, subject to where the CAMA made any provision(s), if at all, in that respect.

In applying the above provisions, a motion for approving a person's appointment as a director of a company or for nominating a person for appointment as such, shall be treated simply as a motion for his appointment. The above provisions do not apply to a resolution that seeks to alter a company's Articles, even if the process will then involve appointing a director along the line (s. 287 (4), (s. 261(3)(4).

Under recommendation 2.1 of principle 2 of the *Australian Principles*, it is stated that 'to facilitate the effective functioning of the board and to promote investor confidence, there should be a formal, rigorous and transparent process for the appointment and reappointment of directors to the board.' On its own part, principle 12.1 NCCG recommends that the board should approve the criteria for appointing directors, as recommended by the relevant committee, that is, the committee responsible for nomination and governance. Such criteria should take into careful consideration the strengths and weaknesses of the existing board, integrity, required competence and skills, knowledge and experience, capacity to undertake the responsibility as well as diversity, including gender diversity. Where the company is involved in a specialized business, for instance, aviation, engineering or computing, then the possession of requisite technical skills by the potential director(s) should be taken into account.

Practically speaking, the role of the company secretary in the process of the appointment of directors in a company is advisory, though it is always continuous. This statement takes for granted situations where a company secretary is also a director, who will then take part in the process of appointing other directors to fill casual vacancies, subject to ratification by the general meeting.

According to the World Bank Group (IFC), the company secretary plays critical advisory role in helping to constitute a functional and effective board by advising the board, through the chairman, on the following areas:

i. ensuring that the requirement for certain numbers or levels of directors to be independent on the board is met;
ii. advising the board on the most effective board size, including all the needed mix in experience, skills and other factors, relative to the size and needs of the company. A good board size is that which will engender quality and effective discussions and decisions on the board, while ensuring efficient operations;
iii. advising the board on the requisite balance on the membership of the board with respect to skills-set, knowledge base and gender balance, etc.

In other routine situations, where the company secretary simply occupies that sole position and not doubling as a director, the role, in this respect, is usually more advisory that substantive, that is, apart from his role in issuing notices of meetings and organizing the general meetings where directors are usually appointed by the members. For instance, the company will rely on the company secretary for advice on any areas of prohibition(s) or restriction(s) on appointing any person or classes of persons as a director(s), for example, an insolvent person or a person previously removed as a director without completing his term. This last category was added by the CAMA 2020.

While appointing directors, backgrounds checks are necessary, in-fact critical, to ensure that only eligible persons are appointed. The company will mostly rely on the company secretary is this respect, who may, in-turn, work with the compliance unit, especially in large public companies, for such checks.

Added to the above, in public companies, the issue of who qualifies as an independent director has now been centralized by the CAMA, in terms of the minimum numbers and who qualifies as such. Previously, it was left for different corporate governance codes (CGCs) to attempt to lay the standards, and the company secretary, as noted above, should play a central role in assessing the proposed independent candidates for appointment, subject to a final decision by the board of directors. The major 'conflict' in this area is that usually the proposed candidates would have been known to most of the existing directors for a long time and the company secretary would almost be left with a *fait accompli*.

Questions do remain. Are there shadow directors around the company, whether known to the company or not? If so, do they need to be formalized as directors with due appointment to comply with the CAMA? Otherwise, the company, that is the directors, will need to know the legal position attributable to shadow directors under the law and the implications.

Close to this is the question as to whether anybody is holding himself out as a director of the company, and if so, what can be done about it? The law allows the company to restrain the person by an injunction. On the flip side, is the company holding out somebody as a director to third parties? If so, would they want to formalize the person's position as a director or otherwise? Either way, the directors should be clearly abreast with what the law says in all these situations, then the company secretary would have correctly performed his responsibilities in these respects.

LEGAL STATUS OF DIRECTORS

Throughout this chapter, particularly, and in-fact, this book, it has been established that the primary responsibilities of directors are to direct and manage the affairs of a company over which they oversee. It is also established that it is immaterial, the terminology with which such directors are described, once their duties to manage and direct a company are carried out effectively. The question now is, having been appointed, what then is the legal status of these directors in carrying out their duties of managing and directing the company?

Section 309(1) CAMA 2020 (s. 283 (1) describes directors as trustees of the company moneys, properties and their powers and as such shall account for all the money over which they exercise control. Directors are also obligated to refund any of the company's money that they are considered to have paid away improperly (s. 283(1). It does not appear that the intention of the directors in paying away any such money would count for anything under this provision, once impropriety has been established against them.

Company directors are obliged to account to the company for 'all the moneys over which they exercise control' and no mention is made of the properties over which they exercise control. This could be implied, however, that having been called trustees of a company's money and properties, the directors are also to account for any properties they misuse. This is based on the principle that a trustee owes fiduciary duties to the beneficiary of any property in his custody and must always act in good faith *(Nasir* v. *Berini (Beirut-Riyad) Nigeria Bank Ltd (1968) All NLR, 269).*A director who misappropriates the properties belonging to a company cannot be said to have acted in good faith, under any guise.

A director is also mandated to exercise all powers honestly and in the interests of the company and its shareholders and not in the director's own or sectional interests. It is also correct that a director may, when acting within his authority and the powers of the company, be regarded as agent of the company (s. 309 (1)(2) CAMA 2020), (s. 283 (1)(2). Calling directors agents of a company would not seem to pose much jurisprudential problems. In fact, in *Mills* v. *Mills (1938) 60 CLR, 150; Charlesworth & Cain, 369)*, directors were called 'fiduciary agents,' being that the powers conferred on them as agents also imports fiduciary duties, by which they cannot be expected to obtain private advantage to themselves. The real question for us is whether, strictly speaking, company directors can be regarded as 'trustees,' in the legal sense of the term?

The consensus opinion seems to be that referring to directors as trustees has to be in a loose sense of the term, being that directors are creations of statutes, mostly, and occupy a position peculiar to themselves. Directors can safely be said to be fiduciaries, that is, persons who have undertaken to act for and on behalf of others in situations that give rise to relationship of trust and confidence *(Bristol & West Building Society* v. *Mothew (1996) 4 All ER 698, 711; Thorne, 208-209).*

POWERS OF COMPANY DIRECTORS

In general, the principal organs through which a company acts are through its members in a general meeting, its board of directors, its officers or agents appointed by, or under authority derived from the members in general meeting (s. 87 CAMA 2020), (s. 63(1). In terms of hierarchy of power, the two main organs of a company's decision making are the board of directors and the members in a general meeting. The details of the division of powers between these organs are usually contractual in nature and matters for the Articles *(Automatic Self-Cleaning Filter Syndicate Co Ltd* v. *Cuninghame (1906) 2 Ch 34; Thorne, 193).*

The board of directors may appoint or authorize the appointment of officers or agents (they always do) to act for the company for its day-to-day management. It is only when such appointment or authorization is validly done that the officers or agents can legitimately act for the company. Subject to the provisions of the CAMA, the nature and extent of powers exercisable by the board of directors are to be regulated by the company's Articles, and this, in all cases. This notwithstanding, except where otherwise provided in a company's Articles, it is usually taken for granted that the board of directors primarily directs a company's business. In doing this, the board may exercise all such powers, to advance its business, that the CAMA or the company's Articles does not require that only members can exercise in a general meeting (s. 87(2)(3) CAMA 2020), (s. 63 (2)(3).

An important point to note is that the powers of directors are not at large and cannot be exercised as such, since they are subject to and curtailed by the provisions of the CAMA and the company's Articles. As will be discussed later, there are instances where directors could incur personal liability for exceeding their powers in managing the company's business.

Another important point to note is that the general powers conferred on directors to manage a company's business does not derogate from the overriding powers vested in the general meeting, to act on behalf of the company in certain specified circumstances. The power of the company to act in such circumstances has been variously described as inherent or as being a default power, though very pervasive. It has been held that such exercise of power by the members in general meeting would be valid and effective, where, for instance:

1. there was a deadlock on the board of directors *(Okeowo* v. *Migliore (1979) 12 NSCC, 210).* In this case, all the six (6) members of the company (Metal Const. West Africa Ltd) (two Nigerians and four Italians) were also directors in the company. One of the Italian directors (the majority shareholder) died and disagreements over who would inherit his shares deadlocked the company's board of directors. Added to this, the company secretary who was a Nigerian took sides with the Nigerian directors and refused to call a meeting of the board, until the Courts intervened and the Supreme Court finally ordered a meeting of the board to be held;
2. there were no directors left in the *company (Alexander Ward & Co. Ltd* v. *Samyang Navigation Co. Ltd (1975) SC (HL), 26*;
3. an effective quorum could not be formed for meetings of the company or the board *(Okeowo* v. *Migliore (1979) 12 NSCC, 210)*;
4. the existing directors were disqualified from voting *(Irvine* v. *Union Bank of Australia (1877) 2 APP. Cas., 366; Gower & Davies, 391)*;
5. the directors fail to commence proceedings, where required;
6. where the directors have purported to borrow money in excess of the amount authorized by the Articles. *(Nzegwu-Danjuma, The Role of the Company Secretary in Corporate Mgt., 43).*

The CAMA also recognizes the inherent power of the general meeting to act on behalf of the company despite the general powers to direct and manage the company that is given to the board of directors. Section 87(5) CAMA 2020, (s. 63(5) provides that notwithstanding the provisions of section 87(3), the members in a general meeting may:

1. act in any matter if the members of the board of directors are disqualified or are unable to act because of a deadlock on the board or otherwise (*Okeowo* v. *Migliore (1979) 12 NSCC, 210)*;
2. institute legal proceedings in the name of and on behalf of the company, if the board of directors refuse or neglect to do so;
3. ratify or confirm any action taken by the board of directors; or

4. make recommendations to the board of directors regarding actions to be taken by the board.

The provisions of section 87(5) CAMA 2020 above appear to be a codification of some of the common law principles on the same points enunciated above, especially in *Okeowo's* case.

Though a company's general meeting has the inherent power to intervene in the running of the company in certain circumstances, the CAMA attempts to prevent an undue interference by the general meeting in the running of the company by the board of directors. In this respect, and to fortify the authority of the board of directors in managing the company, section 87(4) CAMA 2020 (s. 63(4) provides that, unless where the Articles of a company provide to the contrary, the directors, when acting in good faith and with diligence and within the powers conferred on them by the Articles or the Act, are not bound to obey the directions or instructions of the members in general meeting. This provision must be very re-assuring to the directors on the extent of exercise of their managerial powers.

On the other hand, where the directors purport to exercise powers reserved to the company in a general meeting, their actions can be effectively ratified and validated by the ordinary resolution of the company in a general meeting. This must be distinguished from a situation where the general meeting wants to confer on the board of directors, powers vested in the general meeting for the directors' future use. In this case, a properly passed special resolution would be required *(Grant* v. *UK Switchback Rys (1888) 40 Ch. D., 135; Gower & Davies, 391).*

Delegation of Board of Directors' Powers

A company's board of directors is not expected to run the affairs of the company by themselves alone. Whist that may be impossible in practice, especially with respect to large companies, it would be inefficient to even attempt to do so.

In appreciation of the above truism, the directors are at liberty, except where the CAMA or the company's Articles provide to the contrary, to exercise their powers through committees, consisting of such members of the board as they may deem fit (s. 88(a) CAMA 2020, (s. 64(a). This is also a governance issue, as any attempt by the directors to do everything by themselves will lead to inefficiency and low returns on investments. Such committees usually include the credit committee, risk committee, audit committee, the disciplinary committee, and remuneration committee, among others. The size, nature and diversity of the committees could vary from one company to another, depending on their sizes and the nature of their operations.

Principle 11 NCCG, provides that 'to ensure efficiency and effectiveness, the board should delegate some of its functions, duties and responsibilities to well-structured committees without abdicating its responsibilities.' In delegating to the board committees, therefore, the directors are expected to put in place all rules, checks and balances that will guide the committees' work, while allowing the committees enough latitude to carry out the assigned functions efficiently.

Also, when setting up a committee, the board of directors is required to lay ground rules for them, but the other aspects of the committee's proceedings are also regulated by the CAMA. For instance, the board is to fix a quorum for the meetings of any such committee, failing which the whole committee shall meet and act by a majority of its members (s. 290(2) CAMA 2020), (s. 264(2). Also, for its meetings, a committee of the board may elect a chairman, but if no such chairman is elected or if at any meeting of the committee, the chairman is not present within five (5) minutes after the time appointed for holding the meeting, the members present may choose one from among them to preside over the meeting (s. 289(6) CAMA 2020), (s. 263 (6).

It is important to re-iterate that the power to manage and direct the affairs of the company is given to the board of directors, collectively, as a body, and it is only the board, acting as such, that can delegate such power to any of their members. Therefore, in general, the board's power to manage a company cannot validly be exercised or delegated by an individual member of the board without the authority of the board as a body *(Mitchell & Hobbs (UK)* v. *Mill (1996) 2 BCLC, 102, Bhadmus, 189*).

In *Ejekam & Ors* v. *Devon Ind. Ltd (1998) 1 NWLR Pt. 534, 417, 431,* it was held that it is true that only the board of directors or the company in a general meeting may generally authorize an action on behalf of the company. However, that it is also true that a director who enjoys the confidence of the board can, in certain appropriate or emergency circumstances, as events would dictate, commence an action in the name of the company with the intent that such an action would be ratified by the board or the general meeting. It remains to be seen, however, what would amount to a director 'enjoying the confidence of the board,' in absolute terms, and we submit that this must be a matter of fact, to be determined on the peculiar circumstances of each case. In all, care must be taken to avoid a situation of the 'dominant director syndrome' manifesting itself within the company. This is where a director or few directors run the company's affairs, while the rest simply rubber-stamp their decisions, with little or no opinion of their own, on matters before the board *(Re: Westmid Packing Services Ltd, Secretary of State for Trade & Industry* v. *Griffiths (1998) BCLC, 646, 653).*

The Nature of Director's Power to Delegate

Where a director(s) is allowed to delegate his powers or duties under any provision of the CAMA, such a director is not expected to abdicate his powers and duties in the guise of delegation. While a director is not expected to be closely monitoring those to whom he has delegated powers, he is expected to utilize his residual or default supervisory powers to make sure that his instructions are being carried out as delegated, and for the purpose(s) (s. 305(7) CAMA 2020), (s. 279(7). The Courts have continuously stated that the position of a company director is one of inescapable personal responsibility and each director must show enough knowledge and understanding of the company's business, in order to join his colleagues to supervise and control the company's affairs efficiently *(Re: Westmid Packing Services Ltd, Secretary of State for Trade & Industry* v. *Griffiths (1998) BCLC 646, 653; Thorne, 233).*

There are no further provisions or guides with respect to the construction or application of this director's duty under the CAMA. This notwithstanding, it would appear that the principle here is that a director should be aware that the delegation of any of his powers or duties does not absolve him from the consequences of the acts that were performed by the delegate. To this end, certain corporate rules of practice have been developed over the years as guides to the application of this rule:

- directors have, collectively and individually, a duty to acquire and maintain sufficient knowledge and understanding of the company's business to enable them to discharge their duties properly and efficiently;
- while directors are entitled to delegate particular functions to those below them in the management chain, and to trust the integrity and competence of the delegate to a reasonable extent, the directors are not absolved from the duty to supervise the delegated functions;
- for the preceding duty, no rule of universal application can be formulated. The extent of the duty, and the question as to whether it has been

discharged must depend on the fact of each particular case, including the role of the director in the management of the company;

- the key underlying point, therefore, is that directors are able to delegate their authority, but cannot delegate or avoid responsibility (*Re Barings Plc (No. 5) (2001) 1 BCLC 523, ICSA, 39; Hannigan, 211*).

In relation to delegation of duties, we submit that the general prohibition against double delegation, though more prominent in the realm of agency, will also apply in the commercial arena. In essence, where power is delegated to a person, here by a director, it is exercisable by that person himself directly and personally and he lacks the legal power to re-delegate such power on the principle of *delegatus non potest delegare (Okoro* v. *Delta Steel Co. Ltd. (1990) 2 NWLR (Pt. 130, 87).*

It is further submitted, that, when a director delegates power or duty to a subordinate(s) and due to his lack of residual supervisory oversight, he did not discover a further delegation of the power or duty by the delegate, the director would still be liable for any sanctions attributable to the said infraction. This is because the delegating director's lack of effective supervision could actually have amounted to abdication of responsibility, for which he remains responsible, being that there is no break in the chain of his authority down the line.

From all that has been said above, as far as the issue of managing or directing a company is concerned under the CAMA, the nomenclature 'director' signifies a little. The important things are the functions and relationships between the person(s) in question and the company. Once a person is in a position that allows him, directly or indirectly, duly appointed or not, to influence the management and direction of the affairs of a company, he is considered a director under the Act.

As directors, the status imports several duties, responsibilities and more importantly, attendant liabilities to the occupants of the positions. This is whether they be duly appointed by the company or imputed to them by law. The central duty is the directors being 'agents' and 'trustees' of the company when dealing with the company's money and property. The implications of this and other issues allied thereto will be considered in the next chapters.

CHECKPOINTS

✓ A good working relationship between the company secretary and the board of directors is critical to the overall seamless working of the board, and by implication, the company. There are so many governance issues in company law and administration that only a synergy between the company secretary and the directors and senior management will make for efficient company operations. There can no alternative to this.

- ✓ The general duty to direct and manage a company is on the directors and it does not matter what name(s) they are called individually. It is even possible that a person who is regarded as a director by the law may not have been so appointed or even recognized as such by the company. This is a situation where there is a shadow directorship.
- ✓ It is also possible that a person may be deemed to be a director in a company, legally, by holding out, either by himself or by the company. Where a company holds out a person as a director without due appointment, a member is entitled to restrain the company by injunction from continuing to do so. Where, however, it is a person that holds himself out as such, the company is entitled to restrain the person by injunction from continuing to do so.
- ✓ Appointment of directors is procedural and most of their powers are statutory and Articles-based. The first appointment is usually by the subscribers to the Memorandum and Articles, then subsequent appointments could be by the directors themselves in filling up casual vacancies on the board pending approval by the general meeting. The overall responsibility to appoint directors, however, rests on members in general meeting.
- ✓ It is not everyone that can be made a director in a company. People under certain disabilities (age under 18, unsound mind, undischarged bankrupt, etc), cannot be company directors. Where the disability can be remedied, for instance, where a share qualification criterion is provided for in the company's Articles and the potential appointee has not met same, this should be done.
- ✓ Where, for any reason(s), all the company's directors and shareholders die, their personal representatives are entitled to apply to Court for an order to convene a meeting to appoint new directors for the company. Where that is not possible, the company's creditors can make the same application to Court to appoint new directors for the company.
- ✓ Apart from company directors that have been regularly appointed, either at inception by the subscribers to the Memorandum and Articles, those

appointed to fill casual vacancies by the directors or appointed by members in a general meeting, as noted above, there are also shadow directors. These are people, though not formally appointed as directors, but who exert a lot influence on the company that the directors are accustomed to act on their instructions and directions.

- ✓ The law allows a person to be appointed a director for life in a company. However, the person so appointed cannot be officially designated 'director for life.' The person is also removable from office like every other director, that is, by the members of the company in general meeting.
- ✓ There are several classes of directorships in a company: the executive directors, who are those that run the company on a day-to-day basis and the non-executive directors, that are engaged on part-time basis for their expertise and technical know-how. They are not employees of the company.
- ✓ There are also independent and non-independent directors. Independent directors are those that do not have any close affiliation with the company, commercial or filial, close enough that will colour their judgements when advising on any company, board and related issues. The 2020 CAMA (as amended by the BFA) stipulates that a public company must have at least one-third of its directors as independent directors on its board, for balance.
- ✓ For persons who are seventy years (70) and above in age, their appointment as directors in a public company shall be proposed by a special notice, which will disclose the actual age of the person(s) so proposed as a director.
- ✓ Where a company's Articles provide for share qualification for directors, then that condition must be met by any person who is proposed to be a director before being appointed or on other terms stipulated therein. Otherwise, such a term is not to be read into the director's contract, for instance, through their service contract. That will be a breach of the CAMA.
- ✓ The powers of the company as a legal entity are usually exercised through three (3) organs: the general meeting (members), the directors and the officers. The directors are in charge of the day-to-day running of the company's affairs and usually delegate some of their functions to the board committees. Some of these committees, like the audit and remuneration

committees are very sensitive and should be headed by independent directors.

- ✓ Directors should know that they can delegate their powers and duties but not their responsibilities, especially for residual supervision and oversight. In essence, they can delegate but cannot abdicate their powers or duties.
- ✓ There are instances when the general meeting is permitted by law to take over the running of the affairs of the company and make decisions. For instance, where the board of directors is deadlocked and is unable to function and take any decisions concerning the company, the general meeting is entitled to intervene and make decisions for the company. Note that sometimes it may take members going to Court to get an order for directions for the general meeting to take over the management of the company.
- ✓ Directors, generally, are considered as trustees of the company's money and property by the CAMA and the implication is creating fiduciary duties for them. This may not be in the strict meaning of the term 'trustees' as it is under the law of trust, but it is enough to make the directors fiduciaries. This will mean that they are liable to account to the company for the misuse of any of the company's money or property in their care. The directors are also considered agents of the company when acting for the company.
- ✓ There are lots of governance issues with respect to the appointment and functioning of directors on the board. The company secretary is critical to the directors in these areas in terms of advice and guidance on issues regarding appointments to replenish the board and tenure of the directors on the board. In doing this, it is very important to ensure the right mix and balance on the board in these respects.

Chapter 7

DUTIES AND LIABILITIES OF COMPANY DIRECTORS

INTRODUCTION

In general, the CAMA has codified most of what used to be considered as the common law duties of company directors. From section 305 down to 313 CAMA 2020 (ss. 279 to 287) stipulate in great details, what the duties of a company director should be, in addition to other allied duties and responsibilities imposed elsewhere under the Act. These duties, in all cases, are owed to the company as a separate legal entity and not to the individual shareholders of the company or the employees in their own rights *(Percival* v. *Wright (1902) 2 Ch., 421; Peskin* v. *Anderson (2001) 1 BCLC, 372; Charlesworth & Cain, 370).* Also, none of these directors' fiduciary duties is owed to any of the company's creditors, *qua* creditor, as well *(Multinational Gas & Pet. Co.* v. *Multinational Gas & Pet. Serv. Ltd (1983) 2 All ER, 563).*

The most overarching legal implication of the fact of these directors' duties being owed to the company, is that in the event of a breach of any of the duties, the wrong complained of would have been done to the company itself. This presupposes that the company would be the proper person to sue in the event of any breach of duty. Over the years, this principle has been crystallized into the common law rule of *Foss* v. *Harbottle (1843) 2 Hare 461),* which precludes individual shareholders from suing (bar few exceptions) for wrongs alleged to have been committed against a company.

Over the years, for very many years, actually, the common law has been very reluctant, and not surprisingly so, to recognize, as a general rule, that directors' fiduciary duties could be owed to individual shareholders. The immutability of the sanctity of the corporate cloak imposed by law on a company on being incorporated *(Salomon* v. *Salomon (1897) AC, 22),* apart from where the veil is lifted, has always been upheld by common law Courts. A few reasons have been adduced for this judicial approach:

(i) allowing directors' duties to be owed to individual shareholders would, inevitably, undermine the much-cherished principle of collectivity of shareholding in companies;
(ii) it will kill-off derivative actions meant to allow shareholders to enforce the rights of the company, being that individual shareholders would, most likely, sue to enforce their own parallel rights and not the rights of the company;
(iii) it will undermine the good old rule, as was decided in *Salomon* v. *Salomon,* that separated a company and its members and that, in general, the fiduciary duties are owed to and enforceable by the company *(Gower & Davies, 507)*;
(iv) there are bound to be proliferation of shareholder-led litigations against both the directors and the company itself with attendant costs and distractions to the directors in the performance of their duties.

For the foregoing reasons, also, the Courts have resisted and rejected all attempts to create duties owed to individual shareholders by directors via implied terms in the company's Articles *(Towcester Racecourse Co. Ltd* v. *The Racecourse Association Ltd (2003) 1 BCLC, 260; Gower & Davies, 507).*

Sidestepping the fear of the common law Courts on this issue for a moment, there are situations where directors' duties may be owed to individual shareholders, as an exception to the general rule. For example, in takeover bids, where the shareholders are misled by the directors as to the terms of the takeover bids and thereby obtaining undue advantages over the shareholders, duties are enforceable against such directors. This point is made clearer by the learned authors of *Gower and Davies*, in explaining that such a relationship will arise, if, on the facts, the directors place themselves as against the shareholders, individually, in situations where fiduciary duties do normally arise, for instance, agency. A good example will be where the shareholders authorize the directors to sell their shares to a potential bidder in a takeover *(Allen* v. *Hyatt (1914) 30 TLR, 444; Gower & Davies, 507; Breiss* v. *Woolley (1954) AC, 333; Thorne*, 209).

Again, where a director misrepresents the company's financial position to shareholders in order for them to transfer their shares to him for a nominal consideration, he is liable in damages to them individually for negligent misrepresentation *(Gething* v. *Kilner (1972) 1 All ER 1166; Re a Company (1986) BCLC 382; Platt* v. *Platt (2001)1 BCLC, 698; Hannigan, 157, 158).*

In all, it should be pointed out that the jurisprudence on directors' duties being owed to the company as an entity and not to individual shareholders, appears not to be closed to continued evolution. In has been held that, in exceptional circumstances, the Courts may consider the relationships within the company and decide that they give rise to fiduciary relationships as between the directors and the individual shareholders. This is obviously an exception to the rule and we shall see why.

In *Coleman* v. *Myers (1977) 2 NZLR, 225*, it was held that the directors did owe fiduciary duties to the shareholders, including a duty not to mislead them on the sale of their shares. This was a family company, were the minority shareholders habitually looked up to the directors for guidance on matters affecting their interests. It was held that the nature of the relationship gave rise to the fiduciary duties owed the shareholders by the directors. Sound judgment, as the law must evolve with changing circumstances, and not be allowed to be used as instrument to perpetuate fraud.

As already noted, that the directors owe duties to the company as a legal entity does not imply that for all purposes, individual shareholders cannot hold them responsible in certain cases. Depending on the circumstances of any particular case, it has to be said, however, that for any such relationship to confer rights on individual shareholders, it must be distinguished from where the shareholders are attempting to enforce collective rights clandestinely, as the Courts have rejected above. This is because, except the reference is specifically made to individual shareholders in deserving cases, it is without doubt, true, that all the shareholders together constitute the general meeting, which is also the same as the company. Therefore, any attempt to distinguish between individual shareholders acting as body and the company as a legal entity, may become cosmetic and unnecessary hair splitting.

THE NATURE OF DIRECTORS' DUTIES TO THE COMPANY

A company director,at all times, stands in a fiduciary relationship to the company. In consequence, he is mandated to always observe the utmost good faith towards the company in any transaction with it or on its behalf (s. 305(1) CAMA 2020),(s. 279 (1); (*Okeowo* v. *Migliore (1979) 11 SC, 138; Wema Bank* v. *Olutu & Anor (2015) LPELR-42157; FBN Plc* v. *Banjo (2015) 5 NWLR Pt. 1452, 252; Omni Products Nig. Ltd* v. *UBN Plc (2021) 10 NWLR Pt. 1783, 92; UBN Plc* v. *Chimaeze (2014) 9 NWLR Pt. 1411, 166; Agbanelo* v. *UBN Ltd (2000)7 NWLR Pt. 666, 534).*

A director also owes fiduciary duty to a member in the company where:

- he is acting as an agent of a particular shareholder *(Peskin* v. *Anderson (2001) 1 BCLC, 372, 379).*

- though he is not acting as agent of any member(s), such a member(s) or other person is dealing with the company's securities (s. 305 (2) CAMA 2020), (s. 279(2).

What then is the implication of a director being a fiduciary in his relationship with a company? In simple terms, the term 'fiduciary' imports the element of 'trust' and the obligations of a 'trustee' into the relationship between a director and a company. It then imposes consequential liabilities on a director in the event of a breach of any of those duties.

Lord Sankey, in the case of *Regal (Hastings) Ltd.* v. *Gulliver (1942) 1 All ER, 378),* eloquently summarized the import and effect of the term 'fiduciary' as follows:

> as to the duties and liabilities of those occupying such a fiduciary position…in my view, the respondents were in a fiduciary position and their liability to account does not depend upon proof of *mala fides*. The general rule of equity is that no one who has duties of a fiduciary nature to perform is allowed to enter into engagements in which he has or can have a personal interest conflicting with the interests of those whom he is bound to protect.

The pivot, it would appear, with regards to company directors being fiduciary of the powers they wield, is the admonition for them to avoid placing themselves in a position where their personal interests would, in any way, conflict with the interests of the company. This has been a long-established principle in company law, apparently garnered from the rules of equity and the Law of Trusts. In recent years, it has also been amplified as serious corporate governance and ethical issues, that directors cannot abuse their vintage positions in companies, to their own advantage.

Well before the *Regal Hastings* v. *Gulliver* decision above, Clauson J, has had cause, in case of *Re: Thomson v. Allen (1930) 1 Ch., 203), 214*, to articulate the content of fiduciary duties of company directors:

> a corporate body…can only act by agents, and it is of course the duty of those agents so to act as best to promote the interests of the corporation whose affairs they are conducting. Such agents have duties to discharge of a fiduciary nature towards their principal. And it is a rule of universal application, that no one,

> having such duties to discharge, shall be allowed to enter into engagements in which he has, or can have, a personal interest conflicting, or which possibly may conflict, with the interests of those whom he is bound to protect.

A long line of decided cases have held that a fiduciary is under very strict obligations not to profit, in any way, from his fiduciary relationships. If he does, then, subject to certain limited exceptions, he must disgorge any benefit(s) obtained thereby, even if he acted honestly, and in his principal's best interests, or that his principal also got some benefits from his conduct, or that the principal could not have obtained the said benefits, otherwise. He will hold the benefits (profits) as a constructive trustee for his principal *(Boardman & Anor* v. *Phipps (1967) 2 A.C. 46; Nathan & Marshall, Cases and Commentary on the Law of Trusts, 6th edn, 367).* Some of these principles have been captured and reflected under directors' duties in the CAMA.

From a corporate governance perspective, Tricker submits that the duties of company directors are two-fold: the first is a duty of 'trust', which imports the directors' duty to exercise fiduciary responsibility to the shareholders by acting with integrity, honesty and acting fairly for the benefits of the shareholders equally. It also imports protecting the interests of any minority, working for the success of the company and acting solely within their powers, as delegated to them by the company's constitutional documents.

The second is a duty of 'care', which imports directors' exercise of reasonable care, diligence and skill in the performance of their duties to the company. It also imports the directors' exercise of independent judgment, and exhibiting the requisite level of knowledge, skill and experience that the directors possess *(Tricker, 272, 274).*

Whether the segregation of the duties of directors into duty of trust and duty of care, as above, is necessary, is hard to be seen. This is because some of the duties of directors, like the duty to act in the best interests of the company, will be hard to classify, as such strictly. However, the intent for the above classification is noted. As will be seen later, it has to be pointed that there is a serious overlap on the directors' duties to the company. In essence, it will amount to a fruitless exercise to try to strictly compartmentalize directors' duties to a company into well-isolated individual silos. Having said this, we now consider the import of some of these duties individually.

A Director to Act in the Company's Best Interests

A director is mandated to act, at all times, in what he believes is in the best interests of the company as a whole. In so acting, the director would be able to contribute in preserving the company's assets, further its business, and promote the purposes for which it was formed. In this respect, the director is expected to act in such a manner as a faithful, diligent, careful and ordinarily skilful director would act in the circumstances (s. 305(3) CAMA 2020), (s. 279(3). This seems to be an omnibus and all-encompassing duty imposed on the directors, and most of the other duties could conveniently be subsumed under this head. This is because in whatever way a director's duty to the company is couched, the ultimate objective is to manifestly benefit the company the most. In essence, in any exercise of directors' powers, the company must be the entity that must be seen to have benefitted the most.

Section 305 (3) above introduces both an objective test (as faithful, careful and ordinarily skilful director would act) and a subjective test (in what he believes to be in the best interests of the company) in the assessment of a director's actions in relation to managing the affairs of the company. While a director is permitted to use his personal judgment in deciding on issues subjectively, the objective test is open to external scrutiny. However, it has been held that what the law requires is what 'the directors consider' and not 'what the Court may consider' to be in the best interests of the company *(Re Smith & Fawcett Ltd (1942) Ch 304, 306)*. The critical question, it has been held, is not:

> whether, viewed objectively by the Court, the particular act or omission which is challenged was in fact in the interest of the company…rather the question is whether the director honestly believed that his act or omission was in the interest of the company *(Regentcrest Plc* v. *Cohen (2001) BCLC 80, 105 (Thorne, 210).*

The CAMA does not give details as to what would amount to a director acting in the best interests of the company. A persuasive clue could however be taken from section 172 of the English *Companies Act 2006* which deals with the issue under the heading 'Duty to Promote the Success of the Company.' The English *Companies Act* provides a non-exhaustive list of factors that could act as a guide for our Courts to determine when a director(s) has acted in the best interests of the company. In performing his duties, a director should consider:

- the likely consequences of any decision in the long run;
- the interests of the company's employees;
- the need to foster the company's business relationships with sundry stakeholders, including suppliers, customers, consultants and others;
- the impact of the company's operations on the community and the environment;
- the desirability that the company maintains a reputation for high standards of business conduct;
- the need to act fairly as between members of the company (*ICSA, 36).*

It has been held that the test is as to the director's state of the mind during the time of the act being challenged. Where it is clear that the director's act or omission being complained about resulted in a substantial detriment to the company, it would be harder for the director involved to persuade the Court that he believed the act to be in the best interests of the company. However, this fact does not detract from the subjective nature of the test *(Regentcrest Plc* v. *Cohen (2001) 1 BCLC 80, 105, Mayson et al., 519).*

As noted above, directors' duty to act in the best interests of the company is wide in scope and would entail, among other things:

- having a consideration for the interest of the shareholders as a body, balancing the short-term interests of the present members against the long-term interests of future members *(Gaiman* v. *National Assoc. for Mental Health (1971) Ch, 317;*
- where there are classes of shareholders, in taking a decision, the question would then be, as between the classes of shareholders, what is fair in the circumstances *(Howard Smith Ltd* v. *Ampol Pet. Ltd (1974) AC, 821)*;
- the interests of future shareholders become irrelevant when the issue at stake centres squarely and entirely on the interests of the present shareholders, for instance, when the directors are considering rival take-over bids *(Heron Intl Ltd* v. *Grade (1983) BCLC, 244)*;
- having consideration for the interests of the group and subsidiary companies in varying degrees, especially where either of them is having financial difficulties and whose survival might depend on the other *(Facia Footwear Ltd* v. *Hinchcliffe (1998) 1 BCLC, 218)*;

- the general rule is that directors do not owe duties to the company's creditors. However, the directors' duty to act in the best interests of the company will import an obligation to have regards to the interests of the company's creditors, especially where the company is of doubtful solvency or is outrightly insolvent;
- that the directors will act in the best interests of the company imports that they must not fetter their discretion when making decisions concerning the affairs of the company *(Motherwell* v. *Schoof (1949) 4 DLR, 812*). In this wise, they are not allowed to act as mere puppets or rubber-stamps to other director(s) thereby being devoid of any independent judgment *(Selangor United Rubber Estates Ltd* v. *Cradock (a bankrupt) (No. 3) (1968) 2 All ER, 1073; Thorne, 210 - 211).*

The section of the English *Companies Act* referred to above appears to attempt to incorporate elements of modern corporate governance and corporate social responsibility into the realm of directors' decision-making processes. Some of these factors enumerated under the English *Companies Act* are also reflected in the CAMA, which provides in section 305 (4) CAMA 2020, (s. 279(4), that 'the matters to which the director of a company is to have recourse in the performance of his functions include the interests of the company's employees in general as well as the interests of its members.'

Principle 24.3 of the *Nigerian Code of Corporate Governance, 2018 (NCCG)* chose to apply this principle in a broad sense, by providing that directors owe a fiduciary duty to the company, together with a duty of care, skill, diligence and loyalty, in fulfilling the functions of their offices and exercising the powers attached to those offices. Furthermore, that directors and the company's senior management are to act honestly, in good faith and in the best interests of the company, in accordance with legal requirements and agreed ethical standards. This is quite broad and seems to have combined what Tricker called the duty of trust and the duty of care above.

An issue that needs interrogation is the legal effect, if any, of the directors' mandate to have due regards to the interests of the employees in general, under section 305(4) CAMA 2020. Does this confer enforceable rights on the employees against the company, and if so, in what areas of the company's activities? We submit that this must be a persuasive provision, which does not give rise to enforceable rights by the company's employees against the directors. If this be otherwise, especially for large corporations, the process of aggregating the interests of the employees before the directors could take a business decision might prove counter-productive and a disincentive, that is, in terms of ensuring efficiency in decision making.

Directors to Exercise Powers for Proper Purpose

A company director is mandated to exercise his powers for the purpose for which they are specified and shall not do so for a collateral purpose. Furthermore, a director's power, if exercised for the right purpose, does not constitute a breach of duty, even if it incidentally affects a member adversely (s. 305 (5) CAMA 2020), (s. 279 (5).

The CAMA has not detailed out any instance(s) where, or factors that would guide the determination of the proper exercise of directors' power in any event. We must then have to rely on the decisions of the Courts for guidance in this respect, and there are many of such cases in England that could be of persuasive utility.

The requirement that directors must act for a proper purpose in conducting the affairs of a company should not be confused with their duty to act in the best interests of the company. The duties imposed in both instances are not the same. The key ingredient inherent in the exercise of directors' powers for proper purpose is not the purported exercise of the powers that they do not have, but the exercise by them of powers conferred on them for a purpose other than that for which they have been conferred.

More often than not, the exercise of directors' power for improper purpose will be to give the directors an advantage or preserve their control in a company. This would also amount to a breach of duty to act in the best interests of the company *(Howard Smith Ltd* v. *Ampol Pet. Ltd (1974) AC, 821, Gower, 385).* This is where there is a nexus between the two principles.

In *Howard Smith*, the Court found that the allotment of shares by the directors, which was being contested, was made in order to destroy an existing majority and preventing them from taking over the company, while enabling another party to take over. In consequence, therefore, the Court held that the directors' exercise of their powers to make the allotments, which was their legitimate powers in all material particulars, was for an improper purpose and the allotment was set aside.

We noted above the overlapping nature of directors' duties in managing and directing a company. That overlap is also manifest under this head. In-fact, it has been submitted that the prohibition against the exercise of directors' powers for improper purpose applies to all directors' duties to the company, from the power to make allotment of shares *(Bamford* v. *Bamford*

(1969) 1 All ER, 969; making calls on shares *(Galloway* v. *Halle Concert Society (1915) 2 Ch, 233)*; refusing to register share transfers *(Re Smith & Fawcett Ltd (1942) 1 All ER,542)*; ordering the forfeiture of shares *(Re Agriculturalist Cattle Insurance Co, Stanhope's Case (1866) 1 Ch App, 161)*; alienating the company's property *(Ford* v. *Plymer Vision Ltd (2009) 2 BCLC, 160)*; expelling a member *(Gaiman* v. *National Assoc. for Mental Health (1970) 2 All ER, 362)*; to entering into agreement on behalf of the company with third parties *(Lee Panavision Ltd* v. *Lee Lighting Ltd (1992) BCLC, 22; Hannigan, 176-177)*.

From the above, it becomes clear the extent of latitude of this duty of not exercising directors' powers for improper purpose. With this has also come the problems of determining the limits of the powers in its application. In *Howard Smith* above, Lord Wilberforce attempted to give a guide as to the proper approach to the exercise of this power. The first is to consider the nature of the power whose exercise is in question and any limits within which it is to be exercised. Then, the next is to examine the substantial purpose for which the power was exercised and to reach a conclusion whether the purpose was proper or not.

Having given the above guide, Lord Wilberforce went ahead and also acknowledged the difficulties inherent in the Court's approach to interpreting the exercise of this power by directors. This being that the Courts are reluctant to interfere with business decisions by directors and are inclined to respect their judgments in matters relating to managing the company *(Hannigan, 177)*. So, where does this leave us in the interpretation and application of this power by company directors?

The whole scenario might have to be resolved based on provisos to the general rule: provided that the substantial purpose for which the power was exercise is a proper purpose, the exercise of the power is not invalidated by the presence of some other improper, but insubstantial purpose.

For example, it has been held that some incidental benefits obtained by a director does not, *ipso facto,* invalidate the exercise of the power, unless his self-interest was the substantial purpose for the exercise of the power in the first place *(Whitehouse* v. *Carlton Hotel Pty Ltd (1987) 5 ACLC, 421, 427*; *Ngurli* v. *McCann (1954) 90 CLR, 425)*. Conversely, if the substantial purpose was improper, the director's honest belief that he was acting in the best interests of the company will be insufficient to validate the exercise of such power in the material instance *(Re a Company ex p Glossop (1988) BCLC, 570)*. When this happens, the consequence is that the transaction is voidable at the option of the company *(Hogg* v. *Cramphorn Ltd (1967) Ch 254; Thorne, 213)*; meaning that ratification of the director's action by the company is also an option for the company.

In the final analysis, it becomes obvious that the parameters for the application of this duty, in terms of judicial interpretation, are not closed, meaning that it is possible for different Courts to arrive at different answers on a particular scenario. Determining proper purpose, though naturally objective in the present context, therefore, assumes a relatively non-rigid colouration, prone to a slant of judicial subjectivity.

Directors' Proper Exercise of Discretion

In the exercise of his duties owed to a company, a director shall not fetter his discretion to vote in a particular way (305 (6) CAMA 2020), (s. 279 (6). There is no further elaboration on this point. This duty has also been classified as the duty on directors to exercise independent judgment in acting for the company. So, what then is the practical import of this duty, that directors should not fetter their discretion, though the CAMA limits the non-fettering of discretion to instances of voting by the directors? There is a paucity of local judicial authorities on this point, but there are some established common law principles that could guide our present discussions:

- the duty for directors to exercise independent judgment does not preclude them from seeking and acting on the advice from professionals, like solicitors, accountants, investment bankers etc. The board should, however, not take such advice as an instruction and will take responsibility for accepting the advice so given *(Gower & Davies, 536)*;
- there must be a distinction drawn between where company directors are fettering their discretion (which is prohibited) and where the directors are exercising their discretion in a way which restricts their future conducts (which is allowed) *(Thorby* v. *Goldberg (1964) 112 CLR, 597)*.In this case, the company directors agreed, as part of a larger restructuring in the company, to allot shares in particular way at a future date. They later reneged. In an action to force them to allot the shares as earlier agreed, they pleaded that the earlier agreement to allot shares was an invalid fettering of discretion on their part. The Court rejected the directors' argument and held that the directors validly exercised their discretion at the time of entering into the agreement, provided that they had considered the interests of the company at the time. (Also, *Fulham Football Club* v. *Cabra Estates Plc (1994) 1BCLC, 363)*.

- the duty to exercise independent judgment is not infringed where the directors are acting in a way that is authorized by the company's Articles;
- where the company's Articles allow for delegation of duty and functions, the directors are allowed to delegate to the extent allowed by the Articles and cannot be adjudged not to have exercised independent judgment by the fact of such delegation. This does not derogate from the directors' duty of residual supervision, even with the delegation of duty *(Hannigan, 219).*

Over the years, most common law countries have developed many more exceptions to the general rule that directors should not fetter their discretion, especially in entering into contract with third parties. The exceptions concede to company directors the power to bind themselves in contracts for the company with third parties to do particular things in a particular way in the future that would engender a successful performance of the contract. The exceptions to the unfettered discretion rule have been devised to meet the exigency of modern business and avoid portraying companies as unreliable contracting parties. This would have had the effect of denying companies the benefits of long-term contracts and other commercial benefits *(Gower, & Davies, 538).*

Directors' Duty of Care and Skill

In their relationship with a company, every director is obligated to exercise the powers and discharge the duties of his office honestly, in good faith and in the best interests of the company. He is expected to exercise a degree of care, diligence and skill which a reasonably prudent director would exercise in comparable circumstances. Failure to exercise reasonable care in accordance with acceptable parameters is a ground for an action in negligence and breach of duty against such a director (s. 308 (1)(2) CAMA 2020, (s. 282 (1)(2).

This duty seems to be a combination of several of the directors' duties: duty to act in good faith and the allied duty to act in the best interests of the company, affirming, once again, the overlapping nature of these duties

The above provisions seem, in a major sense, to have raised the bar on the elements of the standard of care required from directors in the performance of their duties, away from the principles elaborated in the case of *Re City Equitable Fire Insurance Co. Ltd (1925) Ch., 407,* where it was stated that:

- a director need not exhibit in the performance of his duties a greater degree of skill than may be reasonably expected of a person of his knowledge and experience;
- a director is not bound to give continuous attention to the affairs of his company. His duties are of an intermittent nature to be performed at periodic board meetings...he is not bound to attend all such meetings;
- in respect of duties that may properly be left to some other officials, a director is, in the absence of any ground for suspicion, justified in trusting such officials to perform such duties honestly.

The above case was decided, not surprisingly, in 1925, and it is obvious that times have changed drastically. Most of the postulations above seem to relate to the standard required, to an extent, from non-executive directors, if at all, who work for the company on a part time basis. The modern company law, common law and statutes, coupled with the now-entrenched principles of corporate governance, have since moved on from this era.

The CAMA has, in apparent repudiation of most of the principles enunciated in *Re Equitable Fire* above, streamlined, as it were, the standard of care required from both executive and non-executive directors in their performance of duties to the company, excepting provisions that may be contained in an executive director's contract of service with the company. Section 308(4) CAMA 2020, (s. 282(4) provides that the same standard of care in relation to duties to the company shall be required for both executive and non-executive directors: *provided* that additional liability and benefit may arise under the master and servant law in the case of an executive director, if there is an express or implied contract to that effect.

To further reinforce the need for directors to give constant attention to the company, section 308(3) CAMA 2020, (s. 282 (3), provides that each director shall be individually responsible for the actions of the board in which he participated. Furthermore, that the absence of a director from board deliberations, unless justified, shall not relieve such a director of responsibility.

The provision above introduces the principle of collegiate or collective responsibility into the liability of the board of directors. With the introduction of the CAMA, collegiate or collective responsibility of the board has assumed fundamental importance in Nigerian company law *(Re Westmid Packing Services Ltd (1998) 2 All ER 124, 130)*. It would appear that a director who is dissatisfied with the workings of the board of directors and who could not do anything to remedy the situation would have to resign his membership of the board. A director who stays on the board, although dissatisfied with the workings of such a board, but who deliberately stays away from board deliberations in order to avoid any future liability, is no longer exercising a viable option for a director in Nigeria.

The provisions for directors to exercise the degree of care, diligence and skill which a reasonably prudent director would exercise in comparable circumstances, is all but a statement of the basic minimum standard applicable in such circumstances. The CAMA, like most company legislations, did not go further to enunciate the import or implications of this duty. It is then usually left for the Courts to try to fill-in the gaps.

In *Re Barings Plc (No. 5) Secretary of State for Trade and Industry* v. *Baker (No. 5 (1999) 1 BCLC, 433; Hannigan, 213-214)*, Parker J, enunciated what has been widely accepted as the content of the duty of care, skill and diligence, as follows:

- directors have, both collectively and individually, a continuing duty to acquire and maintain sufficient knowledge and understanding of the company's business to enable them to properly discharge their duties as directors. In essence, if a manager does not properly understand the business which he is seeking to manage, he will be unable to take informed management decisions thereto;
- whilst directors are entitled (subject to the Articles) to delegate particular functions to those below them in the management chain, and to trust their competence and integrity to a reasonable extent, such delegation does not absolve the directors from the duty to supervise the delegated functions. As has been severally mentioned in this chapter, the pivotal point is delegation of duty and not abdication of same *(Re Westminster Property Mgt. Ltd, Official Receiver* v. *Stern (No. 2) (2001) BCC, 305;*
- no rule of universal application can be formulated as to the duty no (ii) above. The extent of the duty and the question as to whether it has been discharged must depend on the facts of each particular case, including the director's role in the management of the company.

In the final analysis, it can safely be said that the duty of care, skill and diligence, therefore, might not be significantly more than the directors being continually abreast of current knowledge requirements for the effective discharge of their duties and the efficient application of same in managing the company. Additionally, when delegating such duties to subordinates, directors must efficiently retain the residual supervisory roles on those functions. There could be some slants to these points, but, we submit, that they form the core of the duty and the ratios in the *Re Barings* propositions.

Directors' Duty not to Misuse Corporate Information

The CAMA imposes a duty on directors not to misuse corporate information, property or opportunity. The duty not to misuse corporate information does not cease by a director or an officer having resigned from the company. He shall still be accountable and can be restrained by an injunction from misusing the information received by virtue of his former position (s. 306 (5) CAMA 2020), (s. 280 (5). The fact that a person holds more than one directorship shall not derogate from his fiduciary duties to each company, including a duty not to use the property, opportunity or information obtained in the course of the management of one company for the benefit of the other company, or to his own or other person's advantage (s. 307 (1) CAMA 2020), (s. 281).

The CAMA seems to have compounded the directors' duty not to misuse corporate information into prohibitions of not only the misuse of corporate information but also misuses of corporate opportunity and property. This is alright. However, what it has done is that it has summed all the duties into the broader one of a director not being allowed to unfairly profit from his position.

It has been submitted that the above, - that is, not unfairly profiting from a director's position - is an inflexible rule of equity, that a person in a fiduciary position, like directors, except where expressly allowed, cannot profit from his position, otherwise, the person will be held responsible to account. This has, in turn, from the time of *Regal (Hastings) Ltd* v. *Gulliver (1967) 2 AC, 134,* metamorphosed into the prohibition against making secret profits by directors, while using their positions *(Cooks* v. *Deeks) (1916) AC, 554; Thorne at 218).*

The CAMA has sought to compound the duties against profiting from corporate information, property and opportunity into one, which has ultimately become the prohibition against directors making secret profits. The real question is: are there clear distinctions amongst all these prohibitions, that is, against abuse of information, property and opportunity? Let us explore some decided cases for assistance.

In *Cooks* v. *Deeks,* three directors of a Canadian railway company had diverted a contract in which the company had an interest, to a company which the directors had incorporated. It was held that the directors were not entitled to take over the contract to themselves, as equity would not allow that, as it will allow the directors to unfairly abuse and profit from their positions as directors and also make secret profits thereby.

In a latter case of *Industrial Development Consultants Ltd (IDC)* v. *Cooley (1972) 2 All ER, 162,* IDC was negotiating a construction contract with another company, who for some unclear reasons, later decided not to deal with IDC on the contract, but were ready, about a year later, to deal directly with Cooley on the contract. The snag was that Cooley was IDC's managing director, who had participated actively in the contract negotiations earlier, but who then promptly resigned his position with IDC, citing ill health. He took up the construction contract offered by the other company. It was held that he abused corporate information by not telling IDC that the other company were ready to contract and with him personally. In consequence, the Court concluded that his fiduciary duties to IDC were breached *(Canadian Aero Service* v. *O'Malley (1973) 40 DLR (3d), 371; Hannigan, 226-227).*

Looking closely at *Cooks and IDC* cases above, they would seem to disclose more of breaches of corporate information and abuse of opportunity, that resulted in secret profits. How then does abuse of property come in?

The case of *CMS Dolphin Ltd* v. *Simonet (2001) 2 BCLC, 704*, attempts to give an answer, especially, as the directors concerned would have resigned their positions and would still be held liable to account for the profits made from the contract. In this case, Collins J, concluded that the answer lies in the proposition that corporate opportunity is treated as the company's property. This implies that a director who resigns his position after learning of the opportunity is just 'as accountable as a trustee, who retires without properly accounting for trust property' *(Gower & Davies, 596).*

The CAMA tries to assist us by classifying the whole scenario discussed above as 'conflict of interests' and that the personal interests of a director shall not conflict with any of his duties as a director. It is submitted that all the duties of directors to a company can be summed up under two heads, maybe three: directors' actions need to be in the best interests of the company; directors need to show care, skill and diligence in the discharge of their duties. The third is that directors must, at all costs, avoid conflict of interests between their personal interests and the company's business. We submit that every other duty owed to a company by directors can comfortably be subsumed into these heads.

The CAMA goes ahead to prohibit the making of secret profits by company directors. However, the prohibition is not in absolute terms, because, where a director discloses his interests to the company in a general meeting, prior to the transaction and before any secret profits, which resulting profits the meeting may or may not authorize, he may escape liability. However, a director shall not escape liability if the disclosure of his interest in a transaction where he made profits occurred after the secret profits had been made. The question is: if the director discloses the profits in a general meeting before they are made: are they still secret profits?

Apparently trying to deal with the directors' shenanigans in cases like *Cooley* and *O'Malley* above, of purportedly resigning their positions before accepting new offers, the CAMA tried to expressly provide against this. To achieve this, the CAMA states that the duty not to misuse corporate information shall not cease by the fact of a director or an officer having resigned from the company. He shall still be accountable and can be restrained by an injunction from misusing the information received by virtue of his former position (s. 309(1)(5)(6) CAMA 2020), (s. 280 (1)(5)(6). The common law principles discussed above under this head have therefore been codified by the CAMA in Nigeria.

Apart from the provisions of the CAMA in the above respects, principle 24.3 of the NCCG asks company directors not make improper or prejudicial use of privileged information and that directors should not take advantage of their position for personal gain or to compete with the company. The terms 'improper' or 'prejudicial use' as used here are very wide and could be stretched to cover any conflict of interests situation wherever corporate information is used by a director to make secret profits or compete with the company in any way.

There has never been any doubt, at least from available literature, in company law and corporate governance, that the position of directors as the managers of a company places them in a sensitive situation of trust and care. This is with respect to how they deal with the company and its properties, both physical and intellectual properties. What seems to be the problem has been the slow or ineffective ways that the law has sought to hold directors responsible for any breach of their duties to the company. The matter is complicated by the fact that it is also the directors that determine, except in limited cases, how and when the company will exercise its right to move against erring directors. The situation is almost like directors being the 'judges,' as it were, in their own causes.

Directors' Duty to Disclose Interests in Transactions

As part of the efforts made by the common law and statutes to avoid company directors putting themselves in situations where conflict of interests with the company may arise, there is a duty on directors to disclose their interests in contracts with the company. Under section 303(1) CAMA 2020, (s. 277 (1), directors are duty bound, when they are, in any way, directly or indirectly, interested in a transaction(s) or proposed transaction(s) with the company, to immediately notify the directors of the company in writing, specifying particulars of the directors' interest(s).

To satisfy the requirement of notice under this section, a general notice given to the directors of the company by a director that he is a member of a specified company or firm and that he should be considered interested in any transaction which may, after the date of the notice, be made with that company or firm, is not considered sufficient declaration of interests in relation to any transaction(s) so made. The exception is, unless the particulars of the transaction are also disclosed by that director to the board upon being known to him and that the director does all things, reasonably necessary, to ensure that it is brought up and read at the next meeting of the directors after it is given (s. 303 (2) CAMA 2020), (s. 277 (3).

Note that under the CAMA 2004, such a general notice by a director, as above, is considered a sufficient declaration of interests to the directors, provided that the notice shall not have effect unless it is given at a meeting of directors, or that the director concerned ensured that it is brought up and read at the next meeting of the directors after the notice is given.

The CAMA 2020 made some changes with respect to the issue of what used to be directors' disclosure of interests in contracts with the company. While some of the changes could be considered far-reaching in their intended effect, others are basically routine changes. Some examples of the major changes would be appropriate here:

- the CAMA 2020 changed the nomenclature of the issue at stake from involving 'contract' with the company to 'transaction.' In essence, a director is required to disclose his interests in a transaction with the company and not necessarily when the transaction is a contract, which is a narrower terminology. A director's contract with a company could, in all respects, be called a transaction, but not all transactions between a director and the company could be considered a contract;

- the CAMA 2020 abolished the dichotomy between the modalities for notice when a director is interested in a transaction and when he is interested in a proposed transaction. The 2004 CAMA made that distinction in the modalities for notice in the two instances, but this was abolished in 2020;
- the CAMA 2004 requires that a director's notice to declare his interests in a contract with the company to the other directors shall be at a meeting of the directors of the company (board meeting). The Act did not state the nature of the notice to be given. For anything, it could be an oral notice to the board and captured in the minutes of the meeting;
- in contrast to the above, the CAMA 2020 requires a director who is interested in a transaction or proposed transaction with the company 'to immediately notify the directors of such company in writing' and specify the nature of his interests. The express requirement that the notice be in writing removes any conjectures as to the modalities for the notice. Also, the notice is to the directors, which, it is submitted, could be individually sent to them, and he does not have to wait for a board meeting to make the disclosure.

The provision of the CAMA 2020 above relating to notice does not prejudice any other law that might restrict, in one way or the other, directors from having contracts with a company. There is a fine imposed, to be specified by the Commission, on any director that fails to give the requisite notice as indicated above. Under the CAMA 2004, the fine was ₦100.00.

The CAMA requires the concerned director to disclose both direct and indirect interests in a transaction with the company. Indirect interest in a transaction means that it is not necessary that the director be the person directly involved as a party with the company. It is enough, for instance, that he is a shareholder in a company that is intended or has transacted with the company he is directing *(Newgate Stud Co.* v. *Penfold (2008) 1 BCLC, 46; Gower & Davies, 565).*

What then should be the nature or content of the disclosure of the director's interest to the company, since this has not been mentioned in the CAMA, apart from saying that it must be in writing? It is actually the common practice, that most company law legislations do not go into such details, leaving same to the common law, through the Courts, to complete the puzzle, as it were. In doing this, the Courts have enunciated a few principles on this:

- the disclosure required is full and frank disclosure as to the nature of the transaction to allow the directors to see the nature and extent of the disclosed interests *(Movitex Ltd* v. *Bulfield (1988) BCLC, 104;*
- the disclosure should be to all the directors (the board), even if they appear to already be aware of the transaction (not a committee of the board)*(Guinness Plc* v. *Saunders (1990) 2 AC, 663; Neptune Vehicle Washing Equipment Ltd* v. *Fitzgerald 1995) 1 BCLC, 352*).

Since the CAMA no longer requires specifically that the notice be sent to the board of directors, a notice to all the directors, without exception, should suffice to satisfy this requirement. It should be noted that non-compliance with the requirement for notice by a director does not invalidate any resulting contract with the company, but makes it voidable at the instance of the company *(Hely-Hutchinson* v. *Brayhead Ltd (1967) 3 All ER, 98).* If the company elects to rescind the contract, that decision must be communicated clearly and promptly, otherwise the contract remains valid and binding *(Re Marini Ltd (2004) BCC, 172*). Undue delay to rescind the contract and the right will be lost, for instance, where the contract is already fully performed, or when third party *bona fide* interests have intervened.

The company may hold the director to account for the profit made from the contract or to indemnify the company for any losses, and this is irrespective of whether the company rescinded the contract or not *(Hannigan, 254).*

This is an area where the company secretary's expertise is needed to guide the directors in complying with a provision on this nature. According to principle 2.10 of the *King Report on Corporate Governance for South Africa 2002 (King Report),* the company secretary should provide a central source of guidance and advice to the board, and within the company, on matters of ethics and good governance. It is possible that a handbook on such compliance issue as this, among others, could be formulated by the company secretary and circulated to the directors, especially those not very experience on the board, during their induction meetings. This could go a long way in meeting the company's corporate governance goals.

Directors' Duty Not to Make Secret Profits

This is one of the duties imposed on company directors that is hydra-headed in terms of its import. A duty not to make secret profits, it is submitted, presupposes a situation where the directors are expected to act 'clean and blameless' in their relationship with the company. This is especially apt in cases where they may gain any inequitable pecuniary benefit(s) at the expense of the company, or in any situation at all, where secret profits would accrue to them.

The duty so imposed here could be stretched to cover the duty to act in the best interests of the company, especially if by not so acting, the director in question makes a profit(s) out of his conduct. It could also cover situations where a director misuses corporate information or did not disclose his interest(s) in a contract or proposed contract with the company, and in any of these latter cases, profits from not acting properly with the company.

The CAMA deals with the issue of directors making secret profits under the omnibus head of conflict of interests, that is, prohibiting the personal interests of a director from conflicting with any of his duties as a director under the Act (s. 306(1) CAMA 2020), (s. 280 (1). The context is that a director must not, in the course of the management of the affairs of the company, or in the utilization of the company's property, make secret profits or achieve other unnecessary and underserved benefits (s. 306(1)(2) CAMA 2020), (s. 280 (1)(2).

As noted earlier, the prohibition against directors making secret profits is tied to their being in a fiduciary relationship with the company, which presupposes that they cannot place themselves, *bona fide* or otherwise, in a situation where conflict of interests with the company results. This common law principle was aptly encapsulated long ago by Lord Herschell, in *Bray* v. *Ford (1896) AC, 44; Thorne, 219)*, as follows:

> it is an inflexible rule of a Court of equity that a person in a fiduciary position…is not, unless otherwise expressly provided, entitled to make a profit; he is not allowed to put himself in a position where his interest and duty conflict. It does not appear to me that this rule is…founded upon principles of morality. I regard it rather as based on the consideration that, human nature being what it is, there is danger in such circumstances, of the person holding a fiduciary position being swayed by interest rather than duty, and thus prejudicing those he was bound to protect *(Gower & Davies at 559)*.

The terms 'secret profits' and 'unnecessary benefits' have not really been defined anywhere in the CAMA, but would, so to say, mean profits made by directors in secret and unearned benefits. A secret profit is also said to be made by a company's director when such a benefit has been made by the director concerned personally, that is, without it being authorized by or disclosed to the company. The golden rule, in relation to directors and secret profits, it would appear, is that a director must not, without the consent of the company, make any personal profits or otherwise benefit from his position as a director in the company beyond his agreed remuneration *(Regal Hastings Ltd* v. *Gulliver (1967) 2 AC, 134; Orojo, 267-268).*

While the determination of what amounts to secret profits by a director might be fairly objective when placed within the context of directors working 'in the best interests of the company,' it would appear that the determination of what amounts to a director acquiring 'unnecessary benefits' also has to be approached from the perspective of benefits that have been earned irregularly or without any proper justification(s).

It is noteworthy that the inability or unwillingness of the company to perform any functions or duties under its Articles and Memorandum shall not constitute a defence to a director's breach of any of the duties imposed by the Act (s. 306(4) CAMA 2020), (s. 280 (4). This provision is meant to forestall a situation whereby company directors would intentionally place the company in a situation where it would be unable to perform certain transactions, while the directors take up those transactions in their individual capacities and then make profits for themselves.

In a further attempt to tighten the gaps around what could loosely be referred to as situations where company directors could 'unjustly enrich' themselves at the expense of the company, the CAMA makes further specific prohibition on directors from making what might have been referred to as 'unnecessary benefits' above. In this wise, directors are prohibited from making secret profits in the form of a bribe, gift, or commission, either in cash or kind, from any person or share in the profits of that person in respect of any transaction involving the director's company in order to introduce the person offering the bribe, gift or other gratification to deal with the company. This latter part is simply a prohibition on directors from engaging in any kind of brokerage activities on the company's transactions (s. 313 (1) CAMA 2020), (s. 287 (1). The main problem with this provision, we submit, is that it is not absolute (and it should have been) and the qualification thereto may actually render same ineffectual in implementation.

As a qualification to the above provision, the CAMA goes ahead to provide that where a director receives a gift in the form of an unsolicited gift that shows gratitude after the transaction has been completed, he may be allowed to keep the gift. The proviso to this is that he declares it before the board of directors and the fact of that declaration shall appear in the directors' minutes book for the meeting (s. 313 (2)(3) CAMA 2020), (s. 287 (2)(3)).

The real question is gratitude for what? Why would a director be receiving gratitude from a third party for a concluded transaction entered into by the company that was not *ex gracias* and on which parties have fulfilled their parts of the bargain?

The above qualification should be applied with caution. This is because, it could, most likely, be subject to abuse. A director could agree to a deferred gratification, gift or bribe with a third party before a transaction but to receive same after the transaction has been concluded, as unsolicited gratification. This would then be declared to the board and most likely approved by the other directors and a precedent is set. This does violence to the original intent of preventing directors from making secret profits and receiving unnecessary benefits and bribes, and could effectively circumvent the intent of the provision.

We submit, that, for the prohibition against receipt of bribes, commissions and gifts by directors to be effective, it has to be total and the qualification under section 313(3) above, should be expunged from the Act. Otherwise, the provision under section 313(2) of the Act authorizing a company to sue a director in breach of the prohibition against illicit gift, bribe and commission for damages, becomes simply otiose. The main purpose, which is to prevent a situation where the taking of bribe, commission or gift, which obscures the loyalty of the directors to the company and skews same to that of the third party, is defeated.

Finally, it should be noted that in all cases concerning directors and the prohibition on their making secret profits and benefits, it is not a defence that the company also benefitted from the transaction or that the gift was accepted in good faith by the director(s) concerned (s. 313(4) CAMA 2020), (s.287(4). In essence, the element of the intention, *bona fide* or *mala fide* of the director concerned in attaching liability under this head is purely irrelevant.

The issues discussed above may appear straight-forward in terms of conceptual analysis, however, in practical terms, the situation gets very complicated with directors, who are usually the engines that drive the companies. Except in large private or publicly quoted companies where activist individual shareholders and shareholders associations do exert serious pressures on the board, strictly enforcing conflict of interest provisions against company directors is usually a difficult task, except where the directors themselves choose to act ethical in such situations. In this respect, principle 25.2 of the NCCG admonishes generically, that, 'directors should promptly disclose any real or potential conflict of interest that they may have by virtue of their membership of the board.' If this is done with fidelity, cases of conflicts of interests between directors and companies, in diverse guises, will be drastically reduced.

The company secretary's duties with respect to the issues discussed in this chapter, have been simplified by the clear rules and regulations of the CAMA and common law principles enunciated above.

In being a sounding board for the directors in their running of the affairs of the company, the company secretary, by his knowledge and training would be in a vantage position to guide the directors in the exercise of their powers and execution of their duties. The major points for the issues discussed in this chapter would be the nature of the power or duty, timelines, and modalities for execution.

The central focus in advising the directors would be the need for the directors to have it in mind to always act in the 'best interests of the company.' And this, not simply in the theoretical sense, as there are parameters, as seen above, as to how directors' actions in this respect can be measured. Why most of the directors may, depending on their background and exposure, be approaching the issues solely from a business perspective, the company secretary will bring in the legal and corporate governance perspectives, in advising the directors on their respective duties, responsibilities and liabilities.

The advice to the directors would be collegiate in certain cases and individualized in others. While the collegiate advice would cover the generic area of the directors' duties to the company, the individualized ones will relate to the specific duty being in issue in the particular instance. An example will be a director's duty not to fetter his discretion in voting in a company's meeting. The company secretary should be in a position to advise the director of the circumstances wherein such a duty would have been deemed to have been violated by a director's action. As noted above, the process of inducting the directors into the board and their continuous engagement with the company secretary will be very helpful in this respect.

Another key area where the company secretary will come in handy for the directors is in relation to the areas where the provisions of the CAMA have been changed, or the modalities for doing an act(s) under the Act have been altered. Apart from, maybe, having a refresher for the directors in respect of such areas of the law, the company secretary will also be continually handy to assist the directors to ensure actual compliance with the provisions of the law. An example is the modalities for the directors to give notice of transactions with the company, which CAMA 2020 has altered considerably.

In the final analysis, we will discover that in most instances where directors are required to give notice to the company or the Commission on particular issue(s), it is actually the company secretary that virtually singularly guides the process for everyone involved. This is especially the case in smaller publicly quoted companies, where there are lots of regulatory requirements imposed on the directors, but where the directors might not be as experienced as those in large publicly quoted companies. The more experienced the directors get on the job, then, the more they would be conversant with regulatory issues and are more inclined to undertake several of the duties with lesser assistance from the company secretary. The exception will be where there are regulatory filings or returns to be executed at the Commission.

Directors' Ancillary Notices to the Company

Aside from the diverse notices required to be given to the company as noted above, the directors have a general duty to give notices to the company on certain other issues. These could be classified as concerning the directors' personal, proprietary or financial interests or relations with the company. This is more germane when a director has just been appointed into the company's board, who may have dealt with the company in other capacities in the past. It also concerns an existing director who then decides to invest in the company or in another entity in which the company has a proprietary or financial interest. He is bound, depending on the nature of the interests so acquired, to disclose same to the company on his being appointed as a director.

The company secretary will be on top of situations of this nature to get prompt notices from the director(s) in question, once a proper situation presents itself to the company.

A few examples on this will suffice for the moment, where it is expected that the company secretary will put an engagement mechanism in place to get the directors, especially those who are not very experienced on the position, to be compliant with these provisions. This is one of the areas where most directors do rely on the guidance of the company secretary to be current with legal requirements.

Under section 302 CAMA 2020, (s. 276) company directors are generally under a duty to give the company notice of such matters relating to themselves, where applicable, for the purposes of sections 301 and 303 CAMA 2020, except in so far as it relates to loans made by the company or by any other person under a guarantee from or on a security provided by the company, to an officer of the company. Section 301 CAMA 2020 deals with register of directors' holdings in shares or debentures in a company which every company is mandated to keep. On the other hand, section 303 of the Act deals with the requirement for the disclosure of a director's interest in a transaction or proposed transaction with the company. This issue has been dealt with extensively earlier above.

Any notice to be given by a director in satisfying the requirement of section 301(to disclose holding in shares or debentures) shall be in writing. It has been argued earlier in this book that a requirement that a notice shall be in writing, in modern business practice, admits a notice sent by e-mail and other electronic forms, once the receipt of same by the recipient can be established by evidence. If such a notice is not given at a board meeting, the director giving the notice shall do everything necessary to ensure that after it has been given, the notice is brought up and read at the next meeting of the board of directors (s.302 (2) CAMA 2020), (s. 276 (2).

The duty to give notice under section 303 above (disclosing interest in a transaction with the company) also applies, in same manner, to other officers of a company who are not directors (s. 302 (3)(a) CAMA 2020), (s. 276 (3) (a). The duty also applies in the same manner to persons who are, or have been, at any time during the preceding five (5) years, officers of the company (section 302 (3)(b) CAMA 2020), (s. 276 (3) (b).

The role of the company secretary in guiding the directors of the company in terms of complying with the provisions of the law as discussed above cannot be over-emphasized. This is because, in all the discussions so far in this book, where fines have been imposed for default in complying with any provision(s) of the Act, with exceptions to where only personal liability was imposed, the fines have always been on the company and each officer (s) in default. We recall that under section 868 2020, an 'officer' is defined as 'a director, manager or secretary.'

In essence, a fine imposed on the company, for example, for failure of the directors to give notice to the company about their shareholdings in the company or of their interests in a transaction or proposed transaction with the company, might be imposed by the Commission on the company, the directors and the company secretary, as an officer, jointly and severally. This would be an unfortunate situation. Apart from the 'red flag' such imposed fines would raise about the capacity or otherwise of the company secretary, especially if the situation becomes persistent, no board or management of any serious-minded company would be comfortable paying consistent fines to the Commission on compliance-related issues.

COMPANY'S POWER TO ENFORCE DIRECTORS' DUTIES

In principle and practice, the duties imposed on company directors by the CAMA are enforceable against the directors by the company, that is, in the event of a breach of any of the duties (s. 305 (9) CAMA 2020), (s. 279 (9). However, that is as far as the principle will go. As we shall see below, enforcing a breach of directors' duties against any of the directors is not usually an easy task, being that the directors are, collectively, the engine that drives the company. Although, the CAMA, flowing from our common law legal ancestry, gives the right to enforce directors' duties to the company itself, it is possible that a member could under some circumstances (for instance while instituting a derivative action or action to protect minority rights) force directors to rescind actions that are not in the best interests of the company. This is especially the case considering that section 305 (4) CAMA 2020, (s. 279(4) urges directors to, among other things, have regard to the interests of the members of the company in performing their duties. There is no suggestion that members, even in a general meeting, would have an easy task in enforcing rights against the directors, especially in situations where the directors themselves are also shareholders, and more often than not, holding controlling shares.

In essence, the difficulties inherent in the company itself or the shareholders (members) enforcing duties against the company directors are two folds, one is legal and the other could be described as administrative.

The legal difficulty in enforcing duties against directors is that it is the company that is expected to enforce the rights, being a separate legal entity. However, the directors, as a collective, are the persons entrusted, by law, with the responsibility of managing and directing the affairs company. Legally speaking, therefore, it is still the same directors that will take the decision to proceed against one of their own. In the spirit of solidarity of directors as a team, this can only happen as a last resort, when every available option, including the option of allowing the director to quietly resign his appointment, has failed.

The second and related difficulty, is administrative in nature. The directors are themselves in charge of the administrative machinery of the company, deciding when to call board meetings, the issue(s) to be discussed at such meetings, time allowed to discuss any issue(s) at meetings, assigning timelines for implementing decisions etc. Therefore, in a situation where the directors do not want to proceed against any member(s) of the board, they may use administrative rigmaroles to frustrate the matter, although there are instances where the general meeting can intervene. That, too, is not as easy as it seems. This is principally because, although CAMA gives the members of a company the inherent right to take far-reaching decisions, including removing directors from office in a general meeting, considering the facts stated above, it is usually difficult and sometimes impossible, for the shareholders to exercise that right against the directors, especially those with substantial or controlling shareholding *(Orojo, 270)*.In the words of Lord Caldcote, the situation is just like where the 'directors are marking their own examination papers,' literally *(Tricker, 38)*.

DIRECTORS CANNOT BE RELIEVED FROM DUTIES

Apparently, in appreciating the enormous powers vested by law in, and exercisable by, the board of directors of companies, the CAMA attempts to thwart a situation where the directors would free themselves, *ab initio*, from any liability for breach of their duties. In this respect, section 305 (8) CAMA 2020, provides that no provisions, whether contained in a company's Articles, resolutions or contract, shall relieve a director from the fiduciary duties imposed under the Act or relieve him from any liability incurred as a result of a breach of such duties (s. 279(8).

Apart from the above provision which deals with potential liability of only company directors, another provision in section 91 CAMA 2020, deals with another aspect of non-relief from liability with respect to officers in general. It is necessary to consider the provisions of section 305 vis-a-vis the provisions of section 91 CAMA 2020, (s. 67) which forbids the exempting of officers of a company from imposed liability.

Section 91(1) of CAMA provides that:

> any provision, whether contained in the Articles of the company or in any contract with a company or otherwise, for exempting any officer of the company or any person (whether an officer of the company or not) employed by the company as an auditor from, or indemnifying him against any liability which by virtue of any rule of law, would otherwise attach to him in respect of

> any negligence, default or breach, or breach of trust of which he may be guilty in relation to the company, shall be void.

Essentially, the above section voids any purported arrangement by a company, either in its Articles or in a contract, with an officer (which definition in section 868 CAMA 2020, (s. 567) includes a director and secretary) or a person employed as an auditor in the company from any liability for negligence, default or breach of trust, which would have otherwise attached to such a person by law. In general, this seems to agree with the intendment of section 305 (8) of the Act which seeks to ensure the sanctity of the performance of directors' fiduciary duties. However, unlike the provisions of section 305(8), the provisions of section 91(1) are not absolute, as there are provisos to them.

The first proviso is in section 91(2)(a) and provides that:

> notwithstanding the provisions of subsection (1) of this section- '(a) person shall not be deprived of any exemption or right to be indemnified in respect of anything done or omitted to be done by him while any such provision as mentioned in that subsection was in force.'

The above proviso saves the actions by officers and the auditor that were done under a provision in the Articles or contract that validly exempted them from liability for negligence, default or breach of trust before the coming into effect of the CAMA. In essence, the position now is that after the commencement of the CAMA, any indemnifying or like provisions would be void.

The second proviso to section 91(1) permits a company to indemnify any officer or auditor for liability incurred:

- in defending any proceedings (civil or criminal) in which judgment is given in his favour; or
- in which he is acquitted; or
- in connection with any application under section 738 CAMA 2020, (s. 558) which provides for where a person applies to Court that even though he had acted in breach of his duty, he had acted honestly and reasonably and should be relieved of liability) and in which relief is granted to him by the

Court. (Note: there is a mistake in section 91 CAMA 2020, which referred to the section above as section 740, instead of section 738).

OPTIONS OPEN TO THE MEMBERS (SHAREHOLDERS)

We have seen above the difficulty inherent in a company enforcing directors' fiduciary duties against directors who are in breach of such duties. While the company might be in dire straits to enforce such duties, the law grants the members, and sometimes, the creditors and other officers, some powers to enforce such duties by themselves against erring directors. In circumstances where the directors are very powerful and hold controlling shares in the company, the shareholders, creditors, or officers may still resort to the following actions:

- petition the Court under section 571 (f) CAMA 2020, (s. 408 (e) to wind-up the company on the ground that it is just and equitable to do so;
- apply to Court for a relief under section 354 CAMA 2020, (s. 311) on the ground that the affairs of the company are being conducted in an illegal, oppressive, unfairly prejudicial or unfairly discriminatory manner, against a member(s) or in a manner that disregards the interests of the members as a whole. This could be against an act or proposed act, resolution or proposed resolution by the company or a class of its members.

On hearing the petition, the Court may make several orders under section 355 CAMA 2020, (s. 312) as it deems fit, including:

- winding-up the company;
- varying or setting aside a particular transaction;
- regulating the affairs of the company in future;
- ordering the purchase of the shares of any member(s) by the company;
- directing the Commission to investigate the company;
- requiring a person to do or refrain from doing a specific act or thing;
- appointing a receiver or receiver and manager of the company's property, among others;

Apart from members in a company, an application to Court under section 354 above can also be brought by an officer or former director or officer, a creditor to the company and the Commission. This is under certain condition(s):

- if a company is in liquidation and it appears that a present or past director or manager, among others, has misapplied the company's money or property that makes him civilly liable to the company, the Court may, on the application of an official receiver, contributor, liquidator, or creditor compel such a director or manager to repay the company for such money or property with interest or to contribute to the assets of the company as compensation for the breach of trust as the Court deems fit (s. 668 CAMA 2020), (s. 507);

- the members may apply to the Commission to investigate the affairs of the company under section 357 CAMA 2020, (s. 314)) and the Commission may appoint one or more inspectors to investigate the company and report on it;
- the members applying to the Commission for the above investigation must be holding not less than one tenth (it was one quarter under the CAMA 2004) of the class of shares issued (for a company with share capital); or not less than one tenth (it was one quarter under CAMA 2004) of persons on the register of members (for companies without a share capital);
- under section 358 CAMA 2020, (s. 315), the Commission shall appoint investigators to investigate a company if a Court gives an order to that effect. However, the Commission may also appoint such inspectors on its own if it appears to it that fraud in any ramification as itemized therein is being committed in or with the company. This is where the Commission may decide to investigate a company on its own volition, but to protect the interests of the members, where it appears to the Commission that cases of fraud, unfairly prejudicial conducts, formation of company for intended illegality, suppression of material information from members, etc., can be established.

Further Remedies for Breach of Directors' Duties

Apart from the options available to the shareholders of a company against directors for breach of their duties to the company, there are other remedies that the company could activate against an erring director(s):

- ***Liability to Account for Profits:*** we have seen that under section 306 (3) CAMA 2020, (s. 280 (3), where a director has unconscionably benefitted from a transaction that would have ordinarily profited the company or misused the company's goodwill or property (including intellectual property) for personal gains, making secret profits thereby, he is bound to account to the company for profits made from such transactions *(Chan* v. *Zacharia (1984) 154 CLR 178, 199;Industrial Development Consultants Ltd* v. *Cooley (1972) 2 All ER, 162; Gray* v. *New Augarita Porcupine Mines*

Ltd (1952) 3 DLR, 1; Nasir v. *Berini Beirut Riyad Nig. Bank Ltd (1967) 2 ALR Comm., 78 (Orojo, 268)* Also, under section 309 CAMA 2020 (s. 283), directors are trustees of the company's money, properties and their powers and shall account for all money over which they exercise control.

- ***Rescission of Contracts***: Where a transaction between a director and a company involves the breach of the director's duty, the company is entitled to rescind the transaction. For instance, if a director, while not disclosing his interest in a transaction with a company as required under section 303 CAMA 2020, (s. 277), goes ahead and sells his property to the company, the company on discovering the fact is entitled to rescind the transaction and claim a refund of the purchase price. The transaction is, however, not void *(Hely-Hutchinson* v. *Brayhead Ltd (1968) 1 QB, 549).* The general rule is that misrepresentation makes the contract voidable at the instance of the representee *(G.H. Treitel, The Law of Contract, 6th ed, 282).*
- ***Constructive Trust***: Any benefit that accrues to a director in breach of his fiduciary duty to a company is held by him as a 'constructive trustee' for the company. This is a kind of relationship created by equity to deal with unconscionable enrichments. The constructive trust arises from the fact that the director has derived a personal gain or profit and it is immaterial that there was absence of bad faith *(Marques* v. *Edematie (1950) 19 NLR 75; AG Federation* v. *AG Abia (2002) 4 SCNJ, 1; Chan* v. *Zacharia (1984) 154 CLR, 178, Mayson et al, 536 -7).*

In *Ibekwe* v. *Nwosu (2011) LPELR-1391*, the Supreme Court explained the concept of constructive trust as 'a remedy that the Court imposes against one who has obtained property by wrongdoing. It is imposed to prevent unjust enrichment and creates a fiduciary relationship…when property has been acquired in circumstances that the holder of the legal title may not in good conscience retain the beneficial interests, equity converts him to a trustee' *(Ecobank* v. *Inyene & Ors (2021) LPELR-53174).*

For a general view on the difficulty that could be posed in using the term 'constructive trust' to describe all directors' breaches of duties that give rise to unjust enrichment, see Millet LJ, in *Paragon Finance Plc* v. *D.B. Thakerar & Co (1999)1 All ER, 400*).

- ***Termination of Directorship***: The members have an unfettered right to remove directors in a general meeting. If the breach of duty by a director amounts to serious misconduct on his part, his service contract with the company may be terminated summarily as a result, where he is an executive director. In other cases, the director could simply be removed from office by the general meeting and replaced, where necessary. However, as noted above, removing directors from their positions is not always very easy at the general meeting, because, apart from the fact that most of the directors are usually members with huge shareholding themselves, they do have their own allies among the members, making their removal difficult.

- ***Restoration of Company's Property*:** Where the assets of a company have been improperly paid away by directors, they will be under a duty to restore such property to the company *(Bairstow* v. *Queen's Moat Houses Plc (2001) 2 BCLC, 531).* This has been the position of the common law, made clearer in the earlier case of *Exchange Banking Co: Re Flitcroft (1882) 21 Ch. D 519)*, where company directors who caused the company to pay out unlawful dividends were held to be under a duty to restore to the company the value of the assets wrongfully paid away. In requiring directors to restore the company to their original position with respect to the assets in question, the issue of whether the directors were at fault, negligent or not, in the situation, is not usually very material *(Gower & Davies, 310).*
- ***Damages:*** Section 308(1) CAMA 2020, (s. 282 (1) requires every director in performing his duties for the company to exercise that degree of care, diligence and skill, which a reasonably prudent director would exercise in comparable circumstances. Directors who are in breach of applying this standard to their functions are liable to be sued for damages for such breach of duty and for negligence under section 308(2), (s. 282 (2).
- ***Injunctions or Declarations to Restrain Action(s):*** An injunction is an equitable order restraining the person to whom it is directed from doing the things specified in the order or requiring, in exceptional situations, the performance of a specified act. A claim for an injunction is a claim in equity. The order for injunction is available to restrain the defendant from the repetition or the continuance of the wrongful act complained of *(Sokari & Ors* v. *Morrison & Ors (2022) LPELR-57310).*

Under section 343 CAMA 2020, on the application of a member, a Court may, by injunction or declaration restrain a company or its officers:

i. from entering into a transaction which is illegal or *ultra vires*;
ii. purporting to do by ordinary resolution what should, by the Articles, be done by a special resolution;

iii. an act affecting the applicant's individual rights as a member;
iv. committing fraud on the company or the minority, or;
v. where a company's meeting cannot be called on time to be of practical use to redress wrong to the company or minority;
vi. where the directors are likely to profit or have profited from their negligence or breach of duty, or where the interests of justice so demand.

A quick observation is that the language of section 343 above is mostly tailored towards acts that are either being planned, threatened or purely futuristic. This is understandable, because injunctions, by their very nature, are, in most cases, not meant to address completed acts or events, except where the acts are continuing *(Kotoye* v. *CBN (1989) 1 NWLR Pt. 98, 419; Obeya Memorial Hospital* v. *AG Federation (1987) 3 NWLR Pt. 60, 325; Ojukwu* v. *Gov. of Lagos State (1986) 3 NWLR Pt. 26, 39.*

While it is cheering that members in a company have the right and avenue to enforce against certain wrongdoings or to stop potential wrongdoings against the company, it has to be noted that there are certain roadblocks against such actions, as considered below.

The first is the source of funding for such action(s), which has to be undertaken solely by the member(s) suing. When matched against a big company with solid financial base, the member(s),in most cases, will be facing an almost insurmountable task.

The second issue has to do with the member's access to relevant information and materials to maintain a successful action(s). Except in cases where the member(s) has insiders who are supporting him with insider information and relevant materials, especially sensitive ones, it is always difficult having access to such information and materials.

The third issue has to do with the effect of such member-led actions on the company itself. It is on record that several, otherwise thriving companies, have been brought down by incessant and protracted shareholder(s) and director(s) related litigations. This is especially so where the shareholders are also directors of the company. A clear example was the protracted case of *Okeowo* v. *Migliore* above, that emanated from shareholders and management crises in Metal Construction (WA) Ltd. It is worthy of note that after the several protracted litigations in that company had gone to the Supreme Court and back, nothing much has been heard about the company ever since.

LIABILITY OF COMPANY DIRECTORS

A company is a juristic person, and that being the case, must act through its directors and officers in carrying on its business. We have seen that directors are regarded as trustees of the properties and powers of company, and are accountable for such to the company. The effect of this postulation, according to 341 CAMA 2020 (s. 299), is that where an irregularity is made in the course of a company's affairs, or any wrong is done to the company, only the company itself can sue to remedy the wrong and only the company can ratify same. This is the almost immortal rule of *Foss* v. *Harbottle.*

The directors are the directing minds of a company and when it is said that a company has to act or take a particular action, it is usually the directors that determine the direction of such actions. In doing this, however, directors do incur certain measures of liability for their action(s), either at the corporate level as agents of the company or at personal level to themselves.

Corporate Liability of Directors

While working for a company, directors could be liable on two levels for actions they undertake. Directors could attract liability to the company when acting within their powers and for the company's business. In this instance, the directors are treated as agents of the company and any liability for their actions attaches to the company as the principal. In this present respect, as agents of a disclosed principal, that is the company, the rule is that the directors cannot incur any personal liability for actions done in furtherance of their duties for the principal, once acting within the ambits of their powers and authority *(Amadiume* v. *Ibok (2006) 6 NWLR Pt. 975, 158; Golden Coast Const. Co. Ltd* v. *Stateco Nig. Ltd (2014) 8 NWLR Pt. 1408, 198; Iyere* v. *Bendel Feed & Flour Mill Ltd (2008) 18 NWLR Pt. 1119, 300).*

Personal Liabilities of Directors

Apart from the corporate-level liability that could attach to directors for their actions, which would, in actual sense, be for the company to deal with as the principal, there are instances where a company's director could assume personal liability for his actions, although still working for the company:

- the first instance is where a director enters into a contract in such a way as to be personally liable on the contract. An instance is where a director enters into a contract in his personal name without disclosing that he is acting for a company. Depending on the nature of the contract being talked about, this could also be a situation of the director concerned either misusing the company's corporate information and property or simply making secret profits. These issues have been discussed extensively earlier in this chapter;

- the second instance is where a director personally perpetrates a fraud or any other form of tort in the course of his duties and is liable to a third party. Fraud being a deliberate deception which is intended to gain undue advantage vitiates every authority of the director concerned *(Ifegwu* v. *Federal Republic of Nigeria (2001) 13 NWLR Pt. 729, 113).*
- o another instance of personal liability is where a director breaches a duty of care imposed on him in the management of the company, he will be personally liable to the company for any loss or damage suffered by the company. The company may also sue the director to recover any lost property and restrain him from committing any further breach of his duty to the company (*Orojo, 271).*
- The CAMA has also made further specific provisions stipulating instances where directors of a company could be personally liable, both for their actions and for their omissions:
- under section 118 CAMA 2020, (s. 93), where the membership of a public company or company limited by guarantee falls below two (2) and the company carries on business for more than six (6) months after that fact, every director or officer of the company during the time at which it had deficient number of members shall be jointly and severally liable with the company for debts contracted during that period. This section creates a strict liability regime for directors and officers and does not require any knowledge of the membership deficit for liability to attach to any director or officer once the number of members in a company falls below two (2). The CAMA 2020 limits this provision to only public companies and companies limited by guarantee and not every company, as it was under CAMA 2004. This is, of course, because the CAMA 2020 recognizes a one-member private company limited by shares.
- section 271 CAMA 2020, (s. 246) mandatorily requires every registered company, not being a small company, to have at least the two (2) directors at any point in time after being registered. If the number of directors in a company, not being a small company, falls below two (2) at any time, the company is mandated to appoint additional director(s) within one (1) month to make-up the deficit or stop carrying on business until the appointment is made. A director or a member of a company, not being a

small company, who knows that this provision is being flouted and has been so for more than 60 days shall be liable personally for all liabilities and debts incurred by the company carrying on business within that period. The qualification 'not being a small company' is germane because CAMA 2020 recognizes that a small company can have a single director.

Unlike section 118 above which adopts a strict liability approach, section 271 introduces the element of *mens rea* into the liability criteria. The directors or members have to know of the deficient number of directors in order to be found culpable under this head. It also penalizes directors and members of a company and not directors and officers as is the case with section 118 of the Act. Furthermore, section 271 imposes sanctions for breach of duties on directors and members specifically, unlike section 118 which imposes joint and several liability on the company and any culpable director(s) or officer(s) of the company.

The strict liability approach adopted by section 118 above seems to emphasize the importance attached to the issue of a company's membership as the substratum of a company's existence. While a director could elect whether or not to be a member in company, he is not usually compelled to be so, except the Articles provides otherwise. Therefore, the issue of proper legal composition of membership of a company is considered fundamental and disposed of the need to require the knowledge of any deficit therein by directors and officers of the company to attract liability.

Section 316 CAMA 2020, (s. 290) targets directors and officers of a company, who, with intent to defraud the company, obtain loans for specific purpose, or, receives money or other property as advance payment purportedly for particular project(s) in the names of the company, and fail to apply such money or other property for the purpose for which it was received. Every director or officer in a company who is in default in failing to apply the money or property for the stated purpose shall be personally liable to the party from which the money or property was received (*PFS Ltd & Anor* v. *Jefia (1998)3 NWLR Pt. 543, 602, 614).* The liability in the above respect does not in any way affect the liability of the company itself.

It is submitted that where fraud is involved, it would not be enough simply that the directors or officers involved refunded the misused funds to the third parties, the company should also be in a position to apply penal sanctions on the officers concerned. This is because the reputational damage that would have been done to the company by the fraudulent acts of the officers could have disastrous consequences, if not well managed. There should also be an option for the company to call in law enforcement agencies to investigate the extent of the directors' culpability in that respect.

The latter suggestion is, however, easier said than done. Most times company directors do look out for one another and would, mostly likely, offer the offending directors the usual option of a 'soft landing' by allowing them tender their 'voluntary' resignations and exit the board quietly, with full benefits. This is especially the case where there is relative amity among the directors.

Relieving Directors of Liability

Although company directors are liable for any breach of duty imposed by the company's Articles or by law, it is not every time that they are in breach of these duties that they are sent to the 'gallows,' as it were. There are several instances where the directors in breach of their duties could be relieved from such liability or would be consequences of such a breach. These are:

- **ratification by the company:** where a director has committed a breach of his fiduciary duty to the company or has the potential of committing such a breach if he goes ahead with a particular transaction and the company endorses the transaction. In this instance, the company would be taken to have ratified or approved the breach and will not be allowed to claim against the director at a latter day *(Bamford* v. *Bamford (1970) Ch, 212 (*s. 341 CAMA 2020), (s. 299*);*
- for the above ratification to hold, the members must understand the full import of the ratification being sought. The Court may, however, still allow the members to claim remedies from the director(s) concerned if it is convinced that the members did not fully understand what they were approving at the time the approval was given. For instance, where the director did not disclose the whole implication of the approval being sought to the company *(Knight* v. *Frost (1999) 1 BCLC, 364; Baillie* v. *Oriental Telephone and Electric Co. Ltd (1915) 1 Ch., 103);*
- the ratification must be by a resolution of the members of the company. Therefore, a resolution of the board of directors would not be enough, except where the directors are also members and ratified the breach while voting as members, not as directors (s. 341 CAMA 2020), (s. 299) *Furs Ltd* v. *Tomkies (1936) 54 CLR, 583; AG Dominion of Canada* v. *Standard Trust Co. New York (1911) AC, 498. Mayson et al, 561);*

- under section 348 CAMA 2020, (s. 305), evidence that members have approved or may approve an irregularity committed against a company shall not be conclusive to stay or dismiss a derivative action under section 346 of the Act, but such evidence may be taken into consideration by the Court in making its orders. (*Note: There is a mistake in section 348 of the CAMA 2020 which referred to the application as being made under section 6, instead section 346*);
- **relief by the Court**: under section 738 CAMA 2020, (s. 558), in any proceeding for negligence or breach of duty against an officer of a company (including directors) or a person employed as an auditor, the Court may grant him relief if it appears to the Court that the person had acted honestly and reasonably considering the whole circumstances of the case and ought to be excused from liability either partly or fully as the Court deems fit;
- an application can also be made when no proceeding is pending but the officer has a reasonable apprehension that a claim may be made against him for negligence, breach of duty, breach of trust or default. The Court has the same power, as above, if convinced, to grant the relief sought;
- in all cases pertaining to this relief, the reasonability of the applicant's act sought to be excused by the Court would depend on the facts of each particular case.

Directors' Unlimited Liability

The CAMA has provided specific provisions on instances and conditions under which the liability of a director, manager or a managing director in a company could be unlimited:

- the company has to be a limited liability company;
- the unlimited liability of the officers and managers in the company must be provided for in the company's Memorandum (s. 314(1) CAMA 2020), (s. 288 (1).

Responsibilities Imposed Where Liability is Unlimited

The CAMA, under section 314(2) (3), (s. 288 (2)(3)) has imposed certain responsibilities on officers and promoters associated with a company where the liability of the officers is unlimited:

- the director, manager and any member who proposes a person to be elected or appointed as a director or manager in such a company is mandated to add to the proposal that the liability of the person holding that office shall be unlimited;

- before the person so proposed to be a director or manager accepts to act in such a position, he must be given a notice of the unlimited liability attached to the position;
- the following persons or one of them is mandated to give the requisite notice to the proposed director, officer or manager: the promoters of the company, any manager, the directors or the company secretary);
- if any person who is required to add a statement to the proposal or give the notice mandated above fails to do so, he is liable to a penalty, to be specified by the Commission, and also liable for any damage which the person so elected or appointed may sustain from the default.

Although, in principle, the notice of the unlimited liability directorship position could be given to a potential director by a promoter, manager, director or the company secretary, in practice, it is usually the company's secretary task to perform. The exception is where no company secretary had been appointed and the matter came up at the point of incorporating the company, otherwise, every other officer mentioned in the section defers to the company secretary on this aspect of directorship position.

In fulfilling that function, what some company secretaries do is to have a standard format of what is required and which includes all other forms that the potential director(s) is expected to execute and have them as a package for incoming directors. In this way, all the difficulties that could be associated with the company complying with this requirement is virtually eliminated.

Further Instances of Directors' Unlimited Liability

The CAMA has gone ahead to provide further instances where, if authorized by its Articles, the liability of directors of a limited liability company could be made unlimited:

- where a company passes a special resolution to alter its Memorandum so as to render as unlimited the liability of its directors or managers, or any managing director (s. 315 (1) CAMA 2020), (s. 289(1); (this section applies to where the liability of the mentioned officers was initially limited but is sought to be rendered unlimited by the company subsequently);
- when the special resolution as required above is passed by the company altering its Memorandum, the provisions of the said resolution shall apply

and be valid in the Memorandum as if they were originally contained in the company's Memorandum (s. 315 (2), (s. 289 (2).

RESTRICTION ON DIRECTORS' CONTRACT WITH A COMPANY

Company directors are the principal managers of the affairs of the company and owe fiduciary duties to the company. Sometimes, especially when working as agents to the company's shareholders, the directors also owe fiduciary duties to the shareholders. The vantage position which directors occupy in relation to a company makes it imperative that they must endeavour not to place themselves in situations that would create a conflict of interests between their personal interests and the corporate interests of the company. To draw a line between what directors could engage in and otherwise, the rule has over the years evolved, limiting what directors could validly do contractually with the company. In general, a director cannot enter into or be interested in a contract with the company, except he has disclosed his interest(s) (where the Articles permit) and the company has affirmed such a transaction *(Nasir* v. *Berini Beirut-Riyad (Nig) Bank Ltd (1967) 2 ALR Comm., 78).*

Section 303 CAMA 2020, (s. 277) requires that directors disclose their interests in a transaction or proposed transaction with the company to the directors. (The CAMA 2004 required that the disclosure be in a meeting of the board of directors). In this respect, a disclosure to a meeting of a sub-committee of the board is invalid to meet this requirement and it is immaterial that all the board members were already aware of the director's interests in the contract *(Guinness Plc* v. *Ward (1988) BCLR, 104, Orojo, 274-5).* In essence, when the Act requires that a disclosure(s) be made to the board of directors, it should be so, and not to some members or committees of the board.

Since the CAMA 2020 has abandoned the requirement that the notice to the directors of interest in a transaction be at a meeting of the board of directors, it should be sufficient that a written notice is sent to the individual directors indicating the nature of the director's interest in the transaction. In this respect, it is submitted that any acceptable formal means or channel of written communication, including e-mail communication, with affirmed evidence of receipt of same by all the directors of the company, should suffice for the purpose.

In summarizing, the CAMA has imposed several duties on company directors with attendant liabilities for breach of same. From the duty not to make secret profits and to account to the company for same, when made, to acting in the best interests of the company, to disclosing interests in transaction(s) with the company, to not misusing corporate opportunity or property, etc, the directors' duties to the company are fiduciary in nature and come with consequences, when breached.

The consequences for the breach of any of the directors' duties are as numerous as the duties themselves. The beauty of the fiduciary nature of these duties is that the directors cannot be relieved from the consequences of any breach by purporting to exculpate themselves either in the Articles or by contract. The company may, therefore, sue for a rescission of the transaction in question, demand for account of any illicit profits, terminate the appointment of the erring director(s), in a general meeting or otherwise, if the Articles so provide, restrain the directors with an injunction from continuing with a breach, or suing the director(s) for damages for a breach that has occurred. The law can also turn the director(s) in question into a constructive trustee for the company for any mismanaged property arising from his fiduciary duty to the company.

It is clear from the discussions above that directors are expected to be above board in the performance of their duties for the company, failing which the company may activate several remedial actions against such directors. Although the difficulties inherent in enforcing these duties against company directors have been highlighted, this is a situation that should not, as much as possible, be allowed to arise in the first place.

In all cases, however, since the duties owed by directors are to the company itself as a separate legal entity, in consequence, it is only the company that can enforce same duties against the directors, save in limited situations. That is, where the members themselves or creditors are allowed by law to institute individual, derivative or collective actions.

For the company secretary, the pivotal duty here is to advise the directors both individually and as a body in areas where they have to avoid conflict of interests with the company. This is because avoidance of conflict of interests seems to be at the very foundation of all the duties owed to the company. Once there is a conflict of interests between a director(s) and the company, it is then very difficult, and in-fact almost impossible, for the director to establish that he is working in the best interests of the company, as a whole.

The company secretary's ultimate loyalty must be to the company as an entity, even if the balancing might prove tough sometimes, especially when the interests of the directors, who are the alter egos of the company, are also in the mix. The minimum standard would be to exhibit high level of professionalism in all situations, for instance, when a director has put himself in a situation that would incur personal liability. Another difficult situation for the company secretary would be a situation where there is a fractured or divided board of directors, as it was in the situation that birthed *Okeowo* v. *Migliore* (above), which proved virtually intractable. In such a situation or one having a semblance to it, the company secretary should endeavour to be as professional as possible, but each case will have to be discussed on its own peculiar circumstances.

In the final analysis, the overall objective should be to ensure an unbroken symbiosis of efforts in the administration of the company as a legal entity: the directors individually and as a collective, the officers, and the members, in whom the ultimate power that is vested in the company as an entity resides. The company secretary must strive to serve each of these interests with equal zeal and professionalism.

CHECKPOINTS

✓ In general, directors in a company owe their duties primarily to the company as a legal entity, although, in limited circumstances, directors may also owe duties to shareholders and even creditors.

✓ Duties owed by directors to a company are fiduciary in nature, requiring a show of utmost good faith, which also imports the element of their being 'trustees' of the company's assets (property) and powers and the responsibility to account for same when mismanaged.

✓ Avoiding any type of conflict of interests in any transaction wherein the company also has an interest is one of the pivots of being a 'good' director. This is because the situation gets complicated, in proving that a director works in best interests of the company, if there be a conflict of interests with the company in a transaction wherein the director also has an interest.

✓ Directors acting in the overall 'best interests of the company' has been noted as the omnibus and all-encompassing duty that encapsulates all the duties owed by directors to the company. This is because a director who has not been sincere in any way in his relationship with the company, cannot work for the best interests of the company.

✓ The CAMA 2020 has made some material changes, in some areas, to the substance and procedures of what directors are required to do in administering a company. For instance, directors need not give a notice of interests in transactions to a board meeting, but a written notice to all the directors (even if individually, we submit) is sufficient.

- ✓ The company secretary should assist and train the directors (if needed) to get familiar with the non-technical changes made by CAMA 2020. This could be part of the induction process for new directors or as part of re-training of the existing directors.
- ✓ In performing his duties for a company, a director is not expected to fetter his discretion in any way. This implies that they must always exercise independent judgement in acting for the company and not be rubber-stamps to either seen or unseen 'hands.'
- ✓ Directors must strive, at all times, to enforce their powers on behalf of the company for proper purpose and not for any collateral or personal purpose, that is, a purpose for which the powers have not been conferred on them. In most cases, but not all, the exercise of powers for improper purposes by directors, result either in oppressing a party or a group within the company or in taking undue advantage of the company by the director(s) concerned.
- ✓ Directors should be aware of instances where personal liability will attach to them solely or jointly with the company. They should do everything possible to avoid incurring such liabilities.
- ✓ A limited liability company can make the liability of the directors unlimited, but the directors must be informed of this fact at the point of being appointed to the board.
- ✓ Directors should be aware that individual members of the company are allowed by law to sue the directors, either individually or collectively, in certain circumstances, for breaching duties owed to the company.
- ✓ Directors' duties are, in some limited instances, also owed to individual shareholders and even creditors, meaning that these persons can enforce same against the directors.
- ✓ Directors owe the company a duty of care and skill that a reasonably prudent person will exercise in similar situations, that is, not being negligent in executing their duties. To do this, a director must acquire enough knowledge and understanding of the job to be able to perform

efficiently. Also, while delegating his duties, a director must supervise the delegated functions and not abdicate same.

- ✓ There is a duty not to misuse corporate opportunity or information, which dovetails into not making secret profits by the directors. This duty continues for some period of time, usually stated in the Articles and now in the CAMA, after the said director has left the company.

- ✓ The directors may apply to Court, in limited instances, for relief from the consequences of a breach of duty owed to the company. The facts and materials placed before the Court will determine the order that the Court will make based on the directors' application. The Court has a wide discretion in this instance.

- ✓ In the final analysis, the directors' duty not to make secret profits has many ramifications (like working in the best interests of the company), and would seem to cover several of the other duties that directors owe to the company, especially where pecuniary benefits accrue to the directors involved. This is because, when the duty is examined, it does seem that every opportunity abused or every trust breached by a director(s) ultimately results in gaining undue advantage, to the company's detriment, and if stretched, will result in gaining secret profits or advantage by the director(s). That is what the law frowns at and prohibits.

Chapter 8

PROCEEDINGS OF COMPANY DIRECTORS

INTRODUCTION

It has been stated severally in this book that the responsibility for directing and managing a company is vested in the directors, acting as a body, that is, the board of directors (s. 269 CAMA 2020, (s. 244). It is the first organ in the hierarchy of actual management of the affairs of a company. The board is, therefore, expected to act collectively as a body for effectiveness and efficiency in running the affairs of the company, even if not all its decisions are expected to be agreed unanimously. However, although the board has to act collectively, the company's Articles or regulations made thereunder by the directors, may provide diverse ways for the exercise of the directors' managerial powers.

The second major organ in the running of the affairs of a company is the general meeting, consisting of the members of the company, as a whole. Although it is legally possible and permissible, it will be practically inefficient and nebulous, for a company, in general meeting, to exercise all the powers vested in it as contained in the CAMA and its Memorandum and Articles. As powerful as it is, and with enormous authority to act, the unwieldy nature of the general meeting as an effective organ to administer a company, implies that delegating such a duty to the board of directors is inevitable (*Nzegwu-Danjuma, 217*). The details on the division of powers between the board of directors and the general meeting is usually spelt out in Articles *(Automatic Self-Cleaning Filter Syndicate Co. Ltd* v. *Cuninghame (1906) 2 Ch., 34; Thorne, 193).* The manner of this division of powers was clearly spelt out in *John Shaw & Sons (Saaford) Ltd* v. *Shaw (1935 2 KB, 113)*, as follows:

> a company is an entity distinct alike from its shareholders and its directors. Some of its powers may, according to its Articles, be exercised by directors, certain other powers may be reserved for the shareholders in the general meeting. If powers of

> management are vested in the directors, they and they alone can exercise these powers. The only way in which the general body of shareholders can control the exercise of the powers vested by the Articles in the directors is by altering the Articles, or…by refusing to re-elect the directors of whose actions they disapprove. They cannot themselves usurp the powers which by the Articles are vested in the directors any more than the directors can usurp the powers vested by the Articles in the general body of shareholders *(Thorne, 193)*.

The above is a succinct description of the nature of division of powers between the board of directors and the general meeting. Though we have noted the pervasive, but residual power, of the general meeting, in practice, the actual function of managing the affairs of the company is for the directors. In carrying out this function, the board usually acts through delegation to different committees to deal with specific issues concerning the company. This ensures effective management of the company's affairs, with the directors reserving the residual powers of supervising the committees. For effectiveness and efficiency of its primary functions of managing the company's affairs, the board is expected to meet regularly to chart strategic course for the company and ensure the overall success of its business.

MEETING OF THE BOARD OF DIRECTORS

The need to act as a collective in administering the affairs of a company, makes imperative regular board of directors' meetings. The frequency of board meetings depends on several factors, including the size of the company and the nature of its business. The management style of the company's executive management may also be a factor in this respect. It should be noted that the advent of modern technology has changed the mode and modalities of meetings and reduced the need for compulsory physical attendance by directors to board meetings.

Under principle 10 of the NCCG, it is stated that 'meetings are the principal vehicle for conducting the business of the board of directors and successfully fulfilling the strategic objectives of the company.' The Code recommends regular meetings for directors, at least every quarter and in which every director should endeavour to participate. This will enable the directors to plan and execute effective strategic directions for the company.

Summoning and Having Board Meetings

The CAMA has given the board of directors the discretion and latitude to decide how, when and where they hold their meetings, including what they choose to discuss in such meetings. Under section 289 (1) CAMA 2020, (s. 263(1), company directors may meet together for the dispatch of the business of the company, adjourn and otherwise regulate their meetings as they deem fit. The first meeting of directors is mandated to be held not later than six (6) months after the company is incorporated. As noted, the Act gives the directors wide latitude to organize their meetings, as long as the proceedings are within the provisions of the Act and the company's Articles.

In terms the frequency of the meetings of the board, the CAMA, still in line with allowing the directors to have a free hand thereto, provides that a director may summon a meeting of the board, at any time. The company secretary shall summon a board meeting at any time, provided that a director requests him to do so (s. 289 (1), (s. 263 (3).

Careful note should be taken of the language used in this section in distinguishing what either a director or the company secretary has the power to do in summoning a board meeting. While a director 'may' summon a meeting of the board, whenever he wishes to do so, the company secretary 'shall' summon a board meeting when requested by a director to do so. This presupposes that the company secretary has no discretion, when requested by a director, in calling a board meeting, as 'shall' when used in statutes, generally imports obligation and not permissiveness *(Nwankwo* v. *Yar'adua (2010) 12 NWLR Pt. 1209, 518; Katto* v. *CBN (1999) 9 NWLR Pt. 214, 126; Kalamu* v. *Gurin (2003) 16 NWLR Pt. 847, 943; Achineku* v. *Ishagba (1988) 4 NWLR Pt. 89, 41; Oraekwe* v. *Chukwuma (2013) 1 NWLR Pt. 1389, 159; Amokoedo* v. *IGP (1999) 6 NWLR Pt. 607,457).* We note that under section 315(2) CAMA 2020, (s. 298(2), the company secretary has no authority, without the authorization of the board, to exercise any of the powers vested in the directors.

It must be re-iterated, that the assertion above that the company secretary has no discretion in summoning a board meeting once requested to do so by a director, is a correct statement of the law. However, in practice, the situation could be very different, especially where there is a divided or fractured board of directors. As was pointed out previously, in the case of *Okeowo* v. *Migliore (1979) 11 SC, 138*, the board of the company, Metal Construction (WA) Ltd, was fractured into two parts, between Nigerian and Italian directors in the company. The company secretary, who was a Nigerian, aligned with the

Nigerian directors and refused persistent requests by the Italian directors to call a meeting of the directors or the members. It took the intervention of the Courts to order a meeting of the company.

According to the World Bank Group (IFC), from a corporate governance perspective, the company secretary has lots of roles to play before the meeting of a company's board, that is, apart from issuing the notice summoning the meeting, as directed by the chairman. The company secretary should maintain an annual calendar of the meetings of the board, communicate the time, date and venue of the meetings to the directors, ensure that the board is properly constituted, including proper appointment of those attending, getting ready any resolution to be passed at the board meetings, getting board papers ready well before time and distributing same to the directors well ahead of the meeting, organizing the allowances of the directors who are entitled to same, among many others.

For decision making at board meetings, under the CAMA 2004, the position was that any question(s) arising at the meeting of a company's board of directors shall be decided by a majority of the votes. Where there is a tie (equality of votes), the chairman of the meeting shall have a second or casting vote (s.263 (2). However, CAMA 2020 has subjected this provision to the company's Articles. In essence, the provision that where there is a tie in votes during a meeting of directors, that the chairman shall cast a second and deciding vote can only be effective if the company's Articles has no provision to the contrary. This presupposes that a company's Articles could provide a totally different course to be taken where there is a tie in votes during a company's board meeting. For example, instead of asking the chairman to cast a second and deciding vote, the Articles may provide that the question be adjourned to the next meeting to be voted on, or that the directors must have voted on the question for a second or third time before the chairman can cast a second or deciding vote, etc.

The above provision on this point in CAMA 2020 is a way to further handover the controls of board of directors' meetings to the company themselves, instead of attempting to centralize same in the Act. However, this will not affect the contrary argument that such a provision is intended to whittle down the powers of the chairmen of the meetings in such situations. This is especially so, being that, as will be seen below, the modalities to change the chairman during a board meeting is extremely flexible.

Chairman of Board Meetings

More often than not, by convention, the chairman of a company is usually the chairman of its board of directors and presides at board meetings. In the absence of the chairman his deputy (where one has been appointed) will chair the meeting or failing that, the board may elect one of its members to preside over the day's deliberations.

Under section 289 (4) CAMA 2020, (s. 263(4), directors may elect a chairman for their meetings and determine the period for which he is to hold office. However, if no chairman has been elected by the company's board or if at any board meeting the chairman is not present within five minutes after the time appointed for the meeting, the directors present may choose one of their members to chair the meeting.

The above provision is more of a provision in principle than it is in practice. This is because, in practice, the synergy between the directors usually implies that they do defer to the chairman during any meeting as to the direction of the meeting and how the meeting proceeds to business. In essence, when the board chairman is indisposed for a meeting, although the CAMA gives the directors the discretionary powers to choose an alternate chair if the chairman is not available five minutes after the meeting is to commence, this is hardly done in practice. Where it has to be done at all, it is usually on the direction of the chairman, who will also nominate the person to preside over the meeting in his absence.

At the board level, in terms of decision-execution, the directors are empowered to delegate any of their powers to a managing director or to board committees, as they deem fit. The managing director and the committees are, in exercising the powers delegated to them by the board of directors, expected to conform to any regulations made by the directors. The procedures for committee meetings mimic those of the board of directors, *mutatis mutandis,* excluding items like notice of meeting and quorum. For quorum for committees' meetings, it is usually fixed by the board, otherwise the committee will meet and act by majority (s. 289 (5) (6) CAMA 2020), (s. 263(5) (6); (s. 290 (2) CAMA 2020), (s. 264 (2). The life, function and structure of board committees are determined by the directors as they deem fit.

In terms of the relevance of board committees, principle 11 of the NCCG states that 'to ensure efficiency and effectiveness, the board delegates some of its functions, duties and responsibilities to well-structured committees, without abdicating its responsibilities.' The NCCG further recommends that certain board committees are indispensable and should almost be compulsory for the board of directors to set up. These are the nomination and governance committee, risk management committee, audit committee and the remuneration committee. This does not mean that this recommendation is cast in stone, as a company's board may add any other committee(s), as deemed fit, and many boards have added the compliance and disciplinary committees. Also, companies that are financial institutions are known to usually have board credit committee, as one of the standing committees.

A point that has been made early on, but which needs re-iteration here, is the fact that any delegation of powers by the directors must not equate to the abdication of their powers, duties and responsibilities to the company. The directors, even with any delegation of functions to the board committees, must retain and effectively exercise the residual power of supervision. That is a non-negotiable decimal and a breach of that duty brings the consequential liabilities to the directors.

The company secretary, except where he is also a director in the company, is not a part of the board, but he is usually the secretary to the board. He should not, under any guise, misinterpret his closeness to the directors and the board to overreach himself in his relationship and interaction with the directors. For instance, the company secretary should not proffer any opinion on an issue being discussed at a board meeting, without being asked to do so by the chairman, or any of the directors. However, as a matter of convention and convenience, he usually acts as the secretary not only to the board of directors but also to the board committees. His involvement with the meetings of the board of directors starts principally with the planning and execution stages of the meetings, in close liaison with the chairman of the board.

Notice of Board of Directors' Meetings

As a matter of law, every director is entitled to receive a notice of meeting of board of directors meeting of that company, unless, for any reason, he is otherwise disqualified under the CAMA from continuing in office as a director (s. 292(1) CAMA 2020), (s. 266(1). The critical importance of serving notice of meeting on all directors to validate the deliberations of the board of directors was re-iterated in *Baffa* v. *Odili (2001) 15 NWLR (Pt. 737) 709, 740),* where it was held that the non-service of the notice of board meeting on some directors (who were actually alternate directors) invalidated the meeting and its outcome.

Now, the question is, what does the expression, 'disqualified for any reason under the Act from continuing with office of director,' imply? To answer this, we have to look at the disqualification provisions of the CAMA as it pertains to directors. Under section 283 CAMA 2020, (s. 257), the following persons are disqualified from being directors:

- an infant (under 18 years);
- a lunatic or person of unsound mind;
- a person suspended or removed under section 288 of the Act (that is a director removed from office by ordinary resolution in a general meeting (for which a special notice is given) before the expiration of his tenure; where such removal was on the ground of fraud, dishonesty or unethical conduct (as amended by section 15 of the schedule to the *Business Facilitation (Miscellaneous Provisions) Act 2022).*
- a person disqualified under sections 279 (being an insolvent person); 280 (person already convicted of fraud in connection with the promotion, formation, or management of a company) and 284 (person failing share qualification requirement, bankrupt person) of the Act;
- a corporation other than its representative appointed to the board for a given term.

Any person caught up with any of the disqualification criteria stated above cannot be a director. However, that is in relation to a person being appointed company director *ab initio.* Having been appointed a director, it presupposes that the person so appointed is entitled to receive notice of every board meeting, as stated above, except otherwise disqualified. So, when is a director, otherwise disqualified? The CAMA does not give a clear answer to this. It was previously thought, in-fact, the Court appeal also held in *Longe* v. *FBN Plc (2006) 3 NWLR Pt. 967, 228*, that a director on suspension is not entitled to receive a notice of board meeting and it fits into this provision (*Orojo* also thought as much at 259fn, although, it would appear that the learned Jurist based his opinion on the Court of Appeal's judgment in the matter, before the Supreme Court's decision was handed down). On appeal to the Supreme Court, that decision of the Court of Appeal was set aside.

The Supreme Court, relying on the decision in *University of Calabar* v. *Esiogu (1997) 4 NWLR Pt. 502, 719, 723*, outlined the nature of the consequences of suspension of an employee, in this case, a director:

> 'suspension' means a temporary privation or deprivation, cessation or stoppage of or from, the privileges and rights of a person. The word carries or conveys a temporary or transient disciplinary procedure which keeps away the victim or person disciplined from his regular occupation or calling either for a fixed or terminal period or indefinitely. The disciplinary procedure gives the initiator of the discipline a period to make up his mind as to what should be done to the person facing the discipline. Although in most cases, suspension, results in a disciplinary action, it is not invariably so. There are instances when the authority decides not to continue with the matter. This could be because the investigations did not result in any disciplinary conduct.

Based on the above reasoning, the Court concluded that Mr. Longe, the suspended director (managing director, actually), was entitled to a notice of the board meeting where his suspension was discussed, failing which, the notice, the meeting and its outcomes, were all invalidated. In essence, a director, even one on suspension, is entitled to the notice of a board meeting, though he might not participate in the board discussions when the issue pertaining to himself is tabled before the board. It is also true that a director will be notified of a meeting even if he is not qualified to vote on the issue to be discussed at the meeting.

From the above discussions, it would be safe to conclude that, except where a company's Articles provide otherwise, as long as a person has not retired, resigned, or been removed as a director, he is entitled to a notice of any meeting of the board of directors. It is difficult to find other disqualifying provisions in the CAMA. Note should, however, be taken of the provisions of section 292(4) CAMA 2020, (s. 266(4), which permits a company not to give a notice of directors' meeting to a director who is outside Nigeria, except where he has advised a Nigerian address for such a notice. The provision is, however, subject to a company's Articles, which may insist that every director should receive a notice of board meeting even while abroad.

Even at that, the provision of section 292(4) above is not a disqualifying provision that disqualifies a director from continuing 'with the office of director', but only relates to giving an existing director a notice of meeting.

A deeper interrogation of the provision on service of notice of meeting on a director who is not in Nigeria is no longer relevant in this age of technology. Although it is understandable that this is a carryover from the CAMA 2004 which was promulgated in 1990, a time when internet and digital technology was at its infancy in Nigeria. That is where the understanding should end. In the present-day Nigeria, where section 240 CAMA 2020 provides that private companies may hold their general meetings electronically, it becomes clear that putting any restriction, no matter how feeble, on the way of a director who is abroad, from receiving notice of meeting is ill-advised. The provision should be expunged from the CAMA.

Unless the company's Articles provide to the contrary, every director that is entitled to receive notice of meeting shall receive a fourteen (14) days' notice in writing summoning a meeting of the board. Failure to give a notice of meeting to a director as stipulated under this section of the CAMA shall invalidate the meeting (s. 292 (2)(3) CAMA 2020, (s. 266 (2)(3). As noted above in *Baffa* v. *Odili and Longe* v. *FBN Plc*, it is immaterial whether the director in question is an alternate director or whether he is suspended from office at the material time of the meeting. The point has also been made earlier that, in this time and age, a written notice would be sufficiently met if same be sent by e-mail and other electronic means where receipt of same by the directors could be confirmed. Providing for this in the company's Articles will make its adoption much easier.

The CAMA's stipulation on length of notice for directors' meeting is subject to any contrary provision in a company Articles. By implication, a company may, by its Articles, provide for a time, longer or shorter than the 14 days provided by the CAMA, as the length of notice for its board meetings. Where, however, a company's Articles have not made contrary provisions regarding the notice period for directors' meetings, any notice that is shorter than the fourteen (14) days stipulated under the CAMA will render the meeting and its outcomes void *(Baffa* v. *Odili (2001) 15 NWLR Pt. 737, 741; Salami* v. *United Foam Products Nig. Ltd (1996) FHCLR 159, 186).*

Agenda for Meeting of Board of Directors

In general, the agenda for a board of directors' meeting, as in every other meeting, is used as a guide to intimate the directors of the issues that would be discussed during the forthcoming meeting. It is usually the company secretary that prepares the agenda for the board meeting, liaising with the chairman. The content of the agenda is often a reflection of what has been agreed among the directors, that is, in normal times. The board chairman usually has the discretion to add whatever extra items he feels should be discussed, before passing them to the company secretary for preparation and circulation to the members of the board.

The modalities for circulating the agenda to the directors vary according to the practice adopted by a particular company. However, it is advisable that supporting documents are delivered with the agenda and referenced by page on the items to maintain conciseness in the documentation. In practice, the commonly adopted pattern is for items to be placed on the agenda in the order that they would be discussed at the meeting, although the meeting (through the chairman) could decide to alter any order of discussing the items on the agenda, as circumstances dictate during the meeting.

Notwithstanding the fact that agendas will vary according to the type of meeting and what is to be discussed therein, typically, an agenda will include:

- apologies for absence;
- minutes of the last meeting, usually circulated with the agenda (with adoption, etc);
- matters arising from the last minutes;
- business of the present meeting-reports, presentations, feedback on same, etc;
- substantive transactions that need to be conducted by the meeting;
- any other business;

When the meeting is the first for a board of directors of a company that has been newly incorporated, there are certain items that are expected to be on the agenda, which ordinarily should not be, if the meeting was for an existing and operational company. The list is not exhaustive, but includes:

- receipt of the certificate of incorporation, formally;
- appointment of first directors- to be noted in the minutes;
- appointment of the chairman of the board;
- appointment of the company secretary (if not already appointed)
- appointment of the company's bankers (this could wait for another meeting, if there is no urgency);
- appointment of external Solicitors (this could wait till another meeting, if there is no urgency);
- appointment of auditors (this could wait until a later date since it's a new company);
- allotment or transfer of shares;

- company's common seal (where company agrees to have one, as CAMA 2020 has now made the common seal optional);
- change of directors and registered office (for former shelf company, if used);
- formal general instructions to the company secretary, going forward (*ICSA, 297).*

The above is simply a sketch of what a standard agenda for a board meeting, and in fact, most meetings, should look like. There is, however, no standard precedent or any hard and fast rule as to what pattern a company must adopt in this respect, as convenience and functionality of the agenda are the key determinants.

Quorum for Directors' Meetings

Simply put, 'quorum' means the minimum number of members who must be present for a body to transact business or take a vote *(Agbeotu* v. *Brisibe (2005) 10 NWLR Pt. 932, 1; Saraki* v. *FRN (2016) LPELR-40013; Wali & Ors* v. *Ogiri & Ors (2021) LPELR-56272).* The quorum for a meeting of the board of directors, therefore, is the number of directors which must be present to make the proceedings of the board valid, in the eye of the law *(Charlesworth & Cain, 348).* It means the minimum number of directors legally considered as sufficient to transact the business of the meeting. In general, the quorum for directors' meetings is usually spelt out in the company's Articles, but where it is not so spelt out, the CAMA provides a default provision.

Section 290(1) CAMA 2020, (s. 264(1), provides that unless the Articles provide otherwise, the quorum necessary for the transaction of business of a company's board of directors shall be two (2) directors, where the directors are not more than six (6) in number. However, where the company has more than six (6) directors, then the quorum shall be one third of the number of directors. Again, where the number of directors is not in a multiple of three (3), then the quorum shall be one third to the nearest number:

Illustration

A company that has a board of directors of twelve (12) will require at least four (4) directors to validly hold a board meeting, which is one-third of the 12 directors. If the number of directors increases to thirteen (13) the quorum will still be four (4) directors. However, if the number of directors rises to fourteen (14), then the quorum for meetings moves to five (5) directors, because fourteen (14) is closer to the next multiple of 3 which is fifteen (15) and one third of fifteen (15) directors, which is 5, will form a quorum for their meeting.

The quorum for a board meeting must be comprised of directors who are entitled to vote on a particular matter tabled before the meeting, and a quorum must be present for each item of business being discussed by the board. In determining whether a quorum is present to discuss and vote on a particular matter, any director(s) who is not competent to vote on the matter being discussed, must not be counted for purposes of the ascertaining the quorum*(Re Greymouth Point Elizabeth Railway and Coal Co. Ltd (1904) 1 Ch., 32).* This notwithstanding, directors who are unable to vote on issues in a particular board meeting can still attend such a meeting, implying that they must have been served a notice of the meeting, whether they are entitled to vote or not *(Grimwade* v. *B.P.S. Syndicate Ltd (1915) 31 TLR, 531*; *Charlesworth & Cain, 349).*

Conventionally, and for obvious reasons, if a director has an interest in a matter that is being discussed by the board, he is not usually permitted by the Articles to vote on the issue and may not be counted for the purposes of the quorum for that item of business. The duty of the director in this respect, is to disclose his interests and nature thereby in the transaction to the directors before the meeting. The immutable rule of natural justice that one should not be a judge in his own cause, will also preclude such a director from voting on a transaction in which he has an interest *(ICSA, 299; Bamgboye* v. *Unilorin & Anor (1999) LPELR-737; Akinfe* v. *State (1988) 3 NWLR Pt. 85, 729).* However, the fact that the director will not be allowed to vote on the matter does not preclude his right to receive the notice of the meeting where the issue will be discussed.

It is important to note that a quorum can only be formed from a board of directors that is properly constituted. Put differently, the proper constitution of the board is a condition precedent before any issue of whether there is a quorum or not for a meeting could even arise. For instance, if a company, not being a small company, has only one director, the issue of quorum for any board meeting would be academic, until the number of the directors on the board is raised to the legally permissible minimum of two directors (depending on the number of directors) to properly constitute the minimum number of directors for the company legally *(Re British Empire Match Co. Ltd (1888) Ch.D., 4, Mayson et al., 483).*

Finally, in all the issues discussed above about directors' meeting and particularly the issue of quorum, it needs to be pointed out that under section 271 CAMA 2020, a small company can actually have a single director (the CAMA 2004 has no such provision). This will imply that the single director will also constitute the company's 'board,' which fact and implications of this development, company law jurisprudence in Nigeria will have to get used to, in the years ahead.

Quorum Failure for Directors' Meeting

There are occasions when, due to a deadlock (as in *Okeowo* v. *Migliore*) or for any other reason(s), a company's board of directors is unable, due to lack a quorum, to meet and take decisions to run the business of the company. In such an instance, except the Articles provide otherwise, any purported exercise of the power of the board by a deficient number of the directors is void *(Martins* v. *Ogungbadero (1967) NCLR, 393; Pricklik* v. *Marsh & Ors (1961) WNLR 59, Orojo, 260).*

The CAMA has made a provision to deal with a situation where company directors could not form a quorum to carry on the business of the board. Section 291 CAMA 2020, (s. 265) provides that where the board is unable to act because a quorum cannot be formed, the general meeting may act in place of the board. Where it is a board committee that could not act because a quorum could not be formed, then, the board of directors may take over and act in place of the committee.

The above is a simple provision aimed at solving the problem of deadlocked boards, which normally arises in corporate circles. However, it is submitted that the provision did not go far enough in anticipating other possible situations in the deadlocking of company boards. For instance, in *Okeowo* v. *Migliore*, all the directors were also the shareholders, and effectively, the board of directors was also the general meeting. This would mean that the provision of section 291 of the Act authorizing the general meeting to act in place of the board when there is a deadlock, will be ineffective and of no consequence to the situation. We suggest an expansion on section 291 of the Act to make an express provision for *ex-parte* application to the Court for direction by any of the directors or shareholders where the board of directors or the general meeting are unable to act.

In all, it is the duty of the company secretary, and critically so, to continually assess the quorum of the meeting from the beginning and as often as is necessary during the duration of the meeting, and to advise the chairman accordingly. If for any reason a board meeting becomes inquorate (the quorum fails during the meeting), the company secretary should advise the chairman to adjourn the meeting immediately until the correct number of directors that would form a quorum is achieved (*ICSA, 299.)* In some jurisdictions, like England, the board meeting is allowed to continue after losing quorum, but only for the purpose of increasing the number of directors to make the quorum valid or to call a general meeting to act. No other issue could be discussed by the meeting at that stage *(Charlesworth & Cain, 349).*In some other jurisdictions, like Malawi, for instance, the law only requires that the meeting has the necessary quorum at the start of the meeting and not subsequently*(World Bank Group, (IFC), 28).* Whatever be the position with respect to quorum, the company secretary should know the applicable laws and rules in the area of jurisdiction and guide the meeting in that direction accordingly.

Directors' Written Resolutions

Company directors are expected to meet regularly and collectively, as a board, to direct the affairs of the company. However, with the advance in technology and modern business practices, the 'meeting of the board' does not have to always involve all the directors physically meeting at a venue to interact and discuss the business of the company. Online meetings, now enabled by various technologies, have made physical meetings less imperative than they previously were. In appreciating the changing trends, under section 289 (8) CAMA 2020, (s. 263 (8), a resolution in writing signed by all the directors for the time being entitled to receive notice of a meeting of directors, shall be as valid and effectual as if it had been passed at a meeting of the directors duly convened and held. This practice is formally called 'resolution in writing', 'circular,' or 'written resolution.' All the directors on a company's board and not a section of them must sign the resolution to make it valid and binding *(Attorney General Enugu State* v. *AVOP Plc (1995) 6 NWLR Pt. 399, 117; Municipal Mutual Insurance Ltd* v. *Harrop (1998) 2 BCLC, 540).*This type of resolution, it is submitted, will gain higher currency in the years to come, being that section 101 CAMA 2020 has now recognized electronic signature as a valid option to execute any document(s) by officers of a company.

A careful reading of provision of section 289(8) above will reveal that it says that those to sign a written resolution are 'all the directors for the time being entitled to receive notice of a meeting of directors.' It has been submitted early on that every director in a company, even those on suspension and those who are not entitled to vote on the issues to be discussed during the board meeting, is entitled to the notice of meeting. In essence, all the directors, who are validly so on the date of the meeting, including alternate directors, will have to sign the resolution to make it valid.

The practice of adopting written resolution is applicable to the board of directors of both private and public companies, as the CAMA makes no distinction on company genre in this respect.

MINUTES OF BOARD MEETINGS

Company directors usually meet and pass resolutions to convey the decisions of their deliberations, just as members do during general meetings. The CAMA does not differentiate between the meetings of directors and the general meetings in its provision relating to minutes of meetings. In essence, the CAMA provisions in this respect relate to meetings of directors, managers and the general meeting. By section 266 (1) CAMA 2020, (s. 241 (1), every company, with the exception of a company having a single member, is mandated to keep minutes of all proceedings at meetings.

Where any such minutes is purported to be signed by the chairman of the meeting at which the proceedings were held, or by the chairman of the next succeeding meeting, such shall be *prima facie* evidence of the proceedings of the meeting. The minutes of any meeting, whether of the directors, managers or the general meeting, may be kept in a book form or in a loose-leaf form in books kept for that particular purpose, as minutes book (*I.A.I. Ltd* v. *Chika Brothers Ltd (1990) 21 NSCC, Pt. 1, 66).*

Where the minutes of meeting of the directors, managers of the general meeting have been duly made in accordance with the provisions of the Act, then until the contrary is proved, the meeting is deemed to have been duly held and convened and all appointment of directors, managers or liquidators shall be deemed valid. There would also be the presumption that all the decisions taken at the meeting were validly done (s. 266 (2)(3) CAMA 2020), (s. 241(2)(3).

In the case of a company that has only one member, as allowed by the CAMA 2020, where that single member takes any decision that:

i. may be taken by the company in general meetings, and
ii. has effect as if agreed by the company in general meeting, he shall provide the board with detail of that decision (s. 266 (4).

The Act imposes a continuing daily penalty to be specified by the Commission on a single shareholder who runs a company and fails to comply with the notification to the directors of the company.

Notwithstanding the fact that minutes of a meeting signed by the chairman of that meeting is considered *prima facie* evidence of the proceedings, it is not usually considered to be conclusive evidence of the proceedings. Where there are valid grounds to do so, the minutes of meeting could be challenged by other evidence to the contrary *(I.A.I Ltd* v. *Chika Brothers Ltd (1990) 21 NSCC, Pt. 1, 66).* It is noteworthy that an unrecorded resolution is not without value. This is because once such a resolution was duly passed at the meeting in question, then, its authenticity may be proved by other evidence *(Re Fireproof Doors Ltd (1916) 7 Ch, 1421*). Specifically, a decision reached at a meeting of a company's board of directors is not invalidated by the fact that it is not recorded in a minutes book *(Re: North Hallenbeagle Mining Co. Knight's Case (1867) LR 2 Ch App, 321, Mayson et al., 483.)* However, where the directors omit to keep minutes of their deliberations in board meetings, then they cannot be heard to complain of any inference(s) drawn from the records, even if it differs from what the directors allege to be correct *(Nasir* v. *Berini-Beirut Riyad (Nig) Bank Ltd (1967) 2 ALR Comm., 78, Orojo 260 -1).*

Finally, minutes constitute credible evidence of the proceedings of the meetings of directors, even if it could be impeached by more credible evidence. It is therefore imperative that the company secretary should take calculated steps to ensure the safety and integrity of the minutes and that the minutes of meetings are not tampered with or falsified in any way. One of the mechanisms for doing this is to glue the minutes into a book, constituting, as it were, the minutes book for board or other meetings. It is also advisable that minutes should be sequentially numbered, either by including the minutes number and the date of the meetings or by including the minutes number and the year of the meetings, or combining both *(World Bank Group (IFC), 42).*

Roles of the Company Secretary

The roles of the company secretary (although some have been highlighted above) before, during and after board meetings are multifarious and vary in some good details from small to large companies. The company secretary is responsible for advising the board, through the chairman, on all governance and compliance matters and for ensuing compliance with board and regulatory procedures. He is also responsible for ensuring good information flows between the board and its committees and between non-executive directors and senior management *(Hannigan, 116).* The ICSA has listed some of the key, but non-exhaustive, roles that the company secretary plays before, during and after board meetings, and we agree with the listing:

Before Board Meetings

- prepare the notice of meeting when instructed by the board of directors, usually through the chairman. The notice should normally include the date, time, venue, proposed resolutions and agenda for the meeting;
- despatch the notice of meeting to directors and all those who are entitled to attend well within the time limited for those concerned to receive it. Where e-mail delivery and service of notices have been agreed to in the company, this will make same very seamless;
- draw up and issue the agenda for the meeting in concert with the chairman of the board of directors;
- circulate the agenda, resolutions, reports and other documents that would need to be studied by the directors and others attending the meeting;
- check that the boardroom or the venue of the meeting is ready (sitting arrangement, name plates, audio visuals, stationery, etc.);
- check that there will be a quorum for the meeting and if in doubt (maybe a director is not attending at the last minute) inform the board chairman;
- arm himself with a copy of the company's Memorandum and Articles, the directors' attendance book (where used), the minutes book, a copy of the CAMA (and other relevant laws depending on the issues before the board) and other necessary documents.

At Board Meetings

- record attendance and report apologies;
- if attendance register is used, get directors to sign;
- ensure that there is quorum for the meeting and that the quorum is maintained throughout the duration of the meeting;
- take the minutes and other relevant notes during the meeting;
- advise the chairman and the meeting on relevant sundry issues (procedure, regulations, laws, etc.);
- contribute informed views, clarifications and opinions to the meeting when requested to do so either by the chairman or any of the directors.

After Board Meetings

- notify the relevant personnel and departments in the company of the decisions of the board affecting them (where applicable);
- file the necessary statutory returns and resolutions at the Commission (if need be);
- make reminder notes on any issues or items that had been deferred by the meeting to avoid it 'slipping through the cracks' and being forgotten altogether, sometimes with disastrous consequences;
- prepare the minutes in draft and circulate, first to the chairman, and then to all the board members for their comment(s);
- produce the final copy of the minutes for approval and the signature of the chairman at the next board meeting;
- once approved, enter the minutes in the minutes book that is kept for directors' meetings (*ICSA, 304-5.*)

The roles of the company secretary in corporate governance in general and in relation to a company's board of directors' meetings in particular, are crucial and indispensable. Even though there are times when a director in a company could also be the company secretary and perform dual functions, the distinctive nature of the roles of the company secretary is why it is now considered an organ of company, especially in public companies. This must why the CAMA 2020 has created an independent register for company secretaries in sections 336, 337 and 338, separating it from being merged with the register of directors. The CAMA has also prohibited a person from doing a thing simultaneously as a director and secretary where the Act requires such a thing to be done by such persons. In essence, one person who is a director and company secretary in a company cannot himself sign a document twice in such dual capacities (s. 331 CAMA 2020), (s. 294). He can either sign as a director or a secretary and another person co-signs in the other capacity.

In closing the discussions here, it is worth re-iterating that the company secretary is not a member of the board of directors (except where he is also a director in the company), but plays almost indispensable roles at the board level, especially where large companies are involved.

Not being a member of the board, it is important that the company secretary appreciates the limits of his participatory authority at board meetings, guarding against any form of interloping during such meetings. For example, good boardroom principles and practice dictate that the company secretary should not join a board debate or offer opinion on any issue being discussed by the directors except where his opinion is sought by any member of the board. Another good practice is that the company secretary should, as much as possible, avoid showing any bias for or against any member of the board, instead, maintaining a stoic posture of neutrality and professionalism. This is especially very important when, for any reason(s), the board of directors is fractured.

During board meetings, the roles of the company secretary are usually and should mainly be procedural and advisory in nature. This should involve, in the main, guiding the meeting to be conducted with the ambits of the relevant laws and rules, keeping the directors abreast with the requirements of relevant laws and regulations, among many others. However, it starts with issuing and service of the notice of meeting on directors, after being advised by the chairman as to the details and timing for the meeting.

On the meeting proper, the company secretary would have to supervise the pre-meeting preparations (securing the venue, arranging tags and stationery, etc.) as noted above. Once the meeting starts, the pivot turns to the chairman, whose responsibility it is to direct and superintend the meeting. The company secretary's roles changes to purely advisory, support and guidance of the board as the meeting progresses, especially on issue of law and compliance. One of the most important issues at this stage is that of quorum, which has to be consistently maintained at three (3) levels: firstly, there has to be a requisite number of directors to form a quorum of directors before the start of the meeting. This is the 'foundational quorum,' without which the meeting would not commence at all. Secondly, there has to be a quorum to sustain the meeting to the end, that is, the 'continuum quorum.' Thirdly, where it is necessary, there has to be a quorum to discuss and vote on particular issue(s) during the meeting, that is, the 'subject quorum.' The effects of the failure of any of these quorums on a meeting are diverse.

When the 'foundational' quorum fails, the meeting would have to be postponed and not started at all. This is because, without 'foundational quorum' the condition precedent to even start the meeting would not have been met. On the other hand, when a 'continuum' quorum fails, the chairman would have to suspend the meeting and make efforts to re-quorate the meeting, failing which, the meeting has to be adjourned to another date. Where a 'subject quorum' fails, the issue would have to be sidestepped and no vote taken thereon until a later date, unless the quorum for it is regained before the meeting ends. If so, the chairman has to decide whether to call up the issue again for concluding discussions and voting or leave it to the next meeting. All these situations must be within the contemplation of the company secretary during a board meeting.

The overall outcomes and decisions of board meetings, like most other company meetings, are captured in resolutions and documented in minutes. Resolutions from board meetings can be 'circular,' conveying decisions taken by the directors without any physical meeting having been convened and held. In capturing the resolutions and writing the minutes, the roles of the company secretary is key. Extensive discussions on resolutions, writing of minutes and incidental issues thereby, are discussed later in the chapter on general meeting.

THE CHECKPOINTS

✓ Directors in a company have the primary duties and responsibility of managing and directing a company, although the general meeting wields residual but pervasive powers over everyone associated with company.

✓ Due to its nature and size, the general meeting is unable to engage in day-to-day management of a company's affairs and often delegates same to the board of directors.

✓ Directors, as a collective, are the engine that drives a company and are to, as a board, meet as frequently as they deem fit, to efficiently plan and further the strategic business objectives of the company. The NCCG suggests that directors meet as a board at least once every quarter.

✓ The company secretary must summon a meeting of the board, when requested to do so by a director. He has no discretion in the matter. When there is a fractured board and the company secretary is conflicted as to whose instructions to follow, he must still be as professional as possible in dealing with the members of the board.

✓ The chairman of the board of directors is usually the chair at board meetings, but the Articles can provide other detailed modalities for adoption by the board. In the absence of the chairman, his deputy will preside (where there is one), otherwise, the board will elect one of the members to preside.

✓ Quorum for directors' meetings, like in most meetings, is critical and must be maintained at all times and dimensions. Otherwise, decisions will be difficult to reach or void, if reached at all. In some instances, without a quorum, like the 'foundational quorum', the meeting cannot even commence at all.

- ✓ Quorum can only be formed from a properly constituted board, and where the board of directors are deadlocked and cannot form a quorum, it gets to a point where the general meeting will intervene to take over the functions of the board. If it is a board committee that is unable to form a quorum for its meetings, the board of directors will intervene to take over its function.
- ✓ The directors may delegate some of their duties to board committees but such delegation should not amount to abdicating the directors' responsibilities. In consequence, the directors must effectively supervise the delegated duties.
- ✓ The company secretary is not usually a member of the board of directors but acts as board secretary and board committee secretary.
- ✓ Except where the Articles provide to the contrary, the length of notice for board meetings must be at least 14 days for the meeting to be valid.
- ✓ Every director, whether an alternate director or one on suspension, is entitled to a notice of meeting, otherwise, the meeting and its outcomes are void. The only exception is where the director(s) is in any way disqualified from continuing as a director under any of the provisions in the CAMA. In that case, he is even no longer a director, strictly speaking.
- ✓ Board resolutions can be written resolutions, without a physical meeting of the board being convened and held. To be effective, however, all the directors that are entitled to receive the notice of the meeting at the time of the meeting must sign the written resolutions. This applies to both private and public companies.
- ✓ Every company, with the exception of single-member companies, is mandated to keep the minutes of its meetings and proceedings. Any such minutes purported to be signed by the chairman of the meeting or the next meeting is *prima facie* evidence of the proceedings of the meeting.
- ✓ The minutes of meetings are very important records and the company secretary must endeavour to protect the safety and integrity of the minutes from any mutilation or manipulation. This can be done, among other means, by numbering the minutes with dates and years of the meetings, among others.

Chapter 9

THE MANAGING DIRECTOR AND PAYMENTS TO DIRECTORS

INTRODUCTION

The managing director is the *primus inter pares* (first among equals) of the board of directors. He is the pivot that manages and directs a company's affairs in conjunction with the other members of the board. In some instances, especially in small private companies, the position of the managing director and chairman of the board are merged in one person. However, this practice is discouraged for purposes of ensuring sound corporate governance and good board oversight on management. The NCCG specifically frowns at this arrangement and advises against it, being an over-concentration of powers in one individual.

The managing director is usually appointed by the board of directors from among themselves, and usually from one of the company's existing executive directors. It is also possible, in some instances, to bring in the managing director from a different entity, especially in situations where there are existing boardroom squabbles and a level of neutrality is required of the person to be appointed. It is also common to bring a managing director from outside the company when the board could not agree on a single candidate from amongst the executive directors to be appointed as the managing director. Either way, however, the ultimate responsibility for his appointment still rests on the board of directors.

THE LEGAL POSITION OF THE MANAGING DIRECTOR

Section 289 (5) CAMA 2020, (s. 263(5), empowers a company's board of directors to appoint one of its members as the managing director and delegate any of their powers to him. The implication of this provision is that for a person to be appointed the managing director of a company, the person must first be a director in such a company, except he is brought in from an outside entity. Even then, a person from outside the company, once he is appointed a managing director, he assumes all the attributes, duties and powers of a director in the company, albeit, with that of managing the company.

The managing director is usually the Chief Executive Officer (CEO) of the company and supervises the day-to-day management of the company. This notwithstanding, except where the company's Articles provide to the contrary, the managing director is not in a more favourable position when compared to the other executive directors of the company. The managing director only has the additional powers of management delegated to him by the board of directors as the leader of the management team (*Nzegwu-Danjuma, 225*). It is possible that the managing director will enjoy a marginally better remuneration package than the other executive directors, but in all cases, all of them are usually treated within the executive director-bracket.

The managing director is generally invested with the apparent authority to carry on the business of the company in the usual way and to do all acts and enter into all contracts necessary for that purpose. Consequently, when a person has been held out to be the managing director of a company, any third party dealing with him as an agent of the company is protected and the company cannot be allowed, at a later date, to deny the authority of the managing director *(S.S. & C. BV* v. *Seymour Energy Ltd (2004) FHCLR 257, 263).* In terms of practical functionality, under principle 4 of the *Nigerian Code of Corporate Governance, 2018 (NCCG)*, the managing director has the responsibility for:

- the day-to-day management of the company's business;
- the proper implementation and achievement of the company's strategic imperatives to ensure the sustainable development and growth of the company;
- ensuring prudent and efficient management of the company's finances and other resources;
- providing the board with complete, accurate and timely information and documentation to enable it make sound business and strategic decisions;
- promoting and protecting the interests of the company; and
- being the company's leading representative in its dealings with all its stakeholders.

It has been held that there is essentially no distinction between the managing director and other directors. However, in terms of their duties and liabilities, the chairman of the board and the managing director have special access to and connection to the company's machinery of control and are expected to be better informed than the other directors on the affairs of the company *(Shonowo* v. *Adebayo (1969) ANLR, 170; Orojo, 262).* In *Southbeach Co. Ltd & Anor* v. *Williams (2021) LPELR-57746,* the Supreme Court summarized the essence of the position of a company's managing director, in saying that, 'the truth, of course, is that under any definition, a managing director is the directing mind and will and the alter ego of the company through which the company acts' *(Ramanchadam* v. *Ekpeyong (1975) 5 SC, 29; Trenco Ltd* v. *African Real Estate Ltd (1978) 4 SC, 9; Delta Steel Nig. Ltd* v. *A.C.T. Incorp. (1999) 4 NWLR Pt. 597, 53; Marine Management Assoc. Inc* v. *National Maritime Authority (2012) 18 NWLR Pt. 1333, 506).*

The managing director is both an officer and a servant to the company. He is an officer by virtue of his being a director and a servant, even if of a special class of sorts, by his contract of service as the managing director. Therefore, the details relating to the duties, powers, remuneration and removal of the managing director are usually based on three sources: the relevant company legislation (here the CAMA), the company's Articles and the managing director's contract of service. The managing director must therefore act and exercise his powers within the limits of these sources (*Nzegwu-Danjuma, 225).* This position finds fortification in the case of *Yalaju-Amaye* v. *AREC (1986) 3 NWLR Pt. 31, 653,* where it was held that 'there is generally the relationship of master and servant between the managing director and his company. As an employee, there is usually a contract of service between him and the company. The managing director relies for his tenure on the company's Articles of Association and any other contract of service supplemental thereto.' As a servant to the company, it has been held that the managing director would have a preferential payment of his salary if a company be wound up *(Re Newspapers Proprietary Syndicate Ltd (1900) 2 Ch. 349; Orojo, 262).*

A company's managing director, whether appointed as a director on subscription to the Memorandum, appointed to fill a casual vacancy by the board, or appointed by members in a general meeting, is considered a director within the meaning of sections 269 and 868 CAMA 2020 (ss. 244 and 567).Therefore, the provisions of section 288 CAMA 2020 (s. 262) must be strictly followed in order to validly remove such a managing director from office *(Longe* v. *First Bank of Nig. Plc (2010) 2 CLRN 21, 51*).

REMUNERATION OF THE MANAGING DIRECTOR

Section 294 (1) CAMA 2020, (s. 268 (1) gives the board of directors the power to fix the remuneration of a company's managing director (whether in the form of salary, commission, profits sharing or a combination of these as the directors may determine).

Where a managing director is removed from office other than as stated under section 288 CAMA 2020, (s. 262), he would have a right to a claim for a breach of contract (if there is a contract or if a contract could be inferred in his favour from the company's Articles). For clarity, the removal of a director under section 288 CAMA 2020 means that he is removed from office before the expiration of his term in office. A company has a right to do this in a general meeting by an ordinary resolution for which a special notice is given. Where, on being removed, the managing director had performed some services for the company without a contract, he shall be entitled to the payment of *quantum meruit* for the services rendered (s. 294 (3) CAMA 2020), (s. 268 (3). This is a claim or right of action for what is considered the reasonable value of services rendered by the claimant (*Black's Law* Dictionary, 7th ed.; 1999, 1255; *FBN Plc* v. *Ozokwere (2014) 3 NWLR Pt 1395, 439; Savannah Bank of Nigeria Plc* v. *Opanubi (2004) 15 NWLR Pt. 896, 437; Oyo* v. *Mercantile Bank (Nig.) Ltd (1989) 3 NWLR Pt. 108, 213.*

REMUNERATION OF DIRECTORS GENERALLY

In Nigeria, generally, the remuneration of company directors is regulated by the CAMA and the company's Articles. Unless so provided, or where there is an agreement approved by the members of the company in general meeting for the purpose, directors are not entitled to any remuneration. This is because, except for executive directors, who are usually employees of the company where they work, directors are generally not considered servants in the company where they serve *(Moriarty* v. *Regent's Garage Co. Ltd (1921) KB, 423; Guinness* v. *Sanders (1990) 2 AC, 663; Wada* v. *Nigerian-Spanish Eng. Co. Ltd & Ors (2000) 1 FHCLR 95, 109).*

Under principle 5 of the *UK Code of Corporate Governance, 2018 (UK Code)*, it has been suggested that, in general, a company's remuneration policies and practices should be designed to support strategy and promote the company's long-term sustainable success. When it pertains to executive remuneration, however, the Code proposes that it should be aligned to the company's purposes and values, and be clearly linked to the successful delivery of the company's long-term strategy. That is not all. Going further on this, the

UK Code proposes that in fixing the remuneration of executive directors (we may simply say directors, and include those of non-executive directors), the process should not be done at large, but that certain items should be addressed by the company's remuneration policy, as follows:

- **clarity** - this points to the fact that a company's remuneration arrangements should be transparent and promote effective engagement with shareholders and the workforce;
- **simplicity** - a company's remuneration structures should avoid complexity and their rationale and operation should be easy to understand by all;
- **risk** - a company's remuneration arrangements should ensure reputational and other risks from excessive rewards, and behavioural risks that can arise from target-based incentive plans, are identified and mitigated at the earliest;
- **predictability** - the range of possible values of rewards to individual directors and any other limits or discretions should be identified and explained in simple details at the time of approving the policies;
- **proportionality** - the link between individual awards, the delivery of strategy and the long-term performance of the company should be clear and well spelt out. Outcomes should not reward poor performances under any guide; and
- **alignment to culture** - all the company's incentive schemes should drive behaviours consistent with the company's purposes, values and strategy.

The above is a positive and well-detailed persuasive guide from the UK Code. However, the *Nigerian Code of Corporate Governance (NCCG), 2018* also made very important and useful provisions on how companies in Nigeria should structure their remuneration in general and their executive remuneration, in particular. Principle 16 of the NCCG provides, among others, that the board should ensure that the company 'remunerates fairly, responsibly and transparently,' in order to be able to 'promote the achievement of strategic objectives and positive outcomes in the short, medium and long term.'

With specific reference to the remuneration of the managing director and other directors in the company, the same principle 16 of the NCCG provides that the remuneration of the managing director and executive directors should be 'structured to link rewards to corporate and individual performances and include a significant component that is related to long-term corporate performance, such as stock options and bonuses.' It is, therefore, clear, that in terms of the underlying objectives and undertones, the provisions of the UK Code and the NCCG on this issue, are not materially different.

It has to be noted that where a company's Articles has made specific stipulations concerning how the remuneration of directors are to be determined, then, the Court will not interfere in order to make its own determination on the issue. The Court also will not award the directors any *quantum meruit* that is at variance with the provisions of the Articles, if such a provision was made therein *(Re Richmond Gate Property Co. Ltd (1965) 1 WLR, 335; Guinness* v. *Sanders (1990) 2 AC, 663; Mayson et al, 488).* The understanding behind the attitude of the Courts to this issue should not be difficult to decipher. We discussed earlier in this book about the statutory contract which the Articles create among the employees, the officers and the company, which binds all of them together. Therefore, once the Articles lawfully provide for a particular thing or a way of doing a thing by a company, the Courts are always very reluctant to interfere.

Section 293 CAMA 2020, (s. 267) makes elaborate provisions relating to the remuneration of directors:

- remuneration of directors is determined by the company in general meeting and such remuneration shall be deemed to accrue from day to day;
- directors may also be paid all travelling, hotel and other expenses properly incurred by them in attending and returning from meetings of the directors or of any committee of directors or the general meetings of the company, or in connection with the business of the company;
- where the remuneration of the directors of a company has been fixed by the Articles, it can only be altered by a special resolution of the members in a general meeting. This is obviously so since altering the provision in the Articles will amount to tacit alteration of the company's Articles, which can only be done by a special resolution;
- a company is not bound to pay remuneration to its directors. However, where the company has agreed to pay its directors, it shall do so from the company's funds and not otherwise;
- the amount of directors' remuneration shall be a debt from the company, therefore, if the directors take office on the basis of the provisions of the Articles, they shall be able to sue the company on account of the debt or prove it, if the company is liquidated;

- a director who receives more money from the company than he is entitled to shall be liable to the company and accountable to it for the excess money so received;
- directors' remunerations are apportionable by the company.

The company secretary has limited roles to play in the context of the directors and their remuneration. This is principally so because much of the dynamics of the determination of the remuneration of directors are already set out in the CAMA and the other aspects are left to the company itself to be determined by the Articles. With respect to the remuneration of the managing director and the executive directors, their service contracts usually contain the details of the terms of their employment and most of times, poses no serious problems of interpretation.

The company secretary will be ready with direction and guidance, if, for instance, in structuring any of the aspects of the remuneration of the directors, there is need to amend the company's Articles. In such an instance, the company secretary must ensure that the principles, earlier discussed, that guide the amendment of company's Articles, are observed. Again, if there be a situation where the directors have gone outside the provisions of the CAMA, the company's Articles and the terms of their service contracts to be receiving remuneration that they were not entitled to, it is the duty of the company secretary to call the attention of the board of directors to the perceived illegality and advise them on ways to restitute, if the situation so warrants.

Prohibition of Tax-Free Payment to Directors

Company directors, especially those working with large corporations, are usually one of the largest groups of tax payers paying high taxes in every tax-paying jurisdiction. With this fact in mind, some companies do structure the remuneration of their directors to avoid paying taxes or to minimize any taxes to be paid by their directors to the tax authorities. The CAMA frowns at any attempt for companies to structure directors' remuneration as tax-free.

Except for remuneration that had accrued to a company director before the coming into effect of the CAMA, or that pertains to a period before the Act, section 295 (1) CAMA 2020, (s. 269 (1), prohibits the payment of any remuneration to a company director (whether as a director or not) that is free of income tax. It is the same fate where a director's remuneration is calculated to be at variance with the amount of his income tax or with the standard rate of income tax within the jurisdiction in question. An exception is where there was a contract which was in force at the commencement of the Act, which provides expressly, and not by reference to the Articles of the company, for a tax-free payment to a director.

With respect to the above prohibition, any provision contained in a company's Articles or in any contract (other than the contract existing before the commencement of the Act) or in any resolution(s) for tax free payment to directors, shall be deemed a gross sum subject to income tax, of the net sum of which it actually provides (s. 295 (2) CAMA 2020), (s. 269(2).

Payment for Directors' Loss of Office

Under section 297 CAMA 2020, (s. 271), it is unlawful for a company to make any payment to a director as a compensation for loss of office, or as a consideration for such a loss. It is also prohibited to offer any such compensation in connection with a director's retirement from office. This is, however, subject to certain exceptions.

For any payment to a director for loss of office or on his retirement to be valid, the particulars of the proposed payment and the amount proposed to be paid must have been disclosed to the members of the company and the proposal approved by the company. The nature of this disclosure is not stated, but it has to be reasoned that it must be in a general meeting. This is because of the further requirement that after the disclosure, the company (that is through the members in a general meeting) is also expected to approve such payment.

Under section 298 CAMA 2020, (s. 272), where due to a process of takeover, merger or acquisition of a company or takeover of its property, any payment is proposed to be made to a director of the company as compensation for loss of office, such payment shall be unlawful. To be validly made, the particulars of such a payment and the amount must have been disclosed to the members (also in a general meeting) and approved by the company as stated above.

Where a payment has been made to a director as compensation for loss of office without the requisite approval of the members, the director receiving such payment shall be treated as having received the sum in trust for the company (s. 298 (2) CAMA 2020), (s. 272 (2)). The director in this instance would be treated as a 'constructive trustee; of such funds until the funds are transferred to the company's coffers (*A.G. Federation* v. *A.G. Abia State & Ors (2002) 4 SCNJ, 1)*. An important point is that, to be valid, the disclosure of the proposed payment to a director must be to all the members of a company and not a section of them. The implication here is that a disclosure to the board of directors, for instance, or a committee of the board will be ineffective for this purpose to validate such payment *(Taupo Totora Timber Co.* v. *Rowe (1977) All ER, 123, Orojo, 278).*

There are general exceptions to the discussions above in section 300 (3) CAMA 2020, (s. 274(3). They provide that the prohibition against payments to directors as compensation for loss of office shall not include any *bona fide* payment by way of damages for breach of contract or by way of pension for past services rendered by the director to the company.

It is not clear why the exceptions became necessary since they do not actually concern payments for directors' loss of office. A payment that is made to pay damages awarded by a Court against a company for breach of contract with a director is not payment made to him for loss of office. In the same way, payments to former director(s) in the form of pensions cannot be termed payment for loss of office in any manner, especially in the present regime in Nigeria, where the pension regime and payments have been standardized and become almost entirely statutory, under the *Pension Reform Act 2014* (as amended).

Loans to Company Directors

Prohibition of loans to company directors has been an issue that regulators have grappled with over the years. This is because loans can be a veritable means of avoiding the rules that regulate the dissipation or tampering with the assets of a company illegally. A transaction can actually be structured and presented as a 'loan' when it is actually a gift to the director concerned, either because the 'loan' was not intended to be repaid to the company *ab initio,* or because the terms are not commercial terms that should attend to a loan of that nature.

Most importantly, given their almost absolute control over the management and direction of companies' affairs, directors are in vantage position to structure any transaction to their benefits, which would have the effect of indirectly increasing their remunerations, to the detriment of the company's wellbeing *(Gower & Davies, 581*).

In Nigeria, section 296 (1) CAMA 2020, (s. 270 (1), prohibits a company from granting loans to its directors or directors of its holding company. It also prohibits the company from entering into any guarantee or providing any security in connection with a loan made to such directors by another person.

In simple terms, a guarantee is a third party obligation where a person is affirming that if the principal debtor (primary obligor) fails to meet the terms of the loan facility and repay the loan, the guarantor will step in and repay *(Trade Bank Plc* v. *Chami (2003) 13 NWLR Pt. 836, 158; Auto Import Export* v. *Adebayo & Ors (2005) 19 NWLR Pt. 959, 44; R.E.A.N.* v. *Aswani Textile Ltd (1992) 3 NWLR Pt. 227, 1; Lingo Nig Ltd* v. *Nwodo (2004) 7 NWLR Pt. 874, 30).*

The above prohibition of loans by a company to its directors has a proviso, and does not extend to anything done to provide a company director with funds to meet expenditure incurred or to be incurred for the purposes of the company. Also, it does not extend to any money given to a director to enable him to properly perform his duties as an officer of the company. However, this exception does not authorize the making of a loan or the entry into a guarantee, or the provision of security, except:

- with the prior approval of the company given at a general meeting at which the purpose of the expenditure, the amount of the loan or the extent of the guarantee or security are disclosed; or
- on the condition that if the approval of the company is not given at or before the next annual general meeting, the loan shall be repaid or the liability under the guarantee or security shall be discharged, within six (6) months from the conclusion of that meeting;
- where the company's approval is not given where it is required, the directors authorizing the giving of the loan, or the entering into the guarantee, or the provision of the security, shall be jointly and severally liable to indemnify the company against any loss arising from the transaction.

This would represent a situation where no approval was given by the company via the general meeting and the transaction actually proceeded to conclusion. In that case, then, the director(s) who approved the loan facility or who entered into the guarantee or provided the security is to assume the liability of indemnifying the company for any loss the company may suffer thereby. It does not appear that there is any sanction provided for a situation where the director(s) went ahead with the transaction(s) without the requisite approval but the company suffered no losses. It is possible that the Act left such an issue to a company's internal disciplinary mechanisms to deal with.

The prohibition against giving loans to company directors does not extend to a company whose ordinary business includes the lending of money or the giving of guarantees in connection with loans made by other persons, for transactions done in the ordinary course of its business (s. 296 (1)(a)(b) and (2) CAMA 2020), (s. 270 (1)(a)(b) and (2). This would seem to be targeted at banks and other financial institutions, who are in the business of granting loans and making other advances. In essence, it then appears that these institutions are free to give loans and advances to their directors, as long as they abide by all the relevant laws and guidelines that regulate such insider-related transactions.

SUBSTANTIAL PROPERTY TRANSACTIONS BY DIRECTORS

A company is prohibited from entering into an arrangement whereby:

- a director (in all cases including a shadow director) or controlling member of the company or its holding company or a person connected with such a director, acquires or is to acquire one or more non-cash assets of the requisite value from the company; (s. 310 (1) CAMA 2020), (s. 284(1)(a).

- o *Note:* the aspect of the prohibition of substantial property transaction by a controlling member is an addition by CAMA 2020, as the CAMA 2004 had no equivalent provision. In this respect, a 'controlling member is a person who, either alone or in understanding with other persons, has more than 50% of the voting power to elect or remove directors of the company (s. 310 (3).
- o The CAMA also prohibits a company from entering into an arrangement whereby the company acquires or:

- is to acquire one or more non-cash assets of the requisite value from its director, controlling member or a director of its holding company or a person connected with such a director, unless the arrangement is first approved by a resolution of the members of the company (or its holding company, if applicable, where the director, controlling member or connected person, is a director of the holding company) in a general meeting, after being informed of all the material facts relating to the transaction(s. 310 (1)(b) CAMA 2020),(s. 284(1)(b).

  Note: the CAMA 2020 introduced the aspect of full disclosure requirement to the general meeting by the director, controlling member or connected person when seeking approval of the property transaction (the CAMA 2004 had no equivalent provision). In doing this, the Act used the phrase 'after being informed of all material facts' relating to the transaction. This presupposes that where a director, controlling member or connected person, suppresses material facts in getting the general meeting to approve any such transaction, the company reserves the right to void any approval and reverse the transaction, when such misrepresentation is subsequently discovered.

Another innovation by the CAMA 2020 is to reserve to the Commission the right to fix, by regulation, the requisite value of the non-cash assets that would qualify for approval by a company's general meeting. Under the CAMA 2004, the requisite value of a non-cash asset prohibited under the Act should not be, at the time the arrangement is entered into, less than ₦2,000.00 (Two thousand naira) but exceed ₦100,000.00 (One hundred thousand naira), or twenty percent of the company's asset value. The value of the company net assets was to be determined by reference to the company's annual account laid before the general meeting for the last preceding year, and where no account has been laid before the time, the amount of the company's called-up share capital is to be used. This approach has now been jettisoned by the 2020 Act.

Section 868 CAMA 2020 (s. 567) defines 'non-cash asset' for the purposes of the above discussions to mean any property or interest in property other than cash and for this purpose, cash is said to include foreign currency.

Who are Persons 'Connected' to a Director?

Several references have been made above to persons who are connected to a director of a company, with respect to directors engaging in substantial property transaction. Such persons are sometimes called related persons, but who are they?

Under section 312 (8) CAMA 2020, (s. 286 (8), for the purposes of knowing whether an approval is needed for any non-cash assets transaction, a person is regarded as being connected to a director of a company, if the person, not being a director himself, is:

- that director's spouse, child or step-child, including illegitimate child;
- a body corporate with which the director is associated; or of a trust whose terms confer the power on the trustees that may be exercised for the benefit of the person, his spouse, or any children or step children of his, or any such body corporate; or
- a person acting in his capacity as a partner to the director or of any person who is connected to the director in any of the ways described above.

It presupposes that any person(s) who does not fall within the bracket of relationships described above, cannot be described as a 'connected person' to a director, at least, in the context of the CAMA and the present discussions.

Exceptions to the Rule for Approval

The requirement for the approval by a company's general meeting for a director's substantial property transaction involving non-cash assets is not absolute. In certain situations, the need for an approval is dispensed with. Section 311 CAMA 2020, (s. 285), provides exceptions to the prohibitions created by section 310 of the Act requiring a company's approval for any non-cash assets acquisition arrangement. There are four (4) exceptions to the prohibitions under section 310 and no approval shall be required where:

- for transactions involving a body corporate, unless it is a company within the meaning of the Act, or is a wholly owned subsidiary of a body corporate;
- where the asset is to be acquired by a holding company from its wholly-owned subsidiaries or from a holding company by any of its wholly-owned subsidiary of a holding company from another wholly-owned subsidiary of the same holding company; or
- where the arrangement is entered into by a company which is being wound up, unless the winding-up is a member's voluntary winding-up;
- a director of a company is permitted to acquire a non-cash asset from the company or its holding company without members' approval, if he is also a member in the company, if the acquisition is made in his capacity as a member.

The problem with the last exception noted above is how to determine when a person is acquiring an asset as a member or a director of a company. This is especially the case when there is no shareholding threshold stated when the person would be qualified to acquire the assets as a member. This implies that a director could simply acquire some insignificant shares in a company and use his status as a member to circumvent the prohibition in section 310 of the Act. We submit that this last exception should be revisited and made a lot more certain as to the criteria to acquire those assets as a member, otherwise it should be expunged from the Act, as it appears prone to abuse.

Offending Transactions to Section 310

Under section 312 CAMA 2020, (s. 286), any arrangement entered into by the company in contravention of the provisions of section 310 of the Act, as indicated above, and any transaction entered into pursuant to the arrangement (whether by the company or any other person), is voidable at the instance of the company. Such an arrangement is also voidable by a Court on a claim by members, unless:

- restitution of any money or the asset, which is the subject matter of the transaction is no longer possible or the company has been indemnified by any other person for any losses it suffered; or
- avoiding the transaction would affect the rights of a *bona fide* acquirer for value without actual notice of the contravention; or
- the arrangement is ratified and affirmed within a reasonable time by the company (or holding company, if applicable) in general meeting.

If a director enters into an arrangement with a company, its holding company or a person connected with the director contrary to section 310 of the Act, the director, controlling member and any other person(s) connected to him and any director who authorized the transaction commits an offence and shall be liable:

- to the company to account for any gain he may have made directly or for any loss suffered by the company, directly or indirectly from the arrangement or transaction;
- directly and derivatively to the members of the company for any loss or damage suffered by them (this is a new provision by the CAMA 2020);
- the director shall be liable jointly and severally (with any other person who is liable) to indemnify the company for any loss resulting from the arrangement or transaction; and, where found guilty and convicted of an offence, he shall be disqualified from serving as a director of the company.

Under section 312 (6) CAMA 2020, (s. 286 (5), a director shall not be liable for any transaction or arrangement with the company if he shows that he took all reasonable steps to ensure that the company complies with section 310 of the Act. Also, a person connected with the director, or any other director that should have been liable under the transaction in question will escape liability if he can show that he took all reasonable steps to secure compliance with the relevant section of the Act.

A few points need to be made about the liability of the director, especially, and the other persons mentioned in this section. The first is that section 312(3) of the Act makes a breach of section 310 an offence, first and foremost. However, the only criminal consequence stated therein is in section

312(3)(c) which bars the director if, convicted, from continuing to serve as a director in the company. The other two remedies: liability to account to the company and account to members for any loss or damages suffered by members, are civil damages.

From the manner of couching section 312 (3), an argument that a director would have to be convicted by a Court first before any of the three remedies avails anybody or the company can be validly made. Although, the word conviction is only used in section 312(3)(c), the drafting of the section in these respects is not elegant enough.

It would appear that the difficulty with couching the provisions of the section is not new. Under section 286 (3) CAMA 2004, which section 312 (3) replaced, it was provided that a director or connected person who contravenes the provisions of the section 'shall be guilty of an offence and liable...' to account and indemnify the company for loss and damages. Apparently realizing that a person cannot be guilty of an offence without a form of trial or judicial intervention, the provision was changed, in the CAMA 2020, to 'commits and offence and liable ...' The problem of clarity of the provision, therefore, persists.

In summarizing the present discussions, the position of a company's managing director is central to the direction and management of a company. He is, in sum, the first among equals and the alter ego of any company. In liaison with and with the assistance of the board, the managing director implements policy and strategic decisions that could make or mar a company as a commercial concern. It is therefore important, especially with large public companies, that a person to be saddled with the position of managing director must have demonstrated both intellectual capacity and business acumen in order to provide efficient leadership to the company.

The managing director, like the executive directors, is a servant of the company, while also having all the attributes and powers of the other directors. He is usually appointed from the pool of executive directors, especially in large companies, but may also be selected from outside the company, as the board deems fit.

While the remuneration of the other directors, especially the non-executive directors, are fixed by the board of directors, that of the managing director (and other executive directors) is usually contained in his service contract based on the company's Articles. The details of his other perks, tenure of office, resignation and removal from office, including other details as to nature and form of notices are also contained therein, flowing from the CAMA.

By virtue of their position, directors occupy vantage positions in relation to the life of any company, include having a total control over the structures of the company including its finances. Having this fact in mind, the CAMA has tried to mitigate the dangers of directors using their positions to structure tax-fee payments under different guises to themselves. Same is the scenario with payment to directors with respect to loss of office, which has to be disclosed and approved by members in general meeting. This is also generally the same with respect to loans to directors and when directors deal with non-cash assets transaction as substantial property transactions with the company.

In all the above situations, the intention of the CAMA is to limit, as much as possible, potential opportunities for abuse of position by directors and against the company. Whether such precautions would achieve the desired result is left to be seen, especially in companies where the directors themselves are also shareholders, with substantial holdings. This means that in some of these situations where a vote is to be taken on particular issues wherein the directors' membership interests are at stake, the results would have been virtually contemplated and agreed before the actual voting.

There are also some far-reaching exceptions by the CAMA that sometimes look as if they were meant to defeat, or at least weaken the main prohibition. An example is where a director is prohibited from doing a particular act but could do same as a member if he is also a shareholder. It would not take the director much efforts or resources to acquire some of the company's shares and use his membership status to defeat the prohibition against directors doing the said act.

For the company secretary, this is one of the situations where his duties to members of the company might seem to be in the face of directors who may want to gain undue advantages in some respects. For instance, where directors would want to structure gifts to themselves in the form of un-repayable loans or where they arrange tax-free payments to themselves, the company secretary should advise the directors that such actions are in direct breach of the provisions of the CAMA and should not be consummated. What the directors decide to do afterwards should not be for the company secretary to intervene directly as confrontation, but for the members to deal with in general meeting.

The same goes to situations where the directors purport to arrange payments for themselves for loss of office or engage in substantial non-cash assets transactions with the company, which, as we have seen, have certain prohibitions. The duty of the company secretary in such instances is to advise and try to guide the directors on the legal implications of the proposed transactions, some of which even have criminal sanctions imposed for breach.

THE CHECKPOINTS

- ✓ The managing director, as the first among equals, is the pivot around which the board of directors, and by implication, the management and direction of the company, revolves. He is a servant of the company, even if a special one, (like the other executive directors) and is usually appointed from among the executive directors, though, sometimes, such an appointment is from outside the company.
- ✓ While, in general, directors' terms and conditions of service are determined by the board of directors, the managing director's terms and conditions of service are usually in his service contract and the Articles, flowing from authorization from the CAMA.
- ✓ Directors occupy very important and powerful positions in a company and the CAMA has tried to avoid or minimize the abuse of such positions by directors in several areas and has imposed restrictions. For instance, directors paying themselves tax-free payments, arranging payments for loss of office for themselves, granting loans to themselves, sometimes in disguised forms, so as not to repay the loans etc.
- ✓ Non-cash property transaction is another means through which directors could dissipate company's assets, disguised as some non-harmful transactions with the company. This is why all the above scenarios are subjected to the approval of the members in general meeting. It is not that this approval requirement will eliminate this abuse entirely, because some of the directors are also powerful members of the company, but, at least, the members will get to see what the directors are up to, and may choose to fight back.
- ✓ In approving any of the transactions noted above between a director (or where connected persons and controlling members feature, themselves also), full disclosures as to the critical nature of and components of the transactions must be disclosed to the general meeting. Where this is not done, the general meeting reserves the right to void the transactions and the approvals earlier given, especially if material facts were suppressed by the director(s) or member(s), when making the earlier disclosure.

- ✓ From the corporate governance perspective, the UK Code and the NCCG gave us persuasive guides in terms of items to be considered in formulating the remuneration packages of company executives. While the items listed may not been exhaustive, they surely appear helpful as useful starting points in that respect.

Chapter 10

VACATION AND REMOVAL OF DIRECTORS FROM OFFICE

INTRODUCTION

The position and office of a company director are undoubtedly exalted ones but the tenure of office for directors is not in any way sacrosanct. This is because directors can be removed from office by the company, at any time, by an ordinary resolution in a general meeting, notwithstanding anything in the Articles or that would have been agreed orally or in writing with the company (s. 288(1) CAMA 2020), (s. 262(1). This rule also applies to those directors that are described as 'directors for life,' as such directors can also be removed from office at any time by an ordinary resolution of the company in general meeting (s. 281 CAMA 2020), (s. 255). Apart from being removed from office by the members, directors can also vacate their offices under several other circumstances, including suspension, resignation and death.

The major roles for the company secretary in any of these respects is to ensure that in either purporting to suspend, remove or otherwise discipline a director, that the relevant provisions of the company's Articles or the CAMA are complied with. For instance, to remove a director before the expiration of his tenure under section 288 (2) CAMA 2020 (s. 262 (2), a special notice (that is, one for which a 28 days' notice has to be given to propose same) is required of any resolution proposed to that effect. That is a non-negotiable condition precedent. There are also post-removal processes that need to be activated by the company secretary for purposes of ensuring efficient corporate governance and regulatory compliance. These issues are discussed further below.

Flowing from the above, where, therefore, a resolution proposed as purporting to remove a director from office before the end of his tenure contravenes the above provision of the CAMA, for instance, because there was no special notice given, the removal of the director would be void and liable to be set aside. It will not be a good answer by the company to rely on the common law right to hire and fire an employee. This being that a statute has made an express provision for the procedure to remove the director, and it has to be followed to the letter for any valid removal of such a director from office (*Awoyemi* v. *Solomon (1976) FRCR, 165*; *Orojo, 255).*

SUSPENSION OF A DIRECTOR FROM OFFICE

One of the most effective means of keeping company directors in check is through disciplinary sanctions that could be meted out to them by the members in general meeting. Among those sanctions, one that is frequently deployed is the suspension of a director from office by the board of directors, pending the ratification or otherwise of such suspension by the general meeting. The CAMA does not make any express provision(s) relating to how and when a company can suspend or otherwise discipline a director, apart from removal from office by the general meeting, as noted above. It is possible, it is submitted, that though there is no express provision to that effect, the general meeting can also suspend a director, but may have to do so through a mandate to the board to exercise such powers. The modalities to deal with these issues are usually detailed in a company's Articles or, for executive directors or the managing director, in a director's contract of service. The procedure stated therein has to be followed to validly discipline such an erring director. It is doubtful, and we submit, problematic, if the provisions of the company's Articles that contradict the express provisions of the CAMA would be effective for compliance, except where such provisions of the CAMA are subject to the Articles.

In the case of *University of Calabar* v. *Esiogu (1997) 4 NWLR (Part 502) 719,723*, the Supreme Court outlined the nature of the consequences of suspension of an employee, in this case, a director, that 'suspension' means a temporary privation or deprivation, cessation or stoppage of or from, the privileges and rights of a person.' In essence, a director on suspension is still, legally speaking, a director, even if some of his rights and privileges are suspended, and that during the period of suspension, he cannot function in his office as such. For instance, while a director on suspension is entitled to notice of board meetings, like the other directors, he is not expected to attend all such meetings, especially where issues concerning him would be discussed. When the director on suspension actually attends boards meetings, he must excuse himself from the meetings' deliberations wherein he features at all (*Longe* v. *FBN Plc (2010) 6 NWLR Pt. 1189, 1).*

The *Black's Law Dictionary's* definition of suspension also comes close to home, in saying that suspension is the 'temporary deprivation of a person's powers or privileges, especially of office or profession' (9th ed, 1584). Our present purpose is on temporary deprivation of a person's powers and privileges relating to an office, that is, the office of a director of a company.

Where it is a company's managing director that is placed on suspension from his duties, he remains a director of the company but without the power to perform his duties as the managing director (or as a director, at all). Therefore, while on suspension from his duties, all of the managing director's rights, privileges and powers that are incidental to his being a director in the company still accrue to him and remain intact. It is his exercise of these rights and powers that would have been suspended *(Longe* v. *First Bank of Nig. Plc (2010) 6 NWLR Pt. 1189, 1).*

VACATION OF THE OFFICE AS DIRECTOR

The rules in CAMA relating to the disqualification of certain persons from being made company directors are aimed at stopping such persons from being appointed as company directors in the first place. On the other hand, the rules relating to the vacation of office by directors are aimed at getting persons who have already been appointed directors to vacate their positions on the occurrence of certain events.

Section 284 (1) CAMA 2020 (s. 258 (1), deals with the issue of vacation of office by directors. In sum, the office of a company director shall be vacated if the director in question:

- ceases to be a director by virtue of section 277 CAMA 2020 (s. 251) (that is a director's inability to meet shareholding qualification where that is required by the company's Articles); or
- becomes bankrupt or makes any arrangement or composition with his creditors; or
- becomes prohibited from being a director by reason of any order made under section 280 CAMA 2020 (s. 254) (an order of Court that could be made to disqualify a fraudulent person from being a director); or
- becomes of unsound mind; or
- resigns his office by notice in writing to the company.

A director in a company, subject to the Articles, may resign his appointment by giving the requisite notice to the company. Such a notice, once given, takes immediate effect and the director concerned cannot withdraw same without the consent of the members *(Kung* v. *General Metalware Co. Ltd & Anor (1987) FHCLR 214, 230; (Glossop* v. *Glossop*

(1907) 2 Ch., 370, Bhadmus, 184). It would appear that the company's consent accepting the withdrawal of any notice of a director's resignation would have to be given in a general meeting. This would give the director's re-engagement the colour of being re-appointed by the members in general meeting, whose responsibility it is, ordinarily, to appoint directors. In essence, it would appear that the remaining directors on the board, for instance, cannot give such consent on behalf or in place of the general meeting.

By section 284(2) CAMA 2020 (s. 258(2), where a director presents himself for a re-election, a record of his attendance at the company's board of directors' meetings during the preceding one year shall be made available to the members at the general meeting where he is to be re-elected. A director that has consistently been absent from board meetings might be evidence of not being committed enough to the business of the company. This is rebuttable, though, and it would be left to the director concerned to convince the members in a general meeting to the contrary, in order to warrant his re-election. This is also a good point, for instance, for a director who after resigning, changed his mind and wants the general meeting to approve his re-engagement into the board. A record of his attendance at board meetings and even his overall performance for the years he was a director should be placed before the general meeting for scrutiny. Issues like these should from part of matters to be detailed in the company's Articles.

Once any of the events stated above under section 284 (1) CAMA 2020 occurs, the director's vacation of office becomes automatic and the company's board of directors does not have the power to waive such an event that triggered the vacation of office *(Re Bodega Co. Ltd. 1904 1 Ch., 276).* If the director purports to continue acting as such after any of such an event(s), he may be restrained by injunction from doing so *(Charlesworth & Cain, 346).*

REMOVAL OF A MANAGING DIRECTOR FROM OFFICE

The managing director is the first among equals in the directorate cadre. He is not the 'regular' director, although he is still removable like the other directors in the company, by an ordinary resolution of the members in a general meeting.

A company's board of directors, acting on the instruction of, or pending the ratification of the general meeting, has the power to terminate the appointment of the managing director in accordance with his contract of service or the provisions of the Articles. Section 288(1) CAMA 2020 (s. 262(1), gives the company the right to remove a director from office by an ordinary resolution (of which special notice shall be given) before the expiration of his tenure of office. This is notwithstanding anything to the contrary in the Articles or in a contract between the director and the company.

Since the managing director is so appointed because of his being a director in the first place, his removal as a director automatically means his relinquishment of the position of the managing director. However, a person may be removed as a managing director and still retain his position as a director in a company. This would mean that the general meeting will have to make such a decision to retain the former managing director on the board, but with a different portfolio.

After appointing a managing director and he assumes his position, if a company alters its Articles to provide for new ground(s) for the removal of directors, such an alteration(s) is not thereby automatically integrated into his contract of service. Any such alteration(s) of the Articles cannot be retroactive in effect and can only be part of the managing director's service contract on re-negotiation of a new service contract with the company. Therefore, in the absence of any such contract re-negotiation, if the managing director is subsequently removed, purportedly based on any of the new grounds, the company would be liable to him for breach of contract (*Nzegwu-Danjuma, 228).*

A managing director that is removed from office is entitled to any compensation or damages that is due to him with the termination of his appointment as a director or any appointment that terminated with his removal as a director (s. 288(6), (s. 262 (6).

REMOVAL OF DIRECTORS FROM OFFICE

The directors of a company may be removed from office by the members in a general meeting, and where the Articles do permit, the board of directors may also vote to remove a fellow director from office. Where the Articles or the contract of appointment of a person as a director does not expressly specify or fix the duration of the director's appointment, such a director holds office at will and may be removed or dismissed by an ordinary resolution passed by the members of the company in general meeting *(Iwuchukwu* v. *Nwizu (1994) 7 NWLR Pt. 357, 379, 402).* The important point to be made about the process of removal of a director is that it is strictly procedural and not *ad hoc.* Any purported removal of a director from office that does not adhere to the laid down procedure(s) is bound to fail, and liable to set aside.

In *Iwuchukwu's* case above, the appellant was first appointed by a company DEC Ltd, as a special assistant to its managing director. He was subsequently made an executive director in the same company, but later made an executive in one of the subsidiaries of DEC Ltd. It was from here that the appellant was 'demoted,' as it were, from executive director to a manager in the same company and his directorship position terminated. He instituted an action that his purported removal as an executive director was *ultra vires* and null and void, without effect.

In its judgment, the Court held that the appellant's removal as a director was null and void, the company having breached the procedural requirements for such removal. The case was also made worse for the company because, while the suit was already in Court, the company hurriedly convened and held a general meeting that purported to 'regularly' remove the director from office. The Court held that such efforts were fruitless and the director was not validly removed.

In companies where the Articles permit, it is possible for directors to be able to remove fellow directors from office. This is usually meant to act as self-checking mechanism against directors' truancy and indiscipline and to aid peer review. The board members are therefore able to remove and replace a truant, incompetent or otherwise non-performing director(s),subject to be ratified by the general meeting, instead of always waiting for the general meeting to hold before taking a decision on such issues. A possible downside to this would be where a few of the directors would collude and form a cartel within the board and lording it over the other directors, determining who stays on the board and who does not. This would be counter-productive and any serious counter-force within the board might lead to a fractured board and stalemate and the company would be the worse for it.

It has to be emphasized that the CAMA does not make any specific provision(s) relating to the removal of a director by fellow directors. Consequently, any attempt by a company to adopt such a practice or procedure to remove directors must be authorized by the company's Articles. The Act however acknowledges that a director could still be removed via other means apart from those specified in section 288. To this end, reference is made in section 288 (6) CAMA 2020, which says that the provision does not purport to derogate 'from any power to remove a director which may exist apart from this section.' Essentially, a company has a right to remove a director from office and the mode for such removal may be stated in the company's Articles, failing which, resort would be had to the provisions of the CAMA *(Omenka* v. *Morrison Ind. Plc (2000)13 NWLR Pt. 683,147, 154).*

Having considered the general principles relating to the removal of directors from office, a review of the specific statutory provisions in this respect would be proper at this stage. Section 288 CAMA 2020, (s. 262) has detailed provisions on the procedure for removal of company directors from office: i) a company is to call a general meeting; ii) an ordinary resolution is required to remove a director; iii) special notice (28 days) is required for such an ordinary resolution to remove a director; iv) such notice to be sent to the director concerned and he may make representations in response and request that same be sent to members.

It has been stated that a company may by an ordinary resolution remove any director from office before the expiration of his tenure of office (section 288(1) CAMA 2020), s. 262 (1). However, failure to strictly follow the provisions of Act in removing a director makes the purported removal null and void *(Pan Ocean Oil Corp. Nig Ltd* v. *Timolini & Ors (2005) 3 FHCLR, 293).*

The more popular and recent case of *Longe* v. *First Bank of Nig. Plc (2010) 6 NWLR Pt. 1189, 1,* deals with almost all the important points regarding the removal of a director from office. As brief facts: the appellant, who was the managing director of major bank in Nigeria, was removed (suspended) from office (later removed by the general meeting) by the board of directors of the bank before his tenure of office expired. This was in line with section 262 (1)(2) CAMA 2004, (now s. 288 (1)(12) CAMA 2020). His removal was consequent upon a business transaction which the bank had engaged in and which went bad and the bank lost a lot of money. Firstly, as noted above, the appellant was placed on suspension by the board and later removed from office, apparently on the approval of the general meeting. He sued for unlawful dismissal. It is instructive that, in appreciating the statutory power of the company to remove him from office, the appellant did not ask the Court to re-instate him to his position as a director (managing director). He only challenged the processes and procedures for his removal.

The appellant's major contention in Court was that the notice of the board meeting where his removal from office was discussed and finalized was not served on him. The High Court and the Court of Appeal agreed with the bank that the appellant was on suspension at the time of the meeting and was not entitled to the notice of board meeting, thereof. The Supreme Court upheld the appeal and set aside the concurrent findings of the two lower

Courts. In the verdict of the Supreme Court, as long as a director in a company has not vacated his office or been validly removed, he is entitled to a notice of any board meeting, for the meeting to be validly convened and held.

As noted earlier, a special notice is required for an ordinary resolution to remove a director from office before the expiration of his tenure. Also, a special notice is required for a resolution to appoint another person to replace the removed director at the meeting in which he is removed. The right of the members to remove any director from office overrides any contrary provision in the Articles or any agreement with a director that forbids that he be removed as such (s. 288(1) CAMA 2020), (s. 262 (1).

It has been argued and held that a director who was removed irregularly could still be considered to have been removed lawfully despite the improper notice and procedure adopted for his removal. This is because the company has a statutory right to remove anybody from being a director on its board, and the Court will not interfere by an injunction in a company's statutory right to remove a director from office *(Bentley-Stevens* v. *Jones & Ors (1974) 2 All ER 653, 655).* It is doubtful what the situation would be if the company expressly breached a statutory provision in order to remove a director and the director went to Court to challenge same, as was the case in *Longe* v. *FBN Plc.* This will be for the Courts to decide, but in most cases, the Court will usually declare the removal of the director void and of no effect but will only award damages to him and not reverse the removal.

Whatever be the case, however, it has to be noted that a director who has been removed through a procedure he considers irregular or void may apply to Court for a winding-up order against the company on the ground that it is just and equitable to make such an order *(A.R.E.C.* v. *Amaye (1986) 3 NWLR Pt. 31, 653, 66; Tika Tore Press & Ors* v. *Abina & Ors (1973) 4 SC. 63).* The facts of the case must have to be very dire for the Court to accede to such a request of winding-up, in the place of award of damages to the removed director.

While a company has the statutory power and can provide for the power to remove directors from office in its Articles, the company cannot validly contract or agree not to remove a director from office. Any such agreement to fetter the company's right of control and discipline over its board will be invalidated by the Court. On the contrary, the shareholders themselves, can validly agree *inter se*, to act in particular way, for instance, not to a remove a director from office. *(Russell* v. *Northern Bank Dev. Corp Ltd (1992) BCLC 1016; Gower & Davies, 715).* The existence of the supremacy of members' right to remove a director from office at any time has been described as a key provision of modern company law (and corporate governance) that confirms that ultimate power rests with the members. This is because it acts as a counterforce to the balance of power in a company which is normally with the directors, whose duty is to direct and manage the company *(Orojo, 254).*

The company secretary's roles in the processes of removing or replacing directors are to ensure that the procedures and processes are followed. In simple terms, to ensure that all due processes are observed, before, during and after the process of removing a director from office.

To remove a director, the starting point is to call a general meeting of the company. This presupposes that the notice of the meeting and the resolution to be proposed will have to be prepared and served. Apart from ensuring that the notice of such a meeting is served on all members and directors who are entitled to receive same, the company secretary must also ensure that a special notice of the proposed resolution to remove the director(s) is also given to all those who are entitled to receive the notice of meeting. In addition, where the director sought to be removed has made representations and has required that same be made available to members, this has to be done. Finally, if the company or a third party makes an application to Court to block the director's representations from being circulated to members for being an abuse of the right to so apply, the company secretary shall ensure that the application is followed-up to resolution by the Court.

The importance of strict adherence to these processes, especially the ones relating to notice of meeting and passing appropriate resolution, is that failure to do so, in most cases, leads to the invalidation of the meeting convened and held and its outcomes. Great care must, therefore, be taken to ensure that valuable time and scare resources are not dissipated on meetings that will ultimately be declared ineffectual and of no consequence by the Courts.

Practical Steps to Remove a Director from Office

Where, for any reason, a company receives a special notice proposing a resolution to remove a director from office before the end of his tenure, it shall immediately forward the notice to the director concerned (whether he is a shareholder in the company or not). The director involved is entitled to be heard at the meeting when the resolution for his removal is to be discussed (s. 288(2) CAMA 2020), (s. 262 (2).

If on the receipt of the notice of resolution to remove him from office, the director concerned makes written representations (of a reasonable length) to the company concerning the notice and requests that his representations be sent to the members, the company shall do so, except if the request from the director came too late with respect to the date that has been fixed for the meeting (s. 288 (3) CAMA 2020), (s. 262(3).

The main problem with the provisions of the above section is the subjective terms used. First is the phrase 'of a reasonable length' in describing the volume of the representations that a director should send to the company before same would be sent to members, on the director's request. The second is the phrase 'too late' in describing the timing of the receipt of the director's representations and it will not be sent to the members. Both terms, 'of a reasonable length' and 'too late' are subjective. Added to this is that, whether a director's representation is of a reasonable length or not or came in too late or not, is to be decided by the company itself. Recall that it is the company that is also the entity that wants to remove the director from office. We submit that there should be better certainty in the process described above with identifiable timelines and terms.

We submit further that certainty of the terms used, especially in statutes, should be guaranteed, instead of leaving rooms for conjectures and guesswork. For instance, a provision in section 288(3) above asking that a director send in his representations but with a two-page summary of same on an A4 size paper to be sent to the members, if he desires, will create certainty in the process. Also, a provision that gives specific timeline, like the representations are to be received by the company, not less than 10 days to the date of the proposed meeting, if same is to be sent to the members. This will create further certainty and clarity in the process. We propose that section 288 (3) CAMA 2020 be re-casted in more certain terms.

Where a company is to send a director's representations to its members, it shall:

- include in the notice of the resolution to the members the fact that representations have been made by the director concerned; and
- then send a copy of the director's representations to every member of the company to whom notice of the meeting is sent (whether before or after receipt of the representations by the company).

If the company did not send the director's representations to the members as he had requested, either because the request came late or because of the company's fault, the director may require that his representations be read out at the meeting. This will not prejudice the director's right to make oral representations during the meeting proper to the members on the resolution seeking to remove him from office as a director.

The company or any person who claims to be aggrieved may apply to Court on the ground that the rights conferred by section 288(3) CAMA 2020, (s. 262 (3) to have the director's representations sent out to members and be read out at the meeting are being abused to secure needless publicity for matters that are defamatory. If the Court is satisfied with the application and agrees that the rights are being abused, then no representations by the director need be sent out to members or be read in the meeting. Additionally, the Court may order that the company's costs in bringing the application be paid wholly or partially by the director. This is notwithstanding the fact that the director was not a party to the application (proviso to s. 288(3)(b), (s. 262(3)(b).

Note that there is no provision in the CAMA for the costs incurred by a person who feels aggrieved, as stated above, and brought a similar application to Court. It is apparent that such a person would have to bear the full costs of such an application. Is this a way to discourage individual applications to Court in this respect and make it a matter for the company to decide when to apply to Court or not? Otherwise, why is the Court only given the powers to award costs to the company, and this is so, even where the company is not made a party to the matter before the Court by the applicant?

After a Director Has Been Removed from Office

Where a director has been removed from office by a company in a general meeting, the vacancy created by such removal, if not filled at the meeting where he was removed, may be subsequently filled by the directors as a casual vacancy. This is usually done via board resolutions and captured in the minutes of the board meetings. The continued efficacy of the replacement of a director by the board is subject to subsequent approval and ratification by the general meeting (s. 288(4) CAMA 2020), (s. 262 (4).

Where a person has been appointed a director in place of the director removed at a general meeting (whether the appointment was made during the general meeting or subsequently by the directors) the person so appointed shall be treated, for purposes of directors' rotation and retirement on the board, as having been appointed on the day the person he replaced as a director was last appointed a director of the company (s. 288(4)(5) CAMA 2020), (s. 262(4)(5).

A director removed from the board of directors is entitled to compensation or damages payable to him in respect of the termination of his appointment. He is also entitled to same on any other appointment(s) that terminates with his directorship. Where, therefore, a company removes a managing director (or an executive director) in breach of his contract of service, the person so removed can recover damages from the company (s. 288 (6) CAMA 2020), (s. 262 (6); *Iwuchukwu* v. *Nwizu (1994) 7 NWLR Pt. 257, 379).*

The question as to whether or not the removal of a managing director is a breach of his service contract with the company depends on the terms of his appointment. In this respect, the terms of each person's (director's) service contract will have to be reviewed before any assessment of a possible breach or otherwise could be made. Where a director has a contract of service, his removal from office other than in accordance with the terms of such a contract entered pursuant to the company's Articles, would be wrongful removal and he would be entitled to recover compensation from the company, including damages, for wrongful dismissal *(Orojo, 255).*

The company secretary would have several official duties to perform after a director(s) has resigned, is removed or vacates his office from the board of a company. The roles are multi-faceted, both in law proper and in corporate governance, and the below are by no means exhaustive, but they include:

- the proper documentation of the fact and process relating to the vacation, resignation or removal of the directors(s);
- the documentation could be in the form of keeping proper minutes of meetings where the decision(s) was taken, keeping safe the resolution passed in such meetings and keeping safe custody of any correspondences relating to the event(s);
- updating the company's register of directors, register of directors' shareholding, register of directors' residential addresses, etc.;
- the fact and details of any changes on the board shall be entered in the register of directors as required by sections 318, 319, 320 & 321 CAMA 2020 (s. 292);
- the company secretary will have to file Form CAC 7 (indicating the appointment of a new director, if the removed director was replaced in the meeting or subsequently);
- the company secretary files the needed *Form CAC 7A* (Notice of Vacation of Office/Removal or Resignation of Director) with the Corporate Affairs

Commission (Commission) to reflect the changes. The Form is to be filed within 14 days from when the change(s) occurred;

- it may be necessary to communicate any change(s) to the company's staff, shareholders, bankers, external solicitors, auditors, consultants, stock exchange (for public companies) and any other relevant stakeholders that might be interested in or affected by the changes in question;
- it might be necessary to print new stationeries, where for instance, the names of the former directors are listed on the existing ones;
- it might be necessary to update the company's website and directors' profiles thereon to keep all stakeholders up to date. This is always a problem with several companies as the names of former directors are usually left on their websites, sometimes for years, after they have ceased to be directors in the company, thereby misleading those seeking information about the company;
- there might be the need for the company secretary to organize a familiarizing tour (induction) of the company for any new director (if the one removed was replaced at the meeting or subsequently).

The company secretary plays pivotal roles with respect to issues bordering on the appointment, the tenure in office, resignation, suspension and removal of directors from office. The process of a director leaving office, either voluntarily or otherwise, is mostly procedural and involves a lot of due process and regulatory compliance activities. It is the duty of the company secretary to ensure that these processes and procedures are complied with. This is because all the statutory notices required to be issued in this respect emanate from the company secretary's office. For instance, where the board of directors intends to summon a particular director for disciplinary purposes or to remove him from office for truancy, incompetence or any other reason(s) (where the company's Articles allow) it is the duty of the company secretary to issue the necessary letters and notices to the director concerned on being instructed by the board, through the chairman.

It is also the duty of the company secretary to write, on the direction of the board chairman, to notify any particular director(s) when circumstances occur that would warrant the director to vacate his office. For instance, where particular threshold of shareholding requirement for directors is mandated by a company's Articles, a director who fails in that respect would have to vacate his office, except he rectifies the deficit. It is the duty of the company secretary, on the instruction of the board chairman, to notify the particular director of the fact of his imminent vacation of office, until the defect is remedied, where possible.

As noted above, the company secretary has the responsibility for diverse notifications when a change occurs on the board. Where there is the need to notify staff members, consultants and other stakeholders about the change(s) on the board and effect any change(s) to the company's identity projection to outsiders, including its website and stationeries, it is the company secretary that undertakes such tasks, sometimes, in liaison with the compliance unit and the corporate branding unit, where these exist independently.

In terms of removal of directors from office before the end of their tenure, this process is also procedural, even technical, in some respects. The CAMA requires that a special notice of the resolution to be proposed at the general meeting should be sent to all the members along with the notice of the meeting. The director sought to be removed is also to be served with these documents and is entitled to make representations, presenting his own case. He may decide to request that his representations be sent to the members, though he will still be afforded the opportunity to make an oral presentation at the meeting.

If the director is removed at the general meeting, the meeting may also replace the director with another director, whose proposal to be appointed would have been communicated by a special notice to the members. Otherwise, the directors may fill the vacancy on the board subsequently as a casual vacancy. However, the efficacy of the replacement director's appointment will be after the general meeting must have approved the appointment made by the board of directors.

THE CHECKPOINTS

✓A director in a company can be removed from office at any time before the end of his tenure by the members in a general meeting, for which special notice of the proposed resolution has been given. This includes directors who have purportedly been appointed by the company as 'directors for life.'

✓In removing a director from office as above, it is imperative to strictly follow the procedures stipulated by the CAMA or the company's Articles, whichever is being relied on to remove him. Otherwise, the removal will be invalidated by the Courts, on the application of the concerned director. It is noted above that the Courts hardly re-instate a removed director back to office, being that the company has a statutory power to remove its directors, but damages for wrongful removal may be awarded.

✓To remove a director from office, the notice of meeting and a notice of the special notice of the proposed resolution to do so must be served on all the members entitled to attend the meeting, and on the director himself.

✓When served with the notice proposing his removal from office, the director concerned is entitled to make representations (concise and promptly) to the company and ask that same be circulated to the members. This aside, he is also entitled to orally address the general meeting on his representations against the resolution to remove him.

✓The company or an aggrieved person can approach the Court to stop the director's representations being read out to the members in general meeting. The Court will so order that the director's representations not be read, if it is satisfied that the representations are an abuse of the right granted by the relevant section of the CAMA, or that they are defamatory. Otherwise, the Court will decline to make the order.

✓Although the most popular route to removing directors from office is through the members in a general meeting, however, where a company's Articles so provide, directors (forming a requisite quorum) may remove a director from office and inform the general meeting for subsequent approval and ratification.

✓Non-compliance with processes and procedures in removing a director will render the removal void and of no effect. Normally, when approached, the Court will set aside such irregular procedures and the outcomes. Strict adherence to the laid down procedures and processes is advised in attempting to remove a director from office.

✓The Courts will usually award damages and other compensations to directors who are considered irregularly removed from office, but, as noted above, very rarely will the Courts grant re-instatement of the director to his position. The directors also rarely ask for re-instatement from the Courts.

✓The company secretary, working mostly with the board chairman, plays pivotal roles in the whole chain of vacation of office by company directors (resignation, suspension and removal). This ranges from initiating notices for the general meeting called to remove a director from office to all post-vacation changes to the internal structures and records within the company, then to regulatory compliance and other external notifications.

✓Once a director(s) has been removed from office, all post-removal notifications to the Commission and to the other regulatory agencies, stakeholders, shareholders, partners (both foreign and local) are within the purview of the duties of the company secretary. So, also, are all post-removal processes and procedures to be adopted or adapted. For instance, changing stationeries and communication channels that have the names of all directors listed thereon, changing the signatories and mandates to the company's bank accounts, if the removed director(s) was one of the signatories, etc.

Chapter 11

MEMBERSHIP IN A COMPANY

INTRODUCTION

In general, every company is composed of members, although the law views a company as a distinct legal entity from these members and directors. With respect to a company limited by shares, the medium of shareholding creates the nexus and proprietary interests in the company and therefore membership in the company.

The terms 'shareholder' and 'member' are then often used synonymously *(Palmers, 527).* The terms are also so used in this chapter, although it has been held that the terms 'shareholder' and 'member' may be synonymous in some cases but may not be so in all cases *(Ponmile* v. *Sparks Electrics Nig. Ltd (1986) 2 NWLR Pt. 23, 519).* In drawing this distinction in *Oilfield Supply Centre Ltd* v. *Johnson (No. 2) (1987) 2 NWLR Pt. 58, 625*, the Court reasoned that, for instance, the share certificate is not the only means of establishing a shareholding in a company, but that oral evidence, when cogent, may suffice. This was distinguished from membership in a company, where the entry of a person's name in the register of members is a *sine qua non for membership (Jethwani & Anor.* v. *Nigeria Wire Ind. Plc (1999) 5 NWLR Pt. 602, 326; Starcola Nig. Ltd* v. *Adeniji & Ors (1972) 1 All NLR, 49).* All things considered, it has been held that, as a fundamental principle of law in this respect, except where there is an express provision to the contrary, the person whose name is on the register of members, is the member, to the exclusion of any other person(s). This remain so unless and until the register is rectified *(Enviroco Ltd* v. *Farstad Supply A/S (2011) 2 BCLC, 165; Hannigan, 303).*

WHAT CONSTITUTES MEMBERSHIP IN A COMPANY?

Under section 105 CAMA 2020, (s. 79), there are two classes of persons who have been statutorily conferred with the status of membership in a company. They are:

- a subscriber of the Memorandum of a company who shall be deemed to have agreed to become a member of the company, and on the registration of the company the subscriber shall be entered as member in the company's register of members;
- every other person who agrees, in writing, to become a member of a company, and whose name is entered in its register of members, shall be a member of the company *(Alalade* v. *Northline Ind. & Agric Serv. Ltd (2003) 14 NWLR Pt. 839, 172, 186; Sparks Electrics (Nig) Ltd* v. *Ponmile (1986) 2 NWLR Pt. 23, 516, 522).*

As it pertains to a company with share capital, each member becomes a shareholder in the company and shall hold at least one share, except in relation to a company with only one shareholder (s. 105 (3) CAMA 2020). (The one- shareholder company is recognized under the CAMA 2020, but not under the repealed CAMA 2004).

It is important to appreciate the distinction between the two ways of becoming a member in a company as stated above. In the case of a subscriber to the Memorandum, his agreement to be a member is deemed by the fact of the subscription to the Memorandum and no other formal agreement is required for his membership. However, in the case of persons who agree in writing to become members, for instance, by having the company's shares transferred to them, the agreement to take the shares is usually not enough for the person to be considered a member. To be effective, the person's name must also be entered in the company's register of members *(Jethwani & Anor.* v. *Nigeria Wire Ind. Plc (1999) 5 NWLR Pt. 602, 326).*

In addition, it is also important to note that the fact that a person's name has been entered in a company's register of members does not automatically make such a person a member in the company. The person in question must have also agreed to be a member and must have authorized that his name be entered in the company's register of members. This emphasizes the element of agreement or authorization for a person's name to be in the register of members, for it to be a validating document as to membership of a company. Where the contrary situation is established, for instance, that a person did not authorize his name to be entered in a company's register of members, such a register must be rectified and the person's name removed.

If the company's share(s) is held jointly by two or more persons, then, each of them is a member in the company *(Permanent Trustee of New South Wales Ltd* v. *Palmer (1929) 42 CLR 277; Mayson et al., 394).*

Avenues to Membership in a Company

There are several ways through which a person may become a member in a company. These ways have been summarized as follows:

- by a person's subscription to the company's Memorandum on the incorporation of the company;
- by a person agreeing with the company to take a share(s) in the company and then have his name being entered in its register of members;
- by a person taking a transfer of the company's share(s) to himself and having his name being subsequently entered in the register of members;
- by a person being a beneficiary of a transmission of shares by operation of law (mostly from the estate of deceased beneficiaries or trusts), then having his name being entered in the register of members *(Palmers, 528).*

The company's secretary's job in terms of the membership of a company is not with any complication. The beginning and the ending of a person's membership in a company is having his name in the register of members. It is key. Though the term 'shareholder' and 'member' are used synonymously in most legal texts, the fact is that without the name of a shareholder being entered in the company's register of members, his membership is inchoate and such a person, most likely, will not be entitled to most of membership benefits that accrue, for instance, receipt of dividends. This will be discussed in full later.

In order to ensure to ensure certainty of the membership base for the company, the company secretary, should, as much as possible, assist to make sure that all those whose names are qualified to be in the register of members are entered into the register. This includes a situation where a member dies, becomes bankrupt or of unsound mind and his shares will have to transmit to his personal representatives or others authorized by law. Conversely, efforts should also be made to ensure that those who are not qualified to be in the register of members are not there. This is to avoid situations where quality time and resources are wasted in dealing with issues surrounding membership and constant requests for the rectification of membership register. All other corporate governance issues that have to do with membership in a company also come under a head like this.

CAPACITY FOR MEMBERSHIP OF A COMPANY

Under section 106 CAMA 2020, (s. 80), every person has a right to be a member in a company, except:

- if he has been found by a Court of law to be of unsound mind. We saw earlier in *Hunpunu-Wusu* v. *Hunpunu-Wusu (1969)1 All NLR, 62*, that the Supreme Court held that the terms 'unsound mind', 'mental illness', 'mental disorder' and 'insanity', among others, are interchangeable and can be used as such. It has to be noted that a person's unsoundness of mind has to be affirmed by a Court of competent jurisdiction to be a disqualifying factor in this respect.
- if he is an undischarged bankrupt;
- if it is a corporate body in liquidation.

It is noteworthy that a person under the age of 18 shall not be counted for the purpose of determining the legal minimum number of members in a company. This is because under common section 20 (2) CAMA 2020 & 2004, a person under 18 years may join in the formation of a company if there are two other persons who are not otherwise disqualified, who are also members. This provision needs to read having in mind the provisions of section 18(2) CAMA 2020, which allows for a single-member private company to be formed by whoever desires to so do, with requisite capacity.

RIGHTS CONFERRED BY MEMBERSHIP IN A COMPANY

The fact of being a member in a company confers certain rights on the member(s), either as stated in the company's Articles, as adopted from the common law or provided by the relevant statutory provisions. These rights are those that can be enforced by the member(s) concerned in Court, either through a declaration or through an injunction to restrain the company from breaching them. Some of these rights are the rights to:

- apply to Court to prohibit the company by injunction from entering into any transaction that is *ultra vires* the company by exceeding the powers conferred by its Memorandum (s. 44 CAMA 2020), (s. 39);
- sue to enforce any right that is owed to him as a member under the company's Memorandum or Articles (s. 46 (4) CAMA 2020), (s. 41 (4);
- receive a copy of the company's Memorandum and Articles, on request (s. 47(1) CAMA 2020), (s. 42 (1);
- attend and vote at any of the company's general meetings and to speak with respect to any resolution before the meeting (s. 107 CAMA 2020), (s. 81); *(Sun Insurance Plc & Anor.* v. *LMB Stockbrokers Ltd & Ors (2005) 12 NWLR Pt. 940, 608, 631);*

- inspect the register of members and index without a fee (s. 112 CAMA 2020), (s. 87 (1);
- object to a notice that is less than 21 days for the company's annual general meeting (s. 241 (2) (a) CAMA 2020), (s. 217 (2)(a);
- receive the notice of a company's general meeting (s. 243 (a) CAMA 2020), (s. 219 (a);
- inspect the minutes book of the company's general meetings (s. 267 (1) CAMA 2020, (s. 242 (1);
- inspect the register of directors kept by the company without a fee (s. 318 (5) CAMA 2020. Unlike section 292 CAMA 2004, which created a combined register for directors and secretaries, CAMA 2020 created separate registers for them. However, the register of secretaries under section 336 is made mandatory for only public companies, which is understandable, as only public companies are under obligation to appoint a company secretary under the CAMA 2020. For private companies that are classified as small companies, appointing a company secretary is optional.
- bring an action to protect the right of minority shareholders by declaration or injunction under section 343 CAMA 2020, (s. 300);
- bring a derivative action on behalf of the company (s. 346 CAMA 2020); (s. 303);
- apply to Court for relief on the ground of unfairly prejudicial or oppressive conduct (ss. 353 – 356 CAMA 2020), (ss. 310-313);
- sue for and recover declared dividends from the company within 12 years of declaration (s. 432 CAMA 2020, (s. 385); *(Re Severn & Wye and Severn Bridge Railway Co. (1896) 1 Ch 559)*;
- sell, mortgage or otherwise dispose of his shares in the company as he deems fit (except as otherwise provided for by the Memorandum and Articles) *(Iwuchukwu* v. *Nwizu (1994) 7 NWLR Pt. 257, 379).*

Under section 82 CAMA 2004, a term of imprisonment of not more than 7 years with an option of fine was imposed on anyone who impersonates another person's membership in a company in obtaining or trying to obtain the benefits conferred by such membership. However, under section 108 CAMA 2020, the punishment template was changed to:

- a term of imprisonment of not more than 7 years or a fine as the Court deems fit;

- pay such additional fine(s) as the Commission may specify by regulation; and
- account to the aggrieved member for any benefit(s) which he directly or indirectly derived as a result of his act of impersonation.

A point needs to be made about the sanctions stipulated above under section 108, wherein after a person has been convicted for impersonation and sent to jail or fined by the Court, the Commission may also specify additional fine for the person to pay for the same breach. Does the provision constitute double jeopardy in favour of the alleged impostor as a defence as was determined in *Nigerian Army v. Aminu Kano (2010) 5 NWLR Pt. 1188, 429?* It would appear so, although a final word on the implication of the provision will have to wait until the Courts pronounce on it.

Still on the issue of membership in a company and rights attached thereto, a clear note should be taken that common section 27 (3) CAMA 2020 and 2004, permits shares in a company to be held in trust by a member for another person. However, such a fact of trust relationship and the name of the beneficiary of the shares must be disclosed in the company's Memorandum.

From a corporate governance perspective, the enforcement of membership rights in a company is an area where the company secretary plays very pivotal roles. According to the *World Bank Group (IFC, 86-92),* the company secretary sits, literally, at the centre of the machinery for the enforcement of membership rights in a company, working with the board and management and also working with the members in symbiotic relationships. Shareholders rights have been listed above.

The company secretary also ensures that the powers of shareholders are protected and allowed to be exercised by members without any restriction(s). Shareholder powers here will include the powers to participate in the amendment of the company's constitutional documents, amending the company's capital structure and object clauses, appointing and removing directors, etc. In some literature, these powers are also classified and discussed as the rights of shareholders, without any dichotomy between their rights and powers as the World Bank Group has adopted.

LIABILITIES OF MEMBERS IN A COMPANY

As the fact of membership in a company confers certain rights on the members, it also entails certain liabilities, depending on the nature of the shareholding and the type of company involved.

For a company limited by shares, common section 21 (1)(a) CAMA 2020 and 2004, states that the liability of its members shall be limited by the Memorandum to the amount, if any, unpaid on the shares held by each member. For a company limited by guarantee, common section 21 (1)(b) CAMA 2020 and 2004, states that the liability of its members shall be limited by the Memorandum to such amount as the members may respectively thereby undertake to contribute to the assets of the company in the event of its being wound up. For an unlimited company, it does not have any limit on the liability of its members and the members have to make full contributions to settle the obligations of the company, if any, unpaid on the shares (common section 21(1)(c) CAMA 2020 and 2004).

Liability of Members Prior to Winding-Up

For a company limited by shares, the liability of the members shall be to contribute the balance, if any, of the amount payable in respect of the shares held by him in accordance with the terms of the agreement under which the shares were issued. It could also be in accordance with a call validly made by the company pursuant to its Articles, at any time prior to the winding-up of the company (s. 117 (1) CAMA 2020), (s. 92 (1).

For a company limited by guarantee, the liability to contribute is activated only when the company is being wound up (s. 117 (4)(d) CAMA 2020), (s. 92 (4)(d).

For a company limited by shares, a member who is due to make a contribution to the company based on a call made and has undertaken personal liability to make future payments for the shares issued to him in the future, will still be liable to pay such sum. This is notwithstanding the fact that the shares were subsequently transferred or forfeited as provided for in the Articles. However, the member's liability in this respect will cease if and when the company receives payment in full in respect of the shares (s. 117(2) CAMA 2020), (s. 92 (2).

Liability of Members on Winding-Up

On the winding-up of a company, every past and present member shall be liable to contribute to the assets of the company to an amount sufficient to meet its debts, liabilities, costs, charges and expenses of winding-up and for adjusting the rights of the members and past members among themselves (s.117 (3) CAMA 2020), (s. 92(3).

The above is a general rule and has certain qualifications and exceptions under section 117 (4) CAMA 2020, (s. 92 (4). These are:

- a past member is excluded from contribution if he ceased to be a member for a period of one (1) year or more before the winding-up proceedings commenced;
- a past member shall not be liable to contribute unless it appears to the Court that the existing members are unable to satisfy the contributions required to be made by them in this regard;
- for a company limited by shares, no contribution is required from any present or past member exceeding the amount, if any, remaining unpaid on the shares for which he is liable;
- for a company limited by guarantee, no contribution is required from any present or past member exceeding the amount undertaken to be contributed by him to the assets of the company on winding-up;
- any sum due from the company to a member in his capacity as a member, by way of dividends or other payments, shall not be set-off against the amount for which he is to contribute in the event of a winding-up; but any such sum is to be taken into account for the purposes of the final adjustment of the rights of the members and past members among themselves.

When Members Will Have Increased Liability

We have seen the liabilities that could attach to members of a company before and during winding-up of the company, depending on the genre. However, there are circumstances where the members of a company will have their liabilities increased beyond what would otherwise be normal:

- where the member agrees in writing under section 54 CAMA 2020 (s. 49) for an increased liability after the alteration of the Memorandum and Articles;
- where the number of directors in a company, not being a small company under section 271 CAMA 2020, falls below two (2) and the company carried on business for more than sixty (60) days, a director or member who is aware of such a situation shall also be liable for the company's liabilities and debts, incurred during the period.

PROTECTION OF CORPORATE AND MEMBERSHIP RIGHTS

A registered company is a distinct legal person separate from the directors and the members and with its own rights and liabilities. It has the right to sue and be sued in its corporate name. As a general rule, the company is the proper plaintiff to bring an action in Court for any wrong that has been done to it. This is provided for under section 341 CAMA 2020, (s. 299), that 'subject to the provisions of this Act, where irregularity has been committed in the course of a company's affairs or any wrong is done to the company, only the company can sue to remedy that wrong and only the company can ratify the irregular conduct.' The phrase 'subject to the provisions of the Act' as used here is crucial, because it subordinates the provision in question to other provisions of the Act *(Oke* v. *Oke (1974) 1 ALL NLR Pt. 1, 443,450; NDIC* v. *Okem Enterprise Limited (2004) 10 NWLR Pt. 880,107, Oloruntoba-Oju* v. *Abdul-Raheem (2009) 13 NWLR Pt. 1157, 83).* In essence, the section presupposes that the Act could contain, and in fact, does contain, other provisions that could confer counter rights on individual members of a company.

Over the years, the above principle has been crystallized in the common law and company law jurisprudence as the rule in *Foss* v. *Harbottle (1843) 2 Hare, 461).* This rule has been applied in Nigeria in a variety of cases by Nigerian Courts including the following cases *(Shodeinde* v. *Registered Trustees of Ahmadiyya Movement in Islam (1980) 1-2 S.C., 163; Amaye* v. *AREC (1990) 4 NWLR Pt. 145, 422; Tanimola* v. *Surveys and Mapping Geodata Ltd (1995) 6 NWLR Pt. 403,617; A-G. Lagos State* v. *Eko Hotels Ltd & Anor. (2006) 18 NWLR Pt. 1011, 378; Elufioye* v. *Halilu (1993) 6 NWLR Pt. 301, 570).* An important point to be made is that the principle does not apply to incorporated companies alone. It was held in *Abubakari & Ors* v. *Smith & Ors (1973) LPELR-56*, that the rule in *Foss* v. *Harbottle* is also applicable to an unincorporated association possessing a constitution or a set of rules and regulations entitling it to sue and be sued as a legal entity. In this case, it was a religious society, the *Jamat-ul-Muslim of Lagos*, that was involved, and the Supreme Court concluded that the rule applies to a religious body in the same way and to the same extent as it does to a limited liability company or a trade union.

In simple terms, the rule in *Foss* v. *Harbottle* as applied by the Courts over years, is that it is only a company (or association), through its majority shareholders, that is the proper plaintiff to sue for any wrong that has been done to the company. It is noteworthy that for the rule to apply, the issue being complained about must relate to a wrong done to the company itself, which would otherwise not be redressed, and not an issue that pertains to shareholders' individual rights in the company, as members *(Okoya* v. *Santili (1990) 2 NWLR Pt. 131, 172, 203).* It has to be noted, as was held by the Supreme Court in *Elufioye & Ors* v. *Halilu & Ors (1993) LPELR-1120*, that the rule applies only where the majority can ratify the irregularity being complained about. In essence, where the act being complained about is incapable of being ratified by the majority, for instance, where it is an absolute illegality, the rule is inapplicable.

The rule in *Foss* v. *Harbottle* can be said to be a rule of *corporate locus standi*, granting only the company, association or entity, in its own right, the authority to commence any action(s) in its own behalf and name, if desired, for any wrong it has suffered. However, there are a few exceptions, under some specific circumstances where the rule will not apply. These circumstances comprise mostly of common law rules, interpreted by the Courts over the years. Some of these exceptions to the rule have been codified in statutes in different common law countries.

Exceptions to the Rule in *Foss* v. *Harbottle*

There have been several exceptions to the rule in *Foss* v. *Harbottle* that have been statutorily provided for and judicially affirmed in Nigeria in several instances. In some instances, these have been incorporated into the CAMA and pronounced on in decided cases. These exceptions come in the form of members' right to individual and derivative actions in deserving cases. In the case of *CBN* v. *Kotoye (1994) 3 NWLR Pt. 330, 66,* the Court restated the rule in *Foss* v. *Harbottle* and then its exceptions, holding that:

- the rule cannot override any clear statutory provision that provides to the contrary;
- the rule does not detract or take away a right conferred by the Constitution;
- the rule does not affect an action instituted to protect the invasion of the personal right of an individual member in a company in his capacity as a member.

In any of the above instances, any attempt to use to the rule in *Foss* v. *Harbottle* as a defence or bar to the action(s) instituted, will fail, without much ado.

Member's Individual Action

The CAMA has provided several remedies for members in a company to protect their individual rights when same are infringed or there is an imminent threat of infringement, in any way. The remedies enunciated below are also considered as exceptions to the general rule in *Foss* v. *Harbottle as* stated above.

Under section 343 (a-g) CAMA 2020, (s. 300 (a)-(f), a member in a company may bring an action to restrain the company either by declaration or injunction from doing anything that could infringe on his right(s) or interest(s) as a member. In this respect, the company could be restrained from:

1. entering into a transaction which is illegal or *ultra vires (Hutton* v. *West Cork Rly Co. (1883) 23 Ch.D., 654; Parke* v. *Daily News (1962) 2 All ER, 929; Edokpolo & Co. Ltd* v. *Sem-Edo Wire Ind. Ltd & Ors (1984) LPELR-1017).* The only seeming drawback to the possibility of enforcing this right would be that of dearth of information to the member(s) on the company's activities, to enable him act on time. Directors usually plan most of the actions for a company and execute same without the members being aware of the plans. Some of the plans would already have been fully executed before the members are notified or become aware, depending on the nature of the project.
2. purporting to do by ordinary resolution any act which by its constitution or the CAMA requires to be done by a special resolution *(Pender* v. *Lushington (1877) Ch.D., 670; Cotter* v. *National Union of Seamen (1929) 2 Ch 58; Edward* v. *Halliwell (1950) 2 All ER, 1064*);
3. any act or omission affecting the applicant's individual right as a member (*Pender* v. *Lushington (1877) Ch.D., 670)*;
4. committing fraud on either the company or minority shareholders where the directors fail to take appropriate action to redress the wrong done *(Menier* v. *Hooper Telegraph Works (1874) 9 Ch. App, 350; Beach* v. *Sullivan (1957) 1 WLR, 1247); Cook* v. *Deeks (1916) 1 A.C., 503);*
5. where a meeting of the company cannot be called in time to be of practical use in redressing a wrong done to the company or to the minority shareholders *(Okeowo* v. *Migliore (1979) 11 SC, 138*; and
6. where the directors are likely to derive a profit or benefit, or have profited or benefitted from their negligence or from their breach of duty *(Orojo, 210).*

Section 343(g) CAMA 2020, adds a new ground on which an action can be maintained against a company by a member, that is, for:

> 'any other act or omission, where the interest of justice so demands.'

This seems to be an omnibus ground for an application, in some respects. In *Ahmad* v. *Barau & Anor (2021) LPELR-56180*, the phrase, 'in the interest of justice' was said to connote 'exercise of discretion by the lower Court,' meaning that it is left to the Court to decide, one way or the other, whether to grant the application or not, jettisoning any hard and fast rules *(Awoyale* v. *Ogunbiyi (1985) NWLR Pt. 10, 861; Contract Resources Nigeria Limited* v. *Standard Trust Bank Ltd (2013) 6 NWLR Pt. 1350, 261; Durbar Hotel Limited* v. *Kasaba United Ltd (2017) 2 NWLR Pt. 1549, 321.*

Under section 344 CAMA 2020, a member who institutes an action under any of the grounds listed above, whether individually or in a representative capacity, is entitled to damages for any loss on account of the breach of that right. The member is also entitled to a declaration or injunction to restrain the company or the directors from doing the particular act(s) complained about. Where the Court finds any director(s) liable for any wrongdoing, the erring director(s) is to be personally liable in damages to the aggrieved member. The Court may also award costs, in its discretion, to the aggrieved member irrespective of whether the suit is successful or not. It is difficult to see how this provision on costs will work in practice, because, in civil litigation, costs are usually awarded against the losing party *(University of Uyo* v. *Akpan (2013) LPELR-1995* (s. 301(1)(2).

The provisions of section 344 above are marked departures from the equivalent provisions under the repealed section 301 CAMA 2004. This is in two major respects: (i). under section 301, a member who sues to enforce his personal right(s) is not entitled to any damages, but simply to declarative and injunctive reliefs against the company and or the directors from doing the act(s) complained about; (ii) section 301 does not hold director(s) who are found liable personally liable to the aggrieved member(s) in damages, which appears to be a way of getting the directors to sit up in the performance of their duties.

It has been shown above that membership in a company comes with diverse rights to the members, but it also comes with attendant liabilities. Membership rights are those rights that enure to the members, as members of the company. Some of the rights are exercisable against the company itself and some simply to assert the membership rights. These rights range from protection of minority rights to preventing the company, for instance, from entering into an ultra vires transaction. There is also the members' right to relief from unfairly prejudicial conduct and the right to prevent, by injunction or declaration, acts that are illegal or *ultra vires*. For instance, where a company decides to do what the law requires to be done by special resolution by using ordinary resolution, the members are entitled to approach the Court to stop such an act.

From the above, it is the duty of the company secretary to ensure, as much as possible, that due processes are adopted in running the company's affairs. This could be achieved by strict adherence to the stipulations of the law and the company's Articles. This is especially important in cases where non-compliance with the Articles and the provisions of the law will invalidate all activities that have been concluded. An example is a failure to give a member the notice of meeting of the company (s. 245 CAMA 2020), which will, in effect, invalidate the meeting, bar the accidental omission exception. But who wants to be relying on such exception to the general rule when a little more diligence would have saved everyone unnecessary stress? The company secretary continuous advisory to the board of directors is also key, since he is the person that will advise the board that particular intended line(s) of action by the board or management is not within the ambits of the law and should be jettisoned. In other cases, it could simply be a case that the proper procedure, although while being followed by the company, but should be followed to the letter, for validity.

Members' Derivative Actions

Notwithstanding the fact that the rule in *Foss* v. *Harbottle* states that it is the company that is the proper party to sue for any wrong done to it, under certain circumstances, it is possible that the company may be unwilling to bring an action to redress such a wrong. In such circumstances, the law has provided avenues where such a wrong would be redressed on the application of another person(s) acting on behalf of the company. This is usually called a derivative action. Under section 352 CAMA 2020, (s. 309), those who can bring the application to Court for redress are:

- a registered holder or a beneficial owner and a former registered holder or beneficial owner of a company's security;
- a director or officer or a former director or officer of a company;
- the Commission; or

- any other person(s) that the Court in its discretion could permit to make an application under section 346.

Commencing or Continuing a Derivative Action

For a derivative action to be effectively commenced or continued by an applicant on behalf of a company, or in the name of a company or its subsidiary, the applicant, first of all, has to apply to Court for leave. This is usually done *ex-parte*, without putting any other party on notice of the application. This first application will be for leave to either bring the action, intervene to prosecute the action or to discontinue same on behalf of the company (s. 346 (1) CAMA 2020), (s. 303 (1).

Under section 346 (2) CAMA 2020, (s. 303), before granting the leave being sought by an applicant to bring or intervene by derivative action on behalf of a company, the Court must satisfy itself that:

- a cause of action has arisen from an actual or proposed act or omission involving negligence, default, breach of duty, or trust by a director or former director of the company;
- the applicant has given reasonable notice to the directors of the company of his intention to apply to Court, as above;
- the directors of the company do not bring, diligently prosecute, defend, or discontinue the action;
- the applicant's notice to the directors contains a factual basis for the claim and the actual or potential damage caused to the company;
- the applicant acted in good faith. It has been held that lack of good faith does not always imply dishonesty, even though dishonesty, on its part, will always imply lack of good faith *(Cannock Chase District Council* v. *Kelly (1978) 1 All ER, 152; West African Breweries Ltd* v. *Savannah Ventures Ltd (2002) LPELR-3475);* and
- it appears to be in the best interests of the company that the action be brought, prosecuted, defended or discontinued.

It is also provided that the action could actually be against a director or any other person, or against both of them. This is one of the innovations brought to this area by CAMA 2020. Another innovation is the requirement that the cause of action would have arisen from the actual or proposed act or omission before even the application for leave could be brought to Court by the applicant.

On hearing any application brought under section 346 CAMA 2020, (s. 303), the Court may make any order(s) as it deems fit, including an order:

- authorizing the applicant or any other person to control the conduct of the action in Court;
- giving directions for the conduct of the action in Court;
- directing that any amount adjudged by the Court as payable by a defendant in the action is paid, in whole or in part, directly to the former and present security holders in the company, instead of to the company itself; and
- requiring the company to pay reasonable legal fees incurred by the applicant in connection with the proceedings in question (s. 347).

An action properly brought as above shall not be stayed or dismissed by the Court simply because it is shown to the Court that the alleged breach of a right or duty owed to the company has been or may be approved (ratified) by the company's shareholders. However, the Court is entitled to take into cognizance evidence of any such approval in deciding on the orders to make in the suit. In the way same, any such derivative application cannot be stayed, settled, discontinued or dismissed for want of diligent prosecution without an order of Court, upon terms. In making any such order, the Court may ask that the applicant be put on notice, if it determines that the applicant may be substantially affected by any such an order (ss. 348 and 349 CAMA 2020), (ss. 305, 306).

Since the nature of a derivative action is that a shareholder wants to enforce a company's right(s) on its behalf, the company is a necessary party and must be joined as a defendant to the action. This would ensure that, as a party to the suit, the company would be bound by any order made or any judgment entered by the Court *(Unipetrol (Nig) Plc* v. *Agip (Nig) Plc (2002) 14 NWLR Pt. 787, 312, 331; Williams* v. *Edu (2002) 3 NWLR Pt. 754, 400; Ferguson* v. *Wall-Bridge (1935) DLR, 66).* Also, it has been held that a derivative claim by a minority shareholder may be joined in the same claim with his direct personal claim, where the claims arise out of the same transaction *(Prudential Assurance Co. Ltd* v. *Newman Ind. Ltd (No. 2) (1980) 2 All ER 841; Wallersteiner* v. *Moir (No. 2) (1975) 1 All ER, 849; Orojo, 214-5).*

APPLICATION TO COURT ON THE GROUND OF UNFAIRLY PREJUDICIAL AND OPPRESSIVE ACTS

An application can be made to Court by a person qualified to do so under the law (by petition) for relief on the ground that the affairs of the company are being or have been conducted in an illegal or oppressive manner (ss. 353 and 354 CAMA 2020), (ss. 310 and 311). Apart from a member in the company (which includes the personal representative(s) of a deceased member and a person(s) who owns shares by the fact of transfer or transmission, (by operation of law), other persons that are entitled to apply to Court to bring this genre of application are:

- a director, officer or a former director or officer of a company;
- a creditor to the company;
- the Commission or;
- any other person(s) that the Court in its discretion finds as being a proper person(s) to make the application-.

Section 354 (2)(a) CAMA 2020, (s. 311 (2)(a) enumerates the grounds on which an application (petition) could be made to Court by an applicant (member) for relief. This is when there is allegation(s) by a member of the company, that:

- the affairs of the company are being or have been conducted in a manner that is oppressive or unfairly prejudicial to, or unfairly discriminatory against, a member(s), or in a manner that is or has been in disregard of the interests of a member or the members as a whole;
- an act or omission or a proposed act or omission, by or on behalf of the company or a resolution, or a proposed resolution, of a class of members, was, is or would be oppressive or unfairly prejudicial to, or unfairly discriminatory against, a member(s), or was, is or would be oppressive or unfairly prejudicial to, or unfairly discriminatory against, a member or members or was, is or would be in a manner which is in disregard of the interests of a member or the members as a whole.

An application by any other person(s) mentioned in section 353, excluding the Commission, may be brought by that person(s) under section 354 (2)(b) of the Act on the allegation(s) that:

- the affairs of the company have been or are being conducted in a manner that is oppressive or unfairly prejudicial to, discriminatory against or in a manner that is in disregard of the interests of that person(s); or

- an act or omission, or a proposed act or omission was, is or would be oppressive or unfairly prejudicial to, or unfairly discriminatory against, or was or is in disregard of the interests of that person(s).
- An application by the Commission can be made under section 354 (2)(c), where it appears to the Commission in the exercise of its powers under the Act, that:
- the affairs of the company were or are being conducted in a manner that was or is oppressive or unfairly prejudicial to, or unfairly discriminatory against, a member(s), or was or is in disregard of the interests of the public; or
- any actual or proposed act or omission of the company (including an act or omission on its behalf) which was, is or would be oppressive, or unfairly prejudicial to, or unfairly discriminatory against a member(s) in a manner which is in disregard of the interests of the public.

PRINCIPLES GUIDING APPLICATIONS UNDER SECTIONS 353 AND 354

Over the years, certain general principles have been developed that act as guide to the Courts when deciding whether or not to grant an application(s) against a company as sought by any person(s) against alleged 'oppressive or unfairly prejudicial conduct.' The principles are not cast in stone and the Courts do have powers to still use their discretion to grant or refuse applications in diverse circumstances. Some of the established principles are:

- the phrase 'unfairly prejudicial' is general in nature and should be applied by the Courts flexibly to meet the circumstances of each particular case *(Re Saul D. Harrison & Sons Plc (1995) 1 BCLC, 14);*
- the prejudice being complained of by the applicant must be 'harm' in the commercial sense and not in any emotional or sentimental sense (*Re Unisoft Group Ltd (No. 3) (1994) 1 BCLC, 609);*
- a petition could be anchored on acts that were in the past, including those that occurred before the person became a member in the company *(Lloyd* v. *Casey (2002) 1 BCLC, 272);*
- the oppression complained of must be 'burdensome, harsh and wrongful' to the other members of the company or some of them, and lacks the probity which they are genuinely entitled to expect in the running of the

company *(Scottish Cooperative Wholesale Society Ltd* v. *Meyer (1958) 3 All ER 66, 71; Mayson et al, 624-6).*

- added to the fact that the oppression being companied about must be considered to be 'burdensome, harsh and wrongful,' to the applicant or other members, it must be a continuing cause of oppressive conduct and not be an isolated act of oppression *(Williams* v. *Williams (1995) 2 NWLR Pt. 375, 1, 18; Ebrahami* v. *Westbourne Galleries Ltd (1972) 2 All ER, 492; Re: Westbourne Galleries Ltd (1970) 3 All ER, 374; Ogunde* v. *Mobile Films (WA) Ltd (1976) 2 FRCR 10; Orojo, 217).*
- the conduct complained of must relate to the conduct of the affairs of the company and must be concerned with acts done by the company or those authorized to act as its organs. It should not be the conduct of an individual shareholder acting in personal capacity *(Re Legal Costs Negotiators Ltd (1999) 2 BCLC, 171);*
- the conduct complained about must be unfairly prejudicial to the interest of the member, *qua member*, as opposed to other interests which the member may possess *(Re a Company (No. 004475 of 1982) (1983) 2 All ER 36, 44).*

In construing these principles, there has to be, in some cases, a flexibility that will accommodate the essence of the grievance(s) and not simply based on technicalities of the terms used. For instance, it has been submitted that prejudice to a member must be seen from the context of the total gamut of the person's membership in the company. If, for example, a person became a member and one of the terms for his membership in the company is that he continues to be a part of the management team, then, removing the person from top management (like from being a director or general manager) is to be considered a prejudice suffered by him as a member *(O'Neil* v. *Phillips (1999) 2 BCLC, 1).* In all, therefore, each case or situation must be determined on its own peculiar facts.

OTHER ORDERS WHICH THE COURT COULD MAKE

When a person's application on any of the grounds under section 354 of the Act is successful, the Court has a wide latitude in making its orders under section 355 of the Act. The Court could make an order:

- winding-up the company;
- regulating the conduct of the affairs of the company in future;
- allowing the purchase of the member's shares by other members;

- allowing the purchase of the member's shares by the company and for the reduction accordingly of the company's capital;
- directing the company to institute, prosecute, defend, discontinue specific proceedings or authorizing a member to do any of these in the name or on behalf of the company;
- varying or setting aside a transaction or contract to which the company is a party and compensating the company or any other party to the transaction or contract;
- directing the Commission to investigate the company;
- appointing a receiver or a receiver and manager for the company's property;
- restraining a person from engaging in specific conduct or from doing a specific act or thing;
- requiring a person to do a specific act or thing.

A review of the discussions above on member's derivative action(s) or action for unfairly prejudicial conduct by a member manifests a single trend, which is, that these actions are embarked on by members on the basis that the affairs of the company are not being managed in the best interests of the members, as a whole. This would imply that where the affairs of the company are managed in a substantially open and transparent manner for the members to see that their interests and the interests of the company as a going concern are the paramount considerations, the spate of derivative actions and actions to correct unfairly prejudicial conducts by the company would be reduced to the minimum.

The company secretary's major role in these respects is simply advisory, being that he cannot force the hands of the directors in one direction or the other, except when his opinion is sought in particular cases. Moreover, as noted earlier, under section 335(2) CAMA 2020, the company secretary cannot, without the authorization of the board, purport to exercise any of the powers vested in the directors. Having said that, however, what the company secretary should not do is not to raise identified 'red flags' to the attention of the directors, that is, when certain obvious breaches of the company's Articles or the CAMA are being committed within the company. This is especially so when the alleged infraction(s) is being perpetrated by directors or senior management staff. For example, where the directors sought to use an ordinary resolution to approve a matter that requires a special resolution, it would be the duty of the company secretary to object or simply intervene and re-direct the directors on the proper legal path and procedure. It does not matter that the directors may still not take and act on the company secretary's advice.

A problematic scenario will be where the company secretary knowingly and actively partakes, either for pecuniary or any other reasons(s), in the breach of laid down laws and the provisions of the Articles and procedures, to the detriment of the company and members. As was noted earlier, in the case of *Okeowo* v. *Migliore*, the company secretary was so involved with and supported one of the factions on the board that he refused to take any instructions at all from the directors on the other side. That type of conduct that projects an abject lack of professionalism by the company secretary should be avoided, at all costs.

INVESTIGATION OF A COMPANY'S AFFAIRS

One of the ways through which members' rights in a company are protected is through the investigation of the company's affairs by the Commission, under certain circumstances. It has to be noted that a company may, on its own volition, petition the Commission to investigate its own affairs. An investigation may also be actuated by a member's application to the Commission or on the order of a competent Court of law.

Investigation on Members' Application

Under section 357 (1)(3) CAMA 2020, (s. 314 (1)(3), an application could be made to the Commission to investigate the affairs of a company. Such an application would be supported by evidence to convince the Commission that the applicant(s) has a good cause for requiring such an investigation. The Commission would then appoint one or more inspectors to investigate the affairs of the company and report to it.

The only catch with respect to this type of application to investigate a company is that the procedure is only available to a member(s) having a certain threshold of shareholding or having a prescribed number of members signing up to the investigation. For instance:

- for a company with a share capital, the application to the Commission would have to be made by members holding not less than one-tenth of the class of shares issued by the company. The CAMA 2020 lowered the shareholding threshold requirement for an application to be made under this head. Under the CAMA 2004, the requisite shareholding threshold was 25% of the class of shares issued;

- in the case of a company without a share capital, the application would have to be by not less one-tenth of the persons on the company's register of members. The CAMA 2020 lowered the membership threshold requirement for an application to be made under this head. Under the CAMA 2004, the threshold was 25% of the persons on the company's register of members.

A company could also, on its own volition, apply to the Commission for its own affairs to be investigated (s. 357 (2)(c) CAMA 2020), (s. 314 (2)(c). This would seem to imply that the directors of the company will authorize the management to make such an application. It is therefore unlikely that such a scenario will arise where the directors themselves are the ones that would be found culpable by any such investigation by the Commission, except in cases where there is a fractured or divided board of directors, and a fraction of the board members petitions the Commission to investigate the company.

Investigation on the Orders of a Court

Under section 355 (2)(g) CAMA 2020, (s. 312 (2)(g), one of the orders a Court could make when it is satisfied that the affairs of a company are being conducted in an unfairly prejudicial manner, is to order the Commission to investigate the affairs of the company. Under section 358 CAMA 2020, (s. 315 (1)(2), when a Court directs the Commission to investigate the affairs of a company, the Commission is mandated to appoint one or more inspectors to undertake such an investigation and report back to it. The Commission can only appoint inspectors if it appears to it that there are circumstances suggesting any of the following, that is:

- the company's affairs are being or have been conducted with intent to defraud its creditors or the creditors of any other person, or in a manner which is unfairly prejudicial to some part of its members;
- any actual or proposed act or omission by the company (including an act or omission on its behalf) is or would be so prejudicial as above; or
- that the company was formed for any fraudulent or unlawful purpose;
- the persons concerned with the company's formation or the management of its affairs have, in connection therewith, been guilty of fraud, misfeasance or other misconduct towards it or towards its members; or
- the company's members have not been given all the information with respect to its affairs, which they might reasonably expect. For instance, a

consistent failure to hold annual general meeting to lay accounts before the members *(Thorne, 352).*

If in the course of the investigation an inspector is of the opinion that a subsidiary or holding company of the company under investigation needs to be investigated also, to be able to accomplish his task, he is entitled to do so. An inspector is entitled to make an informal report to the Commission on his findings, without an interim report, before making a formal report of his findings at the end of the investigations (s. 359 (1)(2) CAMA 2020), (s. 316 (1)(2).

All officers and agents of the company and all officers and agents of any other body being investigated by the inspector(s) are mandated to produce all books and document(s) in their custody to the inspector(s). They are also mandated to attend before the inspector(s), if required, and to give the inspector(s) all the necessary assistance to do his job. Any failure or refusal by any of the person(s) mentioned above to do what is required of him or otherwise cooperate with the inspector(s) may, depending on the circumstances, be treated as a contempt of Court (ss. 360-362 CAMA 2020, (ss. 317-319).

The inspector's report, when certified by the Commission as a true copy, shall be admissible in any legal proceedings as evidence of the opinion of the inspector(s) in relation to any matter contained in the report (s. 368 CAMA 2020), (s. 325).

Finally, in all the inspections above, the basic guiding principle is that the inspectors must act fairly and give any person(s) invited or interviewed the opportunity to make a response before indicting or otherwise criticizing him in their report*(Re Pergamon Press Ltd (1971) Ch, 388; Thorne, 292).* This presupposes that a person who has been indicted or criticized in a report submitted to the Commission and who feels that he has not been afforded a fair opportunity to state his case, can actually approach the Court to set aside the report. This will be a classical case to raise the issue of breach of the person's right to fair hearing, as constitutionally guaranteed under section 36 of the 1999 Constitution (as amended) *(Tunbi* v. *Opawole (2000) 2 NWLR Pt. 644, 275; Ndukauba* v. *Kolomo & Anor (2005) LPELR-1976; Ndu* v. *State (1990) 7 NWLR Pt. 164, 550; Atanda* v. *State (1988) 3 NWLR Pt. 85, 681; Ogundoyin* v. *Adeyemi (2001) 13 NWLR Pt. 730, 403).*

Actions Based on Inspector's Report

When the inspector(s) appointed as above has concluded investigations and handed in a final report to the Commission, it is totally left to the Commission to decide its next line of action. If it appears to the Commission that civil proceedings ought to be commenced by the company or any other body corporate in the public interests, the Commission may bring the action itself on behalf of the company or any other body. However, if it is a criminal proceeding that is to be brought against any person or body corporate for identified infractions, then, the Commission shall refer same to the office of the Attorney General of the Federation (AGF) for any necessary action, as the AGF would deem fit (ss. 364, 365 CAMA 2020), (ss. 321 & 322).

Appointment of Inspectors to Investigate Ownership of a Company

If it appears to the Commission that there is a good reason to appoint inspectors to investigate the ownership of any registered company in Nigeria, it may appoint one or more inspectors to investigate and report to it on the issue. The inspector(s) will report on the membership of the company for the purposes of determining the true persons who are or have been financially interested in the company's success or failure and have been able to control or materially influence the company's policies (s. 369(1) CAMA 2020), (s. 326(1). The Act does not say what the grounds would be that might raise the suspicion of the Commission in order to institute investigations into a company. However, in general, investigations of this nature usually occur when the company's businesses or activities raise concerns to the public or the authorities as to their overall utility to the economy or raise any security or other sensitive concerns. In such cases, where national security is involved, the security agencies would have concluded some level of clandestine investigations before the civil aspects are openly investigated.

On appointing inspectors under this section, the Commission may prescribe the scope and nature of the investigations, including the period and the aspects of the subject matters that should be investigated (s. 369(2) and (s. 326 (2). It is at the discretion of the Commission to decide whether to furnish the company investigated with a full copy or part thereof of the report or not. The expenses for any investigation(s) as above are to be defrayed out of the Consolidated Revenue Fund (s. 370(2) CAMA 2020), (s. 327).

Lawyers and Bankers' Exceptions

The diverse genre of investigations discussed above and powers to carry them out are not, in any way, at large or blanket. There are exceptions. For instance, the need or requirement for an investigation(s) by the Commission does not require a legal practitioner to disclose to the Commission or to an inspector(s) appointed by it any privileged communication he received as a legal practitioner, except the names and addresses of his client(s). This is in line with section 192 of the *Evidence Act 2011*, which states, among others, that:

> no legal practitioner shall at any time be permitted unless with his clients' express consent to disclose any communication made to him in the course and for the purpose of his employment as such legal practitioner by or on behalf of his client or to state the contents or condition of any document with which he has become acquainted in the course and for the purpose of his professional employment, or to disclose any advice given by him to his client in the course and for the purpose of such employment *(Mekwunye* v. *Carnation Registrars Ltd & Anor (2021) LPELR-55187).*

The exceptions to this general rule are when the legal practitioner receives a communication thought to be for the furtherance of an illegal purpose or when he discovers that a crime or fraud has been committed since his services were engaged by the client.

The same rule as above precludes a company's banker(s) from disclosing to the Commission or its appointed inspector(s) any information as to the affairs of any of their customers (s. 373 CAMA 2020), (s. 330).

Reviewing the discussions in this chapter, it could be seen that in any registered company, the members are the bedrock of its existence. The company belongs to the members, not necessarily as individuals, but as a group of shareholders, whose names have been properly entered into the register of members. It is the law that no company, even if not intended to make profit, can exist without having a membership base. The CAMA also penalizes officers of a company where the membership falls below the prescribed threshold, especially where it is not a one-person company as newly introduced under CAMA 2020, and the company continues to carry on business after that fact.

The company secretary, as always, plays major roles relating to the membership of companies. The first is to ensure that whoever is allotted or procures the shares of the company, either by contract or operation of law, is registered as a member in the membership register. This enables the member to enjoy all the benefits that accrue to membership. Aside this, the company secretary also has the statutory duty to maintain the integrity and security of the register of members (in both cases, above, where the duties are not contracted out to professional registrars). Even when a member dies or goes insane or bankrupt, all the legal processes and procedures to regularize the rights and privileges of those who may want to step into the shoes of the dead, insane or bankrupt members, are within the purview, advisory and otherwise, of the company secretary. This is where his expertise as a legal expert and corporate governance anchor for the company also clearly manifest.

In terms of its effect, membership in a company comes with certain individual and corporate rights. While individual rights enure to members in their individual capacities, their corporate rights enure to them as a collective, as members. The CAMA has given members in a company considerable leverage to be able to protect these rights.

The protection of membership rights first of all comes in two major ways: one is a member suing to protect minority rights where the majority are using their powers and numbers to oppress him and maybe the other minority members. The second is when the affairs of the company are being run in unfairly, prejudicial manner, and this comes in several dimensions, as discussed above. There is also a minor route to this, which is a derivative action. Minor, in the sense that it is for the member(s) to sue on behalf of or in the company's name to try and right a wrong(s) that was done to the company, but for which the directors are unwilling to remedy. It is not a direct right to the members, but, in effect, if the company's affairs are well-managed, the members will be the ultimate beneficiaries.

For the company secretary the fundamental responsibility in the present respect is continuously advisory, as noted above. The first is to advise and guide the directors, where necessary, on the right trajectory in dealing with membership issues. In this, the first is to ensure, as much as possible, that membership rights are respected and enhanced by the company. This has to be through deliberate actions by adhering to applicable laws, the Articles and acceptable practice and procedures in running the affairs of the company. The next is through regular engagements with the shareholders through more informal channels that may not necessarily be the annual general meetings only. In this way, members are more readily able to communicate their concerns to the board and management and frictions between members and the company's board and management are reduced to the minimum.

On his own part, the company secretary should ensure that all membership related custodial and compliance issues, especially when they are statutory, are handled well and promptly so. For instance, there is no reason why a member would have to go to Court to have his name to be rectified into the register of members, except in very unavoidable cases. An example is where there is an ownership dispute over the estate of a deceased member from where the share registration request(s) emanated. In this case, extra care should be taken to avoid entering the wrong person's name into the register of members.

The overall aim should be to ensure that members are not forced into unnecessary and avoidable court actions to enforce their membership rights, even in the form of a derivative action, except when it is unavoidable. This is because constant member-related litigations against any company is an early symptom of disequilibrium in the relationship between the members and the company (that is, directors and management) and should strongly be avoided. The company secretary must therefore consistently advise the board and management of situations that could trigger shareholder discontent and ways and actions to avoid them or settle them early.

THE CHECKPOINTS

- ✓ Membership in a company is the backbone of every incorporated company as a separate legal entity, whether limited by shares or otherwise, public or private company.
- ✓ A person can become a member through any of the avenues to membership: subscription to the Memo, transfer and transmission, taking on shares from earlier holders.
- ✓ Being in membership register is key and fundamental to claiming accrued rights, so all efforts must be made to protect the legal sanctity and security of the register of members. The company secretary is statutorily responsible for this important assignment.
- ✓ A person's name does not only have to be in the register to members, which is very important, the person must have consented to have his name entered in the register. Otherwise, the register would have to be rectified to

have the person's name removed, if it was entered therein without his authorization, either in error or fraudulently.

- ✓ There are statutory restrictions to being a member in a company: age, unsound mind, undischarged bankrupt or company in liquidation. None of the entities so impaired should be considered, except they fit into any of the exceptions.
- ✓ Being a member comes with certain rights to the individual member, which rights can be enforced against the company itself, when breached or potentially threatened to so be. A good example is the right to attend a company's general meeting, vote therein, and speak on any of the issues raised at the meeting.
- ✓ Membership also comes with certain liabilities, chief of which is the members' liability to make good their contributions in the event of a winding-up of the company.
- ✓ Unlike the 2004 CAMA under which the Court could not award damages to a member who sues successfully to enforce his personal right(s), but can only order declarations and injunctions, the CAMA 2020 has introduced damages as one of the remedies. Also, a director found liable will have to personally pay damages to the aggrieved member.
- ✓ A member can also sue as a minority to stop by injunction or declaration the company engaging in illegal or ultra vires acts, purporting to use an ordinary resolution to do what the law requires that a special resolution be used, among others.
- ✓ In general, it is the company that has the right to sue to remedy any wrongdoings against it, except when any of the exceptions to the rule in *Foss* v. *Harbottle* applies.
- ✓ Even at that, the rule in *Foss* v. *Harbottle* has its own limitations and will not apply to override clear statutory provisions, detract from a right granted by the Constitution, and does not affect action to protect members' individual rights in a company, etc.
- ✓ The CAMA 2020 has introduced innovations in derivative actions by members, that apart from suing the company a director in the company or any other person can also be sued derivatively.

- ✓ A member can petition the Commission to investigate a company's affairs where he has membership. The CAMA 2020 has lowered the threshold for petitioning from 25% shareholding or membership to holder of one-tenth of the shares or by one-tenth of the members (for company without shares).
- ✓ The Commission can also, on its own, initiate investigations into the affairs of the company to know the persons who are the owners or financially behind the company and what the activities are. This is usually done in the public interests.
- ✓ In all cases, the company secretary greatest task in these respects is to advise and assist the directors, mostly, and senior management, to manage the company's affairs in the best interests of the members as a whole. To that duty imposed on directors, there is no alternative.

Chapter 12

MEETINGS OF MEMBERS

INTRODUCTION

In company law jurisprudence, meetings of members constitute the main vehicle by which a company is administered and where serious issues affecting the company are normally discussed and possibly resolved. In terms of decision making, the members' general meeting is the highest organ in the company. It is also here that final and far-reaching decisions are taken with respect to all issues concerning the company. Decisions in a company's general meetings are usually done by way of resolutions (ordinary or special). The meetings of members are usually referred to as the meetings of a company or shareholders meetings, signifying, in a profound manner, the symbolism of the members being the bedrock on which a company is built.

A major importance of members' meetings is that they are usually the forum for a company to communicate vital information to the shareholders, and sometimes, to communicate to the general public. Such meetings also afford the directors the opportunity to be able to respond directly to the concerns and questions of the members. Additional to the above points is that members' meetings always afford the shareholders a forum for shareholder democracy and activism, where the members can remove the directors and auditors, when desired. Essentially, any members' meeting is where the shareholders are empowered to 'run the show,' as it were, even if for the limited period of the meeting.

The critical importance of members' meeting is not lost on the *Nigerian Code of Corporate Governance (NCCG) 2018,* and it provides in principle 21 that, for companies, general meetings are important platforms for the board to engage the shareholders in order to facilitate greater understanding of the company's business, governance and performance by the members. Apart from this, such meetings usually provide the shareholders with an opportunity to exercise their ownership rights and express their views directly to members of the board of directors and senior management team on any areas of interest that they have concerns.

Principle F2 of Appendix 14 (Corporate Governance Code) to the *Hong Kong Stock Exchange's Listing Rules and Guidance (Hong Kong Rules) 2013* highlights the importance of the meetings of members and provides that the board should be responsible for maintaining an on-going dialogue with shareholders and in particular, using annual general meetings or other general meetings to ensure sustained communications with members, while encouraging their active participation in such meetings.

The Hong Kong Rules also made another important provision which has not been commonly found in other Codes. It provides that apart from giving shareholders sufficient notice of general meetings, that the company should also ensure that the members are familiar with the detailed procedures for conducting a poll, in the event that a poll is needed in any of the meetings. This is an aspect of meetings that sufficient attention has not been paid to, as there is a general assumption, maybe rightly or otherwise, that all those that attend such meetings are conversant with the poll procedures. This is, therefore, a good reminder to companies to pay a closer attention to an aspect like this, among other similar unpopular, but essential, tools of meetings.

In general, the meeting of members is one of the areas where the company secretary is heavily involved in the company's affairs. This involvement is stretched from before, during and after the meetings. From the issuance and service of notice of meeting to all those qualified to receive same to the pre-meeting arrangements of venue, dealing with proxy issues etc., to the meeting proper. From finalizing the agenda for the meeting, in liaison with the chairman, to the taking of minutes during the meeting and post-meeting 'house-cleaning,' activities, the company secretary is a key figure, in-fact, a central figure, in company meetings, whether in private or public companies.

TYPES OF MEMBERS' MEETINGS

The CAMA provides for two major types of meetings that could be held by the members of a company: the statutory meeting and the general meeting. The general meeting, in turn, could be annual general meeting or extra-ordinary general meeting. This classification excludes a class meeting, which is only attended by members who are of a particular class of shareholders in a company.

The Statutory Meeting

This genre of meeting relates only to the activities of public companies. Under section 235 CAMA 2020, (s. 211 (1), when a company has been incorporated as a public company, it shall within a period of six (6) months from the date of being so incorporated, hold a general meeting of the members, more appropriately, the statutory meeting. The main purpose of holding statutory meetings is to afford members of the newly-formed company the opportunity of having the initial progress report from the directors and promoters of the company. Under section 235(8) CAMA 2020, (s. 211 (8), members that attend a company's statutory meeting are at liberty to discuss any matter relating to the formation of the company or arising out of the statutory report. The meeting is also an opportunity for the members to meet and know the directors of the company, senior management and the company secretary personally (*Nzegwu-Danjuma, 154).*

The statutory meeting is a mandatory meeting imposed by the CAMA, and the company (that is a public company) has no discretion with respect to whether to hold the meeting or not. It is important to note that a failure or an omission to hold a statutory meeting is one of the grounds for winding-up a company by the Court under section 571(b) CAMA 2020, (s. 408 (b) CAMA 2004). However, the Court may decide against winding-up a company on this account and instead order that the statutory meeting be held and costs paid by the company *(Re Kent Outcrop Coal Co. (1912) WN 26; Orojo, 229).*

Under section 240 CAMA 2020, with the exception of a small company as defined in the Act and a single-member company, a company's statutory meeting, like the annual general meeting, must be held in Nigeria (now that companies are allowed by the amendment to the CAMA 2020 to hold their general meetings electronically, can we say that such meetings are still held in Nigeria?). The exception for single-member company was not captured in the CAMA 2004 as it did not provide for that type of company. We have noted above that statutory meetings are only for public companies, meaning that the discussions above did not relate to private companies.

The statutory meeting is mandated to be held within six (6) months after a public company is incorporated. However, where a company defaults in holding its statutory meeting within the prescribed period, it requires the leave of Court to extend time to hold such a meeting. The applications for leave of Court are usually done *ex-parte* and, except where there are extenuating circumstances that dictate otherwise, the applications are mostly granted by the Courts almost as a matter of course. This implies that the company cannot, on its own, unilaterally decide when to hold a statutory meeting when they are out of time in holding same. Otherwise, any such unauthorized meeting and its outcomes will be invalid *(Guardian Express Bank* v. *Odukwu & Anor (2007) 4 CLRN 84, 97).*

The Statutory Report

The directors of any newly incorporated public company are mandated by the CAMA to prepare a *statutory report* and forward to every member of the company. This should be done giving at least 21 days interval before the date on which the statutory meeting is to be held (s. 235(2) CAMA 2020), (s. 211 (2). At the company's statutory meeting proper, section 235 (7), (s. 211(7) mandates the directors to prepare a list showing the names, descriptions and addresses of the members of the company and the number of respective shares held by each of them. This is to be produced at the meeting and is to remain open and accessible during the meeting to any of the members of the company.

The statutory report shall be certified by not less than two (2) of the company's directors or a director and the company secretary, and the report must state the following particulars:

- the total number of shares allotted, distinguishing those shares as fully or partly paid-up otherwise than in cash, stating in the case of shares that are partly paid up, the extent to which they are so paid-up, and the consideration for which they have been allotted;
- the total amount of cash received by the company in respect of all the shares allotted, also distinguishing them as above;
- the names, addresses and descriptions of the directors, auditors, managers, if any, and the company secretary;
- the particulars of any pre-incorporation contract(s) together with the particulars of any modification(s) or proposed modification(s) thereon;
- any underwriting contract that has not been carried out and the reasons while it is so;
- the arrears, if any, due on calls from every director; and
- the particulars of any commission or brokerage paid or to be paid in connection with the issue or sale of shares or debentures to any director or to a manager (s. 235(3) CAMA 2020), (s. 211 (3).

Additionally, a statutory report is mandated to contain an abstract of the company's receipts and payments made up to seven (7) days before the date of the report, distinguishing receipts and payments made from shares, debentures and other sources respectively. The report is also to show estimates of expenses and cash balances with the company or estimates of the company's preliminary expenses. In addition to this, the company's auditors are expected to certify as correct, the part of the statutory report that relates to the shares allotted by the company and the cash received in that respect. They are also to certify the company's receipts and payments on its capital account (s. 235 (4)(5) CAMA 2020), (s. 211 (4)(5).

On their part, after certifying the statutory report, the directors are mandated to deliver a copy to the Commission for registration within 14 days, after sending copies to the members of the company. A member who desires to propose a resolution based on any item of the content of the statutory report shall give a 21 days' notice to the company on his intention to so propose. In consequence, the statutory meeting will not hold until the expiration of such a notice period given by a member (if any). At the statutory meeting proper, members are at liberty to discuss any of items contained in the statutory report. The statutory meeting may be adjourned as desired, and at the adjourned meeting, any resolution could be passed and will be as valid as if it was passed at the first meeting (s. 235 (7-10) CAMA 2020), (s. 211 (7-10)

The CAMA 2020 made an effort to introduce certainty into the provision that requires that a copy of the statutory report be sent to the Commission. Under section 211 CAMA 2004, a company is expected to deliver a copy of the statutory report to the Commission for registration, 'forthwith,' after sending copies to the members. In its ordinary usage, 'forthwith' is said to mean 'immediately, without delay, with dispatch,' *(Webster's All-in-One Dictionary and Thesaurus, 256).* The major problem with the use of the word 'forthwith' above is that it could be, and actually is, subject to different interpretations in different situations. For instance, a statutory report that was sent to the Commission by a company, 3, 5, or 7 days after sending same to the members, was it sent forthwith? Answers to this poser will vary. In order to avoid this scenario of subjectivity, section 235(6) CAMA 2020 provides that a company shall send the statutory report to the Commission within 14 days after sending same to the members. This has introduced certainty to the provision and, we submit that, it is a good improvement.

Apart from the fine that could be imposed by the Commission on a company for non-delivery of the statutory report to the Commission, it is also a ground for the company to be wound-up by the Court under section 571 (b) CAMA 2020 (s. 408(b)). Where a company makes an application to Court, the Court may order that, instead of winding-up the company on this ground, time should be extended for the meeting to be held (if not yet held) and the report delivered to the Commission and the company pays costs (*Re Kent Outcrop Coal Co. (1912) WN 26; Orojo, 229).*

THE ANNUAL GENERAL MEETING (AGM)

A company's annual general meeting is one that all members of the company look forward to and are entitled to attend. It is primarily the duty of the directors to call a general meeting of the company. It has been held that directors' power to call general meetings is a fiduciary one, which they must exercise in what they consider to be the best interests of the company and not for any collateral purpose *(Pergamon Press Ltd* v. *Maxwell (1970) 1 WLR 1167; Mayson et al., 407).*

The annual general Meeting is a specific meeting that must be held by every company, with the exception of a small company or single-member company, in each year (these exceptions are under the 2020 CAMA and not under the CAMA 2004, which required every company to hold annual general meeting every year). This is in addition to all other meetings that the company may otherwise hold in the same year. The notice convening an annual general meeting must specifically state that it is an annual general meeting, and there must not be more than a 15 months interval between a company's annual general meeting and the next one; provided that:

- if a company holds its first annual general meeting within 18 months of incorporation, it needs not hold another one in the same year or the year after; or
- except for a company's first annual general meeting, the Commission has the power to extend the time within which any annual general meeting shall be held. The period of such extension shall not exceed three (3) months, so that not more than 18 months shall elapse between the date of the last annual general meeting and the date of any meeting so extended (proviso to s. 237 (1) CAMA 2020), (s. 213 (1).

If there is a default by a company in holding its annual general meeting, the Commission may, on its own, or on the application of any member of the company, call a general meeting of the company. The Commission may, alternatively, direct that such a meeting be called. It may also give other ancillary or consequential directions as it deems fit in the circumstances. The directions that could be given by the Commission could relate to the holding and conducting of the company's annual general meeting, the operation of the company's Articles or that one member present in person or by proxy may apply to Court for an order to take a decision for the company, which decision binds other members of the company (s. 237(2) CAMA 2020), (s. 213 (2).

The above provision is almost on all fours with the corresponding provisions of section 213(2) CAMA 2004, except for one major addition in the 2020 CAMA. That addition is the provision that the Commission may, 'on its own,' that is, without an application by a member of a company, call, or direct, that a general meeting of a company be called. This gives the Commission additional leeway to intervene and save a company where there might be some serious internal issues which needed redress. What is not clear, however, and it does not seem as if it matters in the circumstance, is the source from where the Commission will get the information that the company has defaulted in holding its annual general meeting. This is because a company not filing its annual returns with the Commission could simply be a case of an oversight or tardiness, and not conclusive evidence that the company has not held its annual general meeting.

It is the law that, any general meeting held under the directions of the Commission or called by it, shall be the annual general meeting of the company, except the Commission directs otherwise. If the meeting is not held in the year in which the default occurred, it shall not, unless the company resolves otherwise at the meeting, be treated as an annual general meeting for the year in which it was held. If a company resolves to treat the meeting as its annual general meeting for the year it was held, it shall register such a resolution with the Commission within 15 days of its passing thereof (s. 237 (4) CAMA 2020), (s. 213 (3)(4).

A fine, to be specified by the Commission, is imposed on a company and every officer who is in default by not holding annual general meeting or for failure to comply with directions of the Commission in that respect. Under the CAMA 2004, (s. 213 (5), the fine was ₦500.00 (Five hundred naira only).

Even where it is the Commission that ordered a company's general meeting to be held, the company secretary's pre-meeting, at the meeting, and post-meeting responsibilities as highlighted above (issuing notice and ensuring service of the same, proxy issues, agenda, minutes etc) will still be the same.

Every member of a company has a right to attend any of the company's general meetings. The members also have a right to vote and speak at such a meeting on any resolution, this notwithstanding any provisions in the company's Articles. The Articles may, however, prevent a member from attending a general meeting if he has not paid calls on shares or otherwise owes other sums due to the company in respect of his shares (s. 107 CAMA 2020), (s. 81).

A member who is entitled to attend and vote at a meeting of the company shall be entitled to appoint another person (whether a member or not) as his proxy to attend and vote for him. The proxy has the power to speak at the meeting as the member appointing him. This proxy provision does not apply to a company without a share capital, unless where the company's Articles provide to the contrary. Any provision in the company's Articles requiring that proxy appointing document(s) be returned to the company more than 48 hours before a meeting or adjourned meeting, in order to be valid, is void (s. 254 (1)(3) CAMA 2020), (s. 230(1)(3).

Businesses Transacted at Annual General Meetings

When transacted at a company's annual general meeting, the following businesses are be deemed ordinary businesses:

- the declaration of a dividend;
- the presentation of financial statements and reports of the directors and auditors;
- the election of directors in place of those retiring;
- the appointment and fixing of the remuneration of auditors;
- the appointment of the members of the audit committee;
- the disclosure of remuneration of the company's managers (this is a new addition to list of ordinary businesses by the CAMA 2020).

Apart from the above listed items, every other business transacted at a company's annual general meeting is to be deemed to be special business (s. 238 CAMA 2020), (s. 214). Except for small companies and single-member companies, all annual general meetings must be held in Nigeria. Additionally, the CAMA 2020 also provides that, in terms of modalities for meetings, a private company may hold its general meetings electronically, provided that such meetings are conducted in accordance with the company's Articles (s. 240 (1)(2) CAMA 2020, (s. 216). This was the law before the section was amended by section 11 of the schedule to the *Business Facilitation (Miscellaneous Provisions) Act 2022 (BFA).* The Act now allows all companies in Nigeria, and not only private companies, to be able to hold their general meetings electronically, once the meetings abide by the provisions of the Articles. This is a good improvement which is in tandem with current realities.

The amendment to section 240 CAMA 2020 by the BFA as seen has, however, renders the first part of section, which provides that company annual general meetings shall be held in Nigeria, redundant. This is because if the meetings are held electronically, where participants, which could include the chairman, join from different countries of the world, it would be preposterous to say that any such meeting was held in Nigeria.

In general, however, from the above, the argument could be made, and a strong one it would be, that if a company could conduct its general meetings electronically, then, this should also include the service of notice for the meetings, distribution of the agenda and meeting materials to the members, sending out and receipt of proxy forms, receipt of apologies, etc. All these items should also be done electronically for the meetings, except maybe where the company's Articles specifically provides to the contrary on these items, or some of them.

EXTRAORDINARY GENERAL MEETING (EGM)

Apart from statutory and annual general meetings, any other meeting of members of a company in Nigeria is an extra-ordinary general meeting. The board of directors has the power to convene an extra-ordinary general meeting of a company whenever the board feels it is necessary to discuss pressing company issues, which cannot wait till the next annual general meeting *(Orojo, 231)*. If the board of directors cannot be properly constituted to form a quorum and act as a body in convening such a meeting because of absence of directors from Nigeria, a director is empowered to convene such an extra-ordinary general meeting (s. 239(1) CAMA 2020), (s. 215 (1).

Under section 240 CAMA 2020, (s. 216) an extra-ordinary general meeting is not one of the meetings that must be held within Nigeria. Therefore, such a meeting could be held anywhere around the world that the directors of a company deem fit. In practice, in choosing a venue for a meeting, regard is given to the convenience and accessibility of the venue to those intending to attend such a meeting. However, as seen above, with the provisions of section 240(2) CAMA 2020 allowing companies the liberty to conduct their general meetings electronically, then the burden on the directors in fixing extra-ordinary general meetings is drastically reduced. This is because the meetings can actually be conducted electronically, without regard to the location of those attending, provided that it is done in accordance with the company's Articles.

Any business transacted at a company's extra-ordinary general meeting is to be considered special business (s. 239 (8) CAMA 2020), (s. 215 (8).

Meeting by a Member's Requisition

Apart from the power of a company's board of directors to convene extra-ordinary general meetings, as already noted, a member(s) may requisition such a meeting, if:

- he holds at the date of the requisition, not less than one-tenth of the paid-up capital of the company carrying voting rights; or
- in the case of a company not having a share capital, he represents not less than one-tenth of the total voting rights of all the members having the right to vote at the company's general meetings.

The requisition may be from several sources but may be put together, although each is required to be signed by the person responsible for it and be deposited at the company's registered office. It shall state the object(s) of the meeting. When the directors receive a member's requisition duly made, they are mandated to immediately take steps to convene an extra-ordinary general meeting, and this, notwithstanding anything in the company's Articles (s. 239 (2)(3) CAMA 2020), (s. 215 (2)(3). If the directors do not convene the meeting as requisitioned within 21 days from the date of the deposit of the requisition, the requisitionists(s), or one or more of them representing more than a half of the total voting rights of all of them, may proceed and convene the meeting. The meeting so convened must be held within three (3) months from the date the requisitionist(s) convened the meeting. The meeting so convened by a member(s) must be held, as nearly as possible, as those that directors could have convened, apparently, in line with the provisions of the company's Articles (s. 239(4)(5) CAMA 2020), (s. 215 (4)(5).

The company is mandated to repay all reasonable expenses incurred by the requisitionist(s) by reason of the failure of the directors to call a duly requisitioned meeting (s. 239(6), (s. 215 (6). What is reasonable in any particular instance in terms of expenses, must have to be determined based on the peculiar circumstances of each case.

Over the years, there have been certain principles that are used by the Courts in interpreting issues relating to several aspects of requisitioned meetings.

Firstly, the directors' obligations to convene a meeting can only arise if the requisition is validly submitted by the member(s) to the company, and where it is ineffective, because of a defect in its form, the directors are not obliged to call a meeting *(Rose* v. *McGivern (1998) 2 BCLC at 593; PNC Telecom Plc* v. *Thomas (2003) BCC, 202).*

Secondly, in terms of objects of the meeting to be convened, it has been held that the requirement to 'state the objects of the meeting' does not require those requisitioning a meeting to include proposal for resolution in the requisition. Once the stated object of the meeting is clear enough, the requisitionists could rely on the resolution to be proposed at the meeting proper *(Isle of Wright Railway Co.* v. *Tabourdin (1883) 25 Ch.D., 320; Fruit and Vegetable Growers Association* v. *Kekewich (1912) 2 Ch., 52; Gower, 353).*

Thirdly, where the objects for which members have requisitioned a meeting are not capable of being executed legally in any manner, then the directors would be justified in refusing to act on the requisition *(National Roads & Motorists Association* v. *Parker (1986) 6 NSWLR, 517; Isle of Wright Railway Co.* v. *Tabourdin (1883) 25 Ch.D., 320).* However, if it is only an object in the requisition that could not be legally executed, but there are others that are valid, then, the directors would have to convene a meeting to consider the valid objects *(Totally and Permanently Incapacitated Veterans of NSW Ltd* v. *Gadd (1998) 28 ACSR 549; Mayson et al., 408).*

Next, is that a general meeting convened on a requisition is not permitted to transact any other business other than that covered by the terms of the requisition *(Ball* v. *Metal Industries Ltd (1957) SC, 315).* This can also be taken together with any resolution which the directors of the company might want to put forward, for which the directors must give due notice of the proposed resolution *(Rose* v. *McGivern (1998) 2 BCLC 593; Thorne, 266).*

Finally, on this point, it has been held that a member's right to requisition a meeting is lost if the requisitionists are themselves directors of the company, who have, by failing to attend board meetings, been the cause of the directors' failure to convene a requisitioned meeting *(Thyne* v. *Lauder (1925) SN, 123; Charlesworth & Cain, 304*).

Court Ordered Meetings

Where, for any reason, it is impracticable to call a company's general meeting or board meeting, section 247 CAMA 2020, (s. 223 (1) gives the Court the power to order a meeting of the company or board to be held and conducted as the Court deems fit. The Court could invoke this power on its own motion or on the application of a director or a member who would be entitled to vote at the meeting (for company meeting) and by any director (for a board meeting) *(Iro* v. *Park (1972) 1 All NLR (2), 474; Okeowo* v. *Migliore (1979) 11 SC, 138; Re El Sombrero Ltd (1958) Ch., 900; Re Beckers Pty Ltd (1942) 59 WN (NSW), 206; Re Opera Photographic Ltd (1989) 1 WLR, 634).* The Court's direction in ordering a meeting may include authorizing one member or one director who is present (in person or by proxy) to hold a meeting by himself and take decisions and such shall be binding on the other members of the company or the board (s. 247(2), (s. 223 (2) *(Re H.R. Paul & Son Ltd (1973) 118 SJ, 166*; *Mayson et al., 409).*

From the above discussions, the critical phrase in getting the Court to order a meeting of the board or the company is where 'it is impracticable' to hold either of the meetings through the regular channels. The question is: when would it be considered impracticable, legally, to hold any of these meetings, to warrant the intervention of the Court? A situation where the shareholders refused to attend any of the company's meeting in order to ensure that quorum for the meeting cannot be formed was held a good case for the Court to order a meeting for impracticability to hold normally *(El Sombrero Ltd (1958) Ch., 900; Re HR Paul & Son (1973) 118 Sol Jo. 166; Hannigan, 339).*

In the case of *Okeowo* v. *Migliore (1979) 11 SC 138*, this issue came for consideration before the Supreme Court. Relying on the decision in *Re El Sombrero Ltd (1958) Ch., 900*, the Supreme Court first of all made the point that the word 'impracticable' in the present context is not synonymous with the word 'impossible' and should not be construed as such. The Court then concluded that the word 'impracticable'+ as used is merely to lead the Court to 'examine the circumstances of the particular case and answer the question whether, as a practical matter, the desired meeting of the company can be conducted, there being no doubt, of course, that it can be convened and held.' Once the Court is convinced that the order for a meeting should be made, it should exercise its discretion and order a meeting, notwithstanding that some of the members or directors, whichever is applicable, are opposed to the application being granted.

It should be noted that there are limits to the Court's discretion in intervening to order meetings of the company or the board. The first notable limitation is that a Court will not order a meeting where doing so will alter or negate a class right conferred on a shareholder by his membership of the company or the Articles. Also, an order for a meeting to be held will not be made where the order will shift the balance of power in a shareholding ownership structure that is equal, and which became so, by the agreement of the parties *(Union Music Ltd* v. *Watson (2003) 1 BCLC, 453; Hannigan, 340).*

Whether the general meeting is requisitioned by a member(s) or ordered by the Court, as noted above, the duties and responsibilities of the company secretary thereto, will not change in any material particular. What might change is the nature of the notice to be issued (which must now include the fact that the meeting is requisitioned or that it was ordered by the Court) and the documents to accompany the notice of meeting (the requisition document or the Court order, whichever is applicable).

THE CRITICAL IMPORTANCE OF THE GENERAL MEETINGS

The central importance of general meetings to the overall success and survival of a company's business is predicated on the fact that such meetings afford the members of the company the opportunity to take a stand on critical issues affecting the company. For the company itself, general meetings provide the opportunity to do what it could not otherwise be able to do in another forum. It could be said that, apart from the activities of the board of directors and senior management, which are very crucial, the survival or death of a company depends largely on what happens in its general meetings, over time. For instance, the CAMA has made numerous provisions about what a company can only do in its general meetings and not otherwise. What this implies is that when these things could not be executed in the regular annual general meetings of the company, extra-ordinary general meetings would have to be summoned to address them. Some of the issues are highlighted below.

There are a few things that the company secretary readies in advance of any annual general meeting, while some items are executed during and after the meeting: A few of them are listed below:

Before the Meeting

- to summon the meeting at the instance of the board of directors or those requisitioning a meeting by issuing the relevant notices to all who are entitled to attend;
- to prepare and circulate the agenda for the meeting in liaison with the chairman of the board;
- to assist the chairman (where needed) with the preparation of the outline of any intended speech to be delivered at the meeting;

- to assemble and orderly arrange all reports, documents and correspondences that would be needed at the meeting, especially by the directors;
- to prepare proxy forms for despatch with annual accounts and notice of the general meeting (the packages could differ);
- to invite company advisers (where needed) that are not statutorily required to be invited to company meetings;
- to prepare ballot papers and other materials in the event of a poll being demanded;
- to liaise with the chairman in getting ready the agenda for the meeting;
- to make the register of members available (usually for large companies) in the event that it becomes necessary to identify an attendee as a member and for members who wish to inspect same;
- to prepare and arrange name cards and/or badges for individual directors and other attendees, etc (*Orojo, 288; ICSA, 290).*

At the Meeting

- to attend in good time and ensure that adequate arrangements are made well in advance for the meeting;
- to assist in the registration of proxies for the meeting;
- to read the notice convening the meeting at the commencement of the meeting, once the chairman calls the meeting to order;
- to check that a quorum (foundational and otherwise) for the validity of the meeting deliberations is present at all times during the meeting;
- to bring along all the requisite reports, correspondences and documents to the meeting;
- to ensure that where name tags are used, the directors and advisers are properly seated;
- to take the minutes of the meeting and other notes;
- to assist the chairman in counting the votes during the meeting, especially when a poll is taken;
- to guide any member(s) that has any problem with the poll procedure (if same is taken) during the meeting;

- to continually advise and guide the chairman and other directors as needed during the course of the meeting, especially on legal and compliance related issue;
- to offer all support and legal guidance to the directors and the meeting on any issue or point of law;
- to do all things that would ensure the success of the meeting.

After the Meeting

- to promptly prepare the draft minutes for the attention of the chairman and after the approval of the final copy to maintain the appropriate minute books;
- to carry out any instruction(s) given by the meeting in liaison with members of the board of directors and departmental heads;
- to file the necessary returns, for instance, annual returns, special resolutions (within 15 days) after adoption;
- to send a copy of the minutes of meeting to every member (if that is the practice) or other persons entitled to receive same (members who want copies of minutes of any general meeting are entitled to receive them promptly for a fee);
- to make the necessary arrangements (in collaboration with the other relevant departments) to ensure that members receive their dividend promptly, if and once, approved (*ICSA, 290*).

Apart from the duties of the company secretary in relation to company meetings, there are other duties that a company secretary performs by virtue of his position. The related and intertwined functions are those of regulatory compliance and corporate governance. As was noted at the beginning of this book, the duties and responsibilities of the company secretary have metamorphosed over the years and cannot easily be pigeon-holed into finite itemizations. A few examples, however, will suffice for now:

- in large companies with directors' and employees' share schemes, it is the duty of the company secretary to administer those schemes (except where outsourced or left to the human resources management department to deal with);
- where the company has subsidiaries, the company secretary also acts as the group company secretary;

- the company secretary deals with issues relating to shareholding and share registrations, transmissions and transfers;
- the company secretary is the pivot for communication between the company and its shareholders and other stakeholders;
- where there is a whistle-blower policy in place, the company secretary is always part of the formulation, implementation and reviews of the policy;
- the company secretary is usually a central member of a company's disciplinary and remuneration committees (where non-directors are members);
- he ensures the security and integrity of the company's security documents, resolutions, including all title documents;
- the company secretary keeps custody of and ensures the security and proper use of the company's common seal (the company seal is now optional for companies).

Section 335(1)(a) CAMA 2020, (s. 298(1)(2), mandates the company secretary to ensure that the company complies with all applicable rules and regulations in all its meetings. Apart from compliance that relates to meetings, the company secretary is usually the general compliance officer (the compliance unit usually liaises with the company secretary before proffering any advice, especially those that go outside the company or that has legal element). Some large companies, however, do appoint dedicated compliance officers for compliance and regulatory purposes.

Acts Possible Only at General Meetings

The importance or centrality of the general meetings to companies can be found in the fact certain activities relating to the overall management of a company, can only be executed in general meetings and nowhere else. A few examples below will suffice for our present purposes:

- change of a company's name (special resolution) (s. 30 (3) CAMA 2020), (s. 31 (3);
- alteration of a company's object clause (special resolution) (s. 51 (1) CAMA 2020), (s. 46 (1);
- alteration of a condition in Memorandum which might lawfully have been in the company's Articles (special resolution) (s. 52(1) CAMA 2020), (s. 47 (1);

- alteration of a company's Articles of Association (special resolution) (s. 53 (1) CAMA 2020), (s. 48 (1);
- re-registration of a company from a private to public company and from public company to private (special resolutions) (s. 56 & 62 CAMA 2020), (ss. 50 & 53);
- alteration of a company's share capital by consolidation (s. 125 CAMA 2020), (s. 100);
- increase of a company's share capital (s. 127 CAMA 2020), (s. 102);
- reduction of a company's share capital (special resolution) (s. 131 CAMA 2020), (s. 106);
- creation of reserve liability capital for a company (special resolution) (s. 159 CAMA 2020), (s. 134);
- subsequent appointment or rejection and removal of company directors earlier appointed via casual vacancy (s. 273 CAMA 2020), (s. 248);
- determination of directors' remuneration (s. 293 CAMA 2020), (s. 267);
- affirming an otherwise voidable substantial property transaction entered into by the company with its director(s) (s. 312 (2(c) CAMA 2020), (s. 286 (2)(c);
- rendering unlimited the liability of directors, managers or the managing director (s. 314 CAMA 2020), (s. 289);
- appointment and removal of auditors (s. 401 & 409 CAMA 2020), (ss. 357 & 362);
- declaration of dividends (s. 426 CAMA 2020), (s. 379);
- resolution of a company to be voluntarily wound up (special resolution) (s. 571 CAMA 2020), (s. 457).

Most of the acts that are required to be executed in a general meeting also require special resolutions (that is, to be approved by at least three-fourth of the members who are entitled to vote in the meeting) (s. 258(2) CAMA 2020), (s. 233 (2).

NOTICE OF GENERAL MEETINGS

Except and only in circumstances where a company's Articles provide to the contrary, proper notice of every company's meeting, which is a general meeting, must be given to all the members of the company *(Young* v. *Ladies Imperial Club (1920) 2 KB 523; Onwuka* v. *Taymani (1965) LLR, 62).*To be considered proper, a notice of meeting must contain all the necessary information required, be properly served on the recipients and sufficient time must be allowed between the service of the notice and the date of the meeting (*Orojo, 233).*

A notice of meeting issued by a person who does not have the authority to issue the notice is void, and even if the meeting takes place, its decisions will also be void *(Re State of Wyoming Syndicate (1901) 2 Ch., 431; Orojo, 231).* An instance will be where the company secretary, on his own, that is, without a direction from the directors, purports to call a meeting of the company by issuing a notice thereof. That notice and anything done pursuant thereto would have been invalid. For one, section 335 (2) CAMA 2020, (s. 298 (2) provides that the company secretary shall not, without the authority of the board, exercise any of the powers vested in the director(s). The power to call a meeting of the company is vested in the board of directors, and the company secretary cannot usurp such powers.

It has been held that a Court will not interfere if it is clear that the decisions would have been the same if the notice was issued from the proper source *(Bentley-Stevens* v. *Jones (1974) 1 WLR, 638).* In this case, the Court refused to issue interlocutory injunction to stop a resolution for an action when it was alleged that the applicant was not served with the notice of the meeting. What the majority did in that respect was actually to correct the irregularity with a subsequent vote on the issue and the Court was minded to condone the initial omission that notice was not served. It is our view, that, except in narrow examples of this nature, where the Court was of the opinion that the issue of lack of service of notice could easily be rectified and should not vitiate or stop the meeting, in other cases, the Court must stamp its authority and invalidate the meeting(s) in question. This is especially so when there are no attempts by the company to remedy the flaw or that it would actually be almost as stressful to remedy as to call a new meeting.

Length of Notice

Under section 241(1) CAMA 2020, (s. 217 (1), the notice required for all types of general meetings is 21 days, counting from the date on which the notice was sent out. However, a general meeting may still be called on a shorter notice and be regarded as duly and properly called, if it is so agreed, in the case of:

- a meeting called as an annual general meeting, by all the members entitled to attend and vote at the meeting; and

- any other general meeting (extra-ordinary etc), by a majority in number of members having a right to attend and vote and holding not less than 95 per cent in nominal value of shares giving a right to attend and vote at the meeting, or, in the case of a company not having a share capital, together representing at least 95 per cent of total voting rights at that meeting of all the members (s. 241(2)(a)(b) CAMA 2020), (s. 217 (2)(a)(b).

The Content of Notice of Meeting

Questions often arise as to what should be content of a notice of meeting, for instance, a company's general meeting? It is important because it a legal and foundational issue. In answer, it is a mandatory requirement of the CAMA that a notice of meeting contains:

- the venue, date and time of the meeting. (In this present regime of online meetings, it is submitted, that a notice of meeting that stipulates that the meeting will be online, with all the other coordinates as to time and date, would have satisfied the requirement);
- the general nature of the business to be transacted.

It is required that the above information shall be set out in sufficient details to enable the member receiving the notice of meeting to decide whether to attend the meeting or not. Also, where the meeting is to consider a special resolution, then, the terms of the resolution shall be set out in the notice of meeting. No business may be transacted by a company in a general meeting unless notice of it has been duly given to those receiving the notice of the meeting in question (s. 242 (1)(2) CAMA 2020), (s. 218 (1) (2).

An issue that has agitated company law jurisprudence and corporate governance circles over the years has been the degree of details, aside standard ones for ordinary or special business, which must be given in the notice of meeting to constitute 'sufficient details' as required by law. This is because it is important to avoid issuing a notice that is vague or misleading, which would support an application to restrain the holding of the meeting *(Jackson* v. *Munster Bank (1884) 13 LR 1r, 118; Thorne, 271)*. It has also been held that a proposed resolution whose details were incorrectly notified to a company's meeting will be invalid and not binding on the company *(Baillie* v. *Oriental Telephone and Electric Co. Ltd (1915) 1 Ch, 503; Thorne, 271)*. The key requirement, in terms of the content of notice of meeting, has been held to be the disclosure of all relevant facts so that the member can exercise an informed business judgment as to whether or not he ought to attend the meeting. This will require a fair and candid explanation of the purpose(s) for which the meeting is being summoned. In this respect, while the directors are not expected to disclose every conceivable piece of relevant information to the members, a full and fair disclosure of all matters that will enable the members make informed decisions, will suffice *(Re Royal Automobike Club Ltd (2000) 1BCLC, 307; Thorne, 271).*

Where the notice of meeting being issued is for a company's annual general meeting, then, a statement that the purpose of the meeting is to transact the ordinary business of an annual general meeting shall be sufficient specification that the meeting is for the matters stated as such under section 242(2) CAMA 2020, (s. 214), that is to say:

- the declaration of a dividend;
- the presentation of financial statements and reports of the directors and auditors;
- the election of directors in place of those retiring;
- the appointment and fixing of the remuneration of the auditors;
- the appointment of the members of the audit committee;
- disclosure of remuneration of managers of a company (this is an addition by section 238 CAMA 2020, which was not in the CAMA 2004).

Apart from the above listed businesses, all other businesses, when discussed at a company's general meeting, are deemed to be special businesses. It is important to note that no business may be transacted at a company's annual general meeting unless notice of it has duly been given to the members and all those entitled to receive same (s. 242 (3) CAMA 2020), (s. 218(3).

ERRORS AND OMISSIONS IN NOTICE OF MEETINGS

Where there has been an error or omission in a notice of meeting with respect to the venue, date, time or the general nature of business to be transacted at the meeting, such shall not invalidate the meeting. However, the case will be different where the officer of the company responsible for the default had acted in bad faith or without exercising due diligence, thereby acting in a negligent or reckless manner. In cases omissions or accidental errors, the officer responsible shall effect the necessary correction(s) before or during the meeting, most likely on the direction of the chairman of the meeting (s. 242 (5) CAMA 2020), (s. 218 (5).

Two quick problems manifest from the provisions above. The first is the issue of bad faith. How do we determine when an officer has acted in bad faith in making an error or omission on the notice of meeting? It is even worse that the act of a single officer acting in bad faith would invalidate a company's general meeting when there has been no evidence of either collusion or condonation from the board of directors. The aspect of being negligent or acting without due care and diligence is a matter of fact that could be established by available evidence. However, establishing bad faith is a lot more difficult and prone to more subjectivity.

The second problem is that of the proviso to section 242(5), 'provided that in the case of accidental error or omission…' the officer responsible shall be allowed to effect the necessary correction to the notice of meeting either before or during the meeting. The CAMA did not indicate what incidents would amount to 'accidental error or omission' and the case law on this point has been few.

In the English case of *Musselwhite* v. *C H Musselwhite & Son Ltd (1962) Ch, 964,* the Court had the opportunity to determine this point. It was held that failure to serve a notice of meeting on an otherwise deserving person based on the directors' mistaken belief that the person has ceased being a member of the company did not qualify as accidental omission. In the Nigerian case of *In Re Glaxosmithkline Consumer Nig. Plc (2019) LPELR-47498*, the Court was to determine whether the non-service of the notice of meeting on a member amounted to accidental omission. In the case, the member was not served with the notice of meeting because, according to the company, the courier service engaged to serve the notice could not serve the member and the notice was later posted back to the member about a week after the meeting had been convened and held. It was held, (though the notice was published in some national dailies), that the non-service of the notice of meeting was not an accidental omission but deliberate failure on the part of the company. The meeting was, consequently, invalidated.

What we find is that the cases above have shown the things that were not considered accidental omissions in serving notices of meetings, however, none has shown us what amounts to an accidental omission. Defining the words 'accidental' and 'omission' in their individual meanings and applying them as such might be of help but would not be conclusive. In the final analysis, therefore, each case will have to be determined on its own peculiar facts. From all of the above, what comes out clearly, however, is that acts that are in any way deliberate, negligent, careless or reckless cannot be subsumed to be 'accidental errors or omissions' in the present respect.

It is also important to note that a failure to give a notice of meeting to a person, who is otherwise entitled to the notice, based on the misinterpretation of the provisions of the CAMA by the company, cannot be classified as accidental omission (s. 245(2) CAMA 2020), (s. 221 (2).

PERSONS ENTITLED TO NOTICE OF GENERAL MEETING

Some persons, and them only, are entitled to be served with the notice of a company's general meetings as of right. Under section 243 CAMA 2020, (s. 219) this class of people are:

- every member of the company;
- every person upon whom ownership of shares devolves by reason of his being a legal representative, receiver or a trustee in bankruptcy of a member;
- all directors of the company;
- every of the company's auditors; and
- the company secretary;
- the Commission (that is, with respect to public companies) (this is an addition by CAMA 2020, which was not in CAMA 2004).

Once these persons have been validly served with notice of meeting, then the company would have fulfilled the condition as to service of notice for the meeting in question.

HOW IS THE NOTICE OF MEETING SERVED?

There are several ways recognized by the CAMA through which a company could serve notice of its general meetings on those entitled to receive such notice:

- the notice may be given to a member in person (personal service);
- the notice may be sent to the member by post or to his registered address.

If the member has no registered address within Nigeria, the notice of meeting could be sent to the address given by the member where notices could be served on him. This would seem to imply that even where a member(s) supplied an address abroad, the company has an obligation to send notices of meetings to him there.

Where the notice of meeting is to be sent to a member by post, then, service of the notice shall be deemed to be effected by properly addressing, pre-paying, and posting a letter containing the notice. The notice would be deemed to have been served after seven (7) days of posting of the letter containing the notice. At other times, the notice would be deemed to have been served at the time at which the letter would be delivered in the ordinary course of post (s. 244 (1)(2) CAMA 2020, (s. 220 (1) (2).

The CAMA 2020 (s. 244(3) has made a welcome and overdue provision, that, apart from personal service and service of notices of meetings by post, a member may opt to receive notices of meetings through electronic mail (e-mail messages), by simply providing an e-mail address to the company, which is deemed to be his authorization to so receive. This provision should have been added to the CAMA and implemented decades ago.

The above provision of section 244(3) CAMA 2020 which introduced optional electronic service of notice of meeting on any person who supplies an e-mail address has been expunged from the CAMA. Section 11 of the schedule to the *Business Facilitation (Miscellaneous Provisions) Act 2022 (BFA)* expunged the provisions and instead added electronic service of notice of meeting as one of the ways through which a company may serve notices of meeting. In essence, service of notice of meeting by electronic mail is no longer optional for those that supply their e-mail addresses to the company. It is now one of the statutory ways that a company may serve notice of meetings to those entitled to it.

Where persons have succeeded to an estate of a former member, either through death or bankruptcy, the company may continue to give notice of meeting to that same estate as it used to give to the member until the successors furnish new addresses for receipt of notices. In another respect, where the members are joint holders of a company's shares, then notice of meeting may be given to the joint holder who is named first in the register of members and that would be deemed to be valid and sufficient (s. 244 (4)(5) CAMA 2020), (s. 220 (4)(5).

Additional Notice by Public Companies

Having sent the requisite notice of proposed meeting(s) to all its members and those entitled to same, a company would then be set for the meeting proper. However, there is a further requirement under section 246 CAMA 2020, (s. 222), that in addition to the prescribed notice of meeting to be given to those entitled, every public company shall, at least 21 days before any general meeting, advertise the notice of such a meeting in at least two (2) daily newspapers. There is a question whether non-publication of a notice of meeting by a public company in two (2) daily newspapers can invalidate the meeting and the notice of meeting already given to those entitled to receive same? And in a case where none of the members complained of not receiving the notice of meeting, should the non-publication of the notice in newspapers still invalidate the notice and the meeting? The Courts will have to answer that.

Until the Courts answer the above question, however, we submit that the answer should be in the positive. Non-publication of the notice of meeting by a public company in two (2) national dailies should invalidate the meeting and its outcome. The first reason is that the requirement for publication in newspapers is a mandatory provision of the CAMA, a matter in which the company has no discretion. The second reason is that omitting such a critical requirement for calling a meeting might point to a more sinister fact: that the company is being mismanaged and then closer scrutiny by the members and the regulators is being called for.

The normal practice with public companies is that once the company secretary issues and sends out the notice of meeting to members and all those entitled to attend the meeting, the newspaper publication of the notice is also commissioned. The notices then run *pari passu* and the possibility of an omission or oversight with respect to the newspaper publications of the notice is drastically reduced.

Power of the Court to Order Notice

There are situations whereby it is not possible to hold the meeting of a company, and this could be for several reasons. If a situation arises that makes it impracticable to hold the meeting of a company or of its board of directors in a regular manner as prescribed by the CAMA or the company's Articles, the Court may intervene. On the application of a director of the company or a member who is entitled to vote at the meeting, or of its own motion, the Court may order that a meeting of the company or board be called, held and conducted in a manner that the Court thinks fit.

The Court is empowered to direct that one member or one member of the board of directors applies to Court to take binding decisions on behalf of the company or the board of directors respectively (s. 247 CAMA 2020), (s. 223) (2). Several issues inherent in these provisions have been discussed extensively above and do not warrant repeating here.

PROCEEDINGS AT COMPANY MEETINGS

To a very large extent, proceedings at company meetings are regulated by the relevant Companies Act (the CAMA) and the company's Articles. The specific details of the conduct of the meeting proper are usually decided by the meeting itself, under the direction of the chairman (*Caruth* v. *ICI Ltd (1937) AC, 707*; *Orojo, 236*). As will be seen below, the chairman of the meeting has some levels of powers and discretions usually conceded to him by virtue of his position to enable him perform well in 'carrying the meeting' from inception to conclusion.

Quorum for Meetings

The prevailing acceptable practice in company law and practice globally, that is, in common law jurisdictions, is to allow the company to deal with the issue of quorum for its meetings in its Articles. In general, therefore, the number of persons to form a quorum for a company's general meeting to be validly held and transact its stated business is normally fixed by the company's Articles. This is the same practice under the CAMA, which subordinates its provision on quorum to the Articles of respective companies. Where, however, there is no quorum provision in the Articles, then the CAMA provisions become the default position to be relied on.

The CAMA 2020 confirms the above position in section 256(1), exempting also a single-member company (s. 232 (1). It provides that 'unless otherwise provided in the Articles, no business shall be transacted at any general meeting unless a quorum of members is present at the time when the meeting proceeds to business and throughout the meeting.' Section 256(2) also reconfirms the supremacy of a company's Articles on the issue of quorum. It provides that 'unless otherwise provided in the Articles, the quorum for the meeting of a company is one-third of the total number of members of the company or 25 members (whichever is less) present in person or by proxy. However, where the number of members is not a multiple of three, then the nearest number to one third. Where the number of members is six or less, the quorum shall be two members.' (s. 232 (1)(2).

It is important to note that two members that could form a quorum for a meeting does not mean two persons. In essence, two persons representing a company in a meeting or acting as proxies for the same member cannot constitute a quorum for a company's meeting requiring two members for quorum *(Re Romford Canal Co. Pocock's Claims (1883) 24 Ch.D., 25; Hannigan, 344).*

Determining the Quorum

As a general rule, a meeting that is inquorate (that is, without the requisite quorum) cannot validly transact any business *(Re Cambrian Peat, Fuel, and Charcoal Co. Ltd, De La Mott's and Turner's Case (1875) 31 LT, 773)*; *Mayson et al.*, 421). The CAMA seems to contemplate exceptions to this general rule by inserting the phrase, '*unless otherwise provided in the Articles*,' which presupposes that under certain conditions, a company's Articles could authorize a meeting to proceed to business even without the quorum prescribed under the Act, but elsewhere in the Articles. For the purposes of determining the quorum for a meeting, all members and their proxies must be counted (s. 232 (3) CAMA 2004). It is noteworthy that a quorum for a meeting must be an effective quorum, that is, it has to be formed and constituted only from members and others who are entitled to attend and vote at such a meeting on the business to be transacted *(Henderson* v. *James Loutitt and Co. Ltd (1894) 21 R 674 Mayson et al., 421).*

Some principles on the issue of quorum have been established over the years by the Courts. For instance:

- except in a single-member company, one member alone cannot form a quorum for a company's meeting *(Re London Flats Ltd (1969) 2 All ER, 744)*;
- in a single-member company, one person who is qualified to attend the meeting in person or by proxy can form a quorum;
- for a Court-ordered meeting, a single person can be the quorum for the meeting and take binding decisions (s. 247(2) CAMA 2020), (s. 223);
- where there is only one shareholder in a class of shareholders, the assent of that shareholder is the equivalent of a meeting of the class *(Re RMCA Reinsurance Ltd (1994) BCC, 378).*

Meeting Becoming Inquorate Midway

The CAMA anticipates that the quorum for a meeting, which was otherwise quorate and was transacting its pre-determined business, could be lost midway into the meeting. To deal with this issue, some company's Articles do provide that the quorum for a meeting needs only be present when the meeting proceeds to business and not necessarily throughout the meeting *(Re Hartley Baird Ltd (1955) 3 All ER, 695)(ICSA, 275)*. Although section 256(1) CAMA 2020, (s. 232(1) stipulates that a company's meeting must have a quorum when it proceeds to business and stay so throughout the meeting, it also made provisions to deal with sudden loss of quorum in the course of a meeting.

Under section 256(4), (s. 232 (4) of the Act, where there is a quorum at the beginning of a meeting, but the meeting became inquorate later due some members leaving, in what appears to the chairman of the meeting, to be sufficient reasons, the meeting shall be adjourned to the same place and time in a week's time. If at the adjourned meeting, there be no quorum still, the members present are then the quorum and their decisions shall bind all shareholders. Where it is only one member who is present at the adjourned meeting, he may apply to Court for direction(s) to take a decision(s).

On the other hand, where a meeting became inquorate midway because a member withdrew, for what appears to the chairman to be insufficient reasons, and a ploy to inquorate the meeting and the meeting actually becomes inquorate by that fact, the meeting may continue with the business of the day and its decision shall be binding on the other members. Where, however, it is only one member that is left, he may seek direction(s) of the Court to take a decision(s) (s. 256(3), (s. 232 (4).

In the above respect, the CAMA gives wide discretion to the chairman of a meeting to use his judgment to decide what would happen in such situations as described above. The use of the phrase 'for what appears to the chairman…' in both sub-sections above, shows the wide latitude of discretion, with major subjective undertones, that the CAMA allows the chairman of the meeting to exercise in these situations. The hope is that the chairman of the meeting does not abuse such wide powers, especially in times of crisis in the company. This is especially so since the chairman is not given any parameters or criteria on which to base his opinion of the events.

Agenda for the Meeting

The content, arrangement and presentation of the agenda for a company's general meeting are usually decided by the chairman of the company (same for board of directors' meetings) in consultation with the board and with direction to the company secretary. A detailed agenda prepared for a meeting is a correct practice to avoid aimless discussions and waste of time in trying to rightly steer the discussions during the meeting. It is possible, and in-fact, sometimes almost inevitable, to add items to or subtract from the agenda during the meeting. However, the core businesses of the meeting should be decided upon and reduced into the agenda, well before the start of the meeting.

The common practice is to circulate the agenda to the members few days before meeting proper (some smaller companies circulate the agenda on the floor of the meeting), with the other documents meant for their attention. It is now becoming the practice, and should actually be encouraged, that members that indicate electronic mail addresses do receive the agenda and other documents through such medium (the CAMA, as amended, has now added electronic mailing as a method to serve notice of meetings, and this comes in handy here). An agenda circulated in advance will afford members the time to reflect on the issues to be discussed at the meeting and prepare to contribute meaningfully at the meeting with questions and suggestions. It is also possible for members, especially big institutional members, to give feedback to the board on items on the agenda before the meeting.

It is ordinarily the practice for the company secretary to give the chairman a slightly different agenda for the meeting (slightly in terms of covering the agenda with background notes and additional information and reminders). This is to enable the chairman to conduct the meeting with full authority and mastery of the issues, that is, without reverting to the company secretary for guidance on most of the issues, even if the issues are not ordinarily very familiar to the chairman *(ICSA, 273).*

Chairman of the Meeting

Under section 265(1) CAMA 2020, (s. 240 (1), the chairman of a company's board of directors, if the company has one, shall preside as the chairman of every general meeting of the company. However, where a company's board has no chairman, or if he is not present within one hour after the time appointed for the holding of the meeting or where the chairman is unwilling to act, the directors present shall elect a member of the board of directors to preside at the meeting.

It has been held that it should be taken as a given, that, unless otherwise provided, the chairman of a company is also the chairman of the board of directors *(Chander* v. *Thadani (1980) FHCLR 168; Orojo, 237).* If at any meeting of a company there is no director willing to act as chairman of the meeting, or if no director is present within one hour after the time appointed for holding the meeting, the members present shall choose one of their own to be the chairman of the meeting (s. 265(2), (s. 240 (2).

In practice, it rarely happens, especially in public companies, that a situation will arise where there will be no directors to preside over a meeting or where the ones available will be unwilling to preside over a meeting. The exception will be where there is a fractured or deadlocked board, and even in such cases, the feuding directors would usually apply to Court for directions, instead of allowing a member to preside over a general meeting. The difficulty is that in large public companies, the members do not actually have a lot of personal relationships with one another, and attempting to choose a member to preside over a general meeting, possess several trust-related problems.

The Duties and Powers of the Chairman

Both from legal and corporate governance perspectives, the position of the chairman of a meeting is an important but an onerous one, especially with respect to public companies, with large shareholders base. The chairman takes charge of the meeting and ensures that the scheduled businesses of the meeting are transacted orderly and properly. In doing this, the chairman owes a duty to the meeting primarily and not to the board of directors. This is irrespective of whether he is a director or not *(Gower, 366).* Under principle 22 of the *Nigerian Code of Corporate Governance (NCCG), 2018* the chairman in presiding over members' meetings should use the opportunity to interact personally with shareholders in order to develop a balanced view of shareholders' issues. This will enable the chairman to communicate these observations from the meeting to the whole board.

Under the CAMA, the chairman has statutory duties and powers during a meeting as stipulated under section 265(3) CAMA 2020, (s. 240 (3), but the list is not exhaustive. They include the duties to:

- preserve order during the meeting and with the power to take such measures that are reasonably necessary to be able to do so *(Re Indian Zoedone Co (1884) 26 Ch.D., 70; John* v. *Rees (1970) Ch. 345)*; (*Palmers, 573).* This includes the power to ask that a disruptive member be escorted by security men out of the meeting to allow for a meaningful discourse by the members;
- see that the proceedings are conducted in a regular manner;
- to ensure that the true intention of the meeting is carried out in resolving any issue(s) that arises before it *(National Dwelling Society* v. *Sykes (1894) 3 Ch., 159*);
- ensure that all questions that arise are promptly decided;
- act *bona fide* in the interests of the company *(National Dwellings Society* v. *Sykes (1894) 3 Ch, 159*);

- act, when deciding on any question during a meeting, honestly and fairly to all sectional interests and in the best interests of the company as a going business concern *(Blair* v. *Consolidated Enfield Corp. (1995) 128 DLR (4th), 73;Mayson et al., 422- 3)*;
- act with authority to decide all incidental questions that arise at the meeting and which must be decided at the meeting (*Re Indian Zoedone Co (1884) 26 Ch.D., 70; John* v. *Rees (1970) Ch., 345);*
- act to stop a debate and take a vote on a resolution which has been debated reasonably by the meeting *(Wall* v. *London and Northern Assets Corp. (1898) 2 Ch., 469; Thorne, 273).*

VOTING AT GENERAL MEETINGS

The process of voting at general meetings is usually by a show of hands, except where a poll is demanded (before or when the result of voting by show of hands is declared). (s .248(1) CAMA 2020), (s. 224(1). This was the law until this section of the CAMA 2020 was amended by section 13 of the schedule to the *Business facilitation (Miscellaneous Provisions) Act (BFA),2022* which commendably added electronic voting as an option for voting in general meetings of companies. It should be noted, however, that in advanced economies, electronic voting systems has been introduced into company meetings for some years now, because of the high quality of their internet infrastructure. It is hoped that with advancing technology in the years to come, electronic voting will take a central place as a tool for voting on resolutions in general meetings in Nigeria. This is because it is one thing to provide for electronic voting at meetings, it also another thing altogether to have the infrastructure to make that feasible, without disenfranchising any of the members.

Voting on a Poll

Under section 248(1), (s. 224 (1) those who are entitled to demand a poll during a company's general meeting are:

- the chairman of the meeting, where he is a shareholder or a proxy of a shareholder;
- at least three (3) members present in person or by proxy;

- any member(s) present in person or by proxy and representing not less than one-tenth of the total voting rights of all the members having a right to vote at the meeting; or
- a member(s) holding shares in the company conferring a right to vote at the meeting, being shares on which an aggregate sum has been paid up equal to at least one-tenth of the total sum paid up on all the shares conferring that right.

It is noteworthy that a person who is a proxy has the right to demand or join in demanding a poll at the meeting, but no member has a right to demand a poll on the issue of the election of members of a company's audit committee (s. 249 (2)(3), (s. 225 (2)(3). Unless where a poll is validly demanded, a declaration by the chairman that a resolution has, on show of hands, been carried or lost in a particular manner and entered in the minutes book shall be deemed conclusive evidence of that fact. This is without the need to prove the number or proportion of the votes recorded in favour of or against the resolution (s. 248 (2), (s. 224 (2).

Any provision in a company's Articles shall be void if the effect is to exclude the right to demand a poll at a general meeting on any question other than the election of the chairman or adjournment of the meeting. A provision in a company's Articles that seeks to make ineffective a demand for poll validly made by those qualified shall also be void (s. 249), (s. 225 (1). Where a poll has been duly demanded, it is the duty of the chairman to direct the manner in which the process shall be conducted. The result of the poll shall be deemed to be the resolution of the meeting on the issue being voted on (s. 250(2), (s. 226 (2).

When a poll has been demanded either in a general meeting or in a meeting of a class of members, a member or a member of that class who is entitled to more than one vote, if he votes, is not obliged to use all his votes or use them in the same way (s. 250(1), (s. 226 (1).

It is important to note that when a poll is demanded on the election of the chairman of a meeting or on a question of adjournment, it is to be taken immediately. In any other case(s), the poll is taken as directed by the chairman of the meeting in his discretion (s. 250(4), (s. 226(4).

Chairman's Casting Vote

Where there is an equality of votes cast, either when voting by a show of hands, electronic voting or on a poll, the chairman of the meeting shall have a second or casting vote. However, it should be noted that the chairman does not have an inherent or common law right to a casting vote, and there must be a provision in a company's Articles or the relevant legislation for a right to a casting vote to exist and be exercisable by the chairman *(Nell* v. *Longbottom (1894) 1 Q.B. 767; Charlesworth & Cain, 314).*

OBJECTIONS AS TO QUALIFICATION TO VOTE

Any objection as to the qualification of any voter must be raised at the meeting or adjourned meeting at which the vote objected to is given or tendered and every vote not disallowed at the meeting shall be considered valid. Any objection made shall be referred to the chairman of the meeting whose decision on same shall be final and conclusive (s. 253 CAMA 2020), (s. 229).

ADJOURNMENT OF MEETINGS

The chairman of a meeting has a common law power (now added to the statutory one) to adjourn the meeting. This power must be exercised where it is necessary for the proper transaction of the business of the meeting. For instance:

- where there is disorder during deliberations and it is impossible to adjourn the meeting in an orderly manner with the consent of the meeting *(John* v. *Rees (1970) Ch, 345)*; or
- if it is impossible for the meeting to continue, for example, the venue earlier proposed for the meeting has been otherwise given to another entity *(Jackson* v. *Hamlyn (1953) Ch, 577)*; or
- in order to facilitate the presence in the meeting of those that are entitled to debate and vote on a resolution that is before the meeting *(Byng* v. *London Life Association (1989) BCLC, 400)*;
- a chairman's decision to adjourn a meeting is invalid not only if it is taken in bad faith but also if he fails to take relevant factors into account, or took into account irrelevant factors *(Byng* v. *London Life Association (1989) BCLC, 400; Hannigan, 343).* In this case the chairman the meeting from the morning to the morning of the same day but to a different venue, because the meeting was crowded. The court held that the chairman did not consider, among other factors, that the new venue was inaccessible to many of the members, and the meeting was nullified.

Ways to Adjourn Meetings

Under section 264 (1) CAMA 2020, (s. 239 (1), the chairman of a meeting may, with the consent of the meeting at which a quorum is present, (and shall, if so directed by the meeting), adjourn the meeting from time to time and from place to place. However, no business shall be transacted at any adjourned meeting other than those that were left unfinished at the meeting from which the adjournment took place. This implies that no new items could be introduced into the agenda of an adjourned meeting, being that the meeting's purpose is to conclude unfinished businesses from the previous meeting. What could be rationale for this rule? Most likely because to introduce a new item(s) at the adjourned meeting would require the issuance of a new notice of meeting to all the members who got the previous notice, indicating that such a new item(s) will be discussed at the adjourned meeting. This will equate to calling a new meeting in place of an adjourned meeting.

In terms of notice for adjourned meeting, except where the meeting is adjourned for 30 days or more, there would be no need to give a fresh notice for the adjourned meeting or the business to be transacted at the meeting. However, where the meeting is adjourned for 30 days or more, then, notice of the adjourned meeting shall be given as it was for the original meeting (s. 264(2), (s. 239 (2).

If within one hour from the time appointed for the meeting, a quorum has not been formed, the meeting shall be dissolved if it was convened on members' requisition. Otherwise, the meeting shall stand adjourned to the same day the week after, at the same time and place or to such other time, day, and place as the chairman, or if he be absent, the directors may direct (s. 264(3), (s. 239 (3).

Where a meeting stands adjourned for a lack of quorum to transact the scheduled business as above, then at the adjourned meeting, any two or more members present at the place and time to which it was adjourned shall form a quorum and their decision shall bind all the shareholders. This is meant to deal with situations where some members will deliberately stay away in order to frustrate schedule meetings.

Where it is only one member that is present at the adjourned meeting, he may seek the direction of the Court to take a decision for the company (s. 264(4), (s. 239 (4). Any decision taken by the member on the Court's direction shall be binding on the company and the other members.

While every member(s) has a right to attend a company's general meeting, under sections 251 and 252 CAMA 2020, (ss. 227 & 228) a member who is of unsound mind or in respect of whom an order of competent Court has been made, may not vote in person but by his committee, receiver or *curator bonis* (a guardian appointed to take care of an estate), or persons in the nature of these classes of persons.

In sum, company meetings are crucial fora in the life of any company, being the principal mechanisms through which shareholder solidarity and activism are usually put into effect and far-reaching decisions taken. Therefore, the importance of the meetings cannot be over-emphasized. This is why such meetings are made mandatory by the CAMA and the Court has the power to order a meeting for a company where the prevailing conditions warrant making such an order.

For the company secretary, the roles and responsibilities during company meetings are numerous, ranging from issuing and serving of notices with adequate time for the members to decide whether to attend or not, to serving all those entitled to do so. The company secretary also has a duty in relation to determining and maintaining quorums for meetings, agreeing and preparing the agenda with the chairman, preparing and assisting with proxy forms and votes, taking minutes, preparing resolutions, among many others. These duties are peculiar because failure to execute them diligently portends serious consequences for the company as a legal entity. For instance, failure to serve valid notices for the meeting or to secure a valid quorum invalidates a meeting, with the attendant costs and logistical implications to the company.

The company secretary is also the sounding board for the chairman and the directors during general meetings (we discussed that of the board of directors in previous chapters) advising on all issues with legal and regulatory implications. Even after the meetings, especially with respect to public companies, the company secretary's roles continue with all regulatory notices and returns to the Commission and other regulators.

Finally, company meetings are where companies declare dividends and issue bonus shares and other 'membership sweeteners' to shareholders. They are also the fora where the shareholders have the opportunity to directly interact with the directors and senior management teams. Therefore, when effectively harnessed, a company meeting could be a veritable avenue to enhance the needed synergy between the company's management, its shareholders and other stakeholders for the ultimate success of the company and satisfaction of all stakeholders.

CHECKPOINTS

- ✓ The meeting of members (company's meeting or general meeting) is the highest decision-making organ of the company, although most of its powers are usually delegated to the board of directors, for the day-to-day running of the affairs of the company.
- ✓ Membership in a company guarantees members the right to attend a general meeting (except where the person is otherwise disqualified) by any provisions of the company's Articles.
- ✓ The general meeting is where the members assert their supremacy and also afford the opportunity to members to ask questions and get direct answers from the directors and senior management team.
- ✓ Apart from the statutory meeting, which is a one-off meeting for newly registered public companies, there are also the annual general meeting and the extra-ordinary general meeting, the latter, for dealing with urgent situations that cannot wait for normal general meetings.
- ✓ A 21 days' notice is required to be given for annual general meetings, and additional publications in two (2) national daily newspapers also required for public companies. Failure to give these mandatory notices will invalidate the meeting and its outcomes.
- ✓ The CAMA 2020 has a new provision that empowers the Commission to, on its own, summon a general meeting of a company that has defaulted or has been unable to do so.
- ✓ The CAMA 2020 has also introduced a provision that allows private companies to be able to hold general meetings electronically, which excludes physical attendance, provided the company's Articles are adhered to. An amendment to this section of the CAMA by the BFA 2022 now allows all companies to be able to hold their general meeting electronically.
- ✓ Members with one-tenth of the shareholding or one-tenth of members can requisition a general meeting.
- ✓ The Court can order, on application of a member or on its own accord, that a meeting be held when it is impracticable for the company to organize one by itself. The term 'impracticability,' it has been advised, should not be construed as 'impossibility' in this context.

- ✓ Court ordered meetings have limitations and a meeting will not be ordered where the effect will be to alter class rights conferred on a shareholder or to shift power balance in shareholding, which was earlier agreed to by the parties.
- ✓ The critical importance of general meetings is also supported by the fact that some activities can only be carried out in general meetings like the alteration of the Articles, change of name, change of object clause, increase and reduction in share capital etc.
- ✓ Notice of meetings should have details as to time, date, day, venue, etc and state the general nature of the business to be transacted at the meeting. This is to help members decide whether to attend or not.
- ✓ Notice of meeting must be served on all members and those that are entitled to receive the notice. Failure will invalidate a meeting except for accidental omission, which term has been difficult to precisely establish in decided cases.
- ✓ Quorum for a meeting, in all shades, as determined by the Articles or the CAMA is crucial and a condition precedent for any valid meeting. Lack of quorum will invalidate the meeting and its outcomes.
- ✓ Voting in general meetings is usually be a show of hands, except where a poll is demanded by those qualified to do so. An amendment of the CAMA by the BFA 2022 has introduced electronic voting as an option at companies' general meetings.
- ✓ The chairman of the board normally chairs the general meeting and plays important roles, has a casting vote in the event of a tie but must act in what is in the best interests of the company. He can adjourn the meeting on his own when conditions warrant such, for instance, to restore orderliness or to secure the safety of members or the company's board members and senior management from chaotic situations.
- ✓ However, if the chairman if found to have adjourned a meeting for an improper purpose or without considering all the relevant factors, such an adjournment and meeting (if it has held) will be invalidated.

Chapter 13

RESOLUTIONS AND MINUTES OF MEETINGS

INTRODUCTION

The decisions of a company at its meetings (even for directors' meetings) take the form of resolutions that are agreed to at the meetings by members and other attendees. As a general principle of law, to be valid, all resolutions, subject to some statutory exceptions, must be passed at general meetings proper and not elsewhere (s. 259 CAMA 2020), (s. 234) (*Orojo, 238)* This requirement notwithstanding, being that companies differ in their nature, size and outlook, the law has appreciated these indices and made some limited exceptions to the requirement that all resolutions must be passed at a company's general meetings. That is where written resolutions, also called circular resolutions, become relevant.

WRITTEN OR CIRCULAR RESOLUTIONS

As noted above, for validity, resolutions must be passed at a company's general meetings. To this general rule, however, there is an exception. In the case of a private company, section 259 CAMA 2020, (s. 234) permits a written or circular resolution signed by all the members entitled to attend and vote at the general meeting. Once so executed, it shall be valid as if it was passed at a general meeting duly convened and held *(A.G. Enugu State* v. *A.V.O.P. Plc (1995) 6 NWLR Pt. 399, 90; Baroness Wenlock* v. *River Dee Co. (1883) 36 Ch.D, 675; Re Duomatic Ltd (1969) 2 Ch, 365; Gower & Davies, 443).* This provision has, by implication, disqualified any public company, under any guise, from purporting to use circular resolutions in reaching any decision(s) during its meetings. Any such attempt renders such a resolution ineffective and void, *ab initio.*

Members' Assent Must be Unanimous

The foundation for the validity of any resolution passed as written or circular resolution is the agreement of all the members to so do. In doing this, all the members must sign (assent) to the proposed resolution to indicate their consent thereto and affirm its validity.

It is not enough that a vast majority of the requisite members in a company signed the resolution, as the members' assent must be unanimous in relation to the proposal, to be valid. The principle of unanimity of assent of the members to a proposed circular resolution has been held to be the agreement of those who can vote on the matter being proposed. This has come to be known as the 'Duomatic principle,' from the case of *Re Duomatic Ltd (1969) 2 Ch, 365).* The assent of the members is therefore ineffective if the persons who give the assent could not have made the decision at a meeting of the company, for instance, maybe because they lack a quorum to constitute a meeting or were not qualified to vote at a meeting of the company *(Re Express Engineering Works Ltd (1920) 1 Ch, 466; Re Oxted Motor Co. Ltd (1921) 3 KB, 32; Parker & Cooper* v. *Reading (1926) Ch., 975; Hannigan, 345).*

Finally, the principle of unanimity of assent requires that all persons who are qualified to assent to the resolution must be given the opportunity to do so *(Re Gee and Co. (Woolwich) Ltd (1975) Ch, 52; Mayson et al, 442-3). However,* where an opportunity has been given to a member(s) to assent to a resolution and he acquiesces in doing so, such an action would be taken to mean a positive assent to the resolution *(Re Bailey Hay and Co. Ltd (1971) 1 WLR, 1357).* This is meant to prevent an unwilling or undecided member from using his indecision to frustrate any proposed resolution by a company. It is also the correct position of the law that a member who has assented to a circular resolution cannot successfully object subsequently that the resolution was not validly passed by the company *(Re Pearce, Duff and Co. Ltd (1960) 1 WLR, 1014).* Such a member, in the absence of fraud or other vitiating act(s) by the company, would have been estopped from taking such a line of argument to impeach the already passed resolution.

It is important to note that the 'Duomatic principle' is not usually applied at large, but has a certain limitation, which was established in the case of *Wright* v. *Atlas Wright (Europe) Ltd (1999) 2 BCLC, 301*; *Thorne, 286).* In this case it was established that the application of 'Duomatic principle' cannot be used to override statutory provisions whose purpose and rationale extends beyond the protection of the class which has purported to waive the provision. In essence, the application of the principle must be confined to the very essence of specific purpose that it deals with and not beyond. Otherwise, the application will be ineffective.

The roles of the company secretary in the above respects are, where applicable, to ensure that resolutions are properly prepared and notified, presented, monitored and passed in a general meeting. In the case of a written resolution, the company secretary is to ensure effective unanimity of those to sign and ensure that all assents are gotten before adoption, failing which, all efforts therein will amount to nothing. As will be seen below, different types of resolutions will require different approaches in terms of timing and the requisite number of members and other attendees for passage. Also, there are resolutions that are mandatorily required to be registered with the Commission, and so, within certain time limits.

TYPES OF RESOLUTIONS

A resolution at the general meeting of a company may either be an ordinary or a special resolution. In the absence of a contrary provision in the CAMA or in the Articles of a company, the company acts by ordinary resolutions in its general meetings *(Charlesworth & Cain, 322)*.

The import of the distinction between ordinary and special resolutions is far reaching. For instance, where a company purports to do by an ordinary resolution what its Articles or the CAMA requires to be done by a special resolution, a member is entitled to apply to Court to restrain the company by injunction or declaration from so doing (s. 343 (b) CAMA 2020), (s. 300(b). If the company has already done the proposed act with an irregular type of resolution, the Court, on a member's application, will invalidate the act already done, being based on a faulty foundation.

Ordinary Resolution

This is the type of resolution that is passed by a simple majority of votes cast by those entitled to vote, either in person or through proxy at a company's general meeting (s. 258(1) CAMA 2020), (s. 233 (1) *(Bushell* v. *Faith (1970) AC, 1099)*. Where there is no express provision in the CAMA and the company's Articles, on the requisite resolution to complete a particular act, it is taken that it is an ordinary resolution that is intended and same should be adopted for such purposes.

Special Resolution

This is the type of resolution that is passed by not less than three-fourths of the votes cast by those entitled to attend and vote either in person or by proxy at a general meeting, of which 21 days' notice, specifying the intention to propose the resolution as a special resolution, would have been given (s. 258(2) CAMA 2020), (s. 233 (2). This type of resolution is usually required to effect important changes or to undertake serious businesses for the company, for example, changing a company's name, altering its Articles or its object clause or a resolution to authorize voluntary winding-up of a company, among several others.

A notice of special resolution must set out the text or the entire substance of the resolution, and the resolution adopted by the meeting must be same as that stated in the notice. This means that no amendment of substance can be made to the already notified resolution by the meeting. Any Amendment(s) to an already notified notice of special resolution must be limited to the correction of grammatical or clerical errors, or to reframing the verbiage to a more formal one *(Re Moorgate Mercantile Holdings Ltd (1980) 1 WLR, 227).*In essence, the prayers on the resolution, for instance, cannot be amended after having been notified to members and others who will attend the meeting.

Although a 21 days' notice is required to propose a special resolution, a majority of those entitled to attend and vote at a general meeting and who together hold not less than 95 per cent in nominal value of the shares that gave them such a right, or 95 per cent of total voting right (for a company without a share capital) may agree to propose and pass a resolution as a special resolution. This is even if less than 21 days' notice of such a resolution had been given to those entitled to receive same (s. 258 (2) CAMA 2020), (s. 233 (2).

It has been held that the length of notice stipulated by an Act (in this case the CAMA) to be given for a proposed special resolution cannot be curtailed by a company's Articles *(Re Hector Whaling Ltd (1936) Ch 208; Thompson* v. *Simpson (1961) 1 Q.B. 195; Charlesworth & Cain, 323).* However, a company may by its Articles provide that any matter not required by the Articles or the CAMA to be passed by a special resolution shall be passed by an ordinary resolution of the members (s. 256(6) CAMA 2020), (s. 233 (6).

Resolutions that Require Special Notice

Where a special notice is required for any resolution by the provisions of the CAMA, then, the resolution shall not be effective unless a notice to move it has been given to the company not less than 28 days before the meeting at which the motion for the resolution is to be moved. When a company receives a special notice of a proposed resolution it shall circulate same to its members in the normal manner that it circulates notice of meetings. If this is not practicable, then, it shall advertise the notice in an appropriately circulating newspaper or circulate it in any other way allowed by the Articles, but not less than 21 days before the meeting. Now that notice of meetings can be given electronically to members of a company, it presupposes that this method is also available to the company to use in this instance.

If after notice of intention to move a resolution requiring special notice has been given to a company, a meeting is called 28 days or less after the notice has been given, the notice shall be deemed to be proper even though it did not comply with the requirement of the CAMA as to length of notice required (s. 261 CAMA 2020), (s. 236).

SOME RESOLUTIONS REQUIRING SPECIAL NOTICE

Under the CAMA, some resolutions require that special notice (28 days) of their being moved must be given to the company before any meeting to move same can be convened and held:

- under section 282 CAMA 2020 (s. 256), special notice is required to appoint or approve the appointment of a person that is 70 years or older as a director of a public company;
- under section 288(2) CAMA 2020 (s. 262 (2), special notice is required for a resolution to remove a director before the expiration of his term of office or to appoint another person in place of the removed director;
- under section 411 (a-d) CAMA 2020 (s. 364 (a-d), special notice is required for a resolution to appoint as auditor a person other than a retiring auditor;
- to fill a casual vacancy in the office of auditor; or to re-appoint as auditor a retiring auditor who was appointed by the directors to fill a casual vacancy;
- to remove an auditor before the expiration of his term of office.

RESOLUTIONS PASSED AT ADJOURNED MEETINGS

It has been noted above that an adjourned meeting, in the main, is usually a continuation of the original meeting and can only discuss and conclude on items notified for the previous meeting and nothing more. Flowing from that understanding, therefore, however, a resolution that has been passed at an adjourned meeting of a company, or at a meeting on which it was actually passed. In essence, such a resolution shall not be deemed to have been passed on any earlier date, for instance, on the date from which the meeting could not be concluded and then adjourned (s. 263 CAMA 2020), (s. 238) *(Holmes* v. *Keyes (1959) Ch., 199).*

REGISTRATION OF CERTAIN RESOLUTIONS

Under section 262 CAMA 2020, (s. 237), a printed copy of applicable agreements and resolutions are to be registered with the Commission within 15 days of making the agreement or passing the resolution. The resolutions and agreements concerned are:

- special resolutions;
- resolutions which have been agreed to by all members of a company, but which, if not so agreed to, would not have been effective for their purpose, unless as the case may be, they have been passed as special resolutions;
- resolutions or agreements which have been agreed to by all the members of any class of shareholders but which, if not so agreed to, would not have been effective for their purpose, unless they have been passed by some particular majority or otherwise in some particular manner;
- all resolutions and agreements which effectively bind all the members of any class of shareholders, though not agreed to by all those members; and
- resolutions for the voluntary winding-up of a company under section 620 of the Act (s. 457).

The major attention of the company secretary with resolutions is actually on the issue of notice, that is, the requisite length of notice for particular resolutions. Inadequate notice for a proposed resolution creates unnecessary problems and may invalidate the resolution to be passed. Particular attention should be paid to special resolutions and resolutions requiring special notice to be given and every effort must be made to adhere to the notice requirements.

In another respect, some resolutions are required to be registered, as above, with the Commission within specified days (15) after adoption. While it is correct that non-registration of a resolution, as required here, with the Commission does not invalidate the resolution, a fine is imposed on the company and each officer in respect of any page of the resolution not registered as required.

While a company may be able to pay a fine imposed, it is an incident that most company board of directors detests and such infractions are termed 'avoidable or negligent regulatory infractions.' The company secretary must do all that is possible to avoid this type of regulatory penalty, especially, repeat penalties.

AMENDMENT OF RESOLUTIONS

In simple terms, 'amendment' of a document is a formal revision of the document, and could be by addition, insertion, deletion or substitution, and the amendment of resolutions should be read as such *(CBN* v. *Okonkwo (2013) LPELR-21235; UBN Plc* v. *Lawal) (2011) LPELR-8879).*The CAMA has no express provision(s) concerning the process or conditions for the amendment(s) of resolutions. Even at that, company resolutions, once passed or adopted, are not immutable in themselves. It would seem that most common law jurisdictions actually left this aspect of the company law practice to the common law Courts for direction(s). This lack of statutory provision(s), however, does not imply that amending a resolution is inconceivable in law. The Courts have actually led the way and formulated some guiding rules and principles in relation to the amendment(s) of resolutions:

- first, an amendment of a resolution should be allowed if it is pertinent to the subject matter of the proposed resolution. This is because if the chairman of the meeting refuses to allow a vote on a proper amendment as proposed, then the resolution if passed without the amendment would be invalid *(Henderson* v. *Bank of Australasia (1890) 45 Ch.D, 330*). It is immaterial that the mover of the motion did not challenge the chairman's ruling at the meeting refusing an amendment;
- second, an amendment cannot be proposed that goes beyond the notice of the meeting. For instance, if a notice of the meeting indicated that the resolution would be for 'the reappointment of the company auditors and fixing their fees', then an amendment to 'reappoint company auditors and increase the number of the directors of the company from 5 to 8' is outside the scope of the notice and the meeting and should not be allowed *(Charlesworth & Cain, 324).*

The whole essence of amending resolutions, therefore, is to better bring out the essence of the subject matter proposed to be discussed, and the amendment has to be within what has been proposed. It should not, under any guise at all, be seen to be at large, otherwise, it will go outside the scope of legally permissible amendment(s). In such a case, the amendment(s) will be invalidated by the Court, on application by any aggrieved person(s).

It is for the company secretary, who understands the rules and the principles of amendment, to guide the company and the proponents of the resolution(s) on the need to remain with the allowable scope of amendment(s) to the resolution. Failure to do this will amount to a waste of the company's time and resources, if the amendment(s) is later nullified by the Courts.

DRAFTING RESOLUTIONS FOR MEETINGS

Decisions in meetings are largely in the form of resolutions and kept as minutes of the meeting. Although they are not cast in stone, certain basic rules have been formulated overtime as a guide with respect to the drafting of resolutions:

1. every resolution should commence with the word 'that' for the proposing and the resolution. For instance, 'It was proposed that…' or 'It was resolved 'that...'
2. as far as possible, resolutions should be couched in a positive instead of a negative language;
3. if possible, the resolution should be included in a single sentence, but if it would be too cumbersome, the second sentence should also start with 'that' or 'it was further resolved...
4. the resolution should be numbered serially for certainty;
5. the word 'should' must be avoided and instead definitive phrases like 'it was resolved that ....' should be adopted;
6. the content of a resolution must be legal and not contrary to public policy, for instance, a resolution that 'it was resolved that the company continues evading taxes...' cannot validly be passed, being that it is contrary to public policy;
7. care should be taken with dividend resolutions, which must state the dividend per share, the payment date, and the record date (that is the date for the closure of the register of members for the sake of participating in the dividend);
8. the resolution must be within the powers of the company as authorized by its Memorandum and Articles. In essence, the resolutions cannot be on a matter that is *ultra vires* the company, otherwise it is ineffectual;
9. the resolution must be within the scope of the meeting and covered by the notice of the meeting (*Nzegwu-Danjuma, 196*).

MINUTES OF MEETINGS

Decisions from the deliberations in company meetings and the meetings of its directors, managers or even board committees are usually recorded as minutes of those meetings. Most times it is the company secretary or his designate that is responsible for recording the minutes of meetings and maintaining the minutes book.

The CAMA requires every company operating in Nigeria, (except a company having a single shareholder) to keep minutes of all proceedings at its general meetings and proceedings of its directors and managers (if any). This is to be kept in minutes books. The minutes of any meeting, if purporting to be signed by the chairman of the meeting or of the next meeting, shall be *prima facie* evidence of the proceedings at that meeting (s. 266(1)(2) CAMA 2020), (s. 241(1)(2). Since the minutes are *prima facie* (and not conclusive) evidence of the proceedings of a meeting, it implies that a purported record described as minutes of a meeting can be contradicted by other evidence *(Re Llanharry Hermatite Iron Ore Co. Roney's Case (1864) 4 De G.J. & Sm., 426; Palmers, 594).* The above notwithstanding, when the Articles provide that the minutes, signed by the chairman, shall be 'conclusive evidence without any further proof of the facts therein stated,' as between the company and the members, evidence cannot be called to contradict the minutes unless it is established to be fraudulent *(Kerr* v. *Motram (1940) Ch., 657; Charlesworth & Cain, 321).*

The exemption above, of a single-member company from the mandatory requirement for companies to keep minutes of their meetings, was introduced by the CAMA 2020. Under the CAMA 2004, every company was required to keep minutes of its meetings.

Where minutes have been kept for any of the meetings as stated above, then, until the contrary is proved, the meeting shall be deemed to have been validly held and all appointments of directors, managers or liquidators shall be considered to have been duly made (s. 266(3) CAMA 2020), (s.241 (3). In the case of a single member company, then, the CAMA provides that:

> where the single member takes any decision that (i) may be taken by the company in a general meeting, and (ii) has effect as if agreed by the company in general meeting, the single member shall provide the board with details of that decision (but failure to do this does not affect the decision taken by the single member) (s.266(4).

A failure to enter minutes of meetings in minutes book does not render the proceedings of the meeting void, once such proceedings could be established by other evidence *(Nsirim* v. *Onuma Const. Co. (Nig) Ltd (2001) 7 NWLR Pt. 713, 742, 753).*

The minutes books for proceedings of general meetings of a company are to be kept at the company's registered and shall be open to inspection by members during business hours. This is to be without a charge. A company is entitled to put reasonable restrictions by its Articles or at the general meeting, on such inspections, but access of at least six (6) hours daily should be allowed. A member is also entitled to a copy of the minutes, certified by the company secretary, within 7 seven days of requesting for same and paying the applicable fees thereto (s. 267 (1-3) CAMA 2020), (s. 242 (1-3).

It is the responsibility of the company secretary, from the legal and governance angles, not only to have custody of the company's minutes books but also to protect the integrity of the minutes books from any manipulation. This is because the minutes books, as already noted, are *prima facie* evidence of the proceedings of the meeting they contain and therefore are the primary evidence in any legal proceedings wherein those meetings or their deliberations or outcomes are being challenged.

Penalties are imposed on a company and any of its officers in default by failing to keep minutes of meetings or allowing inspection or making copies available to a member. On application by any aggrieved person, the Court may order an immediate inspection of the minutes books or direct that the company sends copies to the person that requires them (s. 267 (4), (s. 242(4).

Preparing the Minutes of Meetings

It is the responsibility of the company secretary to prepare the initial draft of the minutes of meetings and forward to the chairman of the board for his comments. When the chairman clears the draft minutes, it is then circulated to the directors for their comments. The minutes would then be included in the papers for the next meeting, and if approved by that meeting, to be signed by the chairman.

The process of preparing minutes of meetings requires a measure of skill from the company secretary, since the minutes must reflect accurately the decided issues in sufficient details, yet being concise enough to avoid verbosity. The chairman's preference, except where the company historically has an established pattern of presenting its minutes, will be paramount in the manner the minutes are presented. However, it has to be stated that the rules relating to writing minutes are not static and minutes could be written to suit the peculiarity of a company or a stylistic slant introduced by the company secretary and accepted by the chairman. In any case, however, minutes should of necessity have the following basic elements:

1. name of the company;
2. venue, day and date of the meeting;
3. names of those present and in attendance;
4. apologies for any absences;
5. approval of any previous minutes;
6. record of the proceedings of the instant meeting, (where appropriate a numbering system should be used for each item of business). There is a new pattern being adopted by some company secretaries wherein minutes are written in tabular form with columns that seem to contrast issues discussed in the meeting;
7. conclusion and adjournment;
8. chairman's signature (when the minutes have been approved by the instant meeting) *(ICSA, 302).*

In all events, the form the minutes of meeting take is a function of trying to ensure efficiency of presentation of the minutes and does not affect the substance or legality of the minutes, in any way. Having said that, it should be noted that a badly written minutes that does not bring out the essence of the issues discussed at the meeting or that makes it difficult to appreciate all the issues with minimum efforts, is a disaster for the company secretary.

CHECKPOINTS

- ✓ In general, deliberations in company's meetings are usually agreed in resolutions and recorded in minutes. All company resolutions are to be passed in the company's general meetings, in order to be valid.
- ✓ The law has, however, made exceptions with respect to private companies, which are allowed to use 'written' or 'circular' resolutions, without having to convene and hold a formal meeting.
- ✓ The critical criterion for the validity of 'written' or 'circular' resolution is unanimity of assent of the members, who are entitled to attend the meeting and vote on the resolution. It does not have to be the whole members of

the company signing the resolution to make it valid, but only those who are entitled to attend the meeting.

- ✓ For special resolutions, the key issue for the company secretary is to ensure that the 21 days' notice for its proposal required by law is complied with. Added to this, as much as possible, let the full text of the proposed resolution or the substance of it, be set out in the body of the proposed resolution. Registration of the resolution with the Commission comes after the meeting proper.
- ✓ The same care to be taken in the preceding point above must be taken with resolutions requiring special notice (28 days), ensuring that the length of notice required is fully complied with.
- ✓ Note that where the length of notice for a meeting has been stipulated by the Act (CAMA) it cannot, except where it is made subject to the Articles, be curtailed or elongated by a company's Articles.
- ✓ Notwithstanding the above principle, holders of 95 percent value of shareholding or 95 per cent voting rights (for companies without shares) may agree to validly pass a special resolution with less than 21 days' notice given.
- ✓ A resolution(s) that is passed at an adjourned meeting is deemed to have actually been passed on the day of its actual passage and not on the earlier date of the meeting from which it adjourned.
- ✓ Some resolutions, for example, special resolutions, are required by the CAMA to be registered with the Commission within 15 days after their approval or adoption. Although non-registration will not invalidate the resolution, fines are imposed on the company and any member liable for the non-registration of such registrable resolutions (member here includes a liquidator).
- ✓ Resolutions, when passed, are not immutable, and can be amended. However, any amendment must be within the proposed resolution itself and will not accommodate or introduce external or new matters, which will amount to clandestine new proposition, and is to be rejected.
- ✓ Drafting resolutions and preparing minutes have rules but these rules are not cast in stone. The important thing in all cases is to bring out the real essence of the resolutions or minutes without confusing issues therein.

- ✓ Every company, except a single-member company (created under CAMA 2020), is required to keep minutes of the proceedings of its general meetings (and meetings of its managers and directors) in minutes book.
- ✓ The minutes kept by a company is *prima facie* evidence that the proceedings and matters contained therein actually took place. This presumption can be rebutted by more credible evidence, for instance, if it is established creditably that the minutes book is a forgery.
- ✓ Non-entrance of the minutes of a meeting in a minutes book does not invalidate the minutes, once the proceedings of the meeting can be established by other credible evidence. For instance, if there was an authentic video recording of the meeting with clear audio of the deliberations.
- ✓ Members have a right to inspect a company's minutes book as kept, mostly at the company's registered office, and take copies thereof, after paying the applicable fees for the copies. It is the responsibility of the company secretary to keep and maintain the integrity of the company's minutes books, shielding same from any form of manipulation.
- ✓ If a company refuses or otherwise obstructs the members' rights to inspect the minutes or take copies, on application, a Court may order that immediate access be granted to the member for inspection of the minutes book and to take copies (if also applicable).

Chapter 14

THE SHARE CAPITAL OF A COMPANY

INTRODUCTION

Issues surrounding a company's share capital are ones that confront company secretaries frequently and in diverse dimensions. It is therefore imperative that the company secretary possesses a good knowledge of the company's capital structure where he works and other incidental issues that would aid the secretary's divergent tasks in that respect. This knowledge will also aid the company secretary in giving quality advice to the board of directors, any individual director, members or other stakeholders on any aspect of the company's capital, when needed. And it could be anytime.

For clarity, most big companies do have finance professionals in their employ that deal primarily with the issue of their capital, its structure and content. However, whenever any legal or compliance issues relating to the company's capital arise, the company secretary will have to offer the needed guidance. In that respect, it comes in handy when the company secretary is at home with the capital structure of the company and the attendant implications of each share capital genre, that forms part of the company's share capital structure.

CHARACTERIZATION OF SHARE CAPITAL

The share capital of a company is defined in section 867 CAMA 2020 to mean a company's issued share capital at any given time. A company's share capital could be characterized into several categories depending on the aspect of the company's share capital that is being discussed. However, the CAMA 2020 has made some significant changes in the nomenclature and effects of the classification of some types of share capital. These are:

- minimum issued share capital has replaced the authorized minimum share capital under the CAMA 2004;
- paid-up share capital;
- reserved share capital;

- equity share.

The 'share capital' of a company is 'the issued share capital of a company at any given time' (s. 867 CAMA 2020). This replaces and has the same meaning with 'authorized share capital' under the CAMA 2004) (s. 567). It is, therefore, the total issued share capital of the company at the time it was registered or as it continues its business. It is usually fixed by the Memorandum and no company can be registered with more capital than the issued share capital. The amount of a company's capital can be increased or decreased depending on the terms of the company's Articles. The CAMA 2020 also makes detailed provisions from section 125 through section 135 on the alterations processes of a company's share capital.

The minimum issued share capital replaces the 'authorized minimum share capital' under the CAMA 2004. This means the minimum amount permissible in law with which a particular type of company could be registered. The only distinction is that under the 2020 CAMA, the share amount is issued by the company and not simply on paper. In Nigeria presently, the minimum issued share capital is ₦100,000.00 (One hundred thousand naira only) for a private company and ₦2,000,000.00 (Two million naira only) for a public company (s. 27(2) CAMA 2020). Under section 124 CAMA 2020 (s. 99) no company can be registered with an amount lower than the issued share capital stated in the Memorandum registered with the Commission. An existing company that was registered with a lower minimum issued share capital before the commencement of the CAMA 2020, is mandated, within 180 days of the appointed day, to increase its minimum issued share capital to the new minimum authorized under the CAMA.

The 'paid-up share capital' of a company is the aspect of company's capital that has been subscribed, issued and paid up (the present CAMA uses issued share capital almost exclusively). It is the part of the company's capital that is actively working for the company at any point in time. It is noteworthy that a company's unpaid share capital still forms part of the assets of the company and could be called up at any time to satisfy pressing demands on the company *(Yussuf & Anor* v. *Adewuyi Brothers & Co. (Liquidators to ROTAG Assurance Co Ltd.) (1991) 7 NWLR Pt. 39, 55-56).* It is increasingly uncommon to see companies that allot shares that are not fully paid-up, since most companies do not want to go through the hassles of calling-up shares in diverse situations. This is especially so when the company could get the shares fully paid for on allotment to subscribers.

A company's 'reserve share capital' relates to the re-registration of an unlimited company. Under section 129 CAMA 2020 (s. 104), if an unlimited company resolves to re-register as a limited company, it may:

- increase the nominal amount of its issued share capital by increasing the nominal amount of each of its shares, but subject to the condition that no part of the increased issued share capital shall be capable of being called up except in the event and for the purposes of the company being wound-up; or
- provided that a specified portion of its uncalled share capital shall not be capable of being called up except in the event and for the purposes of the company being wound-up.

The 'equity share' of a company means a share in the company other than a preference share. On its part, a preference share means a share, by whatever name designated, which does not entitle its holder to any right to participate, beyond a specified amount, in any distribution, whether by way of dividend or on redemption, in a winding-up or otherwise (s. 867 CAMA 2020), (s. 567).

There are implications, major and minor, for the changes brought about by CAMA 2020 in this regard. The company secretary should appreciate these changes, especially, the replacement of the authorized minimum share capital with minimum issued share capital and the special utility of the reserve share capital, among others. The real effect(s) of any of the changes on the operations of a company with respect to share capital are not the same, and this fact should be appreciated and internalized by all those concerned, the company secretary mostly to note.

ALTERATION OF COMPANY'S SHARE CAPITAL

Although a company is mandated to be registered with an issued share capital of a particular amount, in virtually every case, the Articles of a company and the CAMA usually give the company the power to alter its share capital. This is either by consolidation, conversion, sub-division or cancellation of some of its share capital. The procedures to do any of these vary, to a large extent.

Consolidation of Share Capital: under section 125 CAMA 2020 (s. 100), a company having a share capital may, in a general meeting only and not otherwise, alter the conditions of its Memorandum to:

- consolidate and divide all or any part of its share capital into shares of larger amount than its existing shares;

- sub-divide its shares or any of them into shares of smaller amount than is fixed by the Memorandum, so that in the sub-division the proportion between the amount paid and the amount, if any, unpaid, on each reduced share shall be the same as it was in the case of the share from which the reduced share is derived.

The CAMA 2020 made two major amendments, by omission, to the process of share capital alteration by consolidation: the first is that the aspect of share capital alteration providing for paid up shares to be converted into stock and then re-converted from stock into paid-up shares has been omitted from the CAMA.

The second thing is the omission of the provision that cancels shares which, at the date of passing of the resolution in that behalf, have been taken or agreed to be taken by a person. Once this is done, the amount of the company's share capital will be diminished by the amount of the shares so cancelled.

The above provisions effectively eliminate the conversion of stocks into shares and the re-conversion of same into stocks. Also eliminated is the issue of cancellation by companies of unissued shares. It is not clear on the face of the CAMA why these provisions were made, although, with respect to unissued shares, it appears that the trend seems to be tilting towards companies using fully issued shares on all occasions.

NOTICE TO COMMISSION OF ALTERATION OF SHARE CAPITAL

If a company having a share capital has altered its share capital in any way by consolidating, dividing or sub-dividing them or part thereof, as stated in section 125 CAMA 2020, (s. 100), then it shall within one (1) month after doing so give notice of the alteration to the Commission, specifying, as the case may be, the shares consolidated, divided or sub-divided. (s.126 CAMA 2020), (s. 101 (1). A continuing daily fine, to be specified by the Commission, is imposed on the company and every officer who is in default for failure to give the requisite notice to the Commission, of the alteration of capital (s.126(2) CAMA 2020), (s. 101(2). Under the CAMA 2004, the penalty was ₦50.00 per day of default.

INCREASE OF A COMPANY'S SHARE CAPITAL

As a going concern, a company may, for different reasons, and in order to meet the exigencies of its business, resolve to increase its share capital at any time. Under section 127 (1) CAMA 2020, (s. 102 (1), a company having a share capital, may, only in a general meeting and not otherwise, increase its issued share capital as it deems fit, by allotment of new shares of such amount as it considers expedient.

The above was the law before this provision of the CAMA was amended by section 3 of the schedule to the *Business Facilitation (Miscellaneous Provisions) Act (BFA) 2022*. Under this amendment, 'a company having a share capital may increase its share capital by allotment of new shares of such amount as it considers expedient (a) in a general meeting, (b) by a resolution of the board of directors, subject to the conditions or direction that may be imposed in the Articles or by the company in a general meeting.' In essence, the new position now is that a company may increase its share capital anytime it wants to do so and does not have to wait only for a general meeting to do so. The board of directors are allowed to pass a resolution to increase a company's share capital. However, this power of the board is subject to any direction or condition that the members may have imposed thereon in general meeting or in the Articles. The provision hands over, in part, the process of increasing a company's share capital, to the directors, but then subjects them also to the powers of the members in general meeting. This is apparently to act as check on the powers of the directors in that respect.

The increase of a company's share capital in a general meeting shall be by an ordinary resolution, which will also make consequential amendments to the company's Memorandum and Articles to reflect the new issued share capital(s. 127(8). A company that has increased its share capital shall give notice to that effect to the Commission within 15 days of passing the resolution authorizing the increase. The Commission is mandated to record the increase so communicated by the company (s. 127(2), (s. 102(2).

It is important to note that, where, in connection with the increase of a company's shares, there is another approval required under any other enactment(s) other than the CAMA, the company shall give notice of that fact to the Commission within 15 days after the passing of the resolution authorizing the increase. This notice is to be accompanied by an affidavit sworn to by a director in the company to that effect. When the Commission receives this notice and the accompanying affidavit, the initial period of 15 days to communicate any increase in shares to the Commission is deemed to be extended by a period of not later than 10 days after the approval required under the other enactment is obtained by the company (s. 127(3).

If after 48 days of a company notifying the Commission that approval is required under another enactment, still, the approval required under that enactment has not been received by the company, then the company shall file another notice and affidavit to that effect to the Commission. The company shall file a new notice on each occasion after the lapse of 48 days and the approval under the other enactment has not been received. However, if after 9 months of the first notification by the company to the Commission, the approval under the other enactment has still not been received and communicated by the company, the resolution increasing the company's issued share capital becomes null and void (s. 127(4)(5). The company will have to start the process afresh if the increase in share capital is still desired.

The above provisions are targeted at companies that report to or deal with two or multiple regulators. For instance, companies in the capital market and insurance sectors will have to obtain approvals to that effect from the Securities and Exchange Commission (SEC) and the National Insurance Commission (NAICOM) respectively to embark on any serious capital restructuring, that is, after or while dealing with the Corporate Affairs Commission (the Commission).

The provisions examined above are extensive additions by the CAMA 2020 to the process of share capital increase by companies. Under the CAMA 2004, the provision was simply that a company that required additional approval under another enactment will apply to the Commission to get an extension to the 15 days required to communicate the increase in share capital to the Commission. Nothing was said of what happens after that request was made, which fact apparently, the CAMA 2020 has dealt with in great details.

The notice of increase to be given to the Commission by any company shall include any particulars prescribed with respect to the classes of shares affected and the conditions subject to which the new shares have been or are being issued. The notice of increase shall be accompanied by a printed copy of the resolution authorizing the increase in share capital (s. 127(6), (s. 102 (4).

A continuing fine, to be prescribed by the Commission, is imposed on any company for failure to comply with the provisions of section.

The basic roles for the company secretary in these respects are mostly notifications and liaisons with the Commission. For instance, when a company increases its shares capital, the requisite notification(s) to the Commission could be one, the 15 days required after passing the resolution to increase. It could be two notifications, where there is an approval under another enactment to be notified. It could also be multiple notifications, depending on the sector of the economy where the company operates and the ease with which the sectoral approval(s) are received and sent to the Commission in matters of this nature.

The attention of the company secretary will therefore be on two critical areas, which is the timing for sending notifications of the approval(s) to the Commission and the regulatory fines imposable by the Commission on any defaulting company. The fines are also imposed on other several fronts, for instance, where the statutory declaration by the directors to confirm an increase in the company's issued share capital was not filed, among others. Where possible, regulatory fines should not be incurred, especially continuing ones.

Increasing Issued Share Capital

Where a company has passed the requisite resolution to allot new shares, thereby increasing its issued share capital, such an increase does not have effect immediately, but shall only take effect, if:

- not less than 25 per cent of the share capital, including the increased portion has been paid up; and
- the directors have delivered a statutory declaration to the Commission verifying that they have fulfilled the above condition (s. 128 CAMA 2020 (s. 103).

A continuing fine, to be prescribed by the Commission, is imposed on any company that defaults in complying with the above provisions.

REDUCTION OF COMPANY'S SHARE CAPITAL

Reduction in the share capital of a registered company is taken seriously by the CAMA and efforts are made in the Act to tighten the procedures for any capital reduction. This is to create certainty and instil confidence in the minds of those that deal with registered companies, especially creditors and other stakeholders, that a company's capital cannot simply be eroded overnight, without stringent procedures being followed.

Therefore, under section 130 (1) CAMA 2020, (s. 105(1), a company having a share capital is prohibited from reducing its issued share capital except as authorized by the Act. To be able to reduce its share capital in any way it wants, a company must meet three important conditions:

- the company's Articles must permit such a reduction of capital *(Carruth v. I.C.I. Ltd (1937) 2 All ER, 422)*;

- the company must pass a special resolution authorizing the reduction (a resolution for reducing share capital);
- the Court must confirm the reduction (s.131(1), (s. 106(1).
- The reduction of a company's capital may be achieved in several ways, and the company may:
- extinguish or reduce the liability on any of its shares in respect of its share capital that has not been paid up; or
- either with or without extinguishing or reducing liability on any of its shares, cancel any paid-up share capital which is lost or unrepresented by available assets; or
- either with or without extinguishing or reducing liability on any of its shares, cancel any paid-up share capital which is in excess of the company's needs, and the company may, if, and in so far as is necessary, alter its Memorandum by reducing the amount of its share capital and of its shares accordingly (s. 131(2), (s. 106(2).

Application to Court to Confirm Capital Reduction

Where a company has passed the requisite special resolution authorizing a reduction of its share capital, it may then apply to Court to issue an order confirming the reduction (s. 132 (1), (s. 107(1). This is said to be one of the ways through which the interests of creditors in a company are protected by the Courts, wherein a company's creditor could object to the process of reduction *(Gower & Davies, 351).*

Creditors' Consent Required for Reduction

If a proposed reduction of a company's share capital involves either:

- a diminution of liability in respect of unpaid share capital, or
- subject to section 132 (6) (s. 107(6), the payment to a shareholder of any paid-up share capital, and in any other case, if the Court so directs, then:

    i. every creditor of the company, who, at the date fixed by the Court is entitled to any debt or claim which, if that date were the commencement of the winding-up of the company, would be admissible in proof against the company, shall be entitled to object to the reduction of capital (s. 132(3), (s.107(3);

The Court shall settle a list of creditors entitled to object and for that purpose:

- shall ascertain as far as possible without requiring an application from any creditor, the names of those creditors and the nature and amount of the debts or claims;
- may publish notices fixing a day or days within which creditors not entered on the list are to claim to be so entered or are to be excluded from the right of objecting to the reduction of the company's capital (s. 132(4) (s. 107(4).
- If a creditor entered on the list whose debt is not discharged or has not been determined does not consent to the reduction, the Court may, if it thinks fit, dispense with the consent of that creditor on the company securing payment of the debt or claim by appropriating (as the Court may direct) the following amount:
- if the company admits the full amount or claim or though not admitting it is willing to provide for the full amount or claim;
- if the company does not admit and is not willing to provide for the full amount of the debt or claim or if the amount is contingent or not ascertained, then an amount fixed by the Court after an inquiry and adjudication as if the company were being wound up by the Court (s. 132(5), (s. 107(5).

The Court may, having regard to the special circumstances of any case, and if it thinks proper to do so, direct that the above provisions in subsections 3 to 5 shall not apply as regards any class or classes of creditors (s. 132(6), (s. 107(6). The Court will only ensure that no creditor who is entitled to object is prejudiced and none of the creditors would be worse off than if they had been allowed to object *(Re Lucania Temperance Billiard Halls (London) Ltd (1965) 3 All ER, 879; Charlesworth & Cain, 237).*

Order of Court Confirming Reduction

The Court has a discretion, with respect to every creditor who is entitled to object to the reduction of a company's share capital, that either:

- the consent of the creditor has been obtained; or
- that his debt or claim has either been determined, discharged or secured; and
- that the company's capital does not by this reduction fall below the minimum issued share capital.

- The Court may then make an order confirming the reduction on such terms and conditions as it deems fit (s. 133 (1), (s. 108(1).
- Where the Court makes an order confirming the reduction of capital, it may also:
- make an order, if for any special reason it thinks proper, directing that the company shall, during such period (commencing on or at the time after the date of the order) as is specified in the order, add to its name as its last words 'and reduced;' and
- make an order requiring the company to publish (as the Court directs) the reason for reduction of capital or such other information in regard to it as the Court considers expedient with a view to giving proper information to the public and (if the Court deems fit) the cause(s) which led to the reduction;
- where 'and reduced' is ordered to be added to the name of a company, until the period specified in the order expires it shall be considered as part of the company's name (s. 132(2)(3), (s. 108 (2)(a) (3).

The Court will exercise its discretion to confirm a reduction of capital only if the reduction is considered fair and equitable *(Trevor v. Whitworth (1887) 12 AC, 409; Re Thomas De La Rue Ltd (1911) 2 Ch, 361; Poole v. National bank of China Ltd (1907) AC, 229; Hannigan, 504).* However, in determining what is fair and equitable in any particular situation, the Court does not usually concern itself, once the laid down rules are followed, with the motive for any capital reduction by a company *(Ex Parte Western Sugar Refineries Ltd (1951) AC, 625; Re David Bell Ltd (1954) SC, 33).*

REGISTRATION OF ORDER AND MINUTES OF REDUCTION

If the order of Court confirming the reduction of a company's capital and a copy of the minutes of the company's meeting (approved by the Court) are delivered to the Commission showing, with respect to the company's altered capital:

- the amount of the share capital;
- the number of shares into which it is to be divided and the amount of each share; and
- the amount (if any) at the date of the registration deemed to be paid-up on each share.

The Commission shall proceed to register the Court order and the minutes, and it is only after their registration that the resolution for reducing the capital of the company, as confirmed by the registered order, shall take effect. A notice of this registration by the Commission shall be published as the Court directs (s. 134 (1-3) CAMA 2020), (s. 109(2)(3). The final point to note here is that any purported reduction in a company's share capital without the sanction of the Court will be declared invalid and of no legal effect *(Consolidated Business Support Serv. Ltd v. Access Bank & Ors (2012) LPELR-8396).*

After registration of the order and minutes as above, the Commission shall then issue a certificate in that respect under the hand of its Registrar-General or authenticated by his official seal, that the order and minutes have been registered. The certificate so issued shall be *prima facie* evidence that all the requisite legal requirements for capital reduction have been met and that the company's share capital is as stated in the minutes (s. 134(4), (s. 109(4). Being *prima facie* evidence, it presupposes that it can still be impeached by credible evidence to the contrary and the whole processes will be voided. For instance, if it is established that no special resolution was actually passed by the company in the process of initiating the share capital reduction procedure, such a discovery, if confirmed true, will vitiate the whole process.

When the minutes has been registered, it shall be deemed to have been substituted for the corresponding part of the company's Memorandum and shall be valid and alterable as if it has always been a part of the Memorandum. The process of substitution shall be deemed to be an alteration of the Memorandum of the company (s. 134(5)(6), (s. 109(5)(6).

From the above discussions, it is obvious that capital reduction in a company is an intricate area with complex processes and procedures to be adopted. If the laid down rules are not followed as expected, there is a possibility that the whole process might be invalidated, especially, the areas that involve dealing with the Courts. This area therefore requires the serious attention of the company secretary. This is because the interactions expected between the company involved and the Courts are numerous, once the notice of decrease and minutes are notified to the Commission, then the application to Court for the order of confirmation of the reduction begins. The company secretary, working with the other relevant departments in the company, is also to ensure the settlement by the Court of the list of creditors entitled to object to the reduction taking cognizance of the interests of these creditors. Even when the Court has confirmed the capital reduction, it is still the duty of the company secretary to forward the Court order to the Commission for registration and conclusion of the process. It is an assignment in which the company secretary plays central and sensitive roles.

THE LIABILITY OF MEMBERS WHEN CAPITAL IS REDUCED

Where a company has reduced its share capital, a member (past or present) is not liable in respect of any share to any call or contribution exceeding in amount the difference (if any) between the amount of the share as fixed by the minutes and the amount paid on the share or reduced amount (if any), which is deemed to have been paid on it, as the case may be (s. 135 (1), (s. 110(1).

Where a creditor is entitled to object to the capital reduction, but due to ignorance of the proceedings, has not been entered on the list and after reduction the company is unable to pay the debts to him, he is still liable to be repaid. In that respect, any person who was a member on the date of registration of the order and minutes of reduction of capital shall be liable to contribute to an amount not exceeding what they would have contributed if the company were to be wound-up on that date (s. 135(2)(3), (s. 110(2)(3). These are the procedures adopted also when a company is wound-up and some creditors have not been paid due to the same reason.

The CAMA imposes a fine, to be prescribed by the Commission, on any officer of a company who wilfully conceals the name of a creditor entitled to object to reduction of capital or wilfully misrepresents the nature or amount of the debt or claim of any creditor. If any officer abets or is a privy to any concealment of misrepresentation, he is equally liable, and on conviction to a fine to be prescribed by the Commission (s. 136 CAMA 2020), (s. 111).

DIRECTOR'S DUTY ON SERIOUS LOSS OF CAPITAL

Loss of capital in any company is always treated as a serious issue, especially when it is of a high degree. Section 137 CAMA 2020, (s. 112) provides that with respect to public companies, where the net assets are half or less of the called-up share capital, the directors shall call an extra-ordinary general meeting not later than 30 days after being aware of that fact. That meeting shall not be more than 60 days farther off from the day it was called. This is to consider whether to take any steps, and if so, which steps to taken to deal with the situation of the loss of capital.

It has to be said that from corporate governance perspectives, this duty on the directors to call an extra-ordinary meeting in this instance is a fiduciary duty, which the directors must oblige without fail. For instance, principle 17 of *Nigerian Code of Corporate Governance (NCCG) 2018* stipulates that one of the major functions of the board of directors is to identify, assess, monitor and manage key business risks to safeguard shareholders' investments and the company's assets. This is an area where the expertise of the directors come in handy, especially non-executive directors, who have been brought on board to bring their diversified wealth of experience to bear on issues of this nature. Another aspect of this duty on the directors, if there be serious loss of capital, is effective communication to stakeholders. A matter that automatically activates an extra-ordinary general meeting of the company must treated as seriously as possible and communicated at the earliest to all stakeholders., This is to show transparency on the part of the company. The company secretary, liaising with the board of directors, has crucial roles to play in this respect.

A fine, to be specified by the Commission, is imposed on any director who defaults in calling the extra-ordinary general meeting mandated under the section.

A company's share capital constitutes the bedrock on which the company sits, that is, in terms of its business strength. A company that is not well capitalized, especially if it intends to engage in large scale transactions, will hardly be able to do so. The importance of a company's share capital is illustrated by section 137 CAMA 2020, (s. 112) which mandates a public company to call an extra ordinary general meeting within 30 days if it suffers serious loss of called-up share capital.

For the company secretary, serious and particular attention should have to be paid to the procedure for the alteration of the company's share capital in any of the ways described above. While all the areas that pertain to alteration of a company's share capital discussed above are important in their respective ways, the aspect of reduction of capital seems to be the most critical, and this for obvious reasons. The CAMA has accorded detailed provisions to this aspect of capital alteration and for good reasons. Once a company's capital base is suspect, or considered weak, except the company recapitalizes, such is usually one of the first symptoms or early warning sign of impending corporate failure(s).

The company secretary should also ensure that all consequential amendments occasioned by the alterations made to the company's Memorandum in altering the share capital (in any manner) are undertaken, and promptly so. Where necessary, new copies of the Memorandum and the

Articles should be printed and copies distributed to those who should have them, for instance, the members, and the old copies retrieved from them.

Due to the continuing fines imposed for default, the company should ensure that the procedures for altering a company's share capital are adhered to and that all returns and notifications to the Commission are undertaken, and within the time limited for doing so, where applicable.

CHECKPOINTS

- ✓ The share capital of a company is a critical aspect of its existence and is defined by the CAMA as the company's issued share capital, at any point in time.
- ✓ Although a company is required by the CAMA to be registered with a particular threshold of minimum issued share capital, the Act also makes provisions on modalities by which a company can alter its share capital so registered.
- ✓ An amendment to the CAMA 2020 by the BFA 2022 has provided that a company can increase its share capital without having to call a general meeting of the company. The directors are now empowered to pass a resolution to increase a company share capital, subject to any direction by the general meeting or condition in the company's Articles.
- ✓ The CAMA 2020 made some significant changes to the processes and nomenclature for share capital alteration by companies. A notable change is the change of the former 'authorized minimum share capital' for incorporation of companies to 'minimum issued share capital,' guaranteeing, as it were, the issuance of all share capital used to register a company.
- ✓ The alteration of a company's share capital could either be by consolidation of the shares and sub-division into larger parts or the same consolidation and sub-division into smaller parts.
- ✓ Of all the processes and procedures to alter a company's share capital under the CAMA, the procedures to reduce a company's share capital is made the most tedious. This is deliberately so. The CAMA made detailed provisions on how to reduce a company's capital and made the route

systematic and thorough in order to avoid easy erosion or dissipation of a company's capital.

- ✓ In terms of initiation of the process of capital reduction, for a start, the company's Articles must permit capital reduction, then a special resolution must have to be passed and, finally, the proposed reduction must be confirmed by the Court to be valid.
- ✓ The interest of the company's creditors is one of the issues that the Court will have to resolve, especially those creditors who are entitled to object to the reduction, before any approval is given to the process of capital reduction by the Court.
- ✓ The order of Court confirming capital reduction and notice of reduction approved by the Court are to be sent to the Commission, which shall then register the order and minutes of reduction. It is after this registration by the Commission that the reduction of capital will take effect.
- ✓ A notice of reduction shall be published by the Commission as directed by the Court.
- ✓ Once the minutes of reduction has been registered by the Commission, it automatically serves as an amendment to the corresponding portion of the company's Memorandum, which shall subsequently be construed accordingly.

Chapter 15

COMPANY SHARES

INTRODUCTION

A 'share' is defined in section 868 CAMA 2020 as a member's interest in the share capital of a company. In simple terms, we saw in the last chapter that a company's share capital is the issued share capital of a company at any given time. It is now a member's level or volume of proprietary interest in that issued share capital that is his share in the company. With this his interest in the company, a member is then entitled to share in the capital or income (profits) of such a company. The provision under section 567 CAMA 2004, that except where there is an express or implied distinction between shares and stocks, that the term shares include stocks, has been omitted by the CAMA 2020.

Put in a different way, a share is a person's interest in a company that is composed of rights and obligations which are defined by the relevant company legislation and the company's Memorandum and Articles *(Borland Trustees* v. *Steel Brothers & Co. Ltd (1901) 1 Ch., 279; Thorne, 63).* A share has also been described as a chose in action and a personal property transferable in the manner provided for in the company's Articles *(*s. 139 CAMA 2020), (*s.* 115)*; Okoya* v. *Santili (1994) 4 NWLR Pt. 338, 256).* Perhaps, one of the most extensive and well-accepted definitions of what 'a share' is must be that of Farwell J, in *Borland Trustee* v. *Steel (1901) 1 Ch., 279*; where he defined 'a share' as:

> the interest of a shareholder in a company measured by a sum of money, for the purpose of liability in the first place, and of interest in the second, but also consisting of a series of mutual covenants entered into by all the shareholders *inter se*...The contract contained in the articles of association is one of the original incidents of the share. A share is not a sum of money...but it is an interest measured by a sum of money and

made up of various rights contained in the contract, including the right to a sum or a more or less amount.

A company's share capital is mostly expressed and denominated in units of shares (companies limited by guarantee are exceptions) to which members subscribe and same allotted proportionally. This makes the members proportional owners of the company to the limits of their ownership of the shares. This ownership of shares by members is distinguished from the ownership of the company's assets, which is vested in the company in its own right and name by virtue of its being incorporated and being a juristic person in law *(Palmers, 332; Co-operative Bank Ltd* v. *Obokhare (1996) 8 NWLR Pt. 468, 579; KSO & Allied Ltd* v. *Kofa (1996) 3 NWLR Pt. 436, 244; NIDB* v. *Fembo (1997) 2 NWLR Pt. 489, 543; Onagoruwa* v. *State (1993) 7 NWLR Pt. 303, 49).*

ISSUANCE OF SHARES BY A COMPANY

A company has the power to issue shares at such times and for a consideration that it shall determine up to the limit of its authorized share capital in its Memorandum. This power to issue shares is subject to any limitation in a company's Articles regarding the number of shares it can issue, and any pre-emptive rights in the Articles in relation to the shares (s. 141 CAMA 2020), (s. 117). It has been held that the term, to 'issue' shares means something different from the 'allotment' of shares, and imports that some subsequent act has been done whereby the title of the allottee had become complete. In a strict sense, it is when unissued shares were applied for, allotted and finally registered. In other words, an allotment creates an enforceable contract for the issue of the shares, which imports application, allotment and notification to the purchaser, followed finally by entry on the company's register of members *(National Westminster Bank Plc* v. *IRC (1994) 3 All ER 1; Hannigan, 454).*

POWER TO ISSUE CLASSES OF SHARES

Where the Articles so authorized, a company may issue classes of shares, and the shares so issued shall not be treated as being of the same class except they rank equally for all purposes (s. 143 CAMA 2020), (s. 118). Class rights are those rights that attach to particular class of shares but not to another class or to a company's shareholders generally. Such rights may be created by the Memorandum, or the Articles of a company, the terms of issue of the shares, or by a unanimous shareholders' agreement. The rights may also relate to such matters as the right to a dividend, right to share in surplus asset and the right to attend and vote at the company's meetings *(Re Old Silkstone Collieries Ltd (1954) Ch., 169; Charlesworth & Cain, 216).* However, it is important to note that a class right must create a 'class' with respect to shareholding in a company to qualify as such. Therefore, a right conferred on an individual member by the Articles, but which was unrelated to shareholding in the company in any way, cannot not be described as a class right *(Re Blue Arrow Plc (1987) BCLC 585; Hannigan, 309.* The opposite of this decision was reached, with justifications, in *Cumbrian Newspapers Group Ltd* v. *Cumberland 7 Westmorland Herald Co. Ltd (1986) 2 All ER 816),* where it was held that class rights include rights to a member in his capacity as a member and which are not attached to any class of shares, but conferring rights on a group of members. From available authorities, this appears to be a one-off exception to the rule.

It has been held that in the absence of any express provision in an agreement between a company and members of a particular class concerning their class rights, all members must be treated equally *(Birch* v. *Gropper (1889) 14 AC, 525, Mayson et al., 180).* Put differently, if all shares in a company fall within a class, either by design or otherwise, there are no class rights, only shareholder rights *(Union Music Ltd* v. *Watson (2003) 1 BCLC, 453; Hannigan, 309).* The source of the rights, privileges and obligations of a particular class of shares may be derived from the company's Articles or the resolution of members that created additional shares for the company.

The rights attaching to each share are interpreted strictly, therefore, except where a particular right is specifically given to a class of shares, such a right will not be implied. For instance, a preferential right to receive dividend will not normally be taken as implying a right to preferential return of capital on winding-up, if the latter is not expressly provided for. There are a number of issues on which the rights of different classes of shares may differ, especially:

- right to share in the distribution of profits;
- right to return of capital in the event of the company being wound up;
- right to attend meetings, vote at meetings, and participate in the governance of the company *(Mason et al., 63).*

Construction of Members' Class Rights

Various rights that attach to different classes of shares are usually stated in a company's Articles and contained in the terms of issue. Details of these rights could vary from one company to the other, and sometimes problems of interpreting the rights and getting to their real import arise. In this respect, over the years, the Courts have developed a set of rules of construction in assisting to construe class rights. Statutorily, also, the CAMA has provided a set of rules of construction to be observed in construing class rights. In practice, both sets of rules are used as outlined below.

Under section 169 CAMA 2020, (s. 144), in construing the provisions of a company's Articles with respect to class rights, the rules are:

- unless the contrary intention appears, no dividend is payable on any shares unless the company resolves to pay such dividend;
- unless the contrary intention appears, a fixed preferential dividend payable on any class of shares is cumulative (even in the absence of any provision in the terms of issue *(Webb* v. *Earle (1875) LR 20 Eq., 556; Gower & Davies, 869)*; and no dividend shall be payable on any share ranking subsequent to them until all the arrears of the fixed dividend have been paid;
- unless the contrary intention appears, in a winding-up, arrears of any cumulative preferential dividend, whether earned or declared or not, are payable up to the date of the actual payment on the winding-up;
- if any class of shares is expressed to have a right to preferential dividend, then, unless the contrary intention appears, such class has no further right to participate in dividends. In essence, the right so attached is exhaustive *(Re National Telephone Co. (1914) 1 Ch, 755; Will* v. *United Lankat Plantations Ltd (1914) AC, 11; Hannigan, 311).*
- if any class of shares is expressed to have a right to preferential payments out of the assets of the company in the event of winding-up, then, unless a contrary intention appears, such class has no further right to participate in the distribution of assets in the winding-up;
- in determining the rights of the various classes to share in the distribution of the company's property on a winding-up, no regards shall be given, unless a contrary intention appears, to whether or not such property represents accumulated profits or surplus, which would have been available for dividend while the company remained a going concern; and
- all shares rank equally in all respects (subject to the Act) unless the contrary intention appears in the company's Articles *(Birch* v. *Cropper, Bridgewater Navigation Co. Ltd (1889) 14 AC, 525; Gower & Davies, 867).*

In the light of these rules and what could be the effect of their interpretation and application by the Courts to respective class rights, what companies usually do is to extensively state all the conditions and presumptions relating to any class of shares in the terms of issue. In doing this, they eliminate, to a large extent, ambiguities and any unintended imputations being read into the terms and conditions by anybody or the Courts. To a great degree, this practice has been successful in achieving the intended purpose.

The detailed rights of members in relation to their shareholdings are usually broken down into finer details in the company's Articles, although there are also provisions of a general nature in the CAMA. The company's secretary role primarily, is to ensure that adherence to processes and procedures as stipulated in the company's Articles, that is, when dealing with members and their rights and duties, as such. This will apply, *mutatis mutandis*, to members of a class of shareholders in the company as well.

PROHIBITION OF NON-VOTING AND WEIGHTED SHARES

Under section 140 (1) CAMA 2020, (s.116(1), except where any other enactment provides otherwise, any shares issued by a company shall carry the right to one vote on a poll in a general meeting of the company in respect of each share. In addition, no company may by its Articles or otherwise authorize the issue of shares which carry more than one vote (weighted) in respect of each share or which do not carry a right to vote at all.

A continuing daily fine, to be specified by the Commission, is imposed on a company and any of its officers in default for contravening the above provisions. Any resolution passed by the company to implement the issue of any weighted or non-voting shares shall be void and of no consequence in any way (s. 140 (2), (s. 116 (2). This notwithstanding, rights attached to a preference share under section 168 CAMA 2020, (s.143) are excluded here, in relation to voting on a poll or for a special resolution to increase the number of shares in a class.

Exceptions to the Prohibition

The prohibition in the CAMA that bars companies from issuing weighted and non-voting shares is not absolute, as the Act provides for some exceptions to the rule:

> Section 140(1) CAMA 2020, (s. 116(1) exempts weighted and non-voting shares, where they are otherwise provided for by any

> other enactment(s). Section 140 (3), (s. 116(3) provides that the prohibition shall not affect any right(s) attached to preference shares under section 168 (s. 143) of the Act. It is therefore possible that if a preference share is weighted in terms of voting during a poll or when a special resolution is proposed to increase the number of shares of a class of shareholders, it would be legally so.

On its part, section 168(1), (s. 143 (1) of Act provides that a company's Articles may permit preference shares to carry more than one vote per share on a poll in a general meeting, only:

> upon any resolution during such period as the preferential dividend or any part of it remains in arrears and unpaid, such period starting from a date not more than 12 months or such lesser period as the Articles may provide, after the due date of the dividend; or
>
> upon any resolution which varies the rights attached to such shares; or
>
> upon any resolution to remove an auditor of the company or to appoint another person in place of such an auditor; or
>
> upon any resolution for the winding-up of the company or during the winding-up of the company.

It is therefore not in every instance that a preference share is allowed to be weighted, and the provisions of section 168 (s. 143) of the CAMA in that respect is also limited and conditional.

Notwithstanding the prohibition against the issue of weighted and non-voting shares in section 140 (s. 116) of the Act, section 168 (2), (s. 143 (2) permits a company while passing a resolution to increase the number of any class of its shares to also resolve that any existing class of preference shares shall carry the right to such votes additional to one vote per share. This would be necessary to preserve the existing ratio which the votes exercisable by the holders of the preference shares at a general meeting bear to the total votes exercisable at the meeting. In essence, this is meant to maintain the balance of power in voting that was attributed to preference shareholders, by the agreements of the parties.

A further example of where another enactment, other than the CAMA, has provided for possible weighted shares is in *section 10 of the Banks and other Financial Institutions Act (BOFIA)* 2020. It provides that notwithstanding the provision of the CAMA, or any agreement or contract, the voting right of every shareholder in a bank shall be proportional to his contribution to the paid-up share capital of the bank. This implies that members' voting rights in Nigerian banks would be proportional to the shares they hold. This practice was confirmed as a common law practice in *(British and American Trustee and Finance Corporation* v. *Couper (1894) AC 399, 417; Mayson et al., 179).*

RIGHTS AND LIABILITIES ATTACHING TO SHARES

Under section 138(a) CAMA 2020, (s. 114 (a), subject to the provisions of the Act, the rights and liabilities attaching to a company's shares or class thereof, shall be dependent on the terms on their issue, and on the company's Articles. However, notwithstanding anything to the contrary in the terms of issue of a company's shares or in its Articles, the rights attaching to its shares include the right to attend and vote at any general meeting of the company. This is virtually non-negotiable (s. 138(b), (s. 114(b) *(Sun Insurance Nig. Plc* v. *LMBS (2005)12 NWLR Pt. 940, 608, 631).* Apart from shareholders' mandatory right to attend and vote at the company's general meeting, they also possess other rights, including:

- the right to earn dividends when any is declared;
- the right to participate in the distribution of the company's assets in the event of a winding-up (if not precluded by the class of shares held);
- the right to receive notice of general meetings;
- the right to receive a copy of the Memorandum and Articles of the company;
- the right to obtain copies of minutes of general meetings (paying any fees applicable thereto);
- the right to bring derivative action on behalf of the company, under appropriate circumstances;
- the right to petition for winding-up in appropriate circumstances (*Orojo, 125).*

- the right to receive share certificates indicating the shares that have been issued to the member *(Standard Trust Bank Plc* v. *Olusola (2007) 9 CLRN, 41).*
- the right to sell, mortgage, or otherwise dispose of the shares belonging to the member *(Kotoye* v. *Saraki (1994) 7 NWLR Pt. 357, 414; Seedorff* v. *Archbode Eng. Ltd (1996)1 NWLR Pt. 423, 223).*

The major liability of a shareholder that is contingent to being a member is to contribute to the capital of the company either for calls on shares made or on winding-up of the company. The amount of the contribution is usually proportionate to the member's shareholding in the company, or as agreed in the Memorandum, for companies without shares.

Power to Vary Class Rights

Under section 166(1) CAMA 2020, (s.141 (1) where a company's share capital is divided into classes, the rights attached to any of the classes thereof may be varied. Although section 167 (6) CAMA 2020 (s. 142 (6), provides that the term 'variation' includes 'abrogation,' however, in *Re House of Fraser Plc (1987) BCLC 293*, it was held that 'variation' of rights presupposes the continuance of rights in a varied state, while 'the abrogation' of such rights presupposes the termination of rights without satisfaction or fulfilment. In essence, once a right is abrogated, the enjoyment of such a right in any form or manner comes to an end. However, we are talking about the CAMA and its provisions will be the guide here.

Under the CAMA, the variation of class rights is carried out either:

- in accordance with the provisions in the company's Articles for the variation of those rights; or
- where the company's Articles contain no such provision, then, with the written consent of holders of three-quarters of the issued shares of that class or by a special resolution passed at a separate general meeting of the members of that class. This power of variation is exercisable even when the company is being wound-up.

The provisions of the CAMA relating to a company's general meetings shall also apply to the general meeting of any class where a special resolution to vary conferred rights is to be passed. The quorum for such a meeting of a class shall be two (2) persons at least holding or representing by proxy, one third of the issued shares of the class in question. In addition, for a class meeting to vary rights, any member of the class who is present in person or by proxy, may demand a poll (s. 166(2), (s. 141(2). A major exception to the right to vary rights attached to a class of shares is where the terms of issue of the class of shares provide otherwise.

What the CAMA 2020 did with the provision is to, first of all, tie any variation of a class right to the provisions of the company's Articles. It is only when there is no provision in this respect in the Articles that a written consent of holders of three-quarter of the shares or a special resolution may be passed by members of the class to vary such a right(s). Under the CAMA 2004, there was no reference to the provisions of the company's Articles in the process of varying class rights, just by three-quarter of the holders or by a special resolution of the members.

Where preferred or other rights are conferred on a class of shares, such rights shall not (except where it is expressly stated in the terms of issue of shares of that class) be deemed to have been varied by the creation or issue of further shares that rank *pari passu* with them(s. 166(3), (s. 141 (3).

Any proposed amendment of a provision contained in a company's Articles for the variation of rights attached to a class of shares, or the insertion of any such provisions into the Articles, shall be treated as a variation of those rights. In that case, it shall require the consent, in writing, of the holders of three-quarters of issued shares of that class, or the sanction of a special resolution passed at a separate general meeting of the holders of the shares of the class, before the procedure for the amendment of the Articles can proceed (s. 166 (4).

The above provision was introduced by the CAMA 2020 to forestall a situation where there could be a surreptitious amendment(s) of class rights by the majority shareholders in a company by simply amending the provisions of the Articles relating to the class rights. As presently constituted, it implies that to amend any provision(s) in the Articles on class rights, there has to be two general meetings: one general meeting will be by the class members to give approval for the proposed amendment to proceed, then, a second meeting by the company for the actual amendment of the Articles to proceed. It is a welcome safeguard to holders of shares that have class rights in respective companies.

Application for a Variation to be cancelled

Where rights attached to any class of shares have been varied in line with section 166 above, the holder(s) of at least fifteen (15%) per cent of the issued shares of that class, being persons who did not consent to or vote in favour of the resolution to vary the rights, may apply to Court to have the variation cancelled. Where such an application for cancellation has been made, the variation of rights will not take effect unless it is confirmed by the Court (ss. 141, 142(1).

However, for the present purposes, any shares held by a company as treasury shares shall not be taken into account for the purpose of computing aggregate per cent of shareholding for those who seek to make application to Court to cancel variation of shares (s. 167). This provision is a new introduction to the process of variation of class rights by the CAMA 2020 seeking to precisely define the place of treasury shares in the whole process.

Those entitled to make an application to cancel a variation of class rights may appoint one of their own in writing to represent them and make the application. The application must be brought to Court within 21 days after the consent to vary was given or the resolution passed. On hearing the application by the applicant(s) and any other person applying to be heard who appears to be interested in the matter, if the Court is satisfied that the variation would unfairly prejudice the shareholders of the class represented by the applicant(s), the Court may disallow the variation. However, if the Court is not satisfied that the applicant(s) has made out a good case for cancellation of the variation of the rights, it may confirm the variation. The decision of the Court on this is final (s. 167) (2)(3)(4), (s. 142 (2)(3)(4).

What then is the implication of the above section saying that the decision of the Court on the matter is final? Does that mean that once the High Court decides on the issue, then no appeal shall lie to the Court of Appeal from the decision by any of the parties to the suit? It is doubtful whether that is the intention of the section, as construing it as such might be going contrary to the constitutional right of appeal granted under section 241 of the 1999 Constitution, as amended *(Diwe* v. *Nwanosike (2017) LPELR-41687; NIWA* v. *SPDC Nig. Ltd (2007) 1 NWLR Pt. 1015, 305).* This, of course, will not be allowed as a statutory provision cannot be allowed to contradict a right guaranteed under the Constitution based on the supremacy of the Constitution *(Lagos State Govt., & Ors* v. *Abdulkareem & Ors (2022) LPELR-58517.*

The company involved in the process of application to Court, as above, is mandated to forward a copy of the order of Court within 15 days of its being made to the Commission. A continuing daily fine, to be specified by the Commission, is imposed on the company and every officer in default (s. 167(5), (s. 142(5).

ISSUE OF SHARES WITH PREFERRED, DEFERRED OR OTHER RIGHTS

Under section 144 CAMA 2020, it is provided that, without prejudice to any special rights previously conferred on the holders of an existing shares or class of shares, a company is permitted to issue shares with preferred, deferred, or such other rights or such restrictions. This could be with regard to dividends, return of capital or otherwise as the company may, from time to time, decide by ordinary resolution in general meeting (s. 119).

The following classes of shares are commonly issued with different rights attached: ordinary shares, preference shares and deferred shares.

If a company has only a class of shares, then they are usually considered as ordinary shares. They are the equity share capital of the company and constitute the residuary class in which is vested everything after the special rights of preference classes, if any, have been satisfied *(Gower & Davies, 870).* As the name implies, ordinary shares ordinarily have no special rights attached to them and rank behind the company's creditors and preference shares in terms of capital on winding-up. They receive after these other classes of holders have been paid.

On the other hand, preference share, according to section 868 CAMA 2020, is the one, irrespective of the term of description that 'does not entitle the holder to any right to participate, beyond specified limit, in any distribution, whether by way of dividend or on redemption, in a winding-up or otherwise.' In their own right, however, preference shares normally have a right to receive a dividend that ranks before the right of ordinary shares. Preference shares may also be convertible to ordinary shares or be redeemable at the option of the company, in both cases, on the occurrence of certain events *(Mason, 64.)*

Section 147(1) CAMA 2020, (s. 122) prohibits a company limited by shares from issuing preference shares that are irredeemable, while sub-section (2) permits a company limited by shares, if authorized by its Articles, to issue redeemable preference shares, subject to such conditions as may be prescribed in the terms of issue or in the company's Articles. Additionally, unless where otherwise expressly stated in the terms of issue, the right of preference shareholders to receive dividend is cumulative, going from year to year *(Webb* v. *Earle (1875) LR 20 Eq 556, Mason, 66).* To avoid any questions or ambiguities on any aspect of the terms, it is more advisable to expressly classify a preference share as cumulative in the Articles or terms of issue, if it is one.

The founders of a company may issue founders or deferred shares to give themselves special rights. The rights attached to the shares are usually deferred and take priority after ordinary shareholders, especially in relation to the sharing of any surplus after all others have been paid. They bear much of the risks of the business, and previously, founders shares were used to confer large proportion of voting rights on the holders.

Deferred shares are considered special kind of shares to be issued by a company. Also, as noted, special rights are usually conferred on deferred shares and for that reason, section 1(a) of the 3rd Schedule to the *Investments and Securities Act (ISA) 2007* requires that particulars of deferred shares be specified in the prospectus as one of the mandatory requirements. This will state important details, including the nature and extent of interest of the holders in the property and profits of the company. This is to ensure transparency and certainty and not to spring surprises on potential investors subsequently, with some outrageous terms and conditions attached to deferred shares.

The above is a good provision from the corporate governance perspective, being that quality and effective disclosures of material information are required from public companies to all stakeholders. According to principle 5 of the Australian *Corporate Governance Principles and Recommendations 2019*, quoted companies should endeavour to make timely and balanced disclosures of all matters concerning it that a reasonable person would expect to have effect on the price or value of its securities. The requirement by the ISA above on deferred shares, although might not appear like a price-sensitive information, is obviously one of those type of information referred to, which may influence investor decision.

ISSUE OF SHARES AT A PREMIUM AND DISCOUNT

A company has the power to issue shares at a premium, but unlike the position under the CAMA 2004, a company has no power under the CAMA 2020 to issue its shares at a discount.

Issue of Shares at a Premium

A company has the power to issues its shares at a premium (s. 145(1) CAMA 2020), (s. 120). When the price at which a company's shares are issued is higher than the nominal value stated for the shares in the company's Memorandum, then, the shares are said to have issued at a premium. Section

145 (2) requires that when shares are issued at a premium, (whether for cash or otherwise) a sum equal to the aggregate amount or value of the shares shall be transferred to the company's share premium account. The relevant provision of the Act relating to the reduction of share capital applies to the share premium account as if it is part of the paid-up share capital of the company (s. 145(3), (s. 120(2)(3).

Application of the Share Premium Account

A company that has established a share premium account after issuing its shares at a premium may apply the account in:

- paying up the company's unissued shares to be issued as fully-paid bonus shares to the members of the company, or
- writing off preliminary expenses of a newly incorporated company; or
- writing off the expense of, or the commission paid on any issue of the company's shares; or
- providing for the premium payable on redemption of any of the company's redeemable shares (s. 145(3), (s. 120(3).

The CAMA 2004 made extensive provisions with regards to the process for a company to issue shares at a discount. However, as alluded to above, section 146 CAMA 2020 makes it unlawful for a company to issue its shares at a discount. The question would be, why the total rejection of the issuance of shares at a discount by CAMA 2020, since no reason is given for this total prohibition in the Act?

The first place to look at for possible answers is the nature of the issuance of shares at a discount. It is the opposite of the issuance of shares at a premium, which means that shares are issued at prices lower than what has been stated as their nominal value, essentially, the shares are issued at a 'loss,' so to say. The rule against issuing shares at a discount was judicially stamped and sealed in *Ooregum Gold Mining Co* v. *Roper (1892) AC, 125; Thorne, 89).*

There have been arguments as to the merits or otherwise of such a prohibition on issuing shares on a discount. Some argue that issuing shares at a discount dilutes the interest of existing shareholders in the company by issuing shares too cheaply to new shareholders. However, others argue that issuing shares at a discount could be used to raise much needed cash in urgent situations, for instance, when a company is facing insolvency. This is especially so, they argue, when the company's shares are trading at below par, as no investor would like to pay for such shares at above market price *(Gower & Davies, 276).* Whatever be the reason(s) for the prohibition of issuing shares at a discount under the CAMA, that position remains the extant law.

VALIDATION OF IMPROPERLY ISSUED SHARES

Where a company has purported to issue or allot shares and the issue or allotment of the shares was invalid for reasons of either non-compliance with the provisions of CAMA, or any other enactment, the company's Articles or the terms of issue of the shares, the issue or allotment of shares is invalid. It may also be that the allotment was inconsistent with or unauthorized by any provision of the CAMA or the Articles, the company may, within 30 days of an application made by a holder, mortgagee of those shares or by the company's creditor, by a special resolution, validate the issue of those shares or confirm the terms of the issue or allotment, whichever is applicable (s. 148(1) CAMA 2020, (s. 123).

Where, in contrast to the above, the company in question refuses to validate the issue or allotment of the shares, or confirm the terms of the issue or allotment, the Court may, upon application made by a holder, mortgagee of those shares or by a creditor of the company, and upon being satisfied that in all cases, it is just and equitable to do so, validate the issue or allotment of those shares or confirm the terms of the issue or allotment, as the case may be 148(2).

Where the Court validates an issue or allotment of shares or confirms the terms of issue or allotment as above, it shall make an order to that effect as proof of such validation or confirmation of terms (s. 148 (3), (s. 123 (3).

The CAMA 2020 took a bold step by primarily granting the powers to the companies to be able to validate invalidly issued shares by themselves. Under the CAMA 2004, the resort was primarily to the Court for validation and the company had no right to do so. However, the CAMA 2020 made the company the primary source of the power to validate invalidly issued shares, and it is only when the company refuses to validate or confirm the terms of issuance that resort to Court may be taken.

Now the question arises whether, if a company issues shares on a discount, though prohibited as unlawful, by section 146 CAMA, can the company or the Court validate the issuance of such shares? The answer must be in the negative. Any issuance of shares by a company on a discount is not an invalid issuance of shares but an illegal issuance, and the contract with the allottee is an illegal contract, which gives rise to no enforceable rights and which the Courts do not enforce *(Sodipo* v. *Lemminkainen & Anor. (1985) 2 NSCC, 1102; Solanke* v. *Abed & Anor (1962) NRNLR, 92).*

It is in this kind of a situation that the company secretary is expected to step in and advise the directors on the need to validate any improperly issued shares on their own, or confirm their terms of issue. Except where there is a genuine reason(s) that will not allow the company to act in that respect, there should be no need to allow an allottee of shares to proceed to Court to obtain an order to get the issue of his shares validated or the terms of issue confirmed. With the attendant costs, in time and resources, of approaching the Court, that should be an avoidable distraction to running of the affairs of the company.

A COMPANY'S AUTHORITY TO ALLOT SHARES

Under section 149 CAMA 2020, (s. 124), the power to allot a company's shares is vested in the company itself, but in a private company, this power may be delegated to the directors, subject to any conditions or directions that the Articles or the general meeting may provide, from time to time *(Anjous* v. *COSEC Services Ltd & Anor. (2006) 6 CLRN, 175, 194; Edokpolor & Co. Ltd* v. *Sam-Edo Wire Ind. Ltd (1984) 7 SC 119).*

The above was the law under the CAMA 2020 until the above provision was amended by section 5 of the schedule to the *Business Facilitation (Miscellaneous Provisions) Act (BFA) 2022.* In the amendment by the BFA, it is provided that the powers to allot the shares of a company are not exercised by the directors of a company unless express authority to do so has been vested in the board of directors by either the general meeting or the Articles.

The amendment by the BFA to the CAMA 2020 has removed the dichotomy of the general meeting or the Articles delegating powers of allotment of shares to the directors in public or private companies. The provision now applies equally to all companies. In essence, without express delegation of powers to allot shares, directors do not have the powers to allot shares. Any such authorization to directors with respect to shares allotment could be for a particular instance or could be general in nature and either conditional or unconditional (s. 149(5).

In addition to the above, section 149(2) CAMA 2020 has removed the blanket subjection of allotment of shares by companies to the provisions of the *Investment and Securities Act (ISA) 2007*, but now limits same to allotment of shares in public companies only. This is because under section 65 of the ISA, where a public offer of 'securities' is made (which term is defined in section 264 of the ISA to include 'shares'), it is the issuer and the issuing house that shall be responsible to allot the company's securities.

Section 142 (1) CAMA 2020, as amended by section 4 of the schedule to the *Business Facilitation (Miscellaneous Provisions) Act (BFA) 2022* provides that a private company shall not in any event allot newly issued shares unless they are offered, in the first instance, to all existing shareholders of the class being issued in the proportion, as nearly as may be, to their existing holding. This means that those with bigger stakes in the class of shares issued will receive bigger offers as against those with marginal holdings. This is the right of pre-emption in favour of existing shareholders in private companies.

The notice offering the shares to the holders will indicate the number of the shares each member is entitled to subscribe to and the price. If the offer of the shares is not accepted by the member within 21 days, the offer is deemed declined by the member. This is a better provision and the clarity was brought by the amendment of the CAMA by the BFA, as noted above. Before the amendment, the provision was that the offer would have to be accepted within a reasonable time or be deemed declined, which expression was subject to several subjective interpretations.

METHOD OF APPLICATION AND ALLOTMENT OF SHARES

Section 150 (1) CAMA 2020, (s. 125 (1), deals with the procedure for allotment of a company's shares and the summary of the process is as follows:

- for a private company or public company where the issue of shares is not public, there shall, if the company so requires, be a written application, signed by the applicant and stating the number of shares desired;
- for a public company, the applicant shall return a duly completed and signed application to the company as stated in company's Articles. This is subject to the condition that the SEC may impose for any public issue of shares;
- if the company wholly or partially accepts the application, it shall make an allotment to the applicant and within 42 days thereafter notify the applicant of the details of the allotment;
- an applicant has the right to write to the company and withdraw his application for its shares, at any time, before an allotment is made to him (s. 150(2).

However, once the company makes an allotment and notifies the applicant, it shall constitute an acceptance of the applicant's offer and a contract is made between the parties on the day the allotment is made (s. 151), (s. 126).

Effect of Irregular Allotment of Shares

There are instances where the process of share allotment by a company could be irregular. For instance, if a public company makes an allotment of shares to an applicant before holding its statutory meeting in breach of the provisions of the CAMA in that respect, such an allotment shall be voidable at the instance of the applicant within one (1) month after the company holds its statutory meeting. Where the allotment was made after the holding of the statutory meeting of the company, it shall be voidable within one (1) month after the allotment (s. 153(1), (s. 128(1). The situation here is the same notwithstanding that the company in question is in the process of being wound-up.

A director who knowingly contravenes or permits the contravention of the CAMA with respect to allotment of shares shall be liable to compensate the allottee and the company for costs, damages or losses they suffered as a result. Any Court proceeding(s) to recover any such costs, losses or damages must be commenced within two (2) years of the allotment, failing which, the cause of action will be statute barred (153(2), (s. 128(2).

Return as to Allotment of Shares

Whenever a company limited by shares makes allotment of its shares to those who applied for the shares and were successful, it shall within 15 days of such allotment deliver to the Commission for registration (the period was one month under section 154 (1) CAMA 2020 before it was amended by section 6 of the schedule to the *Business Facilitation (Miscellaneous Provision) Act (BFA) 2022,* to 15 days):

- a return of the allotments stating the number and nominal amount of the shares comprised in the allotment, the name, addresses and description of the allottees and the amount, if any, paid or payable on each share. It shall also indicate whether the payment is on account of nominal value of the shares or by way of any premium payable in relation to those shares (154 (1)(a) CAMA 2020), (s. 129 (1)(a). This is in Form CAC 5;
- for shares that are allotted as fully or partly paid up otherwise than in cash, then the company shall also forward to the Commission, the following:

i. a written contract constituting the allottee's title to the allotment together with any other duly stamped contract of sale or for services or other consideration in respect of which the shares were allotted;
ii. a return stating the nominal amount of shares so allotted, the extent to which they are to be treated as paid up and the consideration for which they have been allotted (s. 154(1)(6); and

- particulars of the valuation of the consideration in conformity with the provision of section 162 (s. 137) of the Act (which deals with payment for shares allotted than wholly in cash).

The CAMA 2020 limits the requirement to provide this information and particulars only to public companies, unlike under the CAMA 2004, where no such distinction was made. The Commission may require other documents or particulars from the company and where this be the case, the company shall be granted additional time of at least several (7) days within which to send the documents and particulars.

A penalty, to be specified by the Commission, is imposed on any officer in default to comply with the provisions to deliver any requisite return to the Commission relating to return on allotments within the time limited. However, the company or any officer in default may apply to Court for relief, and if the Court is satisfied that the omission was accidental or that it is otherwise just and equitable to grant relief, it will extend time for the company to comply (s. 154(3), (s. 129(2).

The issue of returns to the Commission on any aspect(s) of company law and practice is within the exclusive purview of the company secretary. From instances where only simple notifications are required, to registering documents, like special resolutions, to filing major returns, like annual returns and that on share allotments, there are lots of returns to be made to the Commission. This is especially so with respect to quoted companies. It is solely the responsibility of the company secretary and his team to deal with these issues. If any errors or omissions are made in these respects, they are squarely on the table of the company secretary. As we have seen and will continue to see throughout this book, regulatory filings for compliance and returns, as in this case, are the major duties of the company secretary and must be treated with all due care and attention, being that, most of the time, they are time bound and attract fines and penalties for defaults or delays.

Significant and Substantial Shareholding in a Company

In law, all shareholders are deemed members in a company (with their names in the register of members), although shareholdings are not always equal. The inequality in shareholdings also has consequences, sometimes, far-reaching consequences, depending on the levels of shareholdings. The law appreciates the power and effect that majority shareholders could wield in the affairs of a company and has made efforts to bring in control or oversight in that respect. The CAMA uses the terms 'significant control' and 'substantial shareholder' in different sections.

Under section 119 CAMA 2020, every person with significant control in shareholding in a company, is mandated, within seven (7) day of becoming so, to inform the company in writing indicating the particulars of such significant control. Once the information is received from the member, the company is mandated to inform the Commission of that fact (within one month) with all the details of the member's shareholding. The company is also to include the information in all its annual returns for every year, while indicating same information against the person's name in the register of members. The section does not indicate that this provision applies only to a private or public company and is therefore taken to apply to both of them.

On its part, the Commission is mandated to maintain a register of persons with significant control and populate same with information received from respective companies.

The above provisions which apply to all companies with shares are new additions by the CAMA 2020, as CAMA 2004 made provisions in this respect relating only to persons with substantial shareholding in public companies. Also, the CAMA 2020 used the term 'significant control,' in section 119 but used 'substantial shareholding' in section 120, which relates specifically to public companies.

Under section 868 CAMA 2020, a person with 'significant control' (as a shareholder in a company) is a person:

- directly or indirectly holding at least 5% of the shares or interest in a company or limited liability partnership;
- directly or indirectly holding at least 5% of the voting rights in a company or limited liability partnership;
- directly or indirectly holding the right to appoint or remove a majority of the directors or partners in a company or limited liability partnership;

- otherwise having the right to exercise or actually exercising significant influence or control over a company or limited liability partnership; or
- having the right to exercise or actually exercising significant influence or control over the activities of a trust or firm whether or not it is a legal entity, but would itself satisfy any of the first four conditions, if it were an individual.

Specifically, under section 120 CAMA 2020 (s. 95) a substantial shareholder is a person who holds, in a public company, by himself or by his nominee, shares which entitle him to exercise at least 5 per cent (this was 10 per cent under the CAMA 2004) of unrestricted voting rights at any of the company's general meeting.

A person who is a substantial shareholder is a public company is mandated to give notice in writing, within 14 days after being aware of his status as such, to the company, stating all his particulars (name, address, full particulars of the shares) and for his nominee, if held for him by a nominee. This notice shall still be given to the company even if the member ceases to be a member before the 14 days expires (section 119 above does not have this provision, which seems to imply that the provision applies only to shareholding in public companies).

When the company receives the notice from the member, it shall within 14 days send same notice in writing to the Commission. As noted, the same notification is mandated from a member to the company within 14 days after he ceases to be a substantial shareholder in the company (stating full particulars and circumstances by which he ceased to be a substantial shareholder in the company). The company has 14 days also to inform the Commission in writing that the member has ceased to be a substantial shareholder.

These disclosures and notifications that are required from the significant or substantial shareholders to the company and from the company to the Commission are all corporate governance disclosures. They are meant to ensure transparency and also guide and inform potential and subsisting investors in the company on the true state of affairs. In this respect, principle 28 of the *Nigerian Code of Corporate Governance (NCCG), 2018* recommends that a company shall ensure full and comprehensive disclosures of all matters that are material to investors and stakeholders, while ensuring proper monitoring and implementation of items and materials which engender good corporate governance practice.

There is no doubt that potential and existing investors in a company will be very interested in knowing who has become or stop being a substantial shareholder or a person who has become or stopped having significant control in a company. For some potential investors, the fact of someone having such level of shareholding in a company could be the determining factor as to whether they will invest in such a company or not. Therefore, the importance of corporate governance disclosures of this nature cannot be over-emphasized.

CALLS ON SHARES

Under section 158(1) CAMA 2020 (s. 133 (1), directors of a company have the power, subject to the terms of issue and the Articles, to make calls from time to time on members for shares issued by the company in respect of any unpaid amount on the shares. This is whether it is on account of the nominal value of the shares or by way of premium *(Odesa Tramways Co.* v. *Mendel (1878) 8 Ch.D., 235; Anglo Universal Bank* v. *Baragnon (1881)45 LT 362; Mayson, 194).*

The directors are under a duty to ensure that they do all they can to get every shareholder to pay to the company the amount due from him in respect of a call. It is a fiduciary duty. In this respect, the directors would be breaching their duty of working in the best interests of the company, if they do not take all reasonable steps to enforce payment *(Spackman* v. *Evans (1868) LR 3, 171, Palmer's, 373*). However, under the CAMA, no call shall exceed 25 per cent of the nominal value of the shares. Also, no call shall be payable less than one (1) month from the date fixed for the payment of the last preceding call. The company shall give each member a notice of at least 14 days that will specify the time and place of payment for the call on the shares. Thereafter, each member is mandated to pay the amount of the call to the company at the time and place specified in the notice.

A call on shares shall be deemed to have been made by the directors when they pass the resolution authorizing the call, and joint holders of shares shall be jointly and severally liable to pay for any call on the shares (s. 158(2)(3), (s.133 (2)(3).

A member who does not pay for a call on the day that it is due shall be liable to pay interest on same, except where the directors waive the payment of interest. The directors may accept an advance payment from a member on all or part of the moneys uncalled and unpaid upon any shares held by him and may pay interests to the member on such sums advanced (s. 158 (4) (6), (s.133 (4)(6).

Where a member has made an advance payment for a call, he cannot compel the company to pay back such a sum (*Lock* v. *Queensland Investment and Land Mortgage Co. (1896) 1 Ch., 461; Charlesworth & Cain, 290).* On a related note, the company cannot decide to repay the advance payment made on calls to the shareholder without his consent *(London & North Steamship Co.* v. *Farmer (1914) 111 LT, 20).* Note that in a winding-up, the shareholder who made an advance payment for a call will rank after other creditors, but in priority to other shareholders for that sum that was advanced to the company (*Orojo, 146.)*

The directors have the powers to revoke or postpone a call that has already been made on shares (s. 158 (1), (s. 133(1).

Nature of Directors' Power to Make Calls

Directors' powers to make calls on shares is in the nature of a fiduciary power which must be exercised by them in the best interests of the company and the members as a whole *(Re National Provincial Marine Insurance Co; Gilbert's Case (1870) LR* 5 AC, 559). Therefore, directors are not allowed to abuse their powers to make calls on shares, for instance, by making a call on others while excluding themselves. Such a discriminatory call can only be made with shareholders knowledge and approval in a general meeting *(Alexander* v. *Automatic Telephone Co (1900) 1 Ch., 56; Orojo, 144).*

Irregular Calls on Shares

An irregular call on shares by company directors is *prima facie* invalid *(NBCI & Anor* v. *Balogun & Anor (1989) 2 GRBPL No. 6, 46; Garden Gully United Quartz Mining Co.* v. *McLister (1875) 1 AC, 39; Orojo, 144). Consequently,* a shareholder is not bound to pay for an invalid call and may bring an action for an injunction to restrain the directors from forfeiting his shares on that account *(Lamb* v. *Sambas Rubber Co. Ltd (1906) Ch, 854; Jones* v. *Pacaya Rubber Co. (1911) 1 KB 455).* However, an injunction cannot be granted to restrain a company from the enforcement of a call validly made by directors *(Galloway* v. *Halle Concerts Society (1915) 2 Ch, 233; Gower & Davies, 864).* In the NBCI's case above, the directors made a call on shares without giving some shareholders the 21 days' notice required by the company's Articles, and it was held to be an invalid call. This is notwithstanding the fact that the appellant's representative was at the meeting where the call was made.

It is possible for a company to validate an irregular call on shares made by its directors. This is the case where the company's Articles contain provisions that validate the acts of a board or committee of directors notwithstanding any defect relating to their appointment or qualification that would have otherwise rendered their actions invalid *(British Asbestos Co* v. *Boyd (1903) 2 Ch 439; Orojo, 144,146).*

Statutorily, in Nigeria, section 286 CAMA 2020 (s. 260) also has the effect of validating any irregular call on shares or other acts done by directors of a company if challenged due to any alleged defect in their qualification or appointment. The section will not, however, validate an irregular call that did not comply with a mandatory requirement of the CAMA. For instance, where the minimum 14 days' notice (required by section 158 to validate any call) to be given to members to pay up on a call was not complied with (*NBCI & Anor* v. *Balogun & Anor (1989) 2 GRBPL No. 6, 46).*

NUMBERING OF A COMPANY'S SHARES

Section 170 CAMA 2020, (s. 145) requires that each share in a company having a share capital shall be distinguished by its appropriate number (this is presumed to be a serial number or other form of distinct identification number). However, if at any time all the issued shares of a company, or all of its issued shares of a particular class are fully paid up and rank *pari passu* for all purposes, the requirement for numbering may be dispensed with.

ISSUE OF SHARE CERTIFICATE

The CAMA mandates every company, within 2 months after allotting its shares and within 3 months after an instrument of transfer of shares has been lodged with it, to have ready the certificates for all shares allotted or transferred for delivery to the allottees. An exception is where the condition for the issue of the shares provides otherwise (s.171), (s. 146(1). In such an instance, it is the condition for the issue of the shares that will be followed by the company. The section was amended by section 7 of the schedule to the *Business Facilitation (Miscellaneous Provisions) Act (BFA) 2022*, which provides that a share certificate to be issued by a company after allotting its shares could be in physical or electronic form. The BFA, in essence, has introduced electronic share certificate into the company law regime in Nigeria (although it is mentioned under section 181 CAMA 2020 under instrument of share transfer). This being the case, the necessary changes are also taken for granted, for instance, that a share certificate can now validly be delivered to the allottee electronically. However, this appears not to be an entirely new innovation in Nigeria's financial, corporate and capital market circles. This is because section 315 of the *Investments and Securities Act (ISA) 2007* defines a share certificate to mean 'an instrument of a body corporate certifying that the person named is entitled to a certain number of shares and is *prima facie* evidence of his ownership whether electronically expressed or otherwise as may be approved by the Commission…' This section, in effect, provided for the electronic issuance (and by extension, electronic delivery) of share certificates by quoted companies. Also, under section 181 CAMA 2020, instrument of transfer of shares is said to include certificates issued in electronic form.

Members' Right to a Certificate

Every person whose name has been entered in the register of members shall be entitled to receive a share certificate for all his shares within 3 months of allotment or lodgement of transfer or such period as the conditions of issue may provide. The certificate is to be sent to the member upon the payment of any prescribed fees as the directors shall, from time to time, determine (s. 171(2), (s. 146(2) *(Sharpe* v. *Tophams Ltd (1939)1 All ER 123; Standard Trust Bank Plc* v. *Olusola (2007) 9 CLRN 41, 63).* As noted above, the share certificate can now be in electronic form and the delivery of the certificate to the allottee can also be effected electronically.

A certificate shall be issued under the company's seal (where the company has and uses one) or otherwise signed as a deed by the company. If there are joint holders of shares, a certificate delivered to one of them is considered sufficient for the purpose. In any event, where a share certificate is lost, destroyed or defaced for any reasons, it may be replaced on such terms as the directors may deem fit, including evidence of the incident and indemnity to the company (s. 171(3) 94), (s. 146(3)(4).

REMEDY FOR DEFAULT TO ISSUE CERTIFICATE

If a notice is served on a company requiring it to remedy a default in issuing a share certificate to an allottee or transferee of shares, and the company fails to remedy the default within 10 days of the service of the notice, the Court may, on the application of the person who is entitled to the certificate, make an order directing the company and any of its officers to remedy the default. The Court may, in making the order, prescribe time within which the company may remedy the default. The Court may also award costs against the company or any officer in default incidental to the application (s. 171(5), (s. 146(5) *(Standard Trust Bank Plc* v. *Olusola (2007) 9 CLRN 41, 63).*

LEGAL EFFECTS OF SHARE CERTIFICATE

A share certificate properly issued by a company under its seal (where the company uses one) or signed as a deed by the company, to a member specifying his shareholding, shall be *prima facie* evidence of the title of the member to the shares (s. 172(1) CAMA 2020), (s. 147(1.) This being the case, a share certificate is not considered a conclusive proof of title to the shares and can be impeached by superior title to the shares, if proven (*Oilfield Supply Centre Limited* v. *Johnson (1987) 2 NWLR Pt. 58, 625; Ideh* v. *Zenith Bank Plc & Anor (2020) LPELR-51283).*

Note that if a person changes his position to his detriment in good faith on facts and continued accuracy of the statements made in a share certificate, the company shall be estopped from denying the continued accuracy of such statements. Also, the company shall be liable to compensate the person for losses incurred by relying on such statements, which he would not have suffered had the statements been or continued to be accurate. This is an application of the doctrine of estoppel by representation *(Re Bahia & San Francisco Railway Co. Ltd (1868) LR QB 584; Hannigan, 305; Balkis Consolidated Co. Ltd* v. *Tomkinson (1893) AC, 396; Hannigan, 306).*

In the *Re Bahia's* case, above, the Court reasoned that:

> the power of giving certificate is…for the benefit of the company in general; and it is a declaration by the company to all the world that the person in whose name the certificate is made out, and to whom it is given, is a shareholder in the company, and it is given by the company with the intention that it shall be used by the person to whom it is given, and acted upon in the sale and transfer of shares.

A classic example of the application of this principle is in the case of *Bloomenthal* v. *Ford (1897) AC, 156*) where a lender to a company had taken share certificates from a customer as collateral, which indicated that the shares were full paid-up. It turned out that the shares were not fully paid up. The company was estopped from denying the certificates and essentially could not have been seen to approbate and reprobate on the content of the certificates they issued *(Hannigan, 306).*

PAYMENT FOR ALLOTTED SHARES

Subject to the provision of the CAMA that provides for the payment for shares other than in cash, section 160 CAMA 2020, (s. 135) requires that the shares of any company and any premium on them shall be paid up in cash. Otherwise, where the Articles permit, allotted shares may also be paid for, fully or partly, by a valuable consideration other than in cash. A company's shares shall be deemed to have been paid for in cash, only to the extent that the company actually received cash for them at the time of the agreement to issue the shares or subsequent to that (s. 161(1), (s. 136).

Where shares are issued to a person who has sold or agreed to sell any property to the company or render any service(s), the amount payable to that person from the sale of the property or services rendered shall be deducted from the amount due to be paid by him on the shares. It is the balance (if any) that is to be treated as having been paid for in cash, notwithstanding that cheques or other securities for the money have been exchanged (s. 161(2), (s. 136).

Payment for Shares other than in Cash

Under section 162 (1) CAMA 2020, (s. 137 (1), where a public company agrees to accept payment for its shares in a manner otherwise than wholly in cash, it shall appoint an independent valuer to value the consideration to be used in place of cash and prepare a report on the valuation and submit to the company. The valuer is entitled to ask for and obtain any information and explanation from the officers of the company as he deems necessary to carry out the valuation or prepare the report.

The company shall, not more than three days after the receipt of the valuer's report send a copy of the report to the proposed purchaser of shares, indicating whether or not it intends to accept the consideration as payment or part payment for its shares. However, a public company shall not accept the consideration as any payment unless the value as determined by the valuer is worth at least as much as may be credited as paid up in respect of the shares allowed to the proposed purchaser of its shares (s. 162 (3)(4), (s. 137(3)(4). If a valuer knowingly or recklessly makes a statement that is misleading, false or deceptive in a material particular, he commits an offence and is liable to a term of imprisonment or fine as the Court may impose. A valuer could be an auditor, valuer, engineer, accountant or surveyor who is not an employee of the company or its agent or agent of its employee or director (s. 162 (5)(6), (s.

137 (5)(6). The engineering profession is an addition by the CAMA 2020 as part of the valuers, which was not there under the CAMA 2004.

An important point is that the CAMA 2020 has removed private companies from the rigours of complying with the above procedures. It is now restricted only to public companies.

Power to Pay or Accept Different Amounts on Shares

If permitted by its Articles, under section 163 CAMA 2020, a company may undertake the following actions in relation to its shares:

- make arrangements on the issue of shares for a difference between the shareholders in the amounts and times of payment of calls on their shares;
- accept from any member the whole or part of the amount remaining unpaid on any shares held by him, although no part of that amount has been called up; or
- pay dividends in proportion to the amount paid-up on each share where a larger amount is paid-up on some shares than on others.

As far as the Articles has authorized, the directors are given large discretion and latitude under this section on how to approach the issue of payments on shares, depending on several factors stated therein. Since directors' duties in running a company are fiduciary in nature, it is therefore fair to conclude that even in making a decision in any of the items above to implement, the director must act in what is in the best interests of the company.

COMPANY'S RIGHT TO LIEN ON ITS SHARES

In simple terms, a lien is a right to retain something which is in a person's possession but belonging to another person until certain demand(s) being made by the person in possession from the owner of the thing in question, is satisfied *(Agrotec Tech-Service (Nig) Ltd* v. *MIA & Sons Ltd (2000) 15 NWLR Pt. 692, 730; FBN Plc* v. *Songonuga (2007) 3 NWLR Pt. 1021, 230; Livestock Feeds Plc* v. *Okezie (2000) 10 NWLR Pt. 775, 341*). A lien on shares is an equitable charge on the shares and entitles the company involved to sell the shares in appropriate circumstances *(Orojo, 146).* As a general rule, a company has, *prima facie*, no lien on the shares of its members, but it can be effected by contract between the parties or prescribed by statute (*Pinkett* v. *Wright (1842) 2 Ha., 120; Palmers, 375).*

For instance, section 164(1) CAMA 2020 (s. 139(1) provides that a company has a first and paramount lien on every share, not fully paid-up, for all the money (whether currently payable or not) called or payable at a fixed time in respect of that share. The company also has a first and paramount lien on all shares (other than fully paid shares) standing registered in the name of a single person for all the money presently payable by him or his estate to the company. However, the directors of a company are empowered to declare that the company's lien as described is inapplicable, wholly or in part, to any of its shares *(Champagne Perrier-Jout SA* v. *H Finch Ltd and Others (1982) 3 All ER, 713).*

Note should be taken that a company's lien on any share(s) extends to all dividends payable on and all bonus shares issued in relation to such shares. In essence, as will be seen below, a company's lien on its shares, while the lien remains active, is total in effect (s. 164(2), (s. 139(2). The CAMA 2004 did not include bonus shares as an area wherein a company's lien on shares also has effect, it was introduced in CAMA 2020.

A lien on shares is usually enforced, like any other equitable charge, by a sale. Where the Articles (or statute) does not give the company the power to sell the shares, an application to Court for an order to sell may be necessary. It has been held that a lien on shares cannot be enforced by a forfeiture, even if the power to forfeit shares is in the company's Articles. This is because, among others, forfeiture of debt in a company would amount to an illegal reduction of capital *(Hopkinson* v. *Mortimer, Harley & Co. Ltd (1917) Ch., 646; Charlesworth & Cain, 292 -293).*

A company is empowered to sell, in any way as the directors may deem fit, any shares on which the company has a lien. For any such sale to be valid a sum on which the lien exists must be currently payable and a 14-day written demand notice to the registered holder of the shares or a person otherwise entitled thereto, either by reason of death or bankruptcy, demanding payment would have expired. To give effect to the sale of the shares on which it has a lien, the directors are empowered to authorize the transfer of the shares sold to the purchaser, who shall then be registered as the holder of the shares (s. 164(3), (s. 139(3). The issuance of 14-day demand notice to the registered holder and the fact that the sum over which there is a lien must be currently payable, are conditions precedent to any sale, the absence of either of which will invalidate any purported sale.

In order to give effect to any sale by a company of shares on which it has a lien, the directors of a company may authorize a person to transfer the shares sold to the purchaser and the purchaser shall be registered as the holder of the shares comprised in any such transfer. The purchaser's title is protected and is not affected by internal issues within the company. Under section 164 (5) of the Act, the purchaser is not bound to see to the application of the purchase money and his title to the shares is not affected by any irregularity or invalidity in the proceedings in reference to the sale (s. 164(4)(5), (s. 139(4)(5).

The proceeds of the sale of the shares are to be applied to pay off such part of the amount (presently payable and not so payable) over which the lien exists and the residue shall be paid to the person entitled to the shares at the date of the sale (s. 164 (6). This provision was introduced by CAMA 2020, and there is no equivalent provision under the CAMA 2004.

It has been decided that a shareholder may, by action, compel a company to assign its lien to a person who is willing to pay-off the amount of the lien *(Everitt* v. *Automatic Weighing Machine Co. (1892) 3 Ch. 503, Orojo, 146).* As far as the interests of the company is to get its money which necessitated the lien to be repaid, the reasoning behind this principle then is not far-fetched. The only exception could be where the company discovered a manifest illegality apparent in the process of the repayment sought to be made (for instance, proven case of money laundering) to redeem the lien. In such an instance, the company is entitled to decline to accept such payment.

FORFEITURE OF COMPANY'S SHARES

In general, a company does not have an inherent power to forfeit shares, and such a power must be provided for in the Articles *(Re National Patent Steam Fuel Co., Barton's Case (1859) 4 De G & J 46; Clarke* v. *Hart (1858) 6 HLC, 663*). Due to its overall consequences, one of which is that it is usually viewed as penal in nature, the Courts have always interpreted any provisions for the forfeiture of property strictly, and a failure to follow the procedure laid down in a company's Articles for forfeiture of shares will invalidate the process *(Johnson* v. *Little's Iron Agency (1877) 5 Ch.D, 687; (Mayson et al., 195).*

Under section 165(1), (s. 140 (1), if a member fails to pay any call on shares or instalment on the date due, the directors may, anytime thereafter, where the call remains unpaid, serve a notice on him to pay the outstanding call or instalment and any accrued interests.

In the notice to the member, the directors shall give him another date to pay up the outstanding amount (not being less than 14 days) while stating that in the event that the amount is not paid after the new date the shares shall be liable to be forfeited. If, at the expiry of the period limited in the notice, the member concerned did not comply with the instructions to pay his outstanding on the shares, the directors may pass a resolution forfeiting the shares (s. 140(2) (3). It is important to note that the resolution required to forfeit the shares in this instance is that of the directors and not a resolution of the members. This implies that no general meeting, annual or otherwise, is required for this.

A forfeited share may be sold or otherwise disposed of on such terms as the directors deem fit, even as the directors have the power to cancel the forfeiture before a sale or disposition as they think fit (s. 165 (4), (s. 140(4). When forfeited shares are sold, the purchaser becomes liable for any future calls on the shares, having stepped into the position of the previous owner of the shares. This presupposes that any future payment on the shares by the former owner should be credited to the purchaser *(New Balkis Ferstelling Ltd* v. *Randt Gold and Securities Ltd (1904) AC, 165; Re Randt Gold Mining Co. (1904) 2 Ch., 468; Charlesworth & Cain, 297).*

It has been submitted that the powers conferred on company directors to forfeit shares are fiduciary in nature and must be exercised as such for the company's benefit. Furthermore, forfeiture of shares relates primarily to the inability of the shareholder concerned to fulfil his obligations in relation to the shares, and not otherwise. Therefore, it has been held that the power to forfeit shares for non-payment of debts other than calls or instalments thereof, is invalid as an unauthorized reduction of capital *(Hopkinson* v. *Mortimer, Harley & Co. (1917) 1 Ch, 646 (Palmers, 381).*

LEGAL EFFECT OF FORFEITURE OF SHARES

We have seen that a company has the power to forfeit a holder's shares in deserving circumstances, the question then is, what is the consequence or effect of that forfeiture? A person whose shares have been forfeited ceases to be a member in a company in respect of the forfeited shares. This notwithstanding, the person will still be liable to pay all moneys due from him to the company at the date of forfeiture of the shares. His liability thereto does not cease until the shares are fully paid (s. 165(5) CAMA 2020), (s. 140 (5) *(China Steamship Co, Dawe's Case (1868) LR 6 EQ, 232).* An important point is that any money owed to the company by the former member is subsequently not owed as a member but as a debtor to the company *(Ladies Dress Association Ltd* v. *Pullbrook (1900) 2 QB, 276; Charlesworth & Cain, 298).*

A statutory declaration by a director or the company secretary affirming the person's position in the company and that the shares concerned have been forfeited shall be *prima facie* evidence (rebuttable by superior evidence) of that fact against all persons who claim title to such shares (s. 165(6), (s. 140(6). It is not permissible for a person who is a company secretary but also occupies the position of a director in the company to sign the declaration alone in both capacities, as the declaration must be signed by two persons (s. 331 CAMA 2020), (s. 294).

A company is empowered to receive the consideration for the sale of the shares and execute instrument of transfer in favour of a purchaser, who shall thereupon be registered as the holder of the shares. The purchaser is not bound to see to the application of the purchase money and his title to the shares is not affected by any irregularity or invalidity in the process for the forfeiture, sale or disposal of the shares (s. 165(7), (s. 140(7). For instance, the fact that a director who was not otherwise qualified to vote in the meeting where the directors passed a resolution to forfeit the shares, did actually vote to pass the resolution, is not the business of the purchaser, being that he is not expected to know the internal processes of the company. This is the rule in *Royal British Bank* v. *Turquand (1856) 6E & B, 327*, or the 'indoor management rule', which presumes regularity in a company's internal processes.

SURRENDER OF A COMPANY'S SHARES

There is no express provision in the CAMA for a shareholder to surrender his shares to the company under any circumstance(s). This is understandable, from the point of view of capital maintenance in a company. Surrender of shares by a member is seen as improper, as it releases the member from further liability with respect to the shares so surrendered. Again, a surrender also amounts to a reduction of the company's capital, but this time, without approval of the Court. This is unlawful in ordinary terms. Under section 183 (6) CAMA 2020, (s.160(3) a company may accept from a shareholder, shares in the company which he has surrendered to the company as a gift, but not to reduce or extinguish any liability in respect of amount unpaid thereon.

A company's Articles may authorize the directors to accept a surrender of shares and stipulate the details for the exercise of such powers. A surrender of shares could be appropriate in circumstances where forfeiture would have been the other alternative and any valid surrender of shares to the company would be valid to avert such forfeiture *(Trevor* v. *Whitworth (1887) 12 AC,*

409). There could also be a surrender of fully paid-up shares in exchange for new shares of the same nominal value, but where the shares are partly paid and not liable to forfeiture, they cannot be surrendered *(Bellerby* v. *Rowland Ltd (1902) 2 Ch, 14, Palmers, 386).*

TRANSFER AND TRANSMISSION OF SHARES

It is trite that members in a company have the right to transfer shares belonging to them therein and this right is unfettered, unless there are express restrictions to that effect in the company's Articles or other agreement(s) thereto *(New Resources Intl Ltd* v. *Oranusi (2010) LPELP-4592; Nishbet* v. *Shepherd (1994) 1 BCLC, 300).* Under section 139 CAMA 2020, (s. 115) shares or other interests of a member in a company are in the form of personal property transferable in the manner provided in the company's Articles. Conceptually, transfer of shares is the voluntary conveyance of the rights and, possibly, the duties of a member, as represented in a share in the company, from a shareholder who wishes to cease to be a member (or dilute his shareholding), to a person desirous of becoming a member *(Palmers, 386).*

A company is empowered to transfer its shares by instrument of transfer without any restrictions, except as expressly provided in the company's Articles. However, a company is prohibited, notwithstanding anything in its Articles, from registering a share transfer without receiving a proper instrument of transfer for that purpose. The only exception is where shares have transmitted to any person by operation of law (s. 175(1)(2) CAMA 2020, (s. 151(1)(2). Both the transferor and the transferee of the shares shall execute the instrument of transfer or have it executed for them and the transferor shall be deemed to remain the holder of the shares until the name of the transferee is entered in the register of members in respect of the shares (s. 175(3), (s. 151(3). Therefore, an instrument of transfer that has been executed by one of the parties only would not be valid in transferring shares between the parties *(Inyang & Ors* v. *Ebong (2002) 2 NWLR Pt. 751, 284, 329).*

The processes of transfer and transmission of shares in a company are both legal and corporate governance issues. According to the World Bank Group (IFC, 88) it is the responsibility of the company secretary to organize the processes of transfer and transmission of shares in a company, and in doing this, the company secretary must ensure that there is no restriction(s) against any individual or entity who wants to be a shareholder in the company. Apart from this, it is said that this duty continues with persons who cease to be members in the company and the company secretary must ensure that all post-membership activities are formalized. For instance, once a person ceases to be a member, the company secretary must ensure that the person's name is promptly removed from the register of members for accuracy of the register.

RESTRICTION OF SHARE TRANSFERS

Section 22(2) CAMA 2020 gives a private company, subject to the provisions of its Articles, the right to restrict transfer of its shares and also makes provision that:

- the company shall not without the consent of all its members, sell assets having a value of more than 50 per cent of the total value of the company's assets (this particular aspect requires unanimity of assent of all the members for a sale of this nature to happen and it cannot be sidestepped);
- a member shall not sell the member's shares in the company to a non-member, without first offering those shares to existing members;
- a member or group of members, acting together, shall not sell or agree to sell more than 50 per cent of the shares in the company to a person who is not then a member unless that non-member has offered to buy all the existing members' interests on the same terms.

The CAMA 2020 seems to give a degree of discretion to a private company to restrict, if desired, the transfer of shares in its Articles. This is unlike the situation under the CAMA 2004, which made it mandatory for all private companies to restrict share transfers (s.22(2). Restrictions, like those on transfer of shares, are usually construed strictly as they constitute a fetter on the right to freely transfer property and any deviation from the laid down provisions invalidate the whole process *(Shepherd Trustees* v. *Shepherd (1950) SC, 60)*. In essence, if the provisions in a company's Articles providing for restriction on transfer of shares, or any other property for that matter, is not clearly worded or is in any way ambiguous, it will be construed against enforcing the restriction. The Articles of most private companies contain pre-emption clauses (couched as right of first refusal) to mandate that members first offer any shares they intend to sell to other members at a fair price, and can only sell to non-members if no member is willing to buy. This practice of pre-emption is what the CAMA 2020 has now made statutory (*Ocean Coal Co.* v. *Powell Duffryn Coal Co. (1923) 1 Ch, 654; Lyle and Scott Ltd* v. *Scott's Trustees (1959) SC, 64; Orojo, 150)*.

ENTRY IN THE REGISTER OF TRANSFER

After a transfer of shares between parties, the transferor of the shares shall apply to the company to register the transferee as the new holder of the shares, and the company shall enter the name of the transferee in its register of members as if the transferee had made the application. Until the transferee's name is entered in the register of members, the transferor of the shares is, as far as the company is concerned, deemed to remain the holder of the shares (s. 176 (1)(2), (s. 152 (1)(2). The question, however, is: does the company have a right to refuse to register a transfer of shares sent to it?

Company's Refusal to Register Transfer

When a company's shareholder(s) validly transfers his shares to third parties and lodges the instrument(s) of transfer with the company, the company is obliged to register the transferee(s) as the new holder(s) of the shares and enter his name(s) in the register of members. However, there are instances where a company may validly refuse to register a transfer of shares, (not fully paid-up):

- where the transferee is a person that the company does not approve. The Act does not state on what basis this non-approval of the transferee should be, but it does appear that the company, acting through the directors, has been given the discretion in this respect, to make that decision. There could be an argument that any decision by the directors to refuse to register a person as a shareholder is an exercise of their fiduciary duty (to act in the best interests of the company) and must be grounded in facts and not arbitrary. Otherwise, the transferee has the right to approach the Court for redress;
- where the company has a lien on the share in question (s. 176(3), (s. 152 (3);
- The company may also refuse to recognise an instrument of transfer that has been lodged with it relating to a particular share(s) unless:
- any fee that has been prescribed by the company as payable on the transfer instrument has been paid;
- the instrument of transfer has been accompanied by the share certificate to which it relates and such other evidence that the directors may require to determine the transferor's right to make the transfer; and
- the instrument of transfer was made to cover only one class of shares (s. 176 (4), (s. 152(4).

If a company refuses, for any reason(s), to register a transfer, it shall send a notice of refusal to the transferee within two (2) months after the date on which the transfer was lodged with it (s. 177), (s. 153). It has been held that where the power to refuse to register a transfer is not exercised by the directors within the two (2) months period as prescribed, then it is lost *(Re Swaldale Cleaners Ltd (1968) 1 WLR, 1710; Gower & Davies, 991).* It has also been held that a company that refuses to register a share transfer is obliged to inform the transferee of its decision, but is not required to inform the transferor (*Re Swaldale Cleaners Ltd (1968) 1 WLR, 1710).* It would appear that the CAMA adopted this position on the issue in providing that the transferee should be informed of any refusal to register transfer of shares, but is silent on any notice to the transferor. It is not clear why, but it is possible that the thinking might be that at this point the transferor had already divested himself of his interests in the share(s) (at least in principle) in question and received value for them and the person to be affected by any decision would be the transferee.

Where directors have been given the discretion by the company's Articles in relation to registering transfer of shares, the Court will not normally interfere in their exercise of this discretion. The exception is where it is established that the directors are not exercising the discretion in good faith, or that they are acting oppressively, corruptly or in like manner. In essence, where it does appear that the directors were not exercising their discretion in the best interests of the company as a whole *(Re Smith & Fawcett Ltd (1942) Ch., 304; Re Gresham Society (1872) LR 8 Ch., 446; Re Coalport China Co. (1895) 2 Ch., 404; Re Bell Bros (1891) 65 LT, 245; Charlesworth & Cain, 269)*.

The right given to directors to be able to refuse transfer of shares must be positively exercised in order for it to be effective. Therefore, where the board of directors are evenly divided as to whether to register a transfer or not and no casting vote has been used, then, the transfer has to be registered because the board's refusal has not been positive *(Re Hackney Pavilion (1924) 1 Ch 276; Moodie* v. *Shepherd Bookbinders Ltd (1949) 2 All ER, 1044; Palmers, 396-398).*

It should be noted that where directors of a company have unreasonably failed to register a transfer, the transferee may apply to the Court under section 115 CAMA 2020 (s. 90) to rectify the register of members by substituting his name for that of the transferor *(Abina* v. *Tikatore Press Ltd (1968) 2 ALR Comm., 480, Orojo, 153).*

TRANSFER OF SHARES BY PERSONAL REPRESENTATIVES

Under section178 CAMA 2020, (s. 154) a personal representative of a deceased member may transfer the shares or other interests of the deceased member, even though the personal representative is not himself a member of the company. Such a transfer would be as valid as if the personal representative had been a member when he executed the instrument of transfer. A point that should be noted here, but which did not come out in the provisions of the section on this issue, is that most times, the company would have insisted that the personal representative of the deceased processed and received a Letter of Administration or Probate on the deceased's estate before acting on the shares, at all.

FORGED OR FRAUDULENT TRANSFERS

All the discussions above on the indices of transfer of shares have been on the presumption that the transfer itself was valid and effective. What then happens when a transfer instruction has been forged and presented to the company for registration? Well, in the first place, once a transfer instruction is proven to be a forgery, it is then fraudulent and a nullity. The real owner of the shares can approach the Court to compel the company to restore his name to the register of members *(Barton* v. *Staffordshire Rly. Co (1888) 38 Ch.D, 458; Charlesworth & Cain, 281).* On its own accord, if and when a company discovers the forgery, it may remove the name from the register, without being estopped by the fact that they had registered the name earlier *(Simm* v. *Anglo American Co. (1879) 5 QBD, 188; Gower & Davies, 986).*

Finally, where a company, without notice, registers a forged transfer and sustains any loss thereby, it is entitled to be indemnified by the person who sent in the forged transfer for registration, and indeed, from any agent that sent the transfer to them to register *(Kai Yung* v. *Hong Kong Banking Corp (1981) AC, 787).*

TRANSMISSION OF SHARES

Transmission of shares is the process of the passing of a share by operation of law from a shareholder to another person or body *(Palmers, 386).* The shares 'transmit' to the beneficiary in the sense that no positive act(s) of the beneficiary is required for him to be entitled to the shares, at least in the first instance. Subsequent procedures to get the beneficiary to be entered in the register of members are usually necessary.

Under section 179 CAMA 2020, (s. 155 (1), at the death of a member, his survivor(s) where he is a joint holder, or his legal personal representative where he is a sole holder, shall be the only person(s) recognized by the company as having any title to his interests in the shares, but nothing in the section is capable of releasing the estate of a deceased joint holder from any liability in respect of any share which had been jointly held by him and other persons.

Beneficiary's Right to Elect

When a person upon whom shares have transmitted (on the death or bankruptcy of the holder) has produced evidence (usually a probate or letter of administration is considered sufficient under section 173 CAMA 2020 (s. 148) as required, from time to time, by the directors, he may elect either to be registered himself as a holder of the shares or to have some person nominated by him registered as the transferee of the shares. In either case, the company shall have the same right to decline or suspend registration as they would have before the shares transmitted from the original holder (s. 179(2), (s. 155(2).

If the person who becomes entitled to the transmitted shares on the death of the holder elects to be registered himself, he shall inform the company in writing stating that he has so elected. Where the person elects to have another person(s) registered as the holder of the shares, he shall confirm that election by executing a transfer of the shares concerned to that other person(s). All the restrictions and limitations in the CAMA and the company's Articles relating to the transfer of shares and the registration of transfers shall apply to the notice and transfer mentioned here as if it was a share transfer by the original holder of the shares and the death or bankruptcy had not occurred (s.179 (3)(4), (s. 155 (4)*(Dashfield* v. *Davidson (2009) 1 BCLC, 220).*

Beneficiary's Right to Dividend

A person who becomes entitled to shares due to the death or bankruptcy of the holder shall be entitled to the same dividends and other advantages to which he would have been entitled if he were the registered holder of the shares. However, except such a person is formally registered as a member of the company, or the Articles provide otherwise, (by having his name entered in the register of members) in relation to the shares, he shall not be entitled to exercise any membership rights in relation to the company's meetings (s. 179 (5), (s.155 (5).

The directors may at any time give notice to a person who has become entitled to any shares as described above to elect either to be registered himself or to transfer the shares. If the person concerned fails to make an election within 90 days of receipt of the directors' notice, the directors may thereafter withhold payment of any dividends, bonuses or other money payable in respect of the shares until the person concerned complies with the notice (s. 179(5), (s. 155 (5).

Protection of Beneficiaries

Under section 180 CAMA 2020, (s. 156), any person claiming to be interested in any share, dividend, or interest on them, may protect his interests by serving the company concerned with a notice of his interest (note that the affidavit of interest that was also required to be served on the company under the equivalent portion of CAMA 2004, has been omitted from the 2020 CAMA). Once this is done, the company shall enter the fact of the service of the notice on its register of members, and shall not register any transfer or make any payment or return in respect of the shares until after 42 days' notice of the proposed transfer or payment has been given to the claimant. The company will compensate any person injured, if it does not comply with these provisions.

PROHIBITION OF FINANCIAL ASSISTANCE BY COMPANY

In general, where a person is acquiring or proposing to acquire a company's shares, it is unlawful under the CAMA for the company or its subsidiaries to offer financial assistance, directly or otherwise, to such a person. This is whether it is before or at the time of the transaction, for him to use same finances to acquire the company's shares. The term 'financial assistance' has been defined to mean 'a gift, guarantee, any form of security or indemnity, a loan or any form of credit or any other financial assistance given by a company, the net assets of which are thereby reduced by up to 50 per cent, or which has no net assets.' On the other hand, the term net assets means the aggregate of the company's assets, less the aggregate of its liabilities' (s. 183 (1)(a)(b) CAMA 2020), (s. 159(1). The CAMA 2004 does not define 'net assets.'

Subject to the above, where a person is acquiring or proposing to acquire shares in a company, it shall not be lawful for the company or any of its subsidiaries to give financial assistance, directly or indirectly for the purpose of that acquisition either before or at the time of the acquisition.

Where a person has already acquired shares in a company and any liability has been incurred for the purpose of the acquisition, it shall be unlawful for the company or its subsidiaries to give any financial assistance to a person to discharge or reduce any such liability (s. 183 (2), (159 (2).

Exceptions to the General Prohibitions

The prohibition against companies extending financial assistance to persons to acquire their shares is not absolute, as there are exceptions to the general rule.

Under section 183(3), (s. 159 (3) of the Act, the general prohibition does not extend to:

- a company that lends money in the ordinary course of its business, where money lending is part of the ordinary business of the company;
- where a company provides money in line with an existing scheme, for the purchase of or subscription for fully paid shares in the company or its holding company, the transaction being by the trustees of the shares, to be held by or for the benefit of the employees of the company, including a salaried director in the employment of the company;
- where a company makes loans to persons other than directors, who are *bona fide* employees, to enable them subscribe to fully paid shares in the company or its holding company, to be held by those persons as beneficial owners;
- where the act or transaction is in any way authorized by law, including (i) a distribution of a company's assets by way of dividend lawfully made or a distribution made in the course of the company's winding-up. (ii) the allotment of bonus shares, (iii) a reduction of capital confirmed by order of the Court under the CAMA; and (iv) a redemption or purchase of shares;
- anything done in pursuance of an order of the Court under a scheme of arrangement, scheme of merger or any other scheme or restructuring of a company done with sanction of the Court; or
- an assistance given by the company where the principal purpose is not to reduce or discharge any liability incurred by a person in acquiring shares in a company but an incidental part of a larger purpose of the company and the assistance is given in good faith.

The exceptions that are enumerated in the last three paragraphs above were introduced by the CAMA 2020 and were not mentioned in the repealed CAMA.

WHEN A COMPANY CAN ACQUIRE ITS OWN SHARES

The issue as to whether a company can purchase or in any way acquire its own shares is regulated by section 184 (1) CAMA 2020, (s. 160) and by the company's Articles. It provides that a limited liability company may purchase its shares, including redeemable shares, provided that:

- it is so permitted by its Articles;
- the shareholders shall approve, by special resolution, the shares that the company intends to purchase (in a general meeting);
- only fully paid shares of a company may be purchased by the company, and the terms of purchase shall provide for payment for the purchase;
- within seven days after the passing of the special resolution approving the purchase of the shares, the company shall cause to be published in two national newspapers a notice of the proposed purchase of the company of its own shares;
- within 15 days after the publication above, the company's director shall execute and file with the Commission a statutory declaration of solvency, affirming that the company is solvent and can pay its debts as they fall due and that after the purchase of its shares the company shall remain solvent as such and be able to pay its debts.

A company is not permitted to purchase its own shares if the effect will be to leave the company with only redeemable shares or treasury shares.

Within a period of six weeks following the publication in the national newspapers of its intention to acquire its own shares, any of the company's creditors or a dissenting shareholder who did not vote in favour of the resolution, may make an application to Court for an order cancelling the resolution. Whether the process will proceed to conclusion or not will depend on what the Court orders on hearing the application filed. Payment for its shares bought back by a company can only be paid for out of the company's distributable profits (s. 184(2)(3)(4).

There is an important observation to be made on the approach adopted by the CAMA 2020 and CAMA 2004 with respect to the issue of acquisition of a company of its own shares. As seen above, under section 184 CAMA 2020, in the first place, a company is permitted to acquire its own shares but on certain conditions, as enumerated above.

In contrast to the above, under the CAMA 2004, a company, subject to the provisions of the Act and its Articles, is not permitted to acquire its own shares, but may do so for certain purposes, which included: eliminating factional shares, satisfying the claims of a dissenting shareholder, or settling or compromising a debt or claim against the company, among others.

An intriguing aspect of the provisions of section 184 above, is that, unlike the corresponding provisions in 2004 CAMA (s. 160), it did not bother to state the purposes for which a share buyback could be executed by a company, but only stipulated the procedure to be adopted by a company for achieving same. The implication of this is that the CAMA has ceased to micro-manage companies in this respect by stipulating the purposes for which they could buy back their own shares. In contrast, the Act has given companies themselves the leverage to decide what to do with their share buyback scheme as long they comply with the procedures and conditions stipulated by the Act. Even with this, it is not just from any person or entity that a company could buy-back its shares, as the permissible transactions are limited to buying shares:

- from the existing shareholders or security holders on a proportionate basis;
- from existing shareholders in a manner permitted pursuant to a scheme of arrangement sanctioned by the Court;
- from the open market; and
- by purchasing the securities issued to the company's employees pursuant to a scheme of stock option or any other similar scheme (s. 186 CAMA 2020).

A company is not permitted to buy back more than 15 per cent of issued share capital of any class of its shares as treasury shares. Where a company buys back more than 15 per cent of the issued share capital of any class of its shares, the company shall, before the end of 12 months of exceeding that threshold, put measures in place, either by reissuing, cancelling or both of a number of shares to ensure that it does not exceed the threshold (s. 187).

Rules 13.18 and 14.1 of the *NSE Rule Book 2015* has made extensive provisions with respect to share buy back by listed companies.

Section 190 CAMA 2020 (s. 165) stipulates the conditions to be met for a subsidiary company to acquire shares in a holding company.

MORTGAGING OF SHARES

The mortgage of shares is the process by which the shareholder (the mortgagor) transfers the legal title in the shares as security to another person (the mortgagee) to borrow money. The mortgagor then hands over instrument of transfer and the share certificates to the mortgagee after executing a mortgage deed for the mortgagee to be registered with the shares. This type of mortgage arrangement is usually referred to as a legal mortgage. It usually provides for a right of redemption when the debt is repaid as agreed and no recourse to the security is needed *(BON* v. *Bello (2000) 7 NWLR Pt. 664, 244; Adetona* v. *Zenith Intl Bank Plc (2011) 18 NWLR Pt. 1278, 627; Atiba Iyalamu Savings & Loans Ltd* v. *Suberu (2018) 13 NWLR Pt. 1737, 387; Walker* v. *Jones (1866) LR 1, 50; Rourke* v. *Robinson (1911) Ch. 480, Mayson et al., 341).*

The prime advantage of a legal mortgage is that it gives the mortgagee a complete security over the shares, and if the mortgagor defaults in payment, then the mortgagee can proceed to sell the shares without recourse to the Court. Furthermore, unless the parties to the mortgage deed agree to the contrary, the mortgagee is entitled to claim the dividends that accrue to the shares and to vote at meetings in respect of the shares *(Siemens Brothers & Co. Ltd* v. *Burns (1918) 2 Ch. 324, Orojo, 160).*

There is also the equitable mortgage, which simply involves the deposit of the share certificates with the lender by the borrower. The lender will have to get an order of Court to sell the shares in the event of a default *(Bank of the North* v. *Akintoye (1999) 12 NWLR Pt. 631, 392; UBN Plc* v. *Taylor (2005) 15 NWLR 947, 27; Okuneye* v. *FBN Plc (1996) 6 NWLR Pt. 457, 749; Harold* v. *Plenty (1901) 2 Ch., 314; Fuller* v. *Glyn Mills, Currie & Co. (1914) 2 KB, 168).* The deposit of share certificates with a lender could also be accompanied by the execution of a blank instrument of transfer by the borrower in favour of the lender. In the event of a default the lender will complete the transfer form and register same to give it effect, paying the necessary stamp duties, as assessed by the relevant tax authorities.

The prime disadvantage of an equitable mortgage to the lender is that the borrower would still be registered against the shares in the register and is still entitled to the membership rights attached to the shares. In order to protect his interest in the shares and minimize the creation of any adverse interest(s) thereon, the lender may file a notice of interest with the company under section 180 CAMA 2020 (the requirement under CAMA 2004 for a claimant to also file affidavit of interest has been omitted). The essence of the notice is that the company will not register any transfer or make any payment or return in respect of the shares until after the expiry of a 42-day notice given to the claimant in that respect. This is part of corporate governance disclosures that companies are required to maintain on their shares, helping to inform potential investors on the state of shareholding in the company and adverse interests thereon. If any.

For shares of publicly quoted companies (listed shares), the introduction of the *Central Securities Clearing System (CSCS)* seems to have simplified matters, as share certificates in quoted companies have now been mostly dematerialized (changed to electronic form). The CSCS is a centralized repository of the shares and once they are appropriately notified of any transaction(s) or encumbrance(s) on a share(s), such information is noted on the records against the share(s) in question and the notification in centralized for ease of public access.

There is also the *Scripless Securities Settlement System (S4)*, managed and administered by the Central Bank of Nigeria (CBN), as a central depository for Federal Government bonds, Treasury bonds, CBN Securities etc.

ATTACHMENT OF SHARES

A judgment creditor may apply to Court to attach and sell shares held by a judgment debtor in a public company. This is provided for under the *Judgment Enforcement Rules (the Rules)*, made pursuant to the *Sheriffs and Civil Process Act (Cap. S6 LFN 2004).* In approving an order for attachment of such shares, the Court may prohibit any person holding the shares from making any transfer or receiving dividends on them, and may prohibit any person in the position of making any transfer or payment on the shares from doing so, until the Court issues a contrary order (*Orojo, 161).* The law requires that the judgment debtor be put on notice by serving on him a notice of attachment in the prescribed form. This gives the judgment debtor the opportunity to be aware of the proposed attachment and to act in manner to protect his right, as allowed by law, before the attachment crystallizes.

As it is clearly stated by the Rules above that attachment of shares is applicable only to any shares held by a judgment debtor in a 'public company' or 'corporation' and to which the judgment debtor is entitled, the matter should end there. In consequence, this book is not prepared to follow the decision in *Bank of West Africa Ltd* v. *Fadoul (1960) NNLR 15 (Orojo, 161)* to stretch the provisions of the Rules to also be applicable to shares in private companies, by relying on older English cases and Rules of Court applicable in England. That will be importing extraneous matters into the Nigerian Rules and reading into it what is not there and what was not intended. The Courts frown at such practices *(Action Congress* v. *INEC (2007) 12 NWLR Pt. 1048, 220; A-G Fed.* v. *Abubakar (2007) 10 NWLR Pt. 1041, 1).*

In summing up the discussions above, it is worth re-iterating that shareholding in a company is the bedrock on which membership rights in the company are anchored. There are multifarious aspects to the issue of shareholding, starting from the rights conferred by shareholding: the right to attend a general meeting and vote, right to receive dividends, right to sell the shares, right to bring an action for winding-up in appropriate circumstances, right to a copy of the Memorandum and Articles, right to notice of meetings, among others.

There are also incidences of shareholding, ranging from allotment of shares, to share transfer, transmission, call on shares, lien on shares, payment for allotted shares, payment on calls, forfeiture, mortgaging of shares, attachment of shares, among many others. There are also compulsory corporate governance disclosures, including the disclosures required from person(s) with significant or substantial shareholdings in a company.

As noted above, the duties and responsibilities of the company secretary are mostly procedural, corporate governance-related and regulatory compliance in nature. In a lot of the instances, for example, after allotment of shares by a company, the company is expected to file the necessary returns on allotment with the Commission, and this is time bound. It is the same when a company has passed a special resolution to acquire its own shares, a statutory declaration of solvency, affirming that it is able to pay its debts after the acquisition, will be filed with the Commission. Finally, on this, when a company allots shares that are fully or partly paid up otherwise than in cash, a return is expected to be sent to the Commission forwarding the agreement for the allotment and valuation of the consideration that the company accepted as payment for the shares. These are also corporate governance-related disclosures, although mostly regarded as regulatory compliances. This is because the disclosures give any member(s) of the public who searches the company's file at the Commission, a true picture of the state of affairs in the company. There are lots of returns applicable to companies that carry on business in Nigeria, especially, public quoted companies, and they are continuous.

It has, by now, become clear what the nature of the duties and responsibilities of the company secretary are in this area of company law and practice. It is noteworthy that with respect to shareholding in a company, the possible issues that could arise are so diverse. Although the introduction of de-materialization of share certificates and the role of the CSCS have organized and centralized the processes and streamlined the duties, the company secretary still has to deal with large number of members than in all other areas. This is especially so with publicly quoted companies. To alleviate this situation, some bigger and publicly quoted companies do engage external registrars to take care of some aspects of the diverse issues relating to their shareholding-related matters.

CHECKPOINTS

- ✓ We have seen that a share is a person's interest(s) in a company, measured in terms of money, but also comprised of several rights and obligations, thereto.
- ✓ A company has the power to issue shares of different kinds up to the limits of its share capital and also to issue classes of shares with attached class rights. CAMA has enunciated the rules to assist to construe class rights, usually combined with established common law rules in this respect.
- ✓ The powers to allot shares in a company are not exercisable by the directors except where expressly authorized by the company in a general meeting or by its Articles.
- ✓ For public companies, the right to allot shares cannot be delegated to the directors as a matter of course. It must be expressly given to the directors, either in the Articles or by members in a general meeting, to be valid.
- ✓ Shares can be paid for either wholly in cash (mostly preferred) or by other consideration that are not wholly in cash.
- ✓ Where a public company decides to accept payment for its shares for consideration other than in cash, an independent valuer will have to value the consideration and submit report to the company to use in determining the value to be accorded to the consideration. The CAMA 2020 removed private companies from going through this process of valuation of consideration.
- ✓ In general, both weighted and non-voting shares are prohibited under the CAMA. However, under some legislations, for example, the BOFIA, where members in a bank are allowed to vote according to the number of their respective shareholdings, it is still allowed.
- ✓ There are lot of rights attached to shareholding, including the right to attend a meeting and vote, receive notice of general meetings, receive

dividends, receive a share certificate, transfer shares, sue for winding-up of the company in appropriate cases, etc.

- ✓ With class rights, a company has a right to vary such rights if it is so provided for in the Articles, if not, then by a special resolution is needed, or with the consent of holders of three-quarter of the shares in the class.
- ✓ Any variation of class rights may be cancelled by the Court on the application of members of the class who did not vote for same, or those who hold up to 15 per cent of the shares in that class.
- ✓ A company has the power to issue shares at a premium but not at a discount, which is unlawful under the CAMA 2020. Under the CAMA 2004, shares could be issued at a discount under stringent conditions. The situation now is totally different.
- ✓ The CAMA has made provisions for persons with significant and substantial controls in shareholdings in a company to notify the companies as such within seven (7) and fourteen days (14) days respectively. While the company is to give notice to the Commission of this information within 30 days (for significant holding) and 14 days (for substantial holding) respectively. While the CAMA 2004 seemed to restrict these notifications to holdings in public companies, the CAMA 2020 has brought both private and public companies into the notification net.
- ✓ Unlike under the CAMA 2004, when a person will have to approach the Court to validate improperly issued shares, under the CAMA 2020, a company has the power to do the validation itself. Resort to Court is only when the company refuses to validate the shares improperly issued.
- ✓ The directors have the power, which is fiduciary in nature, to make calls on the company's shares, but are under a duty to ensure that members pay up any amount(s) due on their shares.
- ✓ An irregular call on shares is, *prima facie,* invalid and a member is not bound to pay on it. A member can also approach the Court for an order to restrain a forfeiture of his shares on the account of non-payment on an irregular call on shares.
- ✓ Additionally, an irregular call can be validated by the company if so permitted by the Articles and the CAMA, but an illegal call on shares

cannot be validated. For instance, a call made by the directors without the requisite notice to the members cannot be validated by the company.

- ✓ Every member in a company is entitled to a share certificate evidencing his shareholding in the company (a lot of public companies have dematerialized their shares certificates with CSCS) and the company is estopped from denying the content of a share certificate it issued.
- ✓ By the amendment to the CAMA 2020 by the BFA, electronic (digital) share certificates can now be issued (and obviously so delivered) to members.
- ✓ In general, a company has a first and paramount lien on every of its shares not fully paid-up for all the money called or payable on the shares. However, the directors have the power to declare the lien inapplicable on particular shares issued by the company.
- ✓ A company's lien over its shares, when active, extends to all dividends payable and all bonus shares issued in respect of the shares, and the lien can be enforced by a sale. The addition of bonus shares is by CAMA 2020 and it was not so under CAMA 2004.
- ✓ Under appropriate circumstances, a company has the power to forfeit a member's shares it if it permitted by its Articles. This is permissible, for instance, when a member fails to pay a call, after the directors have served on him a notice to pay up on his shares.
- ✓ The directors' powers to forfeit shares is fiduciary in nature and must be exercised by them in the best interests of the company. For instance, the directors cannot arbitrarily pick and choose which shares to forfeit and which not to.
- ✓ There is no express provision under the CAMA for a member to surrender his shares to the company, except where it is as a gift to the company without affecting his liability or obligations on the shares in any way. However, a company's Articles may provide for surrender, especially where the alternative would be forfeiture of the shares.
- ✓ A member has a right to sell his shares and execute instrument of transfer. However, there are restrictions in private companies, where, among others, a right of pre-emption is given to existing members to buy the shares before offering same to non-members to acquire.

- ✓ A purchaser of shares has the right to have his name entered into the register of members, but the company may, for good reason(s), like where it has a lien on the shares, refuse to register the transfer.
- ✓ A transfer instrument that was forged and sent to a company to transfer shares has no legal effect. In that respect, the original and rightful owner may approach the Court for an order to have his name restored on the company's register of members.
- ✓ Barring certain exceptions, like when a company is in the business of lending money, it is unlawful for a company or its subsidiary to give financial assistance to a person to acquire its own shares.
- ✓ The CAMA permits a limited liability company to acquire its own shares, once the Articles permit and it is fully paid-up shares. A special resolution is required to be duly passed for this purpose. Unlike the CAMA 2004, the CAMA 2020 does not stipulate the purpose(s) for which companies could acquire their shares, leaving that to the discretion of the directors.
- ✓ A member is entitled to mortgage his shares in a company and in this respect, legal mortgage is preferred, for several reasons: one major reason is that the name of the mortgagee is entered in the register of members as the legal owner of the shares, until the mortgage is discharged. In consequence, the mortgagee also has right over any dividends that the company pays on the shares until the mortgage is discharged.
- ✓ In public companies, shares can be attached like other private properties. The CSCS, as a central depository of dematerialized shares, has made the process a lot easier for judgment creditors. In all, the important thing is that the notice of attachment must be served on the owner of the shares (judgment debtor) to put him on notice of the impending attachment and for his possible reaction(s). Presently, there are no express provisions under the Judgment Enforcement Rules to attach shares held by judgment debtors in private companies.

Chapter 16

INSIDER TRADING

INTRODUCTION

One ever-constant index of membership in a company that has been repeatedly mentioned throughout this book, is the unfettered right of a member to sell his shares, subject to the provisions of the CAMA and the company's Articles. This right is unfettered in the sense that nobody is permitted to restrict the member's right to sell his shares, except as provided for in the relevant law(s) and the company's Articles. However, there is a big caveat to this. The member's right to sell his shares must be exercised with the legal and ethical parameters of how he sells, when he sells, and the information on which he based his decision to sell. These otherwise innocuous items are at the centre of the subject of the present chapter: insider trading.

We have now arrived at the position that some learned authors described as 'the margins of company law.' This is because, according to the learned authors, insider trading does not have to involve only an insider in a company for liability to arise, as total strangers to the company have been found liable for insider trading (although, most of the time those involved are company insiders; *Gower & Davies*, 1128).

'Insider trading' or 'insider dealing' is a term that has assumed many dimensions in the perceptions of different people, depending on the perspective from which one approaches the issue. To some people, it is a term that describes capital market or securities market manipulation, to gain undue advantage, while to others, it is simply a category of financial crimes. There are also persons who see insider trading as a term from the corporate governance perspective, describing the abuse of trust and office by company directors and officers, arising from a failure to apply and uphold the tenets of company law appropriately. Although some persons consider the term, insider trading, as a term that describes securities market manipulation by those that play in that market, strictly speaking, market manipulation or market rigging, could be distinguished from insider trading. (While section

106 of the *Investments and Securities Act (ISA) 2007* deals with securities market manipulation, section 111 of the Act deals with insider trading).

In all of the above, it is correct to say that, strictly speaking, none of these perspectives in describing the act of insider trading is totally wrong or totally out of place, as the term, loosely used, covers every aspect described above, maybe, in varying degrees of abuse of critical information. However, the real essence of insider trading is more specific and is based on the two pillars of the 'insider' and 'trading,' which is also termed as dealing or selling. Our focus in this chapter is to consider insider trading within the confines of company law, corporate governance and the roles of the company secretary in all of it. Therefore, our focus will consider the civil and to a lesser extent, the criminal aspects of the subject, which, in truth, is where several jurisdictions would seem to have focused their respective regulatory attention.

In the United States, for instance, from the *Insider Trading Act 1984, Insider Trading and Securities Fraud Enforcement Act 1988, Securities Enforcement Remedies Act 1990,* to the *Financial Disclosures Regulation Act 2000* and the *Sarbanes-Oxley Act 2002*, efforts have been made by the government, by laws and regulations, to try to control the incidence of insider trading in company securities. This is notwithstanding that as far back as the early twentieth century, in the case of *Strong* v. *Rapide (1909) 1213 US, 419*, the US Supreme Court had found a company director guilty of insider trading, but the vice still persists.

In the United Kingdom, the *Companies Act 1980*, the *Companies Securities (Insider Dealing) Act 1985*, the *Criminal Justice Act 1993*, and the *UK Corporate Governance Code 2018*, were also efforts to deal with the issue of insider trading, among other issues dealt with by these laws. The *European Union (EU) Directive on Criminal Sanctions for Market Abuse 2014*, also came in to harmonize criminal sanctions among member countries of the EU for market abuse.

In Nigeria, which is our focus, the *Investment and Securities Act 2007*, the *Securities and Exchange Commission Rules 2013*, the *Nigerian Stock Exchange Rule Book 2015*, the *Companies and Allied Matters Act 2020*, and the *Nigerian Code of Corporate Governance 2018*, are all efforts made to deal with the issue of insider trading in companies, from the perspectives of regulations and criminal sanctions to the area of the duties of those who are termed 'directors' and 'fiduciaries' in companies.

For all these legislative and regulatory efforts, it presupposes that the issue of insider trading must be a serious one, to be able to attract this level of sustained global attention over the years. And it is. Leaving the legal aspects of insider trading momentarily, the moral or ethical reasons for prohibiting insider trading is that the use of the inside information is manifestly unfair to the other persons who deal with the insider. It can be equated, literally, with something like cheating in an examination with already prepared answers to the examination questions, while the other candidates do not have advantage of such secret and beneficial information *(Charlesworth & Cain, 442)*. What then is 'insider trading'?

THE 'INSIDER' AND THE ACT OF 'INSIDER TRADING'

Under the *Investments and Securities Act (ISA) 2007*, the categories of acts that constitute insider trading or dealing, are not closed. Section 315 of the Act stipulates that 'insider dealing' includes 'insider trading' and occurs 'when a person or group of persons, who, being in possession of some confidential and price sensitive information, not generally available to the public, utilizes such information to buy or sell securities for the benefit of himself, itself or any person' *(Ocean Deep Properties Ltd* v. *Access Bank Plc (2021) LPELR-54838)*. It has also been said that 'insider trading' occurs where an individual or organization buys or sell securities, while knowingly in possession of some piece of confidential information which is not generally available and which is likely, if made available to the general public, to materially affect the price of these securities *(Charlesworth & Cain, 442)*. Section 315 of the *ISA 2007* describes the term '*securities*' to encompass debentures, stocks, bonds (private and government issued), shares, notes and any right or option in respect of all of them. The aspect of 'knowingly' being in possession of confidential information is a trajectory also taken by the ISA (s. 111 (2)(a), as it seems that once knowledge of the irregular use of the confidential price sensitive information can be imputed to a person who utilizes same to buy or sell securities and gains benefit thereby, then, liability must attach.

There are some key words and phrases here to be noted: 'confidential and price sensitive information' and 'not generally available to the public.' The latter phrase, we believe, is for emphasis, otherwise, confidential information, in themselves, being confidential, are not usually generally available to the public. While the aspect of the information being confidential can be taken as being amenable to standard understanding, the price sensitive nature of it requires further asking.

What then is 'price sensitive information' in the context of insider trading infraction? The ISA, unfortunately, has not defined this term and we may have to search elsewhere for assistance. Chapter 17 (Information Disclosure) of the *Nigerian Stock Exchange's (NSE) Rule Book 2015* did not define the term 'price sensitive information,' but listed thirteen items, which are non-exhaustive, as price sensitive items, presupposing that any disclosure of any of them, or issues relating to them, by an insider, to a third party, to use for securities trading within the period of the suspect trading activity, would attract liability. The items enumerated are:

- changes in the directorate of the issuer company;
- the death, resignation, dismissal or appointment of a principal officer in the company or any change in the accounting year end;
- annual and interim results or any recommendation or decision that dividends or scrip issues will or will not be made by the company;
- profit warnings or a change in the financial forecast or expectation or where a company proposes to raise capital, restructure or any changes in the capital structure of the company;
- giving or receiving a notice of intention to make a takeover or mergers, or acquisitions or tender offers or divestments involving the company;
- any proposed change in the business model of general character or nature of the business of the company or of the group or where there is a major new development(s) in the company's sphere of activities, including major new products, contract awards and expansion plans;
- any change in voting control or in beneficial ownership of the securities carrying voting control in the company;
- any proposed alteration of the company's Memorandum or Articles of Association within the period in question;
- any other information necessary to enable shareholders to appraise the position of the company and to avoid the establishment of a false market in the shares of the company.

It was posited above that the issue of 'insider trading' is anchored on two pillars of the 'insider' and 'trading' or 'dealing.' Who then is an 'insider' for our present purposes? Section 315 of the *Investments and Securities Act (ISA) 2007*, defines an 'insider' to mean any person who is or is connected with the company in one or more of the following capacities:

- a director or officer of the company or a related company;
- an employer of the company or related company;
- an employee of the company involved in a professional or business relationship to the company;
- any shareholder of the company who owns five percent or more of any class of securities or any person who is or can be deemed to have any relationship with the company or member;
- members of audit committee of a member; and
- any of the persons listed above who is connected with a person or a company in any other way and possess unpublished price sensitive information in relation to the company's securities.

It is stated that the price sensitive information would have to be specific matters relating to the company and not of a general nature. Again, the information would not have been generally known to persons who are accustomed or likely to deal with the company's securities, otherwise, will materially affect the price of the securities. On its part, *Rule 400 (3) SEC Rules and Regulations 2013* virtually repeats the above description of an 'insider.'

From all of the above discussions, it is clear that the whole essence of the prohibition of insider trading, is that none of the persons listed above as insiders should exploit the inside information at their disposal to their own advantage and to the detriment of others, especially the shareholders in the company. The prohibition itself has never been solely a moral issue but has always been from both the legal and ethical perspectives, incorporating, to a large extent, corporate governance considerations. It is the breach of any of these underlying themes, that is, legal and ethical (corporate governance) by a person(s) considered an 'insider' that creates the whole problems of insider trading. In the context of the main plank of this book, the insider breaches will be approached from the perspective of company law, wherein the fiduciary duties of directors and other officers of a company will be on top and corporate governance, wherein the issue of appropriate disclosures by those considered insiders, will be key. A detailed consideration of these issues is appropriate at this point.

INSIDER TRADING AND THE TENETS OF COMPANY LAW

The first point to make here is that there is absolutely nothing wrong, ordinarily, with persons considered insiders in a company, especially directors and other officers, being in possession of inside information or information that are considered price sensitive. Everything is, however, wrong if those insiders make use of these inside information to their own benefit or advantage, without disclosing same to the public. It would appear that the beginning of the infraction by insiders is when the information is used to their benefit, but the infraction would be complete when the information is not disclosed to the public. In essence, if the particular price sensitive information is promptly disclosed to the public by the insiders, even if the insiders also use the information to buy and sell securities after the disclosures, then, no insider trading would have taken place. The major problem is when the insiders keep the public in the dark about the relevant price sensitive development(s) and still proceed to use same information to deal in the company's securities.

The most devastating effect of insider trading in companies, therefore, is that it breaches every conceivable duty that company directors and officers owe to the company, which are fiduciary in nature. From what we have considered to be the omnibus duty of directors exercising their powers in the best interests of the company (s.305(3) CAMA 2020), to the duty not to make secret profits (s.306(2)(3) CAMA 2020); the duty to avoid conflicts of interests with the company (s.306(1) CAMA 2020); to the duty not to misuse the company's information or property for personal gains (s.306(2)(b) CAMA 2020); engaging in insider trading breaches every tenet of the duty to work in the best interests of the company as a whole. The company 'as a whole' includes the shareholders, the creditors, the employees and other stakeholders in the company.

The argument that the duties owed by the directors are to the company as an entity, pales into insignificance, as the matter is even made worse because insider trading has both criminal and civil sanctions. The directors, officers and other insiders involved, may also face criminal prosecutions to the detriment of the company as a whole. Even more serious is the fact that insider trading is both criminal and fraudulent in outcomes *(Adimora* v. *Ajufo (1988) 3 NWLR Pt. 88, 1; Egbo* v. *Nwali (1998) 6 NWLR Pt. 553, 201),* and whatever authority that directors do have to manage and direct the company's affairs will be seriously impaired by the fraud of insider trading committed on the members. On this score, this book submits that an incident of insider trading by directors and other fiduciaries falls within one of the grounds under which an application may be brought by members that the affairs of the company are being run in a manner that is prejudicial to members, under sections 353 and 354 CAMA 2020. Otherwise, what else can be more prejudicial to the interests of the members than where directors and other insiders use confidential information that is not available to the members and the public to deal in the company's securities for personal gains?

Now, if company directors' liability will arise, as it were, from their position as insiders with confidential price sensitive information and their fiduciary duties owed to the company, the question then is, from where does the liability of outsiders who are strangers to the company, arise, with insider trading? The answer is in section 111(2)(a)(b) *ISA 2007.*

At this point, it is crucial to point out that the word 'insider' does not stop at those who are or were physically employees 'inside the company' in question, but extends to those who may be strangers to the company but have access to relevant 'inside information' on the company. In this respect, section 111 (2)(a)(b) *ISA 2007* treats a person who knowingly obtains information (directly or otherwise) from another person who is connected to a company, knowing or having reasonable cause to know that the information was gotten from the source by the first person because of his connection to the company, as an 'insider,' for trading purposes using that information.

In the final analysis therefore, the end point will seem to be that any confidential price sensitive information in the possession of an 'insider,' which has not been disclosed to the public, should remain with the 'insider' and not be used to buy or sell the company's securities. Apart from not being allowed to use this confidential information, the 'insider' is also not allowed to give the information to third parties (usually called 'tippees,' from getting a 'tip' from the insider), to use and deal on the company's securities, otherwise, his connection with the company will convert the third party to an 'insider' and transform the transaction into an 'insider trading'.

A classic example of this is the celebrated American case involving the socialite and businesswoman, Martha Stewart, who was jailed for insider trading in 2004. Ms Stewart had sold her shares in ImClone Systems, a biomedical company, based on a 'tip' from her stockbroker, a day before ImClone's share price crashed. ImClone's managing director, Ms Stewart's stockbroker and the company's general counsel also sold their shares, among many other people. They sold their shares based on the inside information that the expected blockbuster cancer drug from ImClone had been denied approval by the US Food and Drugs Administration (FDA). After investigations by the US Authorities, Ms Stewart, her stockbroker, ImClone's managing director and many others, were convicted for insider trading, for selling their shares based on the negative inside information *(Wikipedia, 5-2023).*

The case is apposite but at least it involved the company's shareholders. The case of Robert Winans, a former columnist for the Wall Street Journal on capital markets and securities, is instructive. He was convicted in *Carpenter* v. *United States (1987)* for insider trading in 1985. His offence was leaking advance price sensitive information of the contents of his newspaper columns to a stockbroker, who then shared same with third parties that used same to deal in securities. Both Winans and the stockbroker were convicted, although totally outsiders to the companies whose securities were traded. Having used the 'inside' price sensitive information, as it were, that were gotten in the line of his duties, to activate other third parties to deal in securities of the concerned companies, they were considered as insiders, for that particular purpose*(Wikipedia, 5-2023).*

It has to be said that the case divided opinion around the world, especially in the United States, as some of the evidence that were used to convict the journalist were gotten from his seized cell phone, raising issues of privacy, police searches and personal liberty. The case, however, illustrates how far the law could go in imputing the 'insider tag' in relation to persons who abuse inside information to deal in company securities.

INSIDER TRADING AND THE TENETS OF CORPORATE GOVERNANCE

The legal issue with insider trading will appear to be mainly the abuse of the relationship with the company or the inside information by insiders and others in using price sensitive information to deal with the company's securities. On the other hand, the corporate governance issue with insider trading is that the price sensitive information in question had not been disclosed to the public. In essence, corporate governance is hinged on disclosures and transparency in the operations of companies and entities. With appropriate disclosures by those concerned, there will be no issues of insider trading in companies, because once the 'inside information' that is price sensitive is disclosed to the public, and promptly so and not after the fact, then, an action for insider trading cannot be maintained against such persons.

Under section *315 ISA 2007*, the operational phrase for insider trading is the use of price sensitive information that is 'not generally available to the public.' In essence, it talks about information that has not been disclosed or published for public consumption, and that if so published, will affect the price of the securities. When such information is used by insiders or those connected to them to buy or sell securities, it creates the insider trading problem. Therefore, as already noted, disclosure or non-disclosure of the price sensitive information to the public and how it is used by those in possession thereto, is key to determining whether insider trading has occurred or not.

Under Rule 17. 2 of the *NSE Rule Book 2015,* every listed company is mandated to ensure that investors and the public are kept fully informed of all factors which might affect their interests and in particular, that immediate disclosure is made of any information concerning their interests which might reasonably be expected to have material effect on market activity in, and the prices or value of, listed securities. This is simply about the disclosure of price sensitive information to the public, to prevent same being used for insider trading.

The *Nigerian Code of Corporate Governance (NCCG) 2018*, provides that full and comprehensive disclosures of all matters material to investors and stakeholders ensures proper monitoring of its implementation which engenders good corporate governance practice (Principle 28). This presupposes that the disclosures in question must not be half-hearted or selective, but full and comprehensive, to qualify as appropriate. The Code goes further to stipulate that insiders are precluded from buying and selling any security in breach of their fiduciary duty and other relationships of trust and confidence, while in possession of material, privileged, non-public and price-sensitive information about the company (Principle 25).

The central issue in this discourse has been 'inside information' and how those persons considered to be insiders in a company, by employment or by association, direct or indirect, handle such information, which is price sensitive. Under Rule 17.4 of the *NSE Rule Book 2015* it is stipulated that a listed company (issuer) shall establish effective arrangements to deny access to inside information to persons other than those who require it for the exercise of their functions within the issuer's organization. This is an interesting aspect of the issue of dealing with inside information, wherein a company is encouraged to, first of all, restrict internal access to such sensitive information to its own staff and allow only those who need the information for their work. That appears to be a good starting point.

Apart from the possession of inside information, Rule 401(a) of the *SEC Rules and Regulations 2013* stipulates that directors and other insiders of public companies shall notify the SEC of the sale of their shares in the company or any purchase of shares in the company not later than 48 hours after the sale activity. Furthermore, Rule 402 of the same SEC Rules mandates a director of a public company to disclose to the SEC any interest he has in any stockbroking or dealing companies engaged by a company in which he is a director. These are all corporate governance disclosure requirements aimed at identifying transactions and relationships that could have been tainted with insider trading violations or had the potential for so being.

Rule 17.15(a) of the *NSE Rule Book 2015* mandates every listed company to establish a securities trading policy which shall apply to all employees and directors. The policy is to be circulated to all the company's employees that may at any time possess any inside or material information about the company. The trading policy is expected to address issues of confidentiality of the information and those who may be allowed to have access to such information.

Under section 301 CAMA 2020 (s. 275), every company is mandated to keep a register of the holding of their directors in shares and debentures, which register is open for inspection at the company's head office, on terms. There are also other disclosures under section 119 and 120 CAMA 2020, wherein a company is mandated to send returns to the Commission and disclose those shareholders that are either significant or substantial shareholders in the company. Under section 262 CAMA 2020 (s. 237) special resolutions, which we know are usually used to effect very important transactions in a company, are required to be registered at the Commission and be made accessible to the public. Then, finally, there are the annual returns, under sections 417 and 418 CAMA 2020 (ss. 370 & 371), which represent the omnibus reports on the activities of the company for the financial year, disclosing sundry matters that are of importance to existing and potential investors. The annual returns usually deal with matters which may guide potential investors to ascertain how well a company is run and whether the application of known corporate governance principles in the company is strong or lax.

In the final analysis, both company law and corporate governance have provided for ways to guard against the incidence of insider trading, usually occasioned by the abuse of price sensitive inside information. One way has been through legislation and fiduciary duties of those considered insiders, the other has been through the insistence on prompt and comprehensive disclosures to the shareholders and the publication of such price sensitive information that are considered prone to abuse. It has to be stated that while legislation and corporate governance principles are very important in attempting to control insider trading, experience over the years has shown that more is still required in this respect. Consistency of application of the laws and rules is required. This has to be done by consistent, intentional and deliberate ethical behaviours by all those that are in a position to abuse confidential and price sensitive inside information, making full disclosures to all stakeholders and the public.

The importance of an entrenched ethical culture in companies in the above respect cannot be over-emphasized. Principle 25 of the *NCCG 2018* captures this well, in stating that the establishment of policies and mechanisms for monitoring insider trading, related party transactions, conflict of interests and other corrupt activities, mitigates the adverse effects of these abuses on the company and promotes good ethical conduct and investor confidence. It needs not be repeated that lack of investor confidence is the worst 'corporate virus' that can infect any company, especially a listed company, and has ruined otherwise erstwhile corporate titans in the past, including the former corporate giant, Enron, in the Unites States.

For the company secretary, his job in respect of the issue of insider trading is central and straightforward, although difficult to implement. Difficult in the sense that the temptation is personal to the director or officer who intends to abuse the inside information and may not even disclose his intention to anyone in the company. The company secretary, therefore, is to ensure, as much as possible, that those insiders, especially the directors and other fiduciaries in the company, do not breach their duty not to use confidential price sensitive information to deal with the company's securities. Continuous engagement is key here. Then again, apart from this, it is also to ensure that the directors live up to the expectations to always work in the best interests of the company, in terms of their use of such confidential non-public, but price sensitive information, to avoid abuse of same.

On his part, the company secretary must ensure that all corporate governance returns and filings to the Commission and other regulators are filed promptly and all statutory registers are kept, and up to date. The disclosure of relevant information to the shareholders and other stakeholders is also critical, especially if they qualify as price sensitive information as seen above.

It should be noted that in practice, it requires persons with high ethical standards and personal discipline to have possession of price sensitive information that will benefit them immensely, and still refuse to use same to their advantage, directly or indirectly. We saw that in the ImClone Systems insider trading case, almost all the senior executives, including the managing director and the general counsel, who were supposed to be the 'gate keeper,' all sold their shares in the company based on inside information. This shows that the fight against insider trading is a tough and a continuing one that requires all hands to be on deck.

CHECKPOINTS

- ✓ Insider trading is the use by company insiders of confidential price sensitive information relating to the company's securities to buy or sell those securities and make gains thereby.
- ✓ Insider trading is as old as when trading in companies' securities began and company insiders, in this context, can be a person who is not an employee of the company, but who is imputed by law to be an insider by association with an insider in the company.
- ✓ There is nothing wrong, ordinarily, when a director or other insiders in a company come into possession of confidential and price sensitive information about their company's securities. However, everything is wrong when they refuse to disclose the same information promptly to shareholders and other stakeholders but use same to deal in the company's securities to their own benefits.
- ✓ Most times, insider trading, when committed by directors or other officers in the company, breaches most of the fiduciary duties that the directors owe the company, especially the duty to work in the best interests of the company as a whole.
- ✓ A total stranger to a company could commit insider trading with respect to the company's securities, if he knowingly receives inside price sensitive information from a person who is connected to the company and uses same to deal in the company's securities.

- ✓ The major plank for insider trading infraction is using price sensitive information 'that is not available to the public' to deal in the securities of a company. It presupposes that if the information is made available to the shareholders and the public promptly but the shareholders and members of the public choose to ignore or did not consider the information blockbuster enough, the directors or other insiders would have discharged the duty that the law imposed on them and no liability will attach to them.
- ✓ From the corporate governance perspective, the major duty is that of transparency and disclosure of the relevant information to all stakeholders and coupled with ethical behaviour in that regard. In essence, ethically, any disclosure to members and the public will have to be clear, prompt and comprehensive enough to make sense to all shareholders and other stakeholders. Disclosures cannot be couched in obfuscated language, slangs or innuendos intended to confuse the audience on the utility of the information being disclosed.
- ✓ The company secretary has a central role to play in continuously engaging those insiders, especially the directors and senior management, on the need to avoid situations that will expose them to insider trading infractions. Continuous education and engagement are key in this respect.

Chapter 17

COMPANY DEBENTURES

INTRODUCTION

A 'debenture' is a document which either creates or acknowledges a debt. It is true that, due to the variety in the types of debentures, no precise legal definition of the term 'debenture' has actually been attempted and it is not clear whether any is actually needed. In most cases, what we have is more like a description of what the term 'debenture' means. In that respect, it has been accepted that the term itself imports a debt or an acknowledgment of a debt. Generally, if not always, the instrument imports an obligation or covenant to pay and relates mostly to transactions by incorporated bodies. This is borne out in the description of a 'debenture' as consisting of a debt owed by a company to another person secured by a deed, which prescribes the conditions for the realization of the debt *(Intercontractors Nig. Ltd* v. *National Provident Fund Mgt. Board (1988) LPELR-1520; Folorunsho* v. *Rosula Nig. Ltd & Anor (2019) LPELR-47339)*. Nowadays, however, this obligation to pay is usually accompanied by some other charge or security *(Fasakin* v. *Fasakin (1994) 4 NWLR Pt. 340, 597; Union Bank Nig. Ltd* v. *Tropic Foods (1992) 3 NWLR Pt. 228, 321; British India Company* v. *I.R.C. (1881) 7 Q.B.D 165, 172; Edmunds* v. *Blaina Co. (1887) 36 Ch. D. 215; Levy* v. *Abercorris Slate & Slab Co. (1887) 37 Ch., 260; Hannigan, 537)*. In essence, therefore, a debenture is a company's security for a loan which usually creates a charge on the company's stocks or property *(NIDB Ltd* v. *Olalomi Ind. Ltd (2002) 5 NWLR Pt. 761, 532, 551)*.

The above descriptions of the term 'debenture' are not far from that of the CAMA 2020, which describes debenture to mean 'a written acknowledgement of indebtedness by the company, setting out the terms and conditions of the indebtedness, and includes debenture stock, bonds and any other securities of a company, whether constituting a charge on the assets of the company or not' (s. 868 CAMA 2020), (s. 567).

A COMPANY'S RIGHT TO CREATE DEBENTURES

As a commercial going concern, a company may, from time to time have the need to raise external finances through borrowing, in order to support its operations. This could be done to any extent as much as a natural person(s) could do. Under section 43 (1) CAMA 2020, (s. 38(1), to the extent permitted by a company's Memorandum and any existing law, a company is given the power of a natural person of full capacity, when furthering its authorized business or objects. This would include borrowing money from any authorized source in order to effectuate its business objectives. This power, however, does not extend to donating money, gift or property to a political party or association, or for any political purpose, which is expressly prohibited (s. 43(2).

Also, as a going concern, a company is deemed to have the inherent power to borrow money, and for that purpose, to give security over any of its properties for the debt(s) that would accrue to it as a result *(Inter-Contractors Nig. Ltd* v. *NPF Mortgage Bank (1988) 2 NWLR Pt. 76, 280, 292).* A company could use any of its property to secure its borrowing, including real, personal, present or future property *(Australian Auxiliary Steam Clipper Co.* v. *Mounsey (1858) 4 K & J, 733; Re Patent File Co (1870) L.R. 6 Ch. 83).* The security could also include a company's uncalled capital, provided that the company's Memorandum and Articles do not prohibit the charging of uncalled capital *(Re Pyle Works (1990) 44 Ch. 534; Palmers, 417).*

All the principles enunciated above have been encapsulated into section 191 CAMA 2020 (s.166). It provides that a company may borrow money for the purpose of its business or objects and may mortgage or charge its undertaking, property and uncalled capital, or any part thereof, and issue debentures, debenture stocks and other securities, whether outright or as security for any debt, liability or obligation of the company or of any third party.

A company is mandated to deliver to the registered holder, within 60 days after allotment of debenture or the transfer of any debentures, the debenture or a certificate of debenture stock, either under seal (if any) or executed as a deed. Where, also a debenture or debenture stock certificate issued by the company is lost, destroyed or defaced, the company is mandated, at the request of the debenture holder, and after paying applicable fees, to issue a certified copy of the debenture or to renew the debenture stock certificate (s. 192(1)(2), (s. 167(1)(2).

TYPES OF DEBENTURES

A company has a right to issue debentures and also has the option on the types of debentures it wants to issue, depending on its circumstances. The CAMA 2020 has categorized them, and a debenture created by a company could be:

- **perpetual debentures:** this is provided for under section 196 CAMA 2020 (s. 171). A company is permitted to issue these types of debentures and they would not be invalid if a condition they contain makes them irredeemable or redeemable only on the happening of a contingency, however remote or on the expiration of any period of time, notwithstanding any rule of equity to the contrary;
- **convertible debentures:** these are debentures issued by a company upon terms that are in lieu of their redemption or repayment, at the option of the holder or the company, they may be converted into shares in the company upon such terms as may be stated in the debentures (s.197), (s.172). It does appear then that a company that does not have share capital might be in difficulty if it intends to issue convertible debentures; or should the question be: is it possible for such a company to issue debentures and then convertible debenture at all?;
- **secured or unsecured (naked) debentures:** debentures are secured if they are secured by a charge over the company's property and are naked when they are unsecured by any charge: secured debentures may be by a fixed charge on certain of the company's property or a floating charge over the whole or a specified part of the company's undertakings and assets, or by both fixed and floating charges (s.198(1)(2), (s.173 (1)(2);
- **redeemable debentures:** a company limited by shares may issue debentures which are to be redeemed, or at the option of the company, are liable to be so redeemed (s. 199), (s.174). A redeemed debenture can still be re-issued on some conditions by the company, either by re-issuing the redeemed one or by issuing new one in place of the redeemed one. In this respect, the person having the earlier priorities on the redeemed debenture shall retain same on the re-issued one (s. 200(1)(2) CAMA 2020), (s. 175(1)(2).

A company is at liberty, depending on its structure, the nature of the transaction involved, the nature of its business and considering other relevant indices, to decide on the type of debenture to adopt to secure its debt. The structure of the types of debentures noted above are basically the same but they differ in terms of their repayment covenants, charging clauses and details of routes to the debt redemption.

Meanwhile, a charge that has been used to secure debentures shall become enforceable on the occurrence of the events specified in the debentures or the deed that secures the debentures. A debenture holder will then need to institute an action to enforce such a charge. Where a debenture holder brings an action to enforce the security of a series of debentures, of which he holds a part thereto, he shall sue in a representative capacity, that is, on behalf of himself and all other holders of that series of debentures (s. 198(3)(4), (s. 173(3)(4). The essence of a representative action, it has been held, is mainly to curtail multiplicity or influx of suits on the same matter. Such representative action is competent once the persons being represented and the person(s) representing them have common or same interest in the same action. It is also important to note that the rules governing representative actions are rules of convenience and a lot of flexibility and liberality are imported in interpreting them to achieve the objective of non-multiplicity of cases *(Ejezie* v. *Nwabeze (2008) 4 SCNJ 113; Anatoye* v. *A-G East Central State (1976) 11 SC, 109).*

STATEMENTS TO BE INCLUDED IN DEBENTURES

Notwithstanding the fact that the detailed form of a debenture could vary in its general format from company to company, section 193 CAMA 2020 (s. 168) has stipulated certain mandatory requirements that are to be included in debentures, and these are:

- the principal amount borrowed by the company;
- the maximum discount which may be allowed on the issue or re-issue of the debenture, and the maximum premium at which the debenture may be redeemable;
- the rate of interests and the date on which interest on the debentures issued shall be paid and the manner in which payment shall be made;
- the date on which the principal amount shall be repaid or the manner in which redemption shall be effected, that is, whether it would be by the payment of instalments of the principal or otherwise;
- with respect to convertible debentures, the date and terms on which the debentures may be converted into shares and the amounts which may be credited as paid-up on those shares. Also required are the dates and terms

on which the holders may exercise any right to subscribe for shares in respect of the debentures held by them;

- the charges securing the debenture and the conditions subject to which the debenture shall take effect.

What then happens when these mandatory requirements are not included as statements in a debenture? Does such an omission invalidate the debenture as issued? These questions came up and were answered by the Court in *Brewtech Nig. Ltd* v. *Akinnawo & Anor (2016) LPELR-40094*, where it was held that since the CAMA did not impose penalties on a failure to include these statements in the body of a debenture, an omission will not make the debenture void, *ab initio*, but simply voidable. A voidable transaction remains in force until a party to it applies to Court to set it aside *(Ordor* v. *Nwosu & Anor (1974) 12 SC., 103).*

Statements contained in debentures or debenture stock certificates shall be *prima facie* evidence of the title to the debentures of the person named therein as the registered holder. The statements are also *prima facie* evidence of the amount secured by the debentures. The statements will therefore constitute an estoppel by conduct against the company that issued the debentures if any person relies on the accuracy of the statements and changes his position to his detriment. The company shall then be estopped from denying the continuing accuracy of the statements and is mandated to compensate the person for any loss suffered (s. 194 (1)(2) CAMA 2020), (s. 169 (1)(2).

ENFORCEMENT OF CONTRACTS RELATING TO DEBENTURES

The CAMA 2020 provides that a contract with a company to take and pay for any debentures of that company may be enforced by an order of Court for specific performance of that contract (s. 195), (s. 170). It is important to note that specific performance is an equitable remedy granted at the discretion of the Court to order the performance of an existing contract *(International Textile Ind. Nig. Ltd* v. *Aderemi & Anor (1999) 8 NWLR Pt. 614, 268).* Also, a person who wants the Court to order specific performance of a contract in his favour must show that his hands are clean and that he has performed his own part of the agreement in question *(Mustapha* v. *Abubakar & Anor (2010) LPELR-4567; Australia Hardwoods Pty. Ltd* v. *Commissioner for Railway (1961)1 All ER, 737).*

RIGHTS OF DEBENTURE HOLDERS

A deep-rooted right vested in a debenture holder by law is that of a creditor, being that he is entitled to the repayment of the money lent to the company with accrued interests *(Orojo, 175).* In consequence of this right, a debenture holder may sue the company which issued the debenture he holds to enforce the payment of any amount payable to him in respect of the debenture. A debenture holder may also sue the trustee of the debenture trust deed covering the debenture he holds for compensation for any breach of the duties which the trustee owes him. In this instance, it shall not be necessary for any other debenture holder of the same class, or the trustee of the trust deed to be joined as a party in such a suit (s. 201(2), (s. 176(2).

In cases where the debenture is covered by a trust deed, the trustee of the debenture trust deed is empowered to hold all contracts, stipulations and undertakings given to him, and all mortgages, charges and securities vested in him in connection with the debentures covered by the deed, or some of those debentures, exclusively for the benefit of the debenture holders concerned (except where the deed provides otherwise). The law requires that the trustee shall exercise due diligence in enforcing these contracts, undertakings, stipulations, mortgages, charges, and securities (s. 201(1), (s. 176(1). What then is due diligence expected of the trustee by the law?

In simple terms, due diligence has been said to mean no more than good care and attention, that is ordinarily exercisable by a reasonable and prudent person under the circumstances *(Subaya Metalware (Nig) Ltd* v. *Toyota Motor Corp. & Anor (2021) LPELR-57346).* The trustee, therefore, is not expected to exhibit or possess super-human abilities or skills in the discharge of his duties in relation to the trust deed.

Where holders of debentures of a class holding at least three-quarters of the value of the debentures issued for that class pass a resolution to that effect, they can:

- where a trustee of the trust deed has breached his duties and liability which must attach to him in consequence, release him from that liability;
- consent to the alteration or abrogation of any of the rights, powers or remedies of debenture holders (except the power to appoint receiver under s. 233 CAMA 2020); or
- consent to the substitution of debenture of different class already issued or the cancellation of debenture issued in consideration of issuing to the

holders, the company or third party's fully paid-up shares (s. 2101 (3) CAMA 2020), (s. 176 (3).

MEETING OF DEBENTURE HOLDERS

A meeting of debenture holders is not compulsory, by law, except if it is by contract. The terms of any debenture or trust deed may provide for the convening of general meeting of the debenture holders and debenture trust deed, the holders could at such a meeting pass resolutions binding on all the holders of the debentures of the same class (s. 202(1) CAMA 2020), (s. 177(1).

However, whether there is a provision in a debenture or trust deed that provides for a meeting of the debenture holders or not, the Commission has the power, at any time, to direct that a meeting of debenture holders of any class be held in any manner as it may direct. This would be to consider issue(s), ancillary or consequential to the debenture, as the Commission may direct.

Furthermore, notwithstanding whether there is any provision in a debenture, trust deed, contract or instrument, relating to holders' meeting(s), the trustee of a debenture deed, shall, on the requisition of persons holding, at the date of the deposit of the requisition, debentures covered by the trust deed which carry at least one tenth of the total voting rights attached to all the issued and outstanding debentures of that class, proceed to convene a meeting of that class of debenture holders (s. 202(2)(3), (s. 177 (2)(3). The CAMA did not clearly state the modalities that will guide any of the meetings of the debenture holders. It would appear, therefore, that where there is a provision for holders' meetings in a debenture, contract, instrument or trust deed, such a document will also provide for the modalities for the meeting. On the other hand, where there is no provision for a meeting or where a meeting is ordered by the Commission, then the Commission will have to advise on the modalities for the meeting.

FIXED AND FLOATING CHARGES

Due to the changing nature of the assets that business concerns employ in their day-to-day activities, the 'floating charge' was developed as a form of security arrangement to charge a company's current assets and undertakings. Such an arrangement allows the company to continue to use the charged assets and undertakings until the charge is discharged or crystallizes *(Jia Ent. Ltd* v. *BICI Ltd (1962) 1 ANLR, 363; Wheatley* v. *Silkstone & Haigh Moor Coal Co. (1885) 29 Ch. D., 715; Illingworth* v. *Houldsworth (1904) AC, 355;*

Thorne, 181). As we shall see below, the fixed charge is the opposite of the floating charge and attaches to specific assets on being created.

The Fixed Charge

A 'fixed charge' is a charge that is not floating. It is also called a 'specific charge' and is a charge granted by a company on its specific assets. In such a case, the company cannot deal with the charged assets unless with the permission of the chargee *(Mayson et al, 347; Omo Dare* v. *New Nigerian Bank Ltd (1978) ALR Comm., 180).* The term 'fixed charge,' it has been held, covers any loan which is secured over a specific asset or a group of specific assets belonging to the company, and even future assets may be subject of a fixed charge *(Siebe Gorman & Co. Ltd* v. *Barclays Bank Ltd (1979) 2 Lloyds Rep., 142; Thorne, 180).* A fixed charge is usually taken over identified or specific assets that are not commonly used in the company's day-to-day business. One major reason for this is that a fixed charge gives the charge holder an immediate proprietary interest in the assets(s) subject to the charge, which makes it inappropriate for assets that a company needs in its ordinary course of business *(Agnew* v. *IRC: Re Brumark) (2001) 2 BCLC, 188).*

The Floating Charge

A floating charge is an equitable creation of company law, allowing companies to charge their movable assets, while still continuing to carry on their businesses with those assets as charged. It was Romer LJ, in *Re Yorkshire Woolcombers Association Ltd (1903) 2 Ch., 284; Charlesworth & Cain, 562),* that outlined the essence and characteristics of a floating charge, while stating that it is:

- a charge on a class of assets of a company, present and future;
- that class is one which, in the ordinary course of the business of the company would be changing from time to time; and
- by the charge it is contemplated that, until some future step is taken by or on behalf of those interested in the charge, the company may carry on its business in the ordinary way.

The description of a floating charge in *Illingworth* v. *Houldworth (1904) AC, 355* is also quite interesting. In this case, a floating charge was described as:

> ambulatory and shifting in its nature, hovering over and, so to speak, floating with the property which it is intended to affect until some event occurs or some act is done, which causes it to settle and fasten on the subject of the charge within its reach and grasp *(Orojo, 176).*

In a classic scenario, a floating charge is typically taken over the company's entire undertaking, both present and future, including assets like plants and machinery, tools, intellectual property rights, trade stocks, etc. *(Agnew* v. *IRC (Re Brumark) (2001) BCLC, 188).* The common thread that runs through all these assets is that they are all circulating assets used in the normal course of the company's business and constantly changing in their nature. Most of them are also wasting assets, that depreciate in value with use *(Re Spectrum Plus Ltd (2005) 2 BCLC, 269).* Most importantly, however, unlike the situation with fixed charges, for a floating charge, the company will continue to have control over and deal with the assets in carrying on their businesses, and this, without the need to obtain the consent of the chargee *(Re Keenan Bros Ltd (1986) BCLC, 242; Hannigan, 535).*

In Nigeria, the CAMA has attempted to encapsulate the principles governing a floating charge into its provisions. By section 203(1) CAMA 2020, (s. 178 (1) a 'floating charge' is said to mean an equitable charge over the whole or a specified part of the company's undertakings and assets, including cash and the company's uncalled capital, both present and future, but so that the charge shall not preclude the company from dealing with such assets, until:

- the security becomes enforceable and the holder thereof, pursuant to a power in that behalf in the debenture or in the deed securing the same, appoints a receiver or manager or enters into possession of the assets;
- the Court appoints a receiver or manager of such assets on the application of the holder;
- the company goes into liquidation.

If any of the incidents indicated above happens, thereby making the security enforceable against the company, then the floating charge shall be deemed to crystallize and become a fixed equitable charge on the company's assets that were subject of the earlier floating charge (*Re Yorkshire Woolcombers Association Ltd (1903) 2 Ch., 284).* However, if the receiver or manager is withdrawn with the consent of the chargee or the chargee withdraws from possession before the charge has been fully discharged, then the charge shall cease to be regarded as a 'fixed charge' and reverts to being a 'floating charge' (*Thorne, 181);* (s. 203(2), (s. 178 (2).

It has been judicially recognized that the nature of the 'floating charge' precludes a company which has created such a charge over its assets from creating another floating charge over all of the same assets ranking equally with or in priority to the first charge, except with the chargee's permission *(Re Benjamin's Cape & Sons Ltd (1914) 1 Ch., 800).* It is, however, possible to create a subsequent floating charge over a part of the assets of a company with priority over the first charge *(Re Automatic Bottle Makers Ltd (1926) Ch. 412; Gower & Davies, 1221).*

A practical approach that has been adopted by modern businesses is to include what has been termed the 'negative pledge' clause in a floating charge. The clause usually provides that the company will not create any charge over the assets covered by the 'floating charge' that will rank in priority over the existing floating charge *(Mayson et al, 348*). It has been postulated that the best option will be to register the restriction(s) on the company not to take a subsequent charge over the property in the company's register of charges. This will constitute a notice to all those who have taken or intends to take registrable charge over the company's asset(s) (*Gower & Davies, 1223).*

Priority of Fixed over Floating Charge

In general, where a fixed charge has been created over a property, it shall have priority over a floating charge created over the same property. Under the CAMA, the only exception to this principle is where the terms of the floating charge prohibit the company from granting any subsequent charge having priority over the floating charge, and the person in whose favour the latter charge was granted had notice of the prohibition at the time when the charge was granted to him (s. 204 CAMA 2020), (s. 179).

The CAMA 2020 removed the word 'actual' from the type of notice of prohibition that is required to have been had by the person who intends to have a subsequent charge over the floating charge. Added to this, to resolve the controversy around the nature or source of the notice in question, the CAMA 2020 provides that a person is deemed to have notice of any prohibition on a floating charge, where a notice indicating the existence of such a prohibition is registered with the Commission. In essence, a potential chargee who then fails to conduct the necessary searches at the Commission for any possible encumbrance(s), will have himself to blame, if subsequently, there were prohibitions registered against the assets or undertakings.

This is a corporate governance notice and disclosure to the world, once registered with the Commission. Whoever intends to deal with the company will get a true picture of the encumbrances or otherwise on the company assets, once a search is conducted on the company at the Commission. It will also be to the person's detriment if no such search is conducted and he proceeds to deal with the company based on other considerations.

Priority between Floating Charges

The CAMA does not have any express provision(s) dealing with the priorities of mutual floating charges created on the same assets, therefore, common law principles on this will come in handy. Where a company has created a floating charge, it is not allowed to create another floating charge over the same property, ranking in priority or *pari passu* with the original charge, unless the original chargee allows it *(Re Automatic Bottle Makers (1926) Ch,. 412*; *Orojo, 177*). If a company grants two floating charges over its assets and undertakings, then, they take priority in order of their creation, being equal equitable charges (*Re Benjamin's Cape & Sons Ltd (1914) 1 Ch., 800).* Note that it is possible that priority between floating charges could be lost by the failure of the chargee, who would otherwise have priority, to register his charge at the Commission as required under sections 222 and 224 CAMA 2020, (ss. 197 & 199),*(Griffiths* v. *Yorkshire Bank Plc (1994) 1 WLR, 1427; Gower & Davies, 1223).*

POWER OF THE COURT REGARDING CHARGES

Whenever a charge becomes enforceable (whether it is a fixed or floating charge), the Court has the power to appoint a receiver. In the case of a floating charge, the Court shall have the power to appoint a receiver and manager of the assets that are the subject of the charge (s. 205 (1) CAMA 2020), (s. 180(1). With specific reference to a floating charge, however, the Court is empowered to appoint a receiver or manager, notwithstanding that the charge has not become enforceable, where the Court is satisfied that the security of the debenture holder is in jeopardy.

The Court will consider the security of the debenture holder to be in jeopardy in relation to the charged assets and undertakings, if it is satisfied that events have occurred or are about to occur which makes it unreasonable in the interest of the debenture holder to allow the company to retain the power to dispose of its charged assets (s. 205 (2), (s. 180 (2).

It is therefore a matter of the nature of evidence that has been placed before the Court that would enable the Court to make a decision one way or the other when called upon to do so in this respect. For instance, if there be credible evidence before the Court, not rebutted by the company, that officers of the company are planning to strip and sell-off the company assets, that would be a ground enough to satisfy the Court that the security of the debenture holder is in jeopardy and the Court will be right to appoint a receiver and manager over the assets. Each case will, however, be decided on its own peculiar facts and merits.

It is noteworthy that where debentures have not been secured by any charge at all, a receiver or manager cannot be appointed as a means of enforcing such debentures (s. 205(3), (s. 180 (3). Where a receiver or manager has been appointed by the Court, he is mandated to advertise the fact of his appointment in the Federal Government Gazette and in two national newspapers. Having been so appointed, he is an officer of the Court and not an agent of any of the parties *(Jannasons Co. Ltd* v. *Uzor & Ors (1991) LPELR-1596)*. In so being appointed, no action can be brought against him or in respect of the property in his hand without the leave of Court, otherwise, such a suit will be incompetent *(Ames* v. *Birkenhead Docks Trustees (1885) 20 Beau* 332; *Orojo, 181*).

EXECUTION OF DEBENTURE TRUST DEED

It is mandatory for every company that offers debentures for subscription or sale to the public to, before issuing the debentures, execute a debenture trust deed in respect of the debentures and to have the deed executed by the trustee of the debenture holders appointed by the deed (s. 208(1) CAMA 2020), (s. 183(1).

A debenture trust deed is not allowed to cover more than one class of debentures, whether or not it is required to be executed (s. 208(2), (s. 183 (2). A debenture is considered to be covered by a trust deed, if:

- the holder of the debenture is entitled to participate in any money payable by the company under the deed; or
- the holder of the debenture is entitled to the benefit of any mortgage, charge or security created by the deed, whether alone or together with other persons [s. 208 (6)].

Where a trust deed is required to be executed but has not been executed, a debenture holder concerned may apply to Court and the Court may (a) order the company to execute a trust deed, or (b) direct that a person nominated by the Court be appointed as a trustee; or (c) give other consequential directions as it deems fit in the circumstances, as to the content of the trust deed and its execution by the trustee (s. 208(3), (s. 183 (3).

A fine, on conviction, is imposed on a defaulting director(s) in a company that issues a debenture under a trust deed that covers two or more classes of debentures or where no trust deed was executed when same is required (s. 208 (7), (s. 183(7).

CONTENTS OF DEBENTURE TRUST DEED

There are mandatory requirements in the CAMA as to what a debenture trust deed has to contain as statements. Section 209 CAMA 2020, (s. 184) states that every such trust deed shall state:

- the maximum sum which the company may raise by issuing debentures of the same class;
- the maximum discount which may be allowed on the issue or re-issue of the debentures and the maximum premium at which the debentures may be made redeemable;
- the nature of any assets over which a mortgage, charge or security is created by the trust deed in favour of the trustee for the benefit of the debenture holders equally, and except the charge is a floating charge, then the identity of the assets subject to it;
- the nature of any asset over which a mortgage, charge or security will be created in favour of any person other than the trustee, for the benefit of the debenture holders equally, and except where the charge is a floating charge, the identity of the assets subject to it;
- any prohibition or restriction on the power of the company to issue debentures or to create mortgages, charges or any security on any of its assets ranking in priority to or equally with the debentures covered by the trust deed;
- whether the company shall have power or not to acquire debentures issued under the deed before the date of their redemption and re-issue the debentures;

- the rate of and the dates on which interests on the debentures issued under the deed shall be payable and the manner of payment;
- the date(s) on which the principal on the debentures issued under the trust deed shall be paid or redeemed and except the whole principal is to repaid to all the debenture holders at the same time, the manner in which redemption is effected whether by payment of equal instalments of principal in respect of each debenture, or by the selection of debentures for redemption by the company, or by drawing ballot or otherwise;
- in the case of convertible debentures, the date and terms on which the debentures will be converted to shares and the amount which may be credited as paid-up on those shares from the debentures converted;
- the circumstances in which the debenture holders shall be entitled to realize any mortgage, charge or security invested in the trustee or any other person for their benefit (other than circumstances under this Act);
- the powers of the company and the trustee to call meetings of debenture holders and the rights of debenture holders to require the company or the trustee to call such meetings;
- whether the rights of debenture holders may be altered or abrogated, and if so, the conditions to be fulfilled and the procedure to be followed to effect such an alteration or abrogation;
- the amount or rate of remuneration to be paid to the trustee and the period for which it is paid, and whether it is paid in priority to the principal interests and costs in respect of the debentures issued under the trust deed; and
- the date on which the principal on the debentures under the deed shall be repaid, and if not paid to all holders at the same time, the manner of any such repayment;
- provisions for the replacement of the trustee, if required (this particular provision is a new addition to requirement by the CAMA 2020. It was not a part of the required statements to be included in a debenture trust deed under CAMA 2004).

The above statements are mandatory requirements. Therefore, it is provided that if debentures are issued without a covering debenture trust deed being executed, the above statements shall be included in each debenture or in a note forming part of the same document endorsed thereon (s. 209(2), (s. 184(2).

Note that a debenture issued by a company is mandated to state legibly on its face that it is unsecured, if no mortgage, charge or security is vested in the holder of the debenture or in any other person for his benefit as security for the payment of the principal or interests (s. 210 (2), (s. 185(2).

TRUSTEE FOR DEBENTURE HOLDERS

Under section 211 (1)(2) CAMA 2020, (s. 186 (1)(2), a debenture may be secured by a trust deed appointing a trustee for the debenture holders, whether or not it is secured by a charge over the company's property. The trustee so appointed shall have the duty of protecting the interests of the debenture holders and exercising on their behalf, rights, powers and discretions conferred on him by the trust deed.

Any provision contained in a trust deed or in any contract with the holders of the debentures secured by a trust deed, is void if it would have the effect of exempting a trustee from or indemnifying him against liability for any breach of trust or failure to show the degree of care and diligence required of him, as a trustee. This is having regard to the powers, authorities or discretions conferred on him by the trust deed (s. 211(4), (s. 186 (4).

A trustee could, however, be released from liability by an agreement of a majority of not less than three-quarter in value of the debenture holders present in person, or where proxies are permitted, by proxy, at a meeting summoned for the purpose. This provision implies that a meeting where the issue will be to relieve a trustee from liability will not be a meeting where other matters concerning the debenture holders will be discussed. It will be a meeting called specifically to discuss the liability of the trustee and the relief thereto.

Notwithstanding the above provision for relief from liability for a trustee, the Court may, on the application of any debenture holder, or on the application of the Commission, remove a trustee and appoint another in his place, if the trustee is conflicted or has an interest that may conflict with those of the debenture holders. A trustee can also be removed by the Court on this head if, for any reason, it is desirable to remove him from so acting (s. 211(6), (s. 186 (5).

DISQUALIFICATION FOR APPOINTMENT AS A TRUSTEE

From all the discussions above, it is clear that the duties and responsibilities that are vested in a trustee of debenture trust deed are quite enormous. In that wise, apparently, it is not everyone that may be appointed as a trustee of a debenture trust deed under the CAMA. Certain categories of persons are disqualified under section 212 (1) CAMA 2020, (s. 187 (1) from acting as trustees of a debenture trust deed. Those disqualified are:

- a person who is an officer or employee of the company that issued the debenture covered by the trust deed or an officer or employee in the group of companies that issued the debenture;
- a person who is less than 18 years;
- a person who has been found to be of unsound mind by a Court in Nigeria or elsewhere;
- a person who is an undischarged bankrupt; or
- a person disqualified from being a company director under section 283 CAMA 2020 (this section additionally disqualifies an insolvent person(s), those convicted of fraud in relation to formation or winding-up of companies. Here, however, a corporation is not disqualified from being a trustee);

Unlike the CAMA 2004, the CAMA 2020 removed a person who is a substantial shareholder in the company from the list of those that are disqualified from being a trustee of a debenture trust deed. This then means that such persons are now qualified to be appointed as such.

If any of the disqualifying events occur after a person has been appointed a trustee, then the person immediately ceases to be qualified to act as such. An offence is created for anyone who acts as a trustee of a debenture trust deed while disqualified as stated above, and on conviction, liable to be punished as the Court deems fit. The Commission may, in the alternative, impose a fine on the person in question (s. 212(3), (s. 187(2)(3). Elsewhere in this book, we have interrogated the legality or otherwise of a fine from the Commission on a person who has been convicted and punished by a Court of law for the same infraction. Although in the present instance, the punishments by the Court and the Commission are in the alternative.

TRANSFERABILITY OF DEBENTURES

In general, debentures are transferable, but not so without limitations. Under the CAMA, except where the terms in any debenture expressly provide to the contrary, debentures are transferable without any restriction(s). Any transfer shall be by way of a written transfer in a common form, or any other form which the company directors may approve, so that the transferee shall be entitled to the debenture and to the money secured by it without regard to any equity, set-off or cross claims between the company and the original or any intermediate holder(s) [(s. 214 (1) CAMA 2020, (s. 189 (1)].

Notwithstanding the fact that debentures are said to be generally transferable without restrictions, the terms of any debentures may impose restrictions on the nature of transferability of debentures. These restrictions may include the company's power to refuse any transfer and may make provisions for compulsory acquisitions or rights of first refusal in favour of other debenture holders, members or officers of the company [s. 214(2), (s. 189 (2)].

It is important to note, as a proviso to the above discussions, that where a restriction(s) has been imposed on the right to transfer any debenture, notice of the restriction must be endorsed on the face of the debenture or debenture stock certificate. If this is not done, such a restriction shall be ineffective against any transferee for value. This is irrespective of whether or not he has notice of the restriction.

Entry of Transfer of Debentures in the Register

When any debenture has been transferred, the transferor applies to the company which shall then enter in its register of debenture holders, the name of the transferee in the same manner and subject to the same conditions as if the application for entry were made by the transferee (s. 220 CAMA 2020), (s. 195). In practice, it is usual that this application be made by the transferee, who is the person that would lose out if, for any reason, the non-entry into the company's register of debenture holders makes the debenture holder to suffer any disability, due to lack of notice of the existence of the debenture to the general public.

This is one of the corporate governance disclosures by companies under the CAMA to alert potential creditors, investors and the general public to the real state of affairs in a company. Once the transfer has been entered into the register of debenture holders, the company would have discharged its own obligations in this respect.

Notice of Refusal to Register Transfer

In the event that a company refuses to register a transfer of any debentures after receiving the application from the transferor (or transferee), it is mandated to send a notice of such refusal to the transferee within two (2) months after the date on which the transfer was lodged with the company for registration. A fine, to be specified by the Commission, is imposed on the company and every officer for any default in sending a notice of refusal to register any transfer to the transferee (s. 221), (s. 196(1)(2).

One noticeable fact is that the CAMA does not say what happens when the notice of refusal to register a transfer of debenture is sent by the company to the transferee. Is such a notice final and conclusive on the matter? Put in another way, what options do the transferee have if the company refuses to register the transfer?

The presumption here is that in refusing to the register the transfer of debenture sent to it, the company would have stated the reason(s) for its refusal. It then appears that the option open to the transferor (transferee) would be to approach the Court, making the transferee a party also, with all relevant facts and evidence to ask for an order to compel the company to register the transfer. This will be on preponderance of positive evidence adduced by the applicant before the Court. It is the order of Court that will then direct further action(s) by the parties. The transferee could also approach the Court on the same basis, making the transferor a party to the suit.

REGISTRATION OF CHARGES WITH THE COMMISSION

Substantial justice was not done to the concept or meaning of a charge by the CAMA 2020. The Act simply states in section 222(13), (s.197 (11), that a charge includes a mortgage. That fact has never been in dispute, but, conceptually, what really is a charge?

In *AIB Ltd* v. *Lee & Tee Ind. Ltd (2003) 7 NWLR Pt. 819, 366*, a 'charge' was defined as 'the appropriation of real or personal property for the discharge of a debt or other obligation, without giving the creditor either a general or special property in, or possession of the subject of the security.' The operative word here is appropriation, because a charge is an index of appropriation of a right(s) exercisable in favour of the chargee. Also, in this direction, in *Canvass Farms (Nig). Ltd* v. *AMCON & Anor (2021) LPELR-54650*, a 'charge' was defined as 'an encumbrance or lien on a property created for the purpose of securing the fulfilment of an obligation.' These definitions give a broad perspective on what a 'charge' is, and it is from that perspective that we approach the matter from here.

Under section 222(1) CAMA 2020, (s. 197 (1), every charge created by a company shall, so far as any security on the company's property or undertaking is conferred, be void against the liquidator and any creditor of the company, unless the particulars of the charge (including any provisions in a floating charge that prohibits or restricts the company from granting any further charge ranking in priority to or *pari passu* with the floating charge) together with the instrument, if any, creating or evidencing the charge, have been or are delivered to or are received by the Commission for registration in the manner required by the Act or by any enactment repealed by the Act, within 90 days after the charge was created.

In practice, where a charge has not been registered within the time allowed (90 days) by the Act, it is possible to approach the Court by an *ex-parte* motion to extend the time within which to register the charge. Once the Court grants the application, the registration of the charge with the Commission on the extended time, will be in order.

When a charge is void for non-registration, as provided for under this section of the CAMA, the charge is as good as could be against the company and without prejudice to any contract or obligation for repayment of the money thereby secured, which becomes immediately repayable; *Independent Automatic Sales Ltd* v. *Knowles & Foster (1962) 1 WLR 974, Palmers, 476).* With respect to the registration as described, once effectively completed, it shall give rise to notice to all and sundry of the matters stated in the particulars of the charge. As noted above, this is also one of the corporate governance disclosures to the public showing the encumbrances on the company's property. This is an invaluable resource and usually the first point of contact for due diligence on companies by potential investors and creditors.

Charges Required to be Registered

As noted above, charges created by a company in Nigeria are required to be registered with the Commission, for notice to interested parties and the general public. However, it is noteworthy that the CAMA did not say that 'all charges' created by a company must be registered, but that 'every charge to which the section applies' and those charges are listed in section 222(2) CAMA 2020, (s. 197 (2) as follows:

- a charge for the purpose of securing any issue of debentures;
- a charge on uncalled share capital of a company;
- a charge created or evidenced by an instrument which if executed by an individual would require registration as a bill of sale;
- a charge on land, wherever situate, or any interest therein, but not including a charge for rent or other periodical sum issuing on the land;

- a charge on book debts of the company (receivables);
- a floating charge on the undertakings or property of a company;
- a charge on calls made but not paid;
- a charge on ship or aircraft or any share in a ship;
- a charge on goodwill, or on any intellectual property (this provision substituted the generic term intellectual property, which is wider, for the itemization of patent, trademark or copyright used under the CAMA 2004).

If a charge requires registration under another law as it is with the CAMA in order to be valid or effectual, then it is sufficient, instead of delivery of the original instrument creating or evidencing the charge, there is delivered to and received by the Commission within the prescribed period of ninety (90) days, or such extended time as the Court may allow, a true of copy of it certified as such by the company secretary (s. 222(3), (s. 197 (3).

The above provision seeks to simplify the process of the second registration of any instrument creating a charge. For instance, where a company has issued a mortgage (debenture) over its property to secure a facility, and the mortgage has been registered with the lands' registry within the state. If the mortgage deed is then sought to be registered with the Commission subsequently against the interest of the mortgagor company, the above procedure simplifies the process to be adopted. In practice, however, the Commission does not seem to appreciate or understand the application of the section, as attempts by this author to use the provision to register a deed of legal mortgage executed by a company were rebuffed by the Commission.

Charges Created Abroad or on Foreign Property

Where a charge has been created outside Nigeria over a property that is also outside Nigeria, then, the delivery and receipt by the Commission of a copy of the instrument, as verified, creating or evidencing the charge shall be sufficient and have the same effect as the delivery of the instrument itself. Also, the period of ninety (90) days after the creation of the charge and the duration of postage to the Commission shall be substituted for requirement of registration within ninety (90) days after the creation of the charge (s. 222 (5), (s. 197 (5).

Where, on the other hand, a charge has been created in Nigeria but affects or relates to a property outside Nigeria, then, the instrument creating or purporting to create the charge may be sent for registration to the Commission within ninety (90) days notwithstanding that further proceedings may be necessary to make the charge valid or effectual according to the law of the country where the property in question is located (s. 222(6), (s. 197 (6).

This provision has to be read while having in mind that section 860 (1) CAMA 2020 provides that any document required to be filed with the Commission for registration, may be filed electronically. It is an area to be explored in this respect.

Certain clarifications are made by the CAMA in terms of interests in some registrable instruments and their significance or effect.

It has been provided that where a negotiable instrument has been given to secure the payment of any book debts (receivables) of a company, the deposit of the instrument for the purpose of securing advance to the company shall not, be treated as a charge on those book debts. Again, the holding of debentures entitling the holder to a charge on land, is not deemed to be an interest in land (s. 222(7)(8) CAMA 2020, (s. 197(7)(8). This presupposes that even if the instruments embodying these could have been registered with the Commission, the incidents mentioned above will not be treated as charges in the excluded respects.

Duty of Company to Register Charges

The CAMA imposes a duty on a company to send to the Commission for registration, within 90 days of creation, the particulars of every charge created by the company as required by section 222, (s. 197) of the Act. The same registration is required when a company issues debentures of a series requiring registration under section 222. However, the registration of the charge may be effected on the application of any person interested in the charge being registered, and the person is entitled to recover from the company any fees paid to the Commission for the registration (s. 224(1)(2), (s. 199 (1)(2).

The Act allows a person interested in the registration of the charge to be able to do so, being that it is the person that stands to lose, if the priority on the charge is lost to other interests that were created subsequently but registered earlier. This is also to avoid the repeat of the instances that led to the decision of the Supreme Court in *Savannah Bank of Nigeria Ltd.* v. *Ajilo (1989) 1 NWLR Pt. 97, 305*, wherein a mortgagor, whose duty it was under the *Land Use Act Cap. L.5 LFN 2004*to procure governor's consent on the alienation of his interest in land, did not do so. When the mortgagee sued for the repayment of the facility and possible realization of the security, the mortgagor went ahead to rely on his dereliction of non-registration of the mortgage (consent) to void the transaction. The decision divided the opinion of legal experts for many years, although some subsequent decisions of the Courts, like *Awojugbagbe Light Ind. Ltd* v. *Chinukwe (1995) 5 NWLR Pt. 390, 379*, and others, have veered away from appearing to follow that trend of thought, because of the perceived injustice of the Ajilo decision.

A fine, to be prescribed by the Commission, is imposed on the company and every officer, who is in default when a charge is not registered, either by the company or a person interested, where registration is mandatory.

Company's Duty to Register Subsisting Charges

Where a company acquires a property that is the subject of an existing charge, subject to registration, the company shall cause the particulars of the charge and a certified copy of the instrument creating or evidencing the charge to be delivered to the Commission for registration within ninety (90) days after the date on which the acquisition of the property was completed (s. 225(1) CAMA 2020), (s. 200 (1). However, if the property is situate and the charge is created outside Nigeria, the period of ninety (90) days after the copy of the instrument could have been received in Nigeria if posted diligently to the Commission shall be substituted for requirement of registration within ninety (90) days after the creation of the charge (s. 225(1), (s. 197 (5). This is also an area where the use of electronic registration procedure should be considered, as noted above.

Where the property acquired by the company is a land and the charge has been registered in a state under a state law, then, it will suffice for the purpose to deliver a certified copy (certified by the company secretary as the one whose original has been duly registered) of the registered charge to the Commission (s. 225(3), (s. 200 (3).

The application of the above proviso to section 225 is what was discussed above in relation to section 222(3), which permits a certified copy of an instrument already registered in a state to simply be sent to the Commission as a fulfilment of the requirement for registration. As was noted above, the Commission had rebuffed this author's attempts to use that provision in the past. It is hoped that, going forward, the Commission will appreciate the essence and import of the provision and put same to good use.

Where a company has property with an existing charge but which had not been registered under the CAMA, the company is mandated, within six (6) months thereof of the Act coming into effect, to send the particulars of the charge and the document creating the charge to the Commission for registration. Failure to do so, however, does not affect the validity of the charge (s. 226 CAMA 2020), (s. 201).

The CAMA 2020, wisely in our view, left out a provision under the CAMA 2004, which required every existing company to deliver a *statutory declaration* made to the Commission, within six (6) months of the commencement of the Act, stating whether they have property with registrable charges and whether the charges have been sent to the Commission for registration.

It was good that the provision was omitted in CAMA 2020, as its utility seems suspect. It is very doubtful if any company that has not registered any registrable charge will choose to 'self-immolate' by reporting themselves to the Commission for punishment.

REGISTER OF PARTICULARS OF CHARGES

The Commission is mandated under section 223(1) CAMA 2020, (s. 198 (1) to maintain, with respect to each company, a register of registrable charges. It is also mandated, on the payment by the company of fees specified by the Commission, to enter in the register the following particulars with respect to such charges:

- in the case of a charge benefitting holders of a series of debentures, then, the particulars enumerated under section 222(9) of the Act (s. 197 (9);
- in the case of any other charge, then:
  i. if the charge is one created by the company, the date of its creation, and if the charge was one existing on a property acquired by the company, the date of its creation and the date of the acquisition of the property;
  ii. the amount secured by the charge;
  iii. brief particulars about the property;
  iv. the persons entitled to the charge; and
  v. for a floating charge, a notice indicating the existence of any provisions in the charge that prohibit or restrict the company from granting any further charge ranking in priority to or *pari passu* with the floating charge. (*Note that this is an addition by the CAMA 2020, which did not exist under the CAMA 2004).*

Once a charge has been registered by the Commission, it shall issue a certificate of registration setting out the parties, amount secured by the charge, and other particulars it considers necessary. The certificate shall be *prima facie* evidence of compliance with the registration requirements by the company. The register of charges kept by the Commission shall be open to inspection by any person(s) on the payment of the prescribed fees (s. 223 (2)(3), (s. 198 (2)(3). The Act left the fees payable for inspection of the register to be prescribed by the Commission, as against the CAMA 2004, which prescribed a fee threshold for such inspection(s).

ENTRIES OF SATISFACTION OF CHARGES

The wish of the parties to an instrument bearing a registered charge, at least theoretically, is that the transaction(s) necessitating the charge be successfully executed and the charge discharged. Therefore, under section 229 CAMA 2020, (s. 204) with respect to a registered charge with the Commission, if the Commission is satisfied that:

- the debt for which the charge was given has been paid or satisfied in whole or in part; or
- part of the property or undertaking charged has been released from the charge or has ceased to form part of the company's property or undertaking, the Commission may enter on the register, a memorandum of satisfaction to the extent necessary to give effect thereto, and when this has been done, if required, furnish the company with a copy of the entry, and the entry shall have effect subject to the requirement of any other enactment regarding registration.

RECTIFICATION OF THE REGISTER

It is only a Court of law that can rectify the register of charges on the presentation of convincing evidence and plausible reasons for the Court to do so. There could be diverse reasons for this. Where the Court is satisfied, on the application of the company or an interested party, that there was an omission to register a charge within the time limited to do so, or that there was a misstatement of any particular with respect to a charge in a memorandum of satisfaction but that it was accidental or due to inadvertence, the Court may extend time for registration or order that the register be rectified. The Court must, however, be satisfied that the delay, misstatement or omission is not in a nature to prejudice the company's creditors or shareholders (s. 230 CAMA 2020), (s. 205). If the application to Court for rectification involves serious issues of facts, then the Court will need all the best information and evidence available in order to be able to make an informed decision *(Re Heathstar Properties Ltd (1966) WLR 993; Charlesworth & Cain, 581).*

REGISTRATION OF APPOINTMENT ORDER

A person who obtains a Court order for the appointment of a receiver or manager or appoints one over a company's property under a power contained in any instrument, shall, within seven (7) days of the order or appointment give notice of the same to the Commission. On its part, the Commission shall, on the payment of the prescribed fees, enter the fact of the appointment of a receiver or manager in the register of charges.

When a person who has been appointed a receiver or manager of a company's property ceases to act as such, he is mandated to send a notice of that fact of the cessation of his appointment to the Commission. The Commission is also mandated to enter such fact into the register of charges (s. 231(1)(2) CAMA 2020), (s.206(1)(2). All these are corporate governance disclosures for public information and use.

REALIZATION OF SECURITY BY DEBENTURE HOLDERS

There are circumstances under which a debenture holder is entitled to realize any security vested in him or vested in another person for his benefit. Section 232 CAMA 2020, (s.208(1) lists the triggering factors for the realization of security by holders, to be, when:

- the company fails to pay any instalment of interest, or the whole or part of the principal or any premium owing under the debenture or debenture trust deed covering the debenture, within one month after it becomes due;
- the company fails to fulfil any of the obligations imposed on it by the debentures or the debenture trust deed;
- any circumstance(s) occur which by the terms of the debentures or debentures trust deed entitled the holder of the debenture to realize his security; or
- the company is wound up.

Where the debenture is secured by a floating charge, the debenture holder or the trustee of the debenture trust deed shall, in addition to the factors stated above, be entitled to realize the security, if:

- any of the company's creditors issue a process of execution against any of its assets or commences proceedings for winding-up the company by order of a Court of competent jurisdiction; or

- the company ceases to pay its debts as they fall due; or
- the company ceases to carry on business; or
- if after the issue of the debenture of the class concerned, the company suffers losses or diminutions in the value of its assets which in the aggregate amounts to more than one-half of the total amount owing in respect of the debenture of the class held by the debenture holder who seeks to enforce his security and debentures whose holder ranks before him for payment of principal or interest; or
- any circumstance(s) occur which entitles a debenture holder who ranks for payment of principal or interest in priority to the debentures secured by the floating charges to realize his security (s. 232(2), (s. 208 (2).

REMEDIES AVAILABLE TO DEBENTURE HOLDERS

When a debenture holder or a class of debenture holders becomes entitled to realize his or their security, a receiver of any asset subject to a mortgage, charge or security in favour of the class of debenture holders or the trustee of the covering trust deed, or any other person, may be appointed by:

- the trustee of a debenture trust deed;
- the holders of debentures of the same class containing power to appoint such a receiver;
- debenture holders having more than one-half of the total amount owing in respect of all the debentures of the same class; or
- the Court on the application of the trustee.
- In order to realize his security, a debenture holder or a trustee in the case of a debenture trust deed (subject to any conditions imposed in a debenture or the debenture trust deed) may undertake any of the following actions:
- bring an action in a representative capacity (approval of Court is needed if company is being wound-up) against the company for the payment and enforcement of the security or realise his security by:
- bringing an action for foreclosure; or
- bring an action for a winding-up of the company (s. 233(2), (s. 209(2);
- a receiver also has the power (subject to any Court order) to take possession and sell the assets that are subject to the mortgage, charge or security, enforce claims vested in the company, compromise, settle or otherwise enter into arrangements in respect of claims by or against the

company, take possession and deal as found fit, the company's intellectual property and licenses thereto and recover any unpaid instalments on company's issued shares (s. 233(3), (s. 209 (3).

The remedies noted above are in addition to, and not as substitute for any other powers or remedies conferred on the trustee of debenture trust deed or debenture holders or in any other instrument by which the debenture holders may exercise their powers to realise their security (s.233(5), (s.209 (5).

Any provision(s) in any instrument that purports to restrict or exclude the remedies provided above for debenture holders shall be invalid to the extent of the exclusions or restrictions (s.233(7), (s.209 (7).

Apart from the remedies stated above, a power of sale may be exercised if it is contained in the debenture or the debenture trust deed. This power is usually contained in a trust deed and there is also an implied power of sale in a mortgage deed, that is, a legal mortgage, once perfected. If the debenture is secured, then the debenture holder is in a position similar to a company's secured creditor. Therefore, if the company is wound up, such a debenture holder may value his security and if it is insufficient, prove for the balance like any other unsecured creditor of the company *(Orojo, 180).*

The duties and responsibilities of the company secretary in relation to company debentures arise immediately debentures are created and are sustained and alive until the particular debenture is realized. Apart from debentures, there are also other charges, registrable as they are that should attract the attention of the company secretary.

The first thing is to comply with the requirement of the CAMA for the registration of company charges with the Commission within 90 days of their creation. Once the charge, including a charge to secure debenture, is created, this duty arises. We are aware that a charge includes a mortgage. As noted above, there are lot of corporate governance disclosures which are meant to inform the public, especially creditors and potential investors on the state of affairs (encumbrances and charges) in the companies concerned.

Added to the duty of registering any charge created by a company, there is also a mandate for a company to register existing charge(s), within 90 days of acquiring any asset(s) with such a charge. The company is to send the particulars of such a charge and the instruments creating the charge to the Commission for registration. There are, therefore, two registers, in this respect. The first register is the one maintained by the company for its charges and the second register is the one maintained for the company by the Commission, both doing the same job of disclosures.

Registration is also required for charges created outside Nigeria on properties that are situate outside Nigeria, so is registration also required for charges created in Nigeria for properties that are situate outside. The charges (instruments creating them) are required to be sent to the Commission for registration within 90 days. However, for charges created outside Nigeria, the 90 days will be calculated to be for the duration that the instrument will take to arrive at the Commission, when posted. We have alluded to the provision of the CAMA 2020, under section 860 that allows electronic means of sending registrable instrument and see how it can be of use in this respect.

Where the terms of issue permit, there could be meetings of debenture holders to discuss pertinent issues relating to the security. Even where the debentures themselves did not make any provisions to this effect, the Commission, on its own, could order that a meeting of debenture holders be held to discuss important matters relevant to the holders.

Apart from the above, it was noted that debentures are transferable. It is the responsibility of the company secretary to maintain and superintend the register of debenture holders and also superintend the incidences of transfer and make same effective. It is also the duty of the company secretary to communicate any refusal to register any transferred debenture to the party that sent in the transfer (transferee, most times), and this has to be done within two (2) months of the company taking the decision to refuse to register the transfer.

A company is expected to deliver a copy of debenture or certificate of debenture stock to the holder within sixty (60) days of the allotment of the debenture or transfer of the debenture stock. Even when delivered to the holder, when a debenture is lost or the debenture stock certificate is lost, destroyed or defaced, the company is mandated to issue a certified copy to the holder on request or renew the debenture stock certificate.

On a final note in this respect, apart from the above duties and responsibilities of the company secretary regarding debentures and charges, which are by no means exhaustive, he is also the anchor point when it comes to realizing the security. Once any of the factors that could trigger the security to be realized is activated, the company secretary takes over, activating both the judicial and non-judicial processes that will lead to the realization of the company's security.

In sum, it is worth reiterating that finance, in various forms, is the bedrock of modern businesses. In this respect, debentures are veritable instruments in the hands of companies, as commercial going concerns, when they need to raise external finances through borrowing.

A lot of matters are connected with the issuing of debentures and in executing debenture trust deed and the terms that they contain are key. Usually, the terms and conditions in debentures are what will determine the rights and liabilities of the parties thereto, and over the years, the contents and terms of debenture trust deeds have become more or less standardized. This is despite the fact that the CAMA has, to a large extent, enunciated what is considered as the critical terms and conditions, in the form of statements, to be included in a deed of debenture.

As noted above, for the company secretary, the focus should start from the statutory requirements for registration and notification of any charges created by the company to the Commission. It is a company's duty to register any charges created over its assets with the Commission. Attention should be paid especially to the time limited for any registration or notification of charges, as any default might deprive the company the priority rights otherwise due to it under any such instrument(s). Having said this, the other issues noted above, including keeping a register of debenture holders, register of charges, registering transfer of debentures, issuing (and replacing where necessary) certificate of debenture stock, superintending the meeting of debenture holders, are not less important. Care should also be taken to execute these items promptly, being that there are continuing fines that are imposed on companies for any default in these respects. No responsible company wants to pay any unnecessary fine(s) or penalties.

In the final analysis, the company secretary must be ready and proactive to realize the company's security when any of the condition(s) that activates such realization occurs.

CHECKPOINTS

- ✓ The term 'debenture' has been accepted to mean an instrument that creates or acknowledges a debt. It is used almost exclusively by corporate bodies.
- ✓ In terms of format, debentures are structurally the same, although there are different types of debentures: perpetual, convertible, redeemable and secured or naked, made so by the terms and conditions they contain and the import of their clauses.

- ✓ As a going commercial concern, a company has inherent powers to borrow money, and in doing so, also has the powers to pledge any of its properties to secure the debt thereby incurred.
- ✓ Every company is mandated to send to the Commission, within ninety (90) days of creation, particulars and instrument creating a charge or used to secure a debenture, for registration.
- ✓ Every company that issued a debenture is mandated to send to the holders, within 60 days of the allotment of debenture or transfer of any debenture, the debenture or certificate of debenture stock, under its common seal (if it has and uses one) or executed as a deed by the company.
- ✓ A company is under obligation, when requested by the holder, to issue a certified copy of a lost debenture or a new certificate for a lost, destroyed or defaced certificate of debenture stock.
- ✓ The CAMA requires certain mandatory statements to be in a debenture, like the amount borrowed, rate of interests, date of redemption of the principal etc. Though mandatory, the Courts have held that the non-inclusion of those statements does not void the debenture, *ab initio*, but only makes it voidable.
- ✓ A contract with a company in relation to its debenture can be enforced by specific performance, which is an equitable remedy and discretionary on the Court to order or not.
- ✓ Debenture holders have several rights attached to their holding a debenture, including the right to the repayment of the money lent and the right to sue thereto to recover same.
- ✓ A debenture holder may also sue the trustee of a debenture trust deed for compensation for breach of any fiduciary duties that the trustee owes him.
- ✓ Where the terms of the debentures or the trust deed permit for meeting of holders, such a meeting may be held and binding resolutions passed. Where otherwise, the Commission may, on its own, direct that a meeting of a class of debentures holders be held and discuss issues that the Commission may direct.

- ✓ Holders of at least one-tenth voting rights attached to a debenture trust deed can requisition a meeting of that class of debentures and the trustee is mandated to call a meeting.
- ✓ It is important to note the peculiar characteristics of a floating charge as the one that 'hovers' over the charged asset(s) of the company while the company retains custody and use of the assets, until events of crystallization happen, to trigger the charge to fix on the assets.
- ✓ The fixed charge is permanently fixed on the assets(s) charged and is more suited to a specific asset(s) that is not used for the company's day-to-day businesses.
- ✓ In terms of priority of charges, generally, a fixed charge once created over an asset(s) has priority over a floating charge, except where the terms of the earlier floating charge prohibit the creation of a subsequent charge with priority over it, and the latter holder has notice of the prohibition on the floating charge. Once the floating charge containing the prohibition has been registered with the Commission, the notice to third parties is conclusively presumed.
- ✓ Between two floating charges, priority is determined by the date of the creation of the charge, once both charges have been registered, meaning that the equities are equal. Where one of the charges has not been registered, it loses priority, even to the one created later but registered.
- ✓ Where a charge has become enforceable, the Court has the power to appoint a manager, and if it is a floating charge, the Court is empowered to appoint a receiver and a manager.
- ✓ The Court is also empowered to appoint a receiver and manager in the case of a floating charge even when the security has not become realizable, but it is established that the security is in jeopardy.
- ✓ Where a receiver or manager is appointed by the Court, there shall be advertisement to this effect in two (2) national newspapers and the Federal Government Gazette.
- ✓ The CAMA enumerates what must be in a debenture trust deed as mandatory statements, including maximum amount a company can raise thereby, nature of the asset(s) over which the security interest will be created, factors that will trigger the realization of security, etc.

- ✓ Some persons are disqualified from being appointed trustees of a debenture trust deed, including persons under 18 years, persons of unsound mind, an officer(s) or employee(s) of the company that issued the debenture, persons disqualified from being a director under the CAMA, etc.
- ✓ Debentures are, in general, transferable, without restrictions, except where the terms of the debenture impose restrictions. In such a case, the restrictions imposed on the debenture will have to be endorsed on the face of the debenture or debenture stock certificate, failing which the restrictions shall be ineffective against any transferee for value. It is immaterial whether the transferee has notice of the prohibition or not, the requisite endorsement is mandatory.
- ✓ Every company that issues a debenture is required to have a register of debenture holders. This is also where incidents of transfer of debenture sent to the company shall be entered for record purposes. This is one of the corporate governance disclosures required from companies to put the public on notice of the state on affairs in the company.
- ✓ A company is empowered to refuse to register a transfer of debenture sent to it, but must inform the person(s) that sent the transfer request, within two (2) months, of its decision not to register the transfer. We posited that a person may approach the Court to reverse this decision.
- ✓ The CAMA has listed several charges, including: charges on a company's intellectual property rights, book debts (receivables), charges on calls made but not paid-up; charges on land, charges on ship, etc., as registrable charges.
- ✓ Every company is mandated to maintain a register of charges it has created, disclosing, among other things, the date of the creation of the charges, amount secured, brief particulars of the assets, the person(s) entitled to the charges, etc.
- ✓ When a charge has been satisfied on being realized, either in whole or in part, and the Commission is notified, the Commission is mandated to enter such fact in its memorandum of satisfaction of charges, and give a copy of the memorandum to the company, that is, if a request is made in that respect.

- ✓ A Court is the only entity that has the power to rectify the register of charges, when satisfied that any delay, misstatement or omission thereto had been through inadvertence. When serious issues of facts are involved, then the Court will require all credible available evidence and information to be able to take a decision.
- ✓ There are factors that trigger the realization of security by a debenture holder, including, company's failure to pay instalment of interests or premium, company being wound-up or failing to fulfil obligations imposed by the debenture or the debenture trust deed, among others.
- ✓ If the debenture is the one secured by a floating charge, other factors, in addition, can also trigger security realization, including, the company stopping to carry-on business, or where a creditor issues execution processes against the company.
- ✓ When the time is ripe to realize their security, debenture holders have several remedies from which to choose, including: bringing an action, with leave of Court, enforce the security, instituting an action for foreclosure, bringing an action to take over and sell the assets secured and suing for winding-up the company.

Chapter 18

STATUTORY REGISTERS, RECORDS AND RETURNS

INTRODUCTION

In modern businesses, one of the most cardinal duties of the company secretary, and for some, arguably the most important, is to make sure that the company complies with all the requirements of relevant existing laws in relation to the company and its businesses. In this respect, the company secretary acts as the company's compliance officer (although the compliance department may still exist independently), in ensuring that all filings, returns and notifications required to be made by the company to relevant authorities are made, and doing so in good time, to avoid any fines or penalties. Things have been fairly simplified in this respect by section 860 CAMA 2020, which provides that any document(s) required to be filed with the Commission for registration, may be filed electronically. This will include but not limited to applicable resolutions, allotments, particulars of different dimensions (charges, directors, company secretary, member's interests in shares etc.). This is an overdue but welcome development.

Section 335(1) (b) CAMA 2020, (s. 298 (1)(b), provides that the company secretary shall be responsible for the maintenance of the registers and other records required to be maintained by the company under the Act. These are the companies' statutory registers and records under the Act, and the details of the contents differ for each register and record. The importance of these registers and records cannot be over-emphasized, this being why the CAMA has always paid due attention, not only to the keeping and maintenance of the registers, but also to the preservation of company records. This is for a reason.

For instance, under section 735 CAMA 2020, (s. 555), where the Attorney General of the Federation applies to a Judge of the Federal High Court, in chambers, that he has reasonable suspicion that a person has committed an offence in the management of a company and that the documents to establish the crime are with the particular company, the Judge may:

- make an order authorizing the person mentioned therein to inspect the document or obtain evidence in that regard; or
- require the company secretary or any other officer named in the order, to produce the said documents to the person named in the order.

We have seen the importance placed on the records of a company and the central place occupied by the company secretary in producing same, when ordered by the Court to do so. In consequence, therefore, it cannot be over-emphasized, the importance of proper keeping of the registers and records of a company and in easily accessible and retrievable condition, when needed, even if not stored in a legible form.

In terms of the forms and structure of keeping company records, section 731 (1) CAMA 2020, (s. 550) provides that any register, record, index, minute book or book of account required to be kept by a company can be kept in bound form or loose leaves, in a photographic film form or any information storage device that will be able to reproduce same without hindrances. Once the storage device is what is acceptable in commercial usage, and the documents stored therein are easily retrievable and usable, the CAMA is not particular about the means of keeping registers or documents in a company's records.

The above notwithstanding, the provision of section 864 CAMA 2020 should be noted carefully. It is to the effect that, companies are mandated to retain documents that are stored pursuant to the Act, in soft copy, for a period of six (6) years from the date of storage. This would seem to suggest that the mandatory requirement for storage of documents in soft copies by a company ends after six (6) and becomes voluntary, except this continues under some other laws and regulations, like the *Nigeria Data Protection Act (NDPA) 2023*, where applicable.

For statutory returns, their importance cannot be over-emphasized, especially within the context of transparency and corporate governance. The public, potential investors and creditors want to know what the state of affairs is in the company they intend to deal with. These returns filed with the Commission is an 'open window' of sorts, through which people can look into the company, before deciding whether to walk in through the door or not for business.

We now consider below some of the specific statutory registers, Returns and records provided for under the CAMA.

REGISTER AND INDEX OF MEMBERS

Under section 109 CAMA 2020, (s. 83), every company is mandated to keep a register of its members. The section does not state categorically the manner in which the register of members is to be kept, but as noted above, section 731 CAMA 2020, (s. 550) has provided a guide as to the form the register or other records will take. The register of members is one of the first and most important corporate governance disclosure instruments in a company, showing the public who the members are, the nature and volume of their shareholdings, etc.

The register of members is very important to a company for many other reasons: it helps a company in putting a tab on who the members are and on its numerical and shareholder base and spread. More importantly, however, the register helps creditors to identify those behind the company, which may affect how they will take a decision either to offer credit facility to or invest in the company. The register of members is also usually under constant monitoring by public companies, in order to detect early enough, persons who are gradually building up their stakes in the company in order to launch a takeover *(Hannigan, 322).*

In all of the above, the most important value of the register of members, it has been held, is that it is the register of members and not the share certificate that is the document of title to shares in a company. The share certificate is only an acknowledgement by the company that the person mentioned in it is duly recorded in the register of members *(Inland Revenue* v. *Wilson (1928) SC 42; Charlesworth & Cain, 194).* It has also been held that a company has no power to create a right of pledge or lien over its register of members, being that doing so would deny the public the right of access to and inspection of the register, which right has been granted to the public by statute *(Liquidator of Garpel Co. Ltd* v. *Andrew (1866) 4 M. 617; Charlesworth & Cain, 194).*

Content of the Register of Members

The register of members maintained by every company in compliance with the CAMA shall contain the following particulars:

- the names and addresses of the members;
- a statement of the shares and class of shares (for companies with share capital) held by each member, each share being distinguished by its

number once it has a number, and of the amount paid or agreed to be paid on the shares of each member;

- the date on which each person became a member of the company;
- the date on which any person ceased to be a member of the company (s. 109(1)(a)(b), (s. 83 (1) (a)(b).

The entries required to be made in the register of members under section 109(1)(a) (b), (83 (1)(a)(b) of the Act shall be made within 28 days after the agreement with the company for the person to be a member was concluded. For a person that subscribed to the Memorandum, then 28 days after the company was formed. In the event of a person ceasing to be a member of a company, the relevant information in that respect is also to be entered in the register of members within 28 days after a person ceased to be a member in a company (s. 109(2)(3), (s. 83 (2)(3).

Where a company incurs liability with respect to the entry in or deletion of any matter from its register of members, an action to enforce same against the company shall be statute barred after a period of 20 years (s. 109(5), (s. 83(5). On face value, it is not clear why the statute bar period for this subject is up to 20 years, which is even more than the period to sue for recovery of dividends in a company or to recover interests in land, which is 12 years, and for enforcement of contractual rights, which is usually 6 years. The register of members is, therefore, a very important legal document in company practice.

Location of Register of Members

Generally, a company's register of members is to be kept at the company's registered office, except under some circumstances, that is:

- where the work of making up the register is done at another office of the company, then, the register may be kept at that office; or
- where a company arranges for another person to make up its register of members, then the register may be kept at that office, once it is not outside of Nigeria (s. 110 (1), (s. 84 (1).

With respect to the location of its register, every company is mandated by the CAMA to send a notice to the Commission regarding any change in the location of its register of members. However, a company is not required to send a notice to the Commission if the register has always been kept at its registered office (s. 110 (2), (s. 84(2). The register is usually treated as *prima facie*, but not conclusive, evidence of any matter the Act requires to be in it. Being *prima facie* evidence, the authenticity of any information therein can be rebutted by superior evidence *(Reese River Silver Mining Co* v. *Smith (1869) LR, 4; Hannigan, 321).*

The prohibition, under the CAMA 2004, of the entry of notice of any trust, whether express, implied or constructive, into the register of members and the receipt of notice of any such trusts by the Commission, has been omitted in CAMA 2020. With this omission, it would appear that shares held in trust are now allowed by the CAMA and same may be sent to the Commission for registration by the trustee.

INDEX OF MEMBERS

By section 111(1)(2) CAMA 2020, (s. 85 (1), where a company has more than 50 members, it shall, except where its register of members is in such a manner as to constitute an index by itself, keep an index of the names of the members of the company. The company shall also make alteration to the index of members within 14 days after an alteration has been made to the register of members.

The index of members shall be located at the same place as the register of members and shall contain sufficient information in relation to a member to make it easy to locate the member's account in the register of members (s. 111(3)(4), (s. 85 (2)(3).

Inspection of the Register and Index

Except in cases where a company closes its register of members under any of the provisions of the CAMA, the register and the index of members shall be open during business hours for inspection by any member without any charge, and by any other person on the payment of the prescribed fees. The company may impose reasonable conditions in a general meeting allowing not less than two (2) hours a day for any inspection to be carried out by a member without a charge (s. 112(1), (s. 87(1).

A member may or any person with the permission of the company, require a copy of the register or part of it. In this respect, on the payment of the prescribed fees the company is mandated to send a copy to the person within 10 days from the day he met the requirement for getting a copy (s. 112(2), (s. 87(2).

As an established principle of company law, a member applying to inspect a company's register of members need not state the reason(s) for the inspection. The fact that his motive(s) for wanting an inspection of the register is hostile to the interests of the company, would not warrant a refusal to allow an inspection *(Holland* v. *Dickson (1888) 27 Ch.D., 679; Mutter* v. *Eastern & Midlands Railway (1888) 28 Ch.D., 92)*. Under the common law, the right to inspect a document, record or register includes a right for the person to make an extract of any portion of the document or register *(Mutter* v. *Eastern & Midlands Railway (1888) 28 Ch.D., 92; Nelson* v. *Anglo American Land Mortgage Agency Co. (1897) 1 Ch, 130; Mayson et al., 132)*.

However, the common law right of taking extracts on inspection of a document, record or register is usually deemed to have been restricted implicitly where the relevant legislation (here the CAMA) imposes a fee for extracts to be taken *(Re Balaghat Mining Co (1901) 2 KB, 665; Palmers, 734)*. This presupposes that although the member's right to take extract of a document or register is intact, it cannot be activated for use if the prescribed fee for inspection and taking of extract is not paid by the person in question (the applicant).

A fine is imposed on the company and any defaulting officer where a member is refused inspection of the register or where a person's request for a copy of the register or part thereof is not sent within the prescribed time. In any case, where inspection of the register is denied, a Court may by order, on the application by the person involved, compel an immediate inspection of the register and index, or direct that copies shall be sent to the person(s) that require them (s. 112(3)(4), (s. 87 (3)(4).

COMPANY'S POWER TO CLOSE REGISTER

A company may close its register of members or any part of it for any time(s), but the period of any such closure shall not exceed thirty (30) days in each year. It is said that this closure of register is usually for the company concerned to have a correct assessment of its membership in order to be able to plan to declare dividends, bonus shares, or other benefits to its members. However, to close its register of members, a company has to give notice of the intended closure of its register by advertisement in a newspaper circulating locally in the area in which the registered office of the company is situate (s. 114 CAMA 2020), (s. 89).

One would have thought that the newspaper publication required here would have been in a national daily newspaper, as against a local newspaper circulating around the location of the company's head office. This is because, for some companies, the membership is spread across the country and a publication in a newspaper circulating only where the head office is situate, will not be effective communication. Another issue will be whether this requirement for publication in a newspaper is necessary and cost-effective for private family-owned companies, where the directors and members are, for instance, a husband, his wife and their children? We even have one-member company now under the CAMA 2020. Communication of the closure of register to those involved is in order but the means of communicating same could also be localized. For instance, instead of publication in a newspaper by all companies, this could be limited to public companies only.

POWER OF THE COURT TO RECTIFY REGISTER

The Court has the power to rectify a company's register of members. It is a discretionary power, which must be exercised as such by the Court. Rectification will be ordered when the Court is satisfied, that:

- the name of a person is, without sufficient cause, entered in or omitted from the register of members; or
- mistake is made or unnecessary delays takes place in entering in the register of members the fact that a person has ceased to be a member in the company.

In either of the instances above, the person aggrieved or any member of the company may apply to Court for a rectification of the company's register of members, and the Court may refuse the application or order that the register of members be rectified (s. 115 CAMA 2020), (s. 90 (1) (2).

As noted above, it should be noted that the Court's power to order rectification of register is a discretionary power and the Court will not exercise such a power if there is a complicated question to be tried *(Pelling* v. *Families Need Fathers Ltd (2002) 2 All ER 440; Re Leo Needham Ltd (1966) 110 SJ, 652*). The same would be the case where injustice would be caused to other members of the company who have not been represented in the proceedings *(Re Sussex Brick Co. (1904) 1 Ch, 598*; *Mayson et al, 399)*. In the latter case, the Court will refuse to order rectification or ask that those that might be prejudiced by any order of rectification be put on notice. Where the persons concerned were already put on notice, the Court may still adjourn the application and insist that the persons should appear to show cause why the order of rectification should not be made, or otherwise.

Note should be taken that an order for rectification of the register can still be made even when the company is being wound-up. The Court also has the discretion, in all cases of rectifying the register, to award damages against the company and in favour of the aggrieved party (Charlesworth & Cain, 195).

REGISTER OF MEMBERS' INTEREST IN SHARES

This genre of register is not required to be kept by a private company as defined under section 22 of the CAMA.

Under section 122 (1) CAMA 2020, (s. 97 (1), a public company is mandated to keep a register in which it shall enter the following particulars:

- an alphabetical order of the name of persons from which it has received a notice under section 121 (s. 96) of the Act (the section relates to a substantial shareholder in a public company, that is, a person who ceases to be a substantial shareholder is required to give a notice in writing to the company stating his name, the day he ceased to be so and the circumstances that led to that. A substantial shareholder is a person who holds shares, by himself or by a nominee, that entitles him to exercise at least five (5) per cent of the unrestricted voting rights at any of the company's general meeting. (The shareholding threshold under the CAMA 2004 was ten (10) per cent).
- against the name of each person in the register the information given in the notice received under section 121 above.

The register of interest in shares shall be kept in the same location and inspected under the same rules as the register of members under sections 109 and 110 above (ss. 84 and 87). The Commission may, at any time, write to a company to furnish it with a copy or part thereof of the register and the company would have 14 days to comply with such a request (s. 122 (2)(3), (s. 97 (2)(3).

A company that ceases to be a public company is still mandated to keep a register of interest in shares until six (6) years after it ceases to be a public company (s. 122(4), (s. 97(4). A fine, to be prescribed by the Commission, is imposed on the company and every defaulting member for failure to comply with the above provisions.

RECORD OF INSTRUMENT CREATING A CHARGE

Every company is mandated to keep a copy of every instrument creating any charge for which registration with the Commission is mandatory. The copy of any such instrument shall be kept at the registered office of the company. Where there are series of uniform debentures, a copy kept of one of the debentures of the series is enough to satisfy this requirement (s. 215 CAMA 2020), (s. 190).

COMPANY'S REGISTER OF CHARGES

Under section 216 CAMA 2020, (s. 191 (1), every company is mandated to keep a register of charges and enter in the register all charges affecting the property of the company and all floating charges on the undertaking or any property of the company. The register is to be kept at the registered head office of the company.

The entries in the register of charges shall give, in each case, the following particulars;

- a short description of the property charged;
- the amount of the charge;
- except in the case of securities to bearer, the name of the persons entitled to the charges.

For a wilful failure by an officer of a company to permit an entry into the register of charges, he is liable to a fine, to be prescribed by the Commission (s. 216 (2), (s. 191 (2). It has been held that a charge does not become ineffective in any way for lack of entry into the register of charges (*Wright* v. *Horton (1887) 12 AC, 371, Mayson et al, 360).* Important information to the public on the state of the company's register of charges may be lost when charges are not entered therein, with attendant legal and corporate governance implications. The thinking is that, apart from the fine that the Commission could imposed on an officer of the company for failure to enter details of charges in the register, the company itself will have to bear the responsibility if the omission misleads a third party into acting to his detriment.

Inspection of the Register and Instrument

A copy of an instrument creating a registrable charge and the register of charges shall be open for inspection during business hours at least two (2) hours in each day by any creditor or member of the company without a fee. Also, the company may, in a general meeting, impose reasonable terms as to the time of the inspections.

The register of charges shall also be open for inspection to any other person who is not a member of the company, on the payment of a fee prescribed by the Commission, even much less so, by the company itself. Note the new provision by the CAMA 2020 that the Commission is entitled to request for and obtain a copy of the register of charges from a company without any fee and without any restriction (s. 217 (1), (s. 192 (1). It was not provided for under the CAMA 2004.

A continuing fine, to be specified by the Commission, is imposed on every officer of the company who is in default in refusing an inspection of the copies of the instrument creating a charge or the register of charges. On application, the Court may, by order, compel an immediate inspection of the copies of instrument or register (s. 217(2)(3), (s. 192 (2)(3).

REGISTER OF DEBENTURE HOLDERS

A company which issues or had issued debentures is mandated to maintain a register of the debenture holders (s. 218 CAMA 2020), (s. 193(1). The register is mandatorily required to contain the following information:

- the names and addresses of the debenture holders;
- the principal of the debentures held by each of them;
- the amount or the highest amount of any premium payable on the redemption of the debentures;
- the issue price of the debenture and the amount paid up on the issue price;
- the date on which the name of each person was entered on the register as a debenture holder; and
- the date on which each person ceased to be a debenture holder (s. 218(2), (s. 193 (2).

The entry required here shall be made in the register of debenture holders within 30 days of the conclusion of the agreement with the company to become a debenture holder or within thirty (30) days of ceasing to be a debenture holder (s. 218(3), (s. 193 (3).

Inspection of the Register of Debenture Holders

Except when the register of debentures is duly closed, it shall be open for inspection at least two (2) hours during business hours by any debenture holder or member of the company without a fee. The company may, in a general meeting, impose reasonable terms as to the time of the inspections. What would amount to reasonable terms is subjective. The register of debenture holders shall also be open to any other person who is not a debenture holder or a member of the company, on the payment of the prescribed fees (s. 219 (1) CAMA 2020), (s. 194 (1). Note the new proviso by the CAMA 2020 that the Commission may apply to a company at any working hours for a copy of the register of debentures and same shall be made available to them without any charge or restriction. This was not provided for under the CAMA 2004.

A debenture holder or any other person may require a copy or part thereof of the company's register of debenture holders on the payment of fees as determined by the Commission or such lesser fess fixed by the company itself. Also, a copy of the trust deed for securing any issue of debentures shall, on request, be forwarded to every holder of any such debenture on payment of prescribed fees (for a copy or for printing the deed and copy thereof) (s. 219(2)(3), (s. 194 (2)(3).

A fine, to be determined by the Commission, is imposed on every officer of a company in default in refusing inspection, copying or for not forwarding copy as required. The Court may, on application, compel immediate inspection of the register or direct that copies shall be forwarded to persons who requested same (s. 219(4)(5), (s. 194 (4)(5).

Entry of Transfers in Register of Debenture Holders

We have seen early on in this book that debentures are generally transferable, although the terms in the debenture could contain some restrictions. When any debenture has been transferred, the transferor applies to the company which shall then enter in its register of debenture holders, the name of the transferee in the same manner and subject to the same conditions as if the application for entry were made by the transferee (s.220 CAMA 2020), (s.195). In the event that a company refuses to register a transfer of any debenture, it shall send a notice of refusal to the transferee within two (2) months after the date the transfer was lodged with the company. A fine, to be specified by the Commission, is imposed on the company and every officer in default of sending to the notice of refusal (s.221), (s.196).

The CAMA did not say what will happen after a transferee is notified by the company (presumably with reasons) that the transfer will not be registered. The position, most likely, will be that the transferee may have to approach the Court with credible evidence, joining the transferor and the company as possible parties, to have the Court to order registration of the transfer. The Court's decision on this issue will most likely be influenced, one way or the other, by the reason(s) to be adduced by the company for its refusal to register the transfer, *ab initio*.

REGISTER OF DIRECTORS' SHAREHOLDING

Every company is mandated under section 301 CAMA 2020, (s. 275 (1) to keep a register, showing, with respect to each director, (not its holding company) the number, description and amount of any shares or debentures in the company, the company's subsidiary or holding company or in a subsidiary of the company's holding company, which are held by, or in trust for him or of which he has a right to become the holder.

The proviso to the above is that the register in question need not include shares in any body corporate which is a wholly owned subsidiary of another body corporate. Also, where a transaction has occurred that made the director's interests not to be entered in the register, but he remains a director, the date, price and other consideration for that transaction shall also be indicated in the register. The nature and extent of the director's interests over the shares and debentures may be indicated in the register, if he so requires.

Location of the Register

The register of directors' shareholding shall be kept at the company's registered office or head office and shall be open for inspection during business hours (the company may by its Articles or in a general meeting, impose reasonable terms as to the time of the inspections) as follows:

- during the period beginning 14 days before the date of the company's annual general meeting and ending 3 days after the date of the conclusion of the meeting, the register shall be open to inspection of any member(s) or holder(s) of the company's debentures (weekends are not included in computing the days); and
- during the period stated above or any other period, the register shall be open to inspection by any person acting on behalf of the Commission. The Commission may, however, at any time request for the register or any part of it (s. 301(5)(7), (s. 275 (5)(7).

A company's register of directors' shareholding shall be produced at the commencement of a company's annual general meeting and shall remain open and accessible during the meeting to any person attending (s. 301(8), (s. 275(8). This is another good instrument of corporate governance disclosure to the members in a general meeting. Members would be able to see the directors who have bought substantial shares in the company and the shareholdings of other directors. This is very useful in publicly quoted companies or large private companies.

A fine, to be specified by the Commission, is imposed on every officer of a company in default with respect to making the necessary entries, allowing inspection, sending a requested copy within a reasonable time, or producing the register during the company's annual general meeting. For any inspection required but which is refused, the Court may by order, compel an immediate inspection of the register (s. 301(9)(10), (s. 275 (9)(10).

REGISTER OF DIRECTORS

The first thing the CAMA 2020 did was to unbundle the register of directors and secretaries under section 292 CAMA 2004, into separate independent registers. Now, section 318 CAMA 2020 has mandated every registered company to keep a register of its directors and has made much wider and comprehensive provisions in this regard than those in the CAMA 2004.

The register is to contain the requisite particulars of each person who is a director of the company and shall be located at the company's registered office. The Commission's registrar shall be notified of the location of the register for inspection and of any change thereto, except it has always been at the registered head office. A member is entitled to inspect the register without any charge but any other person will have to pay a prescribed fee. Where inspection has been refused by the company, on application, the Court may compel inspection.

Particulars Required of a Director in the Register

Section 319 CAMA 2020 specifies the particulars of each director that are required to be in the register of directors, as follows:

- full name and any other former name(s);
- service address (which may be the company's registered office address);
- business occupation (if any); nationality; date of birth
- phone number; and e-mail address.

REGISTER OF DIRECTOR'S RESIDENTIAL ADDRESSES

The CAMA 2020, in section 320, introduced this new register of directors' residential addresses, requiring every company to keep same. If the residential address is the same with the service address supplied in the register of directors, this present register should simply say so, once it is not the company's registered office that was used earlier.

Where a person becomes or ceases to be a director, or if there are changes in the residential address earlier supplied, the company shall, within 14 days thereof, inform the Commission of the change and the date on which such a change occurred. A person who become a director shall include the detail of the directorship and his consent to serve as such (s. 321).

It is not actually clear why the CAMA 2020 created a register of the residential addresses of the company directors. This is because all of the information that are required to be in the register are already in the company's custody, even so, that a director is allowed to use the company's registered office address as his own service address. The matter is even made worse because having asked for the directors' usual residential address and knowing the data protection implication of such an information, sections 324, 325, 326, 327, 328 and 329 of the Act were dedicated in trying to protect the privacy of the directors, and how their sensitive information, otherwise called protected information, may and may not be used in diverse ways. It is the submission of this book that the energy dissipated on the sections that created the register of directors' residential addresses was not worthwhile.

REGISTER OF COMPANY SECRETARIES

This register applies only to public companies, being that the appointment of a company secretary is now optional for private companies, with small companies excluded. Under section 336 CAMA 2020, every public company is mandated to maintain a register of its company secretary, whether individual or corporate. The particulars of the company secretary (for individuals) that are required to be in the register are as follows:

- full names and any former name(s);
- address;
- email address (s. 337).

The former names will not be necessary if they were changed before the company secretary turned 18 years or where the name(s) has not been used by the company secretary in the last 20 years.

Where the company secretary is a corporation, then the register shall contain:

- the registered name of the corporation;
- the corporation's registered office or head office;
- email address (s. 338).

A company shall notify to the Commission as to changes to the particulars in the register, for instance, a person becoming or ceasing to be a company secretary, within 14 days of the event happening. This will be in addition to filing the necessary Forms CAC 8A and CAC 8B, whichever is applicable. In the case of an appointment, to go with particulars of the secretary will be the person's consent to act as such in the company. The Form

CAC 8 for such an appointment will be filed with the Commission for full compliance. The CAMA 2020 does not have any provision for the inspection, either by the members or otherwise, of the register of company secretaries. Apparently, the register is simply meant for regulatory compliance and not for use by members and the public.

COMPANY'S MINUTES BOOKS

The CAMA 2020 exempted single member companies but otherwise requires every company to cause the minutes of all its proceedings at general meetings, all minutes of proceedings of its directors and managers to be entered in minutes books (s. 266(1), (s. 241). Such minutes, if purporting to be signed by the chairman of the meeting or the next meeting, shall be *prima facie* evidence of the proceedings. Therefore, unless where the Articles so provide, minutes of meetings are not conclusive evidence in themselves, other credible evidence may be led to contradict the minutes *(I.A.I Nig. Ltd* v. *Chika Bros Ltd (1990) 1 NWLR Pt. 124, 70).*

Where minutes have been made for any of the meetings as stated above, then, until the contrary is proved, the meeting shall be deemed to have been validly held and all appointments of directors, managers or liquidators duly made (s. 266(3), (s. 241 (3).

In the case of a one-member company, where the single member takes a decision that may be taken by members in a general meeting, and has effect as if agreed by the general meeting, he is obligated to provide the board with the details of that decision (s. 266(4).

A fine, to be specified by the Commission, is imposed on a company and any of its officer(s) in default in keeping minutes of meetings as provided for in this section.

Location and Inspection of Minutes Book

The minutes book of the proceedings of a company's general meetings shall be kept at its registered office, and shall be open during business hours for inspection (at least six (6) hours each day) by members, free of charge. (The company may, however, in its Articles or in a general meeting, impose reasonable restrictions on members' right of inspection) (s. 267 (1), (s. 242 (1). The CAMA did not go into details of what would amount to an unreasonable restriction in this context, and perspectives and interpretations will differ. It might ultimately be for the Courts to fill-in such a gap.

A member is entitled to request for the minutes and certified copies (certified by the company secretary) shall be sent to him within seven (7) days on the payment of the prescribed fees. A fine, to be specified by the Commission, is imposed on every officer of the company in default for not allowing inspection of the minutes book or for not sending the copy of the minutes to a member within the time limited to do so (s. 267(2)(3), (s. 242 (2)(3).

Where there is either a case of failure to allow inspection or to send a copy of the minutes to a member, the Court may, on the member's application, compel an immediate inspection or order that copies required be sent to such a member (s. 267(4), (s. 242 (4).

COMPANIES' ACCOUNTING RECORDS

Every company is mandated to keep its accounting records in the manner as prescribed by section 374 CAMA 2020, (s. 331). The accounting records of a company are not a register in the form of the other standard registers considered above, but they are statutory records that are meant to give a picture of the financial state of the company, as a business concern.

It is the duty of the company directors to prepare annual accounts (financial statements) for each year for the company (s. 377), (s. 334).

The company secretary does not need to be an expert in accounting, (even though a working knowledge of the subject is always handy), but needs to be familiar with the outline requirements concerning the content of the accounts. For instance, it should be taken as a given that a company secretary, especially in publicly quoted companies or large private companies, should be able to read, understand and interpret any company's financial statements, knowing when a company is in good health financially, in trouble or when trouble is looming in the horizon.

Most importantly, however, the company secretary needs to be familiar with the timing, approval, filing and distribution of the accounts, which forms the core of the secretary's duty in this respect, and which may be where the directors will need to rely on his expertise (*Mason, 40).*

A company is mandated to keep its accounting records so that they will be sufficient to show and explain the company's transactions and shall be such as to:

- disclose with reasonable accuracy, at any time, the financial position of the company; and

- enable the directors to ensure that any financial statements prepared by the company comply with the requirements of the CAMA as to the form and content of the company's financial statements (s. 374 (2), (s. 331 (2).

In particular, a company's accounting records shall contain the following information:

- entries from day to day of all sums of money received and expended by the company, and the matter in respect of which the receipt and expenditure took place; and
- a record of the company's assets and liabilities (s. 374(3), (s. 331 (3).
- If the company's business involves dealing in goods, the accounting records are mandated to contain:
- statements of stocks held by the company at the end of each of the company's financial year;
- all statements or stock-takings from which any statement of stock as is mentioned above has been or is to be prepared;
- except for goods sold in the way of ordinary retail trade, statements of all goods sold and purchased, showing the goods and the buyers and sellers in sufficient detail as to enable their identification (s. 374 (4), (s. 331 (4).

Location and Duration of Accounting Records

A company's accounting record shall be kept at its registered office or such other place(s) within Nigeria as the directors of the company think fit. The implication here is that no company can purport to keep its accounting records outside Nigeria while registered and operating in Nigeria. A company's accounting records shall, at all times, be open to inspection by the officers of the company (s. 375(1) CAMA 2020, (s. 332(1). It is curious that the inspection permitted of a company's accounting records under this section is limited only to officers of the company and members are not mentioned. Why are the members excluded from being able to inspect the company's accounting records, even those members who are well versed in accounting and financial matters? Is it meant to avoid issues emanating from such inspections by members constituting distractions to the directors and senior management? There is no clear answer on the face of the CAMA for this. It might be that the members will have to wait for the company's financial results usually presented during the annual general meetings, to have a picture of the company's financial health.

Further, under this section, subject to any direction(s) that may be given under the applicable Companies Winding-up Rules, a company is mandated to preserve its accounting records for a period of six (6) years from the date on which they were first made (s.375(2), (s.332 (2). It should be noted further that section 864 CAMA 2020 mandates every company and corporate bodies registered under the Act to keep documents stored pursuant to the Act in soft copies for six years from the date of storage.

The CAMA 2020 has provided that companies can store original hardcopies of documents but also electronic copies of any document, records or registers that are mandated to be kept under the Act. However, care should be taken to store them with good quality hardware and software, including the protocols, anti-viruses and encryption technologies (s.375(3). This is to ensure that the documents so stored will still be in perfect and uncorrupted conditions, both in their physical state and in content, whenever they are retrieved in the future for use.

ANNUAL RETURNS

Every company is expected, at least, once in a year, to prepare and deliver to the Commission its annual returns that are required under the Act for the company of the type mentioned (s. 417 CAMA 2020), (s. 371). For small companies and companies limited by guarantee, sections 419 and 420 CAMA 2020 (ss. 372 & 373) provide for the form their annual returns should take.

A company is mandated to complete and deliver its annual returns to the Commission not later than 42 days after the annual general meeting (AGM) for the year, whether or not the meeting is the company's first or only meeting for the year. There is room for the Commission, on application, to extend time for any company to file its annual returns. A one-member company is not affected by this provision. The annual return is to be accompanied by a certified copy (by director and company secretary) of the balance sheet and profit and loss account, that were laid before the general meeting held in the year the returns relate. A certified director's and auditor's report on the balance sheet shall also accompany the annual returns, but all the accompanying documents could be sent electronically to the Commission (ss. 421 & 422 CAMA 2020), (ss. 374 & 375).

A private and a small company shall send certificates accompanying their annual returns that they have not each respectively invited the public to subscribe shares (for private company) and has not ceased to maintain the conditions to be a small company (for small companies) (s. 423 CAMA 2020).

Annual returns are the most comprehensive of all the returns required from companies by the CAMA and advisedly so. This is because annual returns present an open source for most of the vital information on a company that anyone may be interested in. This is ranging from the information on the shareholders, their holdings, directors and secretaries, financial state of the company, movement of shares (selling and buying), the company's assets (encumbered or not) etc. For a company limited by shares, which is not a small company, the returns also contain facts on the statutory registers: register of members and debenture holders, shares and debentures, past and present members, and directors and secretary. The form of annual returns has since been standardized by the CAMA as part of the schedule to the Act.

The fact that annual returns are sent only to the Commission but not to the members or other stakeholders, implies that a search at the Commission will give an interested party a full view of the authentic state of affairs in the company. This is why non-filing of annual returns is viewed very seriously by the Commission and could, quite often, but not always, be a signal of mismanaged and troubled company.

The CAMA imposes a fine, to be prescribed by the Commission, on a company and every director or officer for failure to file annual returns.

From this chapter, it becomes clearer that the importance of keeping statutory registers and other statutory records and filing statutory returns by a company cannot be overemphasized. This is actually an aspect of the company law and practice that is almost exclusively under the control of the company secretary. The essence and effect of statutory registers and records differ in material particulars. This is because while some, like the register of directors and the register of secretaries, are mostly for information purposes, some registers, especially those that are for corporate governance disclosures and open to inspection by the members and the public, do have deeper implications, in most cases.

One of the aspects of companies keeping statutory registers to note is the consequences of not keeping them at all or not keeping them properly. Some of the statutory registers are sources of legitimacy in the issue of title, when there is a dispute in a particular area. For instance, it is the register of members that is actually the evidence of title when it comes to members' shareholding in a company. The share certificate is the acknowledgement of that title. Also, a statutory register, like the register of charges gives the public the true picture of the charges, in type and in volume that a company has in its records. This helps potential investors and potential creditors to be able to take informed and important decisions whether to deal with a company or not. There are other dimensions also that diverse fines have been imposed on any company and its officers that are in default in keeping the registers and records or for not sending in the returns to the Commission as prescribed. All these infractions, especially those that come with consequences, should be avoided.

Finally, then, the annual returns are the most comprehensive of the statutory returns filed by companies with the Commission, containing matters that touch on almost all aspects of the company's operations. They are one-stop resource materials for potential investors and creditors who are considering whether to deal with a company or not. When a company's annual returns are reviewed by trained hands, they can easily tell when a company is doing well, in trouble or potentially so. This explains why some companies manipulate the content of their annual returns, especially the aspects relating to their balance sheet and profits and loss accounts, to portray a picture away from the actual.

CHECKPOINTS

- ✓ The maintenance of statutory registers and records is one of the very specific duties that the CAMA prescribed for the company secretary. As has been shown above, it is an important aspect of company law and company administration, which requires detailed and constant attention to execute.
- ✓ The importance of statutory registers and records in the life a company, especially large private and publicly quoted companies, cannot be over-emphasized. This is because dealing with them carries the possibility of dual liability, most of the time, if not handled well: the first is that non-compliance with the terms of keeping the records and registers could attract fines from the Commission. Secondly, it could also expose the company to avoidable problems when the public could not ascertain from the badly kept register(s) that there were actually existing charges that were not entered in the register of charges, for instance, and relied on them to take important decisions about the company.
- ✓ The CAMA 2020 has made provisions that statutory records and registers can now be kept in photo film and electronic forms, once the modes of storage are in forms that are easily retrievable, when needed. This has made keeping of records and registers a lot easier.

- ✓ Equally important are the annual returns, which a company must file within 42 days after its annual general meeting (AGM), opening to the Commission and by implication, the public, the correct state of affairs in the company in the past year.
- ✓ Companies are mandated to retain documents that they have kept as statutory records and registers for a period of six (6) years from the date of the commencement of the storage. There is nothing that says that a company cannot continue to keep the documents after that time, especially with modern technologies simplifying and diversifying ways of documentary storage.
- ✓ Apart from few exceptions, like where a third party maintains the register of members for a company, the register of members is mandated by the CAMA to be kept at the company's registered office.
- ✓ Members have a right to inspect the register of members without a fee and it is a principle of common law that a member applying to inspect the register need not state any reason for wanting to do so. It could even be that the reason for the inspection is for a hostile reason, for example, planning a possible takeover of the company by a third party.
- ✓ The register of members is the central pivot in determining a company's shareholding base, being the actual document of title in determining a member's shareholding in a company. The share certificate is simply an acknowledgement that the member's shareholding has been recorded in the company's register of members.
- ✓ Once in a year, the company has the power to close its register of members (for not more than 30 days) to properly assess its shareholding base for diverse purposes. For example, a company may want to plan for dividends payment or bonus share issue to members.
- ✓ The Court is the only entity that has the power to rectify the register of members (and other statutory registers for that matter) for omissions, wrong insertions or delayed entry of members' information in the register.
- ✓ Court actions to enforce causes of action arising from delay, wrong insertions or omissions into the register of members cannot be maintained after 20 years, as same would have been statute barred. It is not clear why the limitation time is up to 20 years, as actions for most contracts and torts

abate after 6 years, while even actions to recover dividends from companies or for title to land abate after 12 years.

- ✓ There is also the register of members' interests in shares, relating to substantial shareholders in public companies (those having shareholding that gives them 5 per cent or more (reduced from 10 per cent under the CAMA 2004) of the total voting rights of shares of that class. The register is kept in the same location as the register of members.
- ✓ A company that ceases to be a public company is still mandated to maintain its register of members' interests in shares for another six (6) years after ceasing to be so.
- ✓ There is also a company's register of charges, which is kept to give all persons and the public a clear view of all the charges affecting the company's properties and the floating charges affecting its undertakings. Most potential investors and creditors usually start their due diligence on a company from here.
- ✓ The register of debenture holders has the important particulars of the holders: names, addresses, principal sum secured, date a person was entered therein and the date he ceased to be a holder etc. This register is one of the corporate governance disclosures and is open for inspection by a holder without a fee, except when it is closed or based on conditions imposed thereon by the company in a general meeting.
- ✓ A debenture is transferable and the transfer is usually entered in the register of debenture holders on the application of the transferor. If a company declines to register the transfer, it shall inform the transferee within two (2) months of the transfer being lodged with the company for registration.
- ✓ The register of directors' shareholdings is for the details of the shares and interests in debentures held by directors in a company (not being a holding company), or held in trust for them of which they have the right to become the holders. This register is usually kept at the company's registered office.
- ✓ The register of directors and secretaries has now been separated and made into two (2) independent registers. Even as separate registers they still contain basic particulars of the directors and the company secretary

respectively, apart from the addition of email addresses and phone numbers.

- ✓ The CAMA 2020 also introduced the register of directors' residential addresses, the utility of which is not very clear at this point. This is because the details and information about the directors that have to be in it are those that the companies already have in their possession.
- ✓ Every company, except a single member company is mandated to keep minutes book of the meetings of its managers, directors and its general meetings. It is usually kept at the company's registered office and open to inspection by members without a fee at least six (6) hours per day on working days. Minutes books are, *prima facie*, evidence of what is contained therein, except if contradicted successful by superior evidence.
- ✓ The statutory records of accounts are not really registers in the ordinary sense but records that are meant to give, with reasonable accuracy, the financial position or state of the company. It is kept at the company's registered office and officers of the company are allowed to inspect same without a fee. There is no provision in the CAMA for the members to inspect a company's accounting records.
- ✓ Statutory registers, records and returns constitute a bunch of corporate governance disclosure instruments, giving the members and sometimes, the public, a view of the state of affairs of different aspects of the company, from its charges, debentures, and membership, to its shareholdings, among others. They are usually veritable resources for potential investors and creditors for due diligence before taking decisions as to whether to engage in business relations with a company or not.

Chapter 19

DIVIDEND

INTRODUCTION

In simple terms, a dividend has been described as the payment made to shareholders from a company's profits (properly termed 'distributable profits') from time to time *(Kotoye* v. *Saraki (1994) 7 NWLR Pt. 357, 414, 467; Henry* v. *Great Northern Railway Co. (1857)1 De G 7 J,* 606*).* A dividend is also said to be the sum of money that is received by a shareholder as his share of the profits earned by the company. As will be seen below, the materiality of the aspect of paying dividends from 'profits' is pivotal in this discourse. Aside this, the volume of dividend receivable by a shareholder is normally measured by his shareholding in the company. It is usually taken for granted that those who possess larger volumes of shares of the class get higher levels of dividends than those with lesser volumes of shareholding (*Oakbank Oil Co.* v. *Cram (1882) 8 AC 65; Orojo, 323).*

Under section 868 CAMA 2020, (s. 567) dividend is said to mean 'a proportion of the distributed profits of the company which may be a fixed annual percentage, as in the case of preference shares, or it may be variable according to the prosperity or other circumstances of the company, as in the case of equity shares.'

The payment of dividend is one of the commonest ways through which a company, as a going concern, could legally distribute part of its profits to its shareholders. There are other means of making distributions to shareholders, which are not, strictly speaking, dividends, but still offer, ultimately, positive financial gains for shareholders involved. Some examples of these are bonus shares and scrip dividend, which though termed dividend, is actually the issuance of additional shares to the members involved in place of cash dividend. The scrip dividend alternative (some companies even issue enhanced scrip dividend) helps to preserve the liquidity in a company, especially one that is experiencing any issue of cash flow shortages *(Pike & Neale, Corporate Finance & Investment (Decisions and Strategies, 472-473*).

Back to the issue of dividends, it is important to note that there is no rule that makes it mandatory for a company to distribute its profits in a particular year, manner, or within a particular period *(Burland* v. *Earle (1902) AC, 83; Mayson et al., 316)*. The issue of declaring a dividend is always on the recommendation of a company's board of directors and subsequent approval by the general meeting. There are still some principles that guide the declaration of dividend by companies as declarations are not at large. Some of these principles are discussed below.

A COMPANY'S POWER TO PAY DIVIDEND

Except for any restrictions that may have been imposed by a company's Memorandum and Articles, a company has an implied power to transfer distributable profits to its shareholders in the form of dividend. However, as already noted, this implied power does not mean that the company is bound to or could be coerced by judicial action to pay dividend to its shareholders at any given time *(Palmers, 780)*. Under section 426 (1) CAMA 2020), (s. 379) a company is given the discretion to declare a dividend during its general meeting in respect of a particular year or other periods only on the recommendation of its board of directors *(Re Exchange Banking Co. Flitcroft's Case (1882) 21 Ch.D., 519; Charlesworth & Cain, 538)*. This seems to be one of the areas in company law and practice where the exercise of directors' discretion seems to be absolute, in the sense that there appears to be no power inherent in the members in a general meeting, as the owners of the company, to force directors to declare a dividend in a particular year. This is notwithstanding the fact that the company could be very liquid and may be declaring huge operating profits over several years. The solution would appear to be for the members to exercise their overriding powers to remove and replace any director(s), in a general meeting, who appears to be underperforming in his 'duties' to the members.

Although company directors could, acting within their powers, recommend a declaration of dividend during a company's general meeting, a company is however prohibited from declaring or paying dividend to its shareholders if there exists any reasonable ground(s) to believe that the company is, or would be, unable to pay its liabilities as they become due, if it pays any dividend (s. 428 CAMA 2020), (s. 381). As a general principle, in recommending the amount of dividend to be paid to shareholders, the directors must have regard to the general interests of the shareholders in their entirety. In essence, the decision of directors in relation to declaring a dividend should not to be seen to favour one class of shareholders at the expense of the others. Any such discriminatory decision stands to be set aside by the Court on application of a member, being a breach of the directors' fiduciary duty to always act in the best interests of the members, as a whole (*Henry* v. *Great Northern Railway Co. (1857) 1 De G 7 J*, 606; *Mayson et al., 316).*

As noted above, another important point is that a shareholder, even if a preference shareholder, cannot claim any dividend from a company until the company has resolved through its board of directors to pay dividend and has declared same *(Bond* v. *Barrow Haematite Steel Co. (1902) 1 Ch 353; Charlesworth & Cain, 539).*

The wisdom underlying the above principle can be understood from two (2) related perspectives: the first is that to allow a shareholder the right and power to sue a company to declare dividend, notwithstanding the basis for such, will be to create unmitigated chaos in the company. This is because lots of law suits will be filed based on the whims and caprices of the members. This situation will pose serious existential risks to the company. The second is that the company's directors, in deciding either to recommend the payment of dividend to members or not, do usually require and use a complete and detailed financial position of the company, including a detailed information on the company's assets and investments *(Re City Equitable Fire Ins. Co. Ltd (1925) Ch., 407; Charlesworth & Cain, 539).* The members do not have access to such information and will be 'acting blindly and emotionally,' so to say, in demanding for dividend to be declared by the company, based on limited and incomplete financial information.

PAYMENTS OF DIVIDEND FROM DISTRIBUTABLE PROFITS

Under section 426(5) CAMA 2020, (s. 379 (5), every company is mandated, subject to the provisions of the Act, to only pay dividend to its shareholders out of its distributable profits. The term 'distributable profit' is not defined in the Act, and, as will be seen shortly, in attempting to explain what the term means, the Act ended up using several other terminologies that would themselves require definition. It is the submission of this book that the juridical approach, which defines the term 'distributable profits' as a term used to refer to the part of a company's overall profits that has been deemed by the directors to be available for the payment of dividend, that is, after making provisions for past losses, reserves and other purposes, is to be preferred *(Re Buenos Aires Great Southern Railway (1947) Ch., 384; Long*

Acre Press Ltd v. *Oldhams Press (1930) 2 Ch., 196; Charlesworth & Cain, 539).*

What the CAMA 2020 did in terms of isolating what 'distributable profits' are is to say that a company may pay dividends only out of profits available for that purpose (s. 427 (1). The CAMA 2004, on the other hand, itemized revenues and profits from which a company could pay dividend, as:

- profits arising from the use of the company's property, even if it is wasting asset (wasting assets are things like cars, trucks, clothes, shoes, machineries-generally, things that depreciate in value and quality with continued use);
- revenue reserve;
- realized profit on a fixed asset sold, but where more than one asset is sold, the net realized profit on the assets sold.

It could be seen that the term 'wasting assets,' used by the CAMA 2004, in trying to explain the term 'distributable profits' also required a definition or explanation to be generally understood.

The CAMA 2020 in trying to avoid this pitfall that befell the CAMA 2004 on 'distributable profits,' entered even a worse quagmire itself. Under section 427 (2), the Act provides that the profits of a company available for payments of dividends are its accumulated, realized profits (so far as not previously utilized by distribution or capitalization), less its accumulated, realized losses (so far as not previously written off in a lawfully made reduction or reorganization of capital).

So, the question is: for a person who is not deeply versed in business, finance or accounting, what does this section 427 (2) CAMA 2020 actually say, in essence? And this is the CAMA 2020 that created a single member company, where regular, not too literate businessmen that should have normally registered a business name, will now incorporate limited liability companies? What would they make of a provision like this? Even if we are following the principles of common law, sometimes a little bit of local peculiarities should come into play, when adapting and implementing legislation from developed countries. This book submits, that Nigeria of 2023, is not ripe for a single-member company, being that such a company will virtually not be subject to any regulation, or put differently, will not submit itself, to a large extent, to regulatory oversights. This is because to run a single-member company, taking all sensitive legal and corporate governance-related decisions within the ambits of the law and meeting all regulatory compliance requirements, including holding single-member general meetings, require a high level of personal discipline on the part of the single member. This involves a committed show of good faith and fidelity from the single member, to make all the requisite returns to the Commission and keep all requisite registers and records without being pressured to do so. It does not seem an easy ask.

Another question that arises is whether a company that is not a single-member company at inception can now be converted or re-registered, as it were, to a single member company after the coming into effect of CAMA 2020? From the express provision of the Act, it does not appear that conversion or registration from a conventional to a single-member company is envisaged by the CAMA 2020. This is because under section 18(1) of the Act, it started by saying 'as from the commencement of this Act, any two or more persons may form and incorporate a company…' Then section 18(2) states that 'notwithstanding subsection (1), one person may form and incorporate a private company by complying with the requirements of this Act…'

Two things come out from the above provisions: (i) the single-member company regime started with the commencement of CAMA 2020, and applies to companies incorporated after that date. The Act became operational from the 9th of August 2020 when the Bill was assented to by the President of Federal Republic of Nigeria. This being the case, it is clear that companies incorporated under the CAMA, LFN 2004, are not able to benefit from this provision. (ii) Section 869 CAMA 2020 expressly repealed the CAMA, LFN 2004, and incidental legislations. Therefore, there could be no application of its provisions by importation of any sorts into the application of the provisions of CAMA 2020. To do otherwise, will be to read into the Act what the legislators did not put there.

In sum, therefore, any person who operates a conventional incorporated company registered under the CAMA, LFN 2004, and who wants to operate a single-member company would have to incorporate a single-member company afresh under the CAMA 2020 and voluntarily wind-up the existing company.

Further Requirements for Banks on Dividends

Apart from the above general restrictions imposed by the CAMA on companies intending to pay dividend to members, the *Banks and other*

Financial Institutions Act (BOFIA) 2020 and the *Nigerian Deposit Insurance Corporation Act (NDIC)* 2006 (as amended) impose further specific restrictions on any bank that intends to pay dividend to its members. Under section 16 of the BOFIA, no bank is permitted to pay dividend on its shares, until:

- all its preliminary expenses, organizational expenses, shares selling commission, brokerage, amount of losses incurred and other capitalized expenses not represented by tangible assets have been completely written off;
- adequate provisions have been made to the satisfaction of the Central Bank of Nigeria (CBN), for actual and contingent losses on risk assets, liabilities, off balance sheet commitments and such unearned incomes as are derivable from these;
- the bank has complied with any capital ratio requirement specified by the CBN;
- It has satisfied any other corporate governance and prudential requirements that may be stipulated by the CBN;
- section 18 of the NDIC Act 2006 provides that without prejudice to the provisions of the BOFIA, 'no insured institution shall pay any dividend on its capital stock or from profits declared while it remains in default on the payment of any premium obligation due or special contribution due to the corporation.'

The BOFIA imposes a fine and/or term of imprisonment on any director, manager or officer of a bank that contravenes the above provision; while the NDIC Act imposes only a fine on such persons.

GENERAL PRINCIPLES ON PAYMENT OF DIVIDENDS

Over the years, certain cardinal principles that regulate the payment of dividend by companies to their shareholders have crystallized. There have also been judicial pronouncements affirming most of the principles, as shown below:

- dividend may not be paid out of a company's capital (except as authorized by the relevant legislation, which is hardly ever the case as the Courts have always invalidated such attempts). This is because any such payment would amount to an unauthorized reduction of the company's capital *(Ammonia Soda Co.* v. *Chamberlain (1918) 1 Ch., 266; Fisher* v. *Black and White Publishing Co. (1901) 1 Ch., 174).*

- if a payment of dividend out of a company's capital is authorized by the company's Memorandum or Articles, or by a special resolution of the company, it would still be invalid for being in contravention of the relevant legislation as an illegal reduction of the capital of the company *(Trevor* v. *Whitworth (1887) 12 A.C. 409; Gower & Davies, 305).*
- a company's general meeting does not have the power to authorize that dividend be paid out of its capital, in contravention of the relevant legislation and capital maintenance rules *(Re Exchange Banking Co. Flitcroft's Case (1882) 21 Ch.D., 519).*
- all directors of a company who knowingly pay, or are parties to the payment of dividend out of the company's capital, shall be personally liable jointly and severally to refund to the company the amount so paid (s. 433 CAMA 2020), (s. 386 (1); *(Re Exchange Banking Co. Flitcroft's Case (1882) 21 Ch.D., 519; Charlesworth & Cain, 538).* The common law principle is actually based purely on wrongful payment to members by the directors and the 'knowingly' added by the CAMA, which imports *mens rea,* will tend to complicate the application of the rule and is not part of the requirement for liability to attach *(Bairstow* v. *Queens Moat Hose Plc (2001) 2 BCLC, 531; Re Paycheck Services 3 Ltd (2009) 2 BCLC, 309).*
- such directors as above shall have the right to recover the dividend so paid to the shareholders, if the shareholders received same with full knowledge that the company had no power to pay such dividend to them at the time of payment (s. 433), (s. 386(2).

It is difficult to comprehend the intent of the preceding provision, which is to pitch a director(s) against the company shareholders in needless and potentially destructive litigation. It has never been the duty of the shareholders to forensically audit the powers of directors to determine if they are properly exercising same in paying dividends. In the British case, *It's a Wrap (UK) Ltd* v. *Gula (2006) 2 BCLC, 634*; *(Hannigan, 518)*, where the shareholders were held liable to return the dividend paid to them by the company, the peculiarities are huge, in the sense that it was a private company, owned by a husband and wife, who were the only shareholders and were also the only directors. It was therefore easy to make presumptions on their culpability as regards the payment of unauthorized dividend to themselves.

In another case in which the dividend paid to members was asked to be returned to the company by the recipients, that is, *Precision Dippings Ltd* v. *Precision Dippings Marketing Ltd (1985) BCLC, 385*, it was a payment by a subsidiary company to its parent company. Here, also, the directors of the subsidiary company were the only directors and members of the parent company. It was easy to impute and establish knowledge of the illegality of the payment to them. It is unimaginable how the decisions in these cases could be applied, for example, to a publicly quoted company in Nigeria or elsewhere, with thousands of shareholders.

In essence, therefore, it would be wrong, in every material particular, to rely on the decisions in these cases, or on others with such peculiar facts, as precedent, that it is possible to easily determine when members have knowledge that the directors were exceeding their powers. In the *Gula* case above, the directors as managers of the company actually paid dividend to themselves as members knowing, without a doubt, that the company made no profits within the period.

The principle below has tried to deal with that aspect.

> where the shareholders received the dividend on the representations by the company's directors that such dividend being paid is out of the profits of the company, the shareholders shall not be accountable to refund such dividend and may sue the directors to replace the monies so paid out (*Re Exchange Banking Co. Flitcroft's Case (1882) 21 Ch.D., 519; Palmers, 794-5).*

INTERIM AND FINAL DIVIDEND

A company has the power, from time to time, to pay 'interim dividend' to shareholders as recommended by the directors, approved by the general meeting and justified by the profits of the company (s. 426(2) CAMA 2020, (s. 379 (2). This justification is usually based on the state of the company's accounts (finances) and on the estimates and opinion of the directors, as to the overall profitability of the company within the period in question *(Lucas* v. *Fitzgerald (1903) 20 TLR., 16).* An interim dividend is one that is paid to a company's shareholders between two annual general meetings of the company *(Re Jowitt (1922) 2 Ch., 442).* It has been held that an interim dividend declared by the directors may be revoked by them before it is paid. One potential and valid reason for this could be that the directors discovered, after declaration of the interim dividend, but before actual payment to the members, that the company's account on which their decision to declare dividend was based, was seriously inaccurate and misleading (*Re Cleveland Trust Plc (1991) BCLC, 424; Potel* v. *IRC (1971) 2 All ER, 504).*

A final dividend is the additional dividend that is declared and paid to shareholders in addition to the interim dividend paid (if any) both making up the full dividend receipt for the shareholders for the financial year in question. If a company declares no interim dividend for the year, then any dividend declared by the company for that year is the final dividend.

It is important to note that although the responsibility of recommending a declaration of dividend rests with the directors of a company, the general meeting is given the power to reduce the amount of dividend recommended by the directors. However, the general meeting has no power to increase the amount of dividend recommended by the board of directors. Where a company, in a general meeting, reduces the quantum of dividend recommended by its directors, a statement attesting to that fact shall be included in the company's annual returns to be filed at the Commission (s. 426(3)(4), (s. 379 (3)(4).

The possible reasons behind the principle disallowing the general meeting from being able to increase dividend payable to the members are many. The first is that the members, being mostly fixated on the volume of dividend that might come to them, would probably approve a volume of dividend that the company will be unable to pay, considering its finances. Secondly, the members as a body constituting the general meeting do not have the intricate details of, or knowledge, to dissect the company's accounts, to be able to make an informed decision on this subject. Thirdly, it is the directors that run the affairs of the company and are in the best position to determine the volume of dividend to be paid sustainably to the members, and the volume of the profits to be ploughed back into the company's business.

RESERVE AND CONSOLIDATION

It has been established above that a company has the power to transfer its distributable profits to its shareholders in the form of dividend. However, a company need not do that all the time, as it may not be a wise decision for a company to regularly distribute all its profits to the members. There has to be a plan(s) for contingencies and unplanned financial emergencies, and most companies do have it.

Company directors are given the power, before recommending any dividend to the general meeting, to set aside a part of the profits of the company for the year as they think fit, as the company's reserve(s). The directors shall have the discretion to determine the purpose to which the reserve would be applicable. While it appears that the directors have absolute discretion to decide whether or not to set aside any part(s) of the company's yearly profits as reserves, it does not appear that the directors have unfettered discretion with respect to how those reserves will be spent. This is because the CAMA insists that any such purpose(s) must be one of the purposes to which the company's profits may be properly applied.

Where a reserve fund has been established by a company, before the directors exercise their discretion on how to apply the fund, they may decide to channel the money back into the business of the company or into any such investments (other than buying of the company's shares) as the directors may deem fit from time to time. The directors also have the power, without creating any reserve funds for any of the company's profits, to carry forward any such profits which they think should not be distributed to the members at the material time. This is entirely at the directors' discretion (s. 430(1) CAMA 2020), (s. 383 (1).

While section 430 of the CAMA seems to have given company directors the discretion to decide whether to create a reserve fund for a company or not, section 15 of the BOFIA 2020 makes it mandatory for every bank to maintain a reserve fund. The section also provides for mandatory transfers by a bank into its reserve fund before any dividend is declared: (when the reserve fund is less than the company's paid-up share capital, to transfer 30 percent of the net profits to the reserve funds. Where, however, the reserve fund is equal to or more than the paid-up share capital, the company is to transfer a sum not less than 15 percent of the net profits to the reserve fund).

A COMPANY'S POWER TO CAPITALIZE FUNDS

A company is empowered under the CAMA to resolve in its general meeting, on the recommendation of its directors, to capitalize any part of any amount that from time to time stands to the credit of the company's reserve account, its profit and loss account or otherwise available for distribution (s. 430 (2), (s. 383(2). Such sums may be set free for distribution to the members of the company who would have been entitled to receive dividends in the same proportion *(Dimbula Valley (Ceylon) Tea Co. Ltd.* v. *Laurie (1961) Ch., 353; Thorne, 159).* Any distribution to members is subject to three conditions:

- it shall not be paid in cash to members;
- it shall be applied in paying up amounts that for the time being remained unpaid on any shares held by such members respectively; or

- it shall be applied in paying-up in full unissued shares or debentures of the company to be allotted and distributed to creditors as fully paid-up (s.430(3), (s. 383 (3).

The company may decide by a resolution in general meeting (ordinary resolution) what part of the fund set aside is to be distributed in cash or in shares, and the directors would be obliged to give effect to such a resolution by the members. The directors are given the power to issue fractional certificates or to pay in cash or otherwise as they would deem fit in the case of shares or debentures that are distributable in fractions (s. 430(4)(7), (s. 383 (4)(7).

A MEMBER'S RIGHT TO SUE FOR DIVIDEND

Once declared and payable by a company, a dividend is a debt to be paid by the company and any shareholder who is entitled to receive dividend is entitled to sue the company for it (*A.G. Federation & Anor* v. *Ijewere (1986) 4 NWLR Pt. 37, 659, 668; Godfrey Phillips Ltd* v. *Investment Trust Corp. Ltd (1953)1 All ER, 7; Gower & Davies, 869).* A shareholder's right to sue a company for declared dividend must be exercised within 12 years. It has been explained that the effect of a company's Articles with the share certificate, which is either under seal or executed as a deed, is to constitute the right to dividend into a specialty debt, which accordingly the shareholder has 12 years to recover *(Aerobell Nig. Ltd* v. *Fidelity Bank Plc (2018) LPELR-45338; Re Artizans' Land and Mortgage Corp. (1904) 1 Ch., 796; Palmers, 784).*

WHO IS ENTITLED TO DECLARED DIVIDEND?

The general rule is that as between a company and its shareholders, it is the person who is on the register of members as at the date when a dividend is declared that is entitled to such a dividend. This highlights the importance, as noted earlier, of the register of members for every company. Unless a person's name has been entered in the register of members of a particular company, his rights, where they exist at all, are inchoate, and cannot be enforced until his name is entered in the members' register. This includes the right to attend general meetings, receive dividends, apply to Court to wind-up a company, etc.

Also, a transfer of shares after a dividend has been declared by a company does not, as against the company, give the transferee the right to the dividend. However, as between the transferor and the transferee of the shares, the transferee is entitled to the dividend declared after the date of the contract for sale between them was executed, unless the parties agreed otherwise *(Re Wimbush (1940) Ch. 92; Black* v. *Homersham (1878) 4 Ex D, 24*; *Palmers, 784).* This is a slight exception to the exercise of membership rights, in the sense that once a member has sold his shares and executed all the sale documents, then he can no longer receive any benefits from the company, naturally, having exited. Conversely, while the member could be said to have surrendered his membership rights, mostly for value, to the transferee, on the other hand, the transferee cannot enjoy membership rights until his name is entered in the register of members. Until then, his membership rights are inchoate and unenforceable against the company and against other members of the company.

REVOCATION OF DECLARED DIVIDEND

Considering the fact that a dividend properly declared constitutes a debt owed by a company to the shareholders, such a declaration of dividend can, as a general rule, only be revoked with the consent of the shareholders. The consent may be given by the shareholders at any time before the payment of the dividend is made, provided that all the shareholders consent to the revocation (*Orojo, 327).* This would most likely be in a general meeting or by a circular resolution, where it is permissible.

It is possible that circumstances may warrant and justify that company directors decide to revoke an already declared dividend. Such circumstances may include:

- where the declaration of dividend has been found to be illegal;
- where intervening events after the declaration of dividend have seriously depleted the assets of the company and it is inadvisable to complete the payment of the dividend (*Ramaiya, Guide to the Companies Acts of India) 8th edn; Orojo, 327).*
- where a catastrophic event(s), profoundly affecting the company, follows the declaration of dividends, like an outbreak of war.

As discussed above, these circumstances would appear more appropriate in cases of declarations of interim dividends by the directors, however, not ruling out a revocation of declared dividend during catastrophic events, example, an outbreak of war, or a recent example, when the Covid-19 pandemic shut the world down. In the final analysis, therefore, it would appear that each situation will have to be decided on its own peculiar facts and merits.

DIVIDEND AND EMPLOYEE PROFIT SHARING

It has been stated that a cardinal principle of dividend payment is that a company can only pay dividend to its shareholders out of its distributable profits. Another point to make is that an employee profit sharing arrangement is not a distribution in the genre of dividend, cash or scrip dividend. Where, therefore, a person has been employed in a company, and as an incentive under his service contract, he is entitled to share in the profits of the company, he shall always be entitled to share in such profits as agreed. This is irrespective of whether the company has declared a dividend or not, provided that the company declared profits for the particular year in question (s. 431 CAMA 2020), (s. 384).

UNCLAIMED DIVIDENDS

The CAMA 2020 modified the manner with which a company is entitled to handle the issue of unclaimed dividend from what it was under the CAMA 2004. Under the present regime, where a company paid dividends which has not been claimed by those entitled thereto, the company is mandated to publish the list of the unclaimed dividends and those entitled to them in two (2) national newspapers. The list, as published in the newspapers, must accompany notices of annual general meetings sent to members of the company subsequently. The Act did not say for how long such attachment of the list will go on, or if it is in perpetuity. The rational reasoning will be that such notice will continue to the members until the outstanding dividends are claimed by the owners, or forfeited to other shareholders after twelve (12) years (s. 429(1) CAMA 2020), (s. 382(1).

Under the CAMA 2004, it was a simple requirement for the company to send a list of the unclaimed dividends and the names of those entitled thereto to the members with notice of the next annual general meeting. That was all. However, the CAMA 2020 requires that the list and names be sent to members with the notices of subsequent annual general meetings. Also, the 2004 Act did not make any provision(s) for the publication of the list of unclaimed dividends in national newspapers.

Where a company has gone ahead to place publications in two (2) national newspapers and notice of same has been sent to the members as mandated above, then after a period of three (3) months, the company may invest the unclaimed dividends for its own benefit outside the company. The company shall not pay any interest on such invested unclaimed dividends. However, where it is the company that mistakenly omitted to send dividends to some of its members, then the dividends shall earn interest at the current bank rate after three (3) months from the date on which they are supposed to have been sent to the members entitled thereto (s. 429(2)(3), (s. 382 (2)(3).

Where, after all the steps taken by a company to get the owners of unclaimed dividends to come forth and none came forward, after 12 years, the dividends so unclaimed become irrecoverable by the members. The company is then authorized to include these unclaimed dividends as part of the company profits and distribute same to its members (s. 432(2) CAMA 2020). This is an innovation by the 2020 Act and has no equivalent provision under the CAMA 2004.

The logic behind the above provision is sound as there was a major problem of what to do with unclaimed dividends in Nigeria, the amount of which had risen to hundreds of billions of naira. A suggestion from some quarters that the Federal Government could take over the funds and use same for infrastructure development across the country, was vehemently opposed by professionals in the legal and finance sectors, who likened same to illegal expropriation of private assets. The above, therefore, is a welcome development. However, the story did not end there.

Due to the huge volume of unclaimed dividends traceable to shareholders in publicly quoted companies, the Federal Government, working with the Ministry of Finance (MFI) and the Securities and Exchange Commission, (SEC) still went ahead to set up the Unclaimed Dividend Trust Fund (UDTF), to actualize the earlier suggestion of the Federal Government taking over unclaimed dividends in publicly listed companies and in dormant bank accounts. It is said that the funds will be managed by the SEC and the Debt Management Office (DMO). Several shareholder groups have protested vehemently and some have gone to Court to stop the Federal Government from tampering with the funds, which, if done, without any amendment to the CAMA 2020, will be a direct and brazen violation of the provisions of the CAMA as to how to handle such funds.

It is not clear what legal basis the Federal Government relied on to set up the UDTF to take over declared but unclaimed dividends that belong to private individuals. This is because even under the *Proceeds of Crime (Recovery and Management) Act, 2022*, where assets (including cash and property) are suspected to have been acquired through criminal activities, the relevant organization has to apply to Court, *ex parte*, for preservative order on the assets, in the first instance. That has not been the case here. Therefore, for the Federal Government to take over, without a Court order and without any allegation of crime, almost by executive fiat, private assets in unclaimed dividends, against the provisions of extant law, here the CAMA, without repealing same, is proprietary expropriation, in the opinion of this book.

Meanwhile, matters are already in Court on this and it is to wait and see what the ultimate judicial outcomes will be.

In summary, the issue of dividends payment is one that interests most shareholders and stakeholders in a company. This is for two major reasons: first, when a company declares dividends, it is usually taken as an unspoken affirmation that the company has made profits and that the company is financially buoyant and the business is not being run at a loss. That is why dividends can only be paid out of distributable profits. The second reason is that a declaration of dividends is a return on members' investments in the company. It is therefore crucial that care is taken in dealing with issues concerning dividends payment. Most companies that pay good and consistent dividends, especially publicly quoted companies, invariably do see a rise in their share prices as the interests of the members of the public in purchasing their shares are usually high.

Issues concerning dividends, from the recommendation by the board of directors to declaration by the general meeting, and from paying dividends out of distributable profits to who becomes entitled to declared dividends are all regulated by law, statutory and case law.

For the company secretary the major responsibility, as has been in most instances in this book, is advisory, to the board of directors. The principal thing for the company secretary in this area is to ensure that the law is adhered to in anything the company does pertaining to the declaration and payment of dividends. This is because there are lot of things that could go wrong, if not properly addressed. It is taken for granted that the dividends to be declared are from the company's distributable profits, because, determining that fact is an area wherein the directors have exclusive preserve and discretion and in which the company secretary virtually has no say, apart from proffering an opinion when requested by the directors.

The company secretary will offer advice to the board of directors, while ensuring that the declaration and payment of dividends are done within the confines of relevant laws, but he has limits to what he is empowered to do. For instance, it is not the duty of the company secretary to challenge the directors on issues like whether a company should create a reserve fund or not (apart from the BOFIA mandate noted above), how or where to invest unclaimed dividends, whether or not to declare interim dividends, whether or not to revoke declared dividends (except the legal aspects). These are issues for the board of directors and the company secretary should not overreach himself by trying to fish in these waters, uninvited. Those issues are for the board of directors, although the company secretary could offer an advice on them, on the invitation of the directors.

Finally, it is important for the company secretary to advise the board of directors and to ensure that members would not sue the company to recover declared dividend. As much as possible, it is usually advisable to avoid member-related litigation against a company, although sometimes, it is unavoidable. For instance, where a member is simply relying on wrong legal principles to sue and has no legal basis for the action. Otherwise, shareholder-related litigation is usually viewed by the public as symptom of disconnect in communication (especially when a company has been sued by several shareholders) between the company and its members. It is especially not good for the image of publicly quoted companies, that may sometimes have to report these litigations to their members in general meeting and to their regulators.

CHECKPOINTS

✓ Dividend is the payment received by members of a company as a return on their investment(s) in the company and their share of the company's profits. It is also evidence, in principle, that the company is performing well in and making profits in its line of business. The CAMA 2020 calls it, *inter alia,* a 'portion of distributed profits.'

✓ A company has the power to pay both interim and final dividend, provided that the directors recommend that the dividend be paid on each occasion.

✓ Apart from statutory provisions, there are general principles which have been established over the years by the Courts from the common law tradition, that guide the payment of dividend by companies.

✓ One major principle on dividend, which might be the most important, is that dividend cannot be paid out of capital, as this will amount to an unauthorized reduction of the company's capital without a Court order and illegal.

✓ Even a company's general meeting, in the exercise of their ultimate power of control, does not have the power to authorize dividend to be paid out of capital. Any director(s) who participates in such an illegality is liable to repay the company the amount so paid out.

- ✓ Except in cases where the company's Articles place restrictions on distributions by the company, a company has implied powers to pay dividend. However, where a company refuses to pay dividend, even while making profits, they cannot be compelled to do so, not even by a Court order.
- ✓ There is no mandatory rule of law, except where a company's Articles provide, that once profits are made by the company, dividend must be declared and paid to the members.
- ✓ The board of directors has absolute discretion to recommend dividend to the general meeting to declare, and except where it is so recommended by the directors, no dividend can be declared or paid to the members.
- ✓ Where the directors have recommended dividend to the general meeting, but thereafter grounds emerged that make the directors to believe that after the payment of the dividend the company will be unable to meet its obligations, they will have a rethink and not go ahead with paying the dividend. Once the company will be unable to pay its liabilities after paying the dividend, such dividend will not be paid, although already recommended by the directors.
- ✓ It is important to note that dividend can only be paid out of distributable profits, which, simply put, are that part of the company's overall profits that remain after provisions have been made for losses, taxation, reserves, etc.
- ✓ There are further restrictions, before paying dividend, that are imposed on banks by the BOFIA and the NDIC Act, that is, in addition to the provisions of the CAMA.
- ✓ The law is that shareholders that receive illegal dividend, for instance, dividend paid out of capital, knowing that the directors had no power to pay same, are liable to return same to the company. The major problem here is how to establish the knowledge that will be imputed to the shareholders before liability could attach to them.
- ✓ A company is not under any obligation to distribute all of its profits to members as dividend, as it may put away any portion as decided by the

directors as reserves. In actual fact, for banks, the BOFIA makes the reserve fund compulsory with a minimum of 15 percent of the company's profits going into the reserve funds every year.

- ✓ Once dividend has been declared by a company, it becomes payable and a debt that the company owes its members entitled thereto, until they receive same.
- ✓ As a debt owed by the company to them, members who are entitled to declared dividend have a period of 12 years from the date of the declaration of the dividend to sue to recover them from the company. After that period, any such suit would have become statute barred and the dividend irrecoverable. The CAMA provides that after the 12 years the company is to take back the unclaimed dividend as part of its distributable profits and distribute same as dividend to other members.
- ✓ The Federal Government has instituted the Unclaimed Dividends Trust Fund (UDTF) to take over unclaimed dividend from publicly listed companies, allegedly to be managed by the DMO and the SEC. Our position is that without the funds being proceeds of crimes or liable to forfeiture and without a Court order, the Federal Government has no such right and it amounts to expropriation of private property, except the dynamics change.
- ✓ Payments received from employee profits sharing scheme (contract) between a company and an employee are not the same thing as dividend. An employee that is entitled to a profits-sharing payment from his employer is still entitled to receive same, once the company declares profits. This is irrespective of whether the company declares dividend or not.
- ✓ A company is required to publish the names of members with unclaimed dividends in two (2) national newspapers and is mandated to attach the same list to all subsequent notices of annual general meetings to be sent to its members.
- ✓ After three (3) months of issuing the publications and notices above, a company is permitted to invest the unclaimed dividend outside the company, for its own purpose and shall not be liable to pay interests thereon. The company will pay interests on dividend when it was their

fault that they did not send out the dividend to the member(s) when they should have.

- ✓ Finally, after all said and done, it should be noted that it is only the persons whose names appear on the company's register of members as at the date of the close of register that are entitled to receive declared dividend. In essence, even a person who has had shares transferred to him but who has not had his name entered in the register of members, is not legally entitled to dividend declared for that period, but ultimately will, when his name is entered in the register of members.

Chapter 20

THE INTERSECTION OF LAW AND CORPORATE GOVERNANCE: THE ROLE OF THE COMPANY SECRETARY

INTRODUCTION

It is now clear, through the chapters in this book, how issues surrounding the general gamut of company direction, administration and exercise of power of control over companies have become, much more unlike before, topical issues globally. There is no doubt that these issues have always been there, in varying degrees all these years. What changed has been the ascendance of the deliberate application of corporate governance principles to legal principles in company administration and practice. This convergence meant that instead of simply discussing only profits and losses by companies, corporate governance discussions about the powers, or abuse thereof, duties and responsibilities of the board of directors in corporate management, took a centre stage. The company secretary has been at the centre of those managing this change, that is, outside the board members themselves.

In Nigeria, the Adrian Cadbury Report for the British Government on the *Financial Aspects of Corporate Governance*, in 1992, marked the first time that the issue of corporate governance, in its current form, started to garner some levels of serious attention within the corporate circles in the country. On its own part, the Cadbury report was in response to some corporate failures in the United Kingdom and answers were needed thereto. Some of the major recommendations of the report were the need for the independence of the executive directors and the need for stand-alone and strong audit committees, especially in listed companies. The Cadbury report was important to the emergence of other corporate governance reports from around the world: the Vienot report, France, (1995), the King report, South Africa, (1995), the Netherlands report, (1997), report from Hong Kong Society of Accountants on Corporate Governance, (1996), etc. The most critical concern expressed by all these reports was the high potential for abuse of corporate power by company directors. It did not take too long for that prophesy to be fulfilled *(Tricker, 13).*

In the early 2000s, the world woke up to numbing and devastating corporate failures around the world, from Enron, Tyco and WorldCom in the United States, to Parmalat in Italy, and to HIH Insurance in Australia. It was 'corporate mass burials,' literally speaking, and the world had to wake up, willy-nilly, as it were, to conduct a post-mortem on the carcasses of these corporate giants, to identify what went wrong. At the end of the day, everything pointed to some irresistible conclusions: corporate abuses by company directors, financial accounting manipulation by auditors and slack oversight by regulatory authorities. The fears of Adrian Cadbury and others were confirmed, and bitterly so *(Tricker, 13).*

The central place and utility of corporate governance in business was thrown back-up into global consciousness and the pivotal roles of the company secretary in this respect received final affirmation.

The United States' response to the above catastrophic events was swift and firm, with the passing of the *Sarbanes-Oxley Act, 2002.* The Act raised and tightened the standards for financial reporting by companies, especially requiring financial statements to be accurate and must not contain misleading statements, among others. Apart from requiring detailed and accurate statements and disclosures, the Act also imposed jail terms, reaching up to 20 years in some instances, on fraudulent company officials. Several countries around the world followed suit with similar laws and regulations. Apart from these responses, core issues and concepts in corporate governance, as seen below, started to receive renewed attention, even the issue of sustainability, that hitherto was simply discussed but not implemented by most organizations. In most organizations, the effective application of corporate governance principles in general, centred on the effective role of the company secretary, acting on the direction of the board of directors.

Talking about sustainability, as above, the concept, as a corporate governance initiative, although fairly recent, keeps evolving as an organic concept. It has gone beyond the traditional focus of getting business strategies to positively impact the environment and society and now the concept of the 'Tripple Bottom-line' has also emerged within the sustainability discourse. According to the Harvard Business School, the Tripple Bottom-line is a business concept that postulates that businesses should commit to measuring their social and environmental impact, in addition to their financial performance, rather than solely focusing on generating profit, or the standard 'bottom-line.' In terms of its content, it has been submitted that the Triple Bottom-line can be broken down into 'three P's': Profit, People, and the Planet. In its application, the concept posits that businesses are to use these categories to conceptualize their environmental responsibility and determine any negative social impact(s) to which they might be contributing. From whatever reports or feedbacks that they receive, the businesses are then to integrate sustainable practices into every facet of their business operations, including supply chains, business partners, and renewable energy usage. This is to positively impact society and the environment in addition to turning a profit for the business. While it could be said, and correctly too, that, conceptually, this is not too far away from the traditional concept of sustainability, it marks an extension to and further iteration and affirmation of the core sustainability principles (https://online.hbs.edu/blog/post/what-is-the-triple-bottom-line.

CORE ISSUES IN CORPORATE GOVERNANCE

One of the major issues in corporate governance is the reality of the possibility of a conflict of interests between the board of directors (and even among individual directors) and the other stakeholder groups, both within and outside the company. This will include a company's employees and its shareholders.

The key issue here is how to ensure that the directors (being those that are appointed to direct and manage the business of the company) act in the best interests of the company as a whole and not for their personal gains, which will be a breach of their fiduciary duties to the company. In essence, it is how to ensure a seamless operation of the principle that separates the ownership of a company from its management and direction (*Tricker,9).*

This issue is quite germane because of the ever-present potential for malpractices by the board or individual director(s). This is especially the case because company directors, especially executive directors, have unfettered access to most of the company's information systems (as was discussed with insider trading infraction) and are in a position to control or even manipulate the information that is released to the public (*ICSA, 219*). It is therefore essential that a system is put in place that would curtail, if not eliminate, the potential for any abuse of office by directors.

CORE CONCEPTS IN CORPORATE GOVERNANCE

Flowing from the core issues in corporate governance are the core concepts that are germane to sound corporate governance practices in companies. They are the ones that, when applied with fidelity, will reduce the propensity for abuse by directors and other senior managers in a company. They have been listed below and are simply advisory and not exhaustive:

- **transparency**: this is the ease with which a person who is not a company's insider can understand the information (both financial and non-financial) being put out to the public by the company about its activities;
- **independence:** this is the extent to which procedures and structures have been put in place in the company to minimize conflict of interests among the major stakeholders;
- **accountability:** this is the process of ensuring that those who manage and direct the affairs of a company are accountable to the shareholders and other stakeholders, for their actions;
- **responsibility:** this is determining whether, and to what extent, to which directors should be liable or responsible to the shareholders for their actions;
- **fairness**: this is ensuring that all shareholders should be able to receive equal attention and consideration in matters concerning them irrespective of the quantum of their shareholding in the company. This is because institutional shareholders usually do require preferential treatment in certain matters;
- **social responsibility:** a company that practices sound corporate governance should be very aware of and be responsive to issues of social concerns around its geographical area of operation, and beyond.

Apart from these concepts on corporate governance above, one of the global intellectual think tanks on the subject, the *Corporate Governance Institute* (CGI, thecorporategovernanceinstitute.com) also added two (2) more heads, which are 'awareness' and 'impartiality', as explained below:

- **awareness:** this awareness is about the directors and executives having full awareness of the business risks facing the company in its operating environment. The directors are usually at the forefront of pinpointing these risks and articulating the appropriate responses to them, based on their wealth of experience and business versatility;
- **impartiality**: the board of directors must be impartial and seen to be so in their relationship with critical stakeholders: the people who are answerable to them and those they are answerable to. The board should approach every decision-making in the company with an independent mindset,

ensuring that their personal interests or those of their friends and relations do not come between them and sound business decisions.

CORE PRINCIPLES OF CORPORATE GOVERNANCE

Complementing the core concepts of corporate governance, are certain core principles, which are held to be crucial to the application of sound corporate governance practices within any given business organization. This is especially the case with reference to large companies. Some of these principles are, that:

- all company directors should be elected annually by confidential elections superintended by independent individuals;
- a good number of a company's directors should be independent, that is, not have any professional, financial or filial relationship with the company that would colour their judgment. (We saw earlier that the CAMA 2020 as amended, has provided, for the first time, that a public company shall have at least one third of its total number of directors to be independent directors);
- flowing from the above, a company should disclose all available information on a director to the shareholders for them to be able to decide whether the director is independent or not;
- companies should have audit, nominating and remuneration committees, and the members of these committees should be independent directors;
- an ordinary resolution of the shareholders should be required to approve transactions that might have effect on shareholder value, for instance, the sale or pledge of the company's assets. In most cases, in practice, it is the board that usually resolve and decide to enter into these types of transactions (*Fabian Ajogwu, Corporate Governance in Nigeria: Law and Practice, 2007, 6-7*).

KEY GOVERNANCE PRINCIPLES ON THE BOARD OF DIRECTORS

It was noted at the outset, that a successful company is usually one headed by an effective board. It is this board that is responsible for providing entrepreneurial and strategic leadership as well as promoting ethical culture and responsible corporate citizenship. As a link between stakeholders and the company, the board is to exercise oversight and control to ensure that management acts in the best interests of the shareholders and other stakeholders, while sustaining the prosperity of the company (Principle 1 NCCG).

The duty of the company secretary in this respect is to act as link between the board of directors, the shareholders and all the other stakeholders in the company. He is also the pivot in the execution of the decisions of the board with respect to all governance-related issues, taking his traditional company secretarial duties as a given. In some bigger companies, this has included aspects of the application of the company's whistle blower policies and sustainability programmes.

The board is also expected to show leadership, integrity and quality of examples always, in their approach to issues, while ensuring that the company complies, through the office of the company secretary, with all applicable laws in the country. Among many other things, the board should be effectively in charge of the company as an entity that works for the best interests of all the stakeholders. In doing that, the board has responsibility for:

- overall policy formulation and management oversight;
- overseeing the integrity and adequacy of internal controls;
- selection, appraisal and compensation of board members and senior management executives;
- overseeing company's communication and information flows to external audiences;
- ensuring the integrity of annual reports and accounts and all materials that are sent to the regulators;
- ensuring that management systems are in place to identify, early enough, and mitigate social and environmental risks that the company deals with;
- establishing the company's risk management framework to calibrate and manage the company's risk appetite;
- in terms of its composition, to the best possible extent, the board should consider diversity in its membership and be composed in such a way as to ensure diversity of experience, age, gender, professional skills, without compromising compatibility, integrity, availability and independence;
- ensuring that the board is of sufficient size relative to the scale and complexity of the company's operations, and should periodically invigorate itself by injecting new members with new skills, backgrounds and ideas into the board;
- ensuring that the membership of the board is a mix of executive and non-executive directors, each with his core competence and non-executive directors should have independent directors more in number;

- ensuring that the chairman of the board is a non-executive director with the primary responsibility of ensuring the effective operation of the board. The position of the chairman and chief executive should be separated and not held by an individual to avoid undue concentration of power;
- ensuring that the board is not be dominated by an individual or a small group of persons in terms of decision making;
- ensuring that the board meets regularly, at least once every quarter, in a conducive atmosphere that encourages dialogue in order to strategize for the company and maintain effective control over the affairs of the company. Note that the CAMA did not put any possible ratio of meeting for directors, just that they should meet as often as they deem fit for effectiveness;
- ensuring that non-executive directors should be key members of the board and have direct access to the executive directors and the company secretary, however, they should not be involved in the day-to-day running of the company, which is the duty of the managing director and senior management executives. They should be persons of such a calibre to make constructive contribution to the company;
- creating a total and clear disclosure of the remuneration of the chairman and the directors, based on clear principles as earlier discussed;
- ensuring that concurrent or multiple directorships are disclosed to the board and critical stakeholders and should not impair a director's ability to perform on the board engender conflict of interests. However, directorships in too many companies at the same time should also not be encouraged, as it will affect the director's performance, ultimately;
- ensure that decisions reached at the company's general meetings are implemented diligently and fully as governance directives from the members.

KEY GOVERNANCE PRINCIPLES ON THE SHAREHOLDER ENGAGEMENT

The shareholders, as a group, are another important organ in company administration, without which there will be no company to administer. The NCCG emphasizes the importance of shareholder rights and the need for effective shareholder engagement. In essence, that the establishment of a system of regular dialogue with shareholders balances their needs, interests and expectations with the objectives of the company (Principle 22).

In ensuring sound corporate governance practices within an organization, certain shareholders' rights and privileges have been identified as being critical to the achievement of such an objective. Apart from these rights, the right atmosphere has to be created for the shareholders (institutional, majority, minority, etc.) to be able to function effectively in relating with the company. Some of the important issues in this respect are, that:

- the board should develop a policy that ensures appropriate engagement with shareholders. The chairman of the board, or other designated persons as specified in the policy may interact with some shareholders in order to understand their issues;
- the board should encourage institutional investors, to as a matter of principle, positively influence the standard of corporate governance and promote value creation in the companies in which they invest;
- the board should ensure that shareholders at annual general meetings preserve their effective powers to appoint and remove directors of the company and that all shareholders are treated fairly and equitably without any discrimination;
- no shareholder, however large his shareholding, whether institutional or otherwise, should be given preferential treatment or superior access to the company's information or other materials;
- the board should ensure that minority shareholders are adequately protected from abusive actions by controlling shareholders;
- the board should use the company's general meetings as avenues to effectively communicate with the shareholders and also to encourage them to participate in the affairs of the company;
- as far as possible and barring any conflict of interests, majority and minority shareholders should have representatives on the board proportionate to their shareholding;
- shareholder activism by individual or institutional shareholders and others should not be discouraged or suppressed under any guise;
- shareholders' right to vote is inviolable and should not be abridged by a company. Shareholders should have easy and meaningful ability to participate in major decisions affecting the company *(Ajogwu, 12).*

As has been noted throughout this book, the company secretary, especially in large private or publicly quoted companies, plays an almost indispensable role in supporting the effectiveness of the board by assisting the board and management to implement good corporate governance practices within the company. This is just an aspect of the roles that the company secretary play in the area of corporate governance. In terms of practical applicable principles, however, some of the roles, considered key in our present discourse, are apt to note at this point.

KEY GOVERNANCE ROLES FOR THE COMPANY SECRETARY

The roles of the company secretary in corporate governance, part of which have been discussed in earlier chapters, are multi-faceted and diverse, depending on the size and structure of the company. Expectedly, the roles are more complex in larger firms than in smaller ones. The most important point to make here is that the roles are not carried out in isolation, as they are executed at the intersection between law and corporate governance, which sometimes are difficult to segregate. As a generic classification, the key roles of the company secretary are stated below:

- to keep all legal and regulatory developments affecting the company's operations under review continually and ensure that the directors are briefed about them;
- to ensure that the interests of all of the company's stakeholders (employees, shareholders, creditors, etc.) are taken into consideration when important business decisions are being made by the company;
- to act as a confidential 'sounding board' to the chairman of the company and all directors (executive and non-executive directors) on diverse issues;
- to act as an effective channel of communication ensuring good information flow within the board and between the board and the other stakeholders, when the need arises;
- to act as the 'conscience of the company' by providing an additional inquiring voice on the decisions of the board within the context of improving the company's image, regulatory compliance, and business efficiency;
- to ensure and contribute to the implementation of sound corporate governance in the company as agreed to by the board and its committees;
- to manage the company's relationship with investors, especially institutional investors, regarding corporate governance issues and practices within the company;
- to be responsible for assisting new directors to settle down and get acclimatized with the company's business and be inducted as directors;

- as the compliance officer of the company (even where there is a compliance department, to collaborate therewith), to make sure that the company does not commit any compliance or regulatory offences that are otherwise avoidable with due diligence on the part of the company. Otherwise, to work to minimize such infractions;
- to spearhead and effectively ensure the enforcement of the company's whistleblowing programme and sustainability programmes, where these exist.

In summarizing, in modern business circles, corporate governance has assumed a life of its own in recent years. It has now become the norm rather than the exception for companies, especially large publicly quoted companies, to have a detailed and comprehensive policies and practices on corporate governance, now encompassing aspects of sustainability as a component.

In Nigeria, the Financial Reporting Council of Nigeria (FRCN), while acknowledging the existence of earlier sector-specific Codes in the country, in 2018, brought out the Nigerian Code of Corporate Governance (NCCG), as a centralizing Code, in a manner of speaking, for all sectors of the economy. A detailed review of the Code suggests that corporate governance and corporate social responsibility are getting intertwined gradually and consistently, and companies that are proactive would have started to treat them as such. In practice, a lot of companies in Nigeria, especially, publicly quoted companies, actually do treat the subjects as such, and in all these aspects, the role of the company secretary has become central. The company secretary works as the pivot at the intersection between law and corporate governance, which fields are getting increasingly difficult to segregate into distinct components, when discussing company administration.

In the final analysis, from everything that has been discussed from the opening chapter, it is obvious that the duties and responsibilities of the modern company secretary have metamorphosed dramatically, especially in recent decades. The original boundaries of having company secretaries as those only providing support systems to the directors and executives, while maintaining the statutory registers, liaising with external solicitors, arranging meetings (issuing notices and all incidental matters), attending meetings, (board and general meetings) and taking minutes, transactional issues, relating with shareholders and other stakeholders, etc., are still there. However, far beyond these traditional precincts are new areas that the company secretary has quietly taken up responsibility for, especially in large companies, including: whistle-blower policy formulation and implementation (where in place), witness protection programmes incidental to the whistle-blower policy, data protection policies and programmes, aspects of corporate social responsibility (CSR) formulation, etc. In effect, he intersects on the convergence between company law and corporate governance principles. On a final note, therefore, the modern company secretary has become positively ubiquitous in terms of his duties and responsibilities in a modern corporate environment.

Chapter 21

REMOVAL OF THE COMPANY SECRETARY FROM OFFICE

INTRODUCTION

For all his ubiquity, centrality and perceived indispensability to the functions of modern companies, especially large corporations, the company secretary does not have a permanent tenure of office within a company's structure. Even company directors, including those appointed directors 'for life,' do not have permanent tenures of office in a company. In essence, for all his important contributions to the smooth functioning and survival of companies, the company secretary can be removed, just as he was appointed, by the board of directors. The next rational question will be: how? What are really the procedures and processes for the removal of the company secretary from office? We then turn to the CAMA for guidance.

COMPANY SECRETARY IN A PRIVATE COMPANY

It will be correct to say, that with respect to a company secretary in a private company, the CAMA has no express provision(s) on the modalities for his removal from office. The only direction from the Act is that it is at the discretion of the board of directors, who are the appointors, to also remove him, if they so wish. It seems that we have to resort to the terms of the contract that hired the company secretary in a private company to determine the modalities provided therein for terminating his employment.

From a corporate governance point of view, the *World Bank Group (IFC, 8-9)* seriously recommends that the removal of the company secretary should be a matter for the whole board to decide. This, they argue, is for two main reasons: the first is to protect the integrity of the position of the company secretary, from where one or two directors may decide to simply remove him from office on flimsy excuses. The second reason, which is related to the first, is to allow the company secretary to be able to form independent opinion and advise the board as such without fear of being victimized by a few directors.

This may not be as useful in a small private company with few directors as with a large publicly quoted company, with many directors and a large board.

We recall having mentioned severally in previous chapters that the company secretary is a senior officer of the company. It is therefore imperative that the terms and conditions of his engagement are clear on the details of the procedure for his exit from the company, voluntarily or otherwise. This will include details on areas like notice of resignation (length, manner, etc.) or sums in lieu thereof, disciplinary proceedings, incidents warranting termination or dismissal, etc. In essence, for a company secretary in a private company, the procedure for his removal from office can only be based on contractual terms, and where a company breaches same, then they are liable to pay damages. The law is that the object of awarding such damages for breach of contract is to put the injured party, so far as money can do it, in the same position as if the contract had been performed optimally *(Universal Vulcanizing Nig. Ltd* v. *Ijeshah United Trading & Transport Co. & Ors (1992) 5 NWLR Pt. 266, 388; Maiden Electronics Works Ltd* v. *A-G Federation (1974) 1 SC, 53, Shell BP* v. *Jammal Eng. Ltd (1974) 4 SC, 33).*

In essence, as long as the directors of a private company adhered to the terms stipulated in the contract of service to terminate the appointment of a company secretary, that process is in order and final. The motive(s) or reason(s) for the termination is immaterial, the directors' discretion being unfettered in any way in this respect. The only exception is where the company's Articles imposed further conditions on the company secretary's contract of service, in which case, those conditions will have to be complied with also, for any removal of the company secretary to be valid.

COMPANY SECRETARY IN A PUBLIC COMPANY

There is a marked difference in the process of removing a company secretary in a public company from what was just considered above. It has been said that the process of removing a company secretary in a public company is deliberately made stricter in order to better safeguard their tenure of office and ensure that they can effectively protect the interests of the shareholders (usually larger in number than those of most private companies). More importantly, it is also to ensure that the company secretary is able to protect the interests of the investing public *(Orojo, 291)*. In this respect, the two reasons given above for the whole board to be involved in the removal of the company secretary, are more germane with company secretaries in public companies, where the stakes are usually, but not always higher.

For the company secretary in a public company, the process for his removal from office has been standardised under the CAMA. For instance, where he is to be removed, the directors are required to adhere strictly to the provisions of section 333(2) CAMA 2020, (s. 296 (2). The modalities under the section are that:

- the board of directors shall give notice of removal to the company secretary stating that it is intended to remove him from office;
- such a notice shall set out the ground(s) on which it is intended to remove the company secretary;
- the company secretary shall be given a period of not less than seven (7) working days within which to make his defence; and
- the notice shall also give the company secretary an option to resign his appointment within a period of seven (7) working days.

These are mandatory requirements for the removal of the company secretary in a public company and any removal that does not conform to this procedure, stands to be set aside by the Court *(Afolabi* v. *Gateway Insurance Co. Ltd (1997) 1 FHCLR, 84).* As already noted, there is no such requirement for procedural compliance in the case of removing the secretary of a private company, which is entirely at the discretion of the board of directors, subject, always, to the provision of his contract of employment or any terms in the Articles.

After receiving the notice of intention to terminate his appointment from the board of directors, the onus now shifts to the company secretary himself to respond. If the period stated in the notice (minimum of seven (7) working days, which then excludes Saturdays and Sundays) for him to respond, lapses, and the secretary did not resign or put up a defence, the board of directors may remove him from office and report to the next general meeting.

If, in the same situation, the company secretary does not resign within the period as stated in the notice, but puts up a defence to the board, then the board has to consider his defence as submitted and thereafter has two (2) options:

- if the board does not consider the secretary's defence as being sufficient, and the ground for the intended removal borders on fraud or serious misconduct the board may still go ahead and remove him from office and shall report to the next general meeting;
- if on the same situation as above, but the ground for the intended removal of the company secretary does not border on fraud or serious misconduct,

(for instance, if the secretary is sought to be removed for what is considered below-par performance) the board shall not remove him without the approval of the general meeting, but may suspend him and shall report the fact of the suspension to the next general meeting.

If the suspended company secretary is later removed by the general meeting based on the recommendation of the board, then, the removal may take effect from such time as the general meeting may determine.

From the foregoing, it is deducible that the general meeting may, in any event, decide not to remove the company secretary and allow him back to his duty, as it would appear that the ultimate power in this respect rests with the general meeting. In principle, this is what it appears, but in practice, it would be a serious error of judgment for the company and all stakeholders, for the general meeting to foist on the company, a company secretary that has been recommended for a sack by the directors. Boardroom practice will dictate to all that before the board of directors decides to issue a notice of removal to the company secretary, all the members of the board, or the majority of them, including the powerful or influential directors, would have concluded that he should leave the position. Every other thing being done in that respect will simply be to fulfil the requirement of the law.

We recall that one of the primary duties of the board of directors is to direct and manage the affairs of the company, in the best interests of the members as a whole. This duty is fiduciary in nature. Therefore, if the board, in its wisdom, decides that the company secretary is no longer fit and proper for purpose and does not command the respect of the board to continue in such a sensitive position in the company, it is not an area where the general meeting should intervene, although it has the power to do so. In this case, it would not be expedient to do so. After all, it was the board of directors that interviewed, found worthy and hired the company secretary, *ab initio, and* if they decide that he should vacate the office, the directors should be allowed to have their way.

FINANCIAL REPORTING COUNCIL OF NIGERIA
Federal Ministry of Industry, Trade and Investment

ADOPTION AND COMPLIANCE WITH NIGERIAN CODE OF CORPORATE GOVERNANCE 2018

[*Commencement*: January 15, 2019]

In exercise of the powers conferred on me by Section 73 of the Financial Reporting Council of Nigeria Act of 2011, and all other powers enabling me in that behalf and with the advice of the Council, I, Dr. Okechukwu Enyinnaya Enelamah, Minister for Industry, Trade and Investment hereby make the following Regulation:

Application

From the commencement of this Regulation, the following entities shall adopt and comply with Nigerian Code of Corporate Governance 2018, which is the Schedule to this regulation:

(a) all public companies (whether a listed company or not);

(b) all private companies that are holding companies of public companies or other regulated entities;

(c) all concessioned or privatised companies; and

(d) all regulated private companies being private companies that file returns to any regulatory authority other than the Federal Inland Revenue Service (FIRS) and the Corporate Affairs Commission (CAC).

(2) These entities shall report on the application of the Code in their annual reports for financial years ending after January 1, 2020 in the form and manner prescribed by the Financial Reporting Council of Nigeria.

2. ***Miscellaneous***

Words and phrases used in this Regulation bear the same meaning as provided in the Nigerian Code of Corporate Governance, the Schedule to this Regulation.

3. ***Short Title***

This Regulation may be cited as the Regulation on the Adoption and Compliance with Nigerian Code of Corporate Governance 2018.

Made at Abuja this 15th day of January 2019.

Schedule
[Paragraph 1(1)]

NIGERIAN CODE OF CORPORATE GOVERNANCE 2018

Table of Contents

List of Abbreviations

Board	Board of Directors
CBN	Central Bank of Nigeria
Code	Nigerian Code of Corporate Governance 2018
Chairman	Chairman of the Board of Directors
ED	Executive Director
ESG	Environmental, Social and Governance
FRC, Council	Financial Reporting Council of Nigeria
INED	Independent Non-Executive Director
IAS 24	International Accounting Standard 24 (on Related Party Disclosures)
IT	Information Technology
MD/CEO	Managing Director/ Chief Executive Officer
NAICOM	National Insurance Commission
NED	Non-Executive Director
PenCom	National Pension Commission
SEC	Securities and Exchange Commission

Introduction

A. Authority of the Code

Sections 11c and 51c of the Financial Reporting Council of Nigeria Act confer upon the Council, the powers to ensure good corporate governance practices in the public and private sectors of the Nigerian economy and to issue the code of corporate governance and guidelines. The Nigerian Code of Corporate Governance 2018 was approved by the Council pursuant to this authority and commended to the Minister for issuance in accordance with Section 73 of the Act.

B. Aims and Objectives

Corporate Governance is a key driver of corporate accountability and business prosperity. In response to challenges in their respective sectors, a number of industry regulators developed corporate governance codes for companies operating in their sectors. The sectoral codes are:

1. Code of Corporate Governance for the Telecommunication Industry 2016, issued by the Nigerian Communications Commission (replaced 2014 NCC Code);
2. Code of Corporate Governance for Banks and Discount Houses in Nigeria 2014 issued by the Central Bank of Nigeria (replaced 2006 CBN Code);
3. Code of Corporate Governance for Public Companies in Nigeria 2011 issued by the Securities and Exchange Commission (replaced 2003 SEC Code);
4. Code of Good Corporate Governance for Insurance Industry in Nigeria 2009 issued by the National Insurance Commission; and
5. Code of Corporate Governance for Licensed Pension Fund Operators 2008 issued by the National Pension Commission.

The Nigerian Code of Corporate Governance 2018 seeks to institutionalise corporate governance best practices in Nigerian companies. The Code is also to promote public awareness of essential corporate values and ethical practices that will enhance the integrity of the business environment. By institutionalising high corporate governance standards, the Code will rebuild public trust and confidence in the Nigerian economy, thus facilitating increased trade and investment.

Companies with effective boards and competent management that act with integrity and that are engaged with shareholders and other stakeholders are better placed to achieve their business goals and contribute positively to society. In such well managed organisations, the interests of the Board and management are aligned with those of the shareholders and other stakeholders.

By adhering to the principles articulated in this Code, companies will demonstrate a commitment to good governance practices and increase their levels of transparency, trust and integrity, and create an environment for sustainable business operations.

C. Code Philosophy

The Code is aimed at companies of varying sizes and complexities across industries. Consequently, flexibility – the ability to apply the Code in a wide range of circumstances, and scalability – the ability to apply to companies of differing sizes, are of utmost importance for successful implementation. Accordingly, the Code adopts a principle-based approach in specifying minimum standards of practice that companies should adopt.

Where so required, companies should adopt the "Apply and Explain" approach in reporting on compliance with this Code. The '**Apply and Explain**' approach which assumes application of all principles and requires entities to explain how the principles are applied. This requires companies to demonstrate how the specific activities they have undertaken best achieve the outcomes intended by the corporate governance principles specified in the Code. This will help to prevent a 'box ticking' exercise as companies deliberately consider how they have (or have not) achieved the intended outcomes. Although the Code recommends practices to enable companies apply the principles, it recognises that these practices can be tailored to meet industry or company needs. The Code is thus scalable to suit the type, size and growth phase of each company while still achieving the outcomes envisaged by the principles.

D. Monitoring the Implementation of the Code

The implementation of this Code will be monitored by the FRC through the sectoral regulators and registered exchanges who are empowered to impose appropriate sanctions based on the specific deviation noted and the company in question. Additionally, the FRC may conduct reviews on the implementation of the Code where deviations from the Code recur. Other monitoring mechanisms adopted by the FRC will be based on its review of the level of implementation of the Code.

In consonance with the relevant regulatory agencies of the Federal Government of Nigeria, the Council will subsequently issue corporate governance guidelines to assist implementation as may be required to respond to prudential considerations in different sectors of the economy.

E. Structure of the Code

The Code consists of seven (7) parts and twenty-eight (28) principles together with practices recommended by the Code for the implementation of each principle. The highlights of the twenty-eight (28) principles are shown below:

Part	Principle Number	Definition of Principle
A: Board of Directors and Officers of the Board	**Principle 1**	A successful Company is headed by an effective Board which is responsible for providing entrepreneurial and strategic leadership as well as promoting ethical culture and responsible corporate citizenship. As a link between stakeholders and the Company, the Board is to exercise oversight and control to ensure that management acts in the best interest of the shareholders and other stakeholders while sustaining the prosperity of the Company.

	Principle 2	The effective discharge of the responsibilities of the Board and its committees is assured by an appropriate balance of skills and diversity (including experience and gender) without compromising competence, independence and integrity.
A: Board of Directors and Officers of the Board	**Principle 3**	The Chairman is responsible for providing overall leadership of the Company and the Board, and eliciting the constructive participation of all Directors to facilitate effective direction of the Board.
	Principle 4	The Managing Director/Chief Executive Officer is the head of management delegated by the Board to run the affairs of the Company to achieve its strategic objectives for sustainable corporate performance.
	Principle 5	Executive Directors support the Managing Director/Chief Executive Officer in the operations and management of the Company.
	Principle 6	Non-Executive Directors bring to bear their knowledge, expertise and independent judgment on issues of strategy and performance on the Board.
Part	**Principle Number**	**Definition of Principle**
	Principle 7	Independent Non-Executive Directors bring a high degree of objectivity to the Board for sustaining stakeholder trust and confidence.
	Principle 8	The Company Secretary plays an important role in supporting the effectiveness of the Board by assisting the Board and management to develop good corporate governance practices and culture within the Company.

	Principle 9	Directors are sometimes required to make decisions of a technical and complex nature that may require independent external expertise.
	Principle 10	Meetings are the principal vehicle for conducting the business of the Board and successfully fulfilling the strategic objectives of the Company.
	Principle 11	To ensure efficiency and effectiveness, the Board delegates some of its functions, duties and responsibilities to well-structured committees, without abdicating its responsibilities.
	Principle 12	A written, clearly defined, rigorous, formal and transparent procedure serves as a guide for the selection of Directors to ensure the appointment of high quality individuals to the Board.
	Principle 13	A formal induction programme on joining the Board as well as regular training assists Directors to effectively discharge their duties to the Company.
	Principle 14	Annual Board evaluation assesses how each Director, the committees of the Board and the Board are committed to their roles, work together and continue to contribute effectively to the achievement of the Company's objectives.
Part	**Principle Number**	**Definition of Principle**
	Principle 15	Institutionalising a system for evaluating the Company's corporate governance practices ensures that its governance standards, practices and processes are adequate and effective.
	Principle 16	The Board ensures that the Company remunerates fairly, responsibly and transparently so as to promote the achievement of strategic objectives and positive outcomes in the short, medium and long term.

B: Assurance	**Principle 17**	A sound framework for managing risk and ensuring an effective internal control system is essential for achieving the strategic objectives of the Company.
	Principle 18	An effective internal audit function provides assurance to the Board on the effectiveness of the governance, risk management and internal control systems.
	Principle 19	An effective whistle-blowing framework for reporting any illegal or unethical behaviour minimises the Company's exposure and prevents recurrence.
	Principle 20	An external auditor is appointed to provide an independent opinion on the true and fair view of the financial statements of the Company to give assurance to stakeholders on the reliability of the financial statements.
C: Relationship with Shareholders	**Principle 21**	General Meetings are important platforms for the Board to engage shareholders to facilitate greater understanding of the Company's business, governance and performance. They provide shareholders with an opportunity to exercise their ownership rights and express their views to the Board on any areas of interest.
Part	**Principle Number**	**Definition of Principle**
	Principle 22	The establishment of a system of regular dialogue with shareholders balances their needs, interests and expectations with the objectives of the Company.
	Principle 23	Equitable treatment of shareholders and the protection of their statutory and general rights, particularly the interest of minority shareholders, promote good governance.

D: Business Conduct with Ethics	Principle 24	The establishment of professional business and ethical standards underscores the values for the protection and enhancement of the reputation of the Company while promoting good conduct and investor confidence.
	Principle 25	The establishment of policies and mechanisms for monitoring insider trading, related party transactions, conflict of interest and other corrupt activities, mitigates the adverse effects of these abuses on the Company and promotes good ethical conduct and investor confidence.
E: Sustainability	Principle 26	Paying adequate attention to sustainability issues including environment, social, occupational and community health and safety ensures successful long term business performance and projects the Company as a responsible corporate citizen contributing to economic development.
F: Transparency	Principle 27	Communicating and interacting with stakeholders keeps them conversant with the activities of the Company and assists them in making informed decisions.
Part	**Principle Number**	**Definition of Principle**
	Principle 28	Full and comprehensive disclosure of all matters material to investors and stakeholders, and of matters set out in this Code, ensures proper monitoring of its implementation which engenders good corporate governance practice.

Part A. Board of Directors and Officers of the Board

1. **Role of the Board**

Principle 1: *A successful Company is headed by an effective Board which is responsible for providing entrepreneurial and strategic leadership as well as promoting ethical culture and responsible corporate citizenship. As a link between stakeholders and the Company, the Board is to exercise oversight and control to ensure that management acts in the best interest of the shareholders and other stakeholders while sustaining the prosperity of the Company.*

Recommended Practices

The Board, being central in corporate governance and the highest governing body in the Company, should have a charter setting out its responsibilities, which may include the following:

1.1 exercising leadership, enterprise, integrity and judgment in its oversight and control of the Company so as to achieve the Company's continued survival and prosperity;

1.2 ensuring that the Board and its committees act in the best interest of the Company at all times;

1.3 ensuring compliance with the laws of the Federal Republic of Nigeria and other applicable regulations;

1.4 considering and approving the long-term and short-term strategies for the business of the Company and monitoring their implementation by management;

1.5 ensuring the establishment and implementation of a succession plan, appointment process, training mechanism and remuneration structure for both the Board and senior management of the Company;

1.6 being accountable to the Company as well as identifying and managing the relationship with shareholders and other stakeholders;

1.7 establishing and maintaining the Company's values and standards (including an ethical culture) as well as modelling these values and standards;

1.8 overseeing the internal audit function, approving the internal audit plan, and appointing and removing the head of the internal audit function on the recommendation of the committee responsible for audit;

1.9 establishing the Company's risk management framework and monitoring its effectiveness, setting the Company's risk appetite, receiving and reviewing risk reports;

1.10 providing oversight over Information Technology governance;

1.11 defining a formal schedule of matters specifically reserved for Board decision and matters delegated to Board committees and management;

1.12 overseeing the effectiveness and adequacy of the internal control system;

1.13 overseeing the Company's communication and information dissemination policy;

1.14 performing the appraisal of Board members and executive management;

1.15 ensuring the integrity of annual reports and accounts and all material information provided to regulators and other stakeholders; and

1.16 ensuring that management systems are in place to identify and manage environmental and social risks and their impact.

2. Board Structure and Composition

Principle 2: *The effective discharge of the responsibilities of the Board and its committees is assured by an appropriate balance of skills and diversity (including experience and gender) without compromising competence, independence and integrity.*

Recommended Practices

2.1 The Board should be of a sufficient size to effectively undertake and fulfil its business; to oversee, monitor, direct and control the Company's activities and be relative to the scale and complexity of its operations.

2.2 The Board should assume responsibility for its composition by setting the direction and approving the processes for it to attain the appropriate balance of knowledge, skills, experience, diversity and independence to objectively and effectively discharge its governance role and responsibilities.

2.3 The Board should consider the following factors in determining the requisite number of its members:

(a) appropriate mix of knowledge, skills and experience, including the business, commercial and industry experience needed to govern the Company;

(b) appropriate mix of Executive, Non-Executive and Independent Non-Executive members such that majority of the Board are Non-Executive Directors. It is desirable that most of the Non-Executive Directors are independent;

(c) need for a sufficient number of members that qualify to serve on the committees of the Board;

(d) need to secure quorum at meetings; and

(e) diversity targets relating to the composition of the Board.

2.4 The Board should promote diversity in its membership across a variety of attributes relevant for promoting better decision-making and effective governance. These attributes include field of knowledge, skills and experience as well as age, culture and gender. The Board should have a policy to govern this process and establish measurable objectives for achieving diversity in gender and other areas.

2.5 The Board should periodically invigorate its capabilities by ensuring the appointment of new members with relevant skills and fresh perspectives, while retaining valuable knowledge, skills, experience and diversity; and maintaining continuity.

2.6 No individual or small group of individuals should dominate the Board's decision-making.

2.7 The positions of the Chairman of the Board and the Managing Director/Chief Executive Officer (MD/CEO) of the Company should be separate such that no person can combine the two positions.

2.8 Directors may hold concurrent directorships. However, concurrent service on too many Boards may interfere with an individual's ability to discharge his responsibilities. To assist the Board in determining the appropriateness of concurrent directorships:

2.8.1 Prospective Directors should disclose memberships on other Boards, and current Directors should notify the Board of prospective appointments on other Boards. This information should be kept current by serving Board members.

2.8.2 The Board should consider the disclosed directorships, taking into account the number of other directorships and the responsibilities held, and determine whether the individual can discharge his responsibilities and contribute effectively to the performance of the Board before recommending such a person for appointment or continued service.

2.8.3 Directors should not be members of Boards of competing companies to avoid conflict of interest, breach of confidentiality, diversion of corporate opportunity and divulgence of corporate information.

2.9 The Chairman of the Board should not serve as chairman or member of any Board committee. The MD/CEO or an Executive Director should not serve as chairman of any Board committee.

2.10 A person (or group of persons) who is not a serving Director of the Company should not exercise any influence or dominance over the Board and/or Management. Such a person or group of persons would be deemed a shadow director as defined by extant laws.

3. Chairman

Principle 3: *The Chairman is responsible for providing overall leadership of the Company and the Board, and eliciting the constructive participation of all Directors to facilitate effective direction of the Board.*

Recommended Practices

3.1 The Chairman's primary responsibility is to ensure the effective operation of the Board such that the Board works as a group towards achieving the Company's strategic objectives. He should also provide guidance to the MD/CEO and be available to him for regular communication.

3.2 The Chairman of the Board should be a NED and not be involved in the day-to-day operations of the Company, which should be the primary responsibility of the MD/CEO and the management team.

3.3 The MD/CEO or an Executive Director (ED) should not go on to be the Chairman of the same Company. If in very exceptional circumstances the Board decides that a former MD/CEO or an ED should become Chairman, a cool-off period of three years should be adopted.

3.4 The Chairman's functions should include the following:

3.4.1 presiding over meetings of the Board of Directors and general meetings of shareholders;

3.4.2 agreeing an annual Board plan with the Board;

3.4.3 ensuring that the agenda for Board meetings is set;

3.4.4 ensuring that the Board and its committees are composed of individuals with relevant skills, competencies and desired experience;

3.4.5 ensuring that Board meetings are properly conducted;

3.4.6 ensuring that the Board is effective and functions in a cohesive manner;

3.4.7 ensuring that induction programmes are conducted for new Directors and a continuing education programme is in place for all Directors;

3.4.8 ensuring effective communication and relations with the Company's shareholders and other stakeholders; and

3.4.9 taking a lead role in the assessment, improvement and development of the Board.

3.5 The Chairman is responsible for ensuring that management provides the Directors with accurate, timely and adequate information.

3.6 The Chairman may interact with NEDs periodically.

4. Managing Director/Chief Executive Officer

Principle 4: *The Managing Director/Chief Executive Officer is the head of management delegated by the Board to run the affairs of the Company to achieve its strategic objectives for sustainable corporate performance.*

Recommended Practices

4.1 The Board may delegate any of its powers to the MD/CEO as it deems appropriate for the smooth operation of the Company.

4.2 The MD/CEO should have a broad understanding of the Company's business. He should demonstrate entrepreneurial skills, credibility and integrity and have the confidence of the Board and management.

4.3 The MD/CEO should establish a culture of integrity, conformance and performance which should be assimilated by personnel at all levels of the Company.

4.4 The functions and responsibilities of the MD/CEO should include:

4.4.1 day-to-day management of the Company;

4.4.2 proper implementation and achievement of the Company's strategic imperatives to ensure the sustainable development and growth of the Company;

4.4.3 ensuring prudent management of the Company's finances and other resources;

4.4.4 providing the Board with complete, accurate and timely information and documentation to enable it make sound decisions;

4.4.5 promoting and protecting the interests of the Company; and

4.4.6 being the Company's leading representative in its dealings with its stakeholders.

4.5 The authority of the MD/CEO and the relationship between him and the Board should be clearly set out in a contract of employment.

4.6 The MD/CEO should declare any conflict of interest on appointment and annually thereafter. In the event that he becomes aware of any potential conflict of interest at any other point, he should disclose this to the Board at the first possible opportunity. Actions following disclosure should be subject to the Company's Conflict of Interest Policy.

4.7 The MD/CEO should not be a member of the committees responsible for remuneration, audit, or nomination and governance.

4.8 The MD/CEO may be appointed an NED in any other Company, provided such appointment is not detrimental to his responsibilities and is in accordance with Board-approved policy.

5. Executive Directors

Principle 5: *Executive Directors support the Managing Director/Chief Executive Officer in the operations and management of the Company.*

Recommended Practices

5.1 EDs should have a broad understanding of the Company's business in addition to possessing such other qualifications as may be needed for their specific assignments or responsibilities.

5.2 EDs should support the MD/CEO in the proper implementation and achievement of the Company's strategic imperatives, as well as prudent management of the Company's finances and other resources.

5.3 EDs should declare any conflict of interest on appointment and annually thereafter. In the event that they become aware of any potential conflict of interest at any other point, they should disclose this to the Board at the first possible opportunity. Actions following disclosure should be subject to the Company's Conflict of Interest Policy.

5.4 An ED may be appointed NED in any other company, provided such appointment is not detrimental to his responsibilities as an ED and is in accordance with Board-approved policy.

5.5 An ED should not be a member of the committees responsible for remuneration, audit, or nomination and governance.

5.6 The responsibilities and authority of EDs should be clearly set out in a contract of employment.

6. Non-Executive Directors

Principle 6: *Non-Executive Directors bring to bear their knowledge, expertise and independent judgment on issues of strategy and performance on the Board.*

Recommended Practices

6.1 NEDs should be chosen on the basis of their wide experience, knowledge and personal qualities and are expected to bring these qualities to bear on the Company's business and affairs.

6.2 NEDs should constructively contribute to the development of the Company's strategy.

6.3 NEDs should not be involved in the day-to-day operations of the Company, which should be the primary responsibility of the MD/CEO and the management team.

6.4 NEDs should have unfettered access to the EDs, Company Secretary and the Internal Auditor, while access to other senior management should be through the MD/CEO.

6.5 To facilitate the effective discharge of their duties, NEDs should be provided, in a timely manner, with reasonable support as well as quality and comprehensive information relating to the management of the Company and on all Board matters.

7. Independent Non-Executive Directors

Principle 7: *Independent Non-Executive Directors bring a high degree of objectivity to the Board for sustaining stakeholder trust and confidence.*

Recommended Practices

7.1 An Independent Non-Executive Director (INED) should represent a strong independent voice on the Board, be independent in character and judgment and accordingly be free from such relationships or circumstances with the Company, its management, or substantial shareholders as may, or appear to, impair his ability to make independent judgment.

7.2 An INED is a NED who:

7.2.1 does not possess a shareholding in the Company the value of which is material to the holder such as will impair his independence or in excess of 0.01% of the paid up capital of the Company;

7.2.2 is not a representative of a shareholder that has the ability to control or significantly influence Management;

7.2.3 is not, or has not been an employee of the Company or group within the last five years;

7.2.4 is not a close family member of any of the Company's advisers, Directors, senior employees, consultants, auditors, creditors, suppliers, customers or substantial shareholders;

7.2.5 does not have, and has not had within the last five years, a material business relationship with the Company either directly, or as a partner, shareholder, Director or senior employee of a body that has, or has had, such a relationship with the Company;

7.2.6 has not served at directorate level or above at the Company's regulator within the last three years;

7.2.7 does not render any professional, consultancy or other advisory services to the Company or the group, other than in the capacity of a Director;

7.2.8 does not receive, and has not received additional remuneration from the Company apart from a Director's fee and allowances; does not participate in the Company's share option or a performance-related pay scheme, and is not a member of the Company's pension scheme; and

7.2.9 has not served on the Board for more than nine years from the date of his first election.

7.3 The above-mentioned criteria for establishing the independent status of an INED are not exhaustive, but should be considered as examples of some of those relationships or circumstances which may impair, or appear to impair an INED's independent judgment.

7.4 The Board should annually ascertain and confirm the continued independence of each INED of the Company.

7.5 Reclassification of an existing NED into an INED on the same Board is not desirable.

8. Company Secretary

Principle 8: *The Company Secretary plays an important role in supporting the effectiveness of the Board by assisting the Board and management to develop good corporate governance practices and culture within the Company.*

Recommended Practices

8.1 Without prejudice to the provisions of extant laws, the Company Secretary should be a person with relevant qualifications and competence necessary to effectively discharge the duties of his office. The Board should ensure that the person appointed has the gravitas and objectivity to provide independent guidance and support at the highest level of decision-making in the Company.

8.2 Where the Company Secretary is an employee of the Company, he should be a member of senior management and should be appointed through a rigorous selection process similar to that of new Directors.

8.3 The Company Secretary should be properly empowered by the Board to discharge his duties and responsibilities.

8.4 The Company Secretary should have both functional and administrative responsibilities. The functional responsibility is to the Board through the Chairman, while administratively, he reports to the MD/CEO.

8.5 The Board should approve the performance evaluation of the Company Secretary.

8.6 In addition to his statutory functions, the Company Secretary should carry out the following duties and responsibilities:

8.6.1 Provide the Board and Directors individually, with detailed guidance as to how their responsibilities should be properly discharged in the best interest of the Company;

8.6.2 Coordinate the induction and training of new Directors.

8.6.3 Assist the Chairman and MD/CEO in coordinating activities regarding the annual Board plan and with the administration of other strategic issues at the Board level;

8.6.4 Notify Board members of upcoming meetings of the Board and its committees as well as other matters that warrant their attention;

8.6.5 Compile Board papers and ensure that the Board's discussions and decisions are clearly and properly recorded and communicated to relevant persons in a timely manner;

8.6.6 Provide a central source of guidance and advice to the Board and the Company on matters of ethics, conflict of interest and good corporate governance.

8.7 Under the direction of the Chairman, the Company Secretary's responsibilities include ensuring good information flow within the Board and its committees and between senior management and NEDs.

8.8 Subject to the provisions of extant laws, the appointment and removal of the Company Secretary should be a matter for the Board.

9. Access to Independent Advice

Principle 9: *Directors are sometimes required to make decisions of a technical and complex nature that may require independent external expertise.*

Recommended Practices

9.1 The Board should ensure that Directors, especially NEDs, have access to independent professional advice where they consider it necessary to discharge their responsibilities as Directors.

9.2 The Board should ensure that such independent professional advice is obtained as set out in the Company's governance policies and at the Company's expense.

10. Meetings of the Board

Principle 10: *Meetings are the principal vehicle for conducting the business of the Board and successfully fulfilling the strategic objectives of the Company.*

Recommended Practices

10.1 In order to effectively perform its oversight function and monitor management's performance, the Board should meet at least once every quarter.

10.2 Every Director should endeavour to attend all Board meetings. The attendance record of Directors should be among the criteria for the re-election of a Director.

10.3 Minutes of meetings of the Board and its committees, as a record of what transpired at those meetings, should be prepared and sent to Directors on a timely basis. Such minutes should be formally reviewed and approved by the members of the Board or relevant Board committee at its next meeting.

11. Board Committees

Principle 11: *To ensure efficiency and effectiveness, the Board delegates some of its functions, duties and responsibilities to well-structured committees, without abdicating its responsibilities.*

Recommended Practices

11.1 Board Committees

11.1.1 The Board should determine the number and composition of its committees as well as ensure that each is comprised of Directors with relevant skills and competencies.

11.1.2 Only Directors may be members of Board committees, while members of senior management may be required to attend committee meetings.

11.1.3 The terms of reference and composition of such committees should be set out in the Board-approved committee charter, which should be reviewed periodically.

11.1.4 The membership of Board committees should be reviewed and refreshed periodically.

11.1.5 Each committee should be composed of at least three members. Individual Board committee charters will indicate where INEDs are required.

11.1.6 To facilitate adequate oversight, the Board should establish committees responsible for nomination and governance, remuneration, audit and risk management.

11.1.7 The Board may combine any of the responsibilities mentioned in Section 11.1.6 on Board committees, taking into consideration the size, needs and other requirements of the Company.

11.1.8 The chairmen of Board committees should be appointed by the Board.

11.1.9 The Board should ensure that, in appointing members of the Board committees, there is a balanced distribution of power in respect of membership across committees so that no individual has the ability to dominate decision making and undue reliance is not placed on any individual.

11.1.10 The Company Secretary, or any other officer in the office of the Company Secretary, should be the secretary of all Board committees.

11.1.11 The agenda for the meetings of Board committees should be developed in consultation with the respective committee chairmen.

11.1.12 The timing of committee meetings should be well coordinated for the effective discharge of their duties.

11.1.13 At board meetings, the chairman of each Board committee should present a written report of the key recommendations made at all the meetings held by the committee since the last Board meeting.

11.1.14 Members of Board committees should devote sufficient time to the committees' work.

11.1.15 Board Committees may engage a consultant at the expense of the Company for the purpose of obtaining independent external expertise in carrying out their responsibilities. This should be done in line with the Company's policies.

11.1.16 Board Committees should be accountable to the Board for their own activities and performance.

11.2 Committee responsible for Nomination and Governance

11.2.1 The Board should consider assigning the responsibilities for nomination of members and oversight of governance matters to a stand-alone committee, or to any other committee capable of combining it with their existing functions, as is appropriate.

11.2.2 Members of the committee responsible for nomination and governance should be NEDs, and a majority of them should be INEDs where possible.

11.2.3 The chairman of the committee should be a NED.

11.2.4 The committee should meet at least twice a year or such number of times as may be appropriate to discharge its duties.

11.2.5 Among other things, the committee should have the duty to: 11.2.5.1 Review the structure, size, composition and commitment of the Board at least annually and make recommendations on any proposed changes to the Board;

11.2.5.2 Establish a formal and transparent process for Board appointments, including establishing the criteria for appointment to the Board and Board committees, reviewing prospective candidates' qualifications and any potential conflict of interest; assessing the contribution of current Directors against their re-nomination suitability, and making appropriate recommendations to the Board;

11.2.5.3 Identify individuals suitably qualified to become Board members and make recommendations to the Board for nomination and appointment as Directors;

11.2.5.4 Periodically determine the skills, knowledge and experience required on the Board and its committees;

11.2.5.5 Ensure that the Company has a formal programme for the induction and training of Directors;

11.2.5.6 Undertake the annual assessment of the independent status of each INED;

11.2.5.7 Ensure that the Company has a succession policy and plan in place for the Chairman of the Board, the MD/CEO and all other EDs, NEDs and senior management positions to ensure leadership continuity. Succession planning should be reviewed periodically, with provision made for succession in emergency situations as well as long-term vacancies;

11.2.5.8 Deal with all matters pertaining to executive management selection and performance, including an annual evaluation of the performance of the MD/CEO and executive management.

11.2.5.9 Develop a process for, and ensure that the Board undertakes, an annual performance evaluation of itself, its committees, the Chairman and individual Directors, as well as the Company's corporate governance practices.

11.2.5.10 Ensure the development and periodic review of Board charters, Board committee charters and other governance policies, such as the code of ethics, conflict of interest and whistleblowing policies among others.

11.3 Committee responsible for Remuneration

11.3.1 The Board should consider assigning the responsibilities for the determination of remuneration policy and its application to executive management, performance evaluation, the adoption of incentive plans, and various governance responsibilities related to remuneration to a stand-alone committee, or to any other committee capable of combining it with their existing functions, as is appropriate.

11.3.2 Members of the committee responsible for remuneration should be NEDs, and a majority of them should be INEDs where possible.

11.3.3 It is desirable that the chairman of the committee be an INED.

11.3.4 The committee should meet at least once a year or such number of times as may be appropriate to discharge its duties.

11.3.5 The duties of the committee responsible for remuneration should include, among others:

11.3.5.1 Development of a formal, clear and transparent framework for the Company's remuneration policies and procedures;

11.3.5.2 Recommendation to the Board on the Company's remuneration policy and structure for all Directors and senior management employees.

11.4 Committee responsible for Audit

11.4.1 Without prejudice to the provision of extant laws on the Statutory Audit Committee, it is desirable for every Company to have a Board committee responsible for audit.

11.4.2 All members of the committee should be financially literate and should be able to read and understand financial statements. At least one member of the committee should be a financial expert, have current knowledge in accounting and financial management and be able to interpret financial statements.

11.4.3 For private companies, members of the committee responsible for audit should be NEDs, and a majority of them should be INEDs where possible.

11.4.4 In the case of the statutory audit committee, a chairman should be elected from amongst its members, and should have financial literacy.

11.4.5 The committee should meet at least once every quarter.

11.4.6 Subject to the provisions of extant laws, every public company should establish a statutory audit committee which shall perform the following functions:

11.4.6.1 Ascertain whether the accounting and reporting policies of the Company are in accordance with legal requirements and agreed ethical practices.

11.4.6.2 Review the scope and planning of audit requirements.

11.4.6.3 Review the findings in management letter in conjunction with the external auditor and management responses thereon.

11.4.6.4 Keep under review the effectiveness of the Company's system of accounting and internal control.

11.4.6.5 Make recommendations to the Board regarding the appointment, removal and remuneration of the external auditors of the Company.

11.4.6.6 Authorise the internal auditor to carry out investigations into any activities of the Company which may be of interest or concern to the committee.

11.4.7 The Board audit committee should have the following additional responsibilities:

11.4.7.1 Exercise oversight over management's processes to ascertain the integrity of the Company's financial statements, compliance with all applicable legal and other regulatory requirements; and assess the qualifications and independence of the external auditors, and the performance of the Company's internal audit function as well as that of the external auditors;

11.4.7.2 Ensure the establishment of and exercise oversight on the internal audit function which provides assurance on the effectiveness of the internal controls. On a quarterly basis, obtain and review a report by the internal auditor describing the strength and quality of internal controls including identification of any issues or recommendations for improvement raised by the most recent internal audit review of the Company;

11.4.7.3 Ensure the development of a comprehensive internal control framework for the Company, obtain appropriate (internal and/or external) assurance and report annually in the Company's audited financial report, on the design and operating effectiveness of the Company's internal controls over the financial reporting systems;

11.4.7.4 Oversee the process for the identification of fraud risks across the Company and ensure that adequate prevention, detection and reporting mechanisms are in place;

11.4.7.5 Discuss the interim or annual audited financial statements as well as significant financial reporting findings and recommendations with management and external auditors prior to recommending same to the Board for their consideration and appropriate action;

11.4.7.6 Maintain oversight of financial and non-financial reporting.

11.4.7.7 Review and ensure that adequate whistle-blowing policies and procedures are in place and that the issues reported through the whistle-blowing mechanism are summarised and presented to the board;

11.4.7.8 Review, with the external auditors, any audit scope limitations or significant matters encountered and management's responses to same;

11.4.7.9 Develop a policy on the nature, extent and terms under which the external auditors may perform non-audit services;

11.4.7.10 Review the independence of the external auditors in line with the policy referred to in Section 11.4.7.9 above prior to their appointment to perform non-audit services to ensure that where approved non-audit services are provided by the external auditors, there is no real or perceived conflict of interest, or other legal or ethical impediment;

11.4.7.11 Preserve auditor independence, by setting clear hiring policies for employees or former employees of external auditors;

11.4.7.12 Ensure the development of a Related Party Transactions policy and monitor its implementation by management. The Committee should consider any related party transaction that may arise within the Company.

11.4.8 At least once in a year, the committee should hold a discussion with the head of the internal audit function and the external auditors without the presence of management, to facilitate an exchange of views and concerns that may not be appropriate for open discussion.

11.5 Committee responsible for Risk Management

11.5.1 The Board should consider assigning the responsibilities for oversight of matters relating to risk management to a standalone committee, or to any other committee capable of combining it with their existing functions, as is appropriate.

11.5.2 Members of the committee responsible for risk management should include EDs and NEDs, a majority of whom should be NEDs.

11.5.3 Where the committees responsible for audit and risk management are separate, the Board should consider for one or more members to have joint membership of both committees for more effective functioning as this will enhance the discussions at meetings of both committees – the risk implication of audit matters will be discussed more extensively, and a knowledge of findings from the Company's internal audit activities will bring a unique perspective to the discussion of risk issues.

11.5.4 The chairman of the committee should be a NED.

11.5.5 The committee should meet at least twice every financial year or such number of times as may be appropriate to discharge its duties.

11.5.6 The committee should:

11.5.6.1 Review and recommend for approval of the Board, the risk management policies and framework, as well as assist the Board in its oversight of risk management strategy;

11.5.6.2 Review the adequacy and effectiveness of risk management and controls in the Company;

11.5.6.3 Exercise oversight over the process for the identification and assessment of risks across the Company and the adequacy of prevention, detection and reporting mechanisms;

11.5.6.4 Review the level of the Company's compliance with applicable laws and regulatory requirements which may impact the Company's risk profile;

11.5.6.5 Periodically review changes in the economic and business environment, including emerging trends and other factors relevant to the Company's risk profile and those trends which may threaten the Company's business model, key strategies, future performance, solvency and liquidity and make recommendations to the Board as appropriate;

11.5.6.6 Review and recommend for approval of the Board, at least annually, the Company's Information Technology (IT) data governance framework to ensure that IT data risks are adequately mitigated and relevant assets are managed effectively. The framework may include: (a) Development of IT strategy and policy;

(b) Proactive monitoring and management of cyber threats and attacks as well as adverse social media incidents;

(c) Management of risks relating to third-party and outsourced IT service providers;

(d) Assessment of value delivered to the Company through investments in IT; and

(e) Periodic independent assurance on the effectiveness of the Company's IT arrangements.

11.5.7 The person charged with the responsibility for risk management should be a member of senior management of the Company, a professional with relevant qualifications and experience and should be in attendance at meetings of the committee. The direct reporting line of this person should be to the MD/CEO and there should be an indirect reporting line to the committee responsible for risk management.

12. Appointment to the Board

Principle 12: *A written, clearly defined, rigorous, formal and transparent procedure serves as a guide for the selection of Directors to ensure the appointment of high quality individuals to the Board.*

Recommended Practices

12.1 The Board should approve the criteria for appointing Directors, as recommended by the committee responsible for nomination and governance. Such criteria should take into careful consideration the strengths and weaknesses of the existing Board, integrity, required competence and skills, knowledge and experience, capacity to undertake the responsibility as well as diversity, including gender diversity. In the case of specialised businesses, possession of requisite technical skill should be taken into account.

12.2 The committee responsible for nomination and governance should ensure that proposed Directors are fit and proper persons before recommending them to the Board for consideration for directorship positions.

12.3 Shareholders should be provided with biographical information of proposed Directors to guide their decision. Such information should include:
(a) name, age, qualifications, country of primary residence and the ownership interest represented, if any;
(b) whether the appointment is for ED, NED or INED, and any proposed specific area of responsibility or Board committee roles if any;
(c) work experience and occupation;
(d) current directorships and appointments;
(e) direct and/or indirect shareholding in the Company and/or its subsidiaries; and
(f) any other relevant information.

12.4 Every Director should receive a letter of appointment or contract of employment, specifying the terms and conditions of his appointment or employment.

12.5 The letter of appointment or contract of employment should cover the following issues:
(a) duration of the appointment or tenure;
(b) details of the remuneration;
(c) summary of the rights, fiduciary duties and other responsibilities of the Director;
(d) requirement to disclose any material interests in the Company and other entities carrying on business or providing services to the Company;
(e) specific requirements, such as Board or Board committee meeting attendance;
(f) formal induction programme or training for the Director to attend;
(g) Board Charter, Code of Business Conduct and Ethics (attached as separate documents) and the Director's responsibility to observe same;
(h) Board performance evaluation process used by the Company; and
(i) any other relevant information.

12.6 The Company should state the processes used in relation to all Board appointments in its annual report.

12.7 Subject to the provisions of extant laws and the recommendation of the committee responsible for nomination and governance based on the results of the individual Directors' performance appraisal, Board members may offer themselves for re-election.

12.8 NEDs should serve for a reasonable period on the Board. However, it is necessary to reinforce the Board by continually injecting new energy, fresh ideas and perspectives. The Board should ensure the periodic appointment of new Directors to replace existing NEDs.

12.9 The tenure for the MD/CEO and the EDs should be determined by the Board. In determining the tenure of an ED, the Board should take into account his performance, the existing succession planning mechanism, continuity of the Board and the need for continuous refreshing of the Board.

12.10 The tenure for INEDs should not exceed three terms of three years each.

12.11 To resign, Directors should submit a written notice of resignation addressed to the Chairman.

12.12 Where a Director has concerns about the running of the Company which cannot be resolved and he elects to resign from the Board, such concerns should be detailed in a written statement to the Chairman for circulation to the Board.

13. Induction and Continuing Education

Principle 13: *A formal induction programme on joining the Board as well as regular training assists Directors to effectively discharge their duties to the Company.*

Recommended Practices

13.1 The Board should establish a formal induction programme for new Directors of the Company to familiarise them with the Company's, strategic plan, operations, business environment, senior management, and the Directors' fiduciary responsibilities. The induction of new Directors should take place as soon as feasible after their appointment.

13.2 All Directors should participate in periodic, relevant, continuing education programmes to update their knowledge and skills and keep them informed of new developments in the Company's business and operating environment.

13.3 The outcome of the performance evaluation of the individual Directors should be taken into account in developing the Board training programme.

13.4 The training programmes should be at the Company's expense but should not be such that put undue strain on the Company's finances.

14. Board Evaluation

Principle 14: *Annual Board evaluation assesses how each Director, the committees of the Board and the Board are committed to their roles, work together and continue to contribute effectively to the achievement of the Company's objectives.*

Recommended Practices

14.1 The Board should establish a system to undertake a formal and rigorous annual evaluation of its own performance, that of its committees, the Chairman and individual Directors. This process should be externally facilitated by an independent external consultant at least once in three years.

14.2 The evaluation system should include the criteria and key performance indicators and targets for the Board, its committees, the Chairman and each individual Board member.

14.3 The evaluation of the Board should consider the mix of skills, experience, objectivity, competence of members of the Board, its diversity (including gender), knowledge of the Company and its strategic direction, attendance at meetings, how the Board works together and other factors relevant to its effectiveness.

14.4 The result of the Board performance evaluation should be communicated to and discussed by the Board as a whole, while those of individual Directors should be communicated to and discussed with them individually by the Chairman.

14.5 Where the performance of a Director is considered to be unsatisfactory, the Board should provide appropriate training to address the identified gaps.

14.6 The results of a Director's performance evaluation should be considered in the Director re-election process.

15. Corporate Governance Evaluation

Principle 15: *Institutionalising a system for evaluating the Company's corporate governance practices ensures that its governance standards, practices and processes are adequate and effective.*

Recommended Practices

15.1 The Board should ensure that an annual corporate governance evaluation, including the extent of application of this Code, is carried out. The evaluation should be facilitated by an independent external consultant at least once in three years.

15.2 The summary of the report of this evaluation should be included in the Company's annual report and on the investors' portal of the Company.

16. Remuneration Governance

Principle 16: *The Board ensures that the Company remunerates fairly, responsibly and transparently so as to promote the achievement of strategic objectives and positive outcomes in the short, medium and long term.*

Recommended Practices

16.1 The Board should assume responsibility for the governance of remuneration by setting the direction for how remuneration should be addressed on a Company-wide basis.

16.2 The Board should approve policies that articulate and give effect to its direction on fair, responsible and transparent remuneration.

16.3 The remuneration policy should be designed to attract, motivate, reward and retain high performing human capital.

16.4 The Board should periodically confirm that the implementation and execution of the remuneration policy achieves its objectives.

16.5 Remuneration for NEDs should be fixed by the Board and approved by shareholders in the General Meeting.

16.6 The remuneration of the MD/CEO and EDs should be structured to link rewards to corporate and individual performances and include a significant component that is related to long-term corporate performance, such as stock options and bonuses. Mechanisms may be considered to align payment of certain components of the remuneration of the MD/CEO and EDs with the achievement of longer-term goals.

16.7 The MD/CEO and EDs should not be involved in the determination of their remuneration.

16.8 The Company's Remuneration Policy as well as remuneration of all Directors should be disclosed in the Company's annual report.

16.9 Companies should implement a clawback policy to recover excess or undeserved reward, such as bonuses, incentives, share of profits, stock options, or any performance-based reward, from Directors and senior employees.

16.10 Clawback can be triggered if the account or financial performance on which the reward was based is later found to be materially false, misstated, misleading, erroneous, etc. or in instances of misdemeanour, fraud, material violation of Company policy or material regulatory infractions.

16.11 The MD/CEO and EDs should not receive sitting allowances for attending meetings of the Board or its committees and Director's fees from the Company, its holding company or subsidiaries. Their remuneration should however encompass recompense for time spent on the Board, its committees, and related work.

16.12 NEDs should not receive performance-based compensation as it may lead to bias in their decision-making and compromise their objectivity.

16.13 NEDs may be paid sitting allowances, Directors' fees and reimbursable travel and hotel expenses. These payments, in addition to any other allowances and benefits made to NEDs, should be disclosed in the Company's annual report.

16.14 Subject to the provisions of extant laws, the Company may pay compensation for loss of office or retirement to Directors. In the case of the MD/CEO, EDs and senior management, the compensation payable for any loss of office or termination of appointment should be consistent with their contractual terms, fair and not excessive.

Part B. Assurance

17. Risk Management

Principle 17: *A sound framework for managing risk and ensuring an effective internal control system is essential for achieving the strategic objectives of the Company.*

Recommended Practices The Board should:

17.1 ensure the establishment of a risk management framework that:

17.1.1 defines the Company's risk policy, risk appetite and risk limits; and

17.1.2 identifies, assesses, monitors and manages key business risks to safeguard shareholders' investments and the Company's assets;

17.2 formally approve the risk management framework and ensure that it is communicated in simple and clear language to all employees;

17.3 ensure that the risk management framework is integrated into the day-to-day operations of the business and provide guidelines and standards for management of key risks;

17.4 articulate, implement and review the Company's internal control systems to strengthen the risk management framework;

17.5 conduct at least annually, or more often in companies with complex operations, a thorough risk assessment covering all aspects of the Company's business and ensure that mitigating strategies have been put in place to manage identified risks;

17.6 obtain and review relevant reports periodically to ensure the ongoing effectiveness of the Company's risk management framework;

17.7 ensure that the Company's risk management framework is disclosed in the annual report; and

17.8 ensure that the risk management function is headed by a member of senior management who is a professional with relevant qualifications, competence, objectivity and experience.

18. Internal Audit Function

Principle 18: *An effective internal audit function provides assurance to the Board on the effectiveness of the governance, risk management and internal control systems.*

Recommended Practices

18.1 The purpose, authority and responsibility of the internal audit function should be clearly and formally defined in an internal audit charter approved by the Board.

18.2 Where the Board decides not to establish such a function, internally or outsourced, sufficient reasons should be disclosed in the Company's annual report with an explanation as to how the Board has obtained adequate assurance on the effectiveness of the internal processes and systems such as risk management and internal control.

18.3 The internal audit function should be headed by a member of senior management who is a professional with relevant qualifications, competence, objectivity and experience; and is registered with a recognised professional body.

18.4 The Board should ensure that the internal audit function is sufficiently skilled and resourced to address the complexity and volume of risk faced by the organisation.

18.5 The head of the internal audit function should:

18.5.1 Report directly to the committee responsible for audit while having a line of communication with the MD/CEO.

18.5.2 Have unrestricted access to the chairman of the committee responsible for audit as well as the Chairman of the Board.

18.5.3 Report at least once every quarter to the committee responsible for audit, on the adequacy and effectiveness of management, governance, risk and control environment; deficiencies observed and management mitigation plans.

18.5.4 Provide assurance to the Board by conducting periodic evaluations to determine the effectiveness and efficiency of the Company's internal control systems and make recommendations for enhancement or improvement.

18.5.5 Develop an annual risk-based internal audit plan which should be approved by the committee responsible for audit.

18.5.6 Liaise with other internal and external providers of assurance in order to ensure proper coverage and to minimise duplication of efforts.

18.6 There should be an external assessment of the effectiveness of the internal audit function at least once every three years by a qualified independent reviewer to be appointed by the Board.

18.7 The evaluation of the head of the internal audit function should be performed by the committee responsible for audit, and he may only be removed by the Board on the recommendation of the committee responsible for audit.

19. Whistle-blowing

Principle 19: *An effective whistle-blowing framework for reporting any illegal or unethical behaviour minimises the Company's exposure and prevents recurrence.*

Recommended Practices

19.1 The Board should establish a whistle-blowing framework to encourage stakeholders to bring unethical conduct and violations of laws and regulations to the attention of an internal and/or external authority so that action can be taken to verify the allegation and apply appropriate sanctions or take remedial action to correct any harm done. This framework should be known to employees and external stakeholders.

19.2 The Board should ensure the existence of a whistle-blowing mechanism that is reliable, accessible and guarantees the anonymity of the whistle-blower, and that all disclosures resulting from whistleblowing are treated in a confidential manner. The identity of the whistle-blower should be kept confidential.

19.3 The Board should accord priority to the effectiveness of the whistleblowing mechanism and continually affirm publicly, its support for and commitment to the Company's whistle-blower protection mechanism.

19.4 The team responsible for managing disclosures obtained through the whistle-blowing mechanism should:

19.4.1 Review reported cases and bring them to the notice of the committee responsible for audit

19.4.2 Provide the committee responsible for audit with a summary of reported cases, cases investigated, the process of investigation and the results of the investigations.

19.5 A whistle-blower can disclose any information related to a violation or suspected violation of any laws, internal policies, etc. connected with the business of the Company, its employees or stakeholders.

19.6 The Board should ensure that no whistle-blower is subject to any detriment on the grounds that he has made a disclosure. Where a whistle-blower has been subjected to any detriment, he may present a complaint to the Board and/or regulators. A whistle-blower who has suffered any detriment by reason of disclosure may be entitled to compensation and/or reinstatement as appropriate.

20. External Auditors

Principle 20: *An external auditor is appointed to provide an independent opinion on the true and fair view of the financial statements of the Company to give assurance to stakeholders on the reliability of the financial statements.*

Recommended Practices

20.1 Subject to the provisions of any extant laws, the recommendation for the appointment, re-appointment or removal of an external auditor should be made to the Board by the committee responsible for audit.

20.2 External audit firms may be retained for no longer than ten years continuously. External audit firms disengaged after ten years continuous service may not be considered for reappointment until seven years after their disengagement. Where an external auditor's aggregate or cumulative tenure has already exceeded ten years at the date of commencement of this Code, such auditor should cease to hold office as an auditor of the Company at the Annual General Meeting to be held immediately after this Code comes into effect.

20.3 An external auditor may provide to the Company only such other services as are approved by the Board on the recommendation of the committee responsible for audit and such as does not create a self-review threat in line with the provisions of international auditing standards.

20.4 In order to preserve independence, there should be a rotation of the audit engagement partner every five years.

20.5 In order to preserve independence, there should be an appropriate cooling off period spanning at least three years between the retirement of a partner from an audit firm and his appointment to the Board of an audit client. Similarly, there should be a cooling off period before a Company can engage any member of the audit team as a staff member in the financial reporting function.

20.6 In order to ensure quality audit outcomes, the engagement partner and audit team should possess the knowledge, relevant skills and experience. Additionally, they should demonstrate a good understanding of the Company's business, be independent of the Company and approach their work with a high level of objectivity and professionalism – including applying internationally accepted audit standards in their work.

20.7 Where the Board is satisfied that the external auditor has abused its office, acted in a fraudulent manner, colluded in any fraud or engaged in any unethical practice, it may recommend the removal of such external auditor in accordance with the provisions of extant laws. Where a Regulator is satisfied that the external auditor of a Company has abused its office as auditor, it may request the Company to remove such external auditor in line with the provisions of extant laws.

20.8 Where external auditors discover or acquire information during an audit that leads them to believe that the Company or anyone associated with it has committed an indictable offence under any law, they should report this to the

Regulator, whether or not such matter is or will be included in the Management Letter issued to the committee responsible for audit and/or the Board.

Part C. Relationship with Shareholders

21. General Meetings

Principle 21: *General Meetings are important platforms for the Board to engage shareholders to facilitate greater understanding of the Company's business, governance and performance. They provide shareholders with an opportunity to exercise their ownership rights and express their views to the Board on any areas of interest.*

Recommended Practices

21.1 General Meetings should be conducted in an open manner allowing for free discussions on all issues on the agenda. Sufficient time should be allocated to shareholders, particularly minorities, to participate fully and contribute effectively at such meetings.

21.2 The chairmen of all Board committees and of the Statutory Audit Committee should be present at General Meetings of the Company to respond to shareholders' inquiries.

21.3 The venue of a General Meeting should be accessible to shareholders, to ensure that shareholders are not disenfranchised on account of the choice of venue.

21.4 Notices of General Meetings shall be at least 21 days from the date on which the meeting will be held. Copies of the annual reports, audited financial statements and all other information pertaining to any resolution to be voted upon – including voting or proxy instructions and relevant papers – that will enable members prepare adequately for the meeting should be despatched along with the notice.

21.5 The Board should ensure that unrelated issues for consideration are not lumped together at General Meetings. All matters to be considered should be clearly and separately set out. Separate resolutions should be proposed and voted on for each substantive issue.

21.6 The Board should ensure that decisions reached at General Meetings are properly and fully implemented as governance directives.

22. Shareholder Engagement

Principle 22: *The establishment of a system of regular dialogue with shareholders balances their needs, interests and expectations with the objectives of the Company.*

Recommended Practices

22.1 The Board should develop a policy that ensures appropriate engagement with shareholders. The policy should be hosted on the website of the Company.

22.2 The Chairman of the Board, or other designated persons as specified in the policy referred to in Section 22.1, may interact with shareholders in order to help develop a balanced understanding of shareholder issues and ensure that their views are communicated to the Board.

22.3 The Board should encourage institutional investors to:

22.3.1 Positively influence the standard of corporate governance and promote value creation in the companies in which they invest.

22.3.2 Monitor conformance with the provisions of this Code and raise concerns as appropriate.

22.4 The Board should ensure that dealings of the Company with shareholder associations are always transparent and in the best interest of the Company.

23. Protection of Shareholder Rights

Principle 23: *Equitable treatment of shareholders and the protection of their statutory and general rights, particularly the interest of minority shareholders, promote good governance.*

Recommended Practices

23.1 The Board should ensure that:

23.1.1 shareholders at annual general meetings preserve their effective powers to appoint and remove Directors of the Company;

23.1.2 all shareholders are treated fairly and equitably. No shareholder, however large his shareholding or whether institutional or otherwise, should be given preferential treatment or superior access to information or other materials;

23.1.3 minority shareholders are adequately protected from abusive actions by controlling shareholders;

23.1.4 the Company promptly renders to shareholders documentary evidence of ownership interest in the Company and related instruments. Where these are rendered electronically, the Board should ensure that they are rendered to shareholders promptly and in a secure manner; and

23.1.5 all shareholders understand the ownership structure of the Company, and support them in this by making available, current information on the ultimate beneficial owners of the major shareholdings or any shareholders owning, controlling or influencing five percent (5%) or more of the Company's shares.

23.2 At all times, Directors should act in good faith and with integrity in the best interests of all shareholders, and provide adequate information to shareholders to facilitate their investment decisions.

Part D. Business Conduct and Ethics

24. Business Conduct and Ethics

Principle 24: *The establishment of professional business and ethical standards underscores the values for the protection and enhancement of the reputation of the Company while promoting good conduct and investor confidence.*

Recommended Practices

24.1 The Board should clearly model a top-down commitment to professional business and ethical standards by formulating and periodically reviewing the Code of Business Conduct and Ethics.

24.2 The Board should be responsible for monitoring adherence to the Code of Business Conduct and Ethics to ensure that breaches are effectively sanctioned. This may be delegated to the committee responsible for nomination and governance.

24.3 The Code of Business Conduct and Ethics should include the following:

24.3.1 Directors and senior management of the Company should act honestly, in good faith and in the best interests of the Company in accordance with legal requirements and agreed ethical standards;

24.3.2 Directors owe a fiduciary duty to the Company, together with a duty of care, skill, diligence and loyalty in fulfilling the functions of their offices and exercising the powers attached to those offices;

24.3.3 Directors should undertake diligent analysis of all proposals placed before the Board and act with the level of skill expected from Directors;

24.3.4 Directors should not make improper or prejudicial use of privileged information and should not disclose non-public information except where disclosure is authorised or legally mandated;

24.3.5 Directors should not take advantage of their position for personal gain or to compete with the Company;

24.3.6 Directors should not engage in conduct likely to discredit the Company, and should encourage fair dealing by all employees with the Company's customers, suppliers and competitors;

24.3.7 Directors should encourage the reporting of unlawful or unethical behaviours and actively promote ethical behaviours and the protection of those who report violations in good faith; and

24.3.8 Directors, management and other employees shall have an obligation to comply with the principles of the Code of Business Conduct and Ethics at all times.

24.4 The Code of Business Conduct and Ethics should:

(a) commit the Company, its Board, management and other employees, contractors, suppliers (under contractual terms) and other company-controlled entities to the highest standards of professional and ethical behaviour, business conduct and sustainable business practices;

(b) be designed with due consideration of the interests of the Company, its management and employees;

(c) receive its implementation commitment from the MD/CEO and executive management;

(d) be sufficiently detailed as to give clear guidance to users; and (e) be formally communicated to all persons to whom it applies.

24.5 Companies are encouraged to explore formal mechanisms for engagement and communication with stakeholders, including the use of alternative dispute resolution mechanisms and associated processes.

25. Ethical Culture

Principle 25: *The establishment of policies and mechanisms for monitoring insider trading, related party transactions, conflict of interest and other corrupt activities, mitigates the adverse effects of these abuses on the Company and promotes good ethical conduct and investor confidence.*

Recommended Practices

25.1 The Board should ensure:

25.1.1 The establishment of policies on insider trading, related party transactions and conflict of interest.

25.1.2 That insiders are precluded from buying and selling any security in breach of their fiduciary duty and other relationship of trust and confidence while in possession of material, privileged, non-public and price-sensitive information about the Company.

25.1.3 That insiders are precluded from engaging in unlawful or improper transfers of assets and profits out of companies for their personal benefits or for the benefit of those who control the companies.

25.1.4 The disclosure of all transactions between related parties, whether natural persons or bodies corporate, including whether such transactions have been executed at arm's length and on normal market terms. This disclosure should be made prior to the conclusion of the transaction, if they exceed a disclosure threshold as determined by the Board.

25.2 The policy on conflict of interest should be communicated, supported and monitored to provide reasonable assurance that all potential conflict of interest situations will be disclosed. The policy should be guided by the following:

25.2.1 Directors should promptly disclose any real or potential conflict of interest that they may have by virtue of their membership of the Board.

25.2.2 A Director may not be present during the time any matter in which he has an interest is being decided and should not seek to participate or influence any discussions or negotiations relating to that matter.

25.2.3 If a Director is not certain whether he is in a conflict of interest situation, the Director concerned should discuss the matter with the Chairman of the Board, the Company Secretary or the chairman of the committee responsible for nomination and governance for advice and guidance.

25.2.4 If any question arises before the Board as to the existence of a real or perceived conflict, the Board should by a simple majority determine if a conflict exists. The Director or Directors potentially in the conflict of interest situation should not be present during any discussion and voting on the issue.

25.2.5 Directors who are aware of a real, potential or perceived conflict of interest on the part of a fellow Director, have a responsibility to raise the issue promptly for clarification, either with the Director concerned, the Chairman of the Board or the chairman of the committee responsible for nomination and governance.

25.2.6 Disclosure by a Director of a real, potential or perceived conflict of interest or a decision by the Board as to whether or not a conflict of interest exists should be recorded in the minutes of the meeting.

25.2.7 All directors should declare any conflict of interest on appointment and annually thereafter. In the event that they become aware of any potential conflict of interest at any other point, they should disclose this to the Board at the first possible opportunity. Actions following disclosure should be subject to the Company's conflict of interest policy.

25.2.8 No person who has served at directorate level or above, leaving the services of a relevant regulatory institution, for any reason, should be appointed as a Director or top management staff of an institution that has been directly supervised or regulated by the said regulatory institution until after three years of the disengagement of such executive or senior management staff from that regulatory institution.

Part E. Sustainability

26. Sustainability

Principle 26: *Paying adequate attention to sustainability issues including environment, social, occupational and community health and safety ensures successful long term business performance and projects the Company as a responsible corporate citizen contributing to economic development.*

Recommended Practices

26.1 The Board should establish policies and practices regarding its social, ethical, safety, working conditions, health and environmental responsibilities as well as policies addressing corruption.

26.2 The policies should include the following:

26.2.1 the Company's business principles, practices and efforts towards achieving sustainability;

26.2.2 the management of safety issues including workplace accidents, fatalities, occupational and safety incidents;

26.2.3 plans and strategy for addressing and managing the impact of serious diseases on the Company's employees and their families;

26.2.4 the most environmentally beneficial options particularly for companies operating in disadvantaged regions or in regions with delicate ecology, in order to minimise environmental impact of the Company's operations;

26.2.5 the nature and extent of employment equity and diversity (gender and other issues);

26.2.6 training initiatives, employee development and the associated financial investment;

26.2.7 opportunities created for physically challenged persons or disadvantaged individuals;

26.2.8 the environmental, social and governance principles and practices of the Company; and

26.2.9 corruption and related issues.

26.3 The Board should monitor the implementation of sustainability policies and report on the extent of compliance with the policies.

Part F. Transparency

27. Stakeholder Communication

Principle 27: *Communicating and interacting with stakeholders keeps them conversant with the activities of the Company and assists them in making informed decisions.*

Recommended Practices

27.1 The Board should adopt and implement a stakeholder management and communication policy.

27.2 The Board should ensure that the reports and other communication issued to stakeholders are in clear and easily understood language and are posted on the Company's web portal. This information may include description of structures of the Board and management among others, frameworks, policies and other material information about the Company.

27.3 Communication with stakeholders and the general public should be governed by the principle of timely, accurate and continuous disclosure of material information on the activities of the Company so as to give a balanced and fair view of the Company, including its non-financial matters.

27.4 The Board should establish an investors' portal on the Company's website, where the communication policy as well as the Company's annual reports for a minimum of five immediately preceding years and other relevant information about the Company should be published and made accessible to the public in downloadable format.

28. Disclosures

Principle 28: *Full and comprehensive disclosure of all matters material to investors and stakeholders, and of matters set out in this Code, ensures proper monitoring of its implementation which engenders good corporate governance practice.*

Recommended Practices

28.1 The Board should ensure that the Company's annual report includes a corporate governance report that provides clear information on the Company's governance structures, policies and practices as well as environmental and social risks and opportunities.

28.2 The Company's corporate governance report should include the following:

(a) composition of the Board of Directors, stating the names and classification of the Chairman, the MD/CEO, EDs and NEDs as well as INEDs. This information should also be on the Company's website and other publications of the Company;

(b) the plan for achieving gender diversity set by the Board in accordance with its diversity policy, the progress towards achieving them and the proportion of women employees in the whole organisation, including women in executive management positions and women on the Board;

(c) Board appointment process including a summary statement on induction and training of Board members;

(d) evaluation process for the Board, its Committees and individual Directors as well as the assessment of the corporate governance practices in the Company;

(e) Directors standing for re-election;

(f) composition of Board committees including names of chairmen and members of each committee;

(g) description of the roles and responsibilities of the Board committees and how the committees have discharged those responsibilities;
(h) the number of meetings held by the Board and its committees during the year and the attendance of individual Directors at those meetings;
(i) cumulative years of service of each Director, the external auditor and the external consultant who performs the Board Evaluation or Corporate Governance Evaluation at the end of the reporting period;
(j) statement on the availability or otherwise of the Code of Business Conduct and Ethics for Directors, management and other employees;
(k) highlights of human resource policies and internal management structure, including relations with employees, employee share-ownership schemes and other workplace development initiatives;
(l) highlights of sustainability policies and programmes covering social issues such as corruption, community service, including environmental protection, serious diseases and matters of general environmental, social and governance (ESG) initiatives;
(m) highlights of the policy and cases of clawback being pursued by the Company; and
(n) a list of all the fines and penalties (including date, amount, and subject matter) imposed on the Company by regulators at the end of the reporting period.

28.3 The report should specify the nature of any related party relationships and transactions as follows:

28.3.1 their purpose and financial magnitude necessary to understand whether the transactions have been at arm's length and that the Company has not suffered any loss or disadvantage from such transactions.

28.3.2 any Director's interest in contracts either directly or indirectly with the Company or its subsidiaries and holding companies.

28.3.3 the name of the Director, his classification, the nature and details of the transaction and the Director's interest therein: provided that the disclosures required do not include the Director's service contract.

28.3.4 any contracts with controlling shareholder(s), their group networks and associates.

28.3.5 The names of the parties and the nature of the transaction, and the value (monetary or other value) involved in the transaction.

28.4The Board should use its best judgment to disclose any material matter even though not specifically required by this Code to be disclosed if in the opinion of the Board such matter is capable of affecting the present or anticipated financial condition of the Company or its status as a going concern. The onus of proof of such possible negative effect is on the Board.

28.5The annual report should contain a statement by the Board on the Company's level of application of this Code arising from the results of its corporate governance evaluation.

28.6Where the Board has engaged independent experts in evaluating and reporting on the extent of application of this Code, they should name the consultant and include a summary of the report (provided by the consultant) in the Company's annual report.

(a) A Director who has serious concerns about the activities of a Company should ensure that the following are promptly raised to the Board for resolution: any unreported cases of conflict of interest, insider trading, related party transactions, fraud or any illegal or suspected illegal activities;

(b) the impairment of the external auditor's independence and objectivity, or failure to approach his work with an acceptable degree of professional scepticism;

(c) any violation of this Code, extant laws and regulations, and disregard for accounting standards, auditing standards or financial reporting requirements;

(d) the impairment of the independence of the Board or any of its committees; or

(e) condoning of unethical behaviour and conduct in the Company.

28.8 The annual report should contain a statement by the Board on the Company's ESG activities. This should be reviewed by an appropriate Board committee and may be subject to independent review.

28.9 The Company should establish policies and procedures for the identification, communication and response to concerns from stakeholders.

Part G. Definitions

29. Definitions

29.1 In this Code, unless the context otherwise requires:

29.1.1 "chief financial officer" means a person appointed as the chief financial officer of a Company by whatever name designated;

29.1.2 "close family member" means those persons who may be expected to influence, or be influenced by, that person in his dealing with a Company;

29.1.3 "Company" means a Company incorporated under the Companies and Allied Matters Act, Cap. C20, Laws of the Federation of Nigeria 2004;

29.1.4 "concessioned" or "privatised" companies means companies hitherto owned or operated by a government (Federal or State) and ceded or sold to private investors;

29.1.5 "control" refers to a situation where a person is exposed, or has rights, to variable returns from his involvement with a Company and has the ability to affect those returns through his powers over the Company;

29.1.6 "corporate citizenship" means the social responsibility of businesses and the extent to which they meet legal, ethical, economic and environmental responsibilities;

29.1.7 "detriment" includes dismissal, termination, demotion, retirement, redundancy, undue influence duress, withholding of benefits and/or entitlements, blacklisting, withdrawal of patronage and any other act that has a negative impact on the whistle-blower;

29.1.8 "Director" means a person duly appointed by the Company to direct and manage the affairs of the Company;

29.1.9 "ethics" means moral principles that govern a person's behaviour or the conduct of an activity;

29.1.10 "executive management" means the Chief Executive Officer and other persons having authority and responsibility for planning, directing and controlling the day-to-day activities of the Company, whether or not they are members of the Board of Directors of the Company;

29.1.11 "extant laws" means any law or statute in force in the Federal Republic of Nigeria;

29.1.12 "financial expert" means a person who understands and interprets generally accepted accounting principles and financial statements;

29.1.13 "financial literacy" means the possession of the basic set of skills and knowledge that allows an individual to understand financial statements to make effective and informed decisions;

29.1.14 "general meeting" includes the Annual General Meeting, Statutory Meeting and the Extraordinary General Meeting;

29.1.15 "insider" means the following:

(a) any person who is connected with the Company in one or more of the following capacities:

(i) a Director of the Company or a related Company;

(ii) an officer of the Company or a related Company;

(iii) an employee of the Company or a related Company;

(iv) any shareholder of the Company who owns five percent (5%) or more of any class of securities or any person who is or can be deemed to have any relationship with the Company or member;

(v) members of the statutory audit committee of a Company; and

(vi) any person involved in a professional or business relationship who has access to inside information by virtue of his relationship to (i) to (v) above.

(b) any of the persons listed in paragraph (a), who by virtue of having been connected with any such person or connected with the Company in any other way, possesses unpublished price-sensitive information in relation to the securities of the Company, and any reference to unpublished price-sensitive information in relation to any securities of a Company is a reference to information which:

(i) relates to specific matters relating or of concern (directly or indirectly) to that Company, that is, is not of a general nature relating or of concern to that Company; and

(ii) is not generally known to those persons who are accustomed to or would be likely to deal in those securities but which would, if it were generally known to them be likely materially to affect the price of those securities;

29.1.16 "joint control" refers to a situation where more than one person, working together, exercise control over a Company;

29.1.17 "listed Company" means a Company which has any of its securities listed on any recognised stock exchange;

29.1.18 "Managing Director/Chief Executive Officer" means the head of Management delegated by the Board to run the Company;

29.1.19 "regulator" or "regulatory authority" means the Financial Reporting Council of Nigeria and other sectoral regulators as may be appropriate;

29.1.20 "regulated private companies" means private companies that file returns to any regulatory authority other than the Federal Inland Revenue Service and the Corporate Affairs Commission;

29.1.21 "related party/company" means a person or Company that is related to the Company that is preparing its financial statements.

a. A person or a close member of that person's family is related to a reporting Company if that person: i. has control or joint control of the reporting Company; ii. has significant influence over the reporting Company; or iii. is a member of the key management personnel of the reporting Company or of a parent of the reporting Company

b. An entity is related to a reporting Company if any of the conditions in IAS 24 applies.

29.1.22 "significant influence" refers to the power to participate in the financial and operating policy decisions of a Company, but not control them;

29.1.23 "significant shareholder" means a person whose shareholding, directly or indirectly, consists of at least five per cent (5%) of the Company's paid up capital or voting rights;

29.1.24 "stakeholder" includes shareholders, employees, analysts, creditors, customers, regulators, vendors, host community, non-governmental organisations and government;

29.1.25 "Statutory Audit Committee" refers to the committee responsible for audit, which public companies are required to constitute by extant laws;

29.1.26 "whistle-blower" means any person(s) including the employee, management, Directors, customers, service providers, creditors and other stakeholder(s) of a Company who report any form of unethical behaviour or violations of laws and regulations to the appropriate internal authority or regulators.

29.2 In this Code:

29.2.1 words importing the masculine gender include females; and

29.2.2 words in the singular include the plural and words in the plural include the singular.

www.ingramcontent.com/pod-product-compliance
Lightning Source LLC
Chambersburg PA
CBHW050519240926
51846CB00003B/621
* 9 7 8 9 7 8 5 1 5 7 8 9 5 *